Classic
Philosophical
Questions

Third Edition

Classic Philosophical Questions

Third Edition

Edited by
James A. Gould
University of South Florida

Charles E. Merrill Publishing Company
A Bell & Howell Company
Columbus, Ohio 43216

Published by
Charles E. Merrill Publishing Company
A Bell and Howell Company
Columbus, Ohio 43216

This book was set in Times Roman.
The production editor was Rosemary Barnett.
The cover was prepared by Will Chenoweth.

Library of Congress Catalog Card Number: 78–61260
International Standard Book Number: 0–675–08308–7

Printed in the United States of America

1 2 3 4 5 6 7 8 9 10/86 85 84 83 82 81 80 79

Preface

One of the best ways to introduce the student to philosophy is to use a series of problems on familiar topics. This is usually so because it starts where the student's mind is. And if it is the task of philosophy to develop to a greater depth concepts with which one already has some familiarity, then this approach will often meet with success.

This text presents some of the most familiar and fundamental problems in philosophy. I have attempted to present those questions that would interest the student, and that encompass classical questions in which most philosophers are interested. I have avoided very technical articles and concentrated on problems that can be readily grasped by the first- or second-year college student.

The selections are accompanied by study guide questions and thought questions concerning the main ideas of the respective articles. These questions are appropriate for use in classroom discussion or as written assignments. There are also student references that can be used for writing term papers. The appendix correlates the selections with the standard secondary texts in philosophy. A teacher's manual is available; it contains summaries of the articles, critical discussions of them, and some subjective and objective questions.

In the second edition, I included more analytic philosophy than in the first edition, also added were some material on identity, as well as articles representing the women's movement. I hope that both teachers and students found them as informative and exciting as I have.

This third edition takes into account many helpful suggestions from several professors who used the second edition. I have included new selections from Aristotle, Sartre, Rachels, Davis, Taylor, Plato, Pascal, Muller, Blackstone, and Tolstoy. These selections were chosen because they are classic, interesting, and readily readable.

I would like to thank both Camille Genter and Judy Manke as well

as my editors Fred Kinne and Susan Ziegler for their very great help
with the first edition. I wish also to belatedly pay tribute to Beverly
Kolz, who is undoubtedly the finest copy editor in the profession. I
also wish to thank Delma Alvarez, whose patience and humor helped
me through the second edition, and I mustn't fail to mention Lynn
Weissinger. My thanks too, go to Roger Ratliff for the help he gave me
as editor. And for this third edition, my thanks go to my editor Tom
Hutchinson and to Joyce Brown for her cheerful help.

Contents

    "Democracy"

8. Aesthetics   581

one   Are Artistic Judgments Subjective?

    54. *Curt Ducasse:* 4oct 79   583
        "There Can Be No Disputing of Tastes"
    55. *Monroe Beardsley:* 9oct   594
        "Tastes Can Be Disputed"

two   What Is the Function of Art?

    56. *Leo Tolstoy:*   604
        "To Communicate Emotions"
    57. *Meredith Tax:*   616
        "To Communicate Political Views"

three Why Do We Laugh?

    58. *Henri Bergson:*   630
        "Because of Non-Life Actions"
    59. *J. L. Styan:*   641
        "There Are Many Reasons for Laughter"

four   Why Do We Enjoy the Tragic?

    60. *Aristotle:*   651
        "The Catharsis Theory"
    61. *DeWitt Parker:*   660
        "The Catharsis Theory Is Inadequate"

1

The Trial of Socrates and the Value of Philosophy

1

The Apology

Plato (427/8–374/8 B.C.), one of the great Greek philosophers, has exerted more influence upon the development of
Western philosophy than any other writer with the possible
exception of his student, Aristotle. He established the Academy in Athens, the first of the major schools of ancient Greece.
His works, written in dialogue form and featuring his teacher
Socrates as the principal figure, have continued to be widely
read not only for their intellectual content but also for their
literary merit. Among his writings of interest to the student
of ethics are: *Euthyphro, Apology, Crito, Phaedo, The Republic, Protagoras, Gorgias,* and *Philebus.*

The *Apology* is generally thought to be one of Plato's earliest works.
In it Plato portrays the man whom he most revered—Socrates—as he
appeared when he was tried by the citizens of Athens in 399 B.C. The
Apology raises a number of interesting questions about the different
demands of the private and public spheres. It is especially concerned
with the role of the critic in the free society and wi t te difference
between speaking the truth and saying what is merely persuasive and
pleasing. What is central in it is the life and character of Socrates
himself and the attitudes which he judged to be appropriate to a man
who is "free" in the deepest sense.

From *The Apology,* trans. by Jowett, 3rd edition.

TO STUDY

1. What are the charges to which Socrates replies?
2. According to Socrates, how should a man live?

3. Socrates argues that the taker of life injures himself more than his victim. Is this true?

4. What reason does Socrates give for his failure to engage in politics?

5. What does Socrates say should be the chief concern of man? Why?

6. Why doesn't Socrates plead for his life or accept exile?

7. Upon what facts does Socrates base his defense?

8. Why does Socrates refuse exile?

9. What argument does Socrates use to show that death is a good?

CHARACTERS
Socrates
Meletus
Scene—The Court of Justice

Soc. I cannot tell what impression my accusers have made upon you, Athenians. For my own part, I know that they nearly made me forget who I was, so believable were they; and yet they have scarcely uttered one single word of truth. But of all their many falsehoods, the one which astonished me most was when they said that I was a clever speaker, and that you must be careful not to let me mislead you. I thought that it was most impudent of them not to be ashamed to talk in that way; for as soon as I open my mouth they will be refuted, and I shall prove that I am not a clever speaker in any way at all—unless, indeed, by a clever speaker they mean a man who speaks the truth. If that is their meaning, I agree with them that I am a much greater orator than they. My accusers, then I repeat, have said little or nothing that is true; but from me you shall hear the whole truth. Certainly you will not hear an elaborate speech, Athenians, dressed up, like theirs, with words and phrases. I will say to you what I have to say, without preparation, and in the words which come first, for I believe that my cause is just; so let none of you expect anything else. Indeed, my friends, it would hardly be seemingly for me, at my age, to come before you like a young man with his specious phrases. But there is one thing, Athenians, which I do most earnestly beg and entreat of you. Do not be surprised and do not interrupt with shouts if in my defense I speak in the same way that I am accustomed to speak in the market-place, at the tables of the money-changers, where many of you have heard me, and elsewhere. The truth is this. I am more than seventy years old, and this is the first time that I have ever come before a law court; so your manner of speech here is quite strange to me. If I had been really a stranger, you would have forgiven me for speaking in the language and the fashion of my native country; and so now I ask you to grant me what I think I have a right to claim. Never mind the style of my speech—it may be better or it may be worse—give your whole attention to the question, Is what I say just, or is it not? That is what makes a good judge, as speaking the truth makes a good advocate.

I have to defend myself, Athenians, first against the old false accusations of my old accusers, and then against the later ones of my present accusers. For many men have been accusing me to you, and for very many years, who have not uttered a word of truth; and I fear them more than I fear Anytus and his associates, formidable as they are. But, my friends, those others are still more formidable; for they got hold of most of you when you were children, and they have been more persistent in accusing me untruthfully and have persuaded you that there is a certain Socrates, a wise man, who speculates about the heavens, and who investigates things that are beneath the earth, and who can make the weaker reason appear the stronger. These men, Athenians, who spread abroad this report are the accusers whom I fear; for their hearers think that persons who pursue such inquiries never believe in the gods. Then they are many, and their attacks have been going on for a long time, and they spoke to you when you were at the age most readily to believe them, for you were all young, and many of you were children, and there was no one to answer them when they attacked me. And the most unreasonable thing of all is that I do not even know their names: I cannot tell you who they are except when one happens to be a comic poet. But all the rest who have persuaded you, from motives of resentment and prejudice, and sometimes, it may be, from conviction, are hardest to cope with. For I cannot call anyone of them forward in court to cross-examine him. I have, as it were, simply to spar with shadows in my defense, and to put questions which there is no one to answer. I ask you, therefore, to believe that, as I say, I have been attacked by two kinds of accusers—first, by Meletus and his associates, and, then, by those older ones of whom I have spoken. And, with your leave, I will defend myself first against my old accusers; for you heard their accusations first, and they were much more forceful than my present accusers are.

Well, I must make my defense, Athenians, and try in the short time allowed me to remove the prejudice which you have been so long a time acquiring. I hope that I may manage to do this, if it be good for you and for me, and that my defense may be successful; but I am quite aware of the nature of my task, and I know that it is a difficult one. Be the outcome, however, as is pleasing to God, I must obey the law and make my defense.

Let us begin from the beginning, then, and ask what is the accusation which has given rise to the prejudice against me, which was what Meletus relied on when he brought his indictment. What is the prejudice which my enemies have been spreading about me? I must assume that they are formally accusing me, and read their indictment. It would run somewhat in this fashion: Socrates is a wrongdoer, who meddles with inquiries into things beneath the earth and in the heavens, and who makes the weaker reason appear the stronger, and who teaches others these same things. That is what they say; and in the comedy of Aristophanes [*Clouds*] you yourselves saw a man called Socrates swinging round in a basket and saying that he walked the air, and prattling a great deal of nonsense about matters of which I understand nothing, either more or less. I do not mean to disparage that kind of knowledge if there is anyone who is wise about these matters. I trust Meletus may never be able to prosecute me for that. But the truth is, Athenians, I have nothing to do with these matters, and almost all of you are yourselves my witnesses of this. I beg all of you who have heard me discussing, and they are many, to inform your neighbors and tell them if any of you have ever heard me discussing such matters, either more or less. That will show you that the other common stories about me are as false as this one.

But the fact is that not one of these is true. And if you have heard that I undertake to educate men, and make money by so doing, that is not true either, though I think that it would be a fine thing to be able to educate men, as Gorgias of Leontini, and Prodicus of Ceos, and Hippias of Elis do. For each of them, my friends, can go into any city, and persuade the young men to leave the society of their fellow citizens, with any of whom they might associate for nothing, and be only too glad to be allowed to pay money for the privilege of associating with themselves. And I believe that there is another wise man from Paros residing in Athens at this moment. I happened to meet Callias, the son of Hipponicus, a man who has spent more money on sophists than everyone else put together. So I said to him (he has two sons), Callias, if your two sons had been foals or calves, we could have hired a trainer for them who would have made them perfect in the virtue which belongs to their nature. He would have been either a groom or a farmer. But whom do you intend to take to train them, seeing that they are men? Who understands the virtue which belongs to men and to citizens? I suppose that you must have thought of this, because of your sons. Is there such a person, said I, or not? Certainly there is, he replied. Who is he, said I, and where does he come from, and what is his fee? Evenus, Socrates, he replied, from Paros, five minae. Then I thought that Evenus was a fortunate person if he really understood this art and could teach so cleverly. If I had possessed knowledge of that kind, I should have been conceited and disdainful. But, Athenians, the truth is that I do not possess it.

Perhaps some of you may reply: But, Socrates, what is the trouble with you? What has given rise to these prejudices against you? You must have been doing something out of the ordinary. All these stories and reports of you would never have arisen if you had not been doing something different from other men. So tell us what it is, that we may not give our verdict in the dark. I think that that is a fair question, and I will try to explain to you what it is that has raised these prejudices against me and given me this reputation. Listen, then: some of you, perhaps, will think that I am joking, but I assure you that I will tell you the whole truth. I have gained this reputation, Athenians, simply by reason of a certain wisdom. But by what kind of wisdom? It is by just that wisdom which is perhaps human wisdom. In that, it may be, I am really wise. But the men of whom I was speaking just now must be wise in a wisdom which is greater than human wisdom, or else I cannot describe it, for certainly I know nothing of it myself, and if any man says that I do, he lies and speaks to arouse prejudice against me. Do not interrupt me with shouts, Athenians, even if you think that I am boasting. What I am going to say is not my own: I will tell you who says it, and he is worthy of your respect. I will bring the god of Delphi to be the witness of my wisdom, if it is wisdom at all, and of its nature. You remember Chaerephon. From youth upwards he was my comrade; and also a partisan of your democracy, sharing your recent exile and returning with you. You remember, too, Chaerephon's character—how vehement he was in carrying through whatever he took in hand. Once he went to Delphi and ventured to put this question to the oracle—I entreat you again, my friends, not to interrupt me with your shouts—he asked if there was any man who was wiser than I. The priestess answered that there was no one. Chaerephon himself is dead, but his brother here will confirm what I say.

Now see why I tell you this. I am going to explain to you how the prejudice against me has arisen. When I heard of the oracle I began to reflect: What can the god mean by this riddle? I know very well that I am not wise, even the smallest degree. Then what can he mean by saying that I am the wisest of men? It cannot be that he is speaking falsely, for he is a god and cannot lie. For a long time I was at a loss to understand his meaning. Then, very reluctantly, I turned to seek for it in this manner: I went to a man who was reputed to be wise, thinking that there, if anywhere, I should prove the answer wrong, and meaning to point out to the oracle its mistake, and to say, You said that I was the wisest of men, but this man is wiser than I am. So I examined the man—I need not tell you his name, he was a politician—but this was the result, Athenians. When I conversed with him I came to see that, though a great many persons, and most of all he himself, thought that he was wise, yet he was not wise. Then I tried to prove to him that he was not wise, though he fancied that he was; and by so doing I made him indignant, and many of the bystanders. So when I went away, I thought to myself, I am wiser than this man: neither of us knows anything that is really worthwhile, but he thinks that he has knowledge when he has not, while I, having no knowledge, do not think that I have. I seem, at any rate, to be a little wiser than he is on this point: I do not think that I know what I do not know. Next I went to another man who was reputed to be still wiser than the last, with exactly the same result. And there again I made him, and many other men, indignant.

Then I went on to one man after another, seeing that I was arousing indignation every day, which caused me much pain and anxiety. Still I thought that I must set the god's command above everything. So I had to go to every man who seemed to possess any knowledge, and investigate the meaning of the oracle. Athenians, I must tell you the truth; by the god, this was the result of the investigation which I made at the god's bidding: I found that the men whose reputation for wisdom stood highest were nearly the most lacking in it, while others who were looked down on as common people were much more intelligent. Now I must describe to you the wanderings which I undertook, like Heraclean labors, to prove the oracle irrefutable. After the politicians, I went to the poets, tragic, dithyrambic, and others, thinking that there I should find myself manifestly more ignorant than they. So I took up the poems on which I thought that they had spent most pains, and asked them what they meant, hoping at the same time to learn something from them. I am ashamed to tell you the truth, my friends, but I must say it. Almost anyone of the bystanders could have talked about the works of these poets better than the poets themselves. So I soon found that it is not by wisdom that the poets create their works, but by a certain innate power and by inspiration, like soothsayers and prophets, who say many fine things, but who understand nothing of what they say. The poets seemed to me to be in a similar situation. And at the same time I perceived that, because of their poetry, they thought that they were the wisest of men in other matters, too, which they were not. So I went away again, thinking that I had the same advantage over the poets that I had over the politicians.

Finally, I went to the artisans, for I knew very well that I possessed no knowledge at all worth speaking of, and I was sure that I should find that they knew many fine things. And in that I was not mistaken. They knew what I did not know, and so far they were wiser than I. But, Athenians, it seemed to me that the skilled artisans made the same mistake as the poets. Each of them believed himself to be extremely wise in matters of the greatest importance because he was skilful in his own art: and this presumption of theirs obscured their real wisdom. So I asked myself, on behalf of the oracle, whether I would choose to remain as I was, without either their wisdom or their ignorance, or to possess both, as they did. And I answered to myself and to the oracle that it was better for me to remain as I was.

From this examination, Athenians, has arisen much fierce and bitter indignation, and from this a great many prejudices about me, and people say that I am "a wise man." For the bystanders always think that I am wise myself in any matter wherein I refute another. But, my friends, I believe that the god is really wise, and that by this oracle he meant that human wisdom is worth little or nothing. I do not think that he meant that Socrates was wise. He only made use of my name, and took me as an example, as though he would say to men: He among you is the wisest who, like Socrates, knows that in truth his wisdom is worth nothing at all. Therefore I still go about testing and examining every man whom I think wise, whether he be a citizen or a stranger, as the god has commanded me; and whenever I find that he is not wise, I point out to him, on the god's behalf, that he is not wise. I am so busy in this pursuit that I have never had leisure to take any path worth mentioning in public matters or to look after my private affairs. I am in great poverty as the result of my service to the god.

Besides this, the young men who follow me about, who are the sons of wealthy persons and have the most leisure, take pleasure in hearing men cross-examined. They often imitate me among themselves; then they try their hands at cross-examining other people. And, I imagine, they find plenty of men who think that they know a great deal when in fact they know little or nothing. Then the persons who are cross-examined get angry with me instead of with themselves, and say that Socrates is an abomination and corrupts the young. When they are asked, Why, what does he do? what does he teach? they do not know what to say; but, not to seem at a loss, they repeat the stock charges against all philosophers, and allege that he investigates things in the air and under the earth, and that he teaches people to disbelieve in the gods, and to make the weaker reason appear the stronger. For, I suppose, they would not like to confess the truth, which is that they are shown up as ignorant pretenders to knowledge that they do not possess. So they have been filling your ears with their bitter prejudices for a long time, for they are ambitious, energetic, and numerous; and they speak vigorously and persuasively against me. Relying on this, Meletus, Anytus, and Lycon have attacked me. Meletus is indignant with me on the part of the poets, Anytus on the part of the artisans and politicians, and Lycon on the part of the orators. And so, as I said at the beginning, I shall be surprised if I am able, in the short time allowed me for my defense, to remove from your minds this prejudice which has grown so strong. What I have told you, Athenians, is the truth: I neither conceal nor do I suppress anything, small or great. Yet I know that it is just this plainness of speech which rouses indignation. But that is only a proof that my words are true, and that the prejudice against me, and the causes of it, are what I have said. And whether you look for them now or hereafter, you will find that they are so.

What I have said must suffice as my defense against the charges of my first accusers. I will try next to defend myself against Meletus, that "good patriot," as he calls himself, and my later accusers. Let us assume that they are a new set of accusers, and read their indictment, as we did in the case of the others. It runs thus. He says that Socrates is a wrongdoer who corrupts the youth, and who does not believe in the gods whom the state believes in, but in other new divinities. Such is the accusation. Let us examine each point in it separately. Meletus says that I do wrong by corrupting the youth. But I say, Athenians, that he is doing wrong, for he is playing a solemn joke by lightly bringing men to trial, and pretending to have zealous interest in matters to which he has never given a moment's thought. Now I will try to prove to you that it is so.

Come here, Meletus. Is it not a fact that you think it very important that the young should be as excellent as possible?

Mel. It is.

Soc. Come then, tell the judges who is it who improves them? You care so much, you must know. You are accusing me, and bringing me to trial, because, as you say, you have discovered that I am the corrupter of the youth. Come now, reveal to the gentlemen who improves them. You see, Meletus, you have nothing to say; you are silent. But don't you think that this is shameful? Is not your silence a conclusive proof of what I say—that you have never cared? Come, tell us, my good sir, who makes the young better citizens?

Mel. The laws.

Soc. That, my friend, is not my question. What man improves the young, who starts with the knowledge of the laws?

Mel. The judges here, Socrates.

Soc. What do you mean, Meletus? Can they educate the young and improve them?

Mel. Certainly.

Soc. All of them? or only some of them?

Mel. All of them.

Soc. By Hera, that is good news! Such a large supply of benefactors! And do the listeners here improve them, or not?

Mel. They do.

Soc. And do the senators?

Mel. Yes.

Soc. Well then, Meletus, do the members of the assembly corrupt the young or do they again all improve them?

Mel. They, too, improve them.

Soc. Then all the Athenians, apparently, make the young into good men except me, and I alone corrupt them. Is that your meaning?

Mel. Most certainly; that is my meaning.

Soc. You have discovered me to be most unfortunate. Now tell me: do you think that the same holds good in the case of horses? Does one man do them harm and everyone else improve them? On the contrary, is it not one man only, or a very few—namely, those who are skilled with horses—who can improve them, while the majority of men harm them if they use them and have anything to do with them? Is it not so, Meletus, both with horses and with every other animal? Of course it is, whether you and Anytus say yes or no. The young would certainly be very fortunate if only one man corrupted them, and everyone else did them good. The truth is, Meletus, you prove conclusively that you have never thought about the youth in your life. You exhibit your carelessness in not caring for the very matters about which you are prosecuting me.

Now be so good as to tell us, Meletus, is it better to live among good citizens or bad ones? Answer, my friend. I am not asking you at all a difficult question. Do not the bad harm their associates and the good do them good?

Mel. Yes.

Soc. Is there any man who would rather be injured than benefited by his companions? Answer, my good sir; you are obliged by the law to answer. Does any one like to be injured?

Mel. Certainly not.

Soc. Well then, are you prosecuting me for corrupting the young and making them worse, intentionally or unintentionally?

Mel. For doing it intentionally.

Soc. What, Meletus? Do you mean to say that you, who are so much younger than I, are yet so much wiser than I that you know that bad citizens always do evil, and that good citizens do good, to those with whom they come in contact, while I am so extraordinarily stupid as not to know that, if I make any of my companions evil, he will probably injure me in some way, and as to commit this great evil, as you allege, intentionally? You will not make me believe that, nor anyone else either, I should think. Either I do not corrupt the young at all or, if I do, I do so unintentionally: so that you are lying in either case. And if I corrupt them unintentionally, the law does not call upon you to prosecute me for an error which is unintentional, but to take me aside privately and reprove and instruct me. For, of course, I shall cease from doing wrong involuntarily, as soon as I know that I have been doing wrong. But you avoided associating with me and educating me; instead you bring me up before the court, where the law sends persons, not for instruction, but for punishment.

The truth is, Athenians, as I said, it is quite clear that Meletus has never cared at all about these matters. However, now tell us, Meletus, how do you say that I corrupt the young? Clearly, according to your indictment, by teaching them not to believe in the gods the state believes in, but other new divinities instead. You mean that I corrupt the young by that teaching, do you not?

Mel. Yes, most certainly I mean that.

Soc. Then in the name of these gods of whom we are speaking, explain yourself a little more clearly to me and to these gentlemen here. I cannot understand what you mean. Do you mean that I teach the young to believe in some gods, but not in the gods of the state? Do you accuse me of teaching them to believe in strange gods? If that is your meaning, I myself believe in some gods, and my crime is not that of absolute atheism. Or do you mean that I do not believe in the gods at all myself, and I teach other people not to believe in them either?

Mel. I mean that you do not believe in the gods in any way whatever.

Soc. You amaze me, Meletus! Why do you say that? Do you mean that I believe neither the sun nor the moon to be gods, like other men?

Mel. I swear he does not, judges; he says that the sun is a stone, and the moon earth.

Soc. My dear Meletus, do you think that you are prosecuting Anaxagoras? You must have a very poor opinion of these men, and think them illiterate, if you imagine that they do not know that the works of Anaxagoras of Clazomenae are full of these doctrines. And so young men learn these things from me, when they can often buy places in the theatre for a drachma at most, and laugh at Socrates were he to pretend that these doctrines, which are very peculiar doctrines, too, were his own. But please tell me, do you really think that I do not believe in the gods at all?

Mel. Most certainly I do. You are a complete atheist.

Soc. No one believes that, Meletus, not even you yourself. It seems to me, Athenians, that Meletus is very insolent and reckless, and that he is prosecuting me simply out of insolence, recklessness and youthful bravado. For he seems to be testing me, by asking me a riddle that has no answer. Will this wise Socrates, he says to himself, see that I am joking and contradicting myself? or shall I outwit him and everyone else who hears me? Meletus seems to me to contradict himself in his indictment: it is as if he were to say, Socrates is a wrongdoer who does not believe in the gods, but who believes in the gods. But that is mere joking.

Now, my friends, let us see why I think that this is his meaning. Do you answer me, Meletus; and do you, Athenians, remember the request which I made to you at the start, and do not interrupt me with shouts if

I talk in my usual way.

Is there any man, Meletus, who believes in the existence of things pertaining to men and not in the existence of men? Make him answer the question, my friends, without these interruptions. Is there any man who believes in the existence of horsemanship and not in the existence of horses? or in flute-playing and not in flute-players? There is not, my friend. If you will not answer, I will tell both you and the judges. But you must answer my next question. Is there any man who believes in the existence of divine things and not in the existence of divinities?

Mel. There is not.

Soc. I am very glad that these gentlemen have managed to extract an answer from you. Well then, you say that I believe in divine beings, whether they be old or new ones, and that I teach others to believe in them; at any rate, according to your statement, I believe in divine beings. That you have sworn in your indictment. But if I believe in divine beings, I suppose it follows necessarily that I believe in divinities. Is it not so? It is. I assume that you grant that, as you do not answer. But do we not believe that divinities are either gods themselves or the children of the gods? Do you admit that?

Mel. I do.

Soc. Then you admit that I believe in divinities. Now, if these divinities are gods, then, as I say, you are joking and asking a riddle, and asserting that I do not believe in the gods, and at the same time that I do, since I believe in divinities. But if these divinities are the illegitimate children of the gods, either by the nymphs or by other mothers, as they are said to be, then, I ask, what man could believe in the existence of the children of the gods, and not in the existence of the gods? That would be as strange as believing in the existence of the offspring of horses and asses, and not in the existence of horses and asses. You must have indicted me in this manner, Meletus, either to test me or because you could not find any crime that you could accuse me of with truth. But you will never contrive to persuade any man with any sense at all that a belief in divine things and things of the gods does not necessarily involve a belief in divinities, and in the gods, and in heroes.

But in truth, Athenians, I do not think that I need say very much to prove that I have not committed the crime for which Meletus is prosecuting me. What I have said is enough to prove that. But I repeat it is certainly true, as I have already told you, that I have aroused much indignation. That is what will cause my condemnation if I am condemned; not Meletus nor Anytus either, but that prejudice and suspicion of the multitude which have been the destruction of many good men before me, and I think will be so again. There is no fear that I shall be the last victim.

Perhaps someone will say: Are you not ashamed, Socrates, of leading a life which is very likely now to cause your death? I should answer him with justice, and say: My friend, if you think that a man of any worth at all ought to reckon the chances of life and death when he acts, or that he ought to think of anything but whether he is acting rightly or wrongly, and as a good or a bad man would act, you are mistaken. According to you, the demigods who died at Troy would be foolish, and among them the son of Thetis, who thought nothing of danger when the alternative was disgrace. For when his mother—and she was a goddess—addressed him, when he was burning to slay Hector, in this fashion, "My son, if you avenge the death of your comrade Patroclus and slay Hector, you will die yourself, for 'fate awaits you straightway after Hector's death' "; when he heard this, he scorned danger and death; he feared much more to live a coward and not to avenge his friend. "Let me punish the evildoer and straightway die," he said, "that I may not remain here by the beaked ships jeered at, encumbering the earth." Do you suppose that he thought of danger or of death? For this, Athenians, I believe to be the truth. Wherever a man's station is, whether he has chosen it of his own will, or whether he has been placed at it by his commander, there it is his duty to remain and face the danger without thinking of death or of any other thing except dishonor.

When the generals whom you chose to command me, Athenians, assigned me my station at Potidaea and at Amphipolis and at Delium, I remained where they placed me and ran the risk of death, like other men. It would be very strange conduct on my part if I were to desert my station now from fear of death or of any other thing when God has commanded me—as I am persuaded that he has done—to spend my life in searching for wisdom, and in examining myself and others. That would indeed be a very strange thing: then certainly I might with justice be brought to trial for not believing in the gods, for I should be disobeying the oracle, and fearing death and thinking myself wise when I was not wise. For to fear death, my friends, is only to think ourselves wise without really being wise, for it is to think that we know what we do not know. For no one knows whether death may not be the greatest good that can happen to man. But men fear it as if they knew quite well that it was the greatest of evils. And what is this but that shameful ignorance of thinking that we know what we do not know? In this matter, too, my friends, perhaps I am different from the multitude; and if I were to claim to be at all wiser than others, it would be because, not knowing very much about the other world, I do not think I know. But I do know very well that it is evil and disgraceful to do wrong, and to disobey my superior, whoever he is, whether man or god. I will never do what I know to be evil, and shrink in fear from what I do not know to be good or evil. Even if you acquit me now, and do not listen to Anytus' argument that, if I am to be acquitted, I ought never to have been brought to trial at all, and that, as it is, you are bound to put me to death because, as he said, if I escape, all your sons will be utterly corrupted by practising what Socrates teaches. If you were therefore to say to me: Socrates, this time we will not listen to Anytus; we will let you go, but on this condition, that you give up this investigation of yours, and philosophy; if you are found following those pursuits again, you shall die. I say, if you offered to let me go on these terms, I should reply: Athenians, I hold you in the highest regard and affection, but I will be persuaded by the god rather than by you; and as long as I have breath and strength I will not give up philosophy and exhorting you and declaring the truth to every one of you whom I meet, saying, as I am accustomed, "My good friend, you are a citizen of Athens, a city which is very great and very famous for its wisdom and strength—are you not ashamed of caring so much for the making of money and for fame and prestige, when you neither think nor care about wisdom and truth and the improvement of your soul?" And if he disputes my words and says that he does care about these things, I shall not at once release him and go away: I shall question him and cross-examine him and test him. If I think that he does not possess virtue, though he says that he does, I shall reproach him for undervaluing the most valuable things, and overvaluing those that are less valuable. This I shall do to everyone whom I meet, young or old, citizen or stranger, but especially to citizens, for they are more nearly akin to me. For know that the god has commanded me to do so. And I think that no greater good has ever befallen you in Athens than my service to the god. For I spend my whole life in going about and persuading you all to give your first and greatest care to the improvement of your souls, and not till you have done that to think of your bodies or your wealth; and telling you that virtue does not come from wealth, but that wealth, and every other good thing which men have, whether in public or in private, comes from virtue. If then I corrupt the youth by this teaching, these things must be harmful; but if any man says that I teach anything else, there is nothing in what he says. And therefore, Athenians, I say, whether you are persuaded by Anytus or not, whether you acquit me or not, be sure I shall not change my way of life; no, not if I have to die for it many times.

Do not interrupt me, Athenians, with your shouts. Remember the request which I made to you, and do not interrupt my words. I think that it will profit you to hear them. I am going to say something more to you, at which you may be inclined to protest, but do not do that. Be sure that if you put me to death, who am what I have told you that I am, you will do yourselves more harm than me. Meletus and Anytus can do me no harm: that is impossible, for I am sure it is not allowed that a good man be injured by a worse. They may indeed kill me, or drive me into exile, or deprive me of my civil rights; and perhaps Meletus and others think those things great evils. But I do not think so. I think it is a much greater evil to do what he is doing now, and to try to put a man to death unjustly. And now, Athenians, I am not arguing in my own defense at all, as you might expect me to do, but rather in yours in order you may not make a mistake about the gift of the god to you by condemning me. For if you put me to death, you will not easily find another who, if I may use a ludicrous comparison, clings to the state as a sort of gadfly to a horse that is large and well-bred but rather sluggish from its size, and needing to be aroused. It seems to me that the god has attached me like that to the state, for I am constantly alighting upon you at every point to rouse, persuade, and reproach each of you all day long. You will not easily find anyone else, my friends, to fill my place; and if you are persuaded by me, you will spare my life. You are indignant, as drowsy persons are, when they are awakened, and, of course, if you are persuaded by Anytus, you could easily kill me with a single blow, and then sleep on undisturbed for the rest of your lives, unless the god in his care for you sends another to rouse you. And you may easily see that it is the god who has given me to your city; for it is not human the way in which I have neglected all my own interests and permitted my private affairs to be neglected now for so many years, while occupying myself unceasingly in your interests, going to each of you privately, like a father or an elder brother, trying to persuade him to care for virtue. There would have been a reason for it, if I had gained any advantage by this, or if I had been paid for my exhortations; but you see yourselves that my accusers, though they accuse me of everything else without shame, have not had the impudence to say that I ever either exacted or demanded payment. Of that they have no evidence. And I think that I have sufficient evidence of the truth of what I say—my poverty.

Perhaps it may seem strange to you that, though I go about giving this advice privately and meddling in others' affairs, yet I do not venture to come forward in the assembly and advise the state. You have often heard me speak of my reason for this, and in many places: it is that I have a certain divine sign, which is what Meletus has caricatured in his indictment. I have had it from childhood. It is a kind of voice which, whenever I hear it, always turns me back from something which I was going to do, but never urges me to act. It is this which forbids me to take part in politics. And I think it does well to forbid me. For, Athenians, it is quite certain that, if I had attempted to take part in politics, I should have perished at once and long ago without doing any good either to you or to myself. And do not be indignant with me for telling the truth. There is no man who will preserve his life for long, either in Athens or elsewhere, if he firmly opposes the multitude, and tries to prevent the commission of much injustice and illegality in the state. He who would really fight for justice must do so as a private citizen, not as an office-holder, if he is to preserve his life, even for a short time.

I will prove to you that this is so by very strong evidence, not by mere words, but by what you value highly, actions, Listen then to what has happened to me, that you may know that there is no man who could make me consent to do wrong from the fear of death, but that I would perish at once rather than give way. What I am going to tell you may be a commonplace in the law court; nevertheless it is true. The only office that I ever held in the state, Athenians, was that of Senator. When you wished to try the ten generals who did not rescue their men after the battle of Arginusae, as a group, which was illegal, as you all came to think afterwards, the tribe Antiochis, to which I belong, held the presidency. On that occasion I alone of all the presidents opposed your illegal action and gave my vote against you. The speakers were ready to suspend me and arrest me; and you were clamoring against me, and crying out to me to submit. But I thought that I ought to face the danger, with law and justice on my side, rather than join with you in your unjust proposal, from fear of imprisonment or death. That was when the state was democratic. When the oligarchy came in, the Thirty sent for me, with four others, to the council-chamber, and ordered us to bring Leon the Salaminian from Salamis, that they might put him to death. They were in the habit of frequently giving similar orders, to many others, wishing to implicate as many as possible in their crimes. But, then, I again proved, not by mere words, but by my actions, that, if I may speak bluntly, I do not care a straw for death; but that I do care very much indeed about not doing anything unjust or impious. That government with all its powers did not terrify me into doing anything unjust; but when we left the council-chamber, the other four went over to Salamis and brought Leon across to Athens; and I went home. And if the rule of the Thirty had not been destroyed soon afterwards, I should very likely have been put to death for what I did then. Many of you will be my witnesses in this matter.

Now do you think that I could have remained alive all these years if I had taken part in public affairs, and had always maintained the cause of justice like an honest man, and had held it a paramount duty, as it is, to do so? Certainly not, Athenians, nor could any other man. But throughout my whole life, both in private and in public, whenever I have had to take part in public affairs, you will find I have always been the same and have never yielded unjustly to anyone; no, not to those whom my enemies falsely assert to have been my pupils. But I was never anyone's teacher. I have never withheld myself from anyone, young or old, who was anxious to hear me discuss while I was making my investigation; neither do I discuss for payment, and refuse to discuss without payment. I am ready to ask questions of rich and poor alike, and if any man wishes to answer me, and then listen to what I have to say, he may. And I cannot justly be charged with causing these men to turn out good or bad, for I never either taught or professed to teach any of them any knowledge whatever. And if any man asserts that he ever learned or heard anything from me in private which everyone else did not hear as well as he, be sure that he does not speak the truth.

Why is it, then, that people delight in spending so much time in my company? You have heard why, Athenians. I told you the whole truth when I said that they delight in hearing me examine persons who think that they are wise when they are not wise. It is certainly very amusing to listen to that. And, I say, the god has commanded me to examine men, in oracles and in dreams and in every way in which the divine will was ever declared to man. This is the truth, Athenians, and if it were not the truth, it would be easily refuted. For if it were really the case that I have already corrupted some of the young men, and am now corrupting others, surely some of them, finding as they grew older that I had given them bad advice in their youth, would have come forward today to accuse me and take their revenge. Or if they were unwilling to do so themselves, surely their relatives, their fathers or brothers, or others, would, if I had done them any harm, have remembered it and taken their revenge. Certainly I see many of them in Court. Here is Crito, of my own deme and of my own age, the father of Critobulus; here is Lysanias of Sphettus, the father of Aeschines; here is also Antiphon of Cephisus, the father of Epigenes. Then here are others whose brothers have spent their time in my company—Nicostratus, the son of Theozotides and brother of Theodotus—and Theodotus is dead, so he at least cannot entreat his brother to be silent; here is Paralus, the son of Demodocus and the brother of Theages; here is Adeimantus, the son of Ariston, whose brother is Plato here; and Aeantodorus, whose brother is Aristodorus. And I can name many others to you, some of whom Meletus ought to have called as witnesses in the course of his own speech; but if he forgot to call them then, let him call them now—I will yield the floor to him—and tell us if he has any such evidence. No, on the contrary, my friends, you will find all these men ready to support me, the corrupter, the injurer, of their relatives, as Meletus and Anytus call me. Those of them who have been already corrupted might perhaps have some reason for supporting me, but what reason can their relatives have who are grown up, and who are uncorrupted, except the reason of truth and justice—that they know very well that Meletus is a liar, and that I am speaking the truth?

Well, my friends, this, and perhaps more like this, is pretty much what

I have to say in my defense. There may be some one among you who will be indignant when he remembers how, even in a less important trial than this, he begged and entreated the judges, with many tears, to acquit him, and brought forward his children and many of his friends and relatives in Court in order to apppeal to your feelings; and then finds that I shall do none of these things, though I am in what he would think the supreme danger. Perhaps he will harden himself against me when he notices this: it may make him angry, and he may cast his vote in anger. If it is so with any of you—I do not suppose that it is, but in case it should be so—I think that I should answer him reasonably if I said: My friend, I have relatives, too, for, in the words of Homer, "I am not born of an oak or a rock" but of flesh and blood; and so, Athenians, I have relatives, and I have three sons, one of them a lad, and the other two still children. Yet I will not bring any of them forward before you and implore you to acquit me. And why will I do none of these things? It is not from arrogance, Athenians, nor because I lack respect for you—whether or not I can face death bravely is another question—but for my own good name, and for your good name, and for the good name of the whole state. I do not think it right, at my age and with my reputation, to do anything of that kind. Rightly or wrongly, men have made up their minds that in some way Socrates is different from the mass of mankind. And it will be shameful if those of you who are thought to excel in wisdom, or in bravery, or in any other virtue, are going to act in this fashion. I have often seen men of reputation behaving in an extraordinary way at their trial, as if they thought it a terrible fate to be killed, and as though they expected to live for ever if you did not put them to death. Such men seem to me to bring shame upon the state, for any stranger would suppose that the best and most eminent Athenians, who are selected by their fellow citizens to hold office, and for other honors, are no better than women. Those of you, Athenians, who have any reputation at all ought not to do these things, and you ought not to allow us to do them; you should show that you will be much more ready to condemn men who make the state ridiculous by these pitiful pieces of acting, than men who remain quiet.

But apart from the question of reputation, my friends, I do not think that it is right to entreat the judge to acquit us, or to escape condemnation in that way. It is our duty to convince him by reason. He does not sit to give away justice as a favor, but to pronounce judgment; and he has sworn, not to favor any man whom he would like to favor, but to judge according to law. And, therefore, we ought not to encourage you in the habit of breaking your oaths; and you ought not to allow yourselves to fall into this habit, for then neither you nor we would be acting piously. Therefore, Athenians, do not require me to do these things, for I believe them to be neither good nor just nor pious; and, more especially, do not ask me to do them today when Meletus is prosecuting me for impiety. For were I to be successful and persuade you by my entreaties to break your oaths, I should be clearly teaching you to believe that there are no gods, and I should be simply accusing myself by my defense of not believing in them. But, Athenians, that is very far from the truth. I do believe in the gods as no one of my accusers believes in them: and to you and to God I commit my cause to be decided as is best for you and for me.

(He is found guilty by 281 votes to 220.)

I am not indignant at the verdict which you have given, Athenians, for many reasons. I expected that you would find me guilty; and I am not so much surprised at that as at the numbers of the votes. I certainly never thought that the majority against me would have been so narrow. But now it seems that if only thirty votes had changed sides, I should have escaped. So I think that I have escaped Meletus, as it is; and not only have I escaped him, for it is perfectly clear that if Anytus and Lycon had not come forward to accuse me, too, he would not have obtained the fifth part of the votes, and would have had to pay a fine of a thousand drachmae.

So he proposes death as the penalty. Be it so. And what alternative penalty shall I propose to you, Athenians? What I deserve, of course, must I not? What then do I deserve to pay or to suffer for having determined not to spend my life in ease? I neglected the things which most men value, such as wealth, and family interests, and military commands, and popular oratory, and all the political appointments, and clubs, and factions, that there are in Athens; for I thought that I was really too honest a man to preserve my life if I engaged in these matters. So I did not go where I should have done no good either to you or to myself. I went, instead, to each one of you privately to do him, as I say, the greatest of services, and tried to persuade him not to think of his affairs until he had thought of himself and tried to make himself as good and wise as possible, nor to think of the affairs of Athens until he had thought of Athens herself; and to care for other things in the same manner. Then what do I deserve for such a life? Something good, Athenians, if I am really to propose what I deserve; and something good which it would be suitable to me to receive. Then what is a suitable reward to be given to a poor benefactor who requires leisure to exhort you? There is no reward, Athenians, so suitable for him as a public maintenance in the Prytaneum. It is a much more suitable reward for him than for any of you who has won a victory at the Olympic games with his horse or his chariots. Such a man only makes you seem happy, but I make you really happy; and he is not in want, and I am. So if I am to propose the penalty which I really deserve, I propose this—a public maintenance in the Prytaneum.

Perhaps you think me stubborn and arrogant in what I am saying now, as in what I said about the entreaties and tears. It is not so, Athenians; it is rather that I am convinced that I never wronged any man intentionally, though I cannot persuade you of that, for we have discussed together only a little time. If there were a law at Athens, as there is elsewhere, not to finish a trial of life and death in a single day, I think that I could have persuaded you; but now it is not easy in so short a time to clear myself of great prejudices. But when I am persuaded that I have never wronged any man, I shall certainly not wrong myself, or admit that I deserve to suffer any evil, or propose any evil for myself as a penalty. Why should I? Lest I should suffer the penalty which Meletus proposes when I say that I do not know whether it is a good or an evil? Shall I choose instead of it something which I know to be an evil, and propose that as a penalty? Shall I propose imprisonment? And why should I pass the rest of my days in prison, the slave of successive officials? Or shall I propose a fine, with imprisonment until it is paid? I have told you why I will not do that. I should have to remain in prison, for I have no money to pay a fine with. Shall I then propose exile? Perhaps you would agree to that. Life would indeed be very dear to me if I were unreasonable enough to expect that strangers would cheerfully tolerate my discussions and reasonings when you who are my fellow citizens cannot endure them, and have found them so irksome and odious to you that you are seeking now to be relieved of them. No, indeed, Athenians, that is not likely. A fine life I should lead for an old man if I were to withdraw from Athens and pass the rest of my days in wandering from city to city, and continually being expelled. For I know very well that the young men will listen to me wherever I go, as they do here; and if I drive them away, they will persuade their elders to expel me; and if I do not drive them away, their fathers and kinsmen will expel me for their sakes.

Perhaps someone will say, "Why cannot you withdraw from Athens, Socrates, and hold your peace?" It is the most difficult thing in the world to make you understand why I cannot do that. If I say that I cannot hold my peace because that would be to disobey the god, you will think that I am not in earnest and will not believe me. And if I tell you that no better thing can happen to a man than to discuss virtue every day and the other matters about which you have heard me arguing and examining myself and others, and that an unexamined life is not worth living, then you will believe me still less. But that is so, my friends, though it is not easy to persuade you. And, what is more, I am not accustomed to think that I deserve any punishment. If I had been rich, I would have proposed as large a fine as

I could pay: that would have done me no harm. But I am not rich enough to pay a fine unless you are willing to fix it at a sum within my means. Perhaps I could pay you a mina, so I propose that. Plato here, Athenians, and Crito, and Critobulus, and Apollodorus bid me propose thirty minae, and they will be sureties for me. So I propose thirty minae. They will be sufficient sureties to you for the money.

(He is condemned to death.)

You have not gained very much time, Athenians, and, as the price of it, you will have an evil name for all who wish to revile the state, and they will say that you put Socrates, a wise man, to death. For they will certainly call me wise, whether I am wise or not, when they want to reproach you. If you would have waited for a little while, your wishes would have been fulfilled in the course of nature; for you see that I am an old man, far advanced in years, and near to death. I am saying this not to all of you, only to those who have voted for my death. And to them I have something else to say. Perhaps, my friends, you think that I have been convicted because I was wanting in the arguments by which I could have persuaded you to acquit me, if, that is, I had thought it right to do or to say anything to escape punishment. It is not so. I have been convicted because I was wanting, not in arguments, but in impudence and shamelessness—because I would not plead before you as you would have liked to hear me plead, or appeal to you with weeping and wailing, or say and do many other things which I maintain are unworthy of me, but which you have been accustomed to from other men. But when I was defending myself, I thought that I ought not to do anything unworthy of a free man because of the danger which I ran, and I have not changed my mind now. I would very much rather defend myself as I did, and die, than as you would have had me do, and live. Both in a lawsuit and in war, there are some things which neither I nor any other man may do in order to escape from death. In battle, a man often sees that he may at least escape from death by throwing down his arms and falling on his knees before the pursuer to beg for his life. And there are many other ways of avoiding death in every danger if a man is willing to say and to do anything. But, my friends, I think that it is a much harder thing to escape from wickedness than from death, for wickedness is swifter than death. And now I, who am old and slow, have been overtaken by the slower pursuer: and my accusers, who are clever and swift, have been overtaken by the swifter pursuer—wickedness. And now I shall go away, sentenced by you to death; and they will go away, sentenced by truth to wickedness and injustice. And I abide by this award as well as they. Perhaps it was right for these things to be so; and I think that they are fairly measured.

And now I wish to prophesy to you, Athenians, who have condemned me. For I am going to die, and that is the time when men have most prophetic power. And I prophesy to you who have sentenced me to death that a far more severe punishment than you have inflicted on me will surely overtake you as soon as I am dead. You have done this thing, thinking that you will be relieved from having to give an account of your lives. But I say that the result will be very different. There will be more men who will call you to account, whom I have held back, though you did not recognize it. And they will be harsher toward you than I have been, for they will be younger, and you will be more indignant with them. For if you think that you will restrain men from reproaching you for not living as you should, by putting them to death, you are very much mistaken. That way of escape is neither possible nor honorable. It is much more honorable and much easier not to suppress others, but to make yourselves as good as you can. This is my parting prophecy to you who have condemned me.

With you who have acquitted me I should like to discuss this thing that has happened, while the authorities are busy, and before I go to the place where I have to die. So, remain with me until I go: there is no reason why we should not talk with each other while it is possible. I wish to explain to you, as my friends, the meaning of what has happened to me. A wonderful thing has happened to me, judges—for you I am right in calling judges. The prophetic sign has been constantly with me all through my life till now, opposing me in quite small matters if I were not going to act rightly. And now you yourselves see what has happened to me—a thing which might be thought, and which is sometimes actually reckoned, the supreme evil. But the divine sign did not oppose me when I was leaving my house in the morning, nor when I was coming up here to the court, nor at any point in my speech when I was going to say anything; though at other times it has often stopped me in the very act of speaking. But now, in this matter, it has never once opposed me, either in my words or my actions. I will tell you what I believe to be the reason. This thing that has come upon me must be a good; and those of us who think that death is an evil must needs be mistaken. I have a clear proof that that is so; for my accustomed sign would certainly have opposed me if I had not been going to meet with something good.

And if we reflect in another way, we shall see that we may well hope that death is a good. For the state of death is one of two things: either the dead man wholly ceases to be and loses all consciousness or, as we are told, it is a change and a migration of the soul to another place. And if death is the absence of all consciousness, and like the sleep of one whose slumbers are unbroken by any dreams, it will be a wonderful gain. For if a man had to select that night in which he slept so soundly that he did not even dream, and had to compare with it all the other nights and days of his life, and then had to say how many days and nights in his life he had spent better and more pleasantly than this night, I think that a private person, nay, even the great King himself, would find them easy to count, compared with the others. If that is the nature of death, I for one count it a gain. For then it appears that all time is nothing more than a single night. But if death is a journey to another place, and what we are told is true—that there are all who have died—what good could be greater than this, my judges? Would a journey not be worth taking, at the end of which, in the other world, we should be released from the self-styled judges here and should find the true judges who are said to sit in judgment below, such as Minos and Rhadamanthus and Aeacus and Triptolemus, and the other demigods who were just in their own lives? Or what would you not give to discuss with Orpheus and Musaeus and Hesiod and Homer? I am willing to die many times if this be true. And for my own part I should find it wonderful to meet there Palamedes, and Ajax, the son of Telamon, and the other men of old who have died through an unjust judgment, and in comparing my experiences with theirs. That I think would be no small pleasure. And, above all, I could spend my time in examining those who are there, as I examine men here, and in finding out which of them is wise, and which of them thinks himself wise when he is not wise. What would we not give, my judges, to be able to examine the leader of the great expedition against Troy, or Odysseus, or Sisyphus, or countless other men and women whom we could name? It would be an infinite happiness to discuss with them and to live with them and to examine them. Assuredly there they do not put men to death for doing that. For besides the other ways in which they are happier than we are, they are immortal, at least if what we are told is true.

And you, too, judges, must face death hopefully, and believe this as a truth that no evil can happen to a good man, either in life or after death. His fortunes are not neglected by the gods; and what has happened to me today has not happened by chance. I am persuaded that it was better for me to die now, and to be released from trouble; and that was the reason why the sign never turned me back. And so I am not at all angry with my accusers or with those who have condemned me to die. Yet it was not with this in mind that they accused me and condemned me, but meaning to do me an injury. So far I may blame them.

Yet I have one request to make of them. When my sons grow up, punish them, my friends, and harass them in the same way that I have harrassed you, if they seem to you to care for riches or for any other thing more than virtue; and if they think that they are something when they are really nothing, reproach them, as I have reproached you, for not caring for what they should, and for thinking that they are great men when really they are worthless. And if you will do this, I myself and my sons will have received justice from you.

But now the time has come, and we must go away—I to die, and you to live. Whether life or death is better is known to God, and to God only.

─── THINK ABOUT

1. Do you believe Socrates to be entirely guiltless of the charges? Do the Athenians have a case at all?

2. Think about the metaphor of the gadfly. Who are the gadflies in today's world?

3. Socrates said that "An unexamined life is not worth living." What do you think this means? Can you think of people who haven't examined their lives?

4. Do Socrates' reasons for not fearing death satisfy you? Do you fear death? Do your parents?

Readings

1. Hackforth, R. *Composition of Plato's Apology.* Cambridge: Cambridge U. Press, 1933.

2. Livingstone, Sir Rev. *Portrait of Socrates.* Oxford: Clarendon Press, 1953, pp. xxi–xxii.

3. Montgomery, J. D. *Socrates Versus the State.* New York: Beacon Press, 1954.

4. Robinson, R. *Plato's Earlier Dialectic.* 2nd ed.; Oxford: Oxford U. Press, 1953.

5. Winspear, A. D. & T. Silverberg, *Who Was Socrates?* New York: Russell & Russell, 1960.

6. Woodbridge, F. J. E. *The Son of Apollo.* Boston: Houghton Mifflin, 1929, pp. 254–272.

7. Versenyi, L. *Socratic Humanism.* New Haven: Yale Univ. Press, 1963.

8. Vogel, C. J. de, "The Present State of the Socratic Problem," *Phronesis,* 1 (1955), 22 ff.

2

The Value of Philosophy

Bertrand Russell (1872–1970), the grandson of Lord John Russell, a prime minister under Queen Victoria, was born in Wales. He studied mathematics and philosophy at Trinity College, Cambridge from 1890 to 1894. He was a fellow at Trinity from 1895 to 1901, and a lecturer in philosophy there from 1910 to 1916. In 1916, Russell was dismissed from his position because of his pacifist activities. Then, in 1918, he was sentenced to six months in prison because of an allegedly libelous article in which he expressed his opposition to World War I and his desire for peace. Russell was a fellow of the Royal Society, an honorary fellow of the British Academy, and a recipient of the Order of Merit. He was awarded the Nobel Prize for literature in 1950. In the area of logic, Russell has written *Principles of Mathematics* (1903), *Principia Mathematica* (with A. N. Whitehead; three volumes, 1910–13), and *Introduction to Mathematical Philosophy* (1919). His works in epistemology and metaphysics include *Our Knowledge of the External World* (1914), *The Analysis of Matter* (1927), and *Human Knowledge, Its Scope and Limits* (1948). Among his books on social issues are *Marriage and Morals* (1929), and *Education and the Social Order* (1932).

"Practical men" often dismiss philosophy because they see it as vague and uncertain. Russell agrees that philosophy is concerned with issues, the answers to which are not certain. Yet in this he sees its chief value, namely that in contemplating the great questions one is freed from narrow personal interests alone. He believes that unless you free yourself from your narrow practical world—free yourself from your "instinctive self" (a self concerned only with your immediate personal needs), then most probably you will be assaulted and damaged by the events outside of your private world. The "practical man" who scorns philosophy has in fact a philosophy—usually "rugged individualism"—a philosophy Russell argues is inadequate in part because it fails to meet one's mental needs.

TO STUDY

1. Contrast the utility of science with the utility of philosophy.
2. Why must we free ourselves from the prejudices of the practical men?
3. What was the relation between philosophy and science in the past?
4. With what type of questions does philosophy deal? Give an example.
5. In what does the chief value of philosophy lie, according to Russell? Describe the instinctive man.
6. What is the difference between "enlargement of self" and "self-assertion"?
7. What is the relation of the philosophic mind to the world of action and justice? Can you suggest an example?

Having now come to the end of our brief and very incomplete review of the problems of philosophy, it will be well to consider, in conclusion, what is the value of philosophy and why it ought to be studied. It is the more necessary to consider this question, in view of the fact that many men, under the influence of science or of practical affairs, are inclined to doubt whether philosophy is anything better than innocent but useless trifling, hair-splitting distinctions, and controversies on matters concerning which knowledge is impossible.

This view of philosophy appears to result, partly from a wrong conception of the ends of life, partly from a wrong conception of the kind of goods which philosophy strives to achieve. Physical science, through the medium of inventions, is useful to innumerable people who are wholly ignorant of

---

From *Problems of Philosophy* by Bertrand Russell (Oxford: The Clarendon Press, 1912), Chap. 15. Reprinted by permission of the Clarendon Press, Oxford.

it; thus the study of physical science is to be recommended, not only, or primarily, because of the effect on mankind in general. This utility does not belong to philosophy. If the study of philosophy has any value at all for others than students of philosophy, it must be only indirectly, through its effects upon the lives of those who study it. It is in these effects, therefore, if anywhere, that the value of philosophy must be primarily sought.

But further, if we are not to fail in our endeavour to determine the value of philosophy, we must first free our minds from the prejudices of what are wrongly called "practical" men. The "practical" man, as this word is often used, is one who recognises only material needs, who realises that men must have food for the body, but is oblivious of the necessity of providing food for the mind. If all men were well off, if poverty and disease had been reduced to their lowest possible point, there would still remain much to be done to produce a valuable society; and even in the existing world the goods of the mind are at least as important as the goods of the body. It is exclusively among the goods of the mind that the value of philosophy is to be found; and only those who are not indifferent to these goods can be persuaded that the study of philosophy is not a waste of time.

Philosophy, like all other studies, aims primarily at knowledge. The knowledge it aims at is the kind of knowledge which gives unity and system to the body of the sciences, and the kind which results from a critical examination of the grounds of our convictions, prejudices, and beliefs. But it cannot be maintained that philosophy has had any very great measure of success in its attempts to provide definite answers to its questions. If you ask a mathematician, a mineralogist, a historian, or any other man of learning, what definite body of truths has been ascertained by his science, his answer will last as long as you are willing to listen. But if you put the same question to a philosopher, he will, if he is candid, have to confess that his study has not achieved positive results such as have been achieved by other sciences. It is true that this is partly accounted for by the fact that, as soon as definite knowledge concerning any subject becomes possible, this subject ceases to be called philosophy, and becomes a separate science. The whole study of the heavens, which now belongs to astronomy, was once included in philosophy; Newton's great work was called "the mathematical principles of natural philosophy." Similarly, the study of the human mind, which was, until very lately, a part of philosophy, has now been separated from philosophy and has become the science of psychology. Thus, to a great extent, the uncertainty of philosophy is more apparent than real: those questions which are already capable of definite answers are placed in the sciences, while those only to which, at present, no definite answer can be given, remain to form the residue which is called philosophy.

This is, however, only a part of the truth concerning the uncertainty of philosophy. There are many questions—and among them those that are of the profoundest interest to our spiritual life—which, so far as we can see, must remain insoluble to the human intellect unless its powers become of quite a different order from what they are now. Has the universe any unity of plan of purpose, or is it a fortuitous concourse of atoms? Is consciousness a permanent part of the universe, giving hope of indefinite growth in wisdom, or is it a transitory accident on a small planet on which life must ultimately become impossible? Are good and evil of importance to the universe or only to man? Such questions are asked by philosophy, and variously answered by various philosophers. But it would seem that, whether answers be otherwise discoverable or not, the answers suggested by philosophy are none of them demonstrably true. Yet, however slight may be the hope of discovering an answer, it is part of the business of philosophy to continue the consideration of such questions, to make us aware of their importance, to examine all the approaches to them, and to keep alive that speculative interest in the universe which is apt to be killed by confining ourselves to definitely ascertainable knowledge.

Many philosophers, it is true, have held that philosophy could establish the truth of certain answers to such fundamental questions. They have supposed that what is of most importance in religious beliefs could be proved by strict demonstration to be true. In order to judge of such attempts, it is necessary to take a survey of human knowledge, and to form an opinion as to its methods and its limitations. On such a subject it would be unwise to pronounce dogmatically; but if the investigations of our previous chapters have not led us astray, we shall be compelled to renounce the hope of finding philosophical proofs of religious beliefs. We cannot, therefore, include as part of the value of philosophy any definite set of answers to such questions. Hence, once more, the value of philosophy must not depend upon any supposed body of definitely ascertainable knowledge to be acquired by those who study it.

The value of philosophy is, in fact, to be sought largely in its very uncertainty. The man who has no tincture of philosophy goes through life imprisoned in the prejudices derived from common sense, from the habitual beliefs of his age or his nation, and from convictions which have grown up in his mind without the co-operation or consent of his deliberate reason. To such a man the world tends to become definite, finite, obvious; common objects rouse no questions, and unfamiliar possibilities are contemptuously rejected. As soon as we begin to philosophise, on the contrary, we find, as we saw in our opening chapters, that even the most everyday things lead to problems to which only very incomplete answers can be given. Philosophy, though unable to tell us with certainty what is the true answer to the doubts which it raises, is able to suggest many possibilities which enlarge our thoughts and free them from the tyranny of custom. Thus, while diminishing our feeling of certainty as to what things are, it greatly increases our knowledge as to what they may be; it removes the somewhat arrogant dogmatism of those who have never travelled into the region of liberating doubt, and it keeps alive our sense of wonder by showing familiar things in an unfamiliar aspect.

Apart from its utility in showing unsuspected possibilities, philosophy has a value—perhaps its chief value—through the greatness of the objects which it contemplates, and the freedom from narrow and personal aims resulting from this contemplation. The life of the instinctive man is shut up within the circle of his private interests: family and friends may be included, but the outer world is not regarded except as it may help or hinder what comes within the circle of instinctive wishes. In such a life there is something feverish and confined, in comparison with which the philosophic life is calm and free. The private world of instinctive interests is a small one, set in the midst of a great and powerful world which must, sooner or later, lay our private world in ruins. Unless we can so enlarge our interests as to include the whole outer world, we remain like a garrison in a beleaguered fortress, knowing that the enemy prevents escape and that ultimate surrender is inevitable. In such a life there is no peace, but a constant strife between the insistence of desire and the powerlessness of will. In one way or another, if our life is to be great and free, we must escape this prison and this strife.

One way of escape is by philosophic contemplation. Philosophic contemplation does not, in its widest survey, divide the universe into two hostile camps—friends and foes, helpful and hostile, good and bad—it views the whole impartially. Philosophic contemplation when it is unalloyed, does not aim at proving that the rest of the universe is akin to man. All acquisition of knowledge is an enlargement of the Self, but this enlargement is best attained when it is not directly sought. It is obtained when the desire for knowledge is alone operative, by a study which does not wish in advance that its objects should have this or that character, but adapts the Self to the characters which it finds in its objects. This enlargement of Self is not obtained when, taking the Self as it is, we try to show that the world is so similar to this Self that knowledge of it is possible without any admission of what seems alien. The desire to prove this is a form of self-assertion, and like all self-assertion, it is an obstacle to the growth of Self which it desires, and of which the Self knows that it is capable. Self-assertion, in philosophic speculation as elsewhere, views the world as a means to its own ends; thus its makes the world of less account than Self, and the Self sets bounds to the greatness of its goods. In contemplation, on the contrary, we start from the not-Self, and through its greatness the boundaries of Self are enlarged;

through the infinity of the universe the mind which contemplates it achieves some share in infinity.

For this reason greatness of soul is not fostered by those philosophies which assimilate the universe to Man. Knowledge is a form of union of Self and not-Self; like all union, it is impaired by dominion, and therefore by any attempt to force the universe into conformity with what we find in ourselves. There is a widespread philosophical tendency towards the view which tells us that man is the measure of all things, that truth is man-made, that space and time and the world of universals are properties of the mind, and that, if there be anything not created by the mind, it is unknowable and of no account for us. This view, if our previous discussions were correct, is untrue; but in addition to being untrue, it has the effect of robbing philosophic contemplation of all that gives it value, since it fetters contemplation to Self. What it calls knowledge is not a union with the not-Self, but a set of prejudices, habits, and desires, making an impenetrable veil between us and the world beyond. The man who finds pleasure in such a theory of knowledge is like the man who never leaves the domestic circle for fear his word might not be law.

The true philosophic contemplation, on the contrary, finds its satisfaction in every enlargement of the not-Self, in everything that magnifies the objects contemplated, and thereby the subject contemplating. Everything, in contemplation, that is personal or private, everything that depends upon habit, self-interest, or desire, distorts the object, and hence impairs the union which the intellect seeks. By thus making a barrier between subject and object, such personal and private things become a prison to the intellect. The free intellect will see as God might see, without a *here* and *now,* without hopes and fears, without the trammels of customary beliefs and traditional prejudices, calmly, dispassionately, in the sole and exclusive desire of knowledge—knowledge as impersonal, as purely contemplative, as it is possible for man to attain. Hence also the free intellect will value more the abstract and universal knowledge into which the accidents of private history do not enter, than the knowledge brought by the senses, and dependent, as such knowledge must be, upon an exclusive and personal point of view and a body whose sense-organs distort as much as they reveal.

The mind which has become accustomed to the freedom and impartiality of philosophic contemplation will preserve something of the same freedom and impartiality in the world of action and emotion. It will view its purposes and desires as parts of the whole, with the absence of insistence that results from seeing them as infinitesimal fragments in a world of which all the rest is unaffected by any one man's deeds. The impartiality which, in contemplation, is the unalloyed desire for truth, is the very same quality of mind which, in action, is justice, and in emotion is that universal love which can be given to all, and not only to those who are judged useful or admirable. Thus contemplation enlarges not only the objects of our thoughts, but also the objects of our actions and our affections: it makes us citizens of the universe, not only of one walled city at war with all the rest. In this citizenship of the universe consists man's true freedom, and his liberation from the thraldom of narrow hopes and fears.

Thus, to sum up our discussion of the value of philosophy: Philosophy is to be studied, not for the sake of any definite answers to its questions, since no definite answers can, as a rule, be known to be true, but rather for the sake of the questions themselves; because these questions enlarge our conception of what is possible, enrich our intellectual imagination, and diminish the dogmatic assurance which closes the mind against speculation; but above all because, through the greatness of the universe which philosophy contemplates, the mind also is rendered great, and becomes capable of that union with the universe which constitutes its highest good.

Readings

1.   Russell, Bertrand. *Autobiography.* 3 vols. New York: Simon and Schuster, 1967.
2.   Wood, A. *Bertrand Russell.* New York: St. Martin's, 1956.

2

Methodology:
What Is the Best
Approach to Philosophy?

3

Four Approaches
To Philosophy

Charles Sanders Peirce (1839–1914) is regarded by many
as the most profound and original of American philosophers.
His genius was not recognized in his own lifetime, and he
never held a permanent university position. Peirce published
a number of philosophical articles during his career, but no
book on philosophy.

Every individual has a philosophy, or perhaps, a series of beliefs about
particular philosophic issues. For example, everyone has beliefs about
love, the good life, death, the value of money, duty to country, the role
of government, etc. These beliefs are more or less sophisticated, more
or less elementary, more or less constant, etc. A person arrives at these
beliefs by various methods, e.g., one might get his ideas from his parents,
from the church, or from reading Plato.

One cannot delegate the development of one's philosophy to other
people. It is something that each person must do for himself. There is no
escape. A mature philosophy consists of reflecting upon experience in
search of underlying meanings and principles which can afford guidance
in life. Yet not all people use this mature approach.

The particular approach or approaches with which one confronts problems of philosophy in a large measure determine the particular answer one
finds for each problem. There are several approaches to the various problems. In his essay, "The Fixation of Belief," Peirce distinguishes four
methods by which we habitually fix our beliefs. First there is the *method
of tenacity,* which is fixing one's beliefs according to a person's environment

or personal relationships. These beliefs can be of various subjects such as religion, politics, race, economics, sexual involvement, family, etc. The second Peirce calls the *method of authority,* which involves fixing one's beliefs according to a person, an institution, or a state. One believes that what this authority stated is true. Thirdly, Peirce notes the *a priori* method or the *method of intuition.* Those who follow this method arrive at their beliefs independent of experience, that is, by intuition. Peirce rejects each of these three.

Peirce favors what he calls the *method of science.* This method is seen by Peirce to involve both reason and observation as employed in any natural science and, thereby, establishes the nature of the real. He argues that the scientific method alone among the methods can distinguish the true from the false. It alone can settle disagreements in belief.

TO STUDY

1. Why do few people care to study logic?
2. What determines us to draw one inference rather than another one?
3. What distinguishes doubt from belief?
4. What is the role of inquiry?
5. What is the method of tenacity? What are its weaknesses?
6. What is the method of authority? What are its weaknesses?
7. What is the *a priori* method? What are its weaknesses?
8. What is the method of science? What are its advantages?

Few persons care to study logic, because everybody conceives himself to be proficient enough in the art of reasoning already. But I observe that this satisfaction is limited to one's own ratiocination, and does not extend to that of other men.

We come to the full possession of our power of drawing inferences, the last of all our faculties, for it is not so much a natural gift as a long and difficult art. The history of its practice would make a grand subject for a book.

We are, doubtless, in the main logical animals, but we are not perfectly

---

From *Popular Science Monthly,* 1877.

so. Most of us, for example, are naturally more sanguine and hopeful than logic would justify. We seem to be so constituted that, in the absence of any facts to go upon, we are happy and self-satisfied; so that the effect of experience is continually to counteract our hopes and aspirations. Yet a lifetime of the application of this corrective does not usually eradicate our sanguine disposition. Where hope is unchecked by any experience, it is likely that our optimism is extravagant. Logicality in regard to practical matters is the most useful quality an animal can possess, and might, there-fore, result from the action of natural selection; but outside of these, it is probably of more advantage to the animal to have his mind filled with pleasing and encouraging visions, independently of their truth; and thus, upon unpractical subjects, natural selection might occasion a fallacious tendency of thought.

That which determines us, from given premises, to draw one inference rather than another, is some habit of mind, whether it be constitutional or acquired. The habit is good or otherwise, according as it produces true conclusions from true premises or not; and an inference is regarded as valid or not, without reference to the truth or falsity of its conclusion specially, but according as the habit which determines it is such as to produce true conclusions in general or not. The particular habit of mind which governs this or that inference may be formulated in a proposition whose truth depends on the validity of the inferences which the habit determines; and such a formula is called a *guiding principle* of inference. Suppose, for example, that we observe that a rotating disk of copper quickly comes to rest when placed between the poles of a magnet, and we infer that this will happen with every disk of copper. The guiding principle is, that what is true of one piece of copper is true of another. Such a guiding principle with regard to copper would be much safer than with regard to many other substances—brass, for example.

The subject could hardly be treated, however, without being first lim-ited; since almost any fact may serve as a guiding principle. But it so happens that there exists a division among facts, such that in one class are all those which are absolutely essential as guiding principles, while in the other are all those which have any other interest as objects of research. This division is between those which are necessarily taken for granted in asking whether a certain conclusion follows from certain premises, and those which are not implied in that question. A moment's thought will show that a variety of facts are already assumed when the logical question is first asked. It is implied, for instance, that there are such states of mind as doubt and belief—that a passage from one to the other is possible, the object of thought remaining the same, and that this transition is subject to some rules which all minds are alike bound by. As these are facts which we must already know before we can have any clear conception of reasoning at all, it cannot be supposed to be any longer of much interest to inquire into their truth or falsity. On the other hand, it is easy to believe that those rules of reasoning which are deduced from the very idea of the process are the ones which are the most essential; and, indeed, that so long as it conforms to these it will, at least, not lead to false conclusions from true premises. In point of fact, the importance of what may be deduced from the assumptions involved in the logical question turns out to be greater than might be supposed, and this for reasons which it is difficult to exhibit at the outset.

We generally know when we wish to ask a question and when we wish to pronounce a judgment, for there is a dissimilarity between the sensation of doubting and that of believing.

But this is not all which distinguishes doubt from belief. There is a practical difference. Our beliefs guide our desires and shape our actions. The Assassins, or followers of the Old Man of the Mountain, used to rush into death at his least command, because they believed that obedience to him would insure everlasting felicity. Had they doubted this, they would not have acted as they did. So it is with every belief, according to its degree. The feeling of believing is a more or less sure indication of there being established in our nature some habit which will determine our actions. Doubt never has such an effect.

Nor must we overlook a third point of difference. Doubt is an uneasy and dissatisfied state from which we struggle to free ourselves and pass into the state of belief; while the latter is a calm and satisfactory state which we do not wish to avoid, or to change to a belief in anything else. On the contrary, we cling tenaciously, not merely to believing, but to believing just what we do believe.

Thus, both doubt and belief have positive effects upon us, though very different ones. Belief does not make us act at once, but puts us into such a condition that we shall behave in a certain way, when the occasion arises. Doubt has not the least effect of this sort, but stimulates us to action until it is destroyed. This reminds us of the irritation of a nerve and the reflex action produced thereby; while for the analogue of belief, in the nervous system, we must look to what are called nervous associations—for example, to that habit of the nerves in consequence of which the smell of a peach will make the mouth water.

The irritation of doubt causes a struggle to attain a state of belief. I shall term this struggle *inquiry*, though it must be admitted that this is sometimes not a very apt designation.

The irritation of doubt is the only immediate motive for the struggle to attain belief. It is certainly best for us that our beliefs should be such as may truly guide our actions so as to satisfy our desires; and this reflection will make us reject any belief which does not seem to have been so formed as to insure this result. But it will only do so by creating doubt in the place of that belief. With the doubt, therefore, the struggle begins, and with the cessation of doubt it ends. Hence, the sole object of inquiry is the settlement of opinion. We may fancy that this is not enough for us, and that we seek, not merely an opinion, but a true opinion. But put this fancy to the test, and it proves groundless; for as soon as a firm belief is reached we are entirely satisfied, whether the belief be false or true. And it is clear that nothing out of the sphere of our knowledge can be our object, for nothing which does not affect the mind can be a motive for mental effort. The most that can be maintained is that we seek for a belief that we shall *think* to be true. But we think each one of our beliefs to be true, and, indeed, it is mere tautology to say so.

That the settlement of opinion is the sole end of inquiry is a very important proposition. It sweeps away, at once, various vague and erroneous conceptions of proof. A few of these may be noticed here.

1. Some philosophers have imagined that to start an inquiry it was only necessary to utter a question or set it down on paper, and have even recommended us to begin our studies with questioning everything! But the mere putting of a proposition into the interrogative form does not stimulate the mind to any struggle after belief. There must be a real and living doubt, and without this all discussion is idle.

2. It is a very common idea that a demonstration must rest on some ultimate and absolutely indubitable propositions. These, according to one school, are first principles of a general nature; according to another, are first sensations. But, in point of fact, an inquiry, to have that completely satisfactory result called demonstration, has only to start with propositions perfectly free from all actual doubt. If the premises are not in fact doubted at all, they cannot be more satisfactory than they are.

3. Some people seem to love to argue a point after all the world is fully convinced of it. But no further advance can be made. When doubt ceases, mental action on the subject comes to an end; and, if it did go on, it would be without a purpose.

If the settlement of opinion is the sole object of inquiry, and if belief is of the nature of a habit, why should we not attain the desired end by taking any answer to a question, which we may fancy, and constantly reiterating it to ourselves, dwelling on all which may conduce to that belief, and learning to turn with contempt and hatred from anything which might disturb it? This simple and direct method is really pursued by many men. I remember once being entreated not to read a certain newspaper lest it might change my opinion upon free trade. "Lest I might be entrapped by its fallacies and misstatements," was the form of expression. "You are not," my friend said, "a special student of political economy. You might, therefore, easily be deceived by fallacious arguments upon the subject. You might, then, if you read this paper, be led to believe in protection. But you admit that free trade is the true doctrine; and you do not wish to believe what is not true." I have often known this system to be deliberately adopted. Still oftener, the instinctive dislike of an undecided state of mind, exaggerated into a vague dread of doubt, makes men cling spasmodically to the views they already take. The man feels that, if he only holds to his belief without wavering, it will be entirely satisfactory. Nor can it be denied that a steady and immovable faith yields great peace of mind. It may, indeed, give rise to inconveniences, as if a man should resolutely continue to believe that fire would not burn him, or that he would be eternally damned if he received his *ingesta* otherwise than through a stomach-pump. But then the man who adopts this method will not allow that its inconveniences are greater than its advantages. He will say, "I hold steadfastly to the truth and the truth is always wholesome." And in many cases it may very well be that the pleasure he derives from his calm faith overbalances any inconveniences resulting from its deceptive character. Thus, if it be true that death is annihilation, then the man who believes that he will certainly go straight to heaven when he dies, provided he have fulfilled certain simple observances in this life, has a cheap pleasure which will not be followed by the least disappointment. A similar consideration seems to have weight with many persons in religious topics, for we frequently hear it said, "Oh, I could not believe so-and-so, because I should be wretched if I did." When an ostrich buries its head in the sand as danger approaches, it very likely takes the happiest course. It hides the danger, and then calmly says there is no danger; and, if it feels perfectly sure there is none, why should it raise its head to see? A man may go through life systematically keeping out of view all that might cause a change in his opinions, and if he only succeeds—basing his method, as he does, on two fundamental psychological laws—I do not see what can be said against his doing so. It would be an egotistical impertinence to object that his procedure is irrational, for that only amounts to saying that his method of settling belief is not ours. He does not propose to himself to be rational, and, indeed, will often talk with scorn of man's weak and illusive reason. So let him think as he pleases.

But this method of fixing belief, which may be called the method of tenacity, will be unable to hold its ground in practice. The social impulse is against it. The man who adopts it will find that other men think differently from him, and it will be apt to occur to him in some saner moment that their opinions are quite as good as his own, and this will shake his confidence in his belief. This conception, that another man's thought or sentiment may be equivalent to one's own, is a distinctly new step, and a highly important one. It arises from an impulse too strong in man to be suppressed without danger of destroying the human species. Unless we make ourselves hermits, we shall necessarily influence each other's opinions; so that the problem becomes how to fix belief, not in the individual merely, but in the community.

Let the will of the state act, then, instead of that of the individual. Let an institution be created which shall have for its object to keep correct doctrines before the attention of the people, to reiterate them perpetually, and to teach them to the young; having at the same time power to prevent contrary doctrines from being taught, advocated, or expressed. Let all possible causes of a change of mind be removed from men's apprehensions. Let them be kept ignorant, lest they should learn of some reason to think otherwise than they do. Let their passions be enlisted, so that they may regard private and unusual opinions with hatred and horror. Then, let all men who reject the established belief be terrified into silence. Let the people turn out and tar-and-feather such men, or let inquisitions be made into the manner of thinking of suspected persons, and, when they are found guilty of forbidden beliefs, let them be subjected to some signal punishment. When complete agreement could not otherwise be reached, a general massacre of all who have not thought in a certain way has proved a very effective means of settling opinion in a country. If the power to do this be wanting, let a list of opinions be drawn up, to which no man of the least independence of thought can assent, and let the faithful be required to accept all these propositions, in order to segregate them as radically as possible from the influence of the rest of the world.

This method has, from the earliest times, been one of the chief means of upholding correct theological and political doctrines, and of preserving their universal or catholic character. In Rome, especially, it has been practiced from the days of Numa Pompilius to those of Pius Nonus. This is the most perfect example in history; but wherever there is a priesthood—and no religion has been without one—this method has been more or less made use of. Wherever there is an aristocracy, or a guild, or any association of a class of men whose interests depend, or are supposed to depend, on certain propositions, there will be inevitably found some traces of this natural product of social feeling. Cruelties always accompany this system; and when it is consistently carried out, they become atrocities of the most horrible kind in the eyes of any rational man. Nor should this occasion surprise, for the officer of a society does not feel justified in surrendering the interests of that society for the sake of mercy, as he might his own private interests. It is natural, therefore, that sympathy and fellowship should thus produce a most ruthless power.

In judging this method of fixing belief, which may be called the method of authority, we must, in the first place, allow its immeasurable mental and moral superiority to the method of tenacity. Its success is proportionately greater; and, in fact, it has over and over again worked the most majestic results. The mere structures of stone which it has caused to be put together —in Siam, for example, in Egypt, and in Europe—have many of them a sublimity hardly more than rivalled by the greatest works of Nature. And, except the geological epochs, there are no periods of time so vast as those which are measured by some of these organized faiths. If we scrutinize the matter closely, we shall find that there has not been one of their creeds which has remained always the same; yet the change is so slow as to be imperceptible during one person's life, so that individual belief remains sensibly fixed. For the mass of mankind, then, there is perhaps no better method than this. If it is their highest impulse to be intellectual slaves, then slaves they ought to remain.

But no institution can undertake to regulate opinions upon every subject. Only the most important ones can be attended to, and on the rest men's minds must be left to the action of natural causes. This imperfection will be no source of weakness so long as men are in such a state of culture that one opinion does not influence another—that is, so long as they cannot put two and two together. But in the most priest-ridden states some individuals will be found who are raised above that condition. These men possess a wider sort of social feeling; they see that men in other countries and in other ages have held to very different doctrines from those which they themselves have been brought up to believe; and they cannot help seeing that it is the mere accident of their having been taught as they have, and of their having been surrounded with the manners and associations they have, that has caused them to believe as they do and not far differently. Nor can their candor resist the reflection that there is no reason to rate their own views at a higher value than those of other nations and other centuries; thus giving rise to doubts in their minds.

They will further perceive that such doubts as these must exist in their minds with reference to every belief which seems to be determined by the caprice either of themselves or of those who originated the popular opinions. The willful adherence to a belief, and the arbitrary forcing of it upon others, must, therefore, both be given up. A different new method of settling opinions must be adopted, that shall not only produce an impulse to believe, but shall also decide what proposition it is which is to be believed. Let the action of natural preferences be unimpeded, then, and under their influence let men, conversing together and regarding matters in different lights, gradually develop beliefs in harmony with natural causes. This method resembles that by which conceptions of art have been brought to maturity.

The most perfect example of it is to be found in the history of metaphysical philosophy. Systems of this sort have not usually rested upon any observed facts, at least not in any great degree. They have been chiefly adopted because their fundamental propositions seemed "agreeable to reason." This is an apt expression; it does not mean that which agrees with experience, but that which we find ourselves inclined to believe. Plato, for example, finds it agreeable to reason that the distances of the celestial spheres from one another should be proportional to the different lengths of strings which produce harmonious chords. Many philosophers have been led to their main conclusions by considerations like this; but this is the lowest and least developed from which the method takes, for it is clear that another man might find Kepler's theory, that the celestial spheres are proportional to the inscribed and circumscribed spheres of the different regular solids, more agreeable to *his* reason. But the shock of opinions will soon lead men to rest on preferences of a far more universal nature. Take, for example, the doctrine that man only acts selfishly—that is, from the consideration that acting in one way will afford him more pleasure than acting in another. This rests on no fact in the world, but it has had a wide acceptance as being the only reasonable theory.

This method is far more intellectual and respectable from the point of view of reason than either of the others which we have noticed. But its failure has been the most manifest. It makes of inquiry something similar to the development of taste; but taste, unfortunately, is always more or less a matter of fashion, and accordingly metaphysicians have never come to any fixed agreement, but the pendulum has swung backward and forward between a more material and a more spiritual philosophy, from the earliest times to the latest. And so from this, which has been called the *a priori* method, we are driven, in Lord Bacon's phrase, to a true induction. We have examined into this *a priori* method as something which promised to deliver our opinions from their accidental and capricious element. But development, while it is a process which eliminates the effect of some casual circumstances, only magnifies that of others. This method, therefore, does not differ in a very essential way from that of authority. The government may not have lifted its finger to influence my convictions; I may have been left outwardly quite free to choose, we will say, between monogamy and polygamy, and, appealing to my conscience only, I may have concluded that the latter practice is in itself licentious. But when I come to see that the chief obstacle to the spread of Christianity among a people of as high culture as the Hindus has been a conviction of the immorality of our way of treating women, I cannot help seeing that, though governments do not interfere, sentiments in their development will be very greatly determined by accidental causes. Now, there are some people, among whom I must suppose that my reader is to be found, who, when they see that any belief of theirs is determined by any circumstance extraneous to the facts, will from that moment not merely admit in words that that belief is doubtful, but will experience a real doubt of it, so that it ceases in some degree to be a belief.

To satisfy our doubts, therefore, it is necessary that a method should be found by which our beliefs may be caused by nothing human, but by some external permanency—by something upon which our thinking has no effect. Some mystics imagine that they have such a method in a private inspiration from on high. But that is only a form of the method of tenacity, in which the conception of truth as something public is not yet developed. Our external permanency would not be external, in our sense, if it was restricted in its influence to one individual. It must be something which affects, or might affect, every man. And, though these affections are necessarily as various as are individual conditions, yet the method must be such that the ultimate conclusion of every man shall be the same. Such is the method of science. Its fundamental hypothesis, restated in more familiar language, is this: There are Real things, whose characters are entirely independent of our opinions about them; those realities affect our senses according to regular laws, and, though our sensations are as different as are our relations to the objects, yet, by taking advantage of the laws of perception, we can ascertain by reasoning how things really are; and any man, if he have sufficient experience and he reason enough about it, will be led to the one True conclusion. The new conception here involved is that of Reality. It may be asked how I know that there are any realities. If this hypothesis is the sole support of my method of inquiry, my method of inquiry must not be used to support my hypothesis. The reply is this: 1. If investigation cannot be regarded as proving that there are Real things, it at least does not lead to a contrary conclusion; but the method and the conception on which it is based remain ever in harmony. No doubts of the method, therefore, necessarily arise from its practice, as is the case with all the others. 2. The feeling which gives rise to any method of fixing belief is a dissatisfaction at two repugnant propositions. But here already is a vague concession that there is some *one* thing to which a proposition should conform. Nobody, therefore, can really doubt that there are realities, for, if he did, doubt would not be a source of dissatisfaction. The hypothesis, therefore, is one which every mind admits. So that the social impulse does not cause men to doubt it. 3. Everybody uses the scientific method about a great many things, and only ceases to use it when he does not know how to apply it. 4. Experience of the method has not led us to doubt it, but, on the contrary, scientific investigation has had the most wonderful triumphs in the way of settling opinion. These afford the explanation of my not doubting the method or the hypothesis which it supposes; and not having any doubt, nor believing that anybody else whom I could influence has, it would be the merest babble for me to say more about it If there be anybody with a living doubt upon the subject, let him consider it. . . .

This is the only one of the four methods which presents any distinction of a right and a wrong way. If I adopt the method of tenacity, and shut myself out from all influences, whatever I think necessary to doing this, is necessary according to that method. So with the method of authority: the state may try to put down heresy by means which, from a scientific point of view, seem very ill-calculated to accomplish its purposes; but the only test *on that method* is what the state thinks; so that it cannot pursue the method wrongly. So with the *a priori* method. The very essence of it is to think as one is inclined to think. All metaphysicians will be sure to do that, however they may be inclined to judge each other to be perversely wrong. Hegel's system of Nature represents tolerably the science of that day; and one may be sure that whatever scientific investigation has put out of doubt will presently receive *a priori* demonstration on the part of the metaphysicians. But with the scientific method the case is different. I may start with known and observed facts to proceed to the unknown; and yet the rules which I follow in doing so may not be such as investigation would approve. The test of whether I am truly following the method is not an immediate appeal to my feelings and purposes, but, on the contrary, itself involves the application of the method. Hence it is that bad reasoning as well as good reasoning is possible; and this fact is the foundation of the practical side of logic.

It is not to be supposed that the first three methods of settling opinion present no advantage whatever over the scientific method. On the contrary, each has some peculiar convenience of its own. The *a priori* method is distinguished for its comfortable conclusions. It is the nature of the process to adopt whatever belief we are inclined to, and there are certain flatteries to the vanity of man which we all believe by nature, until we are awakened from our pleasing dream by rough facts. The method of authority will always govern the mass of mankind; and those who wield the various forms of organized force in the state will never be convinced that dangerous reasoning ought not to be suppressed in some way. If liberty of speech is to be untrammelled from the grosser forms of constraint, then uniformity of opinion will be secured by a moral terrorism to which the respectability of society will give its thorough approval. Following the method of authority is the path of peace. Certain non-conformities are permitted; certain others (considered unsafe) are forbidden. These are different in different countries and in different ages; but, wherever you are, let it be known that you seriously hold a tabooed belief, and you may be perfectly sure of being treated with a cruelty less brutal but more refined than hunting you like a wolf. Thus, the greatest intellectual benefactors of mankind have never dared, and dare not now, to utter the whole of their thought; and thus a shade of *prima facie* doubt is cast upon every proposition which is considered essential to the security of society. Singularly enough, the persecution does not all come from without; but a man torments himself and is oftentimes most distressed at finding himself believing propositions which he has been brought up to regard with aversion. The peaceful and sympathetic man will, therefore, find it hard to resist the temptation to submit his opinions to authority. But most of all I admire the method of tenacity for its strength, simplicity, and directness. Men who pursue it are distinguished for their decision of character, which becomes very easy with such a mental rule. They do not waste time in trying to make up their minds what they want, but, fastening like lightning upon whatever alternative comes first, they hold it to the end, whatever happens, without an instant's irresolution. This is one of the splendid qualities which generally accompany brilliant, unlasting success. It is impossible not to envy the man who can dismiss reason, although we know how it must turn out at last.

Such are the advantages which the other methods of settling opinion have over scientific investigation. A man should consider well of them; and then he should consider that, after all, he wishes his opinions to coincide with the fact and that there is no reason why the result of those three methods should do so. To bring about this effect is the prerogative of the method of science. Upon such considerations he has to make his choice—a choice which is far more than the adoption of any intellectual opinion, which is one of the ruling decisions of his life, to which, when once made, he is bound to adhere. The force of habit will sometimes cause a man to hold on to old beliefs, after he is in a condition to see that they have no sound basis. But reflection upon the state of the case will overcome these habits, and he ought to allow reflection its full weight. People sometimes shrink from doing this, having an idea that beliefs are wholesome which they cannot help feeling rest on nothing. But let such persons suppose an analogous though different case from their own. Let them ask themselves what they would say to a reformed Mussulman who should hesitate to give up his old notions in regard to the relations of the sexes; or to a reformed Catholic who should still shrink from reading the Bible. Would they not say that these persons ought to consider the matter fully, and clearly understand the new doctrine, and then ought to embrace it, in its entirety? But, above all, let it be considered that what is more wholesome than any particular belief is integrity of belief, and that to avoid looking into the support of any belief from a fear that it may turn out rotten is quite as immoral as it is disadvantageous. The person who confesses that there is such a thing as truth, which is distinguished from falsehood simply by this, that if acted on it will carry us to the point we aim at and not astray, and then, though convinced of this, dares not know the truth and seeks to avoid it, is in a sorry state of mind indeed.

Yes, the other methods do have their merits: a clear logical conscience does cast something—just as any virtue, just as all that we cherish, costs us dear. But we should not desire it to be otherwise. The genius of a man's logical method should be loved and reverenced as his bride, whom he has chosen from all the world. He need not condemn the others; on the contrary, he may honor them deeply, and in doing so he only honors her the more. But she is the one that he has chosen, and he knows that he was right in making that choice. And having made it, he will work and fight for her, and will not complain that there are blows to take, hoping that there may be as many and as hard to give, and will strive to be the worthy knight and champion of her from the blaze of whose splendors he draws his inspiration and his courage.

4

The Scientific Outlook

Herbert Feigl (1902–) was educated at the University of Vienna when the scientific philosophy of logical positivism was at its height. He taught at the University of Minnesota until he retired in 1971. He is very well known for his many publications in the philosophy of science.

Peirce argued that the best approach by which to establish a philosophy was via a scientific approach. Feigl's article is meant to show that approach in more detail. Feigl discusses the relations between science and the humanities as well as the basic characteristics of the scientific method. He sees the aims of science to be description, explanation, and prediction. Furthermore, he conceives science to be regulated by certain criteria: intersubjectiveness, testing ability, sufficient degree of confirmation, precision, coherence, and comprehensiveness. All of these give science its progressive character and sense of experimental certainty. He also contends that science can contribute to making better value judgments.

──TO STUDY

1. Explain the reductive and seductive fallacies.
2. What is the difference between the formal and the factual sciences?
3. What are the three aims of science?
4. Explain "intersubjective test ability."

5. Explain "reliability" in science.
6. Explain both coherence and comprehensiveness as related to a scientific system.
7. Discuss at least one misconception of science with which you either strongly agree or disagree.
8. Discuss Feigl's view of the relation between science and values.

The main purpose of this essay is to dispel certain confusions and misunderstandings which still prevent the much-needed constructive synthesis and mutual supplementation of the scientific and humanistic elements in general education. It is my contention that the philosophical foundations of both science and the humanities are widely misconceived; and that the frequently held claim of their basic incompatibilities arises out of philosophical prejudices which, owing to cultural lag, have unfortunately not as yet been completely relegated to oblivion. Science is still identified with an absurd mechanistic reductionism, but this is the caricature of science drawn by representatives of the humanities who are largely ignorant of the nature of modern science and also of the more recent scientific outlook in philosophy. The defenders of the humanities often enough increase the existing tension by holding an equally distorted view of the philosophical basis of the humanities.

The errors committed may well be characterized respectively as *reductive* and *seductive* fallacies. It is claimed that science either ignores (perhaps by its very method cannot help ignoring) or else explains away the most essential human values. Science is here charged with the reductive fallacy. Usually the same group of thinkers maintains also that there are aspects of the human mind, manifest especially in the domains of morality, religion, and the arts, which contain an irreducible spiritual element and for that reason will never be capable of explanation by the scientific method, no matter how far it advances. I call this fallacy seductive because it is usually committed by those who indulge in what William James called "tender-minded," that is, wishful and sentimental, thinking.

The impasse between seductive thesis and reductive antithesis can be overcome only by a constructive synthesis that retains and develops whatever valid suggestions or emphases we may discover underneath the grandiose verbiage of the first and the harsh austerities of the second. Neither a

From Herbert Feigl, "Naturalism and Humanism," *American Quarterly* 1 (1949), 135–148. Copyright, 1949, Trustees of the University of Pennsylvania. Reprinted with permission of the publisher and the author.

philosophy of the "Something More" nor a philosophy of the "Nothing But" will do for our time. Only an approach that is resolutely guided by the question "What is what?" will avoid reading mysteries into the facts, as well as refrain from impoverishing them by reduction to something less than experience attests them to be. Such a philosophical outlook, if not yet fully achieved, is fortunately very much in the making.

Especially in the melting pot of American thought, we find that the valuable elements of naturalism and humanism are gradually united in a new integration: the pragmatism of Peirce, James, Dewey, Mead, Otto, Kallen, and Hook; the naturalistic realism of Perry, Holt, R. W. Sellars, Drake, and Santayana; the scientific empiricism of Bridgman, Hull, Tolman, Lundberg, N. Wiener, P. Frank, C. Morris, Northrop, Carnap, Reichenbach, Nagel, and others; the liberal ("American Humanist") wing of Unitarianism. All these trends of thought and many others converge in a broad movement that one may well be tempted to regard as the twentieth-century sequel to the enlightenment of the eighteenth century.

The humanism held in common to a very large extent in these scientifically oriented philosophies is too well known to require an elaborate restatement. Suffice it to say that such human values as freedom and responsibility, rights and obligations, creative and appreciative capacities, are here disengaged from the theological and metaphysical ideologies that have traditionally pervaded their conception. Increasingly adequate and nonreductive analyses have been propounded in the last five or six decades. This reconstruction in philosophy has been and still is in the making. Under the impact of modern science philosophy is abandoning some of its earlier grandiose and overambitious claims in favor of a humbler and more useful function: the clarification of the foundations of knowledge and valuation. I shall now attempt to apply what seem to me to be the most important insights and suggestions of these currents of thought to the issues of general education.

Clearly, nothing is more urgent for education today than a social philosophy that will be appropriate and workable in an age of science. Among the various prominent philosophies of education I mention first two currents which may be styled traditionalistic and which have on the whole either ignored the facts of the age of science or have tried (unsuccessfully, I think) to dispute and combat them: Neo-Thomism and Literary Humanism. Reliance on theological or metaphysical presuppositions makes these views incompatible with the modern scientific outlook. More definitely products of the modern scientific attitude are two other schools of thought: Dialectical Materialism, the official philosophy of Soviet Russia, but also fashionable in certain English scientific groups; and, scarcely worthy of being called a philosophy, the attitude of Vocationalism, quite prevalent in American education. The common element of these two views is their exclusive interest in the practical, technological applications of the natural and the social sciences. This, as well as other shortcomings, makes both points of view appear objectionable or at least badly in need of correction or supplementation. A much more acceptable position is that of Scientific Humanism. This view, at least in general outlook, is related to what is known as Progressivism or Reconstructionism in American education: a synthesis of the scientific attitude with an active interest in the whole scale of human values. Education in both the sciences *and* the humanities is the urgent need of our time. But how can these two aims properly be combined? The question reveals an uneasy feeling as to the compatibility of science and humanism.

Misunderstandings of the nature of science are primarily responsible for the appearance of incompatibility here. A proper historical and analytical perspective of the development of the scientific outlook and its distinctive traits as compared with prescientific and nonscientific attitudes helps to show that mankind achieves intellectual adulthood only with the scientific way of thinking.

The scientific view of the world that we have characterized and defended against criticisms from various quarters may with historical and terminological justice be called Naturalism.[4] It differs from mechanistic materialism (too often a mere straw man put up by theologians or idealistic metaphysicians) in that it steers clear of reductive fallacies. If uninformed persons insist on viewing science as essentially materialistic and the humanities as essentially idealistic (not to say spiritualistic) the hopes of fruitful collaboration of both fields in education are slim indeed. But science, properly interpreted, is not dependent on any sort of metaphysics. It merely attempts to cover a maximum of facts by a minimum of laws. On the other side, a mature humanism requires no longer a theological or metaphysical frame either. Human nature and human history become progressively understood in the light of advancing science. It is therefore no longer justifiable to speak of science *versus* the humanities. Naturalism *and* humanism should be our maxim in philosophy and in education. A Scientific Humanism emerges as a philosophy holding considerable promise for mankind—*if* mankind will at all succeed in growing up.

Our age is still replete with remnants of and regressions to such prescientific thought patterns as magic, animism, mythology, theology, and metaphysics. The outstanding characteristics of modern scientific method are mostly absent or at best only adumbrated in those less mature phases of intellectual growth.

---

[4] It should scarcely need mentioning that this meaning of naturalism has only a distant and tenuous relation to the other meaning in which it is applied to a certain type of literature.

Criteria of the Scientific Method

What, then, are the basic characteristics of the scientific method? The often alleged difficulties of an adequate definition of science seem to me mainly a matter of terminology. We must first distinguish between pure mathematics as an exclusively formal-conceptual discipline, and the factual (or empirical, that is, the natural and the social-cultural) sciences. The certainty, complete exactitude, and necessity of pure mathematics depends precisely on its detachment from empirical fact. Mathematics as applied in the factual sciences merely lends its forms and deductive structures to the contents furnished by experience. But no matter how predominant mathematics may be in the formulations and derivations of empirical facts, factual knowledge cannot attain either the absolute precision or necessity of pure mathematics. The knowledge claimed in the natural and the social sciences is a matter of successive approximations and of increasing degrees of confirmation. Warranted assertibility or probability is all that we can conceivably secure in the sciences that deal with the facts of experience. It is empirical science, thus conceived as an unending quest (its truth-claims to be held only "until further notice"), which is under consideration here. Science in this sense differs only in degree from the knowledge accumulated throughout the ages by sound and common sense.

The aims of science are description, explanation, and prediction. The first aim is basic and indispensable, the second and third (closely related to each other) arise as the most desirable fruits of scientific labors whenever inquiry rises beyond the mere fact-gathering stage. History, often and nowadays quite fashionably declared an art, is scientific to the extent that it ascertains its facts concerning past events by a meticulous scrutiny of present evidence. Causal interpretation of these facts (in history, but similarly also in psychology, sociology, cultural anthropology, and economics) is usually much more difficult than, but in principle not logically different from, causal interpretation (that is, explanation) in the natural sciences. The aims of the pure (empirical) sciences are then essentially the same throughout the whole field. What the scientists are seeking are descriptions, explanations, and predictions which are as adequate and accurate as possible in the given context of research.

The quest for scientific knowledge is therefore regulated by certain standards or criteria which may best be formulated in the form of ideals to be approximated, but perhaps never fully attained. The most important of these regulative ideals are:

1. *Intersubjective Testability.*   This is only a more adequate formulation of what is generally meant by the "objectivity" of science. What is here

involved is not only the freedom from personal or cultural bias or partiality, but—even more fundamentally—the requirement that the knowledge claims of science be in principle capable of test (confirmation or disconfirmation, at the least indirectly and to some degree) on the part of any person properly equipped with intelligence and the technical devices of observation or experimentation. The term *intersubjective* stresses the social nature of the scientific enterprise. If there be any "truths" that are accessible only to privileged individuals, such as mystics or visionaries—that is, knowledge-claims which by their very nature cannot independently be checked by anyone else—then such "truths" are not of the kind that we seek in the sciences. The criterion of intersubjective testability thus delimits the scientific from the nonscientific activities of man.

Religious ecstasy, the elations of love, the inspiration of the artist, yes, even the flash of insight on the part of a scientific genius are not in themselves scientific activities. All these processes may eventually become subject matter for scientific study. But in themselves they do not validate knowledge-claims. They may, as in the case of the scientific intuition (or empathy in the psychological-cultural field) be instrumental in the generation of knowledge claims. But it is these knowledge-claims which have to be, first, formulated in an intersubjectively intelligible (or communicable) manner, and, second, subjected to the appropriate kind of tests in order to ascertain their validity. Beliefs transcending all possible tests by observation, self-observation, experiment, measurement, or statistical analysis are recognized as theological or metaphysical and therefore devoid of the type of meaning that we all associate with the knowledge-claims of common sense or factual science. From the point of view of the scientific outlook in philosophy it may be suggested that the sort of significance with which the in-principle-unconfirmable assertions of transcendent theology and metaphysics impress so many people is largely emotive. The pictorial, emotional, and motivational appeals of language, no matter how indispensable or valuable in the contexts of practical life, art, education, persuasion, and propaganda, must, however, not be confused with the cognitive meanings (purely formal- and/or factual-empirical) that are of the essence of science. Each type of significance has its function, and in most uses of language both are combined or even fused. The only point stressed here is that they must not be *con*fused, that is, mistaken for one another, if we wish to be clear as to what we are about.

2. *Reliability, or a Sufficient Degree of Confirmation.*   This second criterion of scientific knowledge enables us to distinguish what is generally called "mere opinion" (or worse still, "superstition") from knowledge (well-substantiated belief). It may be considered as the delimitation of the scientific

from the unscientific knowledge-claims. Clearly, in contrast to the first criterion, we face here a distinction of degree. There is no sharp line of demarcation between the well-confirmed laws, theories, or hypotheses of science, and the only poorly substantiated hunches and ideas-on-trial which may ultimately either be included in the corpus of scientific knowledge or else rejected as unconfirmed. Truth-claims which we repudiate as "superstition," and, quite generally, as judgments based upon hasty generalization or weak analogy (if they fulfill the criterion of testability), differ from what we accept as "scientific truth" in the extremely low degree of probability to which they are supported by the available evidence. Astrology or alchemy, for example, are not factually meaningless, but they are considered false to fact in that all available evidence speaks overwhelmingly against them. Modern techniques of experimentation and of statistical analysis are the most powerful tools we have in the discernment between chance and law and hence the best means of enhancing the reliability of knowledge.

3. *Definiteness and Precision.*   This obvious standard of scientific method requires that the concepts used in the formulation of scientific knowledge-claims be as definitely delimited as possible. On the level of the qualitative-classificatory sciences this amounts to the attempt to reduce all border-zone vagueness to a minimum. On the level of quantitative science the exactitude of the concepts is enormously enhanced through the application of the techniques of measurement. The mensurational devices usually also increase the degree of objectivity. This is especially clear when they are contrasted with purely impressionistic ways of estimating magnitudes. Of course, there is no point in sharpening precision to a higher degree than the problem in hand requires. (You need no razor to cut butter.)

4. *Coherence or Systematic Structure.*   This is what T. H. Huxley had in mind when he defined science as "organized common-sense." Not a mere collection of miscellaneous items of information, but a well-connected account of the facts is what we seek in science. On the descriptive level this results, for example, in systems of classification or division, in diagrams, statistical charts, and the like. On the explanatory levels of science sets of laws, or theoretical assumptions, are utilized. Explanation in science consists in the hypothetico-deductive procedure. The laws, theories, or hypotheses form the premises from which we derive logically, or logico-mathematically, the observed or observable facts. These facts, often belonging to heterogeneous domains, thus become integrated into a coherent, unifying structure. (Theological and metaphysical systems have, frequently enough, ambitiously tried to imitate this feature of science; but even if they succeeded in proceeding *more geometrico,* the important difference from

science remains: they either lack testability or else reliability in the senses specified in our previous points.)

5. *Comprehensiveness or Scope of Knowledge.*   This final point in our enumeration of criteria of science also characterizes scientific knowledge as different in degree (often enormously) from common-sense knowledge. Not only through bold and sweeping hypotheses, but especially through the ingenious devices by means of which they are tested, science acquires a reach far beyond the limits of our unaided senses. With telescopes, microscopes, spectroscopes, Geiger Counters, lie detectors, and the thousands of other contrivances of modern science we manage to amplify our senses and thus open up avenues of at least indirect access to the worlds of the very distant, the very large, the extremely small, or the disguised and concealed. The resulting increase in the completeness of our knowledge is, of course, popularly the most impressive feature of science. It must be kept in mind, however, that the scope thus achieved is a product of hard labor, and not to be confused with the sham completeness metaphysicians procure for their world pictures by verbal magic. Instead of presenting a finished account of the world, the genuine scientist keeps his unifying hypotheses open to revision and is always ready to modify or abandon them if evidence should render them doubtful. This self-corrective aspect of science has rightly been stressed as its most important characteristic and must always be kept in mind when we refer to the comprehensiveness or the unification achieved by the scientific account of the universe. It is a sign of one's maturity to be able to live with an unfinished world view.

The foregoing outline of the criteria of science has been set down in a somewhat dogmatic tone. But this was done only for the sake of brevity.[1] The spirit behind it is that of a humble account of what, I think, an impartial and elaborate study of the history of thought from magic to science would reveal. In any case, these criteria seem unquestionably the guiding ideals of present-day empirical science. They may therefore be used in a definition of science as we understand this term today. It seems rather useless to speculate about just what this term, by a change of meaning, might come to connote in the future.

It should be remembered that the criteria listed characterize the *pure* factual (empirical) sciences. The aims of the *applied* sciences—the technologies, medicine, social and economic planning, and others—are practical control, production, guidance, therapy, reform, and so forth. Responsible activity in the application of science clearly presupposes information which is fairly well substantiated by the methods of the pure sciences. (These

---

[1] A thorough discussion of the logical, epistemological, methodological, and historical issues connected with the criteria would require a whole book, not just another essay.

remarks intend to draw merely a logically important distinction. The obvious practical interpenetration and important mutual fertilization of the pure and the applied disciplines is of course not denied here.)

Critique of Misconceptions

Having indicated at least in broad outline the nature of scientific method we may now turn to the critique of some of the misconceptions to which it is all too commonly exposed. In what follows, a dozen typical charges against science are stated and answered consecutively.[2]

Science arises exclusively out of practical and social needs and has its only value in serving them in turn. (Dialectical Materialism and Vocationalism).

While this is important it does not tell the whole story. Science has always also been the pursuit of knowledge, the satisfaction of a deep-rooted curiosity. It should be recognized as one of the cultural values along with art, literature, and music. Better teaching of the sciences and their history can redress the balance. Fuller utilization of results and suggestions from the history and the philosophy of science would give the student a deeper appreciation of the evolution of scientific knowledge and of the scientific point of view. Through proper instruction, the student could be led to rediscover some of the important results of science. The intellectual gratification that comes with a grasp of the order of nature, with the understanding of its processes by means of laws and theories, is one of the most powerful incentives in the pursuit of pure knowledge.

Science cannot furnish a secure basis for human affairs since it is unstable. It changes its views continually. (Traditionalism)

While there is constant evolution, and occasionally a revolution, in the scientific outlook, the charge is a superficial (usually journalistic) exaggeration. The typical progress of science reveals that later views often contain much of the earlier views (to the extent that these have stood the test of repeated examination). The more radical or revolutionary changes usually amount to a revision of the conceptual frame of a scientific discipline. The criticism often also presupposes other sources of certainty which will simply not bear critical scrutiny. The quest for absolute certainty is an immature, if not infantile, trait of thinking. The best knowledge we have can be established only by the method of trial and error. It is of the essence of

---

[2] These charges are not straw men. In more than twenty years of reading, listening, teaching, and argument I have encountered them again and again in Europe and just as frequently in this country. If space permitted and time were less valuable, I could quote many well-known writers in connection with each charge.

science to make such knowledge as reliable as is humanly and technically possible.

Science rests on uncritical or uncriticized presuppositions. It validates its outlook by its own standards. It therefore begs the question as regards alternative approaches for settling problems of knowledge and action.

Science has been clarifying and revising its basic assumptions throughout its development. Particularly since the beginning of the modern age and still more intensively since the beginning of our century, an increasing awareness of, and critical attitude toward, the fundamental presuppositions has been most fruitfully applied in the repudiation of dogmatic prejudices and in the articulation of the conceptual frame of scientific method. It can be shown (through logical analysis) that the procedure of science is the only one we are *certain* will yield the results (reliable knowledge, that is, valid explanation and predictions) *if* such results can at all be achieved. Any alleged rival method—theology, metaphysics, mysticism, intuition, dialectics—if it made any contributions at all could not be examined and appraised on any basis other than the usual inductive criteria of science. Generally, it seems that these alleged alternatives do not even aim primarily at knowledge but, like the arts, at the enrichment of experience. They may therefore more properly be said to be *non*-scientific, rather than *un*scientific.

Science distorts the facts of reality. In its Procrustean manner it introduces discontinuities where there is continuity (and vice versa). The abstractions and idealizations used in science can never do justice to the richness and complexities of experience.

Since the task of science is to discover reliable and precise knowledge of what happens under what conditions, it always tries to approximate the facts as closely as the problem on hand requires and permits. Both continuity and discontinuity can be formulated mathematically and be given an adequate formulation only with the help of modern mathematics.

Science can deal only with the measurable and therefore tends to "explain away" that which it cannot measure.

While measurement is eminently desirable in order to enhance the precision and objectivity of knowledge, it is not indispensable in many branches of science or, at least, on their more qualitative levels of analysis. Science does not explain away the qualities of experience. It aims at, and often succeeds in, making these qualities more predictable.

Science never explains, it merely describes the phenomena of experience. The reality beyond the appearances is also beyond the reach of science.

This is partly a terminological issue and partly a result of the (traditional but most misleading and useless) metaphysical distinction between appearance and reality. In the sense in which the word *explaining* is used in common life, science *does* explain facts—it deduces them from laws or theoretical assumptions. Questions which are in principle incapable of being answered by the scientific method turn out, on closer analysis, not to be questions of knowledge. They are expressions of emotional tensions or of the wish for soothing (or exciting) experience.

Science and the scientific attitude are incompatible with religion and the religious attitude.

If by religion one refers to an explanation of the universe and a derivation of moral norms from theological premises, then indeed there is logical incompatibility with the results, methods, and general outlook of science. But if religion means an attitude of sincere devotion to human values, such as justice, peace, relief from suffering, there is not only no conflict between religion and science but rather a need for mutual supplementation.

Science is responsible for the evils and maladjustments of our civilization. It is creating ever more powerful weapons of destruction. The employment of scientific techniques in the machine age has contributed to the misery, physical and mental, of the multitudes. Moreover, the biological facts of evolution imply the negation of all morality: the law of the jungle.

These are particularly superficial charges. It is the social-political-economic structure of a society that is responsible for these various evils. Scientific knowledge itself is socially and morally neutral. But the manner in which it is applied, whether for the benefit or to the detriment of humanity, depends entirely on ourselves. Scientists are becoming increasingly aware that they, even more than the average citizen, have to work for enlightenment toward the proper use of knowledge. The facts and theories of evolution have been construed in many ways as regards their implications for ethics. Julian Huxley reads them very differently from the way his grandfather Thomas Henry did.[3] It should be easy to see that the forces active on the level of human civilization and intelligent communal life are not completely reducible to those involved in the ruthless struggle for survival.

The ethical neutrality of scientific truth and the ivory tower situation of the pure researcher is apt to generate an attitude of indifference toward the pressing problems of humanity.

---

[3] Compare Julian Huxley, *Touchstone for Ethics* (Harper, 1947); but see also C. D. Broad, "Review of Julian S. Huxley's Evolutionary Ethics" (*Mind, 53,* 1944), reprinted in H. Feigl and W. Sellars, *Readings in Philosophical Analysis* (Appleton-Century-Crofts, 1949).

Only maladjusted individuals are unable to combine the detachment necessary for the pursuit of truth with an ardent interest in the improvement of the condition of humanity.

Scientific method, while eminently successful in the explanation, prediction, and control of physical phenomena, is distinctly less successful in regard to the facts of organic life and almost altogether hopeless in the mental and social realm. The methods of the physical sciences are essentially mechanistic (if not materialistic) and therefore reductionistic; they cannot do justice to the complex organismic, teleological, and emergent features of life and mind.

"Scientism" as a slogan of criticism and reproach is very fashionable these days. It is true that some scientists and especially some of the popularizers of science have indulged in reductive fallacies of various sorts. But the true scientific spirit as exemplified in some of the foremost researchers is free from that impatience and simple-mindedness that tries to finish the unfinished business of science by hasty speculation. Admittedly, there are tremendous problems yet to be solved. On the other hand what method is there but the method of science to solve them? Explanations of the mechanistic type (in *one* sense of the term) have been abandoned even in physics. But mechanistic explanation in the wider sense of a search for law (deterministic or statistical) is still the indispensable procedure of all sciences that have gone beyond the purely classificatory level. Organic wholeness, teleology, and emergence can be understood, if at all, only by causal analysis on the usual empirical basis. Purposiveness and freedom of choice, far from being incompatible with causality, presuppose causal order.

The methods of science can never replace the intuitive insight or empathic understanding of the practical psychologist, psychiatrist, cultural anthropologist, or historian. This claim is made particularly wherever the object of knowledge is the individual, the unique and unrepeatable.

It is only through the scientific method that the validity and reliability of the intuitive approach can be gauged. There is, on this ground, some doubt as to its more exaggerated claims. However, there is nothing in the principles of scientific method that would deny the occasional, or even frequent, efficacy of intuitive judgments based, as they must be, on a rich (but often not articulated) background of experience in the given field. Aside from the mere artistic contemplation of the unique and individual, knowledge, in the proper sense of the word, always means the subsumption of the specific case under general concepts or laws. This holds in the social sciences just as much as in the natural sciences.

Science cannot determine values. Since scientific knowledge can (at best) find out only what is the case, it can, by its very nature, never tell what ought to be.

This final challenge often comes from theology or metaphysics. It usually maintains that questions of aims, goals, and ideals cannot be settled by the methods of science but rather require recourse either to divine revelation, the voice of conscience, or some metaphysical a priori truths. The answer to this in a scientific age would seem to be that a mature mankind should be able to determine its own value standards on the basis of its needs, wants, and the facts of the social condition of man. But it is true that science cannot dictate value standards. It can, as in social psychology, ascertain the actual evaluations of groups and individuals, study their compatibilities and incompatibilities, and recommend (that is *applied* science!) ways and means of harmonizing conflicting evaluations. True enough, in many of the urgent issues that confront us, we do not possess enough scientific knowledge to warrant a course of action. This means that we have to act, as so often in life, on the highest probabilities available even if these probabilities be low in themselves. But such estimates of probabilities will still be made most reliable by the scientific method. Common life experience and wisdom, when freed from its adherence to prescientific thought patterns, is not fundamentally different from scientific knowledge. In both we find the procedure of self-correction, so essentially needed if knowledge is to be a guide for action. There is an important common element in mature thinking (as we find it in science) and mature social action (as we find it in democracy): progress arises out of the peaceful competition of ideas as they are put to intersubjective test. Cooperative planning on the basis of the best and fullest knowledge available is the only path left to an awakened humanity that has embarked on the adventure of science and civilization.

THINK ABOUT

1. Do you think that either Newton, Darwin, Einstein, or Freud had Feigl's basic aims of science? Give one example. Do their theories attain Feigl's "regulative ideals"?

2. Feigl says "Science cannot dictate value standards." Does this mean that the scientific approach to philosophy is incomplete?

3. Can you cite a recent controversy regarding a scientific matter in which a value judgment was fundamentally involved?

5

How I See Philosophy

Friedrich Waismann (1896–1959) was a member of the Vienna Circle and a friend and disciple of Wittgenstein, whose
views he reported at its meetings. Author of *Introduction to
Mathematical Thinking* (1951), and *The Principles of Linguistic
Philosophy* (1965).

Waismann represents the linguistic methodological approach used by
many contemporary philosophers. He sees two tasks for philosophy. The
first is to clear up philosophical puzzles through careful language analysis.
The second is much rarer, but more important: to develop "a deeper
insight" into the fundamental philosophical puzzles of man.

TO STUDY

1. What is philosophy? What is its source? What is it not?

2. How have philosophers analyzed "time"?

3. What does Waismann see as the real problem of philosophy?
   Explain: "A philosophic question is not solved; it dissolves."

4. What is the *positive* content of philosophy?

5. What is the relation between questions and answers in philosophy?

1

What philosophy is? I don't know, nor have I a set formula to offer. Immediately as I sit down to contemplate the question I am flooded with so many ideas, tumbling over one another, that I cannot do justice to all of them. I can merely make an attempt, a very inadequate one, to sketch with a few strokes what the lie of the land seems to me to be, tracing some lines of thought without entering upon a close-knit argument.

It is, perhaps, easier to say what philosophy is not than what it is. The first thing, then, I should like to say is that philosophy, as it is practised today, is very unlike science; and this in three respects: in philosophy there are no proofs; there are no theorems; and there are no questions which can be decided, Yes or No. In saying that there are no proofs I do not mean to say that there are no arguments. Arguments certainly there are, and first-rate philosophers are recognized by the originality of their arguments; only these do not work in the sort of way they do in mathematics or in the sciences. . . .

What I want to show in this article is that it is quite wrong to look at philosophy as though it had for its aim to provide theorems but had lamentably failed to do so. The whole conception changes when one comes to realize that what philosophers are concerned with is something different —neither discovering new propositions nor refuting false ones nor checking and re-checking them as scientists do. For one thing, proofs require premisses. Whenever such premisses have been set up in the past, even tentatively, the discussion at once challenged them and shifted to a deeper level. Where there are no proofs there are no theorems either. (To write down lists of propositions "proved" by Plato or Kant: a pastime strongly to be recommended.) Yet the failure to establish a sort of Euclidean system of philosophy based on some suitable "axioms" is, I submit, neither a mere accident nor a scandal but deeply founded in the nature of philosophy.

Yet there are questions; (and arguments). Indeed, a philosopher is a man who senses as it were hidden crevices in the build of our concepts where others only see the smooth path of commonplaceness before them.

Questions but no answers? Decidedly odd. The oddness may lessen when we take a look at them at closer range. Consider two famous examples: Achilles and the tortoise, and the astonishment of St. Augustine when confronted with the fact of memory. He is amazed, not at some striking feat of memory, but at there being such a thing as memory at all. A sense-impression, say a smell or a taste, floats before us and disappears. One moment it is here and the next it is gone. But in the galleries of the memory

---

From *Contemporary British Philosopohy*, edited by H. D. Lewis (London: George Allen & Unwin Ltd., 1956), pp. 447–470, with omissions. Reprinted with permission of the publisher.

pale copies of it are stored up after its death. From there I can drag them out when and as often as I wish, like, and yet strangely unlike, the original —unlike in that they are not perishable like the momentary impression: what was transitory has been arrested and has achieved duration. But who can say how this change comes about?

Here the very fact of memory feels mystifying in a way in which ordinary questions asking for information do not; and *of course* it is not a factual question. What is it?

From Plato to Schopenhauer philosophers are agreed that the source of their philosophizing is wonder. What gives rise to it is nothing recondite and rare but precisely those things which stare us in the face: memory, motion, general ideas. (Plato: What does "horse" mean? A single particular horse? No, for it may refer to *any* horse; *all* the horses, the total class? No, for we may speak of this or that horse. But if it means neither a single horse nor all horses, what *does* it mean?) The idealist is shaken in just the same way when he comes to reflect that he has, in Schopenhauer's words, "no knowledge of the sun but only of an eye that sees a sun, and no knowledge of the earth but only of a hand that feels an earth." Can it be, then, that nothing whatever is known to us except our own consciousness?

In looking at such questions, it seems as if the mind's eye were growing dim and as if everything, even that which ought to be absolutely clear, was becoming oddly puzzling and unlike its usual self. To bring out what seems to be peculiar to these questions one might say that they are not so much questions as tokens of a profound uneasiness of mind. Try for a moment to put yourself into the frame of mind of which Augustine was possessed when he asked: How is it possible to measure time? Time consists of past, present and future. The past can't be measured, it is gone; the future can't be measured, it is not yet here; and the present can't be measured, it has no extension. Augustine knew of course how time is measured and this was not his concern. What puzzled him was how it is *possible* to measure time, seeing that the past hour cannot be lifted out and placed alongside the present hour for comparison. Or look at it this way: what is measured is in the past, the measuring in the present: how can that be?

The philosopher as he ponders over some such problem has the appearance of a man who is deeply disquieted. He seems to be straining to grasp something which is beyond his powers. The words in which such a question presents itself do not quite bring out into the open the real point—which may, perhaps more aptly, be described as the recoil from the incomprehensible. If, on a straight railway journey, you suddenly come in sight of the very station you have just left behind, there will be terror, accompanied perhaps by slight giddiness. That is exactly how the philosopher feels when he says to himself, "Of course time can be measured; but how *can* it?" It is as though, up to now, he had been passing heedlessly over the difficulties, and now, all of a sudden, he notices them and asks himself in alarm, "But how can that be?" That is a sort of question which we only ask when it is the very facts themselves which confound us, when something about them strikes us as preposterous. . . .

We all have our moments when something quite ordinary suddenly strikes us as queer—for instance, when time appears to us as a curious thing. Not that we are often in this frame of mind; but on some occasions, when we look at things in a certain way, unexpectedly they seem to change as though by magic: they stare at us with a puzzling expression, and we begin to wonder whether they can possibly be the things we have known all our lives.

"Time flows" we say—a natural and innocent expression, and yet one pregnant with danger. It flows "equably," in Newton's phrase, at an even rate. What can this mean? When something moves, it moves with a definite speed (and speed means: rate of change in time). To ask with what speed time moves, i.e. to ask how quickly time changes in time, is to ask the unaskable. It also flows, again in Newton's phrase, "without relation to anything external." How are we to figure that? Does time flow on irrespective of what happens in the world? Would it flow on even if everything in heaven and on earth came to a sudden standstill as Schopenhauer believed? For if this were not so, he said, time would have to stop with the stopping of the clock and move with the clock's movement. How odd: time flows at the same rate and yet without speed; and perhaps even without anything to occur in it? The expression is puzzling in another way. "I can never catch myself being in the past or in the future," someone might say; "whenever I think or perceive or breathe the word 'now,' I am in the present; therefore I am *always* in the present." In saying this, he may think of the present moment as a bridge as it were from which he is looking down at the "river of time." Time is gliding along underneath the bridge, but the "now" does not take part in the motion. What was future passes into the present (is just below the bridge) and then into the past, while the onlooker, the "self " or the "I," is always in the present. "Time flows *through* the 'now'," he may feel to be a quite expressive metaphor. Yes, it sounds all right—until he suddenly comes to his senses and, with a start, realizes, "But surely the moment flies?". . .

As we all know what time is and yet cannot say what it is it feels mystifying; and precisely because of its elusiveness it catches our imagination. The more we look at it the more we are puzzled: it seems charged with paradoxes. "What is time? What is this being made up of movement only without anything that is moving?" (Schopenhauer). How funny to have it bottled up! "I've got here in my hand the most potent, the most enigmatic, the most fleeting of all essences—Time." (Logan Pearsall Smith of an hour-glass.) For Shelley it is an "unfathomable sea! whose waves are years," a "shoreless flood," for Proust—well, why not leave something to the reader?

But isn't the answer to this that what mystifies us lies in the *noun* form "the time"? Having a notion embodied in the form of a noun almost irresistibly makes us turn round to look for what it is "the name of." We are trying to catch the shadows cast by the opacities of speech. A wrong analogy absorbed into the forms of our language produces mental discomfort; (and the feeling of discomfort, when it refers to language, is a profound one). "All sounds, all colours . . . evoke indefinite and yet precise emotions, or, as I prefer to think, call down among us certain disembodied powers whose footsteps over our hearts we call emotions" (W. B. Yeats).

Yet the answer is a prosaic one: don't ask what time is but how the *word* "time" is being used. Easier said than done; for if the philosopher rectifies the use of language, ordinary language has "the advantage of being in possession of declensions," to speak with Lichtenberg, and thus renews its spell over him, luring him on into the shadow chase. It is perhaps only when we turn to languages of a widely different grammatical structure that the way towards such possibilities of interpretation is entirely barred. "It is highly probable that philosophers within the domain of the Ural-Altaic languages (where the subject-concept is least developed) will look differently 'into the world' and be found on paths of thought different from those of the Indo-Europeans or Mussulmans" (Nietzsche).

2

It may be well at this point to remind ourselves that the words "question" and "answer," "problem" and "solution" are not always used in their most trite sense. It is quite obvious that we often have to do something very different to find the way out of a difficulty. A problem of politics is solved by adopting a certain line of action, the problems of novelists perhaps by the invention of devices for presenting the inmost thoughts and feelings of their characters; there is the painter's problem of how to suggest depth or movement on the canvas, the stylistic problem of expressing things not yet current, not yet turned into cliché; there are a thousand questions of technology which are answered, not by the discovery of some truth, but by a practical achievement; and there is of course the "social question." In philosophy, the real problem is not to find the answer to a given question but to find a sense for it. . . .

A philosophic question is not solved: it *dis*solves. And in what does the "dissolving" consist? In making the meaning of the words used in putting the question so clear to ourselves that we are released from the spell it casts on us. Confusion was removed by calling to mind the use of language or, so far as the use *can* be distilled into rules, the rules: it therefore *was* a confusion about the use of language, or a confusion about rules. It is here that philosophy and grammar meet. . . .

. . . [W]e do not use arguments in order to prove or disprove any "philosophic view." As we have no views we can afford to look at things as they are.

Next, we only describe; we do not "explain." An explanation, in the sense of a deductive proof, cannot satisfy us because it pushes the question "Why just these rules and no other ones?" only one stage back. In following that method, we do not *want* to give reasons. All we do is to describe a use or tabulate rules. In doing this, we are not making any discoveries: there is nothing to be discovered in grammar. Grammar is autonomous and not dictated by reality. Giving reasons, bound as it is to come to an end and leading to something which cannot further be explained, *ought* not to satisfy us. In grammar we never ask the question "why?"

But isn't the result of this that philosophy itself "dissolves"? Philosophy eliminates those questions which *can* be eliminated by such a treatment. Not all of them, though: the metaphysician's craving that a ray of light may fall on the mystery of the existence of this world, or on the incomprehensible fact that it is comprehensible, or on the "meaning of life"—even if such questions *could* be shown to lack a clear meaning or to be devoid of meaning altogether, they are *not silenced*. It does nothing to lessen the dismay they rouse in us. There is something cheap in "debunking" them. The heart's unrest is not to be stilled by logic. Yet philosophy is not dissolved. It derives its weight, its grandeur, from the significance of the questions it destroys. It overthrows idols, and it is the importance of these idols which gives philosophy its importance.

Now it can perhaps be seen why the search for answers fitting the moulds of the questions fails, is *bound* to fail. They are not real questions asking for information but "muddles felt as problems" (Wittgenstein) which wither away when the ground is cleared. If philosophy advances, it is not by adding new propositions to its list, but rather by transforming the whole intellectual scene and, as a consequence of this, by reducing the number of questions which befog and bedevil us. Philosophy so construed is one of the great liberating forces. Its task is, in the words of Frege, "to free the spirit from the tyranny of words by exposing the delusions which arise, almost inevitably, through the use of a word language."

3

What, only criticism and no meat? The philosopher a fog dispeller? If that were all he was capable of I would be sorry for him and leave him to his devices. Fortunately, this is not so. For one thing, a philosophic question, if pursued far enough, may lead to something positive—for instance, to a more profound understanding of language. Take the sceptical doubts as to material objects, other minds, etc. The first reaction is perhaps to say: these doubts are idle. Ordinarily, when I doubt whether I shall finish this article, after a time my doubt comes to an end. I cannot go on doubting forever. It's the destiny of doubt to die. But the doubts raised by the sceptic never die. Are they doubts? Are they pseudo-questions? They appear so only when judged by the twin standards of common sense and common speech. The real trouble lies deeper: it arises from the sceptic casting doubt on the very facts which underlie the use of language, those permanent features of experience which make concept formation possible, which in fact are precipitated in the use of our most common words. Suppose that you see an object in front of you quite clearly, say, a pipe, and when you are going to pick it up it melts into thin air, then you may feel, "Lord, I'm going mad" or something of the sort (unless the whole situation is such that you have reason to suspect that it was some clever trick). But what, the sceptic may press now, if such experiences were quite frequent? Would you be prepared to *dis*solve the connection between different sense experiences which form the hard core of our idea of a solid object, to *un*do what language has done—to part with the category of thing-hood? And would you then be living in a phenomenalist's paradise with colour patches and the other paraphernalia of the sense-datum theory, in a disobjected, desubstantialized world? To say in such circumstances, "Look, it's just tabling now" would be a joke (for even in the weakened verb forms "tabling," "chairing" an element of the thing-category lingers on). That is why the sceptic struggles to express himself in a language which is not fit for this purpose. He expresses himself misleadingly when he says that he doubts such-and-such *facts:* his doubts cut so deep that they affect the fabric of language itself. For what he doubts is already embodied in the very forms of speech, e.g. in what is condensed in the use of thing-words. The moment he tries to penetrate those deep-sunken layers, he undermines the language in which he ventilates his qualms—with the result that he seems to be talking nonsense. He is not. But in order to make his doubts fully expressible, language would first have to go into the melting-pot. (We can get a glimmering of what is needed from modern science where all the long-established categories—thinghood, causality, position—had to be revolutionized. This required nothing less than the construction of some new language, not the expression of new facts with the old one.)

If we look at the matter in this way the attitude of the sceptic is seen in a new light. He considers possibilities which lie far outside the domain of our current experience. If his doubts are taken seriously, they turn into observations which cast a new and searching light on the subsoil of language, showing what possibilities are open to our thought (though not to ordinary language), and what paths might have been pursued if the texture of our experience were different from what it is. These problems are not spurious: they make us aware of the vast background in which any current experiences are embedded, and to which language has adapted itself; thus they bring out the unmeasured sum of experience stored up in the use of our words and syntactical forms.

For another thing, a question may decide to go in for another career than dissolving: it may pass into science. Frege, for instance, was prompted to his inquiries by philosophical motives, namely, to find a definite answer to the question about the nature of arithmetical truths—whether they are analytic[1] or synthetic,[2] *a priori* or *a posteriori*. Starting from this question and pursuing it with all possible rigour, he was led to unearth a whole mine of problems of a scientific nature; and proceeding along these lines, he came to fashion a new instrument, a logic, which in delicacy and range and power far surpassed anything that went by this name before, a subject revealing to this day new and unexpected depths. . . .

The question is the first groping step of the mind in its journeyings that lead towards new horizons. The genius of the philosopher shows itself nowhere more strikingly than in the new kind of question he brings into the world. What distinguishes him and gives him his place is the passion of questioning. That his questions are at times not so clear is perhaps of not so much moment as one makes of it. There is nothing like clear thinking to protect one from making discoveries. It is all very well to talk of clarity, but when it becomes an obsession it is liable to nip the living thought in the bud. This, I am afraid, is one of the deplorable results of Logical Positivism, not foreseen by its founders, but only too striking in some of its followers. Look at these people, gripped by a clarity neurosis, haunted by fear, tongue-tied, asking themselves continually, "Oh dear, now does this make perfectly good sense?" Imagine the pioneers of science, Kepler, Newton, the discoverers of non-Euclidean geometry, of field physics, the unconscious, matter waves or heaven knows what, imagine them asking themselves this question at every step—this would have been the surest means

---

[1] *analytic:* analytic propositions are defined as those which are true in virtue of the meanings of their terms (ED.).

[2] *synthetic:* synthetic propositions are known as true or false through experience (ED.).

of sapping any creative power. No great discoverer has acted in accordance with the motto, "Everything that can be said can be said clearly." And some of the greatest discoveries have even emerged from a sort of primordial fog. (Something to be said for the fog. For my part, I've always suspected that clarity is the last refuge of those who have nothing to say.)

The great mind is the great questioner. . . . But here a new problem presents itself: How do we know what will satisfy a given question? More generally: How does the answer fit the question? Questions of the current sort ("What is the right time?") show already by their form what sort of answer to expect. They are, so to speak, cheques with a blank to be filled. . . . There is no obvious link between question and answer. . . .

The philosopher contemplates things through the prism of language and, misled (say) by some analogy, suddenly sees things in a new strange light. We can cope with these problems only by digging down to the soil from which they spring. What we do is to light up the mental background from which the question has detached itself; in a clearer perception of some of the crucial concepts the question transforms itself into another one. Not that it has been answered in the current sense. Rather we have removed the factors that prompted the question by a more profound and penetrating analysis. The essence of this process is that it leads the questioner on to some new aspect—and leads him with his spontaneous consent. He agrees to be thus led and therefore ends by abandoning his search. We cannot constrain anyone who is unwilling to follow the new direction of a question; we can only extend the field of vision of the asker, loosen his prejudices, guide his gaze in a new direction: but all this can be achieved only with his consent.

By our critical analysis we try to counteract the influence of the language field, or (what comes to the same) we may help the questioner to gain a deeper insight into the nature of what he is seeking first of all,—make him see the build of the concepts and the moulds in which he expresses the question. What matters is more like changing his outlook than proving to him some theorem; or more like increasing his insight. Insight cannot be lodged in a theorem, and this is the deeper reason why the deductive method is doomed to fail: insight cannot be demonstrated by proof.

What it comes to in the end is that the asker of the question, in the course of the discussion, has to make a number of *decisions*. And this makes the philosophical procedure so unlike a logical one. He compares, for instance, the case before him with analogous ones and has to *judge* how far these analogies hold. That is, it is for him to decide how far he is willing to accept these analogies: he has not, like a slave, to follow blindly in their track.

Science is rich in questions of this type. They are not scientific questions properly and yet they exercise scientists, they are philosophic questions and yet they do not exercise philosophers.

What I have wanted to say in this section and have not said, or only half-said:

(1) Philosophy is not only criticism of language: so construed, its aim is too narrow. It is criticizing, dissolving and stepping over *all* prejudices, loosening all rigid and constricting moulds of thought, no matter whether they have their origin in language or somewhere else.

(2) What is essential in philosophy is the breaking through to a *deeper insight*—which is something positive—not merely the dissipation of fog and the exposure of spurious problems.

(3) Insight cannot be lodged in a theorem, and it can therefore not be demonstrated.

(4) Philosophic arguments are, none of them, logically *compelling:* they really screen what actually happens—the quiet and patient undermining of categories over the whole field of thought.

(5) Their purpose is to open our eyes, to bring us to see things in a new way—from a wider standpoint unobstructed by misunderstandings.

(6) The essential difference between philosophy and logic is that logic *constrains* us while philosophy leaves us free: in a philosophic discussion we are led, step by step, to change our angle of vision, e.g. to pass from one way of putting a question to another, and this with our spontaneous agreement—a thing profoundly different from deducing theorems from a given set of premises. Misquoting Cantor one might say: the essence of philosophy lies in its freedom.

THINK ABOUT

1. Waismann says that unlike science there are no proofs in philosophy. Do you think this negates Peirce's hope of a scientific philosophy?

2. Explain, "The essence of philosophy lies in its freedom".

3. Waismann stresses the deep insights of philosophy. Can you think of any deep insights in any field of knowledge?

Readings

General

1. Edman, Irwin. *Four Ways of Philosophy.* New York: Henry Holt Co., 1937.
2. Montague. *The Ways of Knowing.* New York: Humanities Press, 1925.

Peirce

1. Fitzgerald, J. J. "Peirce's Theory of Inquiry," in *Transactions of the Charles Peirce Society,* IV, 3, 130–43.
2. Frankfurt, Harry. "Peirce's Account of Inquiry," *Journal of Philosophy,* 1959, pp. 588–592.

Scientific Method

1. Campbell, Norman. *What Is Science?* New York: Dover, 1930.
2. Copi, Irving. *Introduction to Logic.* 3rd ed. New York: Macmillan, 1968, pp. 373–418. On hypotheses.

Waismann

1. Feigl, H., Sellars, W., and Lehrer, K. *New Readings in Philosophical Analysis.* New York: Appleton Century, 1974.
2. Urmson, J. *Philosophical Analysis.* Oxford: Oxford University Press, 1956.

3

Ethics

one

How Free Is Man?

6

Man Is
Determined

John Stuart Mill (1806–1873) was the most influential British philosopher in the nineteenth century. His major works include *On Liberty* (1859); *Considerations on Representative Government* (1861); *Utilitarianism* (1863); and *The Subjection of Women* (1869).

Nearly everyone believes that he has the free will to choose to do what he wishes. One can freely choose to come to school or stay home. Thus the belief that man has free will is an immediate and a pervasive belief. Yet if one raises a question about what reasons a person would give for avoiding school, then one's will doesn't seem to be so free. One might stay home if one were ill or one's mother died. But if these events *didn't* occur, then given the events that *did* occur (one has an exam at school, one hates to miss a class, etc.), one couldn't have done otherwise. This denial of free will is called the belief in *determinism.* Determinism is the belief that all acts are caused by past events, and given enough knowledge one could predict what a person will do. This is Mill's position. A major question is: Can one be morally blamed if all his acts are determined?

TO STUDY

1. Why do we think every event has a cause? What do the necessitarians say about volition and cause?

2. What is Hamilton's argument about consciousness and freedom?

3. What is Mill's refutation of Hamilton's argument? Do we act in opposition to the strongest desire?

> 4. What is the relation between freedom and moral responsibility? What role does punishment play?
> 5. What are the two kinds of fatalism?

Sir W. Hamilton having thus, as is often the case (and it is one of the best things he does), saved his opponents the trouble of answering his friends, his doctrine is left resting exclusively on the supports which he has himself provided for it. In examining them, let us place ourselves, in the first instance, completely at his point of view, and concede to him the coequal inconceivability of the conflicting hypotheses, an uncaused commencement, and an infinite egress. But this choice of inconceivabilities is not offered to us in the case of volitions only. We are held, as he not only admits but contends, to the same alternative in all cases of causation whatsoever. But we find our way out of the difficulty, in other cases, in quite a different manner. In the case of every other kind of fact, we do not elect the hypothesis that the event took place without a cause: we accept the other supposition, that of a regress, not indeed to infinity, but either generally into the region of the Unknowable, or back to a Universal Cause, regarding which, as we are only concerned with it in respect of attributes bearing relation to what it preceded, and not as itself preceded by anything, we can afford to consider this reference as ultimate.

Now, what is the reason, which, in the case of all things within the range of our knowledge except volitions, makes us choose this side of the alternative? Why do we, without scruple, register all of them as depending on causes, by which (to use our author's language) they are determined necessarily, though, in believing this, we, according to Sir W. Hamilton, believe as utter an inconceivability as if we supposed them to take place without a cause? Apparently it is because the causation hypothesis, inconceivable as he may think it, possesses the advantage of having experience on its side. And how or by what evidence does experience testify to it? Not by disclosing any *nexus* between the cause and the effect, any Sufficient Reason in the cause itself why the effect should follow it. No philosopher now makes this supposition, and Sir W. Hamilton positively disclaims it. What experience makes known, is the fact of an invariable sequence between every event and some special combination of antecedent conditions, in such sort that wherever and whenever that union of antecedents exists, the event does not fail to occur. Any *must* in the case, any necessity, other than the unconditional universality of the fact, we know nothing of. Still,

---

From *An Examination of Sir William Hamilton's Philosophy,* Chap. XXVI, 1867.

this *à posteriori* "does," though not confirmed by an *à priori* "must," decides our choice between the two inconceivables, and leads us to the belief that every event within the phenomenal universe, except human volitions, is determined to take place by a cause. Now, the so-called Necessitarians demand the application of the same rule of judgment to our volitions. They maintain that there is the same evidence for it. They affirm, as a truth of experience, that volitions do, in point of fact follow determinate moral antecedents with the same uniformity, and (when we have sufficient knowledge of the circumstances) with the same certainty, as physical effects follow their physical causes. These moral antecedents are desires, aversions, habits, and dispositions, combined with outward circumstances suited to call those internal incentives into action. All these again are effects of causes, those of them which are mental being consequences of education, and of other moral and physical influences. This is what Necessitarians affirm; and they court every possible mode in which its truth can be verified. They test it by each person's observation of his own volitions. They test it by each person's observation of the voluntary actions of those with whom he comes into contact; and by the power which every one has of foreseeing actions, with a degree of exactness proportioned to his previous experience and knowledge of the agents, and with a certainty often quite equal to that with which we predict the commonest physical events. They test it further, by the statistical results of the observation of human beings acting in numbers sufficient to eliminate the influences which operate only on a few, and which on a large scale neutralise one another, leaving the total result about the same as if the volitions of the whole mass had been affected by such only of the determining causes as were common to them all. In cases of this description the results are as uniform, and may be as accurately foretold, as in any physical inquiries in which the effect depends upon a multiplicity of causes. The cases in which volitions seem too uncertain to admit of being confidently predicted, are those in which our knowledge of the influences antecedently in operation is so incomplete, that with equally imperfect data there would be the same uncertainty in the predictions of the astronomer and the chemist. On these grounds it is contended that our choice between the conflicting inconceivables should be the same in the case of volitions as of all other phenomena: we must reject equally in both cases the hypothesis of spontaneousness, and consider them all as caused. A volition is a moral effect, which follows the corresponding moral causes as certainly and invariably as physical effects follow their physical causes. Whether it *must* do so, I acknowledge myself to be entirely ignorant, be the phenomenon moral or physical; and I condemn, accordingly, the word Necessity as applied to either case. All I know is, that it always *does.*

This argument from experience Sir W. Hamilton passes unnoticed, but urges, on the opposite side of the question, the argument from Consciousness. We are conscious, he affirms, either of our freedom, or at all events (it is odd that, on his theory, there should be any doubt) of something which implies freedom. If this is true, our internal consciousness tells us that we have a power, which the whole outward experience of the human race tells us that we never use. This is surely a very unfortunate predicament we are in, and a sore trial to the puzzled metaphysician. Philosophy is far from having so easy a business before her as our author thinks: the arbiter Consciousness is by no means invoked to turn the scale between two equally balanced difficulties; on the contrary, she has to sit in judgment between herself and a complete induction from experience. Consciousness, it will probably be said, is the best evidence; and so it would be, if we were always certain what is Consciousness. . . .

Let us cross-examine the alleged testimony of consciousness. And, first, it is left in some uncertainty by Sir W. Hamilton whether consciousness makes only one deliverance on the subject, or two: whether we are conscious only of moral responsibility, in which free-will is implied, or are directly conscious of free-will. In his Lectures, Sir W. Hamilton speaks only of the first. In the notes on Reid, which were written subsequently, he seems to affirm both, but the latter of the two in a doubtful and hesitating manner: so difficult, in reality, does he find it to ascertain with certainty what it is that Consciousness certifies. But as there are many who maintain with a confidence far greater than his, that we are directly conscious of free-will, it is necessary to examine that question.

To be conscious of free-will, must mean, to be conscious, before I have decided, that I am able to decide either way. Exception may be taken *in limine* to the use of the word consciousness in such an application. Consciousness tells me what I do or feel. But what I am *able* to do, is not a subject of consciousness. Consciousness is not prophetic; we are conscious of what is, not of what will or can be. We never know that we are able to do a thing, except from having done it, or something equal and similar to it. We should not know that we were capable of action at all, if we had never acted. Having acted, we know, as far as that experience reaches, how we are able to act; and this knowledge, when it has become familiar, is often confounded with, and called by the name of, consciousness. But it does not derive any increase of authority from being misnamed; its truth is not supreme over, but depends on, experience. If our so-called consciousness of what we are able to do is not borne out by experience, it is a delusion. It has no title to credence but as an interpretation of experience, and if it is a false interpretation, it must give way.

But this conviction, whether termed consciousness or only belief, that our will is free—what is it? Of what are we convinced? I am told that whether I decide to do or to abstain, I feel that I could have decided the other way. I ask my consciousness what I do feel, and I find, indeed, that I feel (or am convinced) that I could, and even should, have chosen the other course if I had preferred it, that is, if I had liked it better; but not that I could have chosen one course while I preferred the other. When I say preferred, I of course include with the thing itself, all that accompanies it. I know that I can, because I know that I often do, elect to do one thing, when I should have preferred another in itself, apart from its consequences, or from a moral law which it violates. And this preference for a thing in itself, abstractedly from its accompaniments, is often loosely described as preference for the thing. It is this unprecise mode of speech which makes it not seem absurd to say that I act in opposition to my preference; that I do one thing when I would rather do another; that my conscience prevails over my desires—as if conscience were not itself a desire—the desire to do right. Take any alternative: say to murder or not to murder. I am told, that if I elect to murder, I am conscious that I could have elected to abstain: but am I conscious that I could have abstained if my aversion to the crime, and my dread of its consequences, had been weaker than the temptation? If I elect to abstain: in what sense am I conscious that I could have elected to commit the crime? Only if I had desired to commit it with a desire stronger than my horror of murder; not with one less strong. When we think of ourselves hypothetically as having acted otherwise than we did, we always suppose a difference in the antecedents: we picture ourselves as having known something that we did not know, or not known something that we did know; which is a difference in the external inducements; or as having desired something, or disliked something, more or less than we did; which is a difference in the internal inducements.

In refutation of this it is said, that in resisting a desire, I am conscious of making an effort; that after I have resisted, I have the remembrance of having made an effort; that "if the temptation was long continued, or if I have been resisting the strong will of another, I am as sensibly exhausted by that effort, as after any physical exertion I ever made:" and it is added, "If my volition is wholly determined by the strongest present desire, it will be decided without any effort. . . . When the greater weight goes down, and the lesser up, no effort is needed on the part of the scale." It is implied in this argument, that in a battle between contrary impulses, the victory must always be decided in a moment; that the force which is really the strongest, and prevails ultimately, must prevail instantaneously. The fact is not quite thus even in inanimate nature: the hurricane does not level the house or blow down the tree without resistance; even the balance trembles, and the scales oscillate for a short time, when the difference of the weights is not considerable. Far less does victory come without a contest to the strongest of two moral, or even two vital forces, whose nature it is to be never fixed, but always flowing, quantities. In a struggle between passion, there is not a single instant in which there does not pass across the mind some thought, which adds strength to, or takes it from, one or the other of the contending powers. Unless one of them was, from the beginning, out of all proportion stronger than the other, some time must elapse before the balance adjusts itself between forces neither of which is for any two successive instants the same. During that interval the agent is in the peculiar mental and physical state which we call a conflict of feelings: and we all know that a conflict between strong feelings *is*, in an extraordinary degree, exhaustive of the nervous energies.[1] The consciousness of effort, which we are told of, is this state of conflict. The author I am quoting considers what he calls, I think improperly, an effort, to be only on one side, because he represents to himself the conflict as taking place between me and some foreign power, which I conquer, or by which I am overcome. But it is obvious that "I" am both parties in the contest; the conflict is between me and myself; between (for instance) me desiring a pleasure, and me dreading self-reproach. What causes Me, or, if you please, my Will, to be identified with one side rather than with the other, is that one of the Me's represents a more permanent state of my feelings than the other does. After the temptation has been yielded to, the desiring "I" will come to an end, but the conscience-stricken "I" may endure to the end of life.

I therefore dispute altogether that we are conscious of being able to act in opposition to the strongest present desire or aversion. The difference between a bad and a good man is not that the latter acts in opposition to his strongest desires; it is that his desire to do right, and his aversion to doing wrong, are strong enough to overcome, and in the case of perfect virtue, to silence, any other desire or aversion which may conflict with them. It is because this state of mind is possible to human nature, that human beings are capable of moral government: and moral education consists in subjecting them to the discipline which has most tendency to bring them into this state. The object of moral education is to educate the will: but the will can only be educated through the desires and aversions; by eradicating or weakening such of them as are likeliest to lead to evil; exalting to the highest pitch the desire of right conduct and the aversion to wrong; cultivating all other desires and aversions of which the ordinary operation is auxiliary to right, while discountenancing so immoderate an indulgence of them, as might render them too powerful to be overcome by the moral sentiment, when they chance to be in opposition to it. The other requisites are, a clear intellectual standard of right and wrong, that moral

---

[1] The Battle of the Two Philosophies, pp. 13, 14.

desire and aversion may act in the proper places, and such general mental habits as shall prevent moral considerations from being forgotten or over-looked, in cases to which they are rightly applicable.

Rejecting, then, the figment of a direct consciousness of the freedom of the will, in other words, our ability to will in opposition to our strongest preference; it remains to consider whether, as affirmed by Sir W. Hamilton, a freedom of this kind is implied in what is called our consciousness of moral responsibility. There must be something very plausible in this opinion, since it is shared even by Necessitarians. Many of these—in particular Mr. Owen and his followers—from a recognition of the fact that volitions are effects of causes, have been led to deny human responsibility. I do not mean that they denied moral distinctions. Few persons have had a stronger sense of right and wrong, or been more devoted to the things they deemed right. What they denied was the rightfulness of inflicting punishment. A man's actions, they said, are the result of his character, and he is not the author of his own character. It is made *for* him, not *by* him. There is no justice in punishing him for what he cannot help. We should try to convince or persuade him that he had better act in a different manner; and should educate all, especially the young, in the habits and dispositions which lead to well-doing: though how this is to be effected without any use whatever of punishment as a means of education, is a question they have failed to resolve. The confusion of ideas, which makes the subjection of human volitions to the law of Causation seem inconsistent with accountability, must thus be very natural to the human mind; but this may be said of a thousand errors, and even of some merely verbal fallacies. In the present case there is more than a verbal fallacy, but verbal fallacies also contribute their part.

What is meant by moral responsibility? Responsibility means punish-ment. When we are said to have the feeling of being morally responsible for our actions the idea of being punished for them is uppermost in the speaker's mind. But the feeling of liability to punishment is of two kinds. It may mean, expectation that if we act in a certain manner, punishment will actually be inflicted upon us, by our fellow creatures or by a Supreme Power. Or it may only mean, knowing that we shall deserve that infliction.

The first of these cannot, in any correct meaning of the term, be designated as a consciousness. If we believe that we shall be punished for doing wrong, it is because the belief has been taught to us by our parents and tutors, or by our religion, or is generally held by those who surround us, or because we have ourselves come to the conclusion, by reasoning, or from the experience of life. This is not Consciousness. And, by whatever name it is called, its evidence is not dependent on any theory of the spontan-eousness of volition. The punishment of guilt in another world is believed with undoubting conviction by Turkish fatalists, and by professed Christians who are not only Necessitarians, but believe that the majority of mankind were divinely predestined from all eternity to sin and to be punished for sinning. It is not, therefore, the belief that we shall be *made* accountable, which can be deemed to require or presuppose the free-will hypothesis; it is the belief that we ought so to be; that we are justly accountable; that guilt deserves punishment. It is here that issue is joined between the two opinions. . . .

The real question is one of justice—the legitimacy of retribution, or punishment. On the theory of Necessity (we are told) a man cannot help acting as he does; and it cannot be just that he should be punished for what he cannot help.

Not if the expectation of punishment enables him to help it, and is the only means by which he can be enabled to help it?

To say that he cannot help it, is true or false, according to the qualification with which the assertion is accompanied. Supposing him to be of a vicious disposition, he cannot help doing the criminal act, if he is allowed to believe that he will be able to commit it unpunished. If, on the contrary, the impression is strong in his mind that a heavy punishment will follow, he can, and in most cases does, help it.

The question deemed to be so puzzling is, how punishment can be justified, if men's actions are determined by motives, among which motives punishment is one. A more difficult question would be, how it can be justified if they are not so determined. Punishment proceeds on the assumption that the will is governed by motives. If punishment had no power of acting on the will, it would be illegitimate, however natural might be the inclination to inflict it. Just so far as the will is supposed free, that is, capable of acting *against* motives, punishment is disappointed of its object, and deprived of its justification.

There are two ends which, on the Necessitarian theory, are sufficient to justify punishment: the benefit of the offender himself, and the protection of others. The first justifies it, because to benefit a person cannot be to do him an injury. To punish him for his own good, provided the inflictor has any proper title to constitute himself a judge, is no more unjust than to administer medicine. As far, indeed, as respects the criminal himself, the theory of punishment is, that by counter-balancing the influence of present temptations, or acquired bad habits, it restores the mind to that normal preponderance of the love of right, which many moralists and theologians consider to constitute the true definition of our freedom. In its other aspect, punishment is a precaution taken by society in self-defence. To make this just, the only condition required is, that the end which society is attempting to enforce by punishment, should be a just one. Used as a means of aggression by society on the just rights of the individual, punishment is unjust. Used to protect the just rights of others against unjust aggression by the offender, it is just. If it is possible to have just rights (which is the same thing as to have rights at all), it cannot be unjust to defend them. Free-will or no free-will, it is just to punish so far as is necessary for this purpose, as it is just to put a wild beast to death (without unnecessary suffering) for the same object. . . .

If, indeed, punishment is inflicted for any other reason than in order to operate on the will; if its purpose be other than that of improving the culprit himself, or securing the just rights of others against unjust violation, then, I admit, the case is totally altered. If any one thinks that there is justice in the infliction of purposeless suffering; that there is a natural affinity between the two ideas of guilt and punishment, which makes it intrinsically fitting that wherever there has been guilt, pain should be inflicted by way of retribution; I acknowledge that I can find no argument to justify punishment inflicted on this principle. As a legitimate satisfaction to feelings of indignation and resentment which are on the whole salutary and worthy of cultivation, I can in certain cases admit it; but here it is still a means to an end. The merely retributive view of punishment derives no justification from the doctrine I support. But it derives quite as little from the free-will doctrine. Suppose it true that the will of a malefactor, when he committed an offence, was free, or in other words, that he acted badly, not because he was of a bad disposition, but from no cause in particular: it is not easy to deduce from this the conclusion that it is just to punish him. That his acts were beyond the command of motives might be a good reason for keeping out of his way, or placing him under bodily restraint; but no reason for inflicting pain upon him, when that pain, by supposition, could not operate as a deterring motive.

While the doctrine I advocate does not support the idea that punishment in mere retaliation is justifiable, it at the same time fully accounts for the general and natural sentiment of its being so. From our earliest childhood, the idea of doing wrong (that is, of doing what is forbidden, or what is injurious to others) and the idea of punishment are presented to our mind together, and the intense character of the impressions causes the association between them to attain the highest degree of closeness and intimacy. Is it strange, or unlike the usual processes of the human mind, that in these circumstances we should retain the feeling, and forget the reason on which it is grounded? But why do I speak of forgetting? In most cases the reason has never, in our early education, been presented to the mind. The only ideas presented have been those of wrong and punishment, and an inseparable association has been created between these directly, without the help of any intervening idea. This is quite enough to make the spontaneous feelings of mankind regard punishment and a wrongdoer as naturally fitted to each other—as a conjunction appropriate in itself, independently of any consequences. . .

That a person holding what is called the Necessitarian doctrine should on that account *feel* that it would be unjust to punish him for his wrong actions, seems to me the veriest of chimeras. Yes, if he really "could not help" acting as he did, that is, if it did not depend on his will; if he was under physical constraint, or even if he was under the action of such a violent motive that no fear of punishment could have any effect; which, if capable of being ascertained, is a just ground of exemption, and is the reason why by the laws of most countries people are not punished for what they were compelled to do by immediate danger of death. But if the criminal was in a state capable of being operated upon by the fear of punishment, no metaphysical objection, I believe, will make him feel his punishment unjust. Neither will he feel that because his act was the consequence of motives, operating upon a certain mental disposition, it was not his own fault. For, first, it was at all events his own defect or infirmity, for which the expectation of punishment is the appropriate cure. And secondly, the word fault, so far from being inapplicable, is the specific name for the kind of defect or infirmity which he has displayed—insufficient love of good and aversion to evil. The weakness of these feelings or their strength is in everyone's mind the standard of fault or merit, of degrees of fault and degrees of merit. Whether we are judging of particular actions, or of the character of a person, we are wholly guided by the indications afforded of the energy of these influences. If the desire of right and aversion to wrong have yielded to a small temptation, we judge them to be weak, and our disapprobation is strong. If the temptation to which they have yielded is so great that even strong feelings of virtue might have succumbed to it, our moral reprobation is less intense. If, again, the moral desires and aversions have prevailed, but not over a very strong force, we hold that the action was good, but that there was little merit in it; and our estimate of the merit rises, in exact proportion to the greatness of the obstacle which the moral feeling proved strong enough to overcome.

Mr. Mansel[2] has furnished what he thinks a refutation of the Necessitarian argument, of which it is well to take notice, the more so, perhaps, as it is directed against some remarks on the subject by the present writer in a former work:[3] remarks which were not intended as an argument for so-called Necessity, but only to place the nature and meaning of that ill-understood doctrine in a truer light. With this purpose in view, it was

---

[2] Prolegemena Logica, Note C at the end.
[3] System of Logic, Book vi, ch. 2.

remarked that "by saying that a man's actions necessarily follow from his character, all that is really meant (for no more is meant in any case whatever of causation) is that he invariably does act in conformity to his character, and that any one who thoroughly knew his character, could certainly predict how he would act in any supposable case. No more than this is contended for by any one but an Asiatic fatalist." "And no more than this," observes Mr. Mansel, "is needed to construct a system of fatalism as rigid as any Asiatic can desire."

Mr. Mansel is mistaken in thinking that the doctrine of the causation of human actions is fatalism at all, or resembles fatalism in any of its moral or intellectual effects. To call it by that name is to break down a fundamental distinction. Real fatalism is of two kinds. Pure, or Asiatic fatalism,—the fatalism of the Oedipus,—holds that our actions do not depend upon our desires. Whatever our wishes may be, a superior power, or an abstract destiny, will overrule them, and compel us to act, not as we desire, but in the manner predestined. Our love of good and hatred of evil are of no efficacy, and though in themselves they may be virtuous, as far as conduct is concerned it is unavailing to cultivate them. The other kind, Modified Fatalism I will call it, holds that our actions are determined by our will, our will by our desires, and our desires by the joint influence of the motives presented to us and of our individual character; but that, our character having been made for us and not by us, we are not responsible for it, nor for the actions it leads to, and should in vain attempt to alter them. The true doctrine of the Causation of human actions maintains, in opposition to both, that not only our conduct, but our character, is in part amenable to our will; that we can, by employing the proper means, improve our character; and that if our character is such that while it remains what it is, it necessitates us to do wrong, it will be just to apply motives which will necessitate us to strive for its improvement, and so emancipate ourselves from the other necessity. In other words, we are under a moral obligation to seek the improvement of our moral character. We shall not indeed do so unless we desire our improvement, and desire it more than we dislike the means which must be employed for the purpose. But does Mr. Mansel, or any other of the free-will philosophers, think that we can will the means if we do not desire the end, or if our desire of the end is weaker than our aversion to the means?

Mr. Mansel is more rigid in his ideas of what the free-will theory requires, than one of the most eminent of the thinkers who have adopted it. According to Mr. Mansel, the belief that whoever knew perfectly our character and our circumstances could predict our actions, amounts to Asiatic fatalism. According to Kant, in his Metaphysics of Ethics, such capability of prediction is quite compatible with the freedom of the will.

This seems, at first sight, to be an admission of everything which the rational supporters of the opposite theory could desire. But Kant avoids this consequence, by changing (as lawyers would say) the *venue* of free-will, from our actions generally, to the formation of our character. It is in that, he thinks, we are free, and he is almost willing to admit that while our character is what it is, our actions are necessitated by it. In drawing this distinction, the philosopher of Königsberg saves inconvenient facts at the expense of the consistency of his theory. There cannot be one theory for one kind of voluntary actions, and another theory for the other kinds. When we voluntarily exert ourselves, as it is our duty to do, for the improvement of our character, or when we act in a manner which (either consciously on our part or unconsciously) deteriorates it, these, like all other voluntary acts, presuppose that there was already something in our character, or in that combined with our circumstances, which led us to do so, and accounts for our doing so. The person, therefore, who is supposed able to predict our actions from our character as it now is, would, under the same conditions of perfect knowledge, be equally able to predict what we should do to change our character: and if this be the meaning of necessity, that part of our conduct is as necessary as all the rest. If necessity means more than this abstract possibility of being foreseen; if it means any mysterious compulsion, apart from simple invariability of sequence, I deny it as strenuously as any one in the case of human volitions, but I deny just as much of all other phenomena. To enforce this distinction was the principal object of the remarks which Mr. Mansel has criticised. If an unessential distinction from Mr. Mansel's point of view, it is essential from mine, and of supreme importance in a practical aspect.

The free-will metaphysicians have made little endeavour to prove that we can will in opposition to our strongest desire, but have strenuously maintained that we can will when we have no strongest desire. With this view Dr. Reid formerly, and Mr. Mansel now, have thrown in the teeth of Necessitarians the famous *asinus Buridani.* If, say they, the will were solely determined by motives, the ass, between two bundles of hay, exactly alike, and equally distant from him, would remain undecided until he died of hunger. From Sir W. Hamilton's notes on this chapter of Reid, I infer that he did not countenance this argument; and it is surprising that writers of talent should have seen anything in it. I waive the objection that if it applies at all, it proves that the ass also has free-will; for perhaps he has. But the ass, it is affirmed, would starve before he decided. Yes, possibly, if he remained all the time in a fixed attitude of deliberation; if he never for an instant ceased to balance one against another the rival attractions, and if they really were so exactly equal that no dwelling on them could detect any difference. But this is not the way in which things take place on our planet. From mere lassitude, if from no other cause, he would intermit the process, and cease thinking of the rival objects at all: until a moment arrived when he would be seeing or thinking of one only, and that fact, combined with the sensation of hunger, would determine him to a decision.

But the argument on which Mr. Mansel lays most stress (it is also one of Reid's) is the following. Necessitarians say that the will is governed by the strongest motive: "but I only know the strength of motives in relation to the will by the test of ultimate prevalence; so that this means no more than that the prevailing motive prevails." I have heretofore complimented Mr. Mansel on seeing farther, in some things, than his master. In the present instance I am compelled to remark, that he has not seen so far. Sir W. Hamilton was not the man to neglect an argument like this, had there been no flaw in it. The fact is that there are two. First, those who say that the will follows the strongest motive, do not mean the motive which is strongest in relation to the will, or in other words, that the will follows what it does follow. They mean the motive which is strongest in relation to pain and pleasure; since a motive, being a desire or aversion, is proportional to the pleasantness, as conceived by us, of the thing desired, or the painfulness of the thing shunned. And when what was at first a direct impulse towards pleasure, or recoil from pain, has passed into a habit or a fixed purpose, then the strength of the motive means the completeness and promptitude of the association which has been formed between an idea and an outward act. This is the first answer to Mr. Mansel. The second is, that even supposing there were no test of the strength of motives but their effect on the will, the proposition that the will follows the strongest motive would not, as Mr. Mansel supposes, be identical and unmeaning. We say, without absurdity, that if two weights are placed in opposite scales, the heavier will lift the other up; yet we mean nothing by the heavier, except the weight which will lift up the other. The proposition, nevertheless, is not unmeaning, for it signifies that in many or most cases there *is* a heavier, and that this is always the same one, not one or the other as it may happen. In like manner, even if the strongest motive meant only the motive which prevails, yet if there is a prevailing motive—if, all other antecedents being the same, the motive which prevails to-day will prevail to-morrow and every subsequent day—Sir W. Hamilton was acute enough to see that the free-will theory is not saved. I regret that I cannot, in this instance, credit Mr. Mansel with the same acuteness.

Before leaving the subject, it is worth while to remark, that not only the doctrine of Necessity, but Predestination in its coarsest form—the belief that all our actions are divinely preordained—though, in my view, inconsistent with ascribing any moral attributes whatever to the Deity, yet if combined with the belief that God works according to general laws, which have to be learnt from experience, has no tendency to make us act in any respect otherwise than we should do if we thought our actions really contingent. For if God acts according to general laws, then, whatever he may have preordained, he has preordained that it shall take place through the causes on which experience shows it to be consequent: and if he has predestined that I shall attain my ends, he has predestined that I shall do so by studying and putting in practice the means which lead to their attainment. When the belief in predestination has a paralysing effect on conduct, as is sometimes the case with Mahomedans, it is because they fancy they can infer what God has predestined, without waiting for the result. They think that either by particular signs of some sort, or from the general aspect of things, they can perceive the issue towards which God is working, and having discovered this, naturally deem useless any attempt to defeat it. Because something will certainly happen if nothing is done to prevent it, they think it will certainly happen whatever may be done to prevent it; in a word, they believe in Necessity in the only proper meaning of the term—an issue unalterable by human efforts or desires.

7

Man Is Free

William James (1842–1910), American philosopher and psychologist, received his M.D. from Harvard in 1869. He lectured there on anatomy and physiology until 1880, when he joined the Department of Psychology and Philosophy. He amended and popularized Peirce's pragmatism in a series of books which include *The Will to Believe and Other Essays in Popular Philosophy* (1897), *The Varieties of Religious Experience* (1902), *Pragmatism* (1907), *Essays in Radical Empiricism* (1912).

The *indeterminist* says that some of our acts are not determined by past conditions. This is the position of the believer in free will (James). He holds that some acts of the will are exempt from causal determination. Each of these, determinism and indeterminism, must be distinguished from *predeterminism,* which is the belief that events (either all or some) throughout eternity have been foreordained by some supernatural power (usually God).

James contends that as there is no evidence which is deciding for determinism or indeterminism, then we have the option of holding to that position to which we are temperamentally suited. In James' case, it is the belief in indeterminism. In this case it is argued that one is responsible for his acts for he has the freedom to do otherwise. Hence it is claimed that only indeterminism is compatible with morality.

TO STUDY

1. What is a *genuine* option?

2. According to James, what ought to be our first act if we are free?

3. Distinguish between hard and soft determinism.

4. How does James define indeterminism?

5. What role do facts play as to the determinism-indeterminism issue?

6. What is it that a deterministic world implies? As a corollary, what does an indeterministic world imply? What is James's position?

7. Can you apply the genuine option theory to the free will problem?

. . . I have long defended to my own students the lawfulness of voluntarily adopted faith; but as soon as they have got well imbued with the logical spirit, they have as a rule refused to admit my contention to be lawful philosophically, even though in point of fact they were personally all the time chock-full of some faith or other themselves. I am all the while, however, so profoundly convinced that my own position is correct, that your invitation has seemed to me a good occasion to make my statements more clear. Perhaps your minds will be more open than those with which I have hitherto had to deal. I will be as little technical as I can, though I must begin by setting up some technical distinctions that will help us in the end.

Let us give the name of *hypothesis* to anything that may be proposed to our belief; and just as the electricians speak of live and dead wires, let us speak of any hypothesis as either *live* or *dead*. A live hypothesis is one which appeals as a real possibility to him to whom it is proposed. If I ask you to believe in the Mahdi, the notion makes no electric connection with your nature,—it refuses to scintillate with any credibility at all. As an hypothesis it is completely dead. To an Arab, however (even if he be not one of the Mahdi's followers), the hypothesis is among the mind's possibilities: it is alive. This shows that deadness and liveness in an hypothesis are not intrinsic properties, but relations to the individual thinker. They are measured by his willingness to act. The maximum of liveness in an hypothesis means willingness to act irrevocably. Practically,

From William James, *The Will to Believe.* Reprinted from the Dover Publications edition published in 1960.

that means belief; but there is some believing tendency wherever there is willingness to act at all.

Next, let us call the decision between two hypotheses an *option*. Options may be of several kinds. They may be—1, *living* or *dead;* 2, *forced* or *avoidable;* 3, *momentous* or *trivial;* and for our purposes we may call an option a *genuine* option when it is of the forced, living, and momentous kind.

1. A living option is one in which both hypotheses are live ones. If I say to you: "Be a theosophist or be a Mohammedan," it is probably a dead option, because for you neither hypothesis is likely to be alive. But if I say: "Be an agnostic or be a Christian," it is otherwise: trained as you are, each hypothesis makes some appeal, however small, to your belief.

2. Next, if I say to you: "Choose between going out with your umbrella or without it," I do not offer you a genuine opinion, for it is not forced. You can easily avoid it by not going out at all. Similarly, if I say, "Either love me or hate me," "Either call my theory true or call it false," your option is avoidable. You may remain indifferent to me, neither loving nor hating, and you may decline to offer any judgment as to my theory. But if I say, "Either accept this truth or go without it," I put on you a forced option, for there is no standing place outside of the alternative. Every dilemma based on a complete logical disjunction, with no possibility of not choosing, is an option of this forced kind.

3. Finally, if I were Dr. Nansen and proposed to you to join my North Pole expedition, your option would be momentous; for this would probably be your only similar opportunity, and your choice now would either exclude you from the North Pole sort of immortality altogether or put at least the chance of it into your hands. He who refuses to embrace a unique opportunity loses the prize as surely as if he tried and failed. *Per contra,* the option is trivial when the opportunity is not unique, when the stake is insignificant, or when the decision is reversible if it later prove unwise. Such trivial options abound in the scientific life. A chemist finds an hypothesis live enough to spend a year in its verification: he believes in it to that extent. But if his experiments prove inconclusive either way, he is quit for his loss of time, no vital harm being done.

It will facilitate our discussion if we keep all these distinctions well in mind. . . .

The thesis I defend is, briefly stated, this: *Our passional nature not only lawfully may, but must, decide an option between propositions, whenever it is a genuine option that cannot by its nature be decided on intellectual grounds; for to say, under such circumstances, "Do not decide, but leave the question open," is itself a passional decision,—just like deciding yes or no,—and is attended with the same risk of losing the truth.* . . .

A common opinion prevails that the juice has ages ago been pressed out of the free-will controversy, and that no new champion can do more than warm up stale arguments which everyone has heard. This is a radical mistake. I know of no subject less worn out, or in which inventive genius has a better chance of breaking open new ground,—not, perhaps, of forcing a conclusion or of coercing assent, but of deepening our sense of what the issue between the two parties really is, of what the ideas of fate and of free-will imply. . . . [O]ur first act of freedom, if we are free, ought in all inward propriety to be to affirm that we are free. . . .

With this much understood at the outset, we can advance. But not without one more point understood as well. The arguments I am about to urge all proceed on two suppositions: first, when we make theories about the world and discuss them with one another, we do so in order to attain a conception of things which shall give us subjective satisfaction; and, second, if there be two conceptions, and the one seems to us, on the whole, more rational than the other, we are entitled to suppose that the more rational one is the truer of the two. . . .

To begin, then, I must suppose you acquainted with all the usual arguments on the subject. I cannot stop to take up the old proofs from causation, from statistics, from the certainty with which we can foretell one another's conduct, from the fixity of character, and all the rest. . . . Old-fashioned determinism was what we may call *hard* determinism.* It did not shrink from such words as fatality, bondage of the will, necessitation, and the like. Nowadays, we have a *soft* determinism† which abhors harsh words, and, repudiating fatality, necessity, and even predetermination, says that its real name is freedom; for freedom is only necessity understood, and bondage to the highest is identical with true freedom. . . .

[Determinism] professes that those parts of the universe already laid down absolutely appoint and decree what the other parts shall be. The future has no ambiguous possibilities hidden in its womb: the part we call the present is compatible with only one totality. Any other future complement than the one fixed from eternity is impossible. The whole is in each and every part, and welds it with the rest into an absolute unity, an iron block, in which there can be no equivocation or shadow of turning.

From William James, *The Will to Believe and Other Essays in Popular Philosophy* (New York: Longmans, Green, 1897), pp. 145–183 with omissions.
* *Hard determinism:* All events are caused. [Ed.]
† *Soft determinism:* Man is free when his choices are effective, even though they are caused. [Ed.]

universes to have been from eternity impossible: you believe it to have been impossible because of the intrinsic irrationality or accidentality somewhere involved in it. But looking outwardly at these universes, can you say which is the impossible and accidental one, and which the rational and necessary one? I doubt if the most ironclad determinist among you could have the slightest glimmer of light on this point. In other words, either universe *after the fact* and once there would, to our means of observation and understanding, appear just as rational as the other. There would be absolutely no criterion by which we might judge one necessary and the other matter of chance. Suppose now we relieve the gods of their hypothetical task and assume my choice, once made, to be made forever. I go through Divinity Avenue for good and all. If, as good determinists, you now begin to affirm, what all good determinists punctually do affirm, that in the nature of things I *couldn't* have gone through Oxford Street,—had I done so it would have been chance, irrationality, insanity, a horrid gap in nature,—I simply call your attention to this, that your affirmation is what the Germans call a *Machtspruch*, a mere conception fulminated as a dogma and based on no insight into details. Before my choice, either street seemed as natural to you as to me. Had I happened to take Oxford Street, Divinity Avenue would have figured in your philosophy as the gap in nature; and you would have so proclaimed it with the best deterministic conscience in the world. . . .

And this at last brings us within sight of our subject. We have seen what determinism means: we have seen that indeterminism is rightly described as meaning chance; and we have seen that chance, the very name of which we are urged to shrink from as from a metaphysical pestilence, means only the negative fact that no part of the world, however big, can claim to control absolutely the destinies of the whole. But although, in discussing the word "chance," I may at moments have seemed to be arguing for its real existence, I have not meant to do so yet. We have not yet ascertained whether this be a world of chance or no; at most, we have agreed that it seems so. And I now repeat what I said at the outset, that, from any strict theoretical point of view, the question is insoluble. To deepen our theoretic sense of the *difference* between a world with chances in it and a deterministic world is the most I can hope to do; and this I may now at last begin upon, after all our tedious clearing of the way.

I wish first of all to show you just what the notion that this is a deterministic world implies. The implications I call your attention to are all bound up with the fact that it is a world in which we constantly have to make what I shall, with your permission, call judgments of regret. Hardly an hour passes in which we do not wish that something might be otherwise; and happy indeed are those of us whose hearts have never echoed the wish of Omar Khayam—

> That we might clasp, ere closed, the book of fate,
>   And make the writer on a fairer leaf
> Inscribe our names, or quite obliterate.
>
> Ah! Love, could you and I with fate conspire
> To mend this sorry scheme of things entire,
>   Would we not shatter it to bits, and then
> Remould it nearer to the heart's desire?

Now, it is undeniable that most of these regrets are foolish, and quite on a par in point of philosophic value with the criticisms on the universe of that friend of our infancy, the hero of the fable The Atheist and the Acorn,—

> Fool! had that bough a pumpkin bore,
> Thy whimsies would have worked no more, etc.

Even from the point of view of our own ends, we should probably make a botch of remodelling the universe. How much more then from the point of view of ends we cannot see! Wise men therefore regret as little as they can. But still some regrets are pretty obstinate and hard to stifle,—regrets for acts of wanton cruelty or treachery, for example, whether performed by others or by ourselves. Hardly any one can remain *entirely* optimistic after reading the confession of the murderer at Brockton the other day: how, to get rid of the wife whose continued existence bored him, he inveigled her into a desert spot, shot her four times, and then, as she lay on the ground and said to him, "You didn't do it on purpose, did you, dear?" replied, "No, I didn't do it on purpose," as he raised a rock and smashed her skull. Such an occurrence, with the mild sentence and self-satisfaction of the prisoner, is a field for a crop of regrets, which one need not take up in detail. We feel that, although a perfect mechanical fit to the rest of the universe, it is a bad moral fit, and that something else would really have been better in its place.

But for the deterministic philosophy the murder, the sentence, and the prisoner's optimism were all necessary from eternity; and nothing else for a moment had a ghost of a chance of being put into their place. To admit such a chance, the determinists tell us, would be to make a suicide of reason; so we must steel our hearts against the thought. And here our plot thickens, for we see the first of those difficult implications of determinism and monism which it is my purpose to make you feel. If this Brockton murder was called for by the rest of the universe, if it had to come at its preappointed hour, and if nothing else would have been consistent with the sense of the whole, what are we to think of the universe? Are we stubbornly to stick to our judgment of regret, and say, though it *couldn't* be, yet it *would* have been a better universe with something different from this Brockton murder in it? That, of course, seems the natural and spontaneous thing for us to do; and yet it is nothing short of deliberately espousing a kind of pessimism. The judgment of regret calls the murder bad. Calling a thing bad means, if it mean anything at all, that the thing ought not to be, that something else ought to be in its stead. Determinism, in denying that anything else can be in its stead, virtually defines the universe as a place in which what ought to be is impossible,—in other words, as an organism whose constitution is afflicted with an incurable taint, an irremediable flaw. The pessimism of a Schopenhauer says no more than this,—that the murder is a symptom; and that it is a vicious symptom because it belongs to a vicious whole, which can express its nature no otherwise than by bringing forth just such a symptom as that at this particular spot. Regret for the murder must transform itself, if we are determinists and wise, into a larger regret. It is absurd to regret the murder alone. Other things being what they are, *it* could not be different. What we should regret is that whole frame of things of which the murder is one member. I see no escape whatever from this pessimistic conclusion, if, being determinists, our judgment of regret is to be allowed to stand at all.

The only deterministic escape from pessimism is everywhere to abandon the judgment of regret. That this can be done, history shows to be not impossible. The devil, *quoad existentiam,* may be good. That is, although he be a *principle* of evil, yet the universe, with such a principle in it, may practically be a better universe than it could have been without. On every hand, in a small way, we find that a certain amount of evil is a condition by which a higher form of good is bought. There is nothing to prevent anybody from generalizing this view, and trusting that if we could but see things in the largest of all ways, even such matters as this Brockton murder would appear to be paid for by the uses that follow in their train. An optimism *quand même,* a systematic and infatuated optimism like that ridiculed by Voltaire in his Candide, is one of the possible ideal ways in which a man may train himself to look on life. Bereft of dogmatic hardness and lit up with the expression of a tender and pathetic hope, such an optimism has been the grace of some of the most religious characters that ever lived.

> Throb thine with Nature's throbbing breast,
> And all is clear from east to west.

Even cruelty and treachery may be among the absolutely blessed fruits of time, and to quarrel with any of their details may be blasphemy. The only real blasphemy, in short, may be that pessimistic temper of the soul which lets it give way to such things as regrets, remorse, and grief.

Thus, our deterministic pessimism may become a deterministic optimism at the price of extinguishing our judgments of regret.

But does not this immediately bring us into a curious logical predicament? Our determinism leads us to call our judgments of regret wrong, because they are pessimistic in implying that what is impossible yet ought to be. But how then about the judgments of regret themselves? If they are wrong, other judgments, judgments of approval presumably, ought to be in their place. But as they are necessitated, nothing else *can* be in their place; and the universe is just what it was before,—namely, a place in which what ought to be appears impossible. We have got one foot out of the pessimistic bog, but the other one sinks all the deeper. We have rescued our actions from the bonds of evil, but our judgments are now held fast. When murders and treacheries cease to be sins, regrets are theoretic absurdities and errors. The theoretic and the active life thus play a kind of seesaw with each other on the ground of evil. The rise of either sends the other down. Murder and treachery cannot be good without regret being bad: regret cannot be good without treachery and murder being bad. Both, however, are supposed to have been foredoomed: so something must be fatally unreasonable, absurd, and wrong in the world. It must be a place of which either sin or error forms a necessary part.

But this brings us right back, to the question of indeterminism. . . . For the only consistent way of representing a pluralism and a world whose parts may affect one another through their conduct being either good or bad is the indeterministic way. What interest, zest, or excitement can there be in achieving the right way, unless we are enabled to feel that the wrong way is also a possible and a natural way—nay, more, a menacing and an imminent way? And what sense can there be in condemning ourselves for taking the wrong way, unless we need have done nothing of the sort, unless the right way was open to us as well? I cannot understand the belief that an act is bad, without regret at its happening. I cannot understand regret without the admission of real, genuine possibilities in the world. Only *then* is it other than a mockery to feel, after we have failed to do our best, that an irreparable opportunity is gone from the universe, the loss of which it must forever after mourn. The indeterminism I defend, the free-will theory of popular sense based on the judgment of regret, represents that world as vulnerable, and liable to be injured by certain of its parts if they act wrong. And it represents their acting wrong as a matter of possibility or accident, neither inevitable nor yet to be infallibly warded off. In all this, it is a theory devoid either of transparency or of stability. It gives us a pluralistic, restless universe, in which no single point of view can ever take in the whole scene; and to a mind possessed of the love of unity at any cost, it will, no doubt, remain forever inacceptable. . . . The great point is that the possibilities are really *here*. Whether it be we who solve them or he working through us, at those soul-trying moments when fate's scales seem to quiver, and good snatches the victory from evil or shrinks nerveless from the fight, is of small account, so long as we admit that the issue is decided nowhere else than *here* and *now*. *That* is what gives the palpitating reality to our moral life and makes it tingle, as Mr. Mallock says, with so strange and elaborate an excitement. This reality, this excitement, are what the determinists, hard and soft alike, suppress by their denial that *anything* is decided here and now, and their dogma that all things were foredoomed and settled long ago.

THINK ABOUT

1. Have you ever chosen the weakest of two desires? How could you prove it?

2. Can you think of any act which was not completely determined by past events?

3. The soft determinist says that, "I am free insofar as my actions aren't constrained, even though they are caused by past events." Do you agree that you are free under such circumstances?

4. Are there any indetermined events in nature?

Readings

1. Ayer, A. J. "Freedom and Necessity," in *Philosophical Essays*. London: Macmillan, 1954, pp. 271–284. A clearly written article in behalf of the view that freedom is compatible with determinism.

2. Campbell, C. A. "Is 'Free Will' A Pseudo-Problem?" *Mind*, LX (1951), 446–465. Criticizes the reconciliationist position, especially in the way it is put forward by Nowell-Smith, Schlick, and Stevenson.

3. Clemens, Samuel. "What Is Man?" in *What Is Man? And Other Essays*. New York: Harper, 1917. With typical touches of humor, Mark Twain argues in this essay that man is a machine totally determined by outside influences.

4. Darrow, Clarence. *Plea in Defense of Loeb and Leopold*. Gerard, Kan.: Little Blue Books, 1926, pp. 40–43. A famous lawyer, in the course of defending two killers, argues that determinism is true and therefore man is not responsible for his actions.

5. Lehrer, Keith. "Can We Know That We Have Free Will By Introspection?" *Journal of Philosophy*, LVII (1960), 145–157. Argues that we can know that we have free will by introspection.

6. Wood, Ledger. "The Free-Will Controversy," *Philosophy*, XVI (1941), 386–397. Highly readable statement of arguments in behalf of determinism and against libertarianism.

two

Are Ethics Relative?

8

Ethics Are
Relative

William Sumner (1840–1910) was a sociologist and anthropologist. His books include *Folkways* (1907), *The Challenge of Facts* (1914), and *The Forgotten Man* (1918).

Many people believe that all morals are relative and consequently that all moral principles are equally good. This is especially true of some of the young generation today who reject the customary ethics of the establishment. These youths observe that there is a wide variability in moral standards accepted by people in different societies and during different eras. It is easy to show that there are many actions which are considered right in one society and wrong in another. Hence they say that there is no universal right or wrong. The Hippie statement, "do your own thing," particularly derives from the belief in cultural relativism and is an assertion of belief in relativism.

In the first article which follows, Sumner argues the case for cultural relativism. He observes that, as people seek to satisfy their needs, behavior becomes habitual, which is accepted by all of the members of a given society. He points out that although these "folkways" vary widely among societies, men make their own society from which they make judgments about others. Hence they believe their own mores are the only morally right actions.

---

1. According to Sumner, how did folkways originate? Are they always beneficial?
2. What is the "right" folkway?
3. Define and give an illustration of ethnocentrism.
4. Define mores. What is their significance for society and its institutions?
5. What is the relation, according to Sumner, between mores and morals?
6. How does he explain conscience?
7. What is the meaning of "immoral"?

1. Definition and mode of origin of the folkways. If we put together all that we have learned from anthropology and ethnography about primitive men and primitive society, we perceive that the first task of life is to live. — Men begin with acts, not with thoughts. Every moment brings necessities which must be satisfied at once. Need was the first experience, and it was followed at once by a blundering effort to satisfy it. It is generally taken for granted that men inherited some guiding instincts from their beast ancestry, and it may be true, although it has never been proved. If there were such inheritances, they controlled and aided the first efforts to satisfy needs. Analogy makes it easy to assume that the ways of beasts had produced channels of habit and predisposition along which dexterities and other psychophysical activities would run easily. Experiments with newborn animals show that in the absence of any experience of the relation of means to ends, efforts to satisfy needs are clumsy and blundering. The method is that of trial and failure, which produces repeated pain, loss, and disappointments. Nevertheless, it is a method of rude experiment and selection. The earliest efforts of men were of this kind. Need was the impelling force. Pleasure and pain, on the one side and the other, were the rude constraints which defined the line on which efforts must proceed. The ability to distinguish between pleasure and pain is the only psychical power which is to be assumed. Thus ways of doing things were selected, which were expedient. They answered the purpose better than other ways, or with less toil and pain. Along the course on which efforts were compelled to go, habit, routine, and skill were developed. The struggle to maintain existence

From *Folkways,* by W. G. Sumner, Chaps. 1, 2, 5, and 11. Copyright, 1907, by W. G. Sumner. Published by Ginn and Company.

was carried on, not individually, but in groups. Each profited by the other's experience; hence there was concurrence towards that which proved to be most expedient. All at last adopted the same way for the same purpose; hence the ways turned into customs and became mass phenomena. Instincts were developed in connection with them. In this way folkways arise. The young learn them by tradition, imitation, and authority. The folkways, at a time, provide for all the needs of life then and there. They are uniform, universal in the group, imperative, and invariable. As time goes on, the folkways become more and more arbitrary, positive, and imperative. If asked why they act in a certain way in certain cases, primitive people always answer that it is because they and their ancestors always have done so. A sanction also arises from ghost fear. The ghosts of ancestors would be angry if the living should change the ancient folkways.

3. Folkways are made unconsciously.   It is of the first importance to notice that, from the first acts by which men try to satisfy needs, each act stands by itself, and looks no further than the immediate satisfaction. From recurrent needs arise habits for the individual and customs for the group, but these results are consequences which were never conscious, and never foreseen or intended. They are not noticed until they have long existed, and it is still longer before they are appreciated. Another long time must pass, and a higher stage of mental development must be reached, before they can be used as a basis from which to deduce rules for meeting, in the future, problems whose pressure can be foreseen. The folkways, therefore, are not creations of human purpose and wit. They are like products of natural forces which men unconsciously set in operation, or they are like the instinctive ways of animals, which are developed out of experience, which reach a final form of maximum adaptation to an interest, which are handed down by tradition and admit of no exception or variation, yet change to meet new conditions, still within the same limited methods, and without rational reflection or purpose. From this it results that all the life of human beings, in all ages and stages of culture, is primarily controlled by a vast mass of folkways handed down from the earliest existence of the race, having the nature of the ways of other animals, only the topmost layers of which are subject to change and control, and have been somewhat modified by human philosophy, ethics, and religion, or by other acts of intelligent reflection. . . .

28. Folkways due to false inference.   Furthermore, folkways have been formed by accident, that is, by irrational and incongruous action, based on pseudo-knowledge. In Molembo a pestilence broke out soon after a Portuguese had died there. After that the natives took all possible measures not to allow any white man to die in their country. On the Nicobar islands some natives who had just begun to make pottery died. The art was given up and never again attempted. White men gave to one Bushman in a kraaı a stick ornamented with buttons as a symbol of authority. The recipient died leaving the stick to his son. The son soon died. Then the Bushmen brought back the stick lest all should die. Until recently no building of incombustible materials could be built in any big town of the central province of Madagascar, on account of some ancient prejudice. . . . Soon after the Yakuts saw a camel for the first time smallpox broke out amongst them. They thought the camel to be the agent of the disease. A woman amongst the same people contracted an endogamous marriage. She soon afterwards became blind. This was thought to be on account of the violation of ancient customs. A very great number of such cases could be collected. In fact they represent the current mode of reasoning of nature people. It is their custom to reason that, if one thing follows another, it is due to it. A great number of customs are traceable to the notion of the evil eye, many more to ritual notions of uncleanness. No scientific investigation could discover the origin of the folkways mentioned, if the origin had not chanced to become known to civilized men. We must believe that the known cases illustrate the irrational and incongruous origin of many folkways. In civilized history also we know that customs have owed their origin to "historical accident"—the vanity of a princess, the deformity of a king, the whim of a democracy, the love intrigue of a statesman or prelate. By the institutions of another age it may be provided that no one of these things can affect decisions, acts, or interests, but then the power to decide the ways may have passed to clubs, trades unions, trust, commercial rivals, wire-pullers, politicians, and political fanatics. In these cases also the causes and origins may escape investigation.

29. Harmful folkways.   There are folkways which are positively harmful. Very often these are just the ones for which a definite reason can be given. The destruction of a man's goods at his death is a direct deduction from other-worldliness; the dead man is supposed to want in the other world just what he wanted here. The destruction of a man's goods at his death was a great waste of capital, and it must have had a disastrous effect on the interests of the living, and must have very seriously hindered the development of civilization. With this custom we must class all the expenditure of labor and capital on graves, temples, pyramids, rites, sacrifices, and support of priests, so far as these were supposed to benefit the dead. The faith in goblinism produced other-worldly interests which overruled ordinary worldly interests. Foods have often been forbidden which were plentiful, the prohibition of which injuriously lessened the food supply. There is a tribe of Bushmen who will eat no goat's flesh, although goats are the most numerous domestic animals in the district. Where totemism exists it is regularly accompanied by a taboo on eating the totem animal. Whatever may be the real principle in totemism, it overrules the interest in an abundant food supply. "The origin of the sacred regard paid to the cow must be sought in the primitive nomadic life of the Indo-European race," because it is common to Iranians and Indians of Hindostan. The Libyans ate oxen but not cows. The same was true of the Phoenicians and Egyptians. In some cases the sense of a food taboo is not to be learned. It may have been entirely capricious. Mohammed would not eat lizards, because he thought them the offspring of a metamorphosed clan of Israelites. On the other hand, the protective taboo which forebade killing crocodiles, pythons, cobras, and other animals enemies of man was harmful to his interests, whatever the motive. "It seems to be a fixed article of belief throughout southern India, that all who have willfully or accidentally killed a snake, especially a cobra, will certainly be punished, either in this life or the next, in one of three ways: either by childlessness, or by leprosy, or by ophthalmia " Where this faith exists man has a greater interest to spare a cobra than to kill it. India furnishes a great number of cases of harmful mores. "In India every tendency of humanity seems intensified and exaggerated. No country in the world is so conservative in its traditions, yet no country has undergone so many religious changes and vicissitudes." "Every year thousands perish of disease that might recover if they would take proper nourishment, and drink the medicine that science prescribes, but which they imagine that their religion forbids them to touch.". . .

30. How "true" and "right" are found.   If a savage puts his hand too near the fire, he suffers pain and draws it back. He knows nothing of the laws of the radiation of heat, but his instinctive action conforms to that law as if he did know it. If he wants to catch an animal for food, he must study its habits and prepare a device adjusted to those habits. If it fails, he must try again, until his observation is "true" and his device is "right." All the practical and direct element in the folkways seems to be due to common sense, natural reason, intuition, or some other original mental endowment. It seems rational (or rationalistic) and utilitarian. Often in the mythologies this ultimate rational element was ascribed to the teaching of a god or a culture hero. In modern mythology it is accounted for as "natural."

Although the ways adopted must always be really "true" and "right" in relation to facts, for otherwise they could not answer their purpose, such is not the primitive notion of true and right.

31. The folkways are "right." Rights. Morals.   The folkways are the "right" ways to satisfy all interests, because they are traditional, and exist in fact. They extend over the whole of life. There is a right way to catch game, to win a wife, to make one's self appear, to cure disease, to honor ghosts, to treat comrades or strangers, to behave when a child is born, on the warpath, in council, and so on in all cases which can arise. The ways are defined on the negative side, that is, by taboos. The "right" way is the way which the ancestors used and which has been handed down. The tradition is its own warrant. It is not held subject to verification by experience. The notion of right is in the folkways. It is not outside of them, of independent origin, and brought to them to test them. In the folkways, whatever is, is right. This is because they are traditional, and therefore contain in themselves the authority of the ancestral ghosts. When we come to the folkways we are at the end of our analysis. The notion of right and ought is the same in regard to all the folkways, but the degree of it varies with the importance of the interest at stake. The obligation of conformable and coöperative action is far greater under ghost fear and war than in other matters, and the social sanctions are severer, because group interests are supposed to be at stake. Some usages contain only a slight element of right and ought. It may well be believed that notions of right and duty, and of social welfare, were first developed in connection with ghost fear and other-worldliness, and therefore that, in that field also, folkways were first raised to mores. "Rights" are the rules of mutual give and take in the competition of life which are imposed on comrades in the in-group, in order that the peace may prevail there which is essential to the group strength. Therefore rights can never be "natural" or "God-given," or absolute in any sense. The morality of a group at a time is the sum of the taboos and prescriptions in the folkways by which right conduct is defined. Therefore morals can never be intuitive. They are historical, institutional, and empirical.

World philosophy, life policy, right, rights, and morality are all products of the folkways. They are reflections on, and generalizations from, the experience of pleasure and pain which is won in efforts to carry on the struggle for existence under actual life conditions. The generalizations are very crude and vague in their germinal forms. They are all embodied in folklore, and all our philosophy and science have been developed out of them.

15. Ethnocentrism is the technical name for this view of things in which one's own group is the center of everything, and all others are scaled and rated with reference to it. Folkways correspond to it to cover both the inner and the outer relation. Each group nourishes its own pride and vanity, boasts itself superior, exalts its own divinities, and looks with contempt on outsiders. Each group thinks its own folkways the only right ones, and if it observes that other groups have other folkways, these excite its scorn. Opprobrious epithets are derived from these differences. "Pig-eater," "cow-

eater," "uncircumcised," "jabberers," are epithets of contempt and abomination. The Tupis called the Portuguese by a derisive epithet descriptive
of birds which have feathers around their feet, on account of trousers. For
our present purpose the most important fact is that ethnocentrism leads
a people to exaggerate and intensify everything in their own folkways which
is peculiar and which differentiates them from others. It therefore strengthens the folkways.

16. Illustrations of ethnocentrism.   The Papuans on New Guinea are broken up into village units which are kept separate by hostility, cannibalism,
head hunting, and divergences of language and religion. Each village is
integrated by its own language, religion, and interests. A group of villages
is sometimes united into a limited unity by connubium. A wife taken inside
of this group unit has full status; one taken outside of it has not. The petty
group units are peace groups within and are hostile to all outsiders. The
Mbayas of South America believed that their deity had bidden them live
by making war on others, taking their wives and property, and killing their
men.

17.   When Caribs were asked whence they came, they answered, "We alone
are people." The meaning of the name Kiowa is "real or principal people."
The Lapps call themselves "men," or "human beings." The Greenland
Eskimo think that Europeans have been sent to Greenland to learn virtue
and good manners from the Greenlanders. Their highest form of praise for
a European is that he is, or soon will be, as good as a Greenlander. The
Tunguses call themselves "men." As a rule it is found that nature peoples
call themselves "men." Others are something else—perhaps not defined—
but not real men. In myths the origin of their own tribe is that of the real
human race. They do not account for the others. The Ainos derive their
name from that of the first man, whom they worship as a god. Evidently
the name of the god is derived from the tribe name. When the tribal name
has another sense, it is always boastful or proud. The Ovambo name is a
corruption of the name of the tribe for themselves, which means "the
wealthy." Amongst the most remarkable people in the world for ethnocentrism are the Seri of Lower California. They observe an attitude of suspicion
and hostility to all outsiders, and strictly forbid marriage with outsiders.

18.   The Jews divided all mankind into themselves and Gentiles. They were
the "chosen people." The Greeks and Romans called all outsiders "barbarians." In Euripides' tragedy of *Iphigenia in Aulis* Iphigenia says that it is
fitting that Greeks should rule over barbarians, but not contrariwise, because Greeks are free, and barbarians are slaves. The Arabs regarded themselves as the noblest nation and all others as more or less barbarous. In 1896,

the Chinese minister of education and his counselors edited a manual in which this statement occurs: "How grand and glorious is the Empire of China, the middle kingdom! She is the largest and richest in the world. The grandest men in the world have all come from the middle empire." In all the literature of all the states equivalent statements occur, although they are not so naïvely expressed. In Russian books and newspapers the civilizing mission of Russia is talked about, just as, in the books and journals of France, Germany, and the United States, the civilizing mission of those countries is assumed and referred to as well understood. Each state now regards itself as the leader of civilization, the best, the freest, and the wisest, and all others as inferior. Within a few years our own man-on-the-curbstone has learned to class all foreigners of the Latin peoples as "dagos," and "dago" has become an epithet of contempt. These are all cases of ethnocentrism.

34. Definition of the mores.   When the elements of truth and right are developed into doctrines of welfare, the folkways are raised to another plane. They then become capable of producing inferences, developing into new forms, and extending their constructive influence over men and society. Then we call them the mores. The mores are the folkways, including the philosophical and ethical generalizations as to societal welfare which are suggested by them, and inherent in them, as they grow.

42. Purpose of the present work.   "Ethology" would be a convenient term for the study of manners, customs, usages, and mores, including the study of the way in which they are formed, how they grow or decay, and how they affect the interests which it is their purpose to serve. The Greeks applied the term "ethos" to the sum of the characteristic usages, ideas, standards, and codes by which a group was differentiated and individualized in character from other groups. "Ethics" were things which pertained to the ethos and therefore the things which were the standard of right. The Romans used "mores" for customs in the broadest and richest sense of the word, including the notion that customs served welfare, and had traditional and mystic sanction, so that they were properly authoritative and sacred. It is a very surprising fact that modern nations should have lost these words and the significant suggestions which inhere in them. The English language has no derivative noun from "mores," and no equivalent for it. The French *moeurs* is trivial compared with "mores." The German *Sitte* renders "mores" but very imperfectly. The modern peoples have made morals and morality a separate domain, by the side of religion, philosophy, and politics. In that sense, morals is an impossible and unreal category. It has no existence, and can have none. The word "moral" means what belongs or appertains to the mores. Therefore the category of morals can never be defined without reference to something outside of itself. Ethics, having lost connection with the ethos of a people, is an attempt to systematize the current notions of right and wrong upon some basic principle, generally with the purpose of establishing moral on an absolute doctrine, so that it shall be universal, absolute, and everlasting. In a general way also, whenever a thing can be called moral, or connected with some ethical generality, it is thought to be "raised," and disputants whose method is to employ ethical generalities assume especial authority for themselves and their views. These methods of discussion are most employed in treating of social topics, and they are disastrous to sound study of facts. They help to hold the social sciences under the dominion of metaphysics. The abuse has been most developed in connection with political economy, which has been almost robbed of the character of a serious discipline by converting its discussions into ethical disquisitions.

43. Why use the word mores.   "Ethica," in the Greek sense, or "ethology," as above defined, would be good names for our present work. We aim to study the ethos of groups, in order to see how it arises, its power and influence, the modes of its operation on members of the group, and the various attributes of it (ethica). "Ethology" is a very unfamiliar word. It has been used for the mode of setting forth manners, customs, and mores in satirical comedy. The Latin word "mores" seems to be, on the whole, more practically convenient and available than any other for our purpose, as a name for the folkways with the connotations of right and truth in respect to welfare, embodied in them. The analysis and definition above given show that in the mores we must recognize a dominating force in history, constituting a condition as to what can be done, and as to the methods which can be employed.

44. Mores are a directive force.   Of course the view which has been stated is antagonistic to the view that philosophy and ethics furnish creative and determining forces in society and history. That view comes down to us from the Greek philosophy and it has now prevailed so long that all current discussion conforms to it. Philosophy and ethics are pursued as independent disciplines, and the results are brought to the science of society and to statesmanship and legislation as authoritative dicta. . . . It can be seen also that philosophy and ethics are products of the folkways. They are taken out of the mores, but are never original and creative; they are secondary and derived. They often interfere in the second stage of the sequence—act, thought, act. Then they produce harm, but some ground is furnished for the claim that they are creative or at least regulative. In fact, the real process in great bodies of men is not one of deduction from any great principle of philosophy or ethics. It is one of minute efforts to live well under existing conditions, which efforts are repeated indefinitely by great numbers, getting strength from habit and from the fellowship of united action. The resultant folkways become coercive. All are forced to conform, and the folkways dominate the societal life. Then they seem true and right, and arise into mores as the norm of welfare. Thence are produced faiths, ideas, doctrines, religions, and philosophies, according to the stage of civilization and the fashions of reflection and generalization.

61. The mores and institutions.   Institutions and laws are produced out of mores. An institution consists of a concept (idea, notion, doctrine, interest) and a structure. The structure is a framework, or apparatus, or perhaps only a number of functionaries set to coöperate in prescribed ways at a certain conjuncture. The structure holds the concept and furnishes instrumentalities for bringing it into the world of facts and action in a way to serve the interests of men in society. Institutions are either crescive or enacted. They are crescive when they take shape in the mores, growing by the instinctive efforts by which the mores are produced. Then the efforts, through long use, become definite and specific. Property, marriage, and religion are the most primary institutions. They began in folkways. They became customs. They developed into mores by the addition of some philosophy of welfare, however crude. Then they were made more definite and specific as regards the rules, the prescribed acts, and the apparatus to be employed. This produced a structure and the institution was complete. Enacted institutions are products of rational invention and intention. They belong to high civilization. Banks are institutions of credit founded on usages which can be traced back to barbarism. There came a time when, guided by rational reflection on experience, men systematized and regulated the usages which had become current, and thus created positive institutions of credit, defined by law and sanctioned by the force of the state. Pure enacted institutions which are strong and prosperous are hard to find. It is too difficult to invent and create an institution, for a purpose, out of nothing. The electoral college in the constitution of the United States is an example. In that case the democratic mores of the people have seized upon the device and made of it something quite different from what the inventors planned. All institutions have come out of mores, although the rational element in them is sometimes so large that their origin in the mores is not to be ascertained except by an historical investigation (legislatures, courts, juries, joint stock companies, the stock exchange). Property, marriage, and religion are still almost entirely in the mores. Amongst nature men any man might capture and hold a woman at any time, if he could. He did it by superior force which was its own supreme justification. But his act brought his group and her group into war, and produced harm to his comrades.

They forbade capture, or set conditions for it. Beyond the limits, the individual might still use force, but his comrades were no longer responsible. The glory to him, if he succeeded, might be all the greater. His control over his captive was absolute. Within the prescribed conditions, "capture" became technical and institutional, and rights grew out of it. The woman had a status which was defined by custom, and was very different from the status of a real captive. Marriage was the institutional relation, in the society and under its sanction, of a woman to a man, where the woman had been obtained in a prescribed way. She was then a "wife." What her rights and duties were was defined by the mores, as they are to-day in all civilized society.

62. Laws.   Acts of legislation come out of the mores. In low civilization all societal regulations are customs and taboos, the origin of which is unknown. Positive laws are impossible until the stage of verification, reflection, and criticism is reached. Until that point is reached there is only customary law, or common law. The customary law may be codified and systematized with respect to some philosophical principles, and yet remain customary. The codes of Manu and Justinian are examples. Enactment is not possible until reverence for ancestors has been so much weakened that it is no longer thought wrong to interfere with traditional customs by positive enactment. Even then there is reluctance to make enactments, and there is a stage of transition during which traditional customs are extended by interpretation to cover new cases and to prevent evils. Legislation, however, has to seek standing ground on the existing mores, and it soon becomes apparent that legislation, to be strong, must be consistent with the mores. Things which have been in the mores are put under police regulation and later under positive law. It is sometimes said that "public opinion" must ratify and approve police regulations, but this statement rests on an imperfect analysis. The regulations must conform to the mores, so that the public will not think them too lax or too strict. The mores of our urban and rural populations are not the same; consequently legislation about intoxicants which is made by one of these sections of the population does not succeed when applied to the other. The regulation of drinking places, gambling places, and disorderly houses has passed through the above-mentioned stages. It is always a question of expediency whether to leave a subject under the mores, or to make a police regulation for it, or to put it into criminal law. Betting, horse racing, dangerous sports, electric cars, and vehicles are cases now of things which seem to be passing under positive enactment and out of the unformulated control of the mores. When an enactment is made there is a sacrifice of the elasticity and automatic self-adaptation of custom, but an enactment is specific and is provided with sanctions. Enactments come into use when conscious purposes are formed, and it is believed that specific devices can be framed by which to realize such purposes in the society. Then also prohibitions take the place of taboos, and punishments are planned to be deterrent rather than revengeful. The mores of different societies, or of different ages, are characterized by greater or less readiness and confidence in regard to the use of positive enactments for the realization of societal purposes.

63. How laws and institutions differ from mores.   When folkways have become institutions or laws they have changed their character and are to be distinguished from the mores. The element of sentiment and faith inheres in the mores. Laws and institutions have a rational and practical character, and are more mechanical and utilitarian. The great difference is that institutions and laws have a positive character, while mores are unformulated and undefined. There is a philosophy implicit in the folkways; when it is made explicit it becomes technical philosophy. Objectively regarded, the mores are the customs which actually conduce to welfare under existing life conditions. Acts under the laws and institutions are conscious and voluntary; under the folkways they are always unconscious and involuntary, so that they have the character of natural necessity. Educated reflection and skepticism can disturb this spontaneous relation. The laws, being positive prescriptions, supersede the mores so far as they are adopted. It follows that the mores come into operation where laws and tribunals fail. The mores cover the great field of common life where there are no laws or police regulations. They cover an immense and undefined domain, and they break the way in new domains, not yet controlled at all. The mores, therefore, build up new laws and police regulations in time.

83. Inertia and rigidity of the mores.   We see that we must conceive of the mores as a vast system of usages, covering the whole of life, and serving all its interests; also containing in themselves their own justification by tradition and use and wont, and approved by mystic sanctions until, by rational reflection, they develop their own philosophical and ethical generalizations, which are elevated into "principles" of truth and right. They coerce and restrict the newborn generation. They do not stimulate to thought, but the contrary. The thinking is already done and is embodied in the mores. They never contain any provision for their own amendment. They are not questions, but answers, to the problem of life. They present themselves as final and unchangeable, because they present answers which are offered as "the truth." No world philosophy, until the modern scientific world philosophy, and that only within a generation or two, has ever presented itself as perhaps transitory, certainly incomplete, and liable to be set aside to-morrow by more knowledge. No popular world philosophy or life policy ever can present itself in that light. It would cost too great a mental strain. All the groups whose mores we consider far inferior to our own are quite as well satisfied with theirs as we are with ours. The goodness or badness of mores consists entirely in their adjustment to the life conditions and the interests of the time and place. . . . Therefore it is a sign of ease and welfare when no thought is given to the mores, but all coöperate in them instinctively. The nations of southeastern Asia show us the persistency of the mores, when the element of stability and rigidity in them becomes predominant. Ghost fear and ancestor worship tend to establish the persistency of the mores by dogmatic authority, strict taboo, and weighty sanctions. The mores then lose their naturalness and vitality. They are stereotyped. They lose all relation to expediency. They become an end in themselves. They are imposed by imperative authority without regard to interests or conditions (caste, child marriage, widows). When any society falls under the dominion of this disease in the mores it must disintegrate before it can live again. In that diseased state of the mores all learning consists in committing to memory the words of the sages of the past who established the formulae of the mores. Such words are "sacred writings," a sentence of which is a rule of conduct to be obeyed quite independently of present interests, or of any rational considerations.

232. Mores and morals; social code.   For every one the mores give the notion of what ought to be. This includes the notion of what ought to be done, for all should coöperate to bring to pass, in the order of life, what ought to be. All notions of propriety, decency, chastity, politeness, order, duty, right, rights, discipline, respect, reverence, coöperation, and fellowship, especially all things in regard to which good and ill depend entirely on the point at which the line is drawn, are in the mores. The mores can make things seem right and good to one group or one age which to another seem antagonistic to every instinct of human nature. The thirteenth century bred in every heart such a sentiment in regard to heretics that inquisitors had no more misgivings in their proceedings than men would have now if they should attempt to exterminate rattlesnakes. The sixteenth century gave to all such notions about witches that witch persecutors thought they were waging war on enemies of God and man. Of course the inquisitors and witch persecutors constantly developed the notions of heretics and witches. They exaggerated the notions and then gave them back again to the mores, in their expanded form, to inflame the hearts of men with terror and hate and to become, in the next stage, so much more fantastic and ferocious motives. Such is the reaction between the mores and the acts of the living generation. The world philosophy of the age is never anything but the reflection on the mental horizon, which is formed out of the mores, of the ruling ideas which are in the mores themselves. It is from a failure to recognize the to and fro in this reaction that the current notion arises that mores are produced by doctrines. The "morals" of an age are never anything but the consonance between what is done and what the mores of the age require. The whole revolves on itself, in the relation of the specific to the general, within the horizon formed by the mores. Every attempt to win an outside standpoint from which to reduce the whole to an absolute philosophy of truth and right, based on an unalterable principle, is a delusion. New elements are brought in only by new conquests of nature through science and art. The new conquests change the conditions of life and the interests of the members of the society. Then the mores change by adaptation to new conditions and interests. The philosophy and ethics then follow to account for and justify the changes in the mores; often, also, to claim that they have caused the changes. They never do anything but draw new lines of bearing between the parts of the mores and the horizon of thought within which they are inclosed, and which is a deduction from the mores. The horizon is widened by more knowledge, but for one age it is just as much a generalization from the mores as for another. It is always unreal. It is only a product of thought. The ethical philosophers select points on this horizon from which to take their bearings, and they think that they have won some authority for their systems when they travel back again from the generalization to the specific custom out of which it was deduced. The cases of the inquisitors and witch persecutors who toiled arduously and continually for their chosen ends, for little or no reward, show us the relation between mores on the one side and philosophy, ethics, and religion on the other.

494. Honor, seemliness, common sense, conscience. Honor, common sense, seemliness, and conscience seem to belong to the individual domain. They are reactions produced in the individual by the societal environment. Honor is the sentiment of what one owes to one's self. It is an individual prerogative, and an ultimate individual standard. Seemliness is conduct which befits one's character and standards. Common sense, in the current view, is a natural gift and universal outfit. As to honor and seemliness, the popular view seems to be that each one has a fountain of inspiration in himself to furnish him with guidance. Conscience might be added as another natural or supernatural "voice," intuition, and part of the original outfit of all human beings as such. If these notions could be verified, and if they proved true, no discussion of them would be in place here, but as to honor it is a well-known and undisputed fact that societies have set codes of honor and standards of it which were arbitrary, irrational, and both individually and socially inexpedient, as ample experiment has proved.

These codes have been and are imperative, and they have been accepted and obeyed by great groups of men who, in their own judgment, did not believe them sound. These codes came out of the folkways of the time and place. Then comes the question whether it is not always so. Is honor, in any case, anything but the code of one's duty to himself which he has accepted from the group in which he was educated? Family, class, religious sect, school, occupation, enter into the social environment. In every environment there is a standard of honor. When a man thinks that he is acting most independently, on his personal prerogative, he is at best only balancing against each other the different codes in which he has been educated, e.g., that of the trades union against that of the Sunday school, or of the school against that of the family. What we think "natural" and universal, and to which we attribute an objective reality, is the sum of traits whose origin is so remote, and which we share with so many, that we do not know when or how we took them up, and we can remember no rational selection by which we adopted them. The same is true of common sense. It is the stock of ways of looking at things which we acquired unconsciously by suggestion from the environment in which we grew up. Some have more common sense than others, because they are more docile to suggestion, or have been taught to make judgments by people who were strong and wise. Conscience also seems best explained as a sum of principles of action which have in one's character the most original, remote, undisputed, and authoritative position, and to which questions of doubt are habitually referred. If these views are accepted, we have in honor, common sense, and conscience other phenomena of the folkways, and the notions of eternal truths of philosophy or ethics, derived from somewhere outside of men and their struggles to live well under the conditions of earth, must be abandoned as myths.

438. Specification of the subject.   The ethnographers write of a tribe that the "morality" in it, especially of the women, is low or high, etc. This is the technical use of morality—as a thing pertaining to the sex relation only or especially, and the ethnographers make their propositions by applying our standards of sex behavior, and our form of the sex taboo, to judge the folkways of all people. All that they can properly say is that they find a great range and variety of usages, ideas, standards, and ideals, which differ greatly from ours. Some of them are far stricter than ours. Those we do not consider nobler than ours. We do not feel that we ought to adopt any ways because they are more strict than our traditional ones. We consider many to be excessive, silly, and harmful. A Roman senator was censured for impropriety because he kissed his wife in the presence of his daughter.

439. Meaning of "immoral."   When, therefore, the ethnographers apply condemnatory or depreciatory adjectives to the people whom they study, they beg the most important question which we want to investigate; that is, What are standards, codes, and ideas of chastity, decency, propriety, modesty, etc., and whence do they arise? The ethnographical facts contain the answer to this question. . . . "Immoral" never means anything but contrary to the mores of the time and place. Therefore the mores and the morality may move together, and there is no permanent or universal standard by which right and truth in regard to these matters can be established and different folkways compared and criticised.

Folkways - unconscious
Law - deliberate - thought out -

9

Ethics Aren't
Relative

W. T. Stace (1886–1967), an Anglo-American empirical philosopher, was born in London and studied at Trinity College,
Dublin. From 1910 to 1932 he served in the British civil service
in Ceylon. While in Ceylon, he published *A Critical History
of Greek Philosophy* (1920) and *The Philosophy of Hegel*
(1924). In 1932, he resigned from the civil service and accepted a teaching position at Princeton University, where he
remained until his retirement in 1955. His other works include
The Theory of Knowledge and Existence (1932), *The Concept
of Morals* (1937), *Time and Eternity* (1952), and *Mysticism
and Philosophy* (1960).

In contrast to the view of the cultural relativist, Stace argues that one
cannot conclude that all moral actions are relative from the fact of conflicting mores. He argues that if we believe that morals are relative,
then we cannot make judgments as to which is best, we cannot argue that
there is moral progress, and that we cannot even define the limits of given
"groups" or "societies" between which there are these variable morals.

TO STUDY

1. How does Stace characterize the position of the absolutist?
2. What historical reason has caused the belief in absolutism?
3. How does Stace define ethical relativity? Is it a platitude?

4. Characterize his summation of the difference between the relativist and the absolutist.
5. What is the argument from multiple standards for ethical relativity? What is Stace's refutation?
6. What is the argument in favor of ethical relativity based on the lack of a universally binding code? How does Stace refute it?
7. What is the argument against ethical relativity based on the meaning of critical judgments?
8. What is the argument based on the notion of moral progress?
9. What is the ultimate consequence of the position of the ethical relativist?

There is an opinion widely current nowadays in philosophical circles which passes under the name of "ethical relativity." Exactly what this phrase means or implies is certainly far from clear. But unquestionably it stands as a label for the opinions of a group of ethical philosophers whose position is roughly on the extreme left wing among the moral theorizers of the day. And perhaps one may best understand it by placing it in contrast with the opposite kind of extreme view against which, undoubtedly, it has arisen as a protest. For among moral philosophers one may clearly distinguish a left and a right wing. Those of the left wing are the ethical relativists. They are the revolutionaries, the clever young men, the up to date. Those of the right wing we may call the ethical absolutists. They are the conservatives and the old-fashioned.

Ethical Absolutism

According to the absolutists there is but one eternally true and valid moral code. This moral code applies with rigid impartiality to all men. What is a duty for me must likewise be a duty for you. And this will be true whether you are an Englishman, a Chinaman, or a Hottentot. If cannibalism is an abomination in England or America, it is an abomination in central Africa, notwithstanding that the African may think otherwise. The fact that he sees nothing wrong in his cannibal practices does not make them for him morally right. They are as much contrary to morality for him as they are for

Reprinted with permission of The Macmillan Company from *The Concept of Morals* by W. T. Stace. Copyright 1937 by The Macmillan Company, renewed 1965 by The Macmillan Company.

us. The only difference is that he is an ignorant savage who does not know this. There is not one law for one man or race of men, another for another. There is not one moral standard for Europeans, another for Indians, another for Chinese. There is but one law, one standard, one morality, for all men. And this standard, this law, is absolute and unvarying.

Moreover, as the one moral law extends its dominion over all the corners of the earth, so too it is not limited in its application by any considerations of time or period. That which is right now was right in the centuries of Greece and Rome, nay, in the very ages of the cave man. That which is evil now was evil then. If slavery is morally wicked today, it was morally wicked among the ancient Athenians, notwithstanding that their greatest men accepted it as a necessary condition of human society. Their opinion did not make slavery a moral good for them. It only showed that they were, in spite of their otherwise noble conceptions, ignorant of what is truly right and good in this matter.

The ethical absolutist recognizes as a fact that moral customs and moral ideas differ from country to country and from age to age. This indeed seems manifest and not to be disputed. We think slavery morally wrong, the Greeks thought it morally unobjectionable. The inhabitants of New Guinea certainly have very different moral ideas from ours. But the fact that the Greeks or the inhabitants of New Guinea think something right does not make it right, even for them. Nor does the fact that we think the same things wrong make them wrong. They are *in themselves* either right or wrong. What we have to do is to discover which they are. What anyone thinks makes no difference. It is here just as it is in matters of physical science. We believe the earth to be a globe. Our ancestors may have thought it flat. This does not show that it *was* flat, and is *now* a globe. What it shows is that men having in other ages been ignorant about the shape of the earth have now learned the truth. So if the Greeks thought slavery morally legitimate, this does not indicate that it was for them and in that age morally legitimate, but rather that they were ignorant of the truth of the matter.

The ethical absolutist is not indeed committed to the opinion that his own, or our own, moral code is the true one. Theoretically at least he might hold that slavery is ethically justifiable, that the Greeks knew better than we do about this, that ignorance of the true morality lies with us and not with them. All that he is actually committed to is the opinion that, whatever the true moral code may be, it is always the same for all men in all ages. His view is not at all inconsistent with the belief that humanity has still much to learn in moral matters. If anyone were to assert that in five hundred years the moral conceptions of the present day will appear as barbarous to the people of that age as the moral conceptions of the middle ages appear to us now, he need not deny it. If anyone were to assert that the ethics of Christianity are by no means final, and will be superseded in future ages by vastly nobler moral ideals, he need not deny this either. For it is of the essence of his creed to believe that morality is in some sense objective, not man-made, not produced by human opinion; that its principles are real truths about which men have to learn—just as they have to learn about the shape of the world—about which they may have been ignorant in the past, and about which therefore they may well be ignorant now.

Thus although absolutism is conservative in the sense that it is re-garded by the more daring spirits as an out of date opinion, it is not necessarily conservative in the sense of being committed to the blind sup-port of existing moral ideas and institutions. If ethical absolutists are some-times conservative in this sense too, that is their personal affair. Such conservatism is accidental, not essential to the absolutist's creed. There is no logical reason, in the nature of the case, why an absolutist should not be a communist, an anarchist, a surrealist, or an upholder of free love. The fact that he is usually none of these things may be accounted for in various ways. But it has nothing to do with the sheer logic of his ethical position. The sole opinion to which he is committed is that whatever is morally right (or wrong)—be it free love or monogamy or slavery or cannibalism or vegetarianism—is morally right (or wrong) for all men at all times.

Usually the absolutist goes further than this. He often maintains, not merely that the moral law is the same for all the men on this planet—which is, after all, a tiny speck in space—but that in some way or in some sense it has application everywhere in the universe. He may express himself by saying that it applies to all "rational beings"—which would apparently include angels and the men on Mars (if they are rational). He is apt to think that the moral law is a part of the fundamental structure of the universe. But with this aspect of absolutism we need not, at the moment, concern ourselves. At present we may think of it as being simply the opinion that there is a single moral standard for all human beings.

Historical Causes for the Acceptance of Absolutism.   This brief and rough sketch of ethical absolutism is intended merely to form a background against which we may the more clearly indicate, by way of contrast, the theory of ethical relativity. Up to the present, therefore, I have not given any of the reasons which the absolutist can urge in favour of his case. It is sufficient for my purpose at the moment to state *what* he believes, without going into the question of *why* he believes it. But before proceeding to our next step—the explanation of ethical relativity—I think it will be helpful to indicate some of the historical causes (as distinguished from logical reasons) which have helped in the past to render absolutism a plausible interpretation of morality as understood by European peoples.

Our civilization is a Christian civilization. It has grown up, during nearly two thousand years, upon the soil of Christian monotheism. In this soil our whole outlook upon life, and consequently all our moral ideas, have their roots. They have been moulded by this influence. The wave of religious scepticism which, during the last half century, has swept over us, has altered this fact scarcely at all. The moral ideas even of those who most violently reject the dogmas of Christianity with their intellects are still Christian ideas. This will probably remain true for many centuries even if Christian theology, as a set of intellectual beliefs, comes to be wholly rejected by every educated person. It will probably remain true so long as our civilization lasts. A child cannot, by changing in later life his intellectual creed, strip himself of the early formative moral influences of his childhood, though he can no doubt modify their results in various minor ways. With the outlook on life which was instilled into him in his early days he, in large measure, lives and dies. So it is with a civilization. And our civilization, whatever religious or irreligious views it may come to hold or reject, can hardly escape within its lifetime the moulding influences of its Christian origin. Now ethical absolutism was, in its central ideas, the product of Christian theology.

The connection is not difficult to detect. For morality has been conceived, during the Christian dispensation, as issuing from the will of God. That indeed was its single and all-sufficient source. There would be no point, for the naive believer in the faith, in the philosopher's questions regarding the foundations of morality and the basis of moral obligation. Even to ask such questions is a mark of incipient religious scepticism. For the true believer the author of the moral law is God. What pleases God, what God commands—that is the definition of right. What displeases God, what he forbids, that is the definition of wrong. Now there is, for the Christian monotheist, only one God ruling over the entire universe. And this God is rational, self-consistent. He does not act upon whims. Consequently his will and his commands must be the same everywhere. They will be unvarying for all peoples and in all ages. If the heathen have other moral ideas than ours—inferior ideas—that can only be because they live in ignorance of the true God. If they knew God and his commands, their ethical precepts would be the same as ours.

Polytheistic creeds may well tolerate a number of diverse moral codes. For the God of the western hemisphere might have different views from those entertained by the God of the eastern hemisphere. And the God of the north might issue to his worshippers commands at variance with the commands issued to other peoples by the God of the south. But a mono-theistic religion implies a single universal and absolute morality.

This explains why ethical absolutism, until very recently, was not only believed by philosophers but *taken for granted without any argument.* . . .

Ethical Relativism

We can now turn to the consideration of ethical relativity. . . . The revolt of the relativists against absolutism is, I believe, part and parcel of the general revolutionary tendency of our times. In particular it is a result of the decay of belief in the dogmas of orthodox religion. Belief in absolutism was supported, as we have seen, by belief in Christian monotheism. And now that, in an age of widespread religious scepticism, that support is withdrawn, absolutism tends to collapse. Revolutionary movements are as a rule, at any rate in their first onset, purely negative. They attack and destroy. And ethical relativity is, in its essence, a purely negative creed. It is simply a denial of ethical absolutism. That is why the best way of explaining it is to begin by explaining ethical absolutism. If we understand that what the latter asserts the former denies, then we understand ethical relativity.

Any ethical position which denies that there is a single moral standard which is equally applicable to all men at all times may fairly be called a species of ethical relativity. There is not, the relativist asserts, merely one moral law, one code, one standard. There are many moral laws, codes, standards. What morality ordains in one place or age may be quite different from what morality ordains in another place or age. The moral code of Chinamen is quite different from that of Europeans, that of African savages quite different from both. Any morality, therefore, is relative to the age, the place, and the circumstances in which it is found. It is in no sense absolute.

This does not mean merely—as one might at first sight be inclined to suppose—that the very same kind of action which is *thought* right in one country and period may be *thought* wrong in another. This would be a mere platitude, the truth of which everyone would have to admit. Even the absolutist would admit this—would even wish to emphasize it—since he is well aware that different peoples have different sets of moral ideas, and his whole point is that some of these sets of ideas are false. What the relativist means to assert is, not this platitude, but that the very same kind of action which *is* right in one country and period may *be* wrong in another. And this, far from being a platitude, is a very startling assertion.

It is very important to grasp thoroughly the difference between the two ideas. For there is reason to think that many minds tend to find ethical relativity attractive because they fail to keep them clearly apart. It is so very obvious that moral ideas differ from country to country and from age to age. And it is so very easy, if you are mentally lazy, to suppose that to say this means the same as to say that no universal moral standard exists,—or in other words that it implies ethical relativity. We fail to see that the word "standard" is used in two different senses. It is perfectly true that, in one sense, there are many variable moral standards. We speak of judging a man by the standard of his time. And this implies that different times have different standards. And this, of course, is quite true. But when the word "standard" is used in this sense it means simply the set of moral ideas current during the period in question. It means what people *think* right, whether as a matter of fact it *is* right or not. On the other hand when the absolutist asserts that there exists a single universal moral "standard," he is not using the word in this sense at all. He means by "standard" what *is* right as distinct from what people merely think right. His point is that although what people think right varies in different countries and periods, yet what actually is right is everywhere and always the same. And it follows that when the ethical relativist disputes the position of the absolutist and denies that any universal moral standard exists he too means by "standard" what actually is right. But it is exceedingly easy, if we are not careful, to slip loosely from using the word in the first sense to using it in the second sense; and to suppose that the variability of moral beliefs is the same thing as the variability of what really is moral. And unless we keep the two senses of the word "standard" distinct, we are likely to think the creed of ethical relativity much more plausible than it actually is.

The genuine relativist, then, does not merely mean that Chinamen may think right what Frenchmen think wrong. He means that what is wrong for the Frenchman may *be* right for the Chinaman. And if one enquires how, in those circumstances, one is to know what actually is right in China or in France, the answer comes quite glibly. What is right in China is the same as what people think right in China; and what is right in France is the same as what people think right in France. So that, if you want to know what is moral in any particular country or age all you have to do is to ascertain what are the moral ideas current in that age or country. Those ideas are, *for that age or country,* right. Thus what is morally right is identified with what is thought to be morally right, and the distinction which we made above between these two is simply denied. To put the same thing in another way, it is denied that there can be or ought to be any distinction between the two senses of the word "standard." There is only one kind of standard of right and wrong, namely, the moral ideas current in any particular age or country.

Moral right *means* what people think morally right. It has no other meaning. What Frenchmen think right is, therefore, right *for Frenchmen*. And evidently one must conclude—though I am not aware that relativists are anxious to draw one's attention to such unsavoury but yet absolutely necessary conclusions from their creed—that cannibalism is right for people who believe in it, that human sacrifice is right for those races which practice it, and that burning widows alive was right for Hindus until the British stepped in and compelled the Hindus to behave immorally by allowing their widows to remain alive.

When it is said that, according to the ethical relativist, what is thought right in any social group is right for that group, one must be careful not to misinterpret this. The relativist does not, of course, mean that there actually is an objective moral standard in France and a different objective standard in England, and that French and British opinions respectively give us correct information about these different standards. His point is rather that there are no objectively true moral standards at all. There is no single universal objective standard. Nor are there a variety of local objective standards. All standards are subjective. People's subjective feelings about morality are the only standards which exist.

To sum up. The ethical relativist consistently denies, it would seem, whatever the ethical absolutist asserts. For the absolutist there is a single universal moral standard. For the relativist there is no such standard. There are only local, ephemeral, and variable standards. For the absolutist there are two senses of the word "standard." Standards in the sense of sets of current moral ideas are relative and changeable. But the standard in the sense of what is actually morally right is absolute and unchanging. For the relativist no such distinction can be made. There is only one meaning of the word standard, namely, that which refers to local and variable sets of moral ideas. Or if it is insisted that the word must be allowed two meanings, then the relativist will say that there is at any rate no actual example of a standard in the absolute sense, and that the word as thus used is an empty name to which nothing in reality corresponds; so that the distinction between the two meanings becomes empty and useless. Finally—though this is merely saying the same thing in another way—the absolutist makes a distinction between what actually is right and what is thought right. The relativist rejects this distinction and identifies what is moral with what is thought moral by certain human beings or groups of human beings. . . .

Arguments in Favor of Ethical Relativity. . . .   The first [argument] is that which relies upon the actual varieties of moral "standards" found in the world. It was easy enough to believe in a single absolute morality in older times when there was no anthropology, when all humanity was divided clearly into two groups, Christian peoples and the "heathen." Christian peoples knew and possessed the one true morality. The rest were savages whose moral ideas could be ignored. But all this is changed. Greater knowledge has brought greater tolerance. We can no longer exalt our own morality as alone true, while dismissing all other moralities as false or inferior. The investigations of anthropologists have shown that there exist side by side in the world a bewildering variety of moral codes. On this topic endless volumes have been written, masses of evidence piled up. Anthropologists have ransacked the Melanesian Islands, the jungles of New Guinea, the steppes of Siberia, the deserts of Australia, the forests of central Africa, and have brought back with them countless examples of weird, extravagant, and fantastic "moral" customs with which to confound us. We learn that all kinds of horrible practices are, in this, that, or the other place, regarded as essential to virtue. We find that there is nothing, or next to nothing, which has always and everywhere been regarded as morally good by all men. Where then is our universal morality? Can we, in face of all this evidence, deny that it is nothing but an empty dream?

This argument, taken by itself, is a very weak one. It relies upon a single set of facts—the variable moral customs of the world. But this variability of moral ideas is admitted by both parties to the dispute, and is capable of ready explanation upon the hypothesis of either party. The relativist says that the facts are to be explained by the non-existence of any absolute moral standard. The absolutist says that they are to be explained by human ignorance of what the absolute moral standard is. And he can truly point out that men have differed widely in their opinions about all manner of topics including the subject-matters of the physical sciences—just as much as they differ about morals. And if the various different opinions which men have held about the shape of the earth do not prove that it has no one real shape, neither do the various opinions which they have held about morality prove that there is no one true morality.

Thus the facts can be explained equally plausibly on either hypothesis. There is nothing in the facts themselves which compels us to prefer the relativistic hypothesis to that of the absolutist. And therefore the argument fails to prove the relativist conclusion. If that conclusion is to be established, it must be by means of other considerations.

This is the essential point. But I will add some supplementary remarks. The work of the anthropologists, upon which ethical relativists seem to rely so heavily, has as a matter of fact added absolutely nothing *in principle* to what has always been known about the variability of moral ideas. Educated people have known all along that the Greeks tolerated sodomy, which in modern times has been regarded in some countries as an abominable crime; that the Hindus thought it a sacred duty to burn their widows; that trickery, now thought despicable, was once believed to be a virtue; that terrible torture was thought by our own ancestors only a few centuries ago to be a justifiable weapon of justice; that it was only yesterday that western peoples came to believe that slavery is immoral. Even the ancients knew very well that moral customs and ideas vary—witness the writings of Herodotus. Thus the principle of the variability of moral ideas was well understood long before modern anthropology was ever heard of. Anthropology has added nothing to the knowledge of this principle except a mass of new and extreme examples of it drawn from very remote sources. But to multiply examples of a principle already well known and universally admitted adds nothing to the argument which is built upon that principle. The discoveries of the anthropologists have no doubt been of the highest importance in their own sphere. But in my considered opinion they have thrown no new light upon the special problems of the moral philosopher.

Although the multiplication of examples has no logical bearing on the argument, it does have an immense *psychological* effect upon people's minds. These masses of anthropological learning are impressive. They are propounded in the sacred name of "science." If they are quoted in support of ethical relativity—as they often are—people *think* that they must prove something important. They bewilder and over-awe the simple-minded, batter down their resistance, make them ready to receive humbly the doctrine of ethical relativity from those who have acquired a reputation by their immense learning and their claims to be "scientific." Perhaps this is why so much ado is made by ethical relativists regarding the anthropological evidence. But we must refuse to be impressed. We must discount all this mass of evidence about the extraordinary moral customs of remote peoples. Once we have admitted—as everyone who is instructed must have admitted these last two thousand years without any anthropology at all—the principle that moral ideas vary, all this new evidence adds nothing to the argument. And the argument itself proves nothing for the reasons already given. . . .

[Another] argument in favour of ethical relativity . . . consists in alleging that no one has ever been able to discover upon what foundation an absolute morality could rest, or from what source a universally binding moral code could derive its authority.

If, for example, it is an absolute and unalterable moral rule that all men ought to be unselfish, from whence does this *command* issue? For a command it certainly is, phrase it how you please. There is no difference in meaning between the sentence "You ought to be unselfish" and the sentence "Be unselfish." Now a command implies a commander. An obligation implies some authority which obliges. Who is this commander, what this authority? Thus the vastly difficult question is raised of *the basis of moral obligation.* Now the argument of the relativist would be that it is impossible to find any basis for a universally binding moral law; but that it is quite easy to discover a basis for morality if moral codes are admitted to be variable, ephemeral, and relative to time, place, and circumstance.

. . . I am assuming that it is no longer possible to solve this difficulty by saying naively that the universal moral law is based upon the uniform commands of God to all men. There will be many, no doubt, who will dispute this. But I am not writing for them. I am writing for those who feel the necessity of finding for morality a basis independent of particular religious dogmas. And I shall therefore make no attempt to argue the matter.

The problem which the absolutist has to face, then, is this. The religious basis of the one absolute morality having disappeared, can there be found for it any other, any secular, basis? If not, then it would seem that we cannot any longer believe in absolutism. We shall have to fall back upon belief in a variety of perhaps mutually inconsistent moral codes operating over restricted areas and limited periods. No one of these will be better, or more true, than any other. Each will be good and true for those living in those areas and periods. We shall have to fall back, in a word, on ethical relativity. . . .

Arguments Against Ethical Relativity. . . . Ethical relativity, in asserting that the moral standards of particular social groups are the only standards which exist, renders meaningless all propositions which attempt to compare these standards with one another in respect of their moral worth. And this is a very serious matter indeed. We are accustomed to think that the moral ideas of one nation or social group may be "higher" or "lower" than those of another. We believe, for example, that Christian ethical ideals are nobler than those of the savage races of central Africa. Probably most of us would think that the Chinese moral standards are higher than those of the inhabitants of New Guinea. In short we habitually compare one civilization with another and judge the sets of ethical ideas to be found in them to be some better, some worse. The fact that such judgments are very difficult to make with any justice, and that they are frequently made on very superficial and prejudiced grounds, has no bearing on the question now at issue. The question is whether such judgments have any *meaning.* We habitually assume that they have.

But on the basis of ethical relativity they can have none whatever. For the relativist must hold that there is no *common* standard which can be applied to the various civilizations judged. Any such comparison of moral standards implies the existence of some superior standard which is applicable to both. And the existence of any such standard is precisely what the relativist denies. According to him the Christian standard is applicable only to Christians, the Chinese standard only to Chinese, the New Guinea standard only to the inhabitants of New Guinea.

What is true of comparisons between the moral standards of different races will also be true of comparisons between those of different ages. It is not unusual to ask such questions as whether the standard of our own day is superior to that which existed among our ancestors five hundred years ago. And when we remember that our ancestors employed slaves, practiced barbaric physical tortures, and burnt people alive, we may be inclined to think that it is. At any rate we assume that the question is one which has meaning and is capable of rational discussion. But if the ethical relativist is right, whatever we assert on this subject must be totally meaningless. For here again there is no common standard which could form the basis of any such judgments.

This in its turn implies that the whole notion of moral *progress* is a sheer delusion. Progress means an advance from lower to higher, from worse to better. But on the basis of ethical relativity it has no meaning to say that the standards of this age are better (or worse) than those of a previous age. For there is no common standard by which both can be measured. . . .

If these arguments are valid, the ethical relativist cannot really maintain that there is anywhere to be found a moral standard binding upon anybody against his will. And he cannot maintain that, even within the social group, there is a common standard as between individuals. And if that is so, then even judgments to the effect that one man is morally better than another become meaningless. All moral valuation thus vanishes. There is nothing to prevent each man from being a rule unto himself. The result will be moral chaos and the collapse of all effective standards. . . .

But even if we assume that the difficulty about defining moral groups has been surmounted, a further difficulty presents itself. Suppose that we have not definitely decided what are the exact boundaries of the social group within which a moral standard is to be operative. And we will assume—as is invariably done by relativists themselves—that this group is to be some actually existing social community such as a tribe or nation. How are we to know, even then, what actually *is* the moral standard within that group? How is anyone to know? How is even a member of the group to know? For there are certain to be within the group—at least this will be true among advanced peoples—wide differences of opinion as to what is right, what wrong. Whose opinion, then, is to be taken as representing *the* moral standard of the group? Either we must take the opinion of the majority within the group, or the opinion of some minority. If we rely upon the ideas of the majority, the results will be disastrous. Wherever there is found among a people a small band of select spirits, or perhaps one man, working for the establishment of higher and nobler ideals than those commonly accepted by the group, we shall be compelled to hold that, for that people at that time, the majority are right, and that the reformers are wrong and are preaching what is immoral. We shall have to maintain, for example, that Jesus was preaching immoral doctrines to the Jews. Moral goodness will have to be equated always with the mediocre and sometimes with the definitely base and ignoble. If on the other hand we say that the moral standard of the group is to be identified with the moral opinions of some minority, then what minority is this to be? We cannot answer that it is to be the minority composed of the best and most enlightened individuals of the group. This would involve us in a palpably vicious circle. For by what standard are these individuals to be judged the best and the most enlightened? There is no principle by which we could select the right minority. And therefore we should have to consider every minority as good as every other. And this means that we should have no logical right whatever to resist the claim of the gangsters of Chicago—if such a claim were made— that their practices represent the highest standards of American morality. It means in the end that every individual is to be bound by no standard save his own.

The ethical relativists are great empiricists. *What* is the actual moral standard of any group can only be discovered, they tell us, by an examination on the ground of the moral opinions and customs of that group. But will they tell us how they propose to decide, when they get to the ground, which of the many moral opinions they are sure to find there is *the* right one in that group? To some extent they will be able to do this for the Melanesian Islanders—from whom apparently all lessons in the nature of morality are in future to be taken. But it is certain that they cannot do it for advanced peoples whose members have learnt to think for themselves and to entertain among themselves a wide variety of opinions. They cannot do it unless they accept the calamitous view that the ethical opinion of the majority is always right. We are left therefore once more with the conclusion that, even within a particular social group, anybody's moral opinion is as good as anybody else's, and that every man is entitled to be judged by his own standards.

Finally, not only is ethical relativity disastrous in its consequences for moral theory. It cannot be doubted that it must tend to be equally disastrous in its impact upon practical conduct. If men come really to believe that one moral standard is as good as another, they will conclude that their own moral standard has nothing special to recommend it. They might as well then slip down to some lower and easier standard. It is true that, for a time, it may be possible to hold one view in theory and to act practically upon another. But ideas, even philosophical ideas, are not so ineffectual that they can remain for ever idle in the upper chambers of the intellect. In the end they seep down to the level of practice. They get themselves acted on. . . .

These, then, are the main arguments which the anti-relativist will urge against ethical relativity. And perhaps finally he will attempt a diagnosis of the social, intellectual, and psychological conditions of our time to which the emergence of ethical relativism is to be attributed. His diagnosis will be somewhat as follows.

We have abandoned, perhaps with good reason, the oracles of the past. Every age, of course, does this. But in our case it seems that none of us knows any more whither to turn. We do not know what to put in the place of that which has gone. What ought we, supposedly civilized peoples, to aim at? What are to be our ideals? What is right? What is wrong? What is beautiful? What is ugly? No man knows. We drift helplessly in this direction and that. We know not where we stand nor whither we are going.

There are, of course, thousands of voices frantically shouting directions. But they shout one another down, they contradict one another, and the upshot is mere uproar. And because of this confusion there creeps upon us an insidious scepticism and despair. Since no one knows what the truth is, we will deny that there is any truth. Since no one knows what right is, we will deny that there is any right. Since no one knows what the beautiful is, we will deny that there is any beauty. Or at least we will say—what comes to the same thing—that what people (the people of any particular age, region, society)—think to be true is true *for them;* that what people think morally right is morally right *for them;* that what people think beautiful is beautiful *for them.* There is no common and objective standard in any of these matters. Since all the voices contradict one another, they must be all equally right (or equally wrong, for it makes no difference which we say). It is from the practical confusion of our time that these doctrines issue. When all the despair and defeatism of our distracted age are expressed in abstract concepts, are erected into a philosophy, it is then called relativism —ethical relativism, esthetic relativism, relativity of truth. Ethical relativity is simply defeatism in morals.

And the diagnosis will proceed. Perhaps, it will say, the current pessimism as to our future is unjustified. But there is undoubtedly a wide spread feeling that our civilization is rushing downwards to the abyss. If this should be true, and if nothing should check the headlong descent, then perhaps some historian of the future will seek to disentangle the causes. The causes will, of course, be found to be multitudinous and enormously complicated. And one must not exaggerate the relative importance of any of them. But it can hardly be doubted that our future historian will include somewhere in his list the failure of the men of our generation to hold steadfastly before themselves the notion of an (even comparatively) unchanging moral idea He will cite that feebleness of intellectual and moral grasp which has led them weakly to harbour the belief that no one moral aim is really any better than any other, that each is good and true for those who entertain it. This meant, he will surely say, that men had given up in despair the struggle to attain moral truth. Civilization lives in and through its upward struggle. Whoever despairs and gives up the stuggle, whether it be an individual or a whole civilization, is already inwardly dead.

THINK ABOUT

1. Are you a relativist? If so, how do you answer Stace's arguments?

2. Are the Western religions relativist in any sense?

3. Comment on:

   The great fault of all ethics hitherto has been that they believed themselves to have to deal only with the relations of man to man. In reality, however, the question is what is his attitude to the world and all life that comes within his reach. A man is ethical only when life, as such, is sacred to him, that of plants and animals as that of his fellow men, and when he devotes himself helpfully to all life that is in need of help.

   Albert Schweitzer

4. Comment on:

   (When asked if he had but a single gift to bequeath to the next generation, Ray Bradbury replied:) . . . The gift to see that not all Republicans are evil, that not all Democrats are evil, that not all Communists are evil, that not all Negroes are evil, that not all whites are evil, that not all anything is evil. The ability to see the paradox in every person.

   Ray Bradbury

Readings

1. Brandt, R. "Ethical Relativism," in *Ethical Theory*. Englewood Cliffs, N.J.: Prentice Hall, 1959, Chs. 5, 6, 11.

2. Herskovits, M. "A Defense by an Anthropologist," in *Man and his Works*. New York: Macmillan, 1948.

3. Howard, A. V. "Do Anthropologists Become Moral Relativists by Mistake?" *Inquiry* 11 (1968), 175–189.

4. Ladd, J. *Ethical Relativism.* Belmont, Calif.: Wadsworth Publishing Company, 1973.

5. McClintock, T. "The Definition of Ethical Relativism," *Personalist* 50 (1969), 435–447.

6. Nielsen, K. "Anthropology and Ethics," *Journal of Value Inquiry* 5 (1971), 253–266.

7. Roberts, G. W. "Some Refutations of Private Subjectivism in Ethics," *Journal of Value Inquiry* 5 (1971), 292–309.

three

Is Man Always Selfish?

10

Man Is
Always Selfish

Bernard de Mandeville (1670–1733) was an Anglo-Dutch
moral philosopher and satirist. His reputation rests on his
celebrated work, *A Fable of Peace* (1705).

Some sophisticated college students, as well as many others, believe that
each individual always seeks his own pleasure or his own interest. Such a
belief is called *psychological hedonism*. This refers to the fact that every time
a man does something he does it in order to promote what he conceives
to be his own happiness. Some people go further and believe that even if
this weren't true, everyone ought to seek his own pleasure. This is called
ethical hedonism.

Bernard de Mandeville is an eighteenth-century writer who presents
the classical case for psychological hedonism. He not only argues that
all men always seek their own welfare, but society is better off simply
because they do it.

TO STUDY

1. How do animals differ from man concerning their inclinations
   towards pleasing themselves?
2. What has been the endeavor of law-givers concerning the appetites
   of men? How is this related to honor and shame?
3. How have the skillful politicians defined virtue and vice?
4. What is Mandeville's reply to the charge that many do good to
   others without coveting thanks?

All untaught animals are only solicitous of pleasing themselves, and naturally follow the bent of their own inclinations, without considering the good
or harm that from their being pleased will accrue to others. This is the
reason that, in the wild state of nature, those creatures are fittest to live
peaceably together in great numbers, that discover the least of understanding, and have the fewest appetites to gratify; and consequently no species
of animals is, without the curb of government, less capable of agreeing long
together in multitudes than that of man; yet such are his qualities, whether
good or bad, I shall not determine, that no creature besides himself can ever
be made sociable: but, being an extraordinarily selfish and headstrong, as
well as cunning animal, however he may be subdued by superior strength,
it is impossible by force alone to make him tractable, and receive the
improvements he is capable of.

The chief thing therefore, which lawgivers and other wise men, that
have laboured for the establishment of society, have endeavoured, has been
to make the people they were to govern believe, that it was more beneficial
for every body to conquer than indulge his appetites, and much better to
mind the public than what seemed his private interest. As this has always
been a very difficult task, so no wit or eloquence has been left untried to
compass it; and the moralists and philosophers of all ages employed their
utmost skill to prove the truth of so useful an assertion. But, whether
mankind would have ever believed it or not, it is not likely that any body
could have persuaded them to disapprove of their natural inclinations, or
prefer the good of others to their own, if, at the same time, he had not
showed them an equivalent to be enjoyed as a reward for the violence,
which, by so doing, they of necessity must commit upon themselves. Those
that have undertaken to civilize mankind were not ignorant of this; but
being unable to give so many real rewards as would satisfy all persons for
every individual action, they were forced to contrive an imaginary one, that,
as a general equivalent for the trouble of self-denial, should serve on all
occasions, and without costing any thing either to themselves or others, be
yet a most acceptable recompense to the receivers.

They thoroughly examined all the strength and frailities of our nature,
and observing that none were either so savage as not to be charmed with
praise, or so despicable as patiently to bear contempt, justly concluded that
flattery must be the most powerful argument that could be used to human
creatures. Making use of this bewitching engine, they extolled the excellency of our nature above other animals, and setting forth with unbounded
praises the wonders of our sagacity and vastness of understanding, bestowed

---

First printed in the second edition of Mandeville's *The Fable of the Bees, or Private Vices,*
Public Benefits, Etc., London, 1723.

a thousand encomiums on the rationality of our souls, by the help of which we were capable of performing the most noble achievements. Having, by this artful way of flattery, insinuated themselves into the hearts of men, they began to instruct them in the notions of honour and shame; representing the one as the worst of all evils, and the other as the highest good to which mortals could aspire: which being done, they laid before them how unbecoming it was the dignity of such sublime creatures to be solicitous about gratifying their appetites, which they had in common with brutes, and at the same time unmindful of those higher qualities that gave them the preeminence over all visible beings. They indeed confessed, that those impulses of nature were very pressing; that it was troublesome to resist, and very difficult wholly to subdue them. But this they only used as an argument to demonstrate how glorious the conquest of them was on the one hand and how scandalous on the other not to attempt it.

To introduce, moreover, an emulation amongst men, they divided the whole species into two classes, vastly differing from one another: the one consisted of abject, low-minded people, that always hunting after immediate enjoyment, were wholly incapable of self-denial, and without regard to the good of others, had no higher aim than their private advantage; such as being enslaved by voluptuousness, yielded without resistance to every gross desire, and made no use of their rational faculties but to heighten their sensual pleasure. These wild grovelling wretches, they said, were the dross of their kind, and having only the shape of men, differed from brutes in nothing but their outward figure. But the other class was made up of lofty high-spirited creatures, that free from sordid selfishness, esteemed the improvements of the mind to be their fairest possessions; and, setting a true value upon themselves, took no delight but in embellishing that part in which their excellency consisted; such as despising whatever they had in common with irrational creatures, opposed by the help of reason their most violent inclinations; and making a continual war with themselves, to promote the peace of others, aimed at no less than the public welfare and the conquest of their own passion.

Fortior est qui se quam qui fortissima Vincit Moenia . . .[1]

These they called the true representatives of their sublime species, exceeding in worth the first class by more degrees than that itself was superior to the beasts of the field.

As in all animals that are not too imperfect to discover pride, we find that the finest and such as are the most beautiful and valuable of their kind

---

[1] The man who conquers himself is stronger than the one who conquers the strongest states. [Cf. *Proverbs,* 16:32.]

have generally the greatest share of it; so in man, the most perfect of animals, it is so inseparable from his very essence (how cunningly soever some may learn to hide or disguise it) that without it the compound he is made of would want one of the chiefest ingredients; which, if we consider, it is hardly to be doubted but lessons and remonstrances, so skilfully adapted to the good opinion man has of himself as those I have mentioned, must, if scattered amongst a multitude, not only gain the assent of most of them as to the speculative part, but likewise induce several, especially the fiercest, most resolute, and best among them to endure a thousand inconveniences and undergo as many hardships, that they may have the pleasure of counting themselves men of the second class and consequently appropriating to themselves all the excellencies they have heard of it.

From what has been said, we ought to expect, in the first place, that the heroes who took such extraordinary pains to master some of their natural appetites and preferred the good of others to any visible interest of their own would not recede an inch from the fine notions they had received concerning the dignity of rational creatures; and having ever the authority of the government on their side, with all imaginable vigour assert the esteem that was due to those of the second class, as well as their superiority over the rest of their kind. In the second, that those who wanted a sufficient stock of either pride or resolution to buoy them up in mortifying of what was dearest to them, followed the sensual dictates of nature, would yet be ashamed of confessing themselves to be those despicable wretches that belonged to the inferior class and were generally reckoned to be so little removed from brutes; and that therefore, in their own defence, they would say as others did, and hiding their own imperfections as well as they could, cry up self-denial and public spiritedness as much as any: for it is highly probable, that some of them, convinced by the real proofs of fortitude and self-conquest they had seen, would admire in others what they found wanting in themselves, others be afraid of the resolution and prowess of those of the second class, and that all of them were kept in awe by the power of their rulers; wherefore it is reasonable to think, that none of them (whatever they thought in themselves) would dare openly contradict what by everybody else was thought criminal to doubt of.

This was (or at least might have been) the manner after which savage man was broke; from whence it is evident, that the first rudiments of morality broached by skilful politicians to render men useful to each other, as well as tractable, were chiefly contrived, that the ambitious might reap the more benefit from and govern vast numbers of them with the greater ease and security. This foundation of politics being once laid, it is impossible that man should long remain uncivilized: for even those who only strove to gratify their appetites, being continually crossed by others of the same stamp, could not but observe, that whenever they checked their inclinations or but followed them with more circumspection, they avoided a world of troubles and often escaped many of the calamities that generally attended the too eager pursuit after pleasure.

First, they received, as well as others, the benefit of those actions that were done for the good of the whole society and consequently could not forbear wishing well to those of the superior class that performed them. Secondly, the more intent they were in seeking their own advantage, without regard to others, the more they were hourly convinced that none stood so much in their way as those that were most like themselves.

It being the interest then of the very worst of them, more than any, to preach up public-spiritedness, that they might reap the fruits of the labour and self-denial of others, and at the same time indulge their own appetites with less disturbance, they agreed with the rest to call everything, which, without regard to the public, man should commit to gratify any of his appetites, *vice;* if in that action there could be observed the least prospect that it might either be injurious to any of the society or ever render himself less serviceable to others: and to give the name of *virtue* to every performance, by which man, contrary to the impulse of nature, should endeavour the benefit of others or the conquest of his own passions out of a rational ambition of being good.

It shall be objected that no society was ever any ways civilized before the major part had agreed upon some worship or other of an overruling power and consequently that the notions of good and evil and the distinction between virtue and vice were never the contrivance of politicians, but the pure effect of religion. Before I answer this objection, I must repeat what I have said already, that in this inquiry into the origin of moral virtue, I speak neither of Jews or Christians, but man in his state of nature and ignorance of the true Deity; and then I affirm, that the idolatrous superstitions of all other nations and the pitiful notions they had of the Supreme Being, were incapable of exciting man to virtue and good for nothing but to awe and amuse a rude and unthinking multitude. It is evident from history that in all considerable societies, how stupid or ridiculous soever people's received notions have been as to the deities they worshipped, human nature has ever exerted itself in all its branches and that there is no earthly wisdom or moral virtue, but at one time or other men have excelled in it in all monarchies and commonwealths, that for riches and power have been any ways remarkable.

The Egyptians, not satisfied with having deified all the ugly monsters they could think on, were so silly as to adore the onions of their own sowing; yet at the same time their country was the most famous nursery of arts and sciences in the world and themselves more eminently skilled in the deepest mysteries of nature than any nation has been since.

No states or kingdoms under heaven have yielded more or greater patterns in all sorts of moral virtues than the Greek and Roman empires, more especially the latter; and yet how loose, absurd and ridiculous were their sentiments as to sacred matters? For without reflecting on the extravagant number of their deities, if we only consider the infamous stories they fathered upon them, it is not to be denied but that their religion, far from teaching men the conquest of their passions and the way to virtue, seemed rather contrived to justify their appetites and encourage their vices. But if we would know what made them excel in fortitude, courage, and magnanimity, we must cast our eyes on the pomp of their triumphs, the magnificence of their monuments and arches; their trophies, statues, and inscriptions; the variety of their military crowns, their honours decreed to the dead, public encomiums on the living, and other imaginary rewards they bestowed on men of merit; and we shall find that what carried so many of them to the utmost pitch of self-denial was nothing but their policy in making use of the most effectual means that human pride could be flattered with.

It is visible, then, that it was not any heathen religion or other idolatrous superstition that first put man upon crossing his appetites and subduing his dearest inclinations, but the skilful management of wary politicians; and the nearer we search into human nature, the more we shall be convinced that the moral virtues are the political offspring which flattery begot upon pride

There is no man, of what capacity or penetration soever, that is wholly proof against the witchcraft of flattery, if artfully performed and suited to his abilities. Children and fools will swallow personal praise, but those that are more cunning, must be managed with much greater circumspection; and the more general the flattery is, the less it is suspected by those it is levelled at. What you say in commendation of a whole town is received with pleasure by all the inhabitants: speak in commendation of letters in general, and every man of learning will think himself in particular obliged to you. You may safely praise the employment a man is of or the country he was born in because you give him an opportunity of screening the joy he feels upon his own account under the esteem which he pretends to have for others.

It is common among cunning men that understand the power which flattery has upon pride, when they are afraid they shall be imposed upon, to enlarge, though much against their conscience, upon the honour, fair dealing, and integrity of the family, country, or sometimes the profession of him they suspect; because they know that men often will change their resolution and act against their inclination, that they may have the pleasure of continuing to appear in the opinion of some what they are conscious not to be in reality. Thus sagacious moralists draw men like angels, in hopes that the pride at least of some will put them upon copying after the beautiful originals which they are represented to be.

When the incomparable Sir Richard Steele, in the usual elegance of his easy style, dwells on the praises of his sublime species, and with all the embellishments of rhetoric sets forth the excellency of human nature, it is impossible not to be charmed with his happy turns of thought and the politeness of his expressions. But though I have been often moved by the force of his eloquence and ready to swallow the ingenious sophistry with pleasure, yet I could never be so serious, but, reflecting on his artful encomiums, I thought on the tricks made use of by the women that would teach children to be mannerly. When an awkward girl before she can either speak or go begins after many entreaties to make the first rude essays of curtseying, the nurse falls in an ecstacy of praise; "There is a delicate curtsey! O fine Miss! there is a pretty lady! Mama! Miss can make a better curtsey than her sister Molly!" The same is echoed over by the maids, whilst Mama almost hugs the child to pieces; only Miss Molly, who being four years older, knows how to make a very handsome curtsey, wonders at the perverseness of their judgment, and swelling with indignation, is ready to cry at the injustice that is done her, till, being whispered in the ear that it is only to please the baby and that she is a woman, she grows proud at being let into the secret, and rejoicing at the superiority of her understanding, repeats what has been said with large additions and insults over the weakness of her sister, whom all this while she fancies to be the only bubble among them. These extravagant praises would by anyone above the capacity of an infant be called fulsome flatteries, and, if you will, abominal lies; yet experience teaches us that by the help of such gross encomiums young misses will be brought to make pretty curtseys and behave themselves womanly much sooner, and with less trouble, than they would without them. It is the same with boys, whom they will strive to persuade that all fine gentlemen do as they are bid and that none but beggar boys are rude or dirty their clothes; nay, as soon as the wild brat with his untaught fist begins to fumble for his hat, the mother, to make him pull it off, tells him before he is two years old that he is a man; and if he repeats that action when she desires him, he is presently a captain, a lord mayor, a king, or something higher if she can think of it, till egged on by the force of praise, the little urchin endeavors to imitate man as well as he can and strains all his faculties to appear what his shallow noddle imagines he is believed to be.

The meanest wretch puts an inestimable value upon himself, and the highest wish of an ambitious man is to have all the world, as to that particular, of his opinion: so that the most insatiable thirst after fame that ever hero was inspired with was never more than an ungovernable greediness to engross the esteem and admiration of others in future ages as well as his own; and (what mortification soever this truth might be to the second thoughts of an Alexander or a Caesar) the great recompense in view, for which the most exalted minds have with so much alacrity sacrificed their quiet, health, sensual pleasures, and every inch of themselves, has never been anything else but the breath of man, the aerial coin of praise. Who can forbear laughing when he thinks on all the great men that have been so serious on the subject of that Macedonian madman, his capacious soul, that mighty heart, in one corner of which, according to Lorenzo Gratian, the world was so commodiously lodged that in the whole there was room for six more? Who can forbear laughing, I say, when he compares the fine things that have been said of Alexander with the end he proposed to himself from his vast exploits to be proved from his own mouth; when the vast pains he took to pass the Hydaspes forced him to cry out, Oh ye Athenians, could you believe what dangers I expose myself to, to be praised by you! To define then the reward of glory in the amplest manner, the most that can be said of it is that it consists in a superlative felicity which a man, who is conscious of having performed a noble action, enjoys in self-love, whilst he is thinking on the applause he expects of others.

But here I shall be told that besides the noisy toils of war and public bustle of the ambitious there are noble and generous actions that are performed in silence; that virtue being its own reward, those who are really good have a satisfaction in their consciousness of being so, which is all the recompense they expect from the most worthy performances; that among the heathens there have been men, who, when they did good to others, were so far from coveting thanks and applause, that they took all imaginable care to be forever concealed from those on whom they bestowed their benefits, and consequently that pride has no hand in spurring man on to the highest pitch of self-denial.

In answer to this I say that it is impossible to judge of a man's performance, unless we are thoroughly acquainted with the principle and motive from which he acts. Pity, though it is the most gentle and the least mischievous of all our passions, is yet as much a frailty of our nature as anger, pride, or fear. The weakest minds have generally the greatest share of it, for which reason none are more compassionate than women and children. It must be owned that of all our weaknesses, it is the most amiable and bears the greatest resemblance to virtue; nay, without a considerable mixture of it, the society could hardly subsist: but as it is an impulse of nature that consults neither the public interest nor our own reason, it may produce evil as well as good. It has helped to destroy the honour of virgins and corrupted the integrity of judges; and whoever acts from it as a principle, what good soever he may bring to the society, has nothing to boast of, but that he has indulged a passion that has happened to be beneficial to the public. There is no merit in saving an innocent babe ready to drop into the fire: the action is neither good nor bad, and what benefit soever the infant received, we only obliged ourselves; for to have seen it fall, and not strove to hinder it, would have caused a pain, which self-preservation compelled us to prevent: Nor has a rich prodigal, that happens to be of a commiserating temper and loves to gratify his passions, greater virtue to boast of when he relieves an object of compassion with what to himself is a trifle.

But such men, as without complying with any weakness of their own, can part from what they value themselves and from no other motive but their love to goodness perform a worthy action in silence: such men, I confess, have acquired more refined notions of virtue than those I have hitherto spoke of; yet even in these (with which the world has yet never swarmed) we may discover no small symptoms of pride, and the humblest man alive must confess that the reward of a virtuous action, which is the satisfaction that ensues upon it, consists in a certain pleasure he procures to himself by contemplating on his own worth: which pleasure, together with the occasion of it, are as certain signs of pride as looking pale and trembling at any imminent danger are the symptoms of fear.

If the too scrupulous reader should at first view condemn these notions concerning the origin of moral virtue and think them perhaps offensive to Christianity, I hope he will forbear his censures when he shall consider that nothing can render the unsearchable depth of the Divine Wisdom more conspicuous than that man, whom Providence had designed for society, should not only by his own frailties and imperfections be led into the road to temporal happiness, but likewise receive, from a seeming necessity of natural causes, a tincture of that knowledge, in which he was afterwards to be made perfect by the true religion, to his eternal welfare.

THINK ABOUT

1. "We judge ourselves by what we feel capable of doing, while others judge us by what we have already done."

   Longfellow

2. "Hell is—other people."

   Nietzsche

3. Comment on the following statements:
   (a) "I think; therefore I am."
   (b) "One never really knows other minds."

11

Man Isn't
Always Selfish

James Rachels (1941–), professor of philosophy at the University of Alabama-Birmingham in the areas of ethics and philosophy of action. Among his publications is *Moral Problems* (1971).

Rachels states the classical objections to theories of selfishness argued by such psychological hedonists as de Mandeville. He first challenges the view that everyone always does what he wants to do by showing that we do unpleasant acts for future pleasures and we do some things from feelings of obligation. Next he gives Bishop Butler's famous argument that what we often seek is not pleasure but certain objects such as food, drink, other people's pain, etc. The final part of this section is devoted to clearing up such confusions as the belief that selfishness means the same as self-interest.

Rachels then examines ethical hedonism, the view that man *ought* to seek his own pleasure. He finds that ultimately such a position entails that the advocate not feel compassion, etc. for others. This, Rachels contends, is untenable.

TO STUDY

1. Distinguish psychological egoism from ethical egoism.
2. What are Rachels' arguments against the view that all acts are done for self-interest?
3. If one derives satisfaction from helping others, does it make him selfish: Why or why not?
4. What are the three commonplace confusions which arise about psychological egoism?

5. State the argument against ethical egoism relating to its inability to be universalized.

6. Is there any telling argument against ethical egoism?

1. Our ordinary thinking about morality is full of assumptions that we almost never question. We assume, for example, that we have an obligation to consider the welfare of other people when we decide what actions to perform or what rules to obey; we think that we must refrain from acting in ways harmful to others, and that we must respect their rights and interests as well as our own. We also assume that people are in fact capable of being motivated by such considerations, that is, that people are not wholly selfish and that they do sometimes act in the interests of others.

Both of these assumptions have come under attack by moral sceptics, as long ago as by Glaucon in Book II of Plato's *Republic*. Glaucon recalls the legend of Gyges, a shepherd who was said to have found a magic ring in a fissure opened by an earthquake. The ring would make its wearer invisible and thus would enable him to go anywhere and do anything undetected. Gyges used the power of the ring to gain entry to the Royal Palace where he seduced the Queen, murdered the King, and subsequently seized the throne. Now Glaucon asks us to determine that there are two such rings, one given to a man of virtue and one given to a rogue. The rogue, of course, will use his ring unscrupulously and do anything necessary to increase his own wealth and power. He will recognize no moral constraints on his conduct, and, since the cloak of invisibility will protect him from discovery, he can do anything he pleases without fear of reprisal. So, there will be no end to the mischief he will do. But how will the so-called virtuous man behave? Glaucon suggests that he will behave no better than the rogue: "No one, it is commonly believed, would have such iron strength of mind as to stand fast in doing right or keep his hands off other men's goods, when he could go to the market-place and fearlessly help himself to anything he wanted, enter houses and sleep with any woman he chose, set prisoners free and kill men at his pleasure, and in a word go about among men with the powers of a god. He would behave no better than the other; both would take the same course."[1] Moreover, why shouldn't he? Once he is freed from the fear of reprisal, why shouldn't a man simply do what he pleases, or

---

[1] *The Republic of Plato*, translated by F. M. Cornford (Oxford, 1941), p. 45.

Source: James Rachels, "Egoism and Moral Scepticism," *Ethics*, pp. 423–434. Reprinted by permission of the author.

what he thinks is best for himself? What reason is there for him to continue being "moral" when it is clearly not to his own advantage to do so?

These sceptical views suggested by Glaucon have come to be known as *psychological egoism* and *ethical egoism* respectively. Psychological egoism is the view that all men are selfish in everything that they do, that is, that the only motive from which anyone ever acts is self-interest. On this view, even when men are acting in ways apparently calculated to benefit others, they are actually motivated by the belief that acting in this way is to their own advantage, and if they did not believe this, they would not be doing that action. Ethical egoism is, by contrast, a normative view about how men *ought* to act. It is the view that, regardless of how men do in fact behave, they have no obligation to do anything except what is in their own interests. According to the ethical egoist, a person is always justified in doing whatever is in his own interests, regardless of the effect on others.

Clearly, if either of these views is correct, then "the moral institution of life" (to use Butler's well-turned phrase) is very different than what we normally think. The majority of mankind is grossly deceived about what is, or ought to be, the case, where morals are concerned.

2. Psychological egoism seems to fly in the face of the facts. We are tempted to say: "Of course people act unselfishly all the time. For example, Smith gives up a trip to the country, which he would have enjoyed very much, in order to stay behind and help a friend with his studies, which is a miserable way to pass the time. This is a perfectly clear case of unselfish behavior, and if the psychological egoist thinks that such cases do not occur, then he is just mistaken." Given such obvious instances of "unselfish behavior," what reply can the egoist make? There are two general arguments by which he might try to show that all actions, including those such as the one just outlined, are in fact motivated by self-interest. Let us examine these in turn:

a. The first argument goes as follows. If we describe one person's action as selfish, and another person's action as unselfish, we are overlooking the crucial fact that in both cases, assuming that the action is done voluntarily, *the agent is merely doing what he most wants to do*. If Smith stays behind to help his friend, that only shows that he wanted to help his friend more than he wanted to go to the country. And why should he be praised for his "unselfishness" when he is only doing what he most wants to do? So, since Smith is only doing what he wants to do, he cannot be said to be acting unselfishly.

This argument is so bad that it would not deserve to be taken seriously except for the fact that so many otherwise intelligent people have been taken in by it. First, the argument rests on the premise that people never voluntarily do anything except what they want to do. But this is patently false; there are at least two classes of actions that are exceptions to this generalization. One is the set of actions which we may not want to do, but which we do anyway as a means to an end which we want to achieve; for example, going to the dentist in order to stop a toothache, or going to work every day in order to be able to draw our pay at the end of the month. These cases may be regarded as consistent with the spirit of the egoist argument, however, since the ends mentioned are wanted by the agent. But the other set of actions are those which we do, not because we want to, nor even because there is an end which we want to achieve, but because we feel ourselves *under an obligation* to do them. For example, someone may do something because he has promised to do it, and thus feels obligated, even though he does not want to do it. It is sometimes suggested that in such cases we do the action because, after all, we want to keep our promises; so, even here, we are doing what we want. However, this dodge will not work: if I have promised to do something, and if I do not want to do it then it is simply false to say that I want to keep my promise. In such cases we feel a conflict precisely because we do *not* want to do what we feel obligated to do. It is reasonable to think that Smith's action falls roughly into this second category: he might stay behind, not because he wants to, but because he feels that his friend needs help.

But suppose we were to concede, for the sake of the argument, that all voluntary action is motivated by the agent's wants, or at least that Smith is so motivated. Even if this were granted, it would not follow that Smith is acting selfishly or from self-interest. For if Smith wants to do something that will help his friend, even when it means forgoing his own enjoyments, that is precisely what makes him *un*selfish. What else could unselfishness be, if not wanting to help others? Another way to put the same point is to say that it is the *object* of a want that determines whether it is selfish or not. The mere fact that I am acting on *my* wants does not mean that I am acting selfishly; that depends on *what it is* that I want. If I want only my own good, and care nothing for others, then I am selfish; but if I also want other people to be well-off and happy, and if I act on *that* desire, then my action is not selfish. So much for this argument.

b. The second argument for psychological egoism is this. Since so-called unselfish actions always produce a sense of self-satisfaction in the agent,[2] and since this sense of satisfaction is a pleasant state of consciousness, it follows that the point of the action is really to achieve a pleasant state of consciousness, rather than to bring about any good for others. Therefore, the action is "unselfish" only at a superficial level of analysis. Smith will feel much better with himself for having stayed to help his friend—if he had gone to the country, he would have felt terrible about it—and that is the real point of the action. According to a well-known story, this argument was once expressed by Abraham Lincoln:

> Mr. Lincoln once remarked to a fellow-passenger on an old-time mud-coach that all men were prompted by selfishness in doing good. His fellow-passenger was antagonizing this position when they were passing over a corduroy bridge that spanned a slough. As they crossed this bridge they espied an old razor-backed sow on the bank making a terrible noise because her pigs had got into the slough and were in danger of drowning. As the old coach began to climb the hill, Mr. Lincoln called out, "Driver, can't you stop just a moment?" Then Mr. Lincoln jumped out, ran back, and lifted the little pigs out of the mud and water and placed them on the bank. When he returned, his companion remarked: "Now, Abe, where does selfishness come in on this little episode?" "Why, bless your soul, Ed, that was the very essence of selfishness. I should have had no peace of mind all day had I gone on and left that suffering old sow worrying over those pigs. I did it to get peace of mind, don't you see?"[3]

This argument suffers from defects similar to the previous one. Why should we think that merely because someone derives satisfaction from helping others this makes him selfish? Isn't the unselfish man precisely the one who *does* derive satisfaction from helping others, while the selfish man does not? If Lincoln "got peace of mind" from rescuing the piglets, does this show him to be selfish, or, on the contrary, doesn't it show him to be compassionate and good-hearted? (If a man were truly selfish, why should it bother his conscience that *others* suffer—much less pigs?) Similarly, it is nothing more than shabby sophistry to say, because Smith takes satisfaction in helping his friend, that he is behaving selfishly. If we say this rapidly, while thinking about something else, perhaps it will sound all right; but if we speak slowly, and pay attention to what we are saying, it sounds plain silly.

Moreover, suppose we ask *why* Smith derives satisfaction from help-

---

[2] Or, as it is sometimes said, "It gives him a clear conscience," or "He couldn't sleep at night if he had done otherwise," or "He would have been ashamed of himself for not doing it," and so on.

[3] Frank C. Sharp, *Ethics* (New York, 1928), pp. 74–75. Quoted from the Springfield (Ill.) *Monitor* in the *Outlook*, vol. 56, p. 1059.

ing his friend. The answer will be, it is because Smith cares for him and wants him to succeed. If Smith did not have these concerns, then he would take no pleasure in assisting him; and these concerns, as we have already seen, are the marks of unselfishness, not selfishness. To put the point more generally: if we have a positive attitude toward the attainment of some goal, then we may derive satisfaction from attaining that goal. But the *object* of our attitude is *the attainment of that goal;* and we must want to attain the goal *before* we can find any satisfaction in it. We do not, in other words, desire some sort of "pleasurable consciousness" and then try to figure out how to achieve it; rather, we desire all sorts of different things—money, a new fishing-boat, to be a better chess-player, to get a promotion in our work, etc.—and because we desire these things, we derive satisfaction from attaining them. And so, if someone desires the welfare and happiness of another person, he will derive satisfaction from that; but this does not mean that this satisfaction is the object of his desire, or that he is in any way selfish on account of it.

It is a measure of the weakness of psychological egoism that these insupportable arguments are the ones most often advanced in its favor. Why, then, should anyone ever have thought it a true view? Perhaps because of a desire for theoretical simplicity: In thinking about human conduct, it would be nice if there were some simple formula that would unite the diverse phenomena of human behavior under a single explanatory principle, just as simple formulae in physics bring together a great many apparently different phenomena. And since it is obvious that self-regard is an overwhelmingly important factor in motivation, it is only natural to wonder whether all motivation might not be explained in these terms. But the answer is clearly No; while a great many human actions are motivated entirely or in part by self-interest, only by a deliberate distortion of the facts can we say that all conduct is so motivated. This will be clear, I think, if we correct three confusions which are commonplace. The exposure of these confusions will remove the last traces of plausibility from the psychological egoist thesis.

The first is the confusion of selfishness with self-interest. The two are clearly not the same. If I see a physician when I am feeling poorly, I am acting in my own interest but no one would think of calling me "selfish" on account of it. Similarly, brushing my teeth, working hard at my job, and obeying the law are all in my self-interest but none of these are examples of selfish conduct. This is because selfish behavior is behavior that ignores the interests of others, in circumstances in which their interests ought not to be ignored. This concept has a definite evaluative flavor; to call someone "selfish" is not just to describe his action but to condemn it. Thus, you would not call me selfish for eating a normal meal in normal circumstances (although it may surely be in my self-interest); but you would call me selfish for hoarding food while others about are starving.

The second confusion is the assumption that every action is done *either* from self-interest or from other-regarding motives. Thus, the egoist concludes that if there is no such thing as genuine altruism then all actions must be done from self-interest. But this is certainly a false dichotomy. The man who continues to smoke cigarettes, even after learning about the connection between smoking and cancer, is surely not acting from self-interest, not even by his own standards—self-interest would dictate that he quit smoking at once—and he is not acting altruistically either. He *is*, no doubt, smoking for the pleasure of it, but all that this shows is that undisciplined pleasure-seeking and acting from self-interest are very different. This is what led Butler to remark that "The thing to be lamented is, not that men have so great regard to their own good or interest in the present world, for they have not enough."[4]

The last two paragraphs show (*a*) that it is false that all actions are selfish, and (*b*) that it is false that all actions are done out of self-interest. And it should be noted that these two points can be made, and were, without any appeal to putative examples of altruism.

The third confusion is the common but false assumption that a concern for one's own welfare is incompatible with any genuine concern for the welfare of others. Thus, since it is obvious that everyone (or very nearly everyone) does desire his own well-being, it might be thought that no one can really be concerned with others. But again, this is false. There is no inconsistency in desiring that everyone, including oneself *and* others, be well-off and happy. To be sure, it may happen on occasion that our own interests conflict with the interests of others, and in these cases we will have to make hard choices. But even in these cases we might sometimes opt for the interests of others, especially when the others involved are our family or friends. But more importantly, not all cases are like this: sometimes we are able to promote the welfare of others when our own interests are not involved at all. In these cases not even the strongest self-regard need prevent us from acting considerately toward others.

Once these confusions are cleared away, it seems to me obvious

---

[4] *The Works of Joseph Butler*, edited by W. E. Gladstone (Oxford, 1896), vol. II, p. 26. It should be noted that most of the points I am making against psychological egoism were first made by Butler. Butler made all the important points; all that is left for us is to remember them.

enough that there is no reason whatever to accept psychological egoism. On the contrary, if we simply observe people's behavior with an open mind, we may find that a great deal of it is motivated by self-regard, but by no means all of it; and that there is no reason to deny that "the moral institution of life" can include a place for the virtue of beneficence.[5]

3. The ethical egoist would say at this point, "Of course it is possible for people to act altruistically, and perhaps many people do act that way—but there is no reason why they *should* do so. A person is under no obligation to do anything except what is in his own interests."[6] This is really quite a radical doctrine. Suppose I have an urge to set fire to some public building (say, a department store) just for the fascination of watching the spectacular blaze: according to this view, the fact that several people might be burned to death provides no reason whatever why I should not do it. After all, this only concerns *their* welfare, not my own, and according to the ethical egoist the only person I need think of is myself.

Some might deny that ethical egoism has any such monstrous consequences. They would point out that it is really to my own advantage not to set fire—for, if I do that I may be caught and put into prison (unlike Gyges, I have no magic ring for protection). Moreover, even if I could avoid being caught it is still to my advantage to respect the rights and interests of others, for it is to my advantage to live in a society in which people's rights and interests are respected. Only in such a society can I live a happy and secure life; so, in acting kindly toward others, I would merely be doing my part to create and maintain the sort of society which it is to my advantage to have.[7] Therefore, it is said, the egoist would not be such a bad man; he would be as kindly and considerate as anyone else, because he would see that it is to his own advantage to be kindly and considerate.

This is a seductive line of thought, but it seems to me mistaken. Certainly it is to everyone's advantage (including the egoist's) to preserve a stable society where people's interests are generally protected. But there is no reason for the egoist to think that merely because *he* will not honor the rules of the social game, decent society will collapse. For the vast majority of people are not egoists, and there is no reason to think that

---

[5] The capacity for altruistic behavior is not unique to human beings. Some interesting experiments with rhesus monkeys have shown that these animals will refrain from operating a device for securing food if this causes other animals to suffer pain. See Masserman, Wechkin, and Terris, " 'Altruistic' Behavior in Rhesus Monkeys," *The American Journal of Psychiatry,* vol. 121 (1964), 584–585.

[6] I take this to be the view of Ayn Rand, in so far as I understand her confusing doctrine.

[7] Cf. Thomas Hobbes, *Leviathan* (London, 1651), chap. 17.

they will be converted by his example—especially if he is discreet and does not unduly flaunt his style of life. What this line of reasoning shows is not that the egoist himself must act benevolently, but that he must encourage *others* to do so. He must take care to conceal from public view his own self-centered method of decision-making, and urge others to act on precepts very different from those on which he is willing to act.

The rational egoist, then, cannot advocate that egoism be universally adopted by everyone. For he wants a world in which his own interests are maximized; and if other people adopted the egoistic policy of pursuing their own interests to the exclusion of his interests, as he pursues his interests to the exclusion of theirs, then such a world would be impossible. So he himself will be an egoist, but he will want others to be altruists.

This brings us to what is perhaps the most popular "refutation" of ethical egoism current among philosophical writers—the argument that ethical egoism is at bottom inconsistent because it cannot be universalized.[8] The argument goes like this:

To say that any action or policy of action is *right* (or that it *ought* to be adopted) entails that it is right for *anyone* in the same sort of circumstances. I cannot, for example, say that it is right for me to lie to you, and yet object when you lie to me (provided, of course, that the circumstances are the same). I cannot hold that it is all right for me to drink your beer and then complain when you drink mine. This is just the requirement that we be consistent in our evaluations; it is a requirement of logic. Now it is said that ethical egoism cannot meet this requirement because, as we have already seen, the egoist would not want others to act in the same way that he acts. Moreover, suppose he *did* advocate the universal adoption of egoistic policies: he would be saying to Peter, "You ought to pursue your own interests even if it means destroying Paul"; and he would be saying to Paul, "You ought to pursue your own interest even if it means destroying Peter." The attitudes expressed in these two recommendations seem clearly inconsistent—he is urging the advancement of Peter's interest at one moment, and countenancing their defeat at the next. Therefore, the argument goes, there is no way to maintain the doctrine of ethical egoism as a consistent view about how we ought to act. We will fall into inconsistency whenever we try.

What are we to make of this argument? Are we to conclude that

---

[8] See, for example, Brian Medlin, "Ultimate Principles and Ethical Egoism," *Australasian Journal of Philosophy,* vol. 35 (1957), 111–118; and D. H. Monro, *Empiricism and Ethics* (Cambridge, 1967), chap. 16.

ethical egoism has been refuted? Such a conclusion, I think, would be unwarranted; for I think that we can show, contrary to this argument, how ethical egoism can be maintained consistently. We need only to interpret the egoist's position in a sympathetic way: we should say that he has in mind a certain kind of world which he would prefer over all others; it would be a world in which his own interests were maximized, regardless of the effects on other people. The egoist's primary policy of action, then, would be to act in such a way as to bring about, as nearly as possible, this sort of world. Regardless of however morally reprehensible we might find it, there is nothing *inconsistent* in someone's adopting this as his ideal and acting in a way calculated to bring it about. And if someone did adopt this as his ideal, then he would not advocate universal egoism; as we have already seen, he would want other people to be altruists. So, if he advocates any principles of conduct for the general public, they will be altruistic principles. This would not be inconsistent; on the contrary, it would be perfectly consistent with his goal of creating a world in which his own interests are maximized. To be sure, he would have to be deceitful; in order to secure the good will of others, and a favorable hearing for his exhortations to altrusism, he would have to pretend that he was himself prepared to accept altruistic principles. But again, that would be all right; from the egoist's point of view, this would merely be a matter of adopting the necessary means to the achievement of his goal—and while we might not approve of this, there is nothing inconsistent about it. Again, it might be said: "He advocates one thing, but does another. Surely *that's* inconsistent." But it is not; for what he advocates and what he does are both calculated as means to an end (the *same* end, we might note); and as such, he is doing what is rationally required in each case. Therefore, contrary to the previous argument, there is nothing inconsistent in the ethical egoist's view. He cannot be refuted by the claim that he contradicts himself.

Is there, then, no way to refute the ethical egoist? If by "refute" we mean show that he has made some *logical* error, the answer is that there is not. However, there is something more that can be said. The egoist challenge to our ordinary moral convictions amounts to a demand for an explanation of why we should adopt certain policies of action, namely policies in which the good of others is given importance. We can give an answer to this demand, albeit an indirect one. The reason one ought not to do actions that would hurt other people is: other people would be hurt. The reason one ought to do actions that would benefit other people is: other people would be benefited. This may at first seem like a piece of philosophical sleight-of-hand, but it is not. The point is that the welfare of human beings is something that most of us value *for its own sake,* and not merely for the sake of something else. Therefore, when *further* reasons are demanded for valuing the welfare of human beings, we cannot point to anything further to satisfy this demand. It is not that we have no reason for pursuing these policies, but that our reason *is* that these policies are for the good of human beings.

So: if we are asked "Why shouldn't I set fire to this department store?" one answer would be "Because if you do, people may be burned to death." This is a complete, sufficient reason which does not require qualification or supplementation of any sort. If someone seriously wants to know why this action shouldn't be done, that's the reason. If we are pressed further and asked the sceptical question "But why shouldn't I do actions that will harm others?" we may not know what to say—but this is because the questioner has included in his question the very answer we would like to give: "Why shouldn't you do actions that will harm others? Because, doing those actions would harm others."

The egoist, no doubt, will not be happy with this. He will protest that *we* may accept this as a reason, but *he* does not. And here the argument stops: there are limits to what can be accomplished by argument, and if the egoist really doesn't care about other people—if he honestly doesn't care whether they are helped or hurt by his actions—then we have reached those limits. If we want to persuade him to act decently toward his fellow humans, we will have to make our appeal to such other attitudes as he does possess, by threats, bribes, or other cajolery. That is all that we can do.

Though some may find this situation distressing (we would like to be able to show that the egoist is just *wrong*), it holds no embarrassment for common morality. What we have come up against is simply a fundamental requirement of rational action, namely, that the existence of reasons for action always depends on the prior existence of certain attitudes in the agent. For example, the fact that a certain course of action would make the agent a lot of money is a reason for doing it only if the agent wants to make money; the fact that practicing at chess makes one a better player is a reason for practicing only if one wants to be a better player; and so on. Similarly, the fact that a certain action would help the agent is a reason for doing the action only if the agent cares about his own welfare, and the fact that an action would help others is a reason for doing it only if the agent cares about others. In this respect ethical egoism and what we might call ethical altruism are in exactly the same fix: both require that the agent *care* about himself, or about other people, before they can get started.

So a nonegoist will accept "It would harm another person" as a reason not to do an action simply because he cares about what happens to that other person. When the egoist says that he does *not* accept that as a reason, he is saying something quite extraordinary. He is saying that he has no affection for friends or family, that he never feels pity or compassion, that he is the sort of person who can look on scenes of human misery with complete indifference, so long as he is not the one suffering. Genuine egoists, people who really don't care at all about anyone other than themselves, are rare. It is important to keep this in mind when thinking about ethical egoism; it is easy to forget just how fundamental to human psychological makeup the feeling of sympathy is. Indeed, a man without any sympathy at all would scarcely be recognizable as a man; and that is what makes ethical egoism such a disturbing doctrine in the first place.

4. There are, of course, many different ways in which the sceptic might challenge the assumptions underlying our moral practice. In this essay I have discussed only two of them, the two put forward by Glaucon in the passage that I cited from Plato's *Republic*. It is important that the assumptions underlying our moral practice should not be confused with particular judgments made within that practice. To defend one is not to defend the other. We may assume—quite properly, if my analysis has been correct—that the virtue of beneficence does, and indeed should, occupy an important place in "the moral institution of life"; and yet we may make constant and miserable errors when it comes to judging when and in what ways this virtue is to be exercised. Even worse, we may often be able to make accurate moral judgments, and know what we ought to do, but not do it. For these ills, philosophy alone is not the cure.

Readings

1. Broad, C. D. "Egoism as a Theory of Human Motives" in *Ethics and the History of Philosophy*. London: Routledge and Kegan Paul, 1952. Excellent.

2. Duncan-Jones, Austin. *Butler's Moral Philosophy*. Harmondsworth: Penguin Books, 1952, pp. 95–98.

3. Garvin, Lucius. *A Modern Introduction to Ethics*. Boston: Houghton Mifflin, 1953, Chap. 2.

4. Jackson, R. "Bishop Butler's Refutation of Psychological Hedonism," *Philosophy*, 18 (July 1943), 114–139.

5. McClintock, T. "The Egotists Psychological Argument," *American Philosophical Quarterly*, 8 (January 1971), 79–85.

6. Medlin, Brian. "Ultimate Principles and Ethical Egoism," *Australasian Journal of Philosophy,* XXXV (1957), 111–118.

four

Which Is Basic in Ethics:
Happiness Or Obligation?

12

Happiness Is
Self-fulfillment

Aristotle (384–322 B.C.), son of a physician, studied in Plato's academy for twenty years before founding his own more empirical school, the Lyceum. He tutored Alexander the Great. He wrote on logic, ethics, aesthetics, metaphysics, biology, physics, psychology, politics; had an enormous influence on medieval Hebrew, Arabic, and Christian philosophers, especially on St. Thomas Aquinas and his later scholastic followers. *The Works of Aristotle,* ed. W. D. Ross (1908–28).

Concerning teleological ethics, one must ask himself if it is true that one should measure all action by consequence or whether there are some actions which one should follow simply on the basis of principle, such as promise-keeping. On the other hand, the deontologist must ask whether his rules are adequate for all situations.

Aristotle argues that happiness is one good always sought for its own sake. Happiness itself is an activity of soul in accordance with virtue both intellectual and moral. We achieve the former through knowledge and the latter by habitually seeking the proper mean between the extremes.

-TO STUDY

1. Can you give specific examples which show that honor, pleasure, virtue, etc. are not ends but means?

2. What is Aristotle's argument to show that "The good of man is an activity of the soul in accordance with virtue?"

3. Distinguish moral and intellectual virtue.

4. Explain the role of habit in the achievement of moral virtue.

5. What is the meaning of a given moral virtue?

During his lifetime a person faces many moral problems. One faces problems concerning his parents, siblings, sex, economics, race, the nature of honesty, relating to promise-keeping, divorce, etc. No one can escape all of them. In attempting to deal with these problems one gives two types of answers: one either decides on the basis of principle or on the basis of consequence. One may say that he will not get divorced because he adheres to the basic principle that one ought not to be divorced. This may come from religious scriptures or on the basis of particular principles which one has developed for himself. On the other hand, one may decide to get divorced because of the pain one suffers in his marriage and the consequent pleasure one might find when married to another. If one decides questions on the basis of principles, it is referred to as following *deontological rules.* This involves following what is right as the moral rule. Happiness is not the basic concern here, but the belief that it is a duty to follow one's principles. This is the position of Kant.

If, on the other hand, one decides questions on the basis of consequence, it is referred to as deciding moral matters *teleologically.* This involves following what is good as one's moral rule. This is the position of Aristotle and Bentham, who conceive of good in terms of happiness.

We speak of that which is sought after for its own sake as more final than that which is sought after as a means to something else; we speak of that which is never desired as a means to something else as more final than the things which are desired both in themselves and as means to something else; and we speak of a thing as absolutely final, if it is always desired in itself and never as a means to something else.

It seems that happiness pre-eminently answers to this description, as we always desire happiness for its own sake and never as a means to something else, whereas we desire honor, pleasure, intellect, and every virtue, partly for their own sakes (for we should desire them independently of what might result from them) but partly also as being means to happiness, because we suppose they will prove the instruments of happiness. Happiness, on the other hand, nobody desires for the sake of these things, nor indeed as a means to anything else at all. If we define the function of Man as a kind of life, and this life as an activity of soul, or a course of action in conformity with reason, if the function of a good man is such activity or action of a good and noble kind, and if everything is successfully performed when it is performed in accordance with its proper excellence, it follows that the good of Man is an activity of soul in accordance with virtue or, if there are more virtues than one, in accordance with the best and most complete virtue. But it is necessary to add the words "in a complete life." For as one swallow or one day does not make a spring, so one day or a short time does not make a fortunate or happy man.

Inasmuch as happiness is an activity of soul in accordance with complete or perfect virtue, it is necessary to consider virtue, as this will perhaps be the best way of studying happiness. . . .

Virtue or excellence being twofold, partly intellectual and partly moral, intellectual virtue is both originated and fostered mainly by teaching; it therefore demands experience and time. Moral virtue on the other hand is the outcome of habit, and accordingly its name is derived by a slight deflexion from habit. From this fact it is clear that no moral virtue is implanted in us by nature; a law of nature cannot be altered by habituation. . . . It is neither by nature then nor in defiance of nature that virtues are implanted in us. Nature gives us the capacity of receiving them, and that capacity is perfected by habit. . . . But the virtues we acquire by first exercising them, as is the case with all the arts, for it is by doing what we ought to do when we have learnt the arts that we learn the arts themselves; we become e.g., builders by building and harpists by playing the harp. Similarly it is by doing just acts that we become just, by doing temperate acts that we become temperate, by doing courageous acts that we become courageous. . . . It is by acting in such transactions as take place between man and man that we become either just or unjust. It is by acting in the face of danger and by habituating ourselves to fear or courage that we become either cowardly or courageous. It is much the same with our desires and angry passions. Some people become temperate and gentle, others become licentious and passionate, according as they conduct themselves in one way or another way in particular circumstances. In a word moral states are the results of activities corresponding to the moral states themselves. It is our duty therefore to give a certain character to the activities, as the moral states depend upon the differences of the activities. Accordingly the difference between one training of the habits and another from early days is not a light matter, but is serious or rather all-important. . . .

But it may be asked what we mean by saying that people must become just by doing what is just and temperate by doing what is temperate. For if they do what is just and temperate, they are *ipso facto* proved,

From *The Nicomachean Ethics of Aristotle,* trans. J. E. C. Weldon (London: Macmillan & Co., Ltd., 1892).

it will be said, to be just and temperate in the same way as, if they practise grammar and music, they are proved to be grammarians and musicians. . . .

But actions in accordance with virtue are not e.g. justly or temperately performed [merely] because they are in themselves just or temperate. It is necessary that the agent at the time of performing them should satisfy certain conditions, i.e. in the first place that he should know what he is doing, secondly that he should deliberately choose to do it and to do it for its own sake, and thirdly that he should do it as an instance of a settled and immutable moral state. If it be a question whether a person possesses any art, these conditions, except indeed the condition of knowledge, are not taken into account; but if it be a question of possessing the virtues, the mere knowledge is of little or no avail, and it is the other conditions, which are the results of frequently performing just and temperate actions, that are not of slight but of absolute importance. Accordingly deeds are said to be just and temperate, when they are such as a just or temperate person would do, and a just and temperate person is not merely one who does these deeds but one who does them in the spirit of the just and the temperate. . . .

. . . the virtues are neither emotions nor faculties [but] moral states. . . . But it is not enough to state merely that virtue is a moral state, we must also describe the character of that moral state.

It must be laid down then that every virtue or excellence has the effect of producing a good condition of that of which it is a virtue or excellence, and of enabling it to perform its function well. Thus the excellence of the eye makes the eye good and its function good, as it is by the excellence of the eye that we see well. Similarly, the excellence of the horse makes a horse excellent and good at racing, at carrying its rider and at facing the enemy.

If then this is universally true, the virtue or excellence of man will be such a moral state as makes a man good and able to perform his proper function well. We have already explained how this will be the case, but another way of making it clear will be to study the nature or character of this virtue.

Now in everything, whether it be continuous or discrete, it is possible to take a greater, a smaller, or an equal amount, and this either absolutely or in relation to ourselves, the equal being a mean between excess and deficiency. By the mean in respect of the thing itself, or the absolute mean, I understand that which is equally distinct from both extremes; and this is one and the same thing for everybody By the mean considered relatively to ourselves I understand that which is neither too much nor too little; but this is not one thing, nor is it the same for everybody.

Thus if 10 be too much and 2 too little we take 6 as a mean in respect of the thing itself; for 6 is as much greater than 2 as it is less than 10, and this is a mean in arithmetical proportion. But the mean considered relatively to ourselves must not be ascertained in this way. It does not follow that if 10 pounds of meat be too much and 2 be too little for a man to eat, a trainer will order him 6 pounds, as this may itself be too much or too little for the person who is to take it; it will be too little e.g. for Milo, but too much for a beginner in gymnastics. It will be the same with running and wrestling; the right amount will vary with the individual. This being so, everybody who understands his business avoids alike excess and deficiency; he seeks and chooses the mean, not the absolute mean, but the mean considered relatively to ourselves.

Every science then performs its function well, if it regards the mean and refers the works which it produces to the mean. This is the reason why it is usually said of successful works that it is impossible to take anything from them or to add anything to them, which implies that excess or deficiency is fatal to excellence but that the mean state ensures it. Good artists too, as we say, have an eye to the mean in their works. But virtue, like Nature herself, is more accurate and better than any art; virtue therefore will aim at the mean;—I speak of moral virtue, as it is moral virtue which is concerned with emotions and actions, and it is these which admit of excess and deficiency and the mean. Thus it is possible to go too far, or not to go far enough, in respect of fear, courage, desire, anger, pity, and pleasure and pain generally, and the excess and the deficiency are alike wrong; but to experience these emotions at the right times and on the right occasions and towards the right persons and for the right causes and in the right manner is the mean or the supreme good, which is characteristic of virtue. Similarly there may be excess, deficiency, or the mean, in regard to actions. But virtue is concerned with emotions and actions, and here excess is an error and deficiency a fault, whereas the mean is successful and laudable, and success and merit are both characteristics of virtue.

It appears then that virtue is a mean state, so far at least as it aims at the mean.

Again, there are many different ways of going wrong; for evil is in its nature infinite, to use the Pythagorean figure, but good is finite. But there is only one possible way of going right. Accordingly the former is easy and the latter difficult; it is easy to miss the mark but difficult to hit it. This again is a reason why excess and deficiency are characteristics of vice and the mean state a characteristic of virtue.

"For good is simple, evil manifold."

Virtue then is a state of deliberate moral purpose consisting in a mean that is relative to ourselves, the mean being determined by reason, or as a prudent man would determine it.[1]

It is a mean state firstly as lying between two vices, the vice of excess on the one hand, and the vice of deficiency on the other, and secondly because, whereas the vices either fall short of or go beyond what is proper in the emotions and actions, virtue not only discovers but embraces the mean.

Accordingly, virtue, if regarded in its essence or theoretical conception, is a mean state, but, if regarded from the point of view of the highest good, or of excellence, it is an extreme.

But it is not every action or every emotion that admits of a mean state. There are some whose very name implies wickedness, as e.g., malice, shamelessness, and envy, among emotions, or adultery, theft, and murder, among actions. All these, and others like them, are censured as being intrinsically wicked, not merely the excesses or deficiencies of them. It is never possible then to be right in respect of them; they are always sinful. Right or wrong in such actions as adultery does not depend on our committing them with the right person, at the right time or in the right manner; on the contrary it is sinful to do anything of the kind at all. It would be equally wrong then to suppose that there can be a mean state or an excess or deficiency in unjust, cowardly or licentious conduct; for, if it were so, there would be a mean state of an excess or of a deficiency, an excess of an excess and a deficiency of a deficiency. But as in temperance and courage there can be no excess or deficiency because the mean is, in a sense, an extreme, so too in these cases there cannot be a mean or an excess or deficiency, but, however the acts may be done, they are wrong. For it is a general rule that an excess or deficiency does not admit of a mean state, nor a mean state of an excess or deficiency.

But it is not enough to lay down this as a general rule; it is necessary to apply it to particular cases, as in reasonings upon actions general statements, although they are broader, are less exact than particular statements. For all action refers to particulars, and it is essential that our theories should harmonize with the particular cases to which they apply.

We must take particular virtues then from the catalogue of virtues.

In regard to feelings of fear and confidence, courage is a mean state. On the side of excess, he whose fearlessness is excessive has no name, as often happens, but he whose confidence is excessive is foolhardy, while

---

[1] [That is, moral virtue is a state of character consisting of a disposition to choose the mean relative to oneself in matters of action and feeling, the mean being determined by reason, or as a man of practical wisdom would determine it.—ED.]

he whose timidity is excessive and whose confidence is deficient is a coward.

In respect of pleasures and pains, although not indeed of all pleasures and pains, and to a less extent in respect of pains than of pleasures, the mean state is temperance, the excess is licentiousness. We never find people who are deficient in regard to pleasures; accordingly such people again have not received a name, but we may call them insensible.

As regards the giving and taking of money, the mean state is liberality, the excess and deficiency are prodigality and illiberality. Here the excess and deficiency take opposite forms; for while the prodigal man is excessive in spending and deficient in taking, the illiberal man is excessive in taking and deficient in spending.

(For the present we are giving only a rough and summary account of the virtues, and that is sufficient for our purpose; we will hereafter determine their character more exactly.)

In respect of money there are other dispositions as well. There is the mean state which is magnificence; for the magnificent man, as having to do with large sums of money, differs from the liberal man who has to do only with small sums; and the excess corresponding to it is bad taste or vulgarity, the deficiency is meanness. These are different from the excess and deficiency of liberality; what the difference is will be explained hereafter.

In respect of honour and dishonour the mean state is highmindedness, the excess is what is called vanity, the deficiency littlemindedness. Corresponding to liberality, which, as we said, differs from magnificence as having to do not with great but with small sums of money, there is a moral state which has to do with petty honour and is related to highmindedness which has to do with great honour; for it is possible to aspire to honour in the right way, or in a way which is excessive or insufficient, and if a person's aspirations are excessive, he is called ambitious, if they are deficient, he is called unambitious, while if they are between the two, he has no name. The dispositions too are nameless, except that the disposition of the ambitious person is called ambition. The consequence is that the extremes lay claim to the mean or intermediate place. We ourselves speak of one who observes the mean sometimes as ambitious, and at other times as unambitious; we sometimes praise an ambitious, and at other times an unambitious person. The reason for our doing so will be stated in due course, but let us now discuss the other virtues in accordance with the method which we have followed hitherto.

Anger, like other emotions, has its excess, its deficiency, and its mean state. It may be said that they have no names, but as we call one who observes the mean gentle, we will call the mean state gentleness.

Among the extremes, if a person errs on the side of excess, he may be called passionate and his vice passionateness, if on that of deficiency, he may be called impassive and his deficiency impassivity. . . .

In the matter of truth then, he who observes the mean may be called truthful, and the mean state truthfulness. Pretence, if it takes the form of exaggeration, is boastfulness, and one who is guilty of pretence is a boaster; but if it takes the form of depreciation it is irony, and he who is guilty of it is ironical.

As regards pleasantness in amusement, he who observes the mean is witty, and his disposition wittiness; the excess is buffoonery, and he who is guilty of it a buffoon, whereas he who is deficient in wit may be called a boor and his moral state boorishness.

As to the other kind of pleasantness, viz. pleasantness in life, he who is pleasant in a proper way is friendly, and his mean state friendliness; but he who goes too far, if he has no ulterior object in view, is obsequious, while if his object is self interest, he is a flatterer, and he who does not go far enough and always makes himself unpleasant is a quarrelsome and morose sort of person.

There are also mean states in the emotions and in the expression of the emotions. For although modesty is not a virtue, yet a modest person is praised as if he were virtuous; for here too one person is said to observe the mean and another to exceed it, as e.g. the bashful man who is never anything but modest, whereas a person who has insufficient modesty or no modesty at all is called shameless, and one who observes the mean modest.

Righteous indignation, again, is a mean state between envy and malice. They are all concerned with the pain and pleasure which we feel at the fortunes of our neighbours. A person who is righteously indignant is pained at the prosperity of the undeserving; but the envious person goes further and is pained at anybody's prosperity, and the malicious person is so far from being pained that he actually rejoices at misfortunes. . . .

It is in some cases the deficiency and in others the excess which is the more opposed to the mean. Thus it is not foolhardiness the excess, but cowardice the deficiency which is the more opposed to courage, nor is it insensibility the deficiency, but licentiousness the excess which is the more opposed to temperance. There are two reasons why this should be so. One lies in the nature of the thing itself; for as one of the two extremes is the nearer and more similar to the mean, it is not this extreme, but its opposite, that we chiefly set against the mean. For instance, as it appears that foolhardiness is more similar and nearer to courage than cowardice, it is cowardice that we chiefly set against courage; for things which are further removed from the mean seem to be more opposite to it. This being one reason which lies in the nature of the thing itself, there is a second which lies in our own nature. It is the things to which we ourselves are naturally more inclined that appear more opposed to the mean. Thus we are ourselves naturally more inclined to pleasures than to their opposites, and are more prone therefore to licentiousness than to decorum. Accordingly we speak of those things, in which we are more likely to run to great lengths, as being more opposed to the mean. Hence it follows that licentiousness which is an excess is more opposed to temperance than insensibility.

It has now been sufficiently shown that moral virtue is a mean state, and in what sense it is a mean state; it is a mean state as lying between two vices, a vice of excess on the one side and a vice of deficiency on the other, and as aiming at the mean in the emotions and actions.

That is the reason why it is so hard to be virtuous; for it is always hard work to find the mean in anything, e.g., it is not everybody, but only a man of science, who can find the mean or centre of a circle. So too anybody can get angry—that is an easy matter—and anybody can give or spend money, but to give it to the right persons, to give the right amount of it and to give it at the right time and for the right cause and in the right way, this is not what anybody can do, nor is it easy. That is the reason why it is rare and laudable and noble to do well. Accordingly one who aims at the mean must begin by departing from that extreme which is the more contrary to the mean; he must act in the spirit of Calypso's advice,

"Far from this smoke and swell keep thou thy bark,"

for of the two extremes one is more sinful than the other. As it is difficult then to hit the mean exactly, we must take the second best course, as the saying is, and choose the lesser of two evils, and this we shall best do in the way that we have described, i.e. by steering clear of the evil which is further from the mean. We must also observe the things to which we are ourselves particularly prone, as different natures have different inclinations, and we may ascertain what these are by a consideration of our feelings of pleasure and pain. And then we must drag ourselves in the direction opposite to them; for it is by removing ourselves as far as possible from what is wrong that we shall arrive at the mean, as we do when we pull a crooked stick straight.

But in all cases we must especially be on our guard against what is pleasant and against pleasure, as we are not impartial judges of pleasure. Hence our attitude towards pleasure must be like that of the elders of the people in the *Iliad* towards Helen, and we must never be afraid of applying the words they use; for if we dismiss pleasure as they dismissed Helen, we shall be less likely to go wrong. It is by action of this kind, to put it summarily, that we shall best succeed in hitting the mean.

It may be admitted that this is a difficult task, especially in particular cases. It is not easy to determine e.g. the right manner, objects, occasions, and duration of anger. There are times when we ourselves praise people who are deficient in anger, and call them gentle, and there are other times when we speak of people who exhibit a savage temper as spirited. It is not however one who deviates a little from what is right, but one who deviates a great deal, whether on the side of excess or of deficiency. that is censured; for he is sure to be found out. Again, it is not easy to decide theoretically how far and to what extent a man may go before he becomes censurable, but neither is it easy to define theoretically anything else within the region of perception; such things fall under the head of particulars, and our judgment of them depends upon our perception.

So much then is plain, that the mean state is everywhere laudable, but that we ought to incline at one time towards the excess and at another towards the deficiency; for this will be our easiest manner of hitting the mean, or in other words of attaining excellence.

13

Happiness Is to Do
What Is Good for All

Jeremy Bentham (1748–1832) was the leading figure in the early phase of the British utilitarian movement in philosophy and politics. He was primarily interested in legal reform, and he constantly sought a philosophic basis for the reforms he advocated. In this connection he wrote his highly influential works on the theory of law and on ethics.

Bentham is a teleologist regarding ethical theory. He believes that not only do people seek pleasure, but that they ought to seek it both for themselves and for the wider community. This is the principle of utility. The particular end we should follow is to be calculated via the hedonistic calculus.

TO STUDY

1. Is there any difference, or no difference, between moral value ("what we ought to do") and fact ("what we shall do")? Are moral values and facts determined by the same principles?

2. Bentham puts all the ethical theories before him into two groups: (1) principle of *asceticism* and (2) principle of *sympathy and antipathy*. Do you think his criticism of them convincing?

3. Are pleasures and pains ends or means to ends, according to Bentham?

4. Is Bentham's "hedonistic calculus" practicable? Does he consider the fact that both pleasures and pains vary with different persons, and that they vary even with the same person at different times?

5. Does Bentham believe "motives" to be an exception to his theory? Why?

The Principle of Utility

Nature has placed mankind under the governance of two sovereign masters *pain* and *pleasure*. It is for them alone to point out what we ought to do, as well as to determine what we shall do. On the one hand the standard of right and wrong, on the other the chain of causes and effects, are fastened to their throne. They govern us in all we do, in all we say, in all we think; every effort we can make to throw off our subjection, will serve but to demonstrate and confirm it. In words a man may pretend to abjure their empire: but in reality he will remain subject to it all the while. The *principle of utility* recognizes the subjection, and assumes it for the foundation of that system, the object of which is to tear the fabric of felicity by the hands of reason and of law. Systems which attempt to question it, deal in sounds instead of sense, in caprice instead of reason, in darkness instead of light.

But enough of metaphor and declamation: it is not by such means that moral science is to be improved.

The principle of utility is the foundation of the present work; it will be proper therefore at the outset to give an explicit and determinate account of what is meant by it. By the principle of utility is meant that principle which approves or disapproves of every action whatsoever, according to the tendency which it appears to have to augment or diminish the happiness of the party whose interest is in question; or what is the same thing in other words, to promote or to oppose that happiness. I say of every action whatsoever; and therefore not only of every action of a private individual, but of every measure of government.

By utility is meant that property in any object, whereby it tends to produce benefit, advantage, pleasure, good, or happiness (all this in the present case comes to the same thing) or (what comes again to the same thing) to prevent the happening of mischief, pain, evil, or unhappiness to the party whose interest is considered: if that party be the community in general, then the happiness of the community: if a particular individual, then the happiness of that individual.

The interest of the community is one of the most general expressions that can occur in the phraseology of morals: no wonder that the meaning is often lost. When it has a meaning, it is this. The community is a fictitious *body*, composed of the individual persons who are considered as constituting as it were its *members*. The interest of the community then is, what?—the sum of the interests of the several members who compose it.

It is in vain to talk of the interest of the community, without under-

---

From Bentham: *An Introduction to the Principles of Morals and Legislation,* Chapters 1, 2, 4, and 10.

standing what is the interest of the individual. A thing is said to promote the interest, or to be *for* the interest, of an individual, when it tends to add to the sum total of his pleasures: or, what comes to the same thing, to diminish the sum total of his pains.

An action then may be said to be comformable to the principle of utility, or, for shortness' sake, to utility (meaning with respect to the community at large) when the tendency it has to augment the happiness of the community is greater than any it has to diminish it.

A measure of government (which is but a particular kind of action, performed by a particular person or persons) may be said to be conformable to or dictated by the principle of utility, when in like manner the tendency which it has to augment the happiness of the community is greater than any which it has to diminish it. . . .

Of an action that is comformable to the principle of utility, one may always say either that it is one that ought to be done, or at least that it is not one that ought not to be done. One may also say, that it is right it should be done; at least that it is not wrong it should be done: that it is a right action; at least that it is not a wrong action. When thus interpreted, the words *ought*, and *right* and *wrong*, and others of that stamp, have a meaning: when otherwise, they have none.

Principles Adverse to That of Utility

If the principle of utility be a right principle to be governed by, and that in all cases, it follows from what has been just observed, that whatever principle differs from it in any case must necessarily be a wrong one. To prove any other principle, therefore, to be a wrong one, there needs no more than just to show it to be what it is, a principle of which the dictates are in some point or other different from those of the principle of utility: to state it is to confute it.

A principle may be different from that of utility in two ways: 1. By being constantly opposed to it: this is the case with a principle which may be termed the principle of *asceticism*. 2. By being sometimes opposed to it, and sometimes not, as it may happen: this is the case with another, which may be termed the principle of *sympathy* and *antipathy*.

By the principle of asceticism I mean that principle, which, like the principle of utility, approves or disapproves of any action, according to the tendency which it appears to have to augment or diminish the happiness of the party whose interest is in question; but in an inverse manner: approving of actions in as far as they tend to diminish his happiness; disapproving of them in as far as they tend to augment it. . . .

The principle of asceticism seems originally to have been the reverie of certain hasty speculators, who having perceived, or fancied, that certain pleasures, when reaped in certain circumstances, have, at the long run, been attended with pains more than equivalent to them, took occasion to quarrel with everything that offered itself under the name of pleasure. Having then got thus far, and having forgot the point which they set out from, they pushed on, and went so much further as to think it meritorious to fall in love with pain. Even this, we see, is at bottom but the principle of utility misapplied.

The principle of utility is capable of being consistently pursued; and it is but tautology to say, that the more consistently it is pursued, the better it must ever be for humankind. The principle of asceticism never was, nor never can be, consistently pursued by any living creature. Let but one tenth part of the inhabitants of this earth pursue it consistently, and in a day's time they will have turned it into a hell.

Among principles adverse to that of utility, that which at this day seems to have most influence in matters of government, is what may be called the principle of sympathy and antipathy. By the principle of sympathy and antipathy, I mean that principle which approves or disapproves of certain actions, not on account of their tending to augment the happiness, nor yet on account of their tending to diminish the happiness of the party whose interest is in question, but merely because a man finds himself disposed to approve or disapprove of them: holding up that approbation or disapprobation as a sufficient reason for itself, and disclaiming the necessity of looking out for any extrinsic ground. Thus far in the general department of morals; and in the particular department of politics, measuring out the quantum (as well as determining the ground) of punishment, by the degree of the disapprobation.

It is manifest, that this is rather a principle in name than in reality; it is not a positive principle of itself, so much as a term employed to signify the negation of all principle. What one expects to find in a principle is something that points out some external consideration, as a means of warranting and guiding the internal sentiments of approbation and disapprobation; this expectation is but ill fulfilled by a proposition, which does neither more nor less than hold up each of those sentiments as a ground and standard for itself.

In looking over the catalogue of human actions (says a partizan of this principle) in order to determine which of them are to be marked with the seal of disapprobation, you need but to take counsel of your own feelings: whatever you find in yourself a propensity to condemn, is wrong for that very reason. For the same reason it is also meet for punishment: in what proportion it is adverse to utility, or whether it be adverse to utility at all, is a matter that makes no difference. In that same *proportion* also it is meet for punishment; if you hate much, punish much; if you hate little, punish little; punish as you hate. If you hate not at all; punish not at all; the fine feelings of the soul are not to be overborne and tyrannized by the harsh and rugged dicates of political utility.

The various systems that have been formed concerning the standard of right and wrong, may all be reduced to the principle of sympathy and antipathy. One account may serve for all of them. They consist all of them in so many contrivances for avoiding the obligation of appealing to any external standard, and for prevailing upon the reader to accept of the author's sentiment or opinion as a reason for itself.

The Hedonistic Calculus

Pleasures, then, and the avoidance of pains, are the *ends* which the legislator has in view: it behooves him therefore to understand their *value*. Pleasures and pains are the *instruments* he has to work with: it behooves him therefore to understand their force, which is again, in other words, their value.

To a person considered *by himself*, the value of a pleasure or pain considered *by itself*, will be greater or less, according to the four following circumstances:

1. Its *intensity.*
2. Its *duration.*
3. Its *certainty* or *uncertainty.*
4. Its *propinquity* or *remoteness.*

These are the circumstances which are to be considered in estimating a pleasure or a pain considered each of them by itself. But when the value of any pleasure or pain is considered for the purpose of estimating the tendency of any *act* by which it is produced, there are two other circumstances to be taken into the account; these are,

5. Its *fecundity,* or the chance it has of being followed by sensations of the *same* kind: that is, pleasures, if it be a pleasure: pains, if it be a pain.
6. Its *purity,* or the chance it has of *not* being followed by sensations of the *opposite* kind: that is, pains, if it be a pleasure: pleasures, if it be a pain.

These two last, however, are in strictness scarcely to be deemed properties of the pleasures or the pain itself; they are not, therefore, in strictness to be taken into the account of the value of that pleasure or that pain. They are in strictness to be deemed properties only of the act, or other event, by which such pleasure or pain has been produced; and accordingly are only to be taken into the account of the tendency of such act or such event.

To a *number* of persons, with reference to each of whom the value of a pleasure or a pain is considered, it will be greater or less, according to seven circumstances: to wit, the six preceding ones: viz.

1. Its *intensity.*
2. Its *duration.*
3. Its *certainty* or *uncertainty.*
4. Its *propinquity* or *remoteness.*
5. Its *fecundity.*
6. Its *purity.*

And one other; to wit:

7. Its *extent;* that is, the number of persons to whom it *extends;* or (in other words) who are affected by it.

To take an exact account then of the general tendency of any act, by which the interests of a community are affected, proceed as follows. Begin with any one person of those whose interests seem most immediately to be affected by it: and take an account,

1. Of the value of each distinguishable *pleasure* which appears to be produced by it in the *first* instance.
2. Of the value of each *pain* which appears to be produced by it in the *first* instance.
3. Of the value of each pleasure which appears to be produced by it *after* the first. This constitutes the *fecundity* of the first *pleasure* and the *impurity* of the first *pain.*
4. Of the value of each *pain* which appears to be produced by it after the first. This constitutes the *fecundity* of the first *pain,* and the *impurity* of the first *pleasure.*
5. Sum up all the values of all the *pleasures* on the one side, and those of all the *pains* on the other. The balance, if it be on the side of pleasure, will give the *good* tendency of the act upon the whole, with respect to the interests of that *individual* person; if on the side of pain, the *bad* tendency of it upon the whole.
6. Take an account of the *number* of persons whose interests appear to be concerned; and repeat the above process with respect to each. *Sum up* the numbers expressive of the degrees of *good* tendency, which the act has, with respect to each individual, in regard to whom the tendency of it is *good* upon the whole: do this again with respect to each individual, in regard to whom the tendency of it is *bad* upon the whole. Take the *balance;* which, if on the side of *pleasure,* will give the general *good tendency* of the act, with respect to the total number or community of individuals concerned; if on the side of *pain,* the general *evil tendency,* with respect to the same community.

It is not to be expected that this process should be strictly pursued previously to every moral judgment, or to every legislative or judicial operation. It may, however, be always kept in view: and as near as the process actually pursued on these occasions approaches to it, so near will such process approach to the character of an exact one.

Motives

With respect to goodness and badness, as it is with everything else that is not itself either pain or pleasure, so is it with motives. If they are good or bad, it is only on account of their effects: good, on account of their tendency to produce pleasure, or avert pain: bad, on account of their tendency to produce pain, or avert pleasure. Now the case is, that from one and the same motive, and from every kind of motive, may proceed actions that are good, others that are bad, and others that are indifferent. . . .

It appears then that there is no such thing as any sort of motive which is a bad one in itself: nor, consequently, any such thing as a sort of motive which in itself is exclusively a good one. And as to their effects, it appears too that these are sometimes bad, at other times either indifferent or good, and this appears to be the case with every sort of motive. *If any sort of motive then is either good or bad on the score of its effects, this is the case only on individual occasions, and with individual motives;* and this is the case with one sort of motive as well as with another. *If any sort of motive then can, in consideration of its effects, be termed with any propriety a bad one,* it can only be with reference to the balance of all the effects it may have had of both kinds within a given period, that is, of its most usual tendency.

What then? (it will be said) are not lust, cruelty, avarice, bad motives? Is there so much as any one individual occasion, in which motives like these can be otherwise than bad? No, certainly: and yet the proposition, that there is no one *sort* of motive but what will on many occasions be a good one, is nevertheless true. The fact is, that these are names which, if properly applied, are never applied but in the cases where the motives they signify happen to be bad. The names of these motives, considered apart from their effects, are sexual desire, displeasure, and pecuniary interest. To sexual desire, when the effects of it are looked upon as bad, is given the name of lust. Now lust is always a bad motive. Why? Because if the case be such, that the effects of the motive are not bad, it does not go, or at least ought not to go, by the name of lust. The case is, then, that when I say, "Lust is a bad motive," it is a proposition that merely concerns the import of the word lust; and which would be false if transferred to the other word used for the same motive, sexual desire. Hence we see the emptiness of all those rhapsodies of common-place morality, which consist in the taking of such names as lust, cruelty, and avarice, and branding them with marks of reprobation: applied to the *thing,* they are false; applied to the *name,* they are true indeed, but nugatory. Would you do a real service to mankind, show them the cases in which sexual desire *merits* the name of lust; displeasure, that of cruelty, and pecuniary interest, that of avarice.

14

Equality Means Mediocrity

Friedrich W. Nietzsche (1844–1900), a German romantic philosopher, was born in Rocken, a Prussian province of Saxony. His academic training was in theology and classical languages and literature at the University of Bonn. The influence of Schopenhauer's philosophy led him away from both theological studies and traditional Christianity. Granted a professorship at Basle, he resigned in 1879 because of poor health. He wrote *The Birth of Tragedy* (1872), *Thus Spoke Zarathustra* (1883 ff), *Beyond Good and Evil* (1886), *Genealogy of Morals* (1887).

Nietzsche believes that the uncorrupted aristocratic class gives the meaning and the justification of a society. This master group determines what is good. It creates values; particularly the value of power. The values of the common man, the slave society, are usually pity, humility, friendship, patience, etc. If they are allowed to dominate, then society will decay.

TO STUDY

1. According to Nietzsche how does society advance? What causes society "to decay"?

2. What is the "essential characteristic of a good and healthy aristocracy"?

3. Explain the difference between the master and the slave morality.

4. Why did the early equality of men disappear? What followed "the destruction of equality"?

5. According to Nietzsche how did society and laws originate?

257

Every enhancement of the type "man" has so far been the work of an aristocratic society—and it will be so again and again—a society that believes in the long ladder of an order of rank and differences in value between man and man, and that needs slavery in some sense or other. Without that *pathos of distance* which grows out of the ingrained difference between strata—when the ruling caste constantly looks afar and looks down upon subjects and instruments and just as constantly practices obedience and command, keeping down and keeping at a distance—that other, more mysterious pathos could not have grown up either—the craving for an ever new widening of distances within the soul itself, the development of ever higher, rarer, more remote, further-stretching, more comprehensive states—in brief, simply the enhancement of the type "man," the continual "self-overcoming of man," to use a moral formula in a supra-moral sense.

To be sure, one should not yield to humanitarian illusions about the origins of an aristocratic society (and thus of the presupposition of this enhancement of the type "man"): truth is hard. Let us admit to ourselves, without trying to be considerate, how every higher culture on earth so far has *begun.* Human beings whose nature was still natural, barbarians in every terrible sense of the word, men of prey who were still in possession of unbroken strength of will and lust for power, hurled themselves upon weaker, more civilized, more peaceful races, perhaps traders or cattle raisers, or upon mellow old cultures whose last vitality was even then flaring up in splendid fireworks of spirit and corruption. In the beginning, the noble caste was always the barbarian caste: their predominance did not lie mainly in physical strength but in strength of the soul—they were more *whole* human beings (which also means, at every level, "more whole beasts").

258

Corruption as the expression of a threatening anarchy among the instincts and of the fact that the foundation of the affects, which is called "life," has been shaken: corruption is something totally different depending on the organism in which it appears. When, for example, an aristocracy, like that of France at the beginning of the Revolution, throws away its privileges with a sublime disgust and sacrifices itself to an extravagance of its own moral feelings, that is corruption; it was really only the last act of that centuries-old corruption which had led them to surrender, step by step, their governmental prerogatives, demoting themselves to a mere *function* of the monarchy (finally even to a mere ornament and showpiece). The essential characteristic of a good and healthy aristocracy, however, is that it experiences itself *not* as a function (whether of the monarchy or the commonwealth) but as their *meaning* and highest justification—that it therefore accepts with a good conscience the sacrifice of untold human beings who, *for its sake,* must be reduced and lowered to incomplete human beings, to slaves, to instruments. Their fundamental faith simply has to be that society must *not* exist for society's sake but only as the foundation and scaffolding on which a choice type of being is able to raise itself to its higher task and to a higher state of *being*—comparable to those sun-seeking vines of Java—they are called *Sipo Matador*—that so long and so often enclasp an oak tree with their tendrils until eventually, high above it but supported by it, they can unfold their crowns in the open light and display their happiness.

259

Refraining mutually from injury, violence, and exploitation and placing one's will on a par with that of someone else—this may become, in a certain rough sense, good manners among individuals if the appropriate conditions are present (namely, if these men are actually similar in strength and value standards and belong together in *one* body). But as soon as this principle is extended, and possibly even accepted as the *fundamental principle of society,* it immediately proves to be what it really is—a will to the *denial* of life, a principle of disintegration and decay.

Here we must beware of superficiality and get to the bottom of the matter, resisting all sentimental weakness: life itself is *essentially* appropriation, injury, overpowering of what is alien and weaker; suppression, hardness, imposition of one's own forms, incorporation and at least, at its mildest, exploitation—but why should one always use those words in which a slanderous intent has been imprinted for ages?

Even the body within which individuals treat each other as equals, as suggested before—and this happens in every healthy aristocracy—if it is a living and not a dying body, has to do to other bodies what the individuals within it refrain from doing to each other: it will have to be an incarnate will to power, it will strive to grow, spread, seize, become predominant—not from any morality or immorality but because it is *living* and because life simply *is* will to power. But there is no point on which the ordinary consciousness of Europeans resists instruction as on this: everywhere people are now raving, even under scientific disguises, about coming conditions of society in which "the exploitative aspect" will be removed—which sounds to me as if they promised to invent a way of life that would dispense with all organic functions. "Exploitation" does not belong to a corrupt or imperfect and primitive society: it belongs to the *essence* of what lives, as a basic organic function; it is a consequence of the will to power, which is after all the will of life.

If this should be an innovation as a theory—as a reality it is the *primordial fact* of all history: people ought to be honest with themselves at least that far.

260

Wandering through the many subtler and coarser moralities which have so far been prevalent on earth, or still are prevalent, I found that certain features recurred regularly together and were closely associated—until I finally discovered two basic types and one basic difference.

There are *master morality* and *slave morality*—I add immediately that in all the higher and more mixed cultures there also appear attempts at mediation between these two moralities, and yet more often the interpretation and mutual misunderstanding of both, and at times they occur directly alongside each other—even in the same human being, with a *single* soul. The moral discrimination of values has originated either among a ruling group whose consciousness of its difference from the ruled group was accompanied by delight—or among the ruled, the slaves and dependents of every degree.

In the first case, when the ruling group determines what is "good," the exalted, proud states of the soul are experienced as conferring distinction and determining the order of rank. The noble human being separates from himself those in whom the opposite of such exalted, proud states finds expression: he despises them. It should be noted immediately that in this first type of morality the opposition of "good" and *"bad"* means approximately the same as "noble" and "contemptible." (The opposition of "good" and *"evil"* has a different origin.) One feels contempt for the cowardly, the anxious, the petty, those intent on narrow utility; also for the suspicious with their unfree glances, those who humble themselves, the doglike people who allow themselves to be maltreated, the begging flatterers, above all the liars: it is part of the fundamental faith of all aristocrats that the common people lie. "We truthful ones"—thus the nobility of ancient Greece referred to itself.

It is obvious that moral designations were everywhere first applied to *human beings* and only later, derivatively, to actions. Therefore it is a gross mistake when historians of morality start from such questions as: why was the compassionate act praised? The noble type of man experiences *itself* as determining values; it does not need approval; it judges, "what is harmful to me is harmful in itself"; it knows itself to be that which first accords honor to things; it is *value-creating*. Everything it knows as part of itself it honors: such a morality is self-glorification. In the foreground there is the feeling of fullness, of power that seeks to overflow, the happiness of high tension, the consciousness of wealth that would give and bestow: the noble human being, too, helps the unfortunate, but not, or almost not, from pity, but prompted more by an urge begotten by excess of power. The noble human being honors himself as one who is powerful, also as one who has power over himself, who knows how to speak and be silent, who delights in being severe and hard with himself and respects all severity and hardness. "A hard heart Wotan put into my breast," says an old Scandinavian saga: a fitting poetic expression, seeing that it comes from the soul of a proud Viking. Such a type of man is actually proud of the fact that he is *not* made for pity, and the hero of the saga therefore adds as a warning: "If the heart is not hard in youth it will never harden." Noble and courageous human beings who think that way are furthest removed from that morality which finds the distinction of morality precisely in pity, or in acting for others, or in *désintéressement;* faith in oneself, a fundamental hostility and irony against "selflessness" belong just as definitely to noble morality as does a slight disdain and caution regarding compassionate feelings and a "warm heart."

It is the powerful who *understand* how to honor; this is their art, their realm of invention. The profound reverence for age and tradition—all law rests on this double reverence—the faith and prejudice in favor of ancestors and disfavor of those yet to come are typical of the morality of the powerful; and when the men of "modern ideas," conversely, believe almost instinctively in "progress" and "the future" and more and more lack respect for age, this in itself would sufficiently betray the ignoble origin of these "ideas."

A morality of the ruling group, however, is most alien and embarrassing to the present taste in the severity of its principle that one has duties only to one's peers; that against beings of a lower rank, against everything alien, one may behave as one pleases or "as the heart desires," and in any case "beyond good and evil"—here pity and like feelings may find their place. The capacity for, and the duty of, long gratitude and long revenge—

both only among one's peers—refinement in repaying, the sophisticated concept of friendship, a certain necessity for having enemies (as it were, as drainage ditches for the affects of envy, quarrelsomeness, exuberance—at bottom, in order to be capable of being good *friends*): all these are typical characteristics of noble morality which, as suggested, is not the morality of "modern ideas" and therefore is hard to emphathize with today, also hard to dig up and uncover. [1]

It is different with the second type of morality, *slave morality*. Suppose the violated, oppressed, suffering, unfree, who are uncertain of themselves and weary, moralize: what will their moral valuations have in common? Probably, a pessimistic suspicion about the whole condition of man will find expression, perhaps a condemnation of man along with his condition. The slave's eye is not favorable to the virtues of the powerful: he is skeptical and suspicious, *subtly* suspicious, of all the "good" honored there—he would like to persuade himself that even their happiness is not genuine. Conversely, those qualities are brought out and flooded with light which serve to ease existence for those who suffer: here pity, the complaisant and obliging hand, the warm heart, patience, industry, humility, and friendliness are honored—for here these are the most useful qualities and almost the only means for enduring the pressure of existence. Slave morality is essentially a morality of utility.

Here is the place for the origin of that famous opposition of "good" and "evil": into evil one's feelings project power and dangerousness, a certain terribleness, subtlety, and strength that does not permit contempt to develop. According to slave morality, those who are "evil" thus inspire fear; according to master morality it is precisely those who are "good" that inspire, and wish to inspire, fear, while the "bad" are felt to be contemptible.

The opposition reaches its climax when, as a logical consequence of slave morality, a touch of disdain is associated also with the "good" of this morality—this may be slight and benevolent—because the good human being has to be *undangerous* in the slaves' way of thinking: he is good-natured, easy to deceive, a little stupid perhaps, *un bonhomme*.[2] Wherever slave morality becomes preponderant, language tends to bring the words "good" and "stupid" closer together.

One last fundamental difference: the longing for *freedom*, the instinct for happiness and the subtleties of the feeling of freedom belong just as

---

[1] Clearly master morality cannot be discovered by introspection nor by the observation of individuals who are "masters" rather than "slaves." Both of these misunderstandings are widespread. What is called for is rather a rereading of, say, the *Iliad* and, to illustrate "slave morality," the New Testament.—[W. Kaufmann]

[2] Literally "a good human being," the term is used for precisely the type described here.—[W. Kaufmann]

necessarily to slave morality and morals as artful and enthusiastic reverence and devotion are the regular symptom of an aristocratic way of thinking and evaluating.

This makes plain why love *as passion*—which is our European specialty—simply must be of noble origin: as is well known, its invention must be credited to the Provençal knight-poets, those magnificent and inventive human beings of the *"gai saber"*[3] to whom Europe owes so many things and almost owes itself.—

261

Among the things that may be hardest to understand for a noble human being is vanity: he will be tempted to deny it, where another type of human being could not find it more palpable. The problem for him is to imagine people who seek to create a good opinion of themselves which they do not have of themselves—and thus also do not "deserve"—and who nevertheless end up *believing* this good opinion themselves. This strikes him half as such bad taste and lack of self-respect, and half as so baroquely irrational, that he would like to consider vanity as exceptional, and in most cases when it is spoken of he doubts it.

He will say, for example: "I may be mistaken about my value and nevertheless demand that my value, exactly as I define it, should be acknowledged by others as well—but this is no vanity (but conceit or, more frequently, what is called 'humility' or 'modesty')." Or: "For many reasons I may take pleasure in the good opinion of others: perhaps because I honor and love them and all their pleasures give me pleasure; perhaps also because their good opinion confirms and strengthens my faith in my own good opinion; perhaps because the good opinion of others, even in cases where I do not share it, is still useful to me or promises to become so—but all that is not vanity."

The noble human being must force himself, with the aid of history, to recognize that, since time immemorial, in all somehow dependent social strata the common man *was* only what he was *considered:* not at all used to positing values himself, he also attached no other value to himself than his masters attached to him (it is the characteristic *right of masters* to create values).

It may be understood as the consequence of an immense atavism that even now the ordinary man still always *waits* for an opinion about himself

---

[3] "Gay science": in the early fourteenth century the term was used to designate the art of the troubadours, codified in *Leys d'amors.* Nietzsche subtitled his own *Fröhliche Wissenschaft* (1882), *"la gaya scienza,"* placed a quatrain on the title page, began the book with a fifteen-page "Prelude in German Rhymes," and in the second edition (1887) added, besides a Preface and Book V, an "Appendix" of further verses.—[W. Kaufmann]

and then instinctively submits to that—but by no means only a "good" opinion; also a bad and unfair one (consider, for example, the great majority of the self-estimates and self-underestimates that believing women accept from their father-confessors, and believing Christians quite generally from their church).

In accordance with the slowly arising democratic order of things (and its cause, the intermarriage of masters and slaves), the originally noble and rare urge to ascribe value to oneself on one's own and to "think well" of oneself will actually be encouraged and spread more and more now; but it is always opposed by an older, ampler, and more deeply ingrained propensity—and in the phenomenon of "vanity" this older propensity masters the younger one. The vain person is delighted by *every* good opinion he hears of himself (quite apart from all considerations of its utility, and also apart from truth or falsehood), just as every bad opinion of him pains him: for he submits to both, he *feels* subjected to them in accordance with that oldest instinct of submission that breaks out in him.

It is "the slave" in the blood of the vain person, a residue of the slave's craftiness—and how much "slave" is still residual in woman, for example!—that seeks to *seduce* him to good opinions about himself; it is also the slave who afterwards immediately prostrates himself before these opinions as if he had not called them forth.

And to say it once more: vanity is an atavism.

15

Duty Is Prior
To Happiness

Immanuel Kant (1724–1804) was an immensely innovative and influential philosopher. His *Critique of Pure Reason* (1781) introduced a revolution in thinking which set the tone for all nineteenth-century philosophy, and which is still felt today. Kant lived most of his life in obscurity in Königsberg, East Prussia, teaching at the University of Königsberg.

Kant says that the only good thing in the world is a good will. By this, he does not mean good intentions, but rather a rational will, i.e., one that out of duty wills consistently. This is expressed in terms of the *categorical imperative:* Act only according to that maxim by which you can at the same time will that it should become a universal law. Kant believes this is quite different from the Golden Rule.

TO STUDY

1. According to Kant, what is the only good without qualification?
2. Why are character, gifts of fortune, and happiness not good without qualification?
3. Distinguish between the complete good and the supreme good.
4. What are some of our duties? How does Kant define duty?
5. What law serves the will as a principle? How does promise-keeping exemplify this law?
6. What is the relationship between common men and this law (the

categorical imperative)? Why must common reason take a step into the field of practical philosophy?

7. Do you agree with Kant's criticisms of the Golden Rule?

Nothing can possibly be conceived in the world, or even out of it, which can be called good without qualification, except a Good Will. Intelligence, wit, judgment, and the other *talents* of the mind, however they may be named, or courage, resolution, perseverance, as qualities of temperament, are undoubtedly good and desirable in many respects; but these gifts of nature may also become extremely bad and mischievous if the will which is to make use of them, and which, therefore, constitutes what is called *character*, is not good. It is the same with the *gifts of fortune*. Power, riches, honor, even health, and the general well-being and contentment with one's condition which is called *happiness*, inspire pride, and often presumption, if there is not a good will to correct the influence of these on the mind, and with this also to rectify the whole principle of acting, and adapt it to its end. The sight of a being who is not adorned with a single feature of a pure and good will, enjoying unbroken prosperity, can never give pleasure to an impartial rational spectator. Thus a good will appears to constitute the indispensable condition even of being worthy of happiness.

There are even some qualities which are of service to this good will itself, and may facilitate its action, yet which have no intrinsic unconditional value, but always presuppose a good will, and this qualifies the esteem that we justly have for them, and does not permit us to regard them as absolutely good. Moderation in the affections and passions, self-control and calm deliberation are not only good in many respects, but even seem to constitute part of the intrinsic worth of the person; but they are far from deserving to be called good without qualification, although they have been so unconditionally praised by the ancients. For without the principles of a good will, they may become extremely bad, and the coolness of a villain not only makes him far more dangerous, but also directly makes him more abominable in our eyes than he would have been without it.

A good will is good, not because of what it performs or effects, not by its aptness for the attainment of some proposed end, but simply by virtue of the volition; that is, it is good in itself, and considered by itself is to be esteemed much higher than all that can be brought about by it in favor of any inclination, nay even of the sum total of all inclinations. Even if it should happen that, owing to special disfavor of fortune, or the niggardly

---

From *Fundamental Principles of the Metaphysic of Morals*, trans. by T. K. Abbott (1907).

provision of a stepmotherly nature, this will should wholly lack power to accomplish its purpose, if with its greatest efforts it should yet achieve nothing, and there should remain only the good will (not, to be sure, a mere wish, but the summoning of all means in our power), then, like a jewel, it would still shine by its own light, as a thing which has its whole value in itself. Its usefulness or fruitlessness can neither add to nor take away anything from this value. It would be, as it were, only the setting to enable us to handle it the more conveniently in common commerce or to attract to it the attention of those who are not yet connoisseurs, but not to recommend it to true connoisseurs, or to determine its value.

There is, however, something so strange in this idea of the absolute value of the mere will, in which no account is taken of its utility, that notwithstanding the thorough assent of even common reason to the idea, yet a suspicion must arise that it may perhaps really be the product of mere high-flown fancy, and that we may have misunderstood the purpose of nature in assigning reason as the governor of our will. Therefore, we will examine this idea from this point of view.

In the physical constitution of an organized being, that is, a being adapted suitably to the purposes of life, we assume it as a fundamental principle that no organ for any purpose will be found but what is also the fittest and best adapted for that purpose. Now in a being which has reason and a will, if the proper object of nature were its *conservation,* its *welfare,* in a word, its *happiness,* then nature would have hit upon a very bad arrangement in selecting the reason of the creature to carry out this purpose. For all actions which the creature has to perform with a view to this purpose, and the whole rule of its conduct, would be far more surely prescribed to it by instinct, and that end would have been attained thereby much more certainly than it ever can be by reason. Should reason have been communicated to this favored creature over and above, it must only have served it to contemplate the happy constitution of its nature, to admire it, to congratulate itself thereon, and to feel thankful for it to the beneficent cause, but not that it should subject its desires to that weak and delusive guidance, and meddle bunglingly with the purpose of nature. In a word, nature would have taken care that reason should not break forth into *practical exercise,* nor have the presumption, with its weak insight, to think out for itself the plan of happiness, and of the means of attaining it. Nature would not only have taken on herself the choice of the ends, but also of the means, and with wise foresight would have entrusted both to instinct.

And, in fact, we find that the more a cultivated reason applies itself with deliberate purpose to the enjoyment of life and happiness, so much the more does the man fail of true satisfaction. And from this circumstance there arises in many, if they are candid enough to confess it, a certain degree of *misology*, that is, hatred of reason, especially in the case of those who are most experienced in the use of it, because after calculating all the advantages they derive, I do not say from the invention of all the arts of common luxury, but even from the sciences (which seem to them to be after all only a luxury of the understanding), they find that they have, in fact, only brought more trouble on their shoulders, rather than gained in happiness; and they end by envying, rather than despising, the more common stamp of men who keep closer to the guidance of mere instinct, and do not allow their reason much influence on their conduct. And thus we must admit that the judgment of those who would very much lower the lofty eulogies of the advantages which reason gives us in regard to the happiness and satisfaction of life, or who would even reduce them below zero, is by no means morose or ungrateful to the goodness with which the world is governed, but that there lies at the root of these judgments the idea that our existence has a different and far nobler end, for which, and not for happiness, reason is properly intended, and which must, therefore, be regarded as the supreme condition to which the private ends of man must, for the most part, be postponed.

For as reason is not competent to guide the will with certainty in regard to its objects and the satisfaction of all our wants (which it to some extent even multiplies), this being an end to which an implanted instinct would have led with much greater certainty; and since, nevertheless, reason is imparted to us as a practical faculty, i.e., as one which is to have influence on the *will*, therefore, admitting that nature generally in the distribution of her capacities has adapted the means to the end, its true destination must be to produce a *will*, not merely good as a *means* to something else, but *good in itself*, for which reason was absolutely necessary. This will, then, though not indeed the sole and complete good, must be the supreme good and the condition of every other, even of the desire of happiness. Under these circumstances, there is nothing inconsistent with the wisdom of nature in the fact that the cultivation of the reason, which is requisite for the first and unconditional purpose, does in many ways interfere, at least in this life, with the attainment of the second, which is always conditional, namely, happiness. Nay, it may even reduce it to nothing, without nature thereby failing of her purpose. For reason recognizes the establishment of a good will as its highest practical destination, and in attaining this purpose is capable only of a satisfaction of its own proper kind, namely, that from the attainment of an end, which end again is determined by reason only, notwithstanding that this may involve many a disappointment to the ends of inclination.

We have then to develop the notion of a will which deserves to be highly esteemed for itself, and is good without a view to anything further, a notion which exists already in the sound natural understanding, requiring rather to be cleared up than to be taught, and which in estimating the value of our actions always takes the first place, and constitutes the condition of all the rest. In order to do this we will take the notion of duty, which includes that of a good will, although implying certain subjective restrictions and hindrances. These, however, far from concealing it, or rendering it unrecognizable, rather bring it out by contrast, and make it shine forth so much the brighter.

I omit here all actions which are already recognized as inconsistent with duty, although they may be useful for this or that purpose, for with these the question whether they are done *from duty* cannot arise at all, since they even conflict with it. I also set aside those actions which really conform to duty, but to which men have *no* direct *inclination,* performing them because they are impelled thereto by some other inclination. For in this case we can readily distinguish whether the action which agrees with duty is done *from duty,* or from a selfish view. It is much harder to make this distinction when the action accords with duty, and the subject has besides a *direct* inclination to it. For example, it is always a matter of duty that a dealer should not overcharge an inexperienced purchaser, and wherever there is much commerce the prudent tradesman does not overcharge, but keeps a fixed price for everyone, so that a child buys of him as well as any other. Men are thus *honestly* served; but this is not enough to make us believe that the tradesman has so acted from duty and from principles of honesty: his own advantage required it: it is out of the question in this case to suppose that he might besides have a direct inclination in favor of the buyers, so that, as it were, from love he should give no advantage to one over another. Accordingly the action was done neither from duty nor from direct inclination, but merely with a selfish view.

On the other hand, it is a duty to maintain one's life; and, in addition, everyone has also a direct inclination to do so. But on this account the often anxious care which most men take for it has no intrinsic worth, and their maxim has no moral import. They preserve their life *as duty requires,* no doubt, but not *because duty requires.* On the other hand, if adversity and hopeless sorrow have completely taken away the relish for life, if the unfortunate one, strong in mind, indignant at his fate rather than desponding or dejected, wishes for death, and yet preserves his life without loving it—not from inclination or fear, but from duty—then this maxim has a moral worth.

To be beneficent when we can is a duty; and besides this, there are many minds so sympathetically constituted that, without any other motive of vanity or self-interest, they find a pleasure in spreading joy around them, and can take delight in the satisfaction of others so far as it is their own work. But I maintain that in such a case an action of this kind, however proper, however amiable it may be, has nevertheless no true moral worth, but is on a level with other inclinations, e.g., the inclination to honor, which, if it is happily directed to that which is in fact of public utility and accordant with duty, and consequently honorable, deserves praise and encouragement, but not esteem. For the maxim lacks the moral import, namely, that such actions be done *from duty,* not from inclination. Put the case that the mind of that philanthropist were clouded by sorrow of his own, extinguishing all sympathy with the lot of others, and that while he still has the power to benefit others in distress, he is not touched by their trouble because he is absorbed with his own; and now suppose that he tears himself out of this dead insensibility, and performs the action without any inclination to it, but simply from duty, then only has his action its genuine moral worth. Further still; if nature has put little sympathy in the heart of this or that man; if he, supposed to be an upright man, is by temperament cold and indifferent to the sufferings of others, perhaps because in respect of his own he is provided with the special gift of patience and fortitude, and supposes, or even requires, that others should have the same—and such a man would certainly not be the meanest product of nature—but if nature had not specially framed him for a philanthropist, would he not still find in himself a source from [which to derive a far] higher worth than [any] that a good-natured temperament [might have]? Unquestionably. It is just in this that the moral worth of the character is brought out which is incomparably the highest of all, namely, that he is beneficent, not from inclination, but from duty.

To secure one's own happiness is a duty, at least indirectly; for discontent with one's condition, under a pressure of many anxieties and amidst unsatisfied wants, might easily become a great *temptation to transgression of duty.* But here again, without looking to duty, all men have already the strongest and most intimate inclination to happiness, because it is just in this idea that all inclinations are combined in one total. But the precept of happiness is often of such a sort that it greatly interferes with some inclinations, and yet a man cannot form any definite and certain conception of the sum of satisfaction of all of them which is called happiness. It is not then to be wondered at that a single inclination, definite both as to what it promises and as to the time within which it can be gratified, is often able to overcome such a fluctuating idea, and that a gouty patient, for instance, can choose to enjoy what he likes, and to suffer what he may, since, according to his calculation, on this occasion at least, he has [only] not sacrificed the enjoyment of the present moment to a possibly mistaken expectation of a happiness which is supposed to be found in health. But even in this case, if the general desire for happiness did not influence his will, and supposing that in his particular case health was not a necessary element in his calculation, there yet remains in this, as in all other cases, this law, namely, that he should promote his happiness not from inclination but from duty, and by this would his conduct first acquire true moral worth.

It is in this manner, undoubtedly, that we are to understand those passages of Scripture also in which we are commanded to love our neighbor, even our enemy. For love, as an affection, cannot be commanded, but beneficence for duty's sake may; even though we are not impelled to it by any inclination—nay, are even repelled by a natural and unconquerable aversion. This is *practical* love, and not *pathological*—a love which is seated in the will, and not in the propensions of sense—in principles of action and not of tender sympathy; and it is this love alone which can be commanded.

The second proposition is: That an action done from duty derives its moral worth, *not from the purpose* which is to be attained by it, but from the maxim by which it is determined, and therefore does not depend on the realization of the object of the action, but merely on the *principle of volition* by which the action has taken place, without regard to any object of desire. It is clear from what precedes that the purposes which we may have in view in our actions, or their effects regarded as ends and springs of the will, cannot give to actions any unconditional or moral worth. In what, then, can their worth lie, if it is not to consist in the will and in reference to its expected effect? It cannot lie anywhere but in the *principle of the will* without regard to the ends which can be attained by the action. For the will stands between its *a priori* principle, which is formal, and its *a posteriori* spring, which is material, as between two roads, and as it must be determined by something, it follows that it must be determined by the formal principle of volition when an action is done from duty, in which case every material principle has been withdrawn from it.

The third proposition, which is a consequence of the two preceding, I would express thus: *Duty is the necessity of acting from respect for the law.* I may have *inclination* for an object as the effect of my proposed action, but I cannot have *respect* for it, just for this reason, that it is an effect and not an energy of will. Similarly, I cannot have respect for inclination, whether my own or another's; I can at most, if my own, approve it; if another's, sometimes even love it; i.e., look on it as favorable to my own interest. It is only what is connected with my will as a principle, by no means as an effect—what does not subserve my inclination, but overpowers it, or at least in case of choice excludes it from its calculation—in other words, simply the law of itself which can be an object of respect, and hence a command. Now an action done from duty must wholly exclude the influence of inclination, and with it every object of the will, so that nothing remains which can determine the will except objectively the *law,* and subjectively *pure respect* for this practical law, and consequently the maxim that I should follow this law even to the thwarting of all my inclinations.

Thus the moral worth of an action does not lie in the effect expected from it, nor in any principle of action which requires to borrow its motive from this expected effect. For all these effects—agreeableness of one's condition, and even the promotion of the happiness of others—could have been also brought about by other causes, so that for this there would have been no need of the will of a rational being; whereas, it is in this alone that the supreme and unconditional good can be found. The pre-eminent good which we call moral can, therefore, consist in nothing else than *the conception of law* in itself, *which certainly is only possible in a rational being,* in so far as this conception, and not the expected effect, determines the will. This is a good which is already present in the person who acts accordingly, and we have not to wait for it to appear first in the result.

But what sort of law can that be, the conception of which must determine the will, even without paying any regard to the effect expected from it, in order that this will may be called good absolutely and without qualification? As I have deprived the will of every impulse which could arise to it from obedience to any law, there remains nothing but the universal conformity of its actions to law in general, which alone is to serve the will as a principle, i.e., I am never to act otherwise than so *that I could also will that my maxim should become a universal law.* Here now, it is the simple conformity to law in general, without assuming any particular law applicable to certain actions, that serves the will as its principle, and must so serve it, if duty is not to be a vain delusion and a chimerical notion. The common reason of men in its practical judgments perfectly coincides with this, and always has in view the principle here suggested. Let the question be, for example: May I, when in distress, make a promise with the intention not to keep it? I readily distinguish here between the two significations which the question may have: Whether it is prudent, or whether it is right, to make a false promise. The former may undoubtedly often be the case. I see clearly, indeed, that it is not enough to extricate myself from a present difficulty by means of this subterfuge, but it must be well considered whether there may not hereafter spring from this lie much greater inconvenience than that from which I now free myself, and as, with all my supposed *cunning,* the consequences cannot be so easily foreseen but that credit once lost may be much more injurious to me than any mischief which I seek to avoid at present, it should be considered whether it would not be more *prudent* to act herein according to a universal maxim, and to make it a habit to promise nothing except with the intention of keeping it. But it is soon clear to me that such a maxim will still only be based on the fear of consequences. Now it is a wholly different thing to be truthful from duty, and to be so from apprehension of injurious consequences. In the first case, the very notion of the action already implies a law for me; in the second case, I must first look about elsewhere to see what results may be combined with it which would affect myself. For to deviate from the principle of duty is beyond all doubt wicked; but to be unfaithful to my maxim of prudence may often be very advantageous to me, although to abide by it is certainly safer. The shortest way, however, and an unerring one, to discover the answer to this question whether a lying promise is consistent with duty, is to ask myself, Should I be content that my maxim (to extricate myself from difficulty by a false promise) should hold good as a universal law, for myself as well as for others? and should I be able to say to myself, "Everyone may make a deceitful promise when he finds himself in a difficulty from which he cannot otherwise extricate himself"? Then I presently become aware that while I can will the lie, I can by no means will that lying should be a universal law. For with such a law there would be no promises at all, since it would be in vain to allege my intention in regard to my future actions to those who would not believe this allegation, or if they overhastily did so would pay me back in my own coin. Hence my maxim, as soon as it should be made a universal law, would necessarily destroy itself.

I do not, therefore, need any far-reaching penetration to discern what I have to do in order that my will may be morally good. Inexperienced in the course of the world, incapable of being prepared for all its contingencies, I only ask myself: Canst thou also will that thy maxim should be a universal law? If not, then it must be rejected, and that not because of a disadvantage accruing from it to myself or even to others, but because it cannot enter as a principle into a possible universal legislation, and reason extorts from me immediate respect for such legislation. I do not indeed as yet *discern* on what this respect is based (this the philosopher may inquire), but at least I understand this, that it is an estimation of the worth which far outweighs all worth of what is recommended by inclination, and that the necessity of acting from *pure* respect for the practical law is what constitutes duty, to which every other motive must give place, because it is the condition of a will being good *in itself,* and the worth of such a will is above everything.

Thus, then, without quitting the moral knowledge of common human reason, we have arrived at its principle. And although, no doubt, common men do not conceive it in such an abstract and universal form, yet they always have it really before their eyes, and use it as the standard of their decision. Here it would be easy to show how, with this compass in hand, men are well able to distinguish, in every case that occurs, what is good, what bad, conformably to duty or inconsistent with it, if, without in the least teaching them anything new, we only, like Socrates, direct their attention to the principle they themselves employ; and that, therefore, we do not need science and philosophy to know what we should do to be honest and good, yea, even wise and virtuous. Indeed, we might well have conjectured beforehand that the knowledge of what every man is bound to do, and therefore also to know, would be within the reach of every man, even the commonest. Here we cannot forbear admiration when we see how great an advantage the practical judgment has over the theoretical in the common understanding of men. In the latter, if common reason ventures to depart from the laws of experience and from the perceptions of the senses it falls into mere inconceivabilities and self-contradictions, at least into a chaos of uncertainty, obscurity, and instability. But in the practical sphere, it is just when the common understanding excludes all sensible springs from practical laws that its power of judgment begins to show itself to advantage. It then becomes even subtle, whether it be that it chicanes with its own conscience or with other claims respecting what is to be called right, or whether it desires for its own instruction to determine honestly the worth of actions; and, in the latter case, it may even have as good a hope of hitting the mark as any philosopher whatever can promise himself. Nay, it is almost more sure of doing so, because the philosopher cannot have any other principle, while he may easily perplex his judgment by a multitude of considerations foreign to the matter, and so turn aside from the right way. Would it not, therefore, be wiser in moral concerns to acquiesce in the judgment of common reason, or at most, only to call in philosophy for the purpose of rendering the system of morals more complete and intelligible, and its rules more convenient for use (especially for disputation), but not so as to draw off the common understanding from its happy simplicity, or to bring it by means of philosophy into a new path of inquiry and instruction?

Innocence is indeed a glorious thing, only, on the other hand, it is very sad that it cannot well maintain itself, and is easily seduced. On this account even wisdom—which otherwise consists more in conduct than in knowledge—yet has need of science, not in order to learn from it, but to secure for its precepts admission and permanence. Against all the commands of duty which reason represents to man as so deserving of respect, he feels in himself a powerful counterpoise in his wants and inclinations, the entire satisfaction of which he sums up under the name of happiness. Now reason issues its commands unyieldingly, without promising anything to the inclinations, and, as it were, with disregard and contempt for these claims, which are so impetuous, and at the same time so plausible, and which will not allow themselves to be suppressed by any command. Hence there arises a natural *dialectic*, i.e., a disposition to argue against these strict laws of duty and to question their validity, or at least their purity and strictness;

and, if possible, to make them more accordant with our wishes and inclinations, that is to say, to corrupt them at their very source, and entirely to destroy their worth—a thing which even common practical reason cannot ultimately call good.

Thus is the *common reason of man* compelled to go out of its sphere, and to take a step into the field of a *practical philosophy*, not to satisfy any speculative want (which never occurs to it as long as it is content to be mere sound reason), but even on practical grounds, in order to attain in it information and clear instruction respecting the source of its principle, and the correct determination of it in opposition to the maxims which are based on wants and inclinations, so that it may escape from the perplexity of opposite claims, and not run the risk of losing all genuine moral principles through the equivocation into which it easily falls. Thus, when practical reason cultivates itself, there insensibly arises in it a dialectic which forces it to seek aid in philosophy, just as happens to it in its theoretic use; and in this case, therefore, as well as in the other, it will find rest nowhere but in a thorough critical examination of our reason.

Kant's Criticism Of the Golden Rule

Let it not be thought that the common: *quod tibi non vis fieri,* etc. could serve here as the rule or principle . . . it cannot be a universal law, for it does not contain the principle of duties to oneself, nor of the duties of benevolence to others (for many a one would gladly consent that others should not benefit him, provided only that they might be excused from showing benevolence to them), nor finally that of duties of strict obligation to one another, for on this principle the criminal might argue against the judge who punishes him, etc.

16

Existentialist Ethics

Jean-Paul Sartre (1905–   ), French philosopher, novelist, and playwright generally considered the dean of contemporary existentialism. His massive *Being and Nothingness* (1943) presents a definitive account of his metaphysics, while his literary works, such as *No Exit, Nausea,* and *The Wall,* dramatize various aspects of the existentialist ethic.

Satre's famous essay sets forth the basic tenets of atheistic existentialism: First man is nothing else but what he makes of himself. First man exists and then his essence is developed. Hence, I choose myself and in so doing, I create an image for all men. This necessity of choosing creates anguish, forlornness, and despair in us all. Furthermore, as existence precedes essence, there is no determinism and hence, man is free. He is condemned to be free.

TO STUDY

1. Explain: "Existence precedes essence."
2. Explain: "Man is a being who hurls himself toward a future."
3. Explain: "In choosing myself, I choose man."
4. Why is man put in anguish?
5. Why is forlornness a result of man's condition?
6. Explain: "Man is condemned to be free."
7. Why is despair created in man?

. . . There are two kinds of existentialist; first, those who are Christian, among whom I would include Jaspers and Gabriel Marcel, both Catholic; and on the other hand the atheistic existentialists, among whom I class Heidegger, and then the French existentialists and myself. What they have in common is that they think that existence precedes essence, or, if you prefer, that subjectivity must be the starting point.

Just what does that mean? Let us consider some object that is manufactured, for example, a book or a paper-cutter: here is an object which has been made by an artisan whose inspiration came from a concept. He referred to the concept of what a paper-cutter is and likewise to a known method of production, which is part of the concept, something which is, by and large, a routine. Thus, the paper-cutter is at once an object produced in a certain way and, on the other hand, one having a specific use; and one can not postulate a man who produces a paper-cutter but does not know what it is used for. Therefore, let us say that, for the paper-cutter, essence—that is, the ensemble of both the production routines and the properties which enable it to be both produced and defined—precedes existence. Thus, the presence of the paper-cutter or book in front of me is determined. Therefore, we have here a technical view of the world whereby it can be said that production precedes existence.

When we conceive God as the Creator, He is generally thought of as a superior sort of artisan. Whatever doctrine we may be considering, whether one like that of Descartes or that of Leibnitz, we always grant that will more or less follows understanding or, at the very least, accompanies it, and that when God creates He knows exactly what He is creating. Thus, the concept of man in the mind of God is comparable to the concept of paper-cutter in the mind of the manufacturer, and, following certain techniques and a conception, God produces man, just as the artisan, following a definition and a technique, makes a paper-cutter. Thus, the individual man is the realisation of a certain concept in the divine intelligence.

In the eighteenth century, the atheism of the *philosophes* discarded the idea of God, but not so much for the notion that essence precedes existence. To a certain extent, this idea is found everywhere; we find it in Diderot, in Voltaire, and even in Kant. Man has a human nature; this human nature, which is the concept of the human, is found in all men, which means that each man is a particular example of a universal concept, man. In Kant, the result of this universality is that the wild-man, the natural man, as well as the bourgeois, are circumscribed by the same definition and have the same basic qualities. Thus, here too the essence of man precedes the historical existence that we find in nature.

Atheistic existentialism, which I represent, is more coherent. It states that if God does not exist, there is at least one being in whom existence precedes essence, a being who exists before he can be defined by any concept, and that this being is man, or, as Heidegger says, human reality. What is meant here by saying that existence precedes essence? It means that, first of all, man exists, turns up, appears on the scene, and, only afterwards, defines himself. If man, as the existentialist conceives him, is indefinable, it is because at first he is nothing. Only afterward will he be something, and he himself will have made what he will be. Thus, there is no human nature, since there is no God to conceive it. Not only is man what he conceives himself to be, but he is also only what he wills himself to be after this thrust toward existence.

Man is nothing else but what he makes of himself. Such is the first principle of existentialism. It is also what is called subjectivity, the name we are labeled with when charges are brought against us. But what do we mean by this, if not that man has a greater dignity than a stone or table? For we mean that man first exists, that is, that man first of all is the being who hurls himself toward a future and who is conscious of imagining himself as being in the future. Man is at the start a plan which is aware of itself, rather than a patch of moss, a piece of garbage, or a cauliflower; nothing exists prior to this plan; there is nothing in heaven; man will be what he will have planned to be. Not what he will want to be. Because by the word "will" we generally mean a conscious decision, which is subsequent to what we have already made of ourselves. I may want to belong to a political party, write a book, get married; but all that is only a manifestation of an earlier, more spontaneous choice that is called "will." But if existence really does precede essence, man is responsible for what he is. Thus, existentialism's first move is to make every man aware of what he is and to make the full responsibility of his existence rest on him. And when we say that a man is responsible for himself, we do not only mean that he is responsible for his own individuality, but that he is responsible for all men.

The word subjectivism has two meanings, and our opponents play on the two. Subjectivism means, on the one hand, that an individual chooses and makes himself; and, on the other, that it is impossible for man to transcend human subjectivity. The second of these is the essential meaning of existentialism. When we say that man chooses his own self, we mean that every one of us does likewise; but we also mean by that that in making this choice he also chooses all men. In fact, in creating the man that we want to be, there is not a single one of our acts which does not at the same time create an image of man as we think he ought to be. To choose to be this or that is to affirm at the same time the value of what we choose, because we can never choose evil. We always choose the good, and nothing can be good for us without being good for all.

If, on the other hand, existence precedes essence, and if we grant that we exist and fashion our image at one and the same time, the image is valid for everybody and for our whole age. Thus, our responsibility is much greater than we might have supposed, because it involves all mankind. If I am a workingman and choose to join a Christian trade-union rather than be a communist, and if by being a member I want to show that the best thing for man is resignation, that the kingdom of man is not of this world, I am not only involving my own case—I want to be resigned for everyone. As a result, my action has involved all humanity. To take a more individual matter, if I want to marry, to have children; even if this marriage depends solely on my own circumstances or passion or wish, I am involving all humanity in monogamy and not merely myself. Therefore, I am responsible for myself and for everyone else. I am creating a certain image of man of my own choosing. In choosing myself, I choose man.

This helps us understand what the actual content is of such rather grandiloquent words as anguish, forlornness, despair. As you will see, it's all quite simple.

First, what is meant by anguish? The existentialists say at once that man is anguish. What that means is this: the man who involves himself and who realizes that he is not only the person he chooses to be, but also a law-maker who is, at the same time, choosing all mankind as well as himself, can not help escape the feeling of his total and deep responsibility. Of course, there are many people who are not anxious; but we claim that they are hiding their anxiety, that they are fleeing from it. Certainly, many people believe that when they do something, they themselves are the only ones involved, and when someone says to them, "What if everyone acted that way?" they shrug their shoulders and answer, "Everyone doesn't act that way." But really, one should always ask himself, "What would happen if everybody looked at things that way?" There is no escaping this disturbing thought except by a kind of double-dealing. A man who lies and makes excuses for himself by saying "not everybody does that," is someone with an uneasy conscience, because the act of lying implies that a universal value is conferred upon the lie.

Anguish is evident even when it conceals itself. This is the anguish that Kierkegaard called the anguish of Abraham. You know the story: an angel has ordered Abraham to sacrifice his son; if it really were an angel who has come and said, "You are Abraham, you shall sacrifice your son," everything would be all right. But everyone might first wonder, "Is it really an angel, and am I really Abraham? What proof do I have?"

There was a madwoman who had hallucinations; someone used to speak to her on the telephone and give her orders. Her doctor asked her, "Who is it who talks to you?" She answered, "He says it's God." What proof did she really have that it was God? If an angel comes to me, what proof is there that it's an angel? And if I hear voices, what proof is there that they come from heaven and not from hell, or from the subconscious or a pathological condition? What proves that they are addressed to me? What proof is there that I have been appointed to impose my choice and my conception of man on humanity? I'll never find any proof or sign to convince me of that. If a voice addresses me, it is always for me to decide that this is the angel's voice; if I consider that such an act is a good one, it is I who will choose to say that it is good rather than bad.

Now, I'm not being singled out as an Abraham, and yet at every moment I'm obliged to perform exemplary acts. For every man, everything happens as if all mankind had its eyes fixed on him and were guiding itself by what he does. And every man ought to say to himself, "Am I really the kind of man who has the right to act in such a way that humanity might guide itself by my actions?" And if he does not say that to himself, he is making his anguish.

There is no question here of the kind of anguish which would lead to quietism, to inaction. It is a matter of a simple sort of anguish that anybody who has had responsibilities is familiar with. For example, when a military officer takes the responsibility for an attack and sends a certain number of men to death, he chooses to do so, and in the main he alone makes the choice. Doubtless, orders come from above, but they are too broad; he interprets them, and on this interpretation depend the lives of ten or fourteen or twenty men. In making a decision he can not help having a certain anguish. All leaders know this anguish. That doesn't keep them from acting; on the contrary, it is the very condition of their action. For it implies that they envisage a number of possibilities, and when they choose one, they realize that it has value only because it is chosen. We shall see this kind of anguish, which is the kind that existentialism describes, is explained, in addition, by a direct responsibility to the other men whom it involves. It is not a curtain separating us from action, but is part of action itself.

When we speak of forlornness, a term Heidegger was fond of, we mean only that God does not exist and that we have to face all the consequences of this. The existentialist is strongly opposed to a certain kind of secular ethics which would like to abolish God with the least possible expense. About 1880, some French teachers tried to set up a secular ethics which went something like this: God is a useless and costly hypothesis; we are discarding it; but, meanwhile, in order for there to be an ethics, a society, a civilization, it is essential that certain values be taken seriously and that they be considered as having an *a priori* existence. It must be obligatory, *a priori,* to be honest, not to lie, not to beat your wife, to have children, etc., etc. So we're going to try a little device which will make it possible to show that values exist all the same, inscribed in a heaven of ideas, though otherwise God does not exist. In other words—and this, I believe, is the tendency of everything called reformism in France—nothing will be changed if God does not exist. We shall find ourselves with the same norms of honesty, progress, and humanism, and we shall have made of God an outdated hypothesis which will peacefully die off by itself.

The existentialist, on the contrary, thinks it very distressing that God does not exist, because all possibility of finding values in a heaven of ideas disappears along with Him; there can no longer be an *a priori* Good, since there is no infinite and perfect consciousness to think it. Nowhere is it written that the Good exists, that we must be honest, that we must not lie; because the fact is we are on a plane where there are only men. Dostoievsky said, "If God didn't exist, everything would be possible." That is the very starting point of existentialism. Indeed, everything is permissible if God does not exist, and as a result man is forlorn, because neither within him nor without does he find anything to cling to. He can't start making excuses for himself.

If existence really does precede essence, there is no explaining things away by reference to a fixed and given human nature. In other words, there is no determinism, man is free, man is freedom. On the other hand, if God does not exist, we find no values or commands to turn to which legitimize our conduct. So, in the bright realm of values, we have no excuse behind us, nor justification before us. We are alone, with no excuses.

That is the idea I shall try to convey when I say that man is condemned to be free. Condemned, because he did not create himself, yet, in other respects is free; because, once thrown into the world, he is responsible for everything he does. The existentialist does not believe in the power of passion. He will never agree that a sweeping passion is a ravaging torrent which fatally leads a man to certain acts and is therefore an excuse. He thinks that man is responsible for his passion.

The existentialist does not think that man is going to help himself by finding in the world some omen by which to orient himself. Because he thinks that man will interpret the omen to suit himself. Therefore, he thinks that man, with no support and no aid, is condemned every moment to invent man. Ponge, in a very fine article, has said, "Man is the future of man." That's exactly it. But if it is taken to mean that this future is recorded in heaven, that God sees it, then it is false, because it would really no longer be a future. If it is taken to mean that, whatever a man may be, there is a future to be forged, a virgin future before him, then this remark is sound. But then we are forlorn.

To give you an example which will enable you to understand forlorn-ness better, I shall cite the case of one of my students who came to see me under the following circumstances: his father was on bad terms with his mother, and, moreover, was inclined to be a collaborationist; his older brother had been killed in the German offensive of 1940, and the young man, with somewhat immature but generous feelings, wanted to avenge him. His mother lived alone with him, very much upset by the half-treason of her husband and the death of her older son; the boy was her only consolation.

The boy was faced with the choice of leaving for England and joining the Free French Forces—that is, leaving his mother behind—or remaining with his mother and helping her to carry on. He was fully aware that the woman lived only for him and that his going-off—and perhaps his death—would plunge her into despair. He was also aware that every act that he did for his mother's sake was a sure thing, in the sense that it was helping her to carry on, whereas every effort he made toward going off and fighting was an uncertain move which might run aground and prove completely useless; for example, on his way to England he might, while passing through Spain, be detained indefinitely in a Spanish camp; he might reach England or Algiers and be stuck in an office at a desk job. As a result, he was faced with two very different kinds of action: one, concrete, immediate, but concerning only one individual; the other concerned an incomparably vaster group, a national collectivity, but for that very reason was dubious, and might be interrupted en route. And, at the same time, he was wavering between two kinds of ethics. On the one hand, an ethics of sympathy, of personal devotion; on the other, a broader ethics, but one whose efficacy was more dubious. He had to choose between the two.

Who could help him choose? Christian doctrine? No. Christian doc-trine says, "Be charitable, love your nighbor, take the more rugged path, etc., etc." But which is the more rugged path? Whom should he love as a brother? The fighting man or his mother? Which does the greater good, the vague act of fighting in a group, or the concrete one of helping a particular human being to go on living? Who can decide *a priori*? Nobody. No book of ethics can tell him. The Kantian ethics says, "Never treat any person as a means, but as an end." Very well, if I stay with my mother, I'll treat her as an end and not as a means; but by virtue of this very fact, I'm running the risk of treating the people around me who are fighting, as means; and, conversely, if I go to join those who are fighting, I'll be treating them as an end, and, by doing that, I run the risk of treating my mother as a means.

If values are vague, and if they are always too broad for the concrete and specific case that we are considering, the only thing left for us is to trust our instincts. That's what this young man tried to do; and when I saw him, he said, "In the end, feeling is what counts. I ought to choose whichever pushes me in one direction. If I feel that I love my mother enough to sacrifice everything else for her—my desire for vengeance, for action, for adventure—then I'll stay with her. If, on the contrary, I feel that my love for my mother isn't enough, I'll leave."

But how is the value of a feeling determined? What gives his feeling for his mother value? Precisely the fact that he remained with her. I may say that I like so-and-so well enough to sacrifice a certain amount of money for him, but I may say so only if I've done it. I may say "I love my mother well enough to remain with her" if I have remained with her. The only way to determine the value of this affection is, precisely, to perform an act which confirms and defines it. But, since I require this affection to justify my act, I find myself caught in a vicious circle.

On the other hand, Gide has well said that a mock feeling and a true feeling are almost indistinguishable; to decide that I love my mother and will remain with her, or to remain with her by putting on an act, amount somewhat to the same thing. In other words, the feeling is formed by the acts one performs; so, I can not refer to it in order to act upon it. Which means that I can neither seek within myself the true condition which will impel me to act, nor apply to a system of ethics for concepts which will permit me to act. You will say, "At least, he did go to a teacher for advice." But if you seek advice from a priest, for example, you have chosen this priest; you already knew, more or less, just about what advice he was going to give you. In other words, choosing your adviser is involving yourself. The proof of this is that if you are a Christian, you will say, "Consult a priest." But some priests are collaborating, some are just marking time, some are resisting. Which to choose? If the young man chooses a priest who is resisting or collaborating, he has already decided on the kind of advice he's going to get. Therefore, in coming to see me he knew the answer I was going to give him, and I had only one answer to give: "You're free, choose, that is, invent." No general ethics can show you what is to be done, there are no omens in the world. The Catholics will reply, "But there are." Granted—but, in any case, I myself choose the meaning they have.

As for despair, the term has a very simple meaning. It means that we shall confine ourselves to reckoning only with what depends upon our will, or on the ensemble of probabilities which make our action possible. When we want something, we always have to reckon with probabilities. I may be counting on the arrival of a friend. The friend is coming by rail or street-car; this supposes that the train will arrive on schedule, or that the street-car will not jump the track. I am left in the realm of possibility; but possibilities are to be reckoned with only to the point where my action comports with the ensemble of these possibilities, and no further. The moment the possibilities I am considering are not rigorously involved by my action, I ought to disengage myself from them, because no God, no scheme, can adapt the world and its possibilities to my will. When Descartes said, "Conquer yourself rather than the world," he meant essentially the same thing.

The Marxists to whom I have spoken reply, "You can rely on the support of others in your action, which obviously has certain limits because you're not going to live forever. That means: rely on both what others are doing elsewhere to help you, in China, in Russia, and what they will do later on, after your death, to carry on the action and lead it to its fulfillment, which will be the revolution. You even *have* to rely upon that, otherwise you're immoral." I reply at once that I will always rely on fellow-fighters insofar as these comrades are involved with me in a common struggle, in the unity of a party or a group in which I can more or less make my weight felt; that is, one whose ranks I am in as a fighter and whose movements I am aware of at every moment. In such a situation, relying on the unity and will of the party is exactly like counting on the fact that the train will arrive on time or that the car won't jump the track. But, given that man is free and that there is no human nature for me to depend on, I can not count on men whom I do not know by relying on human goodness or man's concern for the good of society. I don't know what will become of the Russian revolution; I may make an example of it to the extent that at the present time it is apparent that the proletariat plays a part in Russia that it plays in no other nation. But I can't swear that this will inevitably lead to a triumph of the proletariat. I've got to limit myself to what I see.

Given that men are free and that tomorrow they will freely decide what man will be, I can not be sure that, after my death, fellow-fighters will carry on my work to bring it to its maximum perfection. Tomorrow, after my death, some men may decide to set up Fascism, and the others may be cowardly and muddled enough to let them do it. Fascism will then be the human reality, so much the worse for us.

Actually, things will be as man will have decided they are to be.

Does that mean that I should abandon myself to quietism? No. First, I should involve myself; then, act on the old saw, "Nothing ventured, nothing gained." Nor does it mean that I shouldn't belong to a party, but rather that I shall have no illusions and shall do what I can. For example, suppose I ask myself, "Will socialization, as such, ever come about?" I know nothing about it. All I know is that I'm going to do everything in my power to bring it about. Beyond that, I can't count on anything. Quietism is the attitude of people who say, "Let others do what I can't do." The doctrine I am presenting is the very opposite of quietism, since it declares, "There is no reality except in action." Moreover, it goes further, since it adds, "Man is nothing else than his plan; he exists only to the extent that he fulfills himself; he is therefore nothing else than the ensemble of his acts, nothing else than his life."

According to this, we can understand why our doctrine horrifies certain people. Because often the only way they can bear their wretchedness is to think, "Circumstances have been against me. What I've been and done doesn't show my true worth. To be sure, I've had no great love, no great friendship, but that's because I haven't met a man or woman who was worthy. The books I've written haven't been very good because I haven't had the proper leisure. I haven't had children to devote myself to because I didn't find a man with whom I could have spent my life. So there remains within me, unused and quite viable, a host of propensities, inclinations, possibilities, that one wouldn't guess from, the mere series of things I've done."

Now, for the existentialist there is really no love other than one which manifests itself in a person's being in love. There is no genius other than one which is expressed in works of art; the genius of Proust is the sum of Proust's works; the genius of Racine is his series of tragedies. Outside of that, there is nothing. Why say that Racine could have written another tragedy, when he didn't write it? A man is involved in life, leaves his impress on it, and outside of that there is nothing. To be sure, this may seem a harsh thought to someone whose life hasn't been a success. But, on the other hand, it prompts people to understand that reality alone is what counts, that dreams, expectations, and hopes warrant no more than to define a man as a disappointed dream, as miscarried hopes, as vain expectations. In other words, to define him negatively and not positively. However, when we say, "You are nothing else than your life," that does not imply that the artist will be judged solely on the basis of his works of art; a thousand other things will contribute toward summing him up. What we mean is that a man is nothing else than a series of undertakings, that he is the sum, the organization, the ensemble of the relationships which make up these undertakings.

THINK ABOUT

1. Do you have an ultimate ethical principle? What is it? Do you have several? Do they ever conflict? How then do you decide which is the most important?

2. Are religious ethics axiological or deontological? Which are Sartre's ethics?

3. Do you agree?
   "Virtue is its own reward."
   "Happiness is the philosophy of a pig." (Nietzsche)
   "Goodness without knowledge is dangerous."
   "There are no ethical truths; there are just justifications of particular ethical problems." (Kalish)
   "For whoever would save his life will lose it; and whoever loses his life for my sake, he will save it." (Luke 9:24)
   "People are to be loved, and things are to be used . . . . Immorality occurs when things are loved and people are used."

4. Comparing the outlook today with that of some centuries ago, how do you explain the changed views of most members of society on such questions as: hanging for theft, capital punishment, the status of women, slavery, homosexuality, and labor conditions?

Readings

The Pursuit of Happiness

1. Brandt, Richard. *Ethical Theory.* Englewood Cliffs, N.J.: Prentice Hall, 1960. General.

2. Britton, Karl. *Mill.* Baltimore: Penguin Books, 1953.

3. Kaufmann, Walter. *Nietzsche.* New York 1956.

4. Mure, G. R. *Aristotle.* London 1932.

5. Ross, W. D. *Aristotle.* London: Oxford Univ. Press, 1955. The best discussion.

6. Stephen, Leslie. *The English Utilitarians.* New York: Kelley, 1900.

The Pursuit of Duty

1. Broad, C. D. *Five Types of Ethical Theory.* New York: Harcourt, Brace, 1930. Chapter 5: exposition and criticism of hedonism.

2. Desan, Wilfred. *The Tragic Finale*. Cambridge: Harvard Univ. Press, 1954. About Sartre.

3. Korner, S. *Kant*. Baltimore: Penguin Books, 1955. Chapter 6: exposition and criticism.

4. Paton, H. J. *The Categorical Imperative*. Chicago: University of Chicago Press, 1948. Sympathetic exposition.

5. Ross, W. D. *Kant's Ethical Theory*. Oxford: Clarendon Press, 1954. Exposition and criticism.

4

Knowledge

one

Of What Does Knowledge Consist?

17

Knowledge Is Not Ultimately Sense Knowledge

René Descartes (1596–1650) was an important French philosopher, whose *Meditations* became the subject of extended debates and exchanges by philosophers in France and England. He is generally credited with turning modern philosophy toward the problems of self-knowledge.

What are our ultimate grounds for knowing something? If I say that "two plus two equals four," or that "all copper conducts electricity," how are these statements ultimately established? One might reply to the question "how do you know it?" by saying "seeing is believing," but obviously this is insufficient because there is a great deal which we claim to know and have never seen. What, then, is our ultimate basis of knowledge? Descartes was a rationalist. He did not think sense knowledge was the ultimate basis of knowledge, but rather maintained that "whatever is clearly and distinctly perceived is true" is the best general rule for knowledge. This means, as a minimum, that an idea is "clear" if its content includes the nature and essence of it. Similarly, an idea is "distinct" if nothing contradictory to the essence of an object is included within it. For example, your idea of man is clear if you know the nature and essence of man, and your idea of man is distinct if your idea of man is not contradictory. That sense knowledge is not the ultimate criterion for Descartes is brought out by the example of "the piece of wax" in *Meditations* II. With this example Descartes concludes that it is not by sense perception that he understands the nature of the wax, but by the intellect itself.

TO STUDY

1. Why did Descartes undertake the method of doubt? What is it?
2. On what grounds can he doubt his senses?
3. What remains true, even if he is now dreaming?
4. On what grounds is even mathematics possibly false?
5. What is necessarily true each time it is expressed by me?
6. What am I? What is the nature of my mind?
7. What is the nature of material bodies?
8. What important conclusion about the mind does Descartes draw from the example of the piece of wax?

Meditation I

Of the Things Which May Be Brought Within the Sphere of the Doubtful

It is now some years since I detected how many were the false beliefs that I had from my earliest youth admitted as true, and how doubtful was everything I had since constructed on this basis; and from that time I was convinced that I must once for all seriously undertake to rid myself of all the opinions which I had formerly accepted, and commence to build anew from the foundation, if I wanted to establish any firm and permanent structure in the sciences. But as this enterprise appeared to be a very great one, I waited until ı had attained an age so mature that I could not hope that at any later date I should be better fitted to execute my design. This reason caused me to delay so long that I should feel that I was doing wrong were I to occupy in deliberation the time that yet remains to me for action. To-day, then, since very opportunely for the plan I have in view I have delivered my mind from every care [and am happily agitated by no passions] and since I have procured for myself an assured leisure in a peaceable retirement, I shall at last seriously and freely address myself to the general upheaval of all my former opinions.

Now for this object it is not necessary that I should show that all of these are false—I shall perhaps never arrive at this end. But inasmuch as

From *The Philosophical Works of Descartes*, "Meditation VI," trans. by E. S. Haldane and G. R. T. Ross (Cambridge: Cambridge University Press, 1931). Reprinted by permission of the publishers.

reason already persuades me that I ought no less carefully to withhold my assent from matters which are not entirely certain and indubitable than from those which appear to me manifestly to be false, if I am able to find in each one some reason to doubt, this will suffice to justify my rejecting the whole. And for that end it will not be requisite that I should examine each in particular, which would be an endless undertaking; for owing to the fact that the destruction of the foundations of necessity brings with it the downfall of the rest of the edifice, I shall only in the first place attack those principles upon which all my former opinions rested.

All that up to the present time I have accepted as most true and certain I have learned either from the senses or through the senses; but it is sometimes proved to me that these senses are deceptive, and it is wiser not to trust entirely to any thing by which we have once been deceived.

But it may be that although the senses sometimes deceive us concerning things which are hardly perceptible, or very far away, there are yet many others to be met with as to which we cannot reasonably have any doubt, although we recognise them by their means. For example, there is the fact that I am here, seated by the fire, attired in a dressing gown, having this paper in my hands and other similar matters. And how could I deny that these hands and this body are mine, were it not perhaps that I compare myself to certain persons, devoid of sense, whose cerebella are so troubled and clouded by the violent vapours of black bile, that they constantly assure us that they think they are kings when they are really quite poor, or that they are clothed in purple when they are really without covering, or who imagine that they have an earthenware head or are nothing but pumpkins or are made of glass. But they are mad, and I should not be any the less insane were I to follow examples so extravagant.

At the same time I must remember that I am a man, and that consequently I am in the habit of sleeping, and in my dreams representing to myself the same things or sometimes even less probable things, than do those who are insane in their waking moments. How often has it happened to me that in the night I dreamt that I found myself in this particular place, that I was dressed and seated near the fire, whilst in reality I was lying undressed in bed! At this moment it does indeed seem to me that it is with eyes awake that I am looking at this paper; that this head which I move is not asleep, that it is deliberately and of set purpose that I extend my hand and perceive it; what happens in sleep does not appear so clear nor so distinct as does all this. But in thinking over this I remind myself that on many occasions I have in sleep been deceived by similar illusions, and in dwelling carefully on this reflection I see so manifestly that there are no certain indications by which we may clearly distinguish wakefulness from sleep that I am lost in astonishment. And my astonishment is such that it is almost capable of persuading me that I now dream.

Now let us assume that we are asleep and that all these particulars, e.g. that we open our eyes, shake our head, extend our hands, and so on, are but false delusions; and let us reflect that possibly neither our hands nor our whole body are such as they appear to us to be. At the same time we must at least confess that the things which are represented to us in sleep are like painted representations which can only have been formed as the counterparts of something real and true, and that in this way those general things at least, i.e. eyes, a head, hands, and a whole body, are not imaginary things, but things really existent. For, as a matter of fact, painters, even when they study with the greatest skill to represent sirens and satyrs by forms the most strange and extraordinary, cannot give them natures which are entirely new, but merely make a certain medley of the members of different animals; or if their imagination is extravagant enough to invent something so novel that nothing similar has ever before been seen, and that their work represents a thing purely fictitious and absolutely false, it is certain all the same that the colours of which this is composed are necessarily real. And for the same reason, although these general things, to wit, [a body], eyes, a head, hands, and such like, may be imaginary, we are bound at the same time to confess that there are at least some other objects yet more simple and more universal, which are real and true; and of these just in the same way as with certain real colours, all these images of things which dwell in our thoughts, whether true and real or false and fantastic, are formed.

To such a class of things pertains corporeal nature in general, and its extension, the figure of extended things, their quantity or magnitude and number, as also the place in which they are, the time which measures their duration, and so on.

That is possibly why our reasoning is not unjust when we conclude from this that Physics, Astronomy, Medicine and all other sciences which have as their end the consideration of composite things, are very dubious and uncertain; but that Arithmetic, Geometry and other sciences of that kind which only treat of things that are very simple and very general, without taking great trouble to ascertain whether they are actually existent or not, contain some measure of certainty and an element of the indubitable. For whether I am awake or asleep, two and three together always form five, and the square can never have more than four sides, and it does not seem possible that truths so clear and apparent can be suspected of any falsity [or uncertainty].

Nevertheless I have long had fixed in my mind the belief that an all-powerful God existed by whom I have been created such as I am. But how do I know that He has not brought it to pass that there is no earth, no heaven, no extended body, no magnitude, no place, and that nevertheless [I possess the perceptions of all these things and that] they seem to me to exist just exactly as I now see them? And, besides, as I sometimes imagine that others deceive themselves in the things which they think they know best, how do I know that I am not deceived every time that I add two and three, or count the sides of a square, or judge of things yet simpler, if anything simpler can be imagined? But possibly God has not desired that I should be thus deceived, for He is said to be supremely good. If, however, it is contrary to His goodness to have made me such that I constantly deceive myself, it would also appear to be contrary to His goodness to permit me to be sometimes deceived, and nevertheless I cannot doubt that He does permit this.

There may indeed be those who would prefer to deny the existence of a God so powerful, rather than believe that all other things are uncertain. But let us not oppose them for the present, and grant that all that is here said of a God is a fable; nevertheless in whatever way they suppose that I have arrived at the state of being that I have reached—whether they attribute it to fate or to accident, or make out that it is by a continual succession of antecedents, or by some other method—since to err and deceive oneself is a defect, it is clear that the greater will be the probability of my being so imperfect as to deceive myself ever, as is the Author to whom they assign my origin the less powerful. To these reasons I have certainly nothing to reply, but at the end I feel constrained to confess that there is nothing in all that I formerly believed to be true, of which I cannot in some measure doubt, and that not merely through want of thought or through levity, but for reasons which are very powerful and maturely considered; so that henceforth I ought not the less carefully to refrain from giving credence to these opinions than to that which is manifestly false, if I desire to arrive at any certainty [in the sciences].

But it is not sufficient to have made these remarks, we must also be careful to keep them in mind. For these ancient and commonly held opinions still revert frequently to my mind, long and familiar custom having given them the right to occupy my mind against my inclination and rendered them almost masters of my belief; nor will I ever lose the habit of deferring to them or of placing my confidence in them, so long as I consider them as they really are, i.e. opinions in some measure doubtful, as I have just shown, and at the same time highly probable, so that there is much more reason to believe in than to deny them. That is why I consider that I shall not be acting amiss, if, taking of set purpose a contrary belief, I allow myself to be deceived, and for a certain time pretend that all these opinions are entirely false and imaginary, until at least, having thus balanced my former prejudices with my latter [so that they cannot divert my opinions more to one side than to the other], my judgment will no longer be dominated by bad usage or turned away from the right knowledge of the truth. For I am assured that there can be neither peril nor error in this course, and that I cannot at present yield too much to distrust, since I am not considering the question of action, but only of knowledge.

I shall then suppose, not that God who is supremely good and the fountain of truth, but some evil genius not less powerful than deceitful, has employed his whole energies deceiving me; I shall consider that the heavens, the earth, colours, figures, sound, and all other external things are nought but the illusions and dreams of which this genius has availed himself in order to lay traps for my credulity; I shall consider myself as having no hands, no eyes, no flesh, no blood, nor any senses, yet falsely believing myself to possess all these things; I shall remain obstinately attached to this idea, and if by this means it is not in my power to arrive at the knowledge of any truth, I may at least do what is in my power [i.e. suspend my judgment], and with firm purpose avoid giving credence to any false thing, or being imposed upon by this arch deceiver, however powerful and deceptive he may be. But this task is a laborious one, and insensibly a certain lassitude leads me into the course of my ordinary life. And just as a captive who in sleep enjoys an imaginary liberty, when he begins to suspect that his liberty is but a dream, fears to awaken, and conspires with these agreeable illusions that the deception may be prolonged, so insensibly of my own accord I fall back into my former opinions, and I dread awakening from this slumber, lest the laborious wakefulness which would follow the tranquillity of this repose should have to be spent not in daylight, but in the excessive darkness of the difficulties which have just been discussed.

Meditation II

Of the Nature of the Human Mind, and That It Is More Easily Known Than the Body

The Meditation of yesterday filled my mind with so many doubts that it is no longer in my power to forget them. And yet I do not see in what manner I can resolve them; and, just as if I had all of a sudden fallen into very deep water, I am so disconcerted that I can neither make certain of setting my feet on the bottom, nor can I swim and so support myself on the surface. I shall nevertheless make an effort and follow anew the same path as that on which I yesterday entered, i.e. I shall proceed by setting aside all that in which the least doubt could be supposed to exist, just as if I had discovered that it was absolutely false; and I shall ever follow in this road until I have met with something which is certain, or at least, if

I can do nothing else, until I have learned for certain that there is nothing in the world that is certain. Archimedes, in order that he might draw the terrestrial globe out of its place, and transport it elsewhere, demanded only that one point should be fixed and immoveable; in the same way I shall have the right to conceive high hopes if I am happy enough to discover one thing only which is certain and indubitable.

I suppose, then, that all the things that I see are false; I persuade myself that nothing has ever existed of all that my fallacious memory represents to me. I consider that I possess no senses; I imagine that body, figure, extension, movement and place are but the fiction of my mind. What, then, can be esteemed as true? Perhaps nothing at all, unless that there is nothing in the world that is certain.

But how can I know there is not something different from those things that I have just considered, of which one cannot have the slightest doubt? Is there not some God, or some other being by whatever name we call it, who puts these reflections into my mind? That is not necessary, for is it not possible that I am capable of producing them myself? I myself, am I not at least something? But I have already denied that I had senses and body. Yet I hesitate, for what follows from that? Am I so dependent on body and senses that I cannot exist without these? But I was persuaded that there were no minds, nor any bodies: was I not then likewise persuaded that I did not exist? Not at all; of a surety I myself did exist since I persuaded myself of something [or merely because I thought of something]. But there is some deceiver or other, very powerful and very cunning, who ever employs his ingenuity in deceiving me. Then without doubt I exist also if he deceives me, and let him deceive me as much as he will, he can never cause me to be nothing so long as I think that I am something. So that after having reflected well and carefully examined all things, we must come to the definite conclusion that this proposition: I am, I exist, is necessarily true each time that I pronounce it, or that I mentally conceive it.

But I do not yet know clearly enough what I am, I who am certain that I am; and hence I must be careful to see that I do not imprudently take some other object in place of myself, and thus that I do not go astray in respect of this knowledge that I hold to be the most evident of all that I have formerly learned. That is why I shall now consider anew what I believed myself to be before I embarked upon these last reflections; and of my former opinions I shall withdraw all that might even in a small degree be invalidated by the reasons which I have just brought forward, in order that there may be nothing at all left beyond what is absolutely certain and indubitable.

What then did I formerly believe myself to be? Undoubtedly I believed myself to be a man. But what is a man? Shall I say a reasonable animal?

Certainly not; for then I should have to inquire what an animal is, and what is reasonable; and thus from a single question I should insensibly fall into an infinitude of others more difficult; and I should not wish to waste the little time and leisure remaining to me in trying to unravel subtleties like these. But I shall rather stop here to consider the thoughts which of themselves spring up in my mind, and which were not inspired by anything beyond my own nature alone when I applied myself to the consideration of my being. In the first place, then, I considered myself as having a face, hands, arms, and all that system of members composed of bones and flesh as seen in a corpse which I designated by the name of body. In addition to this I considered that I was nourished, that I walked, that I felt, and that I thought, and I referred all these actions to the soul: but I did not stop to consider what the soul was, or if I did stop, I imagined that it was something extremely rare and subtle like a wind, a flame, or an ether, which was spread throughout my grosser parts. As to body I had no manner of doubt about its nature, but thought I had a very clear knowledge of it; and if I had desired to explain it according to the notions that I had then formed of it, I should have described it thus: By the body I understand all that which can be defined by a certain figure: something which can be confined in a certain place, and which can fill a space in such a way that every other body will be excluded from it; which can be perceived either by touch, or by sight, or by hearing, or by taste, or by smell: which can be moved in many ways not, in truth, by itself but by something which is foreign to it, by which it is touched [and from which it receives impressions]: for to have the power of self-movement, as also of feeling or of thinking, I did not consider to appertain to the nature of body: on the contrary, I was rather astonished to find that faculties similar to them existed in some bodies.

But what am I, now that I suppose that there is a certain genius which is extremely powerful, and, if I may say so, malicious, who employs all his powers in deceiving me? Can I affirm that I possess the least of all those things which I have just said pertain to the nature of body? I pause to consider, I revolve all these things in my mind, and I find none of which I can say that it pertains to me. It would be tedious to stop to enumerate them. Let us pass to the attributes of soul and see if there is any one which is in me? What of nutrition or walking [the first mentioned]? But if it is so that I have no body it is also true that I can neither walk nor take nourishment. Another attribute is sensation. But one cannot feel without body, and besides I have thought I perceived many things during sleep that I recognised in my waking moments as not having been experienced at all. What of thinking? I find here that thought is an attribute that belongs to me; it alone cannot be separated from me. I am, I exist, that is certain. But how often? Just when I think; for it might possibly be the case if I ceased entirely to think, that I should likewise cease altogether to exist. I do not now admit anything which is not necessarily true: to speak accurately I am not more than a thing which thinks, that is to say a mind or a soul, or an understanding, or a reason, which are terms whose significance was formerly unknown to me. I am, however, a real thing and really exist; but what thing? I have answered: a thing which thinks.

And what more? I shall exercise my imagination [in order to see if I am not something more]. I am not a collection of members which we call the human body: I am not a subtle air distributed through these members, I am not a wind, a fire, a vapour, a breath, nor anything at all which I can imagine or conceive; because I have assumed that all these were nothing. Without changing that supposition I find that I only leave myself certain of the fact that I am somewhat. But perhaps it is true that these same things which I supposed were non-existent because they are unknown to me, are really not different from the self which I know. I am not sure about this, I shall not dispute about it now; I can only give judgment on things that are known to me. I know that I exist, and I inquire what I am, I whom I know to exist. But it is very certain that the knowledge of my existence taken in its precise significance does not depend on things whose existence is not yet known to me; consequently it does not depend on those which I can feign in imagination. And indeed the very term *feign* in imagination proves to me my error, for I really do this if I image myself a something, since to imagine is nothing else than to contemplate the figure or image of a corporeal thing. But I already know for certain that I am, and that it may be that all these images, and, speaking generally, all things that relate to the nature of body are nothing but dreams [and chimeras]. For this reason I see clearly that I have as little reason to say, 'I shall stimulate my imagination in order to know more distinctly what I am,' than if I were to say, 'I am now awake, and I perceive somewhat that is real and true: but because I do not yet perceive it distinctly enough, I shall go to sleep of express purpose, so that my dreams may represent the perception with greatest truth and evidence.' And, thus, I know for certain that nothing of all that I can understand by means of my imagination belongs to this knowledge which I have of myself, and that it is necessary to recall the mind from this mode of thought with the utmost diligence in order that it may be able to know its own nature with perfect distinctness.

But what then am I? A thing which thinks. What is a thing which thinks? It is a thing which doubts, understands, [conceives], affirms, denies, wills, refuses, which also imagines and feels. . . .

Certainly it is no small matter if all these things pertain to my nature. But why should they not so pertain? Am I not that being who now doubts nearly everything, who nevertheless understands certain things, who affirms that one only is true, who denies all the others, who desires to know more, is averse from being deceived, who imagines many things, sometimes indeed despite his will, and who perceives many likewise, as by the intervention of the bodily organs? Is there nothing in all this which is as true as it is certain that I exist, even though I should always sleep and though he who has given me being employed all his ingenuity in deceiving me? Is there likewise any one of these attributes which can be distinguished from my thought, or which might be said to be separated from myself? For it is so evident of itself that it is I who doubts, who understands, and who desires, that there is no reason here to add anything to explain it. And I have certainly the power of imagining likewise; for although it may happen (as I formerly supposed) that none of the things which I imagine are true, nevertheless this power of imagining does not cease to be really in use, and it forms part of my thought. Finally, I am the same who feels, that is to say, who perceives certain things, as by the organs of sense, since in truth I see light, I hear noise, I feel heat. But it will be said that these phenomena are false and that I am dreaming. Let it be so; still it is at least quite certain that it seems to me that I see light, that I hear noise and that I feel heat. That cannot be false; properly speaking it is what is in me called feeling[1]; and used in this precise sense that is no other thing than thinking.

From this time I begin to know what I am with a little more clearness and distinction than before; but nevertheless it still seems to me, and I cannot prevent myself from thinking, that corporeal things, whose images are framed by thought, which are tested by the senses, are much more distinctly known than that obscure part of me which does not come under the imagination. Although really it is very strange to say that I know and understand more distinctly these things whose existence seems to me dubious, which are unknown to me, and which do not belong to me, than others of the truth of which I am convinced, which are known to me and which pertain to my real nature, in a word, than myself. But I see clearly how the case stands: my mind loves to wander, and cannot yet suffer itself to be retained within the just limits of truth. Very good, let us once more give it the freest rein, so that, when afterwards we seize the proper occasion for pulling up, it may the more easily be regulated and controlled.

Let us begin by considering the commonest matters, those which we believe to be the most distinctly comprehended, to wit, the bodies which we touch and see; not indeed bodies in general, for these general ideas are usually a little more confused, but let us consider one body in particular. Let us take, for example, this piece of wax: it has been taken quite freshly from the hive, and it has not yet lost the sweetness of the honey which it

---

[1] Sentire.

contains; it still retains somewhat of the odour of the flowers from which it has been culled; its colour, its figure, its size are apparent; it is hard, cold, easily handled, and if you strike it with the finger, it will emit a sound. Finally all the things which are requisite to cause us distinctly to recognise a body, are met with in it. But notice that while I speak and approach the fire what remained of the taste is exhaled, the smell evaporates, the colour alters, the figure is destroyed, the size increases, it becomes liquid, it heats, scarcely can one handle it, and when one strikes it, no sound is emitted. Does the same wax remain after this change? We must confess that it remains; none would judge otherwise. What then did I know so distinctly in this piece of wax? It could certainly be nothing of all that the senses brought to my notice, since all these things which fall under taste, smell, sight, touch, and hearing, are found to be changed, and yet the same wax remains.

Perhaps it was what I now think, viz. that this wax was not that sweetness of honey, nor that agreeable scent of flowers, nor that particular whiteness, nor that figure, nor that sound, but simply a body which a little while before appeared to me as perceptible under these forms, and which is now perceptible under others. But what, precisely, is it that I imagine when I form such conceptions? Let us attentively consider this, and, abstracting from all that does not belong to the wax, let us see what remains. Certainly nothing remains excepting a certain extended thing which is flexible and movable. But what is the meaning of flexible and movable? Is it not that I imagine that this piece of wax being round is capable of becoming square and of passing from a square to a triangular figure? No, certainly it is not that, since I imagine it admits of an infinitude of similar changes, and I nevertheless do not know how to compass the infinitude by my imagination, and consequently this conception which I have of the wax is not brought about by the faculty of imagination. What now is this extension? Is it not also unknown? For it becomes greater when the wax is melted, greater when it is boiled, and greater still when the heat increases; and I should not conceive [clearly] according to truth what wax is, if I did not think that even this piece that we are considering is capable of receiving more variations in extension than I have ever imagined. We must then grant that I could not even understand through the imagination what this piece of wax is, and that it is my mind[2] alone which perceives it. I say this piece of wax in particular, for as to wax in general it is yet clearer. But what is this piece of wax which cannot be understood excepting by the [understanding or] mind? It is certainly the same that I see, touch, imagine, and finally it is the same which I have always believed it to be from the beginning. But

---

[2] entendement F., mens L.

what must particularly be observed is that its perception is neither an act of vision, nor of touch, nor of imagination, and has never been such although it may have appeared formerly to be so, but only an intuition[3] of the mind, which may be imperfect and confused as it was formerly, or clear and distinct as it is at present, according as my attention is more or less directed to the elements which are found in it, and of which it is composed.

Yet in the meantime I am greatly astonished when I consider [the great feebleness of mind] and its proneness to fall [insensibly] into error; for although without giving expression to my thoughts I consider all this in my own mind, words often impede me and I am almost deceived by the terms of ordinary language. For we say that we see the same wax, if it is present, and not that we simply judge that it is the same from its having the same colour and figure. From this I should conclude that I knew the wax by means of vision and not simply by the intuition of the mind; unless by chance I remember that, when looking from a window and saying I see men who pass in the street, I really do not see them, but infer that what I see is men, just as I say that I see wax. And yet what do I see from the window but hats and coats which may cover automatic machines? Yet I judge these to be men. And similarly solely by the faculty of judgment which rests in my mind, I comprehend that which I believed I saw with my eyes.

A man who makes it his aim to raise his knowledge above the common should be ashamed to derive the occasion for doubting from the forms of speech invented by the vulgar; I prefer to pass on and consider whether I had a more evident and perfect conception of what the wax was when I first perceived it, and when I believed I knew it by means of the external senses or at least by the common sense[4] as it is called, that is to say by the imaginative faculty, or whether my present conception is clearer now that I have most carefully examined what it is, and in what way it can be known. It would certainly be absurd to doubt as to this. For what was there in this first perception which was distinct? What was there which might not as well have been perceived by any of the animals? But when I distinguish the wax from its external forms, and when, just as if I had taken from it its vestments, I consider it quite naked, it is certain that although some error may still be found in my judgment, I can nevertheless not perceive it thus without a human mind.

But finally what shall I say of this mind, that is, of myself, for up to this point I do not admit in myself anything but mind? What then, I who seem to perceive this piece of wax so distinctly, do I not know myself, not

---

[3] inspectio.
[4] sensus communis.

only with much more truth and certainty, but also with much more distinctness and clearness? For if I judge that the wax is or exists from the fact that I see it, it certainly follows much more clearly that I am or that I exist myself from the fact that I see it. For it may be that what I see is not really wax, it may also be that I do not possess eyes with which to see anything; but it cannot be that when I see, or (for I no longer take account of the distinction) when I think I see, that I myself who think am nought. So if I judge that the wax exists from the fact that I touch it, the same thing will follow, to wit, that I am; and if I judge that my imagination, or some other cause, whatever it is, persuades me that the wax exists, I shall still conclude the same. And what I have here remarked of wax may be applied to all other things which are external to me [and which are met with outside of me]. And further, if the [notion or] perception of wax has seemed to me clearer and more distinct, not only after the sight or the touch, but also after many other causes have rendered it quite manifest to me, with how much more [evidence] and distinctness must it be said that I now know myself, since all the reasons which contribute to the knowledge of wax, or any other body whatever, are yet better proofs of the nature of my mind! And there are so many other things in the mind itself which may contribute to the elucidation of its nature, that those which depend on body such as these just mentioned, hardly merit being taken into account.

But finally here I am, having insensibly reverted to the point I desired, for, since it is now manifest to me that even bodies are not properly speaking known by the senses or by the faculty of imagination, but by the understanding only, and since they are not known from the fact that they are seen or touched, but only because they are understood, I see clearly that there is nothing which is easier for me to know than my mind. But because it is difficult to rid oneself so promptly of an opinion to which one was accustomed for so long, it will be well that I should halt a little at this point, so that by the length of my meditation I may more deeply imprint on my memory this new knowledge.

THINK ABOUT

1. "Anyone who conducts an argument by appealing to authority is not using his intelligence; he is just using his memory."

   Leonardo Da Vinci

2. "Think? Why think! We have computers to do that for us."

   Jean Rostand

3. "Philosophy begins when one learns to doubt—particularly to

doubt one's cherished beliefs, one's dogmas and one's axioms."

Will Durant

4. "Yes, reason is an imperfect instrument, like medical science, or the human eye; we do the best we can with it within the limits which fate and nature set. We do not doubt that some things are better done by instinct than by thought: perhaps it is wiser, in the presence of Cleopatra, to thirst like Antony rather than to think like Caesar; it is better to have loved and lost than to have reasoned well. *But why is it better?*"

Will Durant

5. "Most of our assumptions have outlived their uselessness."

Marshall McLuhan

6. "I have had my solutions for a long time, but I do not yet know how I am to arrive at them."

Karl Friedrich Gauss

7. "The more extensive a man's knowledge of what has been done, the greater will be his power of knowing what to do."

Disraeli

18

Knowledge Is Ultimately Sense Knowledge

John Locke (1632–1704), English empiricist and political philosopher, wrote two major works regarded as classics, *Two Treatises of Government* (1689) and *An Essay Concerning Human Understanding* (1690).

John Locke is an empiricist. He believes that sense perceptions ultimately give us all knowledge and in fact sense perceptions alone are clear and distinct. First he argues that there are no innate ideas because if there were, they would not depend upon experience. All knowledge is founded on experience and ultimately derives from experience. There are two sources for our ideas: sensation, through which the mind is furnished with sense qualities, and reflection, which supplies the mind with ideas of its own operation. The mind itself is a blank tablet upon which the ideas of experience are written.

────────────────── TO STUDY

1. What is the purpose of Locke's essay? What method does he indicate he will pursue?
2. What does Locke mean by the word *idea?*
3. What are innate principles?
4. What is the argument from universal consent as to innate principles? How does Locke refute this argument?

5. What is the argument by "use of reason"? What is Locke's refutation?
6. How does the mind form abstract ideas?
7. By what analogy does Locke describe the mind? From where does the mind get its materials?
8. What are the two general classes of the mind's contents?
9. How does Locke distinguish between simple and complex ideas?

Introduction

1. Since it is the *understanding* that sets man above the rest of sensible beings, and gives him all the advantage and dominion which he has over them; it is certain a subject, even for its nobleness, worth our labour to inquire into. The understanding, like the eye, whilst it makes us see and perceive all other things, takes no notice of itself; and it requires art and pains to set it at a distance and make it its own object. But whatever be the difficulties that lie in the way of this inquiry; whatever it be that keeps us so much in the dark to ourselves; sure I am that all the light we can let in upon our minds, all the acquaintance we can make with our own understandings, will not only be very pleasant, but bring us great advantage, in directing our thoughts in the search of other things.

2. This, therefore, being my purpose—to inquire into the original, certainty, and extent of *human knowledge,* together with the grounds and degrees of *belief, opinion,* and *assent;*—I shall not at present meddle with the physical consideration of the mind; or trouble myself to examine wherein its essence consists; or by what motions of our spirits or alterations of our bodies we come to have any *sensation* by our organs, or any *ideas* in our understandings; and whether those ideas do in their formation, any or all of them, depend on matter or not. These are speculations which, however curious and entertaining, I shall decline, as lying out of my way in the design I am now upon. It shall suffice to my present purpose, to consider the discerning faculties of a man, as they are employed about the objects which they have to do with. And I shall imagine I have not wholly misemployed myself in the thoughts I shall have on this occasion, if, in this historical, plain method, I can give any account of the ways whereby our understandings come to attain those notions of things we have; and can set down any measures of the certainty of our knowledge; or the grounds of

From *An Essay Concerning Human Understanding* by John Locke (1690).

those persuasions which are to be found amongst men, so various, different, and wholly contradictory; and yet asserted somewhere or other with such assurance and confidence, that he that shall take a view of the opinions of mankind, observe their opposition, and at the same time consider the fondness and devotion wherewith they are embraced, the resolution and eagerness wherewith they are maintained, may perhaps have reason to suspect, that either there is no such thing as truth at all, or that mankind hath no sufficient means to attain a certain knowledge of it.

3. It is therefore worth while to search out the bounds between opinion and knowledge; and examine by what measures, in things whereof we have no certain knowledge, we ought to regulate our assent and moderate our persuasion. In order whereunto I shall pursue this following method:—

First, I shall inquire into the original of those *ideas,* notions, or whatever else you please to call them, which a man observes, and is conscious to himself he has in his mind; and the ways whereby the understanding comes to be furnished with them.

Secondly, I shall endeavour to show what *knowledge* the understanding hath by those ideas; and the certainty, evidence, and extent of it.

Thirdly, I shall make some inquiry into the nature and grounds of *faith* or *opinion:* whereby I mean that assent which we give to any proposition as true, of whose truth yet we have not certain knowledge. And here we shall have occasion to examine the reasons and degrees of *assent.*

4. If by this inquiry into the nature of the understanding, I can discover the powers thereof; how far they reach; to what things they are in any degree proportionate; and where they fail us, I suppose it may be of use to prevail with the busy mind of man to be more cautious in meddling with things exceeding its comprehension; to stop when it is at the utmost extent of its tether; and to sit down in a quiet ignorance of those things which, upon examination, are found to be beyond the reach of our capacities. We should not then perhaps be so forward, out of an affectation of an universal knowledge, to raise questions, and perplex ourselves and others with disputes about things to which our understandings are not suited; and of which we cannot frame in our minds any clear or distinct perceptions, or whereof (as it has perhaps too often happened) we have not any notions at all. If we can find out how far the understanding can extend its view; how far it has faculties to attain certainty; and in what cases it can only judge and guess, we may learn to content ourselves with what is attainable by us in this state.

5. For though the comprehension of our understandings comes exceeding short of the vast extent of things, yet we shall have cause enough to magnify the bountiful Author of our being, for that proportion and degree of knowledge he has bestowed on us, so far above all the rest of the

inhabitants of this our mansion. Men have reason to be well satisfied with what God hath thought fit for them, since he hath given them (as St. Peter says) πάντα πρὸς ζωὴν καὶ εὐσέβειαν, whatsoever is necessary for the conveniences of life and information of virtue; and has put within the reach of their discovery, the comfortable provision for this life, and the way that leads to a better. How short soever their knowledge may come of an universal or perfect comprehension of whatsoever is, it yet secures their great concernments, that they have light enough to lead them to the knowledge of their Maker, and the sight of their own duties. Men may find matter sufficient to busy their heads, and employ their hands with variety, delight, and satisfaction, if they will not boldly quarrel with their own constitution, and throw away the blessings their hands are filled with, because they are not big enough to grasp everything. We shall not have much reason to complain of the narrowness of our minds, if we will but employ them about what may be of use to us; for of that they are very capable. And it will be an unpardonable, as well as childish peevishness, if we undervalue the advantages of our knowledge, and neglect to improve it to the ends for which it was given us, because there are some things that are set out of the reach of it. It will be no excuse to an idle and untoward servant, who would not attend his business by candle light, to plead that he had not broad sunshine. The Candle that is set up in us shines bright enough for all our purposes. The discoveries we can make with this ought to satisfy us; and we shall then use our understandings right, when we entertain all objects in that way and proportion that they are suited to our faculties, and upon those grounds they are capable of being proposed to us; and not peremptorily or intemperately require demonstration, and demand certainty, where probability only is to be had, and which is sufficient to govern all our concernments. If we will disbelieve everything, because we cannot certainly know all things, we shall do muchwhat as wisely as he who would not use his legs, but sit still and perish, because he had no wings to fly.

6. When we know our own strength, we shall the better know what to undertake with hopes of success; and when we have well surveyed the *powers* of our own minds, and made some estimate what we may expect from them, we shall not be inclined either to sit still, and not set our thoughts on work at all, in despair of knowing anything; nor on the other side, question everything, and disclaim all knowledge, because some things are not to be understood. It is of great use to the sailor to know the length of his line, though he cannot with it fathom all the depths of the ocean. It is well he knows that it is long enough to reach the bottom, at such places as are necessary to direct his voyage, and caution him against running upon shoals that may ruin him. Our business here is not to know all things, but those which concern our conduct. If we can find out those measures,

whereby a rational creature, put in that state in which man is in this world, may and ought to govern his opinions, and actions depending thereon, we need not to be troubled that some other things escape our knowledge.

7. This was that which gave the first rise to this *Essay* concerning the understanding. For I thought that the first step towards satisfying several inquiries the mind of man was very apt to run into, was, to take a survey of our own understandings, examine our own powers, and see to what things they were adapted. Till that was done I suspected we began at the wrong end, and in vain sought for satisfaction in a quiet and sure possession of truths that most concerned us, whilst we let loose our thoughts into the vast ocean of Being; as if all that boundless extent were the natural and undoubted possession of our understandings, wherein there was nothing exempt from its decisions, or that escaped its comprehension. Thus men, extending their inquiries beyond their capacities, and letting their thoughts wander into those depths where they can find no sure footing, it is no wonder that they raise questions and multiply disputes, which, never coming to any clear resolution, are proper only to continue and increase their doubts, and to confirm them at last in perfect scepticism. Whereas, were the capacities of our understandings well considered, the extent of our knowledge once discovered, and the horizon found which sets the bounds between the enlightened and dark parts of things; between what is and what is not comprehensible by us, men would perhaps with less scruple acquiesce in the avowed ignorance of the one, and employ their thoughts and discourse with more advantage and satisfaction in the other.

8. Thus much I thought necessary to say concerning the occasion of this Inquiry into human Understanding. But, before I proceed on to what I have thought on this subject, I must here in the entrance beg pardon of my reader for the frequent use of the word *idea,* which he will find in the following treatise. It being that term which, I think, serves best to stand for whatsoever is the *object* of the understanding when a man thinks, I have used it to express whatever is meant by *phantasm, notion, species,* or *whatever it is which the mind can be employed about in thinking;* and I could not avoid frequently using it.

I presume it will be easily granted me, that there are such *ideas* in men's minds: every one is conscious of them in himself; and men's words and actions will satisfy him that they are in others.

Our first inquiry then shall be,—how they come into the mind.

No Innate Speculative Principles

I, i,   1. It is an established opinion amongst some men, that there are in the understanding certain *innate principles;* some primary notions, κοιναί ἔννοιαι, characters, as it were stamped upon the mind of man; which the soul receives in its very first being, and brings into the world with it. It would be sufficient to convince unprejudiced readers of the falseness of this supposition, if I should only show (as I hope I shall in the following parts of this Discourse) how men, barely by the use of their natural faculties, may attain to all the knowledge they have, without the help of any innate impressions; and may arrive at certainty, without any such original notions or principles. For I imagine any one will easily grant that it would be impertinent to suppose the ideas of colours innate in a creature to whom God hath given sight, and a power to receive them by the eyes from external objects: and no less unreasonable would it be to attribute several truths to the impressions of nature, and innate characters, when we may observe in ourselves faculties fit to attain as easy and certain knowledge of them as if they were originally imprinted on the mind.

But because a man is not permitted without censure to follow his own thoughts in the search of truth, when they lead him ever so little out of the common road, I shall set down the reasons that made me doubt of the truth of that opinion, as an excuse for my mistake, if I be in one; which I leave to be considered by those who, with me, dispose themselves to embrace truth wherever they find it.

2. There is nothing more commonly taken for granted than that there are certain *principles,* both *speculative* and *practical,* (for they speak of both), universally agreed upon by all mankind: which therefore, they argue, must needs be the constant impressions which the souls of men receive in their first beings, and which they bring into the world with them, as necessarily and really as they do any of their inherent faculties.

3. This argument, drawn from universal consent, has this misfortune in it, that if it were true in matter of fact, that there were certain truths wherein all mankind agreed, it would not prove them innate, if there can be any other way shown how men may come to that universal agreement, in the things they do consent in, which I presume may be done.

4. But, which is worse, this argument of universal consent, which is made use of to prove innate principles, seems to me a demonstration that there are none such: because there are none to which all mankind give an universal assent. I shall begin with the speculative, and instance in those magnified principles of demonstration, 'Whatsoever is, is,' and 'It is impossible for the same thing to be and not to be'; which, of all others, I think have the most allowed title to innate. These have so settled a reputation of maxims universally received, that it will no doubt be thought strange if any one should seem to question it. But yet I take liberty to say, that these propositions are so far from having an universal assent, that there are a great part of mankind to whom they are not so much as known.

5. For, first, it is evident, that all children and idiots have not the least apprehension or thought of them. And the want of that is enough to destroy that universal assent which must needs be the necessary concomitant of all innate truths: it seeming to me near a contradiction to say, that there are truths imprinted on the soul, which it perceives or understands not: imprinting, if it signify anything, being nothing else but the making certain truths to be perceived. For to imprint anything on the mind without the mind's perceiving it, seems to me hardly intelligible. If therefore children and idiots have souls, have minds, with those impressions upon them, *they* must unavoidably perceive them, and necessarily know and assent to these truths; which since they do not, it is evident that there are no such impressions. For if they are not notions naturally imprinted, how can they be innate? and if they are notions imprinted, how can they be unknown? To say a notion is imprinted on the mind, and yet at the same time to say, that the mind is ignorant of it, and never yet took notice of it, is to make this impression nothing. No proposition can be said to be in the mind which it never yet knew, which it was never yet conscious of. For if any one may, then, by the same reason, all propositions that are true, and the mind is capable ever of assenting to, may be said to be in the mind, and to be imprinted: since, if any one can be said to be in the mind, which it never yet knew, it must be only because it is capable of knowing it; and so the mind is of all truths it ever shall know. Nay, thus truths may be imprinted on the mind which it never did, nor ever shall know; for a man may live long, and die at last in ignorance of many truths which his mind was capable of knowing, and that with certainty. So that if the capacity of knowing be the natural impression contended for, all the truths a man ever comes to know will, by this account, be every one of them innate; and this great point will amount to no more, but only to a very improper way of speaking; which, whilst it pretends to assert the contrary, says nothing different from those who deny innate principles. For nobody, I think, ever denied that the mind was capable of knowing several truths. The capacity, they say, is innate; the knowledge acquired. But then to what end such contest for certain innate maxims? If truths can be imprinted on the understanding without being perceived, I can see no difference there can be between any truths the mind is *capable* of knowing in respect of their original: they must all be innate or all adventitious: in vain shall a man go about to distinguish them. He therefore that talks of innate notions in the understanding, cannot (if he intend thereby any distinct sort of truths) mean such truths to be in the understanding as it never perceived, and is yet wholly ignorant of. For if these words 'to be in the understanding' have any propriety, they signify to be understood. So that to be in the understanding, and not to be understood; to be in the mind and never to be perceived, is all one as to say

anything is and is not in the mind or understanding. If therefore these two propositions, 'Whatsoever is, is,' and 'It is impossible for the same thing to be and not to be,' are by nature imprinted, children cannot be ignorant of them: infants, and all that have souls, must necessarily have them in their understandings, know the truth of them, and assent to it.

6. To avoid this, it is usually answered, that all men know and assent to them, *when they come to the use of reason;* and this is enough to prove them innate. I answer:

7. Doubtful expressions, that have scarce any significance, go for clear reasons to those who, being prepossessed, take not the pains to examine even what they themselves say. For, to apply this answer with any tolerable sense to our present purpose, it must signify one of these two things: either that as soon as men come to the use of reason these supposed native inscriptions come to be known and observed by them; or else, that the use and exercise of men's reason, assists them in the discovery of these principles, and certainly makes them known to them.

8. If they mean, that by the use of reason men may discover these principles, and that this is sufficient to prove them innate; their way of arguing will stand thus, viz. that whatever truths reason can certainly discover to us, and make us firmly assent to, those are all naturally imprinted on the mind; since that universal assent, which is made the mark of them, amounts to no more but this,—that by the use of reason we are capable to come to a certain knowledge of and assent to them; and, by this means, there will be no difference between the maxims of the mathematicians, and theorems they deduce from them: all must be equally allowed innate; they being all discoveries made by the use of reason, and truths that a rational creature may certainly come to know, if he apply his thoughts rightly that way.

9. But how can these men think the use of reason necessary to discover principles that are supposed innate, when reason (if we may believe them) is nothing else but the faculty of deducing unknown truths from principles of propositions that are already known? That certainly can never be thought innate which we have need of reason to discover; unless as I have said, we will have all the certain truths that reason ever teaches us, to be innate. We may as well think the use of reason necessary to make our eyes discover visible objects, as that there should be need of reason, or the exercise thereof, to make the understanding see what is originally engraven on it, and cannot be in the understanding before it be perceived by it. So that to make reason discover those truths thus imprinted, is to say, that the use of reason discovers to a man what he knew before: and if men have those innate impressed truths originally, and before the use of reason, and yet are always ignorant of them till they come to the use of reason, it is in effect

to say, that men know and know them not at the same time.

10. It will here perhaps be said that mathematical demonstrations, and other truths that are not innate, are not assented to as soon as proposed, wherein they are distinguished from these maxims and other innate truths. I shall have occasion to speak of assent upon the first proposing, more particularly by and by. I shall here only, and that very readily, allow, that these maxims and mathematical demonstrations are in this different: that the one have need of reason, using of proofs, to make them out and to gain our assent; but the other, as soon as understood, are, without any the least reasoning, embraced and assented to. But I withal beg leave to observe, that it lays open the weakness of this subterfuge, which requires the use of reason for the discovery of these general truths: since it must be confessed that in their discovery there is no use made of reasoning at all. And I think those who give this answer will not be forward to affirm that the knowledge of this maxim, 'That it is impossible for the same thing to be and not to be,' is a deduction of our reason. For this would be to destroy that bounty of nature they seem so fond of, whilst they make the knowledge of those principles to depend on the labour of our thoughts. For all reasoning is search, and casting about, and requires pains and application. And how can it with any tolerable sense be supposed, that what was imprinted by nature, as the foundation and guide of our reason, should need the use of reason to discover it?

11. Those who will take the pains to reflect with a little attention on the operations of the understanding, will find that this ready assent of the mind to some truths, depends not, either on native inscription, or the use of reason, but on a faculty of the mind quite distinct from both of them, as we shall see hereafter. Reason, therefore, having nothing to do in procuring our assent to these maxims, if by saying, that 'men know and assent to them, when they come to the use of reason,' be meant, that the use of reason assists us in the knowledge of these maxims, it is utterly false; and were it true, would prove them not to be innate.

12. If by knowing and assenting to them 'when we come to the use of reason,' be meant, that this is the time when they come to be taken notice of by the mind; and that as soon as children come to the use of reason, they come also to know and assent to these maxims; this also is false and frivolous. First, it is false; because it is evident these maxims are not in the mind so early as the use of reason; and therefore the coming to the use of reason is falsely assigned as the time of their discovery. How many instances of the use of reason may we observe in children, a long time before they have any knowledge of this maxim, 'That it is impossible for the same thing to be and not to be?' And a great part of illiterate people and savages pass many years, even of their rational age, without ever thinking on this and

the like general propositions. I grant, men come not to the knowledge of these general and more abstract truths, which are thought innate, till they come to the use of reason; and I add, nor then neither. Which is so, because, till after they come to the use of reason, those general abstract ideas are not framed in the mind, about which those general maxims are, which are mistaken for innate principles, but are indeed discoveries made and verities introduced and brought into the mind by the same way, and discovered by the same steps, as several other propositions, which nobody was ever so extravagant as to suppose innate. This I hope to make plain in the sequel of this Discourse. I allow therefore, a necessity that men should come to the use of reason before they get the knowledge of those general truths; but deny that men's coming to the use of reason is the time of their discovery.

13. In the mean time it is observable, that this saying, that men know and assent to these maxims 'when they come to the use of reason,' amounts in reality of fact to no more but this,—that they are never known nor taken notice of before the use of reason, but may possibly be assented to some time after, during a man's life; but when is uncertain. And so may all other knowable truths, as well as these; which therefore have no advantage nor distinction from others by this note of being known when we come to the use of reason; nor are thereby proved to be innate, but quite the contrary.

14. But, secondly, were it true that the precise time of their being known and assented to were, when men come to the use of reason; neither would that prove them innate. This way of arguing is as frivolous as the supposition itself is false. For, by what kind of logic will it appear that any notion is originally by nature imprinted in the mind in its first constitution, because it comes first to be observed and assented to when a faculty of the mind, which has quite a distinct province, begins to exert itself? And therefore the coming to the use of speech, if it were supposed the time that these maxims are first assented to, (which it may be with as much truth as the time when men come to the use of reason,) would be as good a proof that they were innate, as to say they are innate because men assent to them when they come to the use of reason. I agree then with these men of innate principles, that there is no knowledge of these general and self-evident maxims in the mind, till it comes to the exercise of reason: but I deny that the coming to the use of reason is the precise time when they are first taken notice of; and if that were the precise time, I deny that it would prove them innate. All that can with any truth be meant by this proposition, that men 'assent to them when they come to the use of reason,' is no more but this,—that the making of general abstract ideas, and the understanding of general names, being a concomitant of the rational faculty, and growing up with it, children commonly get not those general ideas, nor learn the names that stand for them, till, having for a good while exercised their

reason about familiar and more particular ideas, they are, by their ordinary discourse and actions with others, acknowledged to be capable of rational conversation. If assenting to these maxims, when men come to the use of reason, can be true in any other sense, I desire it may be shown; or at least, how in this, or any other sense, it proves them innate.

15. The senses at first let in *particular* ideas, and furnish the yet empty cabinet, and the mind by degrees growing familiar with some of them, they are lodged in the memory, and names got to them. Afterwards, the mind proceeding further, abstracts them, and by degrees learns the use of general names. In this manner the mind comes to be furnished with ideas and language, the *materials* about which to exercise its discursive faculty. And the use of reason becomes daily more visible, as these materials that give it employment increase. But though the having of general ideas and the use of general words and reason usually grow together, yet I see not how this any way proves them innate. The knowledge of some truths, I confess, is very early in the mind; but in a way that shows them not to be innate. For, if we will observe, we shall find it still to be about ideas, not innate, but acquired; it being about those first which are imprinted by external things, with which infants have earliest to do, which make the most frequent impressions on their senses. In ideas thus got, the mind discovers that some agree and others differ, probably as soon as it has any use of memory; as soon as it is able to retain and perceive distinct ideas. But whether it be then or no, this is certain, it does so long before it has the use of words; or comes to that which we commonly call 'the use of reason.' For a child knows as certainly before it can speak the difference between the ideas of sweet and bitter (i.e. that sweet is not bitter), as it knows afterwards (when it comes to speak) that wormwood and sugarplums are not the same thing. . . .

Of Ideas in General, And Their Original

II, i,   1. Every man being conscious to himself that he thinks; and that which his mind is applied about whilst thinking being the *ideas* that are there, it is past doubt that men have in their minds several ideas,—such as are those expressed by the words *whiteness, hardness, sweetness, thinking, motion, man, elephant, army, drunkenness,* and others: it is in the first place then to be inquired, *How he comes by them?*

I know it is a received doctrine, that men have native ideas, and original characters, stamped upon their minds in their very first being. This opinion I have at large examined already; and, I suppose what I have said in the foregoing Book will be much more easily admitted, when I have shown whence the understanding may get all the ideas it has; and by what

ways and degrees they may come into the mind;—for which I shall appeal
to every one's own observation and experience.

2. Let us then suppose the mind to be, as we say, white paper, void
of all characters, without any ideas:—How comes it to be furnished?
Whence comes it by that vast store which the busy and boundless fancy
of man has painted on it with an almost endless variety? Whence has it all
the *materials* of reason and knowledge? To this I answer, in one word, from
experience. In that all our knowledge is founded; and from that it ultimately
derives itself. Our observation employed either, about external sensible
objects, or about the internal operations of our minds perceived and reflected on by ourselves, is that which supplies our understandings with all
the *materials* of thinking. These two are the fountains of knowledge, from
whence all the ideas we have, or can naturally have, do spring.

3. First, our Senses, conversant about particular sensible objects, do
convey into the mind several distinct perceptions of things, according to
those various ways wherein those objects do affect them. And thus we come
by those *ideas* we have of *yellow, white, heat, cold, soft, hard, bitter, sweet,*
and all those which we call sensible qualities; which when I say the senses
convey into the mind, I mean, they from external objects convey into the
mind what produces there those perceptions. This great source of most of
the ideas we have, depending wholly upon our senses, and derived by them
to the understanding, I call *sensation.*

4. Secondly, the other fountain from which experience furnisheth the
understanding with ideas is,—the perception of the operations of our own
mind within us, as it is employed about the ideas it has got;—which operations, when the soul comes to reflect on and consider, do furnish the
understanding with another set of ideas, which could not be had from things
without. And such are *perception, thinking, doubting, believing, reasoning,
knowing, willing,* and all the different actings of our own minds;—which
we being conscious of, and observing in ourselves, do from these receive
into our understandings as distinct ideas as we do from bodies affecting our
senses. This source of ideas every man has wholly in himself; and though
it be not sense, as having nothing to do with external objects, yet it is very
like it, and might properly enough be called *internal sense.* But as I call
the other Sensation, so I call this *reflection,* the ideas it affords being such
only as the mind gets by reflecting on its own operations within itself. By
reflection then, in the following part of this discourse, I would be understood to mean, that notice which the mind takes of its own operations, and
the manner or not; and the operations of our minds will not let us be
without, at least, some obscure notions of them. No man can be wholly
ignorant of what he does when he thinks. These simple ideas, when offered
to the mind, the understanding can no more refuse to have, nor alter when

they are imprinted, nor blot them out and make new ones itself, than a mirror can refuse, alter or obliterate the images or ideas which the objects set before it do therein produce. As the bodies that surround us do diversely affect our organs, the mind is forced to receive the impressions; and cannot avoid the perception of those ideas that are annexed to them.

Of Simple Ideas

II, ii,   1. The better to understand the nature, manner, and extent of our knowledge, one thing is carefully to be observed concerning the ideas we have; and that is, that some of them are *simple* and some *complex.*

Though the qualities that affect our senses are, in the things themselves, so united and blended, that there is no separation, no distance between them; yet it is plain, the ideas they produce in the mind enter by the senses simple and unmixed. For, though the sight and touch often take in from the same object, at the same time, different ideas;—as a man sees at once motion and colour; the hand feels softness and warmth in the same piece of wax: yet the simple ideas thus united in the same subject, are as perfectly distinct as those that come in by different senses. The coldness and hardness which a man feels in a piece of ice being as distinct ideas in the mind as the smell and whiteness of a lily; or as the taste of sugar, and smell of a rose. And there is nothing can be plainer to a man than the clear and distinct perception he has of those simple ideas; which, being each in itself uncompounded, contains in it nothing but *one uniform appearance, or conception in the mind,* and is not distinguishable into different ideas.

2. These simple ideas, the materials of all our knowledge, are suggested and furnished to the mind only by those two ways above mentioned, viz. sensation and reflection. When the understanding is once stored with these simple ideas, it has the power to repeat, compare, and unite them, even to an almost infinite variety, and so can make at pleasure new complex ideas. But it is not in the power of the most exalted wit, or enlarged understanding, by any quickness or variety of thought, to *invent* or *frame* one new simple idea in the mind, not taken in by the ways before mentioned: nor can any force of the understanding *destroy* those that are there. The dominion of man, in this little world of his own understanding being muchwhat the same as it is in the great world of visible things; wherein his power, however managed by art and skill, reaches no farther than to compound and divide the materials that are made to his hand; but can do nothing towards the making the least particle of new matter, or destroying one atom of what is already in being. The same inability will every one find in himself, who shall go about to fashion in his understanding one simple idea, not received in bv his senses from external objects, or by reflection from the

operations of his own mind about them. I would have any one try to fancy any taste which had never affected his palate; or frame the idea of a scent he had never smelt: and when he can do this, I will also conclude that a blind man hath ideas of colours, and a deaf man true distinct notions of sounds.

3. This is the reason why—though we cannot believe it impossible to God to make a creature with other organs, and more ways to convey into the understanding the notice of corporeal things than those five, as they are usually counted, which he has given to man—yet I think it is not possible for any *man* to imagine any other qualities in bodies, howsoever constituted, whereby they can be taken notice of, besides sounds, tastes, smells, visible and tangible qualities. And had mankind been made but with four senses, the qualities then which are the objects of the fifth sense had been as far from our notice, imagination, and conception, as now any belonging to a sixth, seventh, or eighth sense can possibly be;—which, whether yet some other creatures, in some other parts of this vast and stupendous universe, may not have, will be a great presumption to deny. He that will not set himself proudly at the top of all things, but will consider the immensity of this fabric, and the great variety that is to be found in this little and inconsiderable part of it which he has to do with, may be apt to think that, in other mansions of it, there may be other and different intelligent beings, of whose faculties he has as little knowledge or apprehension as a worm shut up in one drawer of a cabinet hath of the senses or understanding of a man; such variety and excellency being suitable to the wisdom and power of the Maker. I have here followed the common opinion of man's having but five senses; though, perhaps, there may be justly counted more;—but either supposition serves equally to my present purpose.

19

Knowledge Is
Ultimately Intuitive

Henri Bergson (1859–1941) dominated French philosophy
for a considerable part of the twentieth century. His philosophy
focused on evolutionary process and interpreted it in terms
of a fundamental life force; it had wide international influence.
Among his books are: *Creative Evolution* (1944); *The Two
Sources of Morality and Religion* (1935); *Time and Free Will*
(1950); *Introduction to MetaPhysics* (1949); and *Matter and
Memory* (1950).

The method of intuition seeks to establish philosophical beliefs via certain
truths directly perceived. Intuition means to know directly. One sometimes
speaks of knowing these truths "self-evidently." Recall the Declaration
of Independence, "We hold these truths to be self-evident. . . ." Others
have maintained that such ethical propositions as "You ought to keep
promises" are self evidently or intuitively known. From such propositions
these philosophers seek to construct a system of philosophy.

Some intuitionists often claim that in addition to knowing the truth
of certain propositions it is also possible to directly know the existence
of certain states of affairs. For example, mystics often have claimed to
have direct experience of God. In the following essay Bergson claims
that one can directly experience one's mind. Man can intuitively know
that he has a mind. Such direct knowledge of the mind does not require
symbols. What one knows is a reality which Bergson says "endures."
Reality endures, that is, it changes ceaselessly and continuously rather
than discontinuously, cumulatively, irreversibly, and unforseeably. Thus,
Bergson's philosophic method seeks to establish a system of philosophy
based upon the intuitive knowledge of reality.

TO STUDY

1. How does Bergson distinguish between absolute and relative knowledge?

2. What does Bergson mean by intuition? Is there any way you see of relating this to the notion of the self-evident?

3. How does Bergson define metaphysics? What does he mean?

4. Describe what is perceived when one directs his attention inward to contemplate his own self. What metaphors does Bergson use when he finally wishes to discuss his enduring self?

5. Describe what Bergson means by his important concept, "duration."

6. What is Bergson trying to explain with the example of the sketch of Paris?

A comparison of the definitions of metaphysics and the various conceptions of the absolute leads to the discovery that philosophers, in spite of their apparent divergencies, agree in distinguishing two profoundly different ways of knowing a thing. The first implies that we move round the object; the second that we enter into it. The first depends on the point of view at which we are placed and on the symbols by which we express ourselves. The second neither depends on a point of view nor relies on any symbol. The first kind of knowledge may be said to stop at the *relative;* the second, in those cases where it is possible, to attain the *absolute.*

Consider, for example, the movement of an object in space. My perception of the motion will vary with the point of view, moving or stationary, from which I observe it. My expression of it will vary with the systems of axes, or the points of reference, to which I relate it; that is, with the symbols by which I translate it. For this double reason I call such motion *relative:* in the one case, as in the other, I am placed outside the object itself. But when I speak of an *absolute* movement, I am attributing to the moving object an interior and, so to speak, states of mind; I also imply that I am in sympathy with those states, and that I insert myself in them by an effort of imagination. Then, according as the object is moving or stationary, according as it adopts one movement or another, what I experience will vary. And what I experience will depend neither on the point of view I may take up in regard to the object, since I am inside the object itself, nor on the symbols by which I may translate the motion, since I have rejected all

From *An Introduction to Metaphysics.*

translations in order to possess the original. In short, I shall no longer grasp the movement from without, remaining where I am, but from where it is, from within, as it is in itself. I shall possess an absolute.

Consider, again, a character whose adventures are related to me in a novel. The author may multiply the traits of his hero's character, may make him speak and act as much as he pleases, but all this can never be equivalent to the simple and indivisible feeling which I should experience if I were able for an instant to identify myself with the person of the hero himself. Out of that indivisible feeling, as from a spring, all the words, gestures, and actions of the man would appear to me to flow naturally. They would no longer be accidents which, added to the idea I had already formed of the character, continually enriched that idea, without ever completing it. The character would be given to me all at once, in its entirety, and the thousand incidents which manifest it, instead of adding themselves to the idea and so enriching it, would seem to me, on the contrary, to detach themselves from it, without, however, exhausting it or impoverishing its essence. All the things I am told about the man provide me with so many points of view from which I can observe him. All the traits which describe him, and which can make him known to me only by so many comparisons with persons or things I know already are signs by which he is expressed more or less symbolically. Symbols and points of view, therefore, place me outside him; they give me only what he has in common with others, and not what belongs to him and to him alone. But that which is properly himself, that which constitutes his essence, cannot be perceived from without, being internal by definition, nor be expressed by symbols, being incommensurable with everything else. Description, history, and analysis leave me here in the relative. Coincidence with the person himself would alone give me the absolute.

It is in this sense, and in this sense only, that *absolute* is synonymous with *perfection*. Were all the photographs of a town, taken from all possible points of view, to go on indefinitely completing one another, they would never be equivalent to the solid town in which we walk about. Were all the translations of a poem into all possible languages to add together their various shades of meaning and, correcting each other by a kind of mutual retouching, to give a more and more faithful image of the poem they translate, they would yet never succeed in rendering the inner meaning of the original. A representation taken from a certain point of view, a translation made with certain symbols, will always remain imperfect in comparison with the object of which a view has been taken, or which the symbols seek to express. But the absolute, which is the object and not its representation, the original and not its translation, is perfect, by being perfectly what it is.

It is doubtless for this reason that the *absolute* has often been identified with the *infinite.* Suppose that I wished to communicate to someone who did not know Greek the extraordinarily simple impression that a passage in Homer makes upon me; I should first give a translation of the lines, I should then comment on my translation, and then develop the commentary; in this way, by piling up explanation on explanation, I might approach nearer to what I wanted to express; but I should never quite reach it. When you raise your arm, you accomplish a movement of which you have, from within, a simple perception; but for me, watching it from the outside, your arm passes through one point, then through another, and between these two there will be still other points; so that, if I began to count, the operation would go on forever. Viewed from the inside, then, an absolute is a simple thing; but looked at from the outside, that is to say, relatively to other things, it becomes, in relation to these signs which express it, the gold coin for which we never seem able to finish giving small change. Now, that which lends itself at the same time both to an indivisible apprehension and to an inexhaustible enumeration, is, by the very definition of the word, an infinite.

It follows from this that an absolute could only be given in an *intuition,* while everything else falls within the province of *analysis.* By intuition is meant the kind of *intellectual sympathy* by which one places oneself within an object in order to coincide with what is unique in it and consequently inexpressible. Analysis, on the contrary, is the operation which reduces the object to elements already known, that is, to elements common both to it and other objects. To analyze, therefore, is to express a thing as a function of something other than itself. All analysis is thus a translation, a development into symbols, a representation taken from successive points of view from which we note as many resemblances as possible between the new object which we are studying and others which we believe we know already. In its eternally unsatisfied desire to embrace the object around which it is compelled to turn, analysis multiplies without end the number of its points of view in order to complete its always incomplete representation, and ceaselessly varies its symbols that it may perfect the always imperfect translation. It goes on, therefore, to infinity. But intuition, if intuition is possible, is a simple act.

Now it is easy to see that the ordinary function of positive science is analysis. Positive science works, then, above all, with symbols. Even the most concrete of the natural sciences, those concerned with life, confine themselves to the visible form of living beings, their organs and anatomical elements. They make comparisons between these forms, they reduce the more complex to the more simple; in short, they study the workings of life in what is, so to speak, only its visual symbol. If there exists any means of possessing a reality absolutely instead of knowing it relatively, of placing oneself within it instead of looking at it from outside points of view, of having the intuition instead of making the analysis: in short, of seizing it without any expression, translation, or symbolic representation—metaphysics is that means. *Metaphysics, then, is the science which claims to dispense with symbols.*

There is one reality, at least, which we all seize from within, by intuition and not by simple analysis. It is our own personality in its flowing through time—our self which endures. We may sympathize intellectually with nothing else, but we certainly sympathize with our own selves.

When I direct my attention inward to contemplate my own self (supposed for the moment to be inactive), I perceive at first, as a crust solidified on the surface, all the perceptions which come to it from the material world. These perceptions are clear, distinct, juxtaposed, or juxtaposable one with another; they tend to group themselves into objects. Next, I notice the memories which more or less adhere to these perceptions and which serve to interpret them. These memories have been detached, as it were, from the depth of my personality, drawn to the surface by the perceptions which resemble them; they rest on the surface of my mind without being absolutely myself. Lastly, I feel the stir of tendencies and motor habits—a crowd of virtual actions, more or less firmly bound to these perceptions and memories. All these clearly defined elements appear more distinct from me, the more distinct they are from each other. Radiating, as they do, from within outwards, they form, collectively, the surface of a sphere which tends to grow larger and lose itself in the exterior world. But if I draw myself in from the periphery toward the center, if I search in the depth of my being that which is most uniformly, most constantly, and most enduringly myself, I find an altogether different thing.

There is, beneath these sharply cut crystals and this frozen surface, a continuous flux which is not comparable to any flux I have ever seen. There is a succession of states, each of which announces that which follows and contains that which precedes it. They can, properly speaking, only be said to form multiple states when I have already passed them and turn back to observe their track. While I was experiencing them they were so solidly organized, so profoundly animated with a common life, that I could not have said where any one of them finished or where another commenced. In reality no one of them begins or ends, but all extend into each other.

This inner life may be compared to the unrolling of a coil, for there is no living being who does not feel himself coming gradually to the end of his role; and to live is to grow old. But it may just as well be compared to a continual rolling up, like that of a thread on a ball, for our past follows us, it swells incessantly with the present that it picks up on its way; and consciousness means memory.

But actually it is neither an unrolling nor a rolling up, for these two similes evoke the idea of lines and surfaces whose parts are homogeneous and superposable on one another. Now, there are no two identical moments in the life of the same conscious being. Take the simplest sensation, suppose it constant, absorb in it the entire personality: the consciousness which will accompany this sensation cannot remain identical with itself for two consecutive moments, because the second moment always contains, over and above the first, the memory that the first has bequeathed to it. A consciousness which could experience two identical moments would be a consciousness without memory. It would die and be born again continually. In what other way could one represent unconsciousness?

It would be better, then, to use as a comparison the myriad-tinted spectrum, with its insensible gradations leading from one shade to another. A current of feeling which passed along the spectrum, assuming in turn the tint of each of its shades, would experience a series of gradual changes, each of which would announce the one to follow and would sum up those which preceded it. Yet even here the successive shades of the spectrum always remain external one to another. They are juxtaposed; they occupy space. But pure duration, on the contrary, excludes all idea of juxtaposition, reciprocal externality, and extension.

Let us, then, rather, imagine an infinitely small elastic body, contracted, if it were possible, to a mathematical point. Let this be drawn out gradually in such a manner that from the point comes a constant lengthening line. Let us fix our attention not on the line as a line, but on the action by which it is traced. Let us bear in mind that this action, in spite of its duration, is indivisible if accomplished without stopping, that if a stopping point is inserted, we have two actions instead of one, that each of these separate actions is then the indivisible operation of which we speak, and that it is not the moving action itself which is divisible, but, rather, the stationary line it leaves behind it as its track in space. Finally, let us free ourselves from the space which underlies the movement in order to consider only the movement itself, the act of tension or extension; in short, pure mobility. We shall have this time a more faithful image of the development of our self in duration.

However, even this image is incomplete, and, indeed, every comparison will be insufficient, because the unrolling of our duration[1] resembles in some of its aspects the unity of an advancing movement and in others the multi-

---

[1] "Duration" means a change that changes ceaselessly and continuously rather than discontinuously, cumulatively, irreversibly, and unforseeably (ED.).

plicity of expanding states; and, clearly, no metaphor can express one of these two aspects without sacrificing the other. If I use the comparison of the spectrum with its thousand shades, I have before me a thing already made, while duration is continually in the making. If I think of an elastic which is being stretched, or of a spring which is extended or relaxed, I forget the richness of color, characteristic of duration that is lived, to see only the simple movement by which consciousness passes from one shade to another. The inner life is all this at once; variety of qualities, continuity of progress and unity of direction. It cannot be represented by images.

But it is even less possible to represent it by *concepts,* that is, by abstract, general, or simple ideas. It is true that no image can reproduce exactly the original feeling I have of the flow of my own conscious life. But it is not even necessary that I should attempt to render it. If a man is incapable of getting for himself the intuition of the constitutive duration of his own being, nothing will ever give it to him, concepts no more than images. Here the single aim of the philosopher should be to promote a certain effort, which in most men is usually fettered by habits of mind more useful to life. Now the image has at least this advantage, that it keeps us in the concrete. No image can replace the intuition of duration, but many diverse images, borrowed from very different orders of things, may, by the convergence of their action, direct consciousness to the precise point where there is a certain intuition to be seized. By choosing images as dissimilar as possible, we shall prevent any one of them from usurping the place of the intuition it is intended to call up, since it would then be driven away at once by its rivals. By providing that, in spite of their differences of aspect, they all require from the mind the same kind of attention, and in some sort the same degree of tension, we shall gradually accustom consciousness to a particular and clearly defined disposition—that precisely which it must adopt in order to appear to itself as it really is, without any veil. But, then, consciousness must at least consent to make the effort. For it will have been shown nothing: it will simply have been placed in the attitude it must take up in order to make the desired effort, and so come by itself to the intuition. Concepts on the contrary—especially if they are simple—have the disadvantage of being in reality symbols substituted for the object they symbolize, and demand no effort on our part. Examined closely, each of them, it would be seen, retains only that part of the object which is common to it and to others, and expresses, still more than the image does, a *comparison* between the object and others which resemble it. But as the comparison has made manifest a resemblance, as the resemblance is a property of the object, and as a property has every appearance of being a *part* of the object which possesses it, we easily persuade ourselves that by setting concept beside concept we are reconstructing the whole of the object with its parts, thus obtaining, so to speak, its intellectual equivalent. In this way we believe that we can form a faithful representation of duration by setting in line the concepts of unity, multiplicity, continuity, finite or infinite divisibility, etc. There precisely is the illusion. There also is the danger. Just insofar as abstract ideas can render service to analysis, that is, to the scientific study of the object in its relations to other objects, so far are they incapable of replacing intuition, that is, the metaphysical investigation of what is essential and unique in the object. For on the one hand these concepts, laid side by side, never actually give us more than an artificial reconstruction of the object, of which they can only symbolize certain general, and, in a way, impersonal aspects; it is, therefore, useless to believe that with them we can seize a reality of which they present to us the shadow alone. And, on the other hand, besides the illusion there is also a very serious danger. For the concept generalizes at the same time as it abstracts. The concept can only symbolize a particular property by making it common to an infinity of things. It therefore always more or less deforms the property by the extension it gives to it. Replaced in the metaphysical object to which it belongs, a property coincides with the object, or at least moulds itself on it, and adopts the same outline. Extracted from the metaphysical object, and presented in a concept, it grows indefinitely larger, and goes beyond the object itself, since henceforth it has to contain it, along with a number of other objects. Thus the different concepts that we form of the properties of a thing inscribe round it so many circles, each much too large and none of them fitting it exactly. And yet, in the thing itself the properties coincided with the thing, and coincided consequently with one another. So that, if we are bent on reconstructing the object with concepts, some artifice must be sought whereby this coincidence of the object and its properties can be brought about. For example, we may choose one of the concepts and try, starting from it, to get round to the others. But we shall then soon discover that, according as we start from one concept or another, the meeting and combination of the concepts will take place in an altogether different way. According as we start, for example, from unity or from multiplicity, we shall have to conceive differently the multiple unity of duration. Everything will depend on the weight we attribute to this or that concept, and this weight will always be arbitrary, since the concept extracted from the object has no weight, being only the shadow of a body. In this way, as many different *systems* will spring up as there are external points of view from which the reality can be examined, or larger circles in which it can be enclosed. Simple concepts have, then, not only the inconvenience of dividing the concrete unity of the object into so many symbolical expressions; they also divide philosophy into distinct schools, each of which takes its seat, chooses its counters, and carries on with the others a game that will never end. Either metaphysics is only this play of ideas, or else, if it is a serious occupation of the mind, if it is a science and not simply an exercise, it must transcend concepts in order to reach intuition. Certainly, concepts are necessary to it, for all the other sciences work as a rule with concepts, and metaphysics cannot dispense with the other sciences. But it is only truly itself when it goes beyond the concept, or at least when it frees itself from rigid and ready-made concepts in order to create a kind very different from those which we habitually use; I mean supple, mobile, and almost fluid representations, always ready to mould themselves on the fleeting forms of intuition. We shall return later to this important point. Let it suffice us for the moment to have shown that our duration can be presented to us directly in an intuition, that it can be suggested to us indirectly by images, but that it can never—if we confine the word concept to its proper meaning—be enclosed in a conceptual representation.

Let us try for an instant to consider our duration as a multiplicity. It will then be necessary to add that the terms of this multiplicity, instead of being distinct, as they are in any other multiplicity, encroach on one another; and that, while we can no doubt, by an effort of imagination, solidify duration once it has elapsed, divide it into juxtaposed portions and count all these portions, yet this operation is accomplished on the frozen memory of the duration, on the stationary trace which the mobility of duration leaves behind it, and not on the duration itself. We must admit, therefore, that if there is a multiplicity here, it bears no resemblance to any other multiplicity we know. Shall we say, then, that duration has unity? Doubtless, a continuity of elements which prolong themselves into one another participates in unity as much as in multiplicity; but this moving, changing, colored, living unity has hardly anything in common with the abstract, motionless, and empty unity which the concept of pure unity circumscribes. Shall we conclude from this that duration must be defined as unity and multiplicity at the same time? But singularly enough, however much I manipulate the two concepts, portion them out, combine them differently, practice on them the most subtle operations of mental chemistry, I never obtain anything which resembles the simple intuition that I have of duration; while, on the contrary, when I replace myself in duration by an effort of intuition, I immediately perceive how it is unity, multiplicity, and many other things besides. These different concepts, then, were only so many standpoints from which we could consider duration. Neither separated nor reunited have they made us penetrate into it.

We do penetrate into it, however, and that can only be by an effort of intuition. In this sense, an inner, absolute knowledge of the duration of the self by the self is possible. But if metaphysics here demands and can obtain an intuition, science has none the less need of an analysis. Now it is a confusion between the function of analysis and that of intuition which gives birth to the discussions between the schools and the conflicts between systems.

Psychology, in fact, proceeds like all the other sciences by analysis. It resolves the self, which has been given to it at first in a simple intuition, into sensations, feelings, ideas, etc., which it studies separately. It substitutes, then, for the self a series of elements which form the facts of psychology. But are these *elements* really *parts?* That is the whole question, and it is because it has been evaded that the problem of human personality has so often been stated in insoluble terms.

It is incontestable that every psychical state, simply because it belongs to a person, reflects the whole of a personality. Every feeling, however simple it may be, contains virtually within it the whole past and present of the being experiencing it, and, consequently, can only be separated and constituted into a "state" by an effort of abstraction or of analysis. But it is no less incontestable that without this effort of abstraction or analysis there would be no possible development of the science of psychology. What, then, exactly, is the operation by which a psychologist detaches a mental state in order to erect it into a more or less independent entity? He begins by neglecting that special coloring of the personality which cannot be expressed in known and common terms. Then he endeavors to isolate, in the person already thus simplified, some aspect which lends itself to an interesting inquiry. If he is considering inclination, for example, he will neglect the inexpressible shade which colors it, and which makes the inclination mine and not yours; he will fix his attention on the movement by which our personality *leans towards* a certain object: he will isolate this attitude, and it is this special aspect of the personality, this snapshot of the mobility of the inner life, this "diagram" of concrete inclination, that he will erect into an independent fact. There is in this something very like what an artist passing through Paris does when he makes, for example, a sketch of a tower of Notre Dame. The tower is inseparably united to the building, which is itself no less inseparably united to the ground, to its surroundings, to the whole of Paris, and so on. It is first necessary to detach it from all these; only one aspect of the whole is noted, that formed by the tower of Notre Dame. Moreover, the special form of this tower is due to the grouping of the stones of which it is composed; but the artist does not concern himself with these stones, he notes only the silhouette of the tower. For the real and internal organization of the thing he substitutes, then, an external and schematic representation. So that, on the whole, his sketch corresponds to an observation of the object from a certain point of view and to the choice of a certain means of representation. But exactly the same thing holds true of the operation by which the psychologist extracts a single mental state from the whole personality. This isolated psychical state is hardly anything but a sketch, the commencement of an artificial reconstruction; it is the whole considered under a certain elementary aspect in which we are specially interested and which we have carefully noted. It is not a part, but an element. It has not been obtained by a natural dismemberment, but by analysis.

Now beneath all the sketches he has made at Paris the visitor will probably, by way of memento, write the word "Paris." And as he has really seen Paris, he will be able, with the help of the original intuition he had of the whole, to place his sketches therein, and so join them up together. But there is no way of performing the inverse operation; it is impossible, even with an infinite number of accurate sketches, and even with the word "Paris" which indicates that they must be combined together, to get back to an intuition that one has never had, and to give oneself an impression of what Paris is like if one has never seen it. This is because we are not dealing here with real *parts,* but with mere *notes* of the total impression. To take a still more striking example, where the notation is more completely symbolic, suppose that I am shown, mixed together at random, the letters which make up a poem I am ignorant of. If the letters were *parts* of the poem, I could attempt to reconstitute the poem with them by trying the different possible arrangements, as a child does with the pieces of a Chinese puzzle. But I should never for a moment think of attempting such a thing in this case, because the letters are not *component parts,* but only *partial expressions,* which is quite a different thing. That is why, if I know the poem, I at once put each of the letters in its proper place and join them up without difficulty by a continuous connection, while the inverse operation is impossible. Even when I believe I am actually attempting this inverse operation, even when I put the letters end to end, I begin by thinking of some plausible meaning. I thereby give myself an intuition, and from this intuition I attempt to redescend to the elementary symbols which would reconstitute its expression. The very idea of reconstituting a thing by operations practiced on symbolic elements alone implies such an absurdity that it would never occur to anyone if [he] recollected that [he was] not dealing with fragments of the thing, but only, as it were, with fragments of its symbol.

Such is, however, the undertaking of the philosophers who try to reconstruct personality with psychical states, whether they confine themselves to those states alone, or whether they add a kind of thread for the purpose of joining the states together. Both empiricists and rationalists are victims of the same fallacy. Both of them mistake *partial notations* for *real parts,* thus confusing the point of view of analysis and of intuition, of science and of metaphysics.

Readings

1. Aaron, R. I. *John Locke.* Rev. ed. New York: Oxford Univ. Press, 1955. A good discussion of Locke.

2. Bouwsma, O. K. "Descartes' Evil Genius," *Philosophical Review* (1949), pp. 141–157.

3. Doney, Willis, ed. *Descartes.* Notre Dame: Univ. of Notre Dame Press, 1968. An anthology of recent essays on Descartes.

4. Gibson, A. B. *The Philosophy of Descartes.* New York: Russell, 1932. A classic discussion of Descartes.

5. Hamlyn, D. W. *Sensation and Perception.* New York: Humanities, 1961. A history of perception theory.

6. Hintikka, Jaako. "Cogito, Ergo Sum," *Philosophical Review* (1962), pp. 3–32.

7. Lecky, W. E. H. *History of the Rise and Influence of the Spirit of Rationalism in Europe.* London, 1865. Rev. ed., London, 1910.

8. Malcolm, Norman. "Dreaming and Skepticism," *Philosophical Review* (1956), pp. 14–37.

9. Miller, L. G. "Descartes, Mathematics, and God," *Philosophical Review* (1957), pp. 451–465.

10. Russell, Bertrand. *The Problems of Philosophy.* New York: Oxford Univ. Press, 1912. A twentieth-century empiricist.

11. Santillana, Giorgio de, and Edgar Zilsel. "The Development of Rationalism and Empiricism" in *International Encyclopedia of Unified Science.* Chicago: Univ. of Chicago Press, 1941, Vol. II.

12. Woozley, A. D. *Theory of Knowledge.* London: Hutchinson, 1949. A discussion of the various problems of epistemology.

Bergson

13. Lindsay, A. D. *The Philosophy of Bergson.* New York: Kennikat Press, 1968.

14. Luce, A. A. *Bergson's Doctrine of Intuition.* New York: Macmillan, 1922.

two

Do We Have Knowledge
of an Identical Self?

20

Yes, by Consciousness

John Locke (1632–1704), English empiricist and political philosopher, wrote two major works regarded as classics, *Two Treatises of Government* (1689) and *An Essay Concerning Human Understanding* (1690).

One often notes that another person is different than he was. In fact, sometimes we say "he is not the same person." But we seldom, if ever, mean that he is a completely different person such that we don't identify him with the same past acts. If we believe that we are the same person today as we were yesterday and a year ago, then how do we know this? Locke defines a person as a "thinking intelligent being, that has reason and reflection, and can consider itself as itself, the same thinking thing, in different times and places . . . ," and it can do this "by consciousness which is inseparable from thinking . . . ." Since it is by this immediate self-awareness that "everyone is to himself that which he calls self . . . ," it follows that this self-consciousness constitutes the essence of personality, and consequently that the identity of the person is to be found in the identity of consciousness. Of course, we are not always conscious, as for example when we are sleeping. Because we are morally responsible in cases where we are not conscious, our identity has to be established on forensic or legal means.

TO STUDY

1. According to Locke, what does "person" stand for?
2. In what alone consists personal identity?
3. What is the difficulty created when consciousness is the test of the same identical substance?
4. If our bodies change do we have the same personal identity?

If our minds change do we have the same personal identity?

5. Can two thinking substances be one person? Explain.
6. Can one immaterial substance be two persons? Explain.
7. Upon which does the self depend: consciousness or substance?
8. Who is the object of punishment: persons or substances? Should a sleepwalker be punished for his bad deeds?
9. What is meant by the same *man*?
10. Is a drunk and sober man the same person?
11. What alone unites separate existences into the same person? Could two distinct consciousnesses occupy the same body?
12. Why is "person" a forensic term?
13. What does Locke conclude?

This being premised, to find wherein personal identity consists, we must consider what *person* stands for;—which, I think, is a thinking intelligent being, that has reason and reflection, and can consider itself as itself, the same thinking thing, in different times and places; which it does only by that consciousness which is inseparable from thinking, and, as it seems to me, essential to it: it being impossible for any one to perceive without *perceiving* that he does perceive. When we see, hear, smell, taste, feel, meditate, or will anything, we know that we do so. Thus it is always as to our present sensations and perceptions: and by this every one is to himself that which he calls *self*:—it not being considered, in this case, whether the same self be continued in the same or divers substances. For, since consciousness always accompanies thinking, and it is that which makes every one to be what he calls self, and thereby distinguishes himself from all other thinking things, in this alone consists personal identity, i.e. the sameness of a rational being: and as far as this consciousness can be extended backwards to any past action or thought, so far reaches the identity of that person; it is the same self now it was then; and it is by the same self with this present one that now reflects on it, that that action was done.

But it is further inquired, whether it be the same identical substance. This few would think they had reason to doubt of, if these perceptions, with their consciousness, always remained present in the mind, whereby the

From *An Essay Concerning Human Understanding* by John Locke (1690), Book II, Chap. XXVII.

same thinking thing would be always consciously present, and, as would be thought, evidently the same to itself. But that which seems to make the difficulty is this, that this consciousness being interrupted always by forgetfulness, there being no moment of our lives wherein we have the whole train of all our past actions before our eyes in one view, but even the best memories losing the sight of one part whilst they are viewing another; and we sometimes, and that the greatest part of our lives, not reflecting on our past selves, being intent on our present thoughts, and in sound sleep having no thoughts at all, or at least none with that consciousness which remarks our waking thoughts,—I say, in all these cases, our consciousness being interrupted, and we losing the sight of our past selves, doubts are raised whether we are the same thinking thing, i.e. the same *substance* or no. Which, however reasonable or unreasonable, concerns not *personal* identity at all. The question being what makes the same person; and not whether it be the same identical substance, which always thinks in the same person, which, in this case, matters not at all: different substances, by the same consciousness (where they do partake in it) being united into one person, as well as different bodies by the same life are united into one animal, whose identity is preserved in that change of substances by the unity of one continued life. For, it being the same consciousness that makes a man be himself to himself, personal identity depends on that only, whether it be annexed solely to one individual substance, or can be continued in a succession of several substances. For as far as any intelligent being *can* repeat the idea of any past action with the same consciousness it had of it at first, and with the same consciousness it has of any present action; so far it is the same personal self. For it is by the consciousness it has of its present thoughts and actions, that it is *self to itself* now, and so will be the same self, as far as the same consciousness can extend to actions past or to come; and would be by distance of time, or change of substance, no more two persons, than a man be two men by wearing other clothes to-day than he did yesterday, with a long or a short sleep between: the same consciousness uniting those distant actions into the same person, whatever substances contributed to their production.

That this is so, we have some kind of evidence in our very bodies, all whose particles, whilst vitally united to this same thinking conscious self, so that *we feel* when they are touched, and are affected by, and conscious of good or harm that happens to them, are a part of ourselves; i.e. of our thinking conscious self. Thus, the limbs of his body are to every one a part of himself; he sympathizes and is concerned for them. Cut off a hand, and thereby separate it from that consciousness he had of its heat, cold, and other affections, and it is then no longer a part of that which is himself, any more than the remotest part of matter. Thus, we see the *substance* whereof personal self consisted at one time may be varied at another, without the change of personal identity; there being no question about the same person, though the limbs which but now were a part of it, be cut off.

But the question is, Whether if the same substance which thinks be changed, it can be the same person; or, remaining the same, it can be different persons?

And to this I answer: First, This can be no question at all to those who place thought in a purely material animal constitution, void of an immaterial substance. For, whether their supposition be true or no, it is plain they conceive personal identity preserved in something else than identity of substance; as animal identity is preserved in identity of life, and not of substance. And therefore those who place thinking in an immaterial substance only, before they can come to deal with these men, must show why personal identity cannot be preserved in the change of immaterial substances, or variety of particular immaterial substances, as well as animal identity is preserved in the change of material substances, or variety of particular bodies: unless they will say, it is one immaterial spirit that makes the same life in brutes, as it is one immaterial spirit that makes the same person in men . . .

But next, as to the first part of the question, Whether, if the same thinking substance (supporting immaterial substances only to think) be changed, it can be the same person? I answer, that cannot be resolved but by those who know what kind of substances they are that do think; and whether the consciousness of past actions can be transferred from one thinking substance to another. I grant were the same consciousness the same individual action it could not: but it being a present representation of a past action, why it may not be possible, that that may be represented to the mind to have been which really never was, will remain to be shown. And therefore how far the consciousness of past actions is annexed to any individual agent, so that another cannot possibly have it, will be hard for us to determine, till we know what kind of action it is that cannot be done without a reflex act of perception accompanying it, and how performed by thinking substances, who cannot think without being conscious of it. But that which we call the same consciousness, not being the same individual act, why one intellectual substance may not have represented to it, as done by itself, what *it* never did, and was perhaps done by some other agent—why, I say, such a representation may not possibly be without reality of matter of fact, as well as several representations in dreams are, which yet whilst dreaming we take for true—will be difficult to conclude from the nature of things. . . . But yet, to return to the question before us, it must be allowed, that, if the same consciousness (which, as has been shown, is quite a different thing from the same numerical figure or motion in body) can be transferred from one thinking substance to another, it will be possible that two thinking substances may make but one person. For the same consciousness being preserved, whether in the same or different substances, the personal identity is preserved.

As to the second part of the question, Whether the same immaterial substance remaining, there may be two distinct persons; which question seems to me to be built on this,—Whether the same immaterial being, being conscious of the action of its past duration, may be wholly stripped of all the consciousness of its past existence, and lose it beyond the power of ever retrieving it again: and so as it were beginning a new account from a new period, have a consciousness that *cannot* reach beyond this new state. All those who hold pre-existence are evidently of this mind; since they allow the soul to have no remaining consciousness of what it did in that pre-existent state, either wholly separate from body, or informing any other body; and if they should not, it is plain experience would be against them. So that personal identity, reaching no further than consciousness reaches, a pre-existent spirit not having continued so many ages in a state of silence, must needs make different persons. . . . I once met with one, who was persuaded his had been the *soul* of Socrates . . . would any one say, that he, being not conscious of any of Socrates's actions or thoughts, could be the same *person* with Socrates? Let any one reflect upon himself, and conclude that he has in himself an immaterial spirit, which is that which thinks in him, and, in the constant change of his body keeps him the same: and is that which he calls *himself:* let him also suppose it to be the same soul that was in Nestor or Thersites, at the siege of Troy, . . . which it may have been, as well as it is now the soul of any other man: but he now having no consciousness of any of the actions either of Nestor or Thersites, does or can he conceive himself the same person with either of them? Can he be concerned in either of their actions? attribute them to himself, or think them his own, more than the actions of any other men that ever existed? So that this consciousness, not reaching to any of the actions of either of those men, he is no more one *self* with either of them than if the soul or immaterial spirit that now informs him had been created, and began to exist, when it began to inform his present body; though it were never so true, that the same *spirit* that informed Nestor's or Thersites' body were numerically the same that now informs his. For this would no more make him the same person with Nestor, than if some of the particles of matter that were once a part of Nestor were now a part of this man; the same immaterial substance, without the same consciousness, no more making the same person, by being united to any body, than the same particle of matter, without consciousness, united to any body, makes the same person. But let him once find himself conscious of any of the actions of Nestor, he then finds himself the same person with Nestor. . . .

But though the same immaterial substance or soul does not alone, wherever it be, and in whatsoever state, make the same *man;* yet it is plain, consciousness, as far as ever it can be extended—should it be to ages past—unites existences and actions very remote in time into the same *person,* as well as it does the existences and actions of the immediately preceding moment: so that whatever has the consciousness of present and past actions, is the same person to whom they both belong. Had I the same consciousness that I saw the ark and Noah's flood, as that I saw an over-flowing of the Thames last winter, or as that I write now, I could no more doubt that I who write this now, that saw the Thames overflowed last winter, and that viewed the flood at the general deluge, was the same *self,* —place that self in what *substance* you please—than that I who write this am the same *myself* now whilst I write (whether I consist of all the same substance, material or immaterial, or no) that I was yesterday. For as to this point of being the same self, it matters not whether this present self be made up of the same or other substances—I being as much concerned, and as justly accountable for any action that was done a thousand years since, appropriated to me now by this self-consciousness, as I am for what I did the last moment.

Self is that conscious thinking thing,—whatever substance made up of, (whether spiritual or material, simple or compounded, it matters not)— which is sensible or conscious of pleasure and pain, capable of happiness or misery, and so is concerned for itself, as far as that consciousness extends. Thus every one finds that, whilst comprehended under that consciousness, the little finger is as much a part of himself as what is most so. Upon separation of this little finger, should this consciousness go along with the little finger, and leave the rest of the body, it is evident the little finger would be the person, the same person; and self then would have nothing to do with the rest of the body. As in this case it is the consciousness that goes along with the substance, when one part is separate from another, which makes the same person, and constitutes this inseparable self: so it is in reference to substances remote in time. That with which the consciousness of this present thinking thing *can* join itself, makes the same person, and is one self with it, and with nothing else; and so attributes to itself, and owns all the actions of that thing, as its own, as far as that consciousness reaches, and no further; as every one who reflects will perceive.

In this personal identity is founded all the right and justice of reward and punishment; happiness and misery being that for which every one is concerned for *himself,* and not mattering what becomes of any *substance,* not joined to, or affected with that consciousness. For, as it is evident in the instance I gave but now, if the consciousness went along with the little finger when it was cut off, that would be the same self which was concerned for the whole body yesterday, as making part of itself, whose actions then it cannot but admit as its own now. Though, if the same body should still live, and immediately from the separation of the little finger have its own peculiar consciousness, whereof the little finger knew nothing, it would not at all be concerned for it, as a part of itself, or could own any of its actions, or have any of them imputed to him.

This may show us wherein personal identity consists: not in the identity of substance, but, as I have said, in the identity of consciousness, wherein if Socrates and the present mayor of Queinborough agree, they are the same person: if the same Socrates waking and sleeping do not partake of the same consciousness, Socrates waking and sleeping is not the same person. And to punish Socrates waking for what sleeping Socrates thought, and waking Socrates was never conscious of, would be no more of right, than to punish one twin for what his brother-twin did, whereof he knew nothing, because their outsides were so like, that they could not be distinguished; for such twins have been seen.

But yet possibly it will still be objected,—Suppose I wholly lose the memory of some parts of my life, beyond a possibility of retrieving them, so that perhaps I shall never be conscious of them again; yet am I not the same person that did those actions, had those thoughts that I once was conscious of, though I have now forgot them? To which I answer, that we must here take notice what the word *I* is applied to; which, in this case, is the *man* only. And the same man being presumed to be the same person, I is easily here supposed to stand also for the same person. But if it be possible for the same man to have distinct incommunicable consciousness at different times, it is past doubt the same man would at different times make different persons; which, we see, is the sense of mankind in the solemnest declaration of their opinions, human laws not punishing the mad man for the sober man's actions, nor the sober man for what the mad man did,—thereby making them two persons: which is somewhat explained by our way of speaking in English when we say such an one is 'not himself,' or is 'beside himself'; in which phrases it is insinuated, as if those who now, or at least first used them, thought that self was changed; the selfsame person was no longer in that man.

But yet it is hard to conceive that Socrates, the same individual man, should be two persons. To help us a little in this, we must consider what is meant by Socrates, or the same individual *man*.

First, it must be either the same individual, immaterial, thinking substance; in short, the same numerical soul, and nothing else.

Secondly, or the same animal, without any regard to an immaterial soul.

Thirdly, or the same immaterial spirit united to the same animal.

Now, take which of these suppositions you please, it is impossible to make personal identity to consist in anything but consciousness; or reach any further than that does.

For, by the first of them, it must be allowed possible that a man born of different women, and in distant times, may be the same man. A way of speaking which, whoever admits, must allow it possible for the same man to be two distinct persons, as any two that have lived in different ages without the knowledge of one another's thoughts.

By the second and third, Socrates, in this life and after it, cannot be the same man any way, but by the same consciousness; and so making human identity to consist in the same thing wherein we place personal identity, there will be no difficulty to allow the same man to be the same person. But then they who place human identity in consciousness only, and not in something else, must consider how they will make the infant Socrates the same man with Socrates after the resurrection. But whatsoever to some men makes a man, and consequently the same individual man, wherein perhaps few are agreed, personal identity can by us be placed in nothing but consciousness, (which is that alone which makes what we call *self*,) without involving us in great absurdities.

But is not a man drunk and sober the same person? why else is he punished for the fact he commits when drunk, though he be never afterwards conscious of it? Just as much the same person as a man that walks, and does other things in his sleep, is the same person, and is answerable for any mischief he shall do in it. Human laws punish both, with a justice suitable to *their* way of knowledge;—because, in these cases, they cannot distinguish certainly what is real, what counterfeit: and so the ignorance in drunkenness or sleep is not admitted as a plea. [For, though punishment be annexed to personality, and personality to consciousness, and the drunkard perhaps be not conscious of what he did, yet human judicatures justly punish him; because the fact is proved against him, but want of consciousness cannot be proved for him.] . . .

Nothing but consciousness can unite remote existences into the same person: the identity of substance will not do it; for whatever substance there is, however framed, without consciousness there is no person: and a carcass may be a person, as well as any sort of substance be so, without consciousness.

Could we suppose two distinct incommunicable consciousnesses acting the same body, the one constantly by day, the other by night; and, on the other side, the same consciousness, acting by intervals, two distinct bodies: I ask, in the first case, whether the day and the night—man would not be two as distinct persons as Socrates and Plato? And whether, in the second case, there would not be one person in two distinct persons bodies, as much as one man is the same in two distinct clothings? Nor is it at all material to say, that this same, and this distinct consciousness, in the cases above mentioned, is owing to the same and distinct immaterial substances, bringing it with them to those bodies; which, whether true or no, alters not the case: since it is evident the personal identity would equally be determined by the consciousness, whether that consciousness were annexed to some individual immaterial substance or no. For, granting that the thinking substance in man must be necessarily supposed immaterial, it is evident that immaterial thinking thing may sometimes part with its past consciousness, and be restored to it again: as appears in the forgetfulness men often have of their past actions; and the mind many times recovers the memory of a past consciousness, which it had lost for twenty years together. Make these intervals of memory and forgetfulness to take their turns regularly by day and night, and you have two persons with the same immaterial spirit, as much as in the former instance two persons with the same body. So that self is not determined by identity or diversity of substance, which it cannot be sure of, but only by identity of consciousness.

Indeed it may conceive the substance whereof it is now made up to have existed formerly, united in the same conscious being: but, consciousness removed, that substance is no more itself, or makes no more a part of it, than any other substance; as is evident in the instance we have already given of a limb cut off, of whose heat, or cold, or other affections, having no longer any consciousness, it is no more of a man's self than any other matter of the universe. In like manner it will be in reference to any immaterial substance, which is void of that consciousness whereby I am myself to myself: [if there be any part of its existence which] I cannot upon recollection join with that present consciousness whereby I am now myself, it is, in that part of its existence, no more *myself* than any other immaterial being. For, whatsoever any substance has thought or done, which I cannot recollect, and by my consciousness make my own thought and action, it will no more belong to me, whether a part of me thought or did it, than if it had been thought or done by any other immaterial being anywhere existing.

I agree, the more probable opinion is, that this consciousness is annexed to, and the affection of, one individual immaterial substance.

But let men, according to their diverse hypotheses, resolve of that as they please. This every intelligent being, sensible of happiness or misery, must grant—that there is something that is *himself,* that he is concerned for, and would have happy; that this self has existed in a continued duration more than one instant, and therefore it is possible may exist, as it has done, months and years to come, without any certain bounds to be set to its duration; and may be the same self, by the same consciousness continued on for the future. And thus, by this consciousness he finds himself to be the same self which did such and such an action some years since, by which he comes to be happy or miserable now. In all which account of self, the same numerical *substance* is not considered as making the same self; but the same continued consciousness, in which several substances may have been united, and again separated from it, which, whilst they continued in a vital union with that wherein this consciousness then resided, made a part of that same self. Thus any part of our bodies, vitally united to that which is conscious in us, makes a part of ourselves: but upon separation from the vital union by which that consciousness is communicated, that which a moment since was part of ourselves, is now no more so than a part of another man's self is a part of me: and it is not impossible but in a little time may become a real part of another person. And so we have the same numerical substance become a part of two different persons; and the same person preserved under the change of various substances. Could we suppose any spirit wholly stripped of all its memory or consciousness of past actions, as we find our minds always are of a great part of ours, and sometimes of them all; the union or separation of such a spiritual substance would make no variation of personal identity, any more than that of any particle of matter does. Any substance vitally united to the present thinking being is a part of that very same self which now is; anything united to it by a consciousness of former actions, makes also a part of the same self, which is the same both then and now.

Person, as I take it, is the name for this self. Wherever a man finds what he calls himself, there, I think, another may say is the same person. It is a forensic term, appropriating actions and their merit; and so belongs only to intelligent agents, capable of a law, and happiness, and misery. This personality extends itself beyond present existence to what is past, only by consciousness,—whereby it becomes concerned and accountable; owns and imputes to itself past actions, just upon the same ground and for the same reason as it does the present. All which is founded in a concern for happiness, the unavoidable concomitant of consciousness; that which is conscious of pleasure and pain, desiring that that self that is conscious should be happy. And therefore whatever past actions it cannot reconcile or *appropriate* to that present self by consciousness, it can be no more concerned in than if they had never been done: and to receive pleasure or pain, i.e. reward or punishment, on the account of any such action, is all one as to be made happy or miserable in its first being, without any demerit at all. For, supposing a *man* punished now for what he had done in another life, whereof he could be made to have no consciousness at all, what difference is there between that punishment and being *created* miserable? And therefore, conformable to this, the apostle tells us, that, at the great day, when every one shall 'receive according to his doings, the secrets of all hearts shall be laid open.' The sentence shall be justified by the consciousness all persons shall have, that *they themselves,* in what bodies soever they appear, or what substances soever that consciousness adheres to, are the *same* that committed those actions, and deserve that punishment for them. . . .

To conclude: Whatever substance begins to exist, it must, during its existence, necessarily be the same: whatever compositions of substances begin to exist, during the union of those substances, the concrete must be the same: whatsoever mode begins to exist, during its existence it is the same: and so if the composition be of distinct substances and different modes, the same rule holds. Whereby it will appear, that the difficulty or obscurity that has been about this matter rather rises from the names ill-used, than from any obscurity in things themselves. For whatever makes the specific idea to which the name is applied, if that idea be steadily kept to, the distinction of anything into the same and divers will easily be conceived, and there can arise no doubt about it.

For, supposing a rational spirit be the idea of a *man,* it is easy to know what is the same man, viz. the same spirit—whether separate or in a body—will be the *same man.* Supposing a rational spirit vitally united to a body of a certain conformation of parts to make a man; whilst that rational spirit, with that vital conformation of parts, though continued in a fleeting successive body, remains, it will be the *same man.* But if to any one the idea of a man be but the vital union of parts in a certain shape; as long as that vital union and shape remain in a concrete, no otherwise the same but by a continued succession of fleeting particles, it will be the *same man.* For, whatever be the composition whereof the complex idea is made, whenever existence makes it one particular thing under any denomination, *the same existence continued* preserves it the *same* individual under the same denomination.

THINK ABOUT

1. In his book *Reality* (New York: Macmillan, 1926), p. 36, B. H. Streeter says that what a person really knows of the "inner quality of life" depends primarily on the following three things: "first, the depth and the range of his own personal experience; secondly, how far he has the imaginative sympathy to penetrate into the inner experience of others; thirdly, the extent to which he has reflected on the material so presented." Give reasons for agreeing or disagreeing with Streeter.

2. A man's skull is opened, under local anesthetic, so that he remains

conscious. The ridges of the whitish-grey matter (the cortex) of the brain are exposed to view. The movements or changes that take place in the brain are shown in magnifying mirrors, so that the man is able to watch these brain changes while he perceives and thinks. Who or what is doing the watching?

3. Report on views of the self and man as found in modern literature. You may prefer to pick out one or two writers, such as Ibsen, Sartre, or. others.

4. Much of a person's sense of self is related to that person's biological sex and to the sex-roles assigned by society. To what extent do you feel that you define yourself in terms of your sex? What limitations do you see in this kind of personal definition?

5. "The member of a primitive clan might express his identity in the formula 'I am we'; he cannot yet conceive of himself as an 'individual,' existing apart from his group . . . When the feudal system broke down, this sense of identity was shaken and the acute question 'who am I?' arose."

21

There Is No
Identical Self

David Hume (1711–1776) is a British philosopher, historian,
and essayist whose views on causality stimulated Kant to
construct his "critical philosophy"; noted for his development
of the empiricism of Locke and Berkeley and for his skepticism. He is the author of *Treatise on Human Nature*.

In contrast, Hume does not believe there is an identical self. He argues
that there is no impression of such self, that there are no constant
and invariable impressions, and finally that introspection does not discover
anything else except particular perceptions. I have particular sensations and
emotions, but no impression of a self. Hume says "the identity which we
ascribe to the mind of man is a fictitious one . . . (this because) it . . . is
not able to run the several different perceptions into one, and make them
lose their character of distinction and difference, which are essential to
them."

TO STUDY

1. What is it about the Self some philosophers believe?
2. What does Hume believe about the ideas of *self*? Why?
3. What does Hume say occurs when he "enters most intimately
   into what I call my self"?
4. According to Hume, what is the Self?
5. Why do we believe there is a personal identity?

There are some philosophers, who imagine we are every moment intimately conscious of what we call our Self; that we feel its existence and its continuance in existence; and are certain, beyond the evidence of a demonstration, both of its perfect identity and simplicity. The strongest sensation, the most violent passion, say they, instead of distracting us from this view, only fix it the more intensely, and make us consider their influence on *self* either by their pain or pleasure. To attempt a farther proof of this were to weaken its evidence; since no proof can be derived from any fact, of which we are so intimately conscious; nor is there any thing, of which we can be certain, if we doubt of this.

Unluckily all these positive assertions are contrary to that very experience, which is pleaded for them, nor have we any idea of *self*, after the manner it is here explained. For from what impression could this idea be derived? This question it is impossible to answer without a manifest contradiction and absurdity; and yet it is a question, which must necessarily be answered, if we would have the idea of self pass for clear and intelligible. It must be some one impression, that gives rise to every real idea. But self or person is not any one impression, but that to which our several impressions and ideas are supposed to have a reference. If any impression gives rise to the idea of self, that impression must continue invariably the same, through the whole course of our lives; since self is supposed to exist after that manner. But there is no impression constant and invariable. Pain and pleasure, grief and joy, passions and sensations succeed each other, and never all exist at the same time. It cannot, therefore, be from any of these impressions, or from any other, that the idea of self is derived; and consequently there is no such idea.

But farther, what must become of all our particular perceptions upon this hypothesis? All these are different, and distinguishable, and separable from each other, and may be separately considered, and may exist separately, and have no need of any thing to support their existence. After what manner, therefore, do they belong to self; and how are they connected with it? For my part, when I enter most intimately into what I call *myself*, I always stumble on some particular perception or other, of heat or cold, light or shade, love or hatred, pain or pleasure. I never can catch *myself* at any time without a perception, and never can observe any thing but the perception. When my perceptions are removed for any time, as by sound sleep; so long am I sensible of *myself*, and may truly be said not to exist. And were all my perceptions removed by death, and could I neither think, nor feel, nor see, nor love, nor hate after the dissolution of my body, I should

From David Hume, "Of Personal Identity," from *A Treatise of Human Nature*, Book I, Part 4.

be entirely annihilated, nor do I conceive what is farther requisite to make me a perfect non-entity. If anyone upon serious and unprejudiced reflexion, thinks he has a different notion of *himself,* I must confess I can reason no longer with him. All I can allow him is, that he may be in the right as well as I, and that we are essentially different in this particular. He may, perhaps, perceive something simple and continued, which he calls *himself;* though I am certain there is no such principle in me.

But setting aside some metaphysicians of this kind, I may venture to affirm of the rest of mankind, that they are nothing but a bundle or collection of different perceptions, which succeed each other with an inconceivable rapidity, and are in a perpetual flux and movement. Our eyes cannot turn in their sockets without varying our perceptions. Our thought is still more variable than our sight; and all our other senses and faculties contribute to this change; nor is there any single power of the soul, which remains unalterably the same, perhaps for one moment. The mind is a kind of theatre, where several perceptions successively make their appearance; pass, re-pass, glide away, and mingle in an infinite variety of postures and situations. There is properly no *simplicity* in it at one time, nor *identity* in different; whatever natural propension we may have to imagine that simplicity and identity. The comparison of the theatre must not mislead us. They are the successive perceptions only, that constitute the mind; nor have we the most distant notion of the place, where these scenes are represented, or of the materials, of which it is composed.

What then gives us so great a propension to ascribe an identity to these successive perceptions, and to suppose ourselves possest of an invariable and uninterrupted existence through the whole course of our lives? . . .

We have a distinct idea of an object, that remains invariable and uninterrupted through a supposed variation of time; and this idea we call that of *identity* or *sameness.* We have also a distinct idea of several different objects existing in succession, and connected together by a close relation; and this to an accurate view affords as perfect a notion of *diversity,* as if there was no manner of relation among the objects. But though these two ideas of identity, and a succession of related objects be in themselves perfectly distinct, and even contrary, yet it is certain, that in our common way of thinking they are generally confounded with each other. That action of the imagination, by which we consider the uninterrupted and invariable object, and that by which we reflect on the succession of related objects, are almost the same to the feeling, nor is there much more effort of thought required in the latter case than in the former. The relation facilitates the transition of the mind from one object to another, and renders its passage as smooth as if it contemplated one continued object. This resemblance is the case of the confusion and mistake, and makes us substitute the notion of identity, instead of that of related objects. However at one instant we may consider the related succession as variable or interrupted, we are sure the next to ascribe to it a perfect identity, and regard it as invariable and uninterrupted. Our propensity to this mistake is so great from the resemblance above-mentioned, that we fall into it before we are aware; and though we incessantly correct ourselves by reflexion, and return to a more accurate method of thinking, yet we cannot long sustain our philosophy, or take off this bias from the imagination. Our last resource is to yield to it, and boldly assert that these different related objects are in effect the same, however interrupted and variable. In order to justify to ourselves this absurdity, we often feign some new and unintelligible principle, that connects the objects together, and prevents their interruption or variation. Thus we feign the continued existence of the perceptions of our senses, to remove the interruption; and run into the notion of a *soul,* and *self,* and *substance,* to disguise the variation. But we may farther observe, that where we do not give rise to such a fiction, our propension to confound identity with relation is so great, that we are apt to imagine[1] something unknown and mysterious, connecting the parts, beside their relation; and this I take to be the case with regard to the identity we ascribe to plants and vegetables. And even when this does not take place, we still feel a propensity to confound these ideas, though we are not able fully to satisfy ourselves in that particular, nor find any thing invariable and uninterrupted to justify our notion of identity.

Thus the controversy concerning identity is not merely a dispute of words. For when we attribute identity, in an improper sense, to variable or interrupted objects, our mistake is not confined to the expression, but is commonly attended with a fiction, either of something invariable and uninterrupted, or of something mysterious and inexplicable, or at least with a propensity to such fictions. . . .

We now proceed to explain the nature of *personal identity,* which has become so great a question in philosophy, especially of late years in *England,* where all the abstruser sciences are studied with a peculiar ardour and application. . . .

It is evident, that the identity, which we attribute to the human mind, however perfect we may imagine it to be, is not able to run the several different perceptions into one, and make them lose their characters of distinction and difference, which are essential to them. It is still true, that every distinct perception, which enters into the composition of the mind,

---

[1] If the reader is desirous to see how a great genius may be influenced by these seemingly trivial principles of the imagination, as well as the mere vulgar, let him read my Lord *Shaftsbury's* reasonings concerning the uniting principle of the universe, and the identity of plants and animals. See his *Moralists:* or, *Philosophical Rhapsody.*

is a distinct existence, and is different, and distinguishable, and separable from every other perception, either contemporary or successive. But, as, notwithstanding this distinction and separability, we suppose the whole train of perceptions to be united by identity, a question naturally arises concerning this relation of identity; whether it be something that really binds our several perceptions together, or only associates their ideas in the imagination. That is, in other words, whether in pronouncing concerning the identity of a person, we observe some real bond among his perceptions, or only feel one among the ideas we form of them. This question we might easily decide, if we would recollect what has been already proved at large, that the understanding never observes any real connexion among objects, and that even the union of cause and effect, when strictly examined, resolves itself into a customary association of ideas. For from thence it evidently follows, that identity is nothing really belonging to these different perceptions, and uniting them together; but is merely a quality, which we attribute to them, because of the union of their ideas in the imagination, when we reflect upon them. Now the only qualities, which can give ideas an union in the imagination, are these three relations above-mentioned. These are the uniting principles in the ideal world, and without them every distinct object is separable by the mind, and may be separately considered, and appears not to have any more connexion with any other object, than if disjoined by the greatest difference and remotences. It is, therefore, on some of these three relations of resemblance, contiguity and causation, that identity depends; and as the very essence of these relations consists in their producing an easy transition of ideas; it follows, that our notions of personal identity, proceed entirely from the smooth and uninterrupted progress of the thought along a train of connected ideas, according to the principles above-explained.

The only question, therefore, which remains, is, by what relations this uninterrupted progress of our thought is produced, when we consider the successive existence of a mind or thinking person. And here it is evident we must confine ourselves to resemblance and causation, and must drop contiguity, which has little or no influence in the present case.

To begin with *resemblance;* suppose we could see clearly into the breast of another, and observe that succession of perceptions, which constitutes his mind or thinking principle, and suppose that he always preserves the memory of a considerable part of past perceptions; it is evident that nothing could more contribute to the bestowing a relation on this succession amidst all its variations. For what is the memory but a faculty, by which we raise up the images of past perceptions? And as an image necessarily resembles its object, must not the frequent placing of these resembling perceptions in the chain of thought, convey the imagination more easily from one link to another, and make the whole seem like the continuance of one object? In this particular, then, the memory not only discovers the identity, but also contributes to its production, by producing the relation of resemblance among the perceptions. The case is the same whether we consider ourselves or others.

As to *causation;* we may observe, that the true idea of the human mind, is to consider it as a system of different perceptions or different existences, which are linked together by the relation of cause and effect, and mutually produce, destroy, influence, and modify each other. Our impressions give rise to their correspondent ideas; and these ideas in their turn produce other impressions. One thought chases another, and draws after it a third, by which it is expelled in its turn. In this respect, I cannot compare the soul more properly to anything than to a republic or commonwealth, in which the several members are united by the reciprocal ties of government and subordination, and give rise to other persons, who propagate the same republic in the incessant changes of its parts. And as the same individual republic may not only change its members, but also its laws and constitutions; in like manner the same person may vary his character and disposition, as well as his impressions and ideas, without losing his identity. Whatever changes he endures, his several parts are still connected by the relation of causation. And in this view our identity with regard to the passions serves to corroborate that with regard to the imagination, by the making our distant perceptions influence each other, and by giving us a present concern for our past or future pains or pleasures.

As memory alone acquaints us with the continuance and extent of this succession of perceptions, it is to be considered, upon that account chiefly, as the source of personal identity. Had we no memory, we never should have any notion of causation, nor consequently of that chain of causes and effects, which constitute our self or person. But having once acquired this notion of causation from the memory, we can extend the same chain of causes, and consequently the identity of our persons beyond our memory, and can comprehend times, and circumstances, and actions, which we have entirely forgot, but suppose in general to have existed. For how few of our past actions are there, of which we have memory? Who can tell me, for instance, what were his thoughts and actions on the first of *January* 1715, the 11th of *March* 1719, and the 3rd of *August* 1733? Or will he affirm, because he has entirely forgot the incidents of these days, that the present self is not the same person with the self of that time; and by that means overturn all the most established notions of personal identity? In this view, therefore, memory does not so much *produce* as *discover* personal identity, by shewing us the relation of cause and effect among our different perceptions. It will be incumbent on those, who affirm that memory produces entirely our personal identity, to give a reason why we can thus extend our identity beyond our memory.

The whole of this doctrine leads us to a conclusion, which is of great importance in the present affair, *viz.*, that all the nice and subtle questions concerning personal identity can never possibly be decided.

22

Man Can Have An Identity

Keith E. Davis (1936–   ) received his Ph.D. from Duke University in 1961 and has written on the problem of personal interaction.

Davis's particular concern with identity is different from Hume's. It is not only important in itself; it is also interesting to contrast his emphasis with Hume's. Davis's formulation of the problem of self-identity can be seen as not denying Hume's position that there is no inner, substantial, unalterable core, but rather that one's self must be viewed as developing in time as one "consolidates" the self and world through the process of self-awareness reflecting on self-identity.

William James found his sense of identity through an invigorating sameness and continuity:

> A man's character is discernible in the mental or moral attitude in which, when it came upon him, he felt himself most deeply and intensely active and alive. At such moments there is a voice inside which speaks and says: *"This* is the real me!"[1]

Such experience always includes

> . . . an element of active tension, of holding my own, as it were, and trusting outward things to perform their part so as to make it a full harmony, but without any *guaranty* that they will. Make it a guaranty . . . and the attitude immediately becomes to my consciousness stagnant and stingless. Take away the guaranty, and I feel (provided I am *ueberhaupt* (totally or generally) in vigorous condition) a sort of deep enthusiastic bliss, of bitter willingness

---

[1] *The Letters of William James,* edited by Henry James (his son), vol. I, Boston: The Atlantic Monthly Press, 1920, p. 199.

to do and suffer anything . . . and which, although it is a mere mood or emotion to which I can give no form in words, authenticates itself to me as the deepest principle of all active and theoretic determination which I possess . . .

In addition to James's *subjective* sense of identity, one can obtain a unity of *personal and cultural identity* through his cultural heritage and/or religious commitment. This is reflected in a speech by Sigmund Freud:

What bound me to Jewry was (I am ashamed to admit) neither faith nor national pride, for I have always been an unbeliever and was brought up without any religion though not without a respect for what are called the "ethical" standards of human civilization. Whenever I felt an inclination to national enthusiasm I strove to suppress it as being harmful and wrong, alarmed by the warning examples of the peoples among whom we Jews live. But plenty of other things remained over to make the attraction of Jewry and Jews irresistible—many obscure emotional forces, which were the more powerful the less they could be expressed in words, as well as a clear consciousness of inner identity, the safe privacy of a common mental construction. And beyond this there was a perception that it was to my Jewish nature alone that I owed two characteristics that had become indispensable to me in the difficult course of my life. Because I was a Jew, I found myself free from many prejudices which restricted others in the use of their intellect; and as a Jew I was prepared to join the Opposition, and to do without agreement with the "compact majority."[2]

In his article, Davis not only reflects these two sources of identity, but he continues by pointing out that a society whose people don't have a strong sense of identity can readily experience chaos. A society full of contradictions is a society without an identity. A society with a common ideology is a society with an identity. As an individual adopts an ideology—personal or social—so he develops an identity. The confident individual needs both a personal and a social ideology.

---

[2] Sigmund Freud, "Address to the Society of B'nai B'rith" (1926), Standard Edition, 20:273, London: Hogarth Press, 1959.

TO STUDY

1. According to Davis, at rock bottom, what holds society together? Do you agree?
2. What fosters social disorganization? Can you give an example?
3. What is the social pathology thesis?

4. According to Kenniston why is there a student drug culture?

5. What is the difference between identity and self-concept?

6. What is required for development of a sense of identity?

The aim of this final section is to remove some of the mystery from a set of related concepts—*identity, alienation, commitment*—that are bandied about in both popular and scholarly discussions of man's place in contemporary society. Of necessity, these concepts extend beyond purely psychological considerations because the phenomena are social, historical, and cultural. Thus our starting place is the social reality that gives substance to personal identities.

What Holds a Society Together?

If society is held together by more than fear, then the positive basis must consist in some *appreciation* by the individual of his own place in it and of what everyone is getting out of the society's practices and institutions—a sense that the arrangement benefits those taking part in it. Actually, in most complex societies, there may be few who appreciate the full range of society's practices and many for whom certain practices are unacceptable. In the actual case then, the social fabric must be held together by a narrower perspective. Probably the rock bottom requirement is that a person appreciate his own options and his own place in society. Such an appreciation gives one a reason to accept norms and rules that do not confer immediate personal advantage.

When this condition is not met for a sufficient number of persons, there is widespread social chaos and pervasive identity confusion and alienation. When people cease to think that their interests and their values are being protected by the larger social pattern, then each significant social subgroup is tempted to take the enforcement of norms or the protection of its own interests into its own hands. Witness the recent concern for "law and order."

Many conditions can foster social disorganization. Perhaps the most critical one is the existence of genuine contradictions in the social system. A self-contradictory system cannot in fact be understood: thus it can hardly be fully appreciated.

A particularly pernicious form of self-contradiction has been labeled

Source: Michael Wertheimer, *Confrontation* (Glenview, Ill.: Scott, Foresman, 1970), pp. 51–56.

value-access disjunction by sociologists (Merton, 1957). To the degree that people come to cherish values and strive for goals that are not in fact open to them (or, in the case of values, are not adhered to by those in power), one has the conditions for *anomie*—a sense of social chaos and individual confusion of self and values. In a very concrete sense, the members of the society are being taught to live a way of life that cannot be lived, and this state of affairs has serious implications for psychological functioning—particularly with respect to the kinds of identities that can be developed.

Contradictions in a social system are likely to be a matter of degree, in that some contradictions affect more people than others, and affect them more severely. For example the contradiction between our ideal of equality before the law and the actual absence of effective legal services for the poor has its greatest detrimental effect on the poor—others in the society do not feel the impact of the contradiction and may even be unaware of it. The same is true of the discrepancy between our ideals of freedom and equality and the systematic, unthinking anti-Negro policies that have been so prevalent in our society.

When a person does not appreciate his options and his place in society, it may be because he is inadequate or pathological in some way, so that he suffers a *reduced ability to appreciate a way of life*. This personal pathology interpretation is reflected in Keniston's "Inburn." There we see a person who distrusts men, who anticipates only harm, injustice, and abuse from his fellow men. He wishes to return to the womb. He rejects society, has no definite plans; he is unable to relate to women of his own age. In short, he has no appreciation for what the society has to offer in the way of ideals, careers, and personal satisfaction, nor does he appreciate his place in society. The opportunities and possibilities of youth and adulthood have no zest for him. Rather they are nothing more than uncertainties and difficulties when he compares them to his special relationship with his mother.

But another general possibility is that the person's society has offered him a *reduced opportunity to participate meaningfully in its practices*. On this view, there is nothing to appreciate: one's place in the society really *is* unacceptable. Again, it is Keniston who most clearly articulates the relevance of this alternative. There he shows conditions which are conducive to social pathology. In his analysis, rapid, chronic social change is the key, for it contributes to the irrelevance of parents as sources of positive identities, and to a cult of the present. Also produced by these kinds of social changes are (1) a fragmentation of work and of communities in ways that make the development of a stable identity more difficult, and (2) family tensions which are reflected in the difficulty that men have in reconciling the demands of career and family and that women have in the severe frustrations of their artistic and intellectual strivings because of the sheer fact of motherhood.

With rapid social change, the potential for self-contradiction increases. It is a commonplace idea of sociological theory that social change will have unanticipated consequences. Because any change, planned or not, has this potential to produce results that conflict with other practices or values of the society, we sometimes must live with our new practices for a generation or more to know just what they will bring. An example of unintended and undesired consequences of a new practice is described in Bettelheim's *Children of the Dream* (1969), which deals with what the second- and third-generation children of the Israeli kibbutzim are like. While the intent of the communal child-rearing was to reduce the extremely close family ties and the subtle controlling power of the family (now almost a cliché in the form of the "Jewish-mother" stereotype), Bettelheim has found evidence that the collective child rearing has resulted in a person who is less guilt-ridden and less psychologically disturbed but also more shallow and less complex.

In Keniston's view the prevalence of alienation and protest among those students in the best social positions—from affluent backgrounds, at the best colleges and universities—argues for the social pathology thesis. The depth of the alienation, identity crises, and despair are such that the society itself must be contributing to the problem. In a recent article on student drug use (1969) he says:

> Political and historical events do not have a direct, one-to-one relationship with drug use: the war in Vietnam does not *cause* students to smoke marijuana or experiment with LSD. But the political climate of the past few years has created a negative view of the possibility of meaningful involvement within the established institutions of the society, at the same time that it has convinced many students that society is in desperate need of reform. This climate of opinion in turn contributes to the assumption that if meaning, excitement, and dignity are to be found in the world, they must be found within one's own cranium. Drug use can indeed be a kind of cop-out, not from perversity or laziness, but simply because there seems to be no other alternative. Student drug use is indeed a commentary upon American society, but it is above all an indirect criticism of our society's inability to offer the young exciting, honorable and effective ways of using their intelligence and idealism to reform our society.

While the relative contribution of the two sources—personal and societal—is unclear, we have a situation in which too few people appreciate what the society actually does have to offer them, and in which our society, to some extent, really does offer bitterly conflicting values and social practices. And it is just this situation that shows us the relationship of *alienation* and *commitment* to each other and to a way of life. To be alienated from one's way of life is to go through the motions of participating in some (or all) of its practices while seeing no meaning or value in them. For example, the individual gets a job and works not because work is a human good containing the possibility of self-realization, productivity, and service to others but simply because he must live. The commitments normally associated with one's work are nonexistent, or they are held only mechanically. Alienation is, therefore, a distinctive kind of identity confusion that has its roots jointly in the individual's experience and capacities and in the society's structuring of his experience and opportunities.

Sense of Identity and One's Place in Society

It is a commonplace finding in research on the self-concept that for most people, status concepts such as age, sex, religion, career, and the like play a central role in their concepts of themselves—of "who they are." A person tends to think of himself in terms of the positions he occupies and the roles he has in the society. Such a fact raises a number of interesting questions: (1) What is the relation between self-concept and sense of identity? (2) What is the role of ideology in identity development? (3) What explains the dramatic changes of identity that occasionally occur? Let us deal with these in order.

Identity and Self-Concept

In many respects the notions of self-concept and identity have the same conceptual implications, but in one important way they differ. The self-concept—how a particular person views himself and how he treats himself—can be reproduced by a list of characteristics and statuses. An identity, however, involves a unity of the self as object and actor. In the same way that a physical object is a unity—not a fragment, part, or incomplete element of another structure—the self has a unity and completeness. So conceptually a sense of identity includes the idea of the unified totality, which no list of characteristics could ever capture.

One of the favorite assessment devices for self-concept involves having the person answer the question, "Who am I?" by listing 20 items. One of the common complaints by persons taking this instrument is, "But I am more than a list of the 20 most important things about me." And of course the complaint is justified. But though the list structure is inappropriate to capture that sense of unity, it is needed for specifying what identity crisis the person is suffering or in what respect he is alienated; thus the classic self-concept research can be useful in understanding identities.

Ideology and Identity

One might wonder whether a person at the bottom of the social order— say, an untouchable in nineteenth-century India—could have anything but a negative view of himself. The answer is that, even though his position is the lowest in the society, he may yet have a partially positive self-image and identity through sharing his society's ideology. In fact, one might argue that only brute force could hold together a society with severe inequities if an ideology did not exist which justified the social order and which was accepted by most of its members. In the case of the untouchable, the Hindu religious way of life contains the possibility of reincarnation in animal and human forms. Thus the lowly untouchable was still a person with the possibility, in the next life, of a much higher social station and the ultimate possibility of perfection or oneness with God and nature (Nirvana).

Also important is the fact that a social oder, too, is a totality. Just as the lowest position on any team is still an intrinsic part of the team, so even the lowest social position is required by the society for it to exist in its current form. An ideology or religion that justifies the entire way of life will, then, contain a justification for even the lowest social position and a statement of its importance.

But just as an ideology provides the resources for reconciling people to the social order, so it can provide the resources for rebellion, protest, and reform. It is the youth who take the values of justice, equality, and moral commitment seriously who are most likely to protest the discrepancies they see between what is preached and what is practiced.

Erikson, in his studies of Luther and Gandhi, has shown how the creative resolution of identity crises can be the source of significant alterations of a way of life. Luther's innovation was the idea of the freedom of the human spirit and the pre-eminence of the individual conscience over the structure of the Church—ideas which were to fuel the fires both of the reformation and, later, of liberalism. Gandhi's innovation was the idea of militant nonviolence as a tool of social revolution by the weak. In both cases, the ideas, when acted upon, were to lead to significant political and social change.

Conversions and Dramatic Identity Changes

Perhaps no other aspect of identity is more puzzling than the dramatic changes of the convert to a new way of life. Malcolm X (1964), a hustler, drug addict, and thief, down and out in jail, was converted to Black Muslimism and became a Puritan in his gratification of physical pleasures and an extraordinarily adept preacher, proselytizer, and political debater. Furthermore, he had the psychological flexibility to profit from his experiences in Mecca and with white student audiences to begin to rethink the Muslim separatist doctrine. Bertrand Russell, after devoting ten years to intense intellectual work (with Whitehead) on the *Principia Mathematica,* largely withdrawn from society and for most of the period without any intimate relations (emotional or sexual) with his first wife, came out of his isolation into a love affair and into an active life of political, social, and moral combat. In his autobiography, Russell (1968) comments on some of the changes he underwent as a result.

> Ottoline had a great influence upon me, which was almost wholly beneficial. She laughed at me when I behaved like a don or a prig, and when I was dictatorial in conversation. She gradually cured me of the belief that I was seething with appalling wickedness which could only be kept under by an iron self-control. She made me less self-centered, and less self-righteous. Her sense of humour was very great, and I became aware of the danger of rousing it unintentionally. She made me much less of a Puritan, and much less censorious than I had been. And of course the mere fact of happy love after the empty years made everything easier. Many men are afraid of being influenced by women, but as far as my experience goes, this is a foolish fear. It seems to me that men need women, and women need men, mentally as much as physically. For my part, I owe a great deal to women whom I have loved, and without them I should have been far more narrow-minded.

Identity changes can range all the way from the major sort experienced by Malcolm X and Martin Luther through the moderate changes described by Russell to minor changes such as the giving up of a bad habit or vice like cigarette smoking or profanity.

Anthony Wallace (1961), the cultural anthropologist, described the general features of a case of identity change that is typical. The focus in this excerpt is not an individual, as in the illustrations we have used so far, but an entire people.

> The severe disorganization of a sociocultural system may be caused by the impact of any one or combination of a variety of forces which push the system beyond the limits of equilibrium. Some of these forces are: climatic or faunal changes which destroy the economic basis of its existence; epidemic disease which grossly alters the population structure; wars which exhaust the society's resources of manpower or result in defeat or invasion; internal conflict among interest groups which results in extreme disadvantage for at least one group; and, very commonly, a position of perceived subordination

and inferiority with respect to an adjacent society. The latter, by the use of more or less coercion (or even no coercion at all, as in situations where the mere example set by the dominant society raises too-high levels of aspiration), brings about uncoordinated cultural changes. Under conditions of disorganization, the system, from the standpoint of at least some of its members, is unable to make possible the reliable satisfaction of certain values which are held to be essential to continued well-being and self-respect. The [world view] of a culturally disillusioned person, accordingly, is an image of a world that is unpredictable, or barren in its simplicity, or both. His mood (depending on the precise nature of the disorganization) will be one of panic-stricken anxiety, shame, guilt, depression, or apathy.

An example of the kind of disorganization to which we refer is given by the two thousand or so Seneca Indians of New York at the close of the eighteenth century. Among these people, a supreme value attached to the conception of the absolutely free and autonomous individual, unconstrained by and indifferent to his own and others' pain and hardship. This individual was capable of free indulgence of emotional impulses but, in crises, freely subordinated his own wishes to the needs of his community. Among the men, especially, this ego-ideal was central in personality organization. Men defined the roles of hunting, of warfare, and of statesmanship as the conditions of achievement of this value; thus, the stereotypes of "the good hunter," "the brave warrior," and "the forest statesman" were the images of masculine success. But the 43 years from 1754, when the French and Indian War began, to 1797, when the Seneca sold their last hunting grounds and became largely confined to tiny, isolated reservations, brought with them changes in their situation which made achievement of these ideals virtually impossible. The good hunter could no longer hunt; the game was scarce, and it was almost suicidally dangerous to stray far from the reservation among the numerous hostile white men. The brave warrior could no longer fight, being under-supplied, abandoned by his allies, and his women and children threatened by growing military might of the United States. The forest statesman was an object of contempt, and this disillusionment was perhaps more shattering than the rest. The Iroquois chiefs, for nearly a century, had been able to play off British and French, then Americans and British, against one another, extorting supplies and guarantees of territorial immunity from both sides. They had maintained an extensive system of alliances and hegemonies among surrounding tribal groups. Suddenly they were shorn of their power. White men no longer spoke of the League of the Iroquois with respect; their western Indian dependents and allies regarded them as cowards for having made peace with the Americans.

The initial Seneca response to the progress of sociocultural disorganization was quasi-pathological: many became drunkards; the fear of witches increased; squabbling factions were unable to achieve a common policy. But a revitalization movement developed in 1799, based on the religious revelations reported by one of the disillusioned forest statesman, one Handsome Lake, who preached a code of patterned religious and cultural reform.

The drinking of whiskey was proscribed; witchcraft was to be stamped out; various outmoded rituals and prevalent sins were to be abandoned. In addition, various syncretic cultural reforms, amounting to a reorientation of the socioeconomic system, were to be undertaken, including the adoption of agriculture (hitherto a feminine calling) by the men, and the focusing of kinship responsibilities within the nuclear family (rather than in the clan and lineage). The general acceptance of Handsome Lake's Code, within a few years, wrought seemingly miraculous changes. A group of sober, devout, partly literate, and technologically up-to-date farming communities suddenly replaced the demoralized slums in the wilderness.

Such dramatic transformations are, as a matter of historical fact, very common in human history, and probably have been the medium of as much culture change as the slower equilibrium processes. (pp. 144–146)[1]

In the more dramatic cases of identity change, the change is a matter of adopting (Malcolm X) or creating a new way of life (Handsome Lake and Luther) with a basis for self-respect. Wallace continues.

Revitalization depends on the successful completion of the following functions:

1. *Formulation of a code.* An individual, or a group of individuals, constructs a new, utopian image of sociocultural organization. This model is a blueprint of an ideal society or "goal culture." Contrasted with the goal culture is the existing culture, which is presented as inadequate or evil in certain respects. Connecting the existing culture and the goal culture is a transfer culture: a system of operations which, if faithfully carried out, will transform the existing culture into the goal culture. Failure to institute the transfer operations will, according to the code, result in either the perpetuation of the existing misery or the ultimate destruction of the society (if not of the whole world). Not infrequently the code, or the core of it, is formulated by one individual in the course of a hallucinatory revelation; such prophetic experiences are apt to launch religiously oriented movements, since the source of the revelation is apt to be regarded as a supernatural being. Nonhallucinatory formulations usually are found in politically oriented movements. In either case, the formulation of the code constitutes a reformulation of the author's own [world view], and often brings to him a renewed confidence in the future and a remission of the complaints. . . .

2. *Communication.* The formulators of the code preach the code to other people in an evangelistic spirit. The aim of the communication is to make converts. The code is offered as the means of spiritual salvation for the individual and of cultural salvation for the society. Promises of benefit to the target population need not be immediate or materialistic, for the basis of the code's appeal is the attractiveness of identification with a more

---

[1] From *Culture and Personality* by Anthony Wallace, pp. 144–146 and 148–149. Copyright © 1961 by Random House, Inc. Reprinted by permission of the publisher.

highly organized system, with all that this implies in the way of self-respect. Indeed, in view of the extensiveness of the changes in values often implicit in such codes, appeal to currently held values would often be pointless. Religious codes offer spiritual salvation, identification with God, elect status; political codes offer honor, fame; the respect of society for sacrifices made in its interest. But refusal to accept the code is usually defined as placing the listener in immediate spiritual, as well as material, peril with respect to his existing values. In small societies, the target population may be the entire community; but in more complex societies, the message may be aimed only at certain groups deemed eligible for participation. . . .

Wallace's other characteristics of a successful revitalization movement need not be given here in detail. They deal with conversions, social organization, and the eventual routinization of the code. A very useful source for the study of identity change specifically in college students is Madison's *Personality Development in College* (1969).

Conclusion

A central theme here has been the connection between one's sense of identity and the ways of life available to him. The development of a sense of identity requires not only inner values and a sense of selfhood but a commitment to certain social practices and to the implications of certain standards of performance and evaluation. To appreciate these practices is to be inclined to participate in the way of life that embodies them. If a significant minority does not appreciate the practices of the larger society, then the conditions are ripe for social disorganization and identity confusion. When these conditions exist, one of the possible results is ideological change and the creation of new identities. Whether or how generally we are now at that stage in our society is difficult to say.

Readings

1. Butchvarov, Panayot. "The Self and Perceptions: A Study in Human Philosophy," *The Philosophical Quarterly* 9 (1959).
2. Flew, Antony. "Locke and the Problem of Personal Identity," *Philosophy* XXVI (1951).
3. Frondizi, Risieri. *The Nature of the Self.* Carbondale, Ill.: Southern Illinois Univ. Press, 1971. A discussion of Locke and Hume.
4. Gould, J. and Iorio, J. *Love, Sex and Identity.* San Francisco: Boyd and Fraser, 1972, pp. 41–51.
5. Ogilvy, James. *Self and World.* New York: Harcourt, 1973.

6. Penelhum, T. "Hume on Personal Identity." *The Philosophical Review* LXIV (1955), 571–589.

three

How Is Truth Established?

23

By Correspondence

Bertrand Russell (1872–1970), the grandson of Lord John Russell, a prime minister under Queen Victoria, was born in Wales. He studied mathematics and philosophy at Trinity College, Cambridge from 1890 to 1894. He was a fellow at Trinity from 1895 to 1901, and a lecturer in philosophy there from 1910 to 1916. In 1916, Russell was dismissed from his position because of his pacifist activities. Then, in 1918, he was sentenced to six months in prison because of an allegedly libelous article in which he expressed his opposition to World War I and his desire for peace. Russell was a fellow of the Royal Society, an honorary fellow of the British Academy, and a recipient of the Order of Merit. He was awarded the Nobel Prize for literature in 1950. In the area of logic, Russell has written *Principles of Mathematics* (1903), *Principia Mathematica* (with A. N. Whitehead; three volumes, 1910–13), and *Introduction to Mathematical Philosophy* (1919). His works in epistemology and metaphysics include *Our Knowledge of the External World* (1914), *The Analysis of Matter* (1927), and *Human Knowledge, Its Scope and Limits* (1948). Among his books on social issues are *Marriage and Morals* (1929), and *Education and the Social Order* (1932).

Centuries ago, when Jesus stood trial before him, Pilate asked, "What is truth?" Before this, Socrates, Plato, and others sought to answer the same question. Philosophers are still seeking the answer.

In attempting to determine which beliefs are true, philosophers have mainly relied on three tests of truth. Russell holds to the correspondence theory of truth. He believes that what we say is true if it corresponds to reality. There is a realm of *facts* independent of any of us ("San Francisco is in California," "my mother is alive," etc.), and our beliefs are *true* if they correspond with these facts.

─── TO STUDY

1. According to Russell, what is the difference between our knowledge of things and our knowledge of truth?
2. In this chapter, of what basic question is Russell seeking the meaning?
3. What are the three requisites of any theory of truth?
4. What is Russell's criticism of the coherence theory of truth?
5. According to Russell, what distinguishes a true judgment from a false one?

Our knowledge of truths, unlike our knowledge of things, has an opposite, namely *error*. So far as things are concerned, we may know them or not know them, but there is no positive state of mind which can be described as erroneous knowledge of things, so long, at any rate, as we confine ourselves to knowledge by acquaintance. Whatever we are acquainted with must be something: we may draw wrong inference from our acquaintance, but the acquaintance itself cannot be deceptive. Thus there is no dualism as regards acquaintance. But as regards knowledge of truths, there is a dualism. We may believe what is false as well as what is true. We know that on very many subjects different people hold different and incompatible opinions: hence some beliefs must be erroneous. Since erroneous beliefs are often held just as strongly as true beliefs, it becomes a difficult question how they are to be distinguished from true beliefs. How are we to know, in a given case, that our belief is not erroneous? This is a question of the very greatest difficulty, to which no completely satisfactory answer is possible. There is, however, a preliminary question which is rather less difficult, and that is: What do we *mean* by truth and falsehood? It is this preliminary question which is to be considered in this chapter.

In this chapter we are not asking how we can know whether a belief is true or false: we are asking what is meant by the question whether a belief is true or false. It is to be hoped that a clear answer to this question may help us to obtain an answer to the question what beliefs are true, but for

---

From "Truth and Falsehood" in *The Problems of Philosophy* by Bertrand Russell (Oxford: The Clarendon Press, 1912). Reprinted by permission of the publisher.

the present we ask only "What is truth?" and "What is falsehood?" not "What beliefs are true?" and "What beliefs are false?" It is very important to keep these different questions entirely separate, since any confusion between them is sure to produce an answer which is not really applicable to either.

There are three points to observe in the attempt to discover the nature of truth, three requisites which any theory must fulfill.

(1) Our theory of truth must be such as to admit of its opposite, falsehood. A good many philosophers have failed adequately to satisfy this condition: they have constructed theories according to which all our thinking ought to have been true, and have then had the greatest difficulty in finding a place for falsehood. In this respect our theory of belief must differ from our theory of acquaintance, since in the case of acquaintance it was not necessary to take account of any opposite.

(2) It seems fairly evident that if there were no beliefs there could be no falsehood, and no truth either, in the sense in which truth is correlative to falsehood. If we imagine a world of mere matter, there would be no room for falsehood in such a world, and although it would contain what may be called "facts," it would not contain any truths, in the sense in which truths are things of the same kind as falsehoods. In fact, truth and falsehood are properties of beliefs and statements: hence a world of mere matter, since it would contain no beliefs or statements, would also contain no truth or falsehood.

(3) But, as against what we have just said, it is to be observed that the truth or falsehood of a belief always depends upon something which lies outside the belief itself. If I believe that Charles I. died on the scaffold, I believe truly, not because of any intrinsic quality of my belief, which could be discovered by merely examining the belief, but because of an historical event which happened two and a half centuries ago. If I believe that Charles I. died in his bed, I believe falsely: no degree of vividness in my belief, or of care in arriving at it, prevents it from being false, again because of what happened long ago, and not because of any intrinsic property of my belief. Hence, although truth and falsehood are properties of beliefs, they are properties dependent upon the relations of the beliefs to other things, not upon any internal quality of the beliefs.

The third of the above requisites leads us to adopt the view—which has on the whole been commonest among philosophers—that truth consists in some form of correspondence between belief and fact. It is, however, by no means an easy matter to discover a form of correspondence to which there are no irrefutable objections. By this partly—and partly by the feeling that, if truth consists in a correspondence of thought with something outside thought, thought can never know when truth has been attained—many philosophers have been led to try to find some definition of truth which shall not consist in relation to something wholly outside belief. The most important attempt at a definition of this sort is the theory that truth consists in *coherence.* It is said that the mark of falsehood is failure to cohere in the body of our beliefs, and that it is the essence of a truth to form part of the completely rounded system which is The Truth.

There is, however, a great difficulty in this view, or rather two great difficulties. The first is that there is no reason to suppose that only *one* coherent body of beliefs is possible. It may be that, with sufficient imagination, a novelist might invent a past for the world that would perfectly fit on to what we know, and yet be quite different from the real past. In more scientific matters, it is certain that there are often two or more hypotheses which account for all the known facts on some subject, and although, in such cases, men of science endeavor to find facts which will rule out all the hypotheses except one, there is no reason why they should always succeed.

In philosophy, again, it seems not uncommon for two rival hypotheses to be both able to account for all the facts. Thus, for example, it is possible that life is one long dream, and that the outer world has only that degree of reality that the objects of dreams have; but although such a view does not seem inconsistent with known facts, there is no reason to prefer it to the common-sense view, according to which other people and things do really exist. Thus coherence as the definition of truth fails because there is no proof that there can be only one coherent system.

The other objection to this definition of truth is that it assumes the meaning of "coherence" known, whereas, in fact, "coherence" presupposes the truth of the laws of logic. Two propositions are coherent when both may be true, and are incoherent when one at least must be false. Now in order to know whether two propositions can both be true, we must know such truths as the law of contradiction. For example, the two propositions "this tree is a beech" and "this tree is not a beech," are not coherent, because of the law of contradiction. But if the law of contradiction itself were subjected to the test of coherence, we should find that, if we choose to suppose it false, nothing will any longer be incoherent with anything else. Thus the laws of logic supply the skeleton or framework within which the test of coherence applies, and they themselves cannot be established by this test.

For the above two reasons, coherence cannot be accepted as giving the *meaning* of truth, though it is often a most important *test* of truth after a certain amount of truth has become known.

Hence we are driven back to *correspondence with fact* as constituting the nature of truth. It remains to define precisely what we mean by "fact," and what is the nature of the correspondence which must subsist between belief and fact, in order that belief may be true.

In accordance with our three requisites, we have to seek a theory of truth which (1) allows truth to have an opposite, namely falsehood, (2) makes truth a property of beliefs, but (3) makes it a property wholly dependent upon the relation of the beliefs to outside things.

The necessity of allowing for falsehood makes it impossible to regard belief as a relation of the mind to a single object, which could be said to be what is believed. If belief were so regarded, we should find that, like acquaintance, it would not admit of the opposition of truth and falsehood, but would have to be always true. This may be made clear by examples. Othello believes falsely that Desdemona loves Cassio. We cannot say that this belief consists in a relation to a single object, "Desdemona's love for Cassio," for if there were such an object, the belief would be true. There is in fact no such object, and therefore Othello cannot have any relation to such an object. Hence his belief cannot possibly consist in a relation to this object.

It might be said that his belief is a relation to a different object, namely "that Desdemona loves Cassio"; but it is almost as difficult to suppose that there is such an object as this, when Desdemona does not love Cassio, as it was to suppose that there is "Desdemona's love for Cassio." Hence it will be better to seek for a theory of belief which does not make it consist in a relation of the mind to a single object.

It is common to think of relations as though they always held between *two* terms, but in fact this is not always the case. Some relations demand three terms, some four, and so on. Take, for instance, the relation "between." So long as only two terms come in, the relation "between" is impossible: three terms are the smallest number that render it possible. York is between London and Edinburgh; but if London and Edinburgh were the only places in the world, there could be nothing which was between one place and another. Similarly *jealousy* requires three people: there can be no such relation that does not involve three at least. Such a proposition as "A wishes B to promote C's marriage with D" involves a relation of four terms; that is to say, A and B and C and D all come in, and the relation involved cannot be expressed otherwise than in a form involving all four. Instances might be multiplied indefinitely, but enough has been said to show that there are relations which require more than two terms before they can occur.

The relation involved in *judging* or *believing* must, if falsehood is to be duly allowed for, be taken to be a relation between several terms, not between two. When Othello believes that Desdemona loves Cassio, he must not have before his mind a single object, "Desdemona's love for Cassio," or "that Desdemona loves Cassio," for that would require that there should be objective falsehoods, which subsist independently of any minds; and this, though not logically refutable, is a theory to be avoided if possible. Thus it is easier to account for falsehood if we take judgment to be a relation in which the mind and the various objects concerned all occur severally; that is to say, Desdemona and loving and Cassio must all be terms in the relation which subsists when Othello believes that Desdemona loves Cassio. This relation, therefore, is a relation of four terms, since Othello also is one of the terms of the relation. When we say that it is a relation of four terms, we do not mean that Othello has a certain relation to Desdemona, and has the same relation to loving and also to Cassio. This may be true of some other relation than believing; but believing, plainly, is not a relation which Othello has to *each* of the three terms concerned, but to *all* of them together: there is only one example of the relation of believing involved, but this one example knits together four terms. Thus the actual occurrence, at the moment when Othello is entertaining his belief, is that the relation called "believing" is knitting together into one complex whole the four terms Othello, Desdemona, loving, and Cassio. What is called belief or judgment is nothing but this relation of believing or judging, which relates a mind to several things other than itself. An *act* of belief or of judgment is the occurrence between certain terms at some particular time, of the relation of believing or judging.

We are now in a position to understand what it is that distinguishes a true judgment from a false one. For this purpose we will adopt certain definitions. In every act of judgment there is a mind which judges, and there are terms concerning which it judges. We will call the mind the *subject* in the judgment, and the remaining terms the *objects*. Thus, when Othello judges that Desdemona loves Cassio, Othello is the subject, while the objects are Desdemona and loving and Cassio. The subject and the objects together are called the *constituents* of the judgment. It will be observed that the relation of judging has what is called a "sense" or "direction." We may say, metaphorically, that it puts its objects in a certain *order*, which we may indicate by means of the order of the words in the sentence. (In an inflected language, the same thing will be indicated by inflections, e.g., by the difference between nominative and accusative.) Othello's judgment that Cassio loves Desdemona differs from his judgment that Desdemona loves Cassio, in spite of the fact that it consists of the same constituents, because the relation of judging places the constituents in a different order in the two cases. Similarly, if Cassio judges that Desdemona loves Othello, the constituents of the judgment are still the same, but their order is different. This property of having a "sense" or "direction" is one which the relation of judging shares with all other relations. The "sense" of relations is the ultimate source of order and series and a host of mathematical concepts; but we need not concern ourselves further with this aspect.

We spoke of the relation called "judging" or "believing" as knitting together into one complex whole the subject and the objects. In this respect, judging is exactly like every other relation. Whenever a relation holds between two or more terms, it unites the terms into a complex whole. If Othello loves Desdemona, there is such a complex whole as "Othello's love for Desdemona." The terms united by the relation may be themselves complex, or may be simple, but the whole which results from their being united must be complex. Wherever there is a relation which relates certain terms, there is a complex object formed of the union of those terms; and conversely, wherever there is a complex object, there is a relation which relates its constituents. When an act of believing occurs, there is a complex, in which "believing" is the uniting relation, and subject and objects are arranged in a certain order by the "sense" of the relation of believing. Among the objects, as we saw in considering "Othello believes that Desdemona loves Cassio," one must be a relation—in this instance, the relation "loving." But this relation, as it occurs in the act of believing, is not the relation which creates the unity of the complex whole consisting of the subject and the objects. The relation "loving," as it occurs in the act of believing, is one of the objects—it is a brick in the structure, not the cement. The cement is the relation "believing." When the belief is *true*, there is another complex unity, in which the relation which was one of the objects of the belief relates the other objects. Thus, e.g., if Othello believes *truly* that Desdemona loves Cassio, then there is a complex unity, "Desdemona's love for Cassio," which is composed exclusively of the *objects* of the belief, in the same order as they had in the belief, with the relation which was one of the objects occurring now as the cement that binds together the other objects of the belief. On the other hand, when a belief is *false*, there is no such complex unity composed only of the objects of the belief. If Othello believes *falsely* that Desdemona loves Cassio, then there is no such complex unity as "Desdemona's love for Cassio."

Thus a belief is *true* when it *corresponds* to a certain associated complex, and *false* when it does not. Assuming, for the sake of definiteness, that the objects of the belief are two terms and a relation, the terms being put in a certain order by the "sense" of the believing, then if the two terms in that order are united by the relation into a complex, the belief is true; if not, it is false. This constitutes the definition of truth and falsehood that we were in search of. Judging or believing is a certain complex unity of which a mind is a constituent; if the remaining constituents, taken in the order which they have in the belief, form a complex unity, then the belief is true; if not, it is false.

Thus although truth and falsehood are properties of beliefs, yet they are in a sense extrinsic properties, for the condition of the truth of a belief is something not involving beliefs, or (in general) any mind at all, but only the *objects* of the belief. A mind, which believes, believes truly when there is a *corresponding* complex not involving the mind, but only its objects. This correspondence ensures truth, and its absence entails falsehood. Hence we account simultaneously for the two facts that beliefs (*a*) depend on minds for their *existence,* (*b*) do not depend on minds for their *truth.*

We may restate our theory as follows: If we take such a belief as "Othello believes that Desdemona loves Cassio," we will call Desdemona and Cassio the *object-terms,* and loving the *object-relation.* If there is a complex unity "Desdemona's love for Cassio," consisting of the object-terms related by the object-relation in the same order as they have in the belief, then this complex unity is called the *fact corresponding to the belief.* Thus a belief is true when there is a corresponding fact, and is false when there is no corresponding fact.

It will be seen that minds do not *create* truth or falsehood. They create beliefs, but when once the beliefs are created, the mind cannot make them true or false, except in the special case where they concern future things which are within the power of the person believing, such as catching trains. What makes a belief true is a *fact,* and this fact does not (except in exceptional cases) in any way involve the mind of the person who has the belief.

THINK ABOUT

1. "We have to live today by what truth we can get today, and be ready tomorrow to call it falsehood."

   William James

2. "If you cannot convince me that there is some kind of knowable ultimate reality, or if you cannot convince me that there are certain absolute values by which I can live my life, I shall commit psychological suicide. That is, either convince me that there is 'one truth' or one right way of doing things, or I shall conclude that everything is meaningless and I will not try any more."

   Joseph Royce

3. How would you answer the student who asked, "How do we know whether the intelligent life is really the best?"

4. State as clearly as you can the distinction among reason, rationalism, and rationalization. Why do people frequently confuse these terms?

5. In court, witnesses are asked to swear "to tell the truth, the whole truth, and nothing but the truth." What assumptions underlie this oath? Are you able to accept these assumptions?

24

By Coherence

Francis H. Bradley (1846–1924) was the most distinguished of the British Absolute Idealists who dominated Anglo-American philosophy in the late nineteenth century.

Bradley holds to the coherence theory of truth and he believes that the correspondence theory of truth is inadequate. He contends that our judgments are not like the physical things to which they refer. Furthermore, how can we know "the reality" to which our beliefs correspond? The coherence theory of truth is better. It maintains that if our ideas are consistent or comprehensive, then they should be said to be true since there is no other way of testing them.

─TO STUDY

1. According to Bradley, what is the test of truth we apply to facts of perception and memory?
2. In what sense is the doctrine that perception gives us infallible truth sound, and in what sense is it defective?
3. On what grounds is my experience solid? Why does no fact possess an absolute right?
4. How do we establish facts of memory and of history?
5. What are the characteristics of Bradley's own theory of truth?

. . . What I maintain is that in the case of facts of perception and memory the test [of truth] which we do apply, and which we must apply, is that of system. I contend that this test works satisfactorily, and that no other test will work. And I argue in consequence that there are no judgements of sense which are in principle infallible. . . .

The reason for maintaining independent facts and infallible judgements, as I understand it, is twofold. (1) Such data, it may be said, can be actually shown. And (2) in any case they must exist, since without them the intelligence cannot work. . . .

(1) I doubt my ability to do justice to the position of the man who claims to show ultimate given facts exempt from all possible error. In the case of any datum of sensation or feeling, to prove that we have this wholly unmodified by what is called 'apperception' seems a hopeless undertaking. And how far it is supposed that such a negative can be proved I do not know. What, however, is meant must be this, that we somehow and somewhere have verifiable facts of perception and memory, and also judgements, free from all chance of error.

I will begin hereby recalling a truth familiar but often forgotten. . . . In your search for independent facts and for infallible truths you may go so low that, when you have descended beyond the level of error, you find yourself below the level of any fact or of any truth which you can use. What you seek is particular facts of perception or memory, but what you get may be something not answering to that character. I will go on to give instances of what I mean, and I think that in every case we shall do well to ask this question, 'What on the strength of our ultimate fact are we able to contradict?'

(a) If we take the instance of simple unrelated sensations or feelings, a, b, c—supposing that there are such things—what judgement would such a fact enable us to deny? We could on the strength of this fact deny the denial that a,b and c exist in any way, manner or sense. But surely this is not the kind of independent fact of which we are in search.

(b) From this let us pass to the case of a complex feeling containing, at once and together, both a and b. On the ground of this we can deny the statement that a and b cannot or do not ever anyhow co-exist in feeling. This is an advance, but it surely leaves us far short of our goal.

(c) What we want, I presume, is something that at once is infallible and that also can be called a particular fact of perception or memory. And we want, in the case of perception, something that would be called a fact

From "On Truth and Coherence" in *Essays on Truth and Reality* by Francis Herbert Bradley (Oxford: The Clarendon Press, 1914), pp. 202–218. Reprinted by permission of the publisher.

for observation. We do not seem to reach this fact until we arrive some-where about the level of 'I am here and now having a sensation or complex of sensations of such or such a kind.' The goal is reached; but at this point, unfortunately, the judgement has become fallible, so far at least as it really states particular truth.

(α) In such a judgement it is in the first place hard to say what is meant by the 'I.' If, however, we go beyond feeling far enough to mean a self with such or such a real existence in time, then memory is involved, and the judgement at once, I should urge, becomes fallible. . . . Thus the statement made in the judgement is liable to error, or else the statement does not convey particular truth.

(β) And this fatal dilemma holds good when applied to the 'now' and 'here.' If these words mean a certain special place in a certain special series or order, they are liable to mistake. But, if they fall short of this meaning, then they fail to state individual fact. My feeling is, I agree, not subject to error in the proper sense of that term, but on the other side my feeling does not of itself deliver truth. And the process which gets from it a deliverance as to individual fact is fallible.

Everywhere such fact depends on construction. And we have here to face not only the possibility of what would commonly be called mistaken interpretation. We have in addition the chance of actual sense-hallucina-tion. And, worse than this, we have the far-reaching influence of abnormal suggestion and morbid fixed idea. This influence may stop short of halluci-nation, and yet may vitiate the memory and the judgement to such an extent that there remains no practical difference between idea and perceived fact. And, in the face of these possibilities, it seems idle to speak of perceptions and memories secure from all chance of error. Or on the other side banish the chance of error, and with what are you left? You then have something which (as we have seen) goes no further than to warrant the assertion that such and such elements can and do co-exist—somehow and somewhere, or again that such or such a judgement happens—without any regard to its truth and without any specification of its psychical context. And no one surely will contend that with this we have particular fact.

The doctrine that perception gives us infallible truth rests on a founda-tion which in part is sound and in part fatally defective. That what is felt is felt, and cannot, so far as felt, be mistaken—so much as this must be accepted. But the view that, when I say 'this,' 'now,' 'here,' or 'my,' what I feel, when so speaking, is carried over intact into my judgement, and that my judgement in consequence is exempt from error, seems wholly indefen-sible. It survives, I venture to think, only because it never has understood its complete refutation. That which I designate, is not and cannot be carried over into my judgement. The judgement may in a sense answer to that which I feel, but none the less it fails to contain and to convey my feeling. And on the other hand, so far as it succeeds in expressing my meaning, the judgement does this in a way which makes it liable to error. Or, to put it otherwise, the perceived truth, to be of any use, must be particularized. So far as it is stated in a general form, it contains not only that which you meant to say but also, and just as much, the opposite of that which you meant. And to contend for the infallibility of such a truth seems futile. On the other side so far as your truth really is individualized, so far as it is placed in a special construction and vitally related to its context, to the same extent the element of interpretation or implication is added. And, with this element obviously comes the possibility of mistake. And we have seen above that, viewed psychologically, particular judgements of perception immune from all chance of error seem hardly tenable.

(2) I pass now to the second reason for accepting infallible data of perception. Even if we cannot show these (it is urged) we are bound to assume them. For in their absence our knowledge has nothing on which to stand, and this want of support results in total scepticism.

It is possible of course here to embrace both premises and conclusion, and to argue that scepticism is to be preferred to an untrue assumption. And such a position I would press on the notice of those who uphold infallible judgements of sense and memory. But personally I am hardly concerned in this issue, for I reject both the conclusion and the premises together. Such infallible and incorrigible judgements are really not required for our knowledge, and, since they cannot be shown, we must not say that they exist. . . .

I agree that we depend vitally on the sense-world, that our material comes from it, and that apart from it knowledge could not begin. To this world, I agree, we have for ever to return, not only to gain new matter but to confirm and maintain the old. I agree that to impose order from without on sheer disorder would be wholly impracticable, and that, if my sense-world were disorderly beyond a certain point, my intelligence would not exist. And further I agree that we cannot suppose it possible that *all* the judgements of perception and memory which for me come first, could in fact for me be corrected. I cannot, that is, imagine the world of my experience to be so modified that in the end none of these accepted facts should be left standing. But so far, I hasten to add, we have not yet come to the real issue. There is still a chasm between such admissions and the conclusion that there are judgements of sense which possess truth absolute and infallible.

We meet here a false doctrine largely due to a misleading metaphor. My known world is taken to be a construction built upon such and such foundations. It is argued, therefore, to be in principle a superstructure which rests upon these supports. You can go on adding to it no doubt, but only so long as the supports remain; and, unless they remain, the whole building comes down. But the doctrine, I have to contend, is untenable, and the metaphor ruinously inapplicable. The foundation in truth is provisional merely. In order to begin my construction I take the foundation as absolute—so much certainly is true. But that my construction continues to rest on the beginnings of my knowledge is a conclusion which does not follow. It does not follow that, if these are allowed to be fallible, the whole building collapses. For it is in another sense that my world rests upon the data of perception.

My experience is solid, not so far as it is a superstructure but so far as in short it is a system. My object is to have a world as comprehensive and coherent as possible, and, in order to attain this object, I have not only to reflect but perpetually to have recourse to the materials of sense. I must go to this source both to verify the matter which is old and also to increase it by what is new. And in this way I must depend upon the judgements of perception. Now it is agreed that, if I am to have an orderly world, I cannot possibly accept all 'facts.' Some of these must be relegated, as they are, to the world of error, whether we succeed or fail in modifying and correcting them. And the view which I advocate takes them all as in principle fallible. On the other hand, that view denies that there is any necessity for absolute facts of sense. Facts for it are true, we may say, just so far as they work, just so far as they contribute to the order of experience. If by taking certain judgements of perception as true, I can get more system into my world, then these 'facts' are so far true, and if by taking certain 'facts' as errors I can order my experience better, then so far these 'facts' are errors. And there is no 'fact' which possesses an absolute right. Certainly there are truths with which I begin and which I personally never have to discard, and which therefore remain in fact as members of my known world. And of some of these certainly it may be said that without them I should not know how to order my knowledge. But it is quite another thing to maintain that every single one of these judgements is in principle infallible. The absolute indispensable fact is in my view the mere creature of false theory. Facts are valid so far as, when taken otherwise than as 'real,' they bring disorder into my world. And there are today for me facts such that, if I take them as mistakes, my known world is damaged and, it is possible, ruined. But how does it follow that I cannot tomorrow on the strength of new facts gain a wider order in which these old facts can take a place as errors? The supposition may be improbable, but what you have got to show is that it is in principle impossible. A foundation used at the beginning does not in short mean something fundamental at the end, and there is no single 'fact' which in the end can be called fundamental absolutely. It is all a question of relative contribution to my known world-order.

'Then no judgement of perception will be more than probable?' Certainly that is my contention. 'Facts' are justified because and as far as, while taking them as real, I am better able to deal with the incoming new 'facts' and in general to make my world wider and more harmonious. The higher and wider my structure, and the more that any particular fact or set of facts is implied in that structure, the more certain are the structure and the facts. And, if we could reach an all-embracing ordered whole, then our certainty would be absolute. But, since we cannot do this, we have to remain content with relative probability. Why is this or that fact of observation taken as practically certain? It is so taken just so far as it is *not* taken in its own right. (i) Its validity is due to such and such a person perceiving it under such and such conditions. This means that a certain intellectual order in the person is necessary as a basis, and again that nothing in the way of sensible or mental distortion intervenes between this order and what is given. And (ii) the observed fact must agree with our world as already arranged, or at least must not upset this. If the fact is too much contrary to our arranged world we provisionally reject it. We eventually accept the fact only when after confirmation the hypothesis of its error becomes still more ruinous. We are forced then more or less to rearrange our world, and more or less perhaps to reject some previous 'facts.' The question throughout is as to what is better or worse for our order as a whole.

Why again to me is a remembered fact certain, supposing that it is so? Assuredly not because it is infallibly delivered by the faculty of Memory, but because I do not see how to reconcile the fact of its error with my accepted world. Unless I go on the principle of trusting my memory, apart from any special reason to the contrary, I cannot order my world so well, if indeed I can order it at all. The principle here again is system. . . .

The same account holds with regard to the facts of history. For instance, the guillotining of Louis XVI is practically certain, because, to take this as error, would entail too much disturbance of my world. Error is possible here of course. Fresh facts conceivably might come before me such as would compel me to modify in part my knowledge as so far arranged. And in this modified arrangement the execution of Louis would find its place as an error. But the reason for such a modification would have to be considerable, while, as things are, no reason exists. . . . To take memory as in general trustworthy, where I have no special reason for doubt, and to take the testimony of those persons, whom I suppose to view the world as I view it, as being true, apart from special reason on the other side—these are principles by which I construct my ordered world, such as it is. And because by any other method the result is worse, therefore for me these principles are true. On the other hand to suppose that any 'fact' or perception or memory is so certain that no possible experience could justify me in taking it as error, seems to me injurious if not ruinous. On such a principle my world of knowledge would be ordered worse, if indeed it could be ordered at all. For to accept all the 'facts,' as they offer themselves, seems obviously impossible; and, if it is we who have to decide as to which facts are infallible, then I ask how we are to decide. The ground of validity, I maintain, consists in successful contribution. That is a principle of order, while any other principle, so far as I see, leads to chaos.

'But,' it may still be objected, 'my fancy is unlimited. I can therefore invent an imaginary world even more orderly than my known world. And further this fanciful arrangement might possibly be made so wide that the world of perception would become for me in comparison small and inconsiderable. Hence, my perceived world, so far as not supporting my fancied arrangement, might be included within it as *error*. Such a consequence would or might lead to confusion in theory and to disaster in practice. And yet the result follows from your view inevitably, unless after all you fall back upon the certainty of perception.'

To this possible objection, I should reply first, that it has probably failed to understand rightly the criterion which I defend. The aspect of comprehensiveness has not received here its due emphasis. The idea of system demands the inclusion of all possible material. Not only must you include everything to be gained from immediate experience and perception, but you must also be ready to act on the same principle with regard to fancy. But this means that you cannot confine yourself within the limits of this or that fancied world, as suits your pleasure or private convenience. You are bound also, so far as is possible, to recognize and to include the opposite fancy.

This consideration to my mind ruins the above hypothesis on which the objection was based. The fancied arrangement not only has opposed to it the world of perception. It also has against it any opposite arrangement and any contrary fact which I can fancy. And, so far as I can judge, these contrary fancies will balance the first. Nothing, therefore, will be left to outweigh the world as perceived, and the imaginary hypothesis will be condemned by our criterion.

. . . I may state the view which has commended itself to my mind. Truth is an ideal expression of the Universe, at once coherent and comprehensive. It must not conflict with itself, and there must be no suggestion which fails to fall inside it. Perfect truth in short must realize the idea of a systematic whole. And such a whole . . . possesses essentially the two characters of coherence and comprehensiveness.

25

On Pragmatic Grounds

William James (1842–1910), American philosopher and psychologist, received his M.D. from Harvard in 1869. He lectured there on anatomy and physiology until 1880, when he joined the Department of Psychology and Philosophy. He amended and popularized Peirce's pragmatism in a series of books which include *The Will to Believe and Other Essays in Popular Philosophy* (1897), *The Varieties of Religious Experience* (1902), *Pragmatism* (1907), *Essays in Radical Empiricism* (1912).

James holds to the pragmatic theory of truth. He believes that the coherence theory cannot distinguish between consistent truth and consistent error, and the best way to define truth is in terms of beliefs that "work." For the pragmatist the test of truth is utility, workability, or satisfactory consequences. There is no such thing as static or absolute truth, rather, truth is made in the processes of human adjustment. What works in practice will decide which of our alternative beliefs are true.

TO STUDY

1. According to James, what are the classic stages of a theory's careeer?
2. What is James' argument against the correspondence theory?
3. How does James define true and false ideas?

4. According to James, what is the value of the possession of true thoughts?
5. What does James mean when he says "Truth is made"? What is the rationalist's argument against this? What is James' reply?
6. According to James, what is the "absolutely" true?
7. According to James, what is the relationship between the good and the true?

I

. . . I fully expect to see the pragmatist view of truth run through the classic stages of a theory's career. First, you know, a new theory is attacked as absurd; then it is admitted to be true, but obvious and insignificant; finally it is seen to be so important that its adversaries claim that they themselves discovered it. Our doctrine of truth is at present in the first of these three stages, with symptoms of the second stage having begun in certain quarters. I wish that this lecture might help it beyond the first stage in the eyes of many of you.

Truth, as any dictionary will tell you, is a property of certain of our ideas. It means their "agreement," as falsity means their disagreement, with "reality." Pragmatists and intellectualists both accept this definition as a matter of course. They begin to quarrel only after the question is raised as to what may precisely be meant by the term "agreement," and what by the term "reality," when reality is taken as something for our ideas to agree with.

In answering these questions the pragmatists are more analytic and painstaking, the intellectualists more offhand and irreflective. The popular notion is that a true idea must copy its reality. Like other popular views, this one follows the analogy of the most usual experience. Our true ideas of sensible things do indeed copy them. Shut your eyes and think of yonder clock on the wall, and you get just such a true picture or copy of its dial. But your idea of its "works" (unless you are a clock-maker) is much less of a copy, yet it passes muster, for it in no way clashes with the reality. Even though it should shrink to the mere word "works," that word still serves you truly; and when you speak of the "time-keeping function" of the clock, or of its spring's "elasticity," it is hard to see exactly what your ideas can copy.

From *Pragmatism* (1907). Part I is from Lecture VI, pp. 198–209; part II from Lecture VI, pp. 218–223; and part III from Lecture II, pp. 75–78.

You perceive that there is a problem here. Where our ideas cannot copy definitely their object, what does agreement with that object mean? Some idealists seem to say that they are true whenever they are what God means that we ought to think about that object. Others hold the copy-view all through, and speak as if our ideas possessed truth just in proportion as they approach to being copies of the Absolute's eternal way of thinking.

These views, you see, invite pragmatistic discussion. But the great assumption of the intellectualists is that truth means essentially an inert static relation. When you've got your true idea of anything, there's an end of the matter. You're in possession; you *know;* you have fulfilled your thinking destiny. You are where you ought to be mentally; you have obeyed your categorical imperative; and nothing more need follow on that climax of your rational destiny. Epistemologically you are in stable equilibrium.

Pragmatism, on the other hand, asks its usual question. "Grant an idea or belief to be true," it says, "what concrete difference will its being true make in any one's actual life? How will the truth be realized? What experiences will be different from those which would obtain if the belief were false? What, in short, is the truth's cash-value in experiential terms?"

The moment pragmatism asks this question, it sees the answer: *True ideas are those that we can assimilate, validate, corroborate and verify. False ideas are those that we cannot.* That is the practical difference it makes to us to have true ideas; that, therefore, is the meaning of truth, for it is all that truth is known-as.

This thesis is what I have to defend. The truth of an idea is not a stagnant property inherent in it. Truth *happens* to an idea. It *becomes* true, is *made* true by events. Its verity *is* in fact an event, a process: the process namely of its verifying itself, its veri-*fication.* Its validity is the process of its valid-*ation.*

But what do the words verification and validation themselves pragmatically mean? They again signify certain practical consequences of the verified and validated idea. It is hard to find any one phrase that characterized these consequences better than the ordinary agreement-formula—just such consequences being what we have in mind whenever we say that our ideas "agree" with reality. They lead us, namely, through the acts and other ideas which they instigate, into or up to, or towards, other parts of experience with which we feel all the while—such feeling being among our potentialities—that the original ideas remain in agreement. The connections and transitions come to us from point to point as being progressive, harmonious, satisfactory. This function of agreeable leading is what we mean by an idea's verification. . . .

. . . The possession of true thoughts means everywhere the possession of invaluable instruments of action; and . . . our duty to gain truth, so far from being a blank command from out of the blue, or a "stunt" self-imposed by our intellect, can account for itself by excellent practical reasons.

The importance to human life of having true beliefs about matters of fact is a thing too notorious. We live in a world of realities that can be infinitely useful or infinitely harmful. Ideas that tell us which of them to expect count as the true ideas in all this primary sphere of verification, and the pursuit of such ideas is a primary human duty. The possession of truth, so far from being here an end in itself, is only a preliminary means towards other vital satisfactions. If I am lost in the woods and starved, and find what looks like a cow-path, it is of the utmost importance that I should think of a human habitation at the end of it, for if I do so and follow it, I save myself. The true thought is useful here because the house which is its object is useful. The practical value of true ideas is thus primarily derived from the practical importance of their objects to us. Their objects are, indeed, not important at all times. I may on another occasion have no use for the house; and then my idea of it, however verifiable, will be practically irrelevant, and had better remain latent. Yet since almost any object may some day become temporarily important, the advantage of having a general stock of *extra* truths, of ideas that shall be true of merely possible situations, is obvious. We store such extra truths away in our memories, and with the overflow we fill our books of reference. Whenever such an extra truth becomes practically relevant to one of our emergencies, it passes from cold-storage to do work in the world and our belief in it grows active. You can say of it then either that "it is useful because it is true" or that "it is true because it is useful." Both these phrases mean exactly the same thing, namely that here is an idea that gets fulfilled and can be verified. True is the name for whatever idea starts the verification-process, useful is the name for its completed function in experience. True ideas would never have been singled out as such, would never have acquired a class-name, least of all a name suggesting value, unless they had been useful from the outset in this way.

From this simple cue pragmatism gets her general notion of truth as something essentially bound up with the way in which one moment in our experience may lead us towards other moments which it will be worthwhile to have been led to. Primarily, and on the common-sense level, the truth of a state of mind means this function of *a leading that is worthwhile.* When a moment in our experience, of any kind whatever, inspires us with a thought that is true, that means that sooner or later we dip by that thought's guidance into the particulars of experience again and make advantageous connection with them. This is a vague enough statement, but I beg you to retain it, for it is essential.

Our experience meanwhile is all shot through with regularities. One bit of it can warn us to get ready for another bit, can "intend" or be "significant of" that remoter object. The object's advent is the significance's verification. Truth, in these cases, meaning nothing but eventual verification, is manifestly incompatible with waywardness on our part. Woe to him whose beliefs play fast and loose with the order which realities follow in his experience; they will lead him nowhere or else make false connections.

By "realities" or "objects" here, we mean either things of common sense, sensibly present, or else common-sense relations, such as dates, places, distances, kinds, activities. Following our mental image of a house along the cow-path, we actually come to see the house; we get the image's full verification. *Such simply and fully verified leadings are certainly the originals and prototypes of the truth-process.* Experience offers indeed other forms of truth-process, but they are all conceivable as being primary verifications arrested, multiplied or substituted one for another.

Take, for instance, yonder object on the wall. You and I consider it to be a "clock," altho no one of us has seen the hidden works that make it one. We let our notion pass for true without attempting to verify. If truths mean verification-process essentially, ought we then to call such unverified truths as this abortive? No, for they form the overwhelmingly large number of the truths we live by. Indirect as well as direct verifications pass muster. Where circumstantial evidence is sufficient, we can go without eye-witnessing. Just as we here assume Japan to exist without ever having been there, because it *works* to do so, everything we know conspiring with the belief, and nothing interfering, so we assume that thing to be a clock. We *use* it as a clock, regulating the length of our lecture by it. The verification of the assumption here means its leading to no frustration or contradiction. Verifi-*ability* of wheels and weights and pendulum is as good as verification. For one truth-process completed there are a million in our lives that function in this state of nascency. They turn us *towards* direct verification; lead us into the *surroundings* of the objects they envisage; and then, if everything runs on harmoniously, we are so sure that verification is possible that we omit it, and are usually justified by all that happens.

Truth lives, in fact, for the most part on a credit system. Our thoughts and beliefs "pass," so long as nothing challenges them, just as bank-notes pass so long as nobody refuses them. But this all points to direct face-to-face verifications somewhere, without which the fabric of truth collapses like a financial system with no cash-basis whatever. You accept my verification of one thing, I yours of another. We trade on each other's truth. But beliefs verified concretely by *somebody* are the posts of the whole super-structure.

Another great reason—beside economy of time—for waiving complete verification in the usual business of life is that all things exist in kinds and not singly. Our world is found once for all to have that peculiarity. So that when we have once directly verified our ideas about one specimen of a kind, we consider ourselves free to apply them to other specimens without verification. A mind that habitually discerns the kind of thing before it, and acts by the law of the kind immediately, without pausing to verify, will be a "true" mind in ninety-nine out of a hundred emergencies, proved so by its conduct fitting everything it meets, and getting no refutation.

Indirectly or only potentially verifying processes may thus be true as well as full verification-processes. They work as true processes would work, give us the same advantages, and claim our recognition for the same reasons. . . .

II

Our account of truth is an account of truths in the plural, of processes of leading, realized *in rebus,*[1] and having only this quality in common, that they *pay.* They pay by guiding us into or towards some part of a system that dips at numerous points into sense-percepts, which we may copy mentally or not, but with which at any rate we are now in the kind of commerce vaguely designated as verification. Truth for us is simply a collective name for verification-processes, just as health, wealth, strength, etc., are names for other processes connected with life, and also pursued because it pays to pursue them. Truth is *made,* just as health, wealth and strength are made, in the course of experience.

Here rationalism is instantaneously up in arms against us. I can imagine a rationalist to talk as follows:

"Truth is not made," he will say; "it absolutely obtains, being a unique relation that does not wait upon any process, but shoots straight over the head of experience, and hits its reality every time. Our belief that yon thing on the wall is a clock is true already, altho no one in the whole history of the world should verify it. The bare quality of standing in that transcendent relation is what makes any thought true that possesses it, whether or not there be verification. You pragmatists put the cart before the horse in making truth's being reside in verification-processes. These are merely signs of its being, merely our lame ways of ascertaining after the fact, which of our ideas already has possessed the wondrous quality. The quality itself is timeless, like all essences and natures. Thoughts partake of it directly, as they partake of falsity or of irrelevancy. It can't be analyzed away into pragmatic consequences."

The whole plausibility of this rationalist tirade is due to the fact to which we have already paid so much attention. In our world, namely,

---

[1] [In things—ed. note.]

abounding as it does in things of similar kinds and similarly associated, one verification serves for others of its kind, and one great use of knowing things is to be led not so much to them as to their associates, especially to human talk about them. The quality of truth, obtaining *ante rem*,[2] pragmatically means, then, the fact that in such a world innumerable ideas work better by their indirect or possible than by their direct and actual verification. Truth *ante rem* means only verifiability, then; or else it is a case of the stock rationalist trick of treating the *name* of a concrete phenomenal reality as an independent prior entity, and placing it behind the reality as its explanation. . . .

In the case of "wealth" we all see the fallacy. We know that wealth is but a name for concrete processes that certain men's lives play a part in, and not a natural excellence found in Messrs. Rockefeller and Carnegie, but not in the rest of us.

Like wealth, health also lives *in rebus*. It is a name for processes, as digestion, circulation, sleep, etc., that go on happily, tho in this instance we are more inclined to think of it as a principle and to say the man digests and sleeps so well *because* he is so healthy.

With "strength" we are, I think, more rationalistic still, and decidedly inclined to treat it as an excellence pre-existing in the man and explanatory of the herculean performances of his muscles.

With "truth" most people go over the border entirely, and treat the rationalistic account as self-evident. But really all these words in *th* are exactly similar. Truth exists *ante rem* just as much and as little as the other things do.

The scholastics, following Aristotle, made much of the distinction between habit and act. Health *in actu*[3] means, among other things, good sleeping and digesting. But a healthy man need not always be sleeping, or always digesting, any more than a wealthy man need be always handling money, or a strong man always lifting weights. All such qualities sink to the status of "habits" between their times of exercise; and similarly truth becomes a habit of certain of our ideas and beliefs in their intervals of rest from their verifying activities. But those activities are the root of the whole matter, and the condition of there being any habit to exist in the intervals.

"The true," to put it very briefly, is only the expedient in the way of our thinking, just as "the right" is only the expedient in the way of our behaving. Expedient in almost any fashion; and expedient in the long run and on the whole of course; for what meets expediently all the experience in sight won't

---

[2] [Before the thing—ed. note.]

[3] [In actuality—ed. note.]

necessarily meet all farther experiences equally satisfactorily. Experience, as we know, has ways of *boiling over*, and making us correct our present formulas.

The "absolutely" true, meaning what no farther experience will ever alter, is that ideal vanishing-point towards which we imagine that all our temporary truths will some day converge. It runs on all fours with the perfectly wise man, and with the absolutely complete experience; and, if these ideals are ever realized, they will all be realized together. Meanwhile we have to live today by what truth we can get today, and be ready tomorrow to call it falsehood. Ptolemaic astronomy, Euclidean space, Aristotelian logic, scholastic metaphysics, were expedient for centuries, but human experience has boiled over those limits, and we now call these things only relatively true, or true within those borders of experience. "Absolutely" they are false; for we know that those limits were casual, and might have been transcended by past theorists just as they are by present thinkers. . . .

III

. . . Truth is *one species of good*, and not, as is usually supposed, a category distinct from good, and coordinate with it. *The true is the name of whatever proves itself to be good in the way of belief, and good, too, for definite, assignable reasons.* Surely you must admit this, that if there were *no* good for life in true ideas, or if the knowledge of them were positively disadvantageous and false ideas the only useful ones, then the current notion that truth is divine and precious, and its pursuit a duty, could never have grown up or become a dogma. In a world like that, our duty would be to *shun* truth, rather. But in this world, just as certain foods are not only agreeable to our taste, but good for our teeth, our stomach, and our tissues; so certain ideas are not only agreeable to think about, or agreeable as supporting other ideas that we are fond of, but they are also helpful in life's practical struggles. If there be any life that it is really better we should lead, and if there be any idea which, if believed in, would help us to lead that life, then it would be really *better for us* to believe in that idea, *unless, indeed, belief in it incidentally clashed with other greater vital benefits.*

"What would be better for us to believe!" This sounds very like a definition of truth. It comes very near to saying "what we *ought* to believe:" and in *that* definition none of you would find any oddity. Ought we ever not to believe what it is *better for us* to believe? And can we then keep the notion of what is better for us, and what is true for us, permanently apart?

Pragmatism says no, and I fully agree with her. Probably you also agree, so far as the abstract statement goes, but with a suspicion that if we practically did believe everything that made for good in our own personal lives, we should be found indulging all kinds of fancies about this world's affairs, and all kinds of sentimental superstitions about a world hereafter. Your suspicion here is undoubtedly well founded, and it is evident that something happens when you pass from the abstract to the concrete that complicates the situation.

I said just now that what is better for us to believe is true *unless the belief incidentally clashes with some other vital benefit.* Now in real life what vital benefits is any particular belief of ours most liable to clash with? What indeed except the vital benefits yielded by *other beliefs* when these *prove* incompatible with the first ones? In other words, the greatest enemy of any one of our truths may be the rest of our truths. Truths have once for all this desperate instinct of self-preservation and of desire to extinguish whatever contradicts them. . . .

Readings

1. Blanshard, Brand. *The Nature of Thought,* Vol. 2, Chap. 25, "The Tests of Truth"; Chap. 26, "Coherence as the Nature of Truth." New York: Macmillan, 1939.

2. Khatchadourian, Haig. *The Coherence Theory of Truth.* (Beirut: American University Press, 1961).

3. Murphy, Arthur E. *The Uses of Reason,* "The Pragmatic Theory of Truth." New York: Macmillan, 1943, pp. 85–95.

4. Pepper, Stephen. *World Hypotheses: A Study in Evidence,* Chap. 1, "The Utter Skeptic" (esp. pp. 3–10); Chap. 2, "Dogmatists." Los Angeles: U. of California Press, 1942.

5. Russell, Bertrand. *Human Knowledge: Its Scope and Limits,* Pt. 2, Chap. 11, "Fact, Belief, Truth, and Knowledge." New York: Simon and Schuster, 1948.

6. Woozley, A. D. *Theory of Knowledge.* London: Allen and Unwin, 1949, pp. 146–169.

four

Can We Know The Nature of Cause?

26

Cause Means Regular Association

David Hume (1711–1776) is a British philosopher, historian,
and essayist whose views on causality stimulated Kant to
construct his "critical philosophy"; noted for his development
of the empiricism of Locke and Berkeley and for his skepticism. He is the author of *Treatise on Human Nature*.

There are two main views concerning the relationship of cause and effect.
The first, represented by Hume, states that two events are causally related
if the three following conditions are satisfied: (1) the two events are spatially
contiguous; (2) one event precedes the other; (3) these two events have been
associated in such spatial and temporal conditions many times. Thus if one
says that smoking causes cancer one means that smoking and cancer are
spatially contiguous, that smoking precedes cancer, and that there are many
cases of smoking being associated with cancer. Hume denies that there is
any necessary connection between smoking and cancer. We have no impression of any necessary connection between the two events. Hence the ordinary belief that one event necessarily causes the second is false.

TO STUDY

1. What is Hume trying to illustrate by the example of the billiard
   balls?
2. What is the difference between the "will" and the example of
   the billiard balls?

3. What three arguments does Hume give against the idea of "willing" proving the idea of power or necessary connection?

4. How does Hume believe the idea of necessary connection arises among events?

5. How does he define cause?

Part I

There are no ideas, which occur in metaphysics, more obscure and uncertain, than those of *power, force, energy* or *necessary connexion,* of which it is every moment necessary for us to treat in all our disquisitions. We shall, therefore, endeavor, in this section, to fix, if possible, the precise meaning of these terms, and thereby remove some part of that obscurity, which is so much complained of in this species of philosophy.

It seems a proposition, which will not admit of much dispute, that all our ideas are nothing but copies of our impressions, or, in other words, that it is impossible for us to *think* of any thing, which we have not antecedently *felt,* either by our external or internal senses. . . . To be fully acquainted, therefore, with the idea of power or necessary connexion, let us examine its impression with greater certainty, let us search for it in all the sources, from which it may possibly be derived.

When we look about us towards external objects, and consider the operation of causes, we are never able, in a single instance, to discover any power or necessary connexion; any quality, which binds the effect to the cause, and renders the one an infallible consequence of the other. We only find, that the one does actually, in fact, follow the other. The impulse of one billiard-ball is attended with motion in the second. This is the whole that appears to the *outward* senses. The mind feels no sentiment or *inward* impression from this succession of objects: Consequently, there is not, in any single, particular instance of cause and effect, any thing which can suggest the idea of power or necessary connexion.

From the first appearance of an object, we never can conjecture what effect will result from it. But were the power or energy of any cause discoverable by the mind, we could foresee the effect, even without experience; and might, at first, pronounce with certainty concerning it, by mere dint of thought and reasoning.

In reality, there is no part of matter, that does ever, by its sensible qualities, discover any power or energy, or give us ground to imagine. that

From Hume: *An Enquiry Concerning Human Understanding,* Sections 7 and 5.

it could produce any thing, or be followed by any other object, which we could denominate its effect. Solidity, extension, motion; these qualities are all complete in themselves, and never point out any other event which may result from them. The scenes of the universe are continually shifting, and one object follows another in an uninterrupted succession; but the power or force, which actuates the whole machine, is entirely concealed from us, and never discovers itself in any of the sensible qualities of body. We know, that, in fact, heat is a constant attendant of flame; but what is the connexion between them, we have no room so much as to conjecture or imagine. It is impossible, therefore, that the idea of power can be derived from the contemplation of bodies, in single instances of their operation; because no bodies ever discover any power, which can be the original of this idea.

Since, therefore, external objects as they appear to the senses, give us no idea of power or necessary connexion, by their operation in particular instances, let us see, whether this idea be derived from reflection on the operations of our own minds, and be copied from any internal impression. It may be said, that we are every moment conscious of internal power; while we feel, that, by the simple command of our will, we can move the organs of our body, or direct the faculties of our mind. An act of volition produces motion in our limbs, or raises a new idea in our imagination. This influence of the will we know by consciousness. Hence we acquire the idea of power or energy; and are certain, that we ourselves and all other intelligent beings are possessed of power. . . .

We shall proceed to examine this pretension; and first with regard to the influence of volition over the organs of the body. This influence, we may observe, is a fact, which, like all other natural events, can be known only by experience, and can never be foreseen from any apparent energy or power in the cause, which connects it with the effect, and renders the one an infallible consequence of the other. The motion of our body follows upon the command of our will. Of this we are every moment conscious. But the means, by which this is effected; the energy, by which the will performs so extraordinary an operation; of this we are so far from being immediately conscious, that it must for ever escape our most diligent enquiry.

For *first;* is there any principle in all nature more mysterious than the union of soul with body; by which a supposed spiritual substance acquires such an influence over a material one, that the most refined thought is able to actuate the grossest matter? Were we empowered, by a secret wish, to remove mountains, or control the planets in their orbit; this extensive authority would not be more extraordinary, nor more beyond our comprehension. But if by consciousness we perceived any power or energy in the will, we must know this power; we must know its connexion with the effect; we must know the secret union of soul and body, and the nature of both these substances; by which the one is able to operate, in so many instances, upon the other.

Secondly, We are not able to move all the organs of the body with a like authority; though we cannot assign any reason besides experience, for so remarkable a difference between one and the other. Why has the will an influence over the tongue and fingers, not over the heart or liver? This question would never embarrass us, were we conscious of a power in the former case, not in the latter. . . .

Thirdly, We learn from anatomy, that the immediate object of power in voluntary motion, is not the member itself which is moved, but certain muscles, and nerves, and animal spirits, and, perhaps, something still more minute and more unknown, through which the motion is successively propagated, ere it reach the member itself whose motion is the immediate object of volition. Can there be a more certain proof, that the power, by which this whole operation is performed, so far from being directly and fully known by an inward sentiment or consciousness, is, to the last degree, mysterious and unintelligible? Here the mind wills a certain event: Immediately another event, unknown to ourselves, and totally different from the one intended, is produced: This event produces another, equally unknown: Till at last, through a long succession, the desired event is produced. But if the original power were felt, it must be known: Were it known, its effect also must be known; since all power is relative to its effect. And *vice versa,* if the effect be not known, the power cannot be known nor felt. How indeed can we be conscious of a power to move our limbs, when we have no such power; but only that to move certain animal spirits, which, though they produce at last the motion of our limbs, yet operate in such a manner as is wholly beyond our comprehension?

We may, therefore, conclude . . . that our idea of power is not copied from any sentiment or consciousness of power within ourselves, when we give rise to animal motion, or apply our limbs to their proper use and office. That their motion follows the command of the will is a matter of common experience, like other natural events: But the power or energy by which this is effected, like that in other natural events, is unknown and inconceivable. . . .

The generality of mankind never find any difficulty in accounting for the more common and familiar operations of nature—such as the descent of heavy bodies, the growth of plants, the generation of animals, or the nourishment of bodies by food: But suppose that, in all these cases, they perceive the very force or energy of the cause, by which it is connected with its effect, and is for ever infallible in its operation. They acquire, by long habit, such a turn of mind, that, upon the appearance of the cause, they immediately expect with assurance its usual attendant, and hardly conceive it possible that any other event could result from it. It is only on the discovery of extraordinary phaenomena, such as earthquakes, pestilence, and prodigies of any kind, that they find themselves at a loss to assign a proper cause, and to explain the manner in which the effect is produced by it. It is usual for men, in such difficulties to have recourse to some invisible intelligent principle as the immediate cause of that event which surprises them, and which, they think, cannot be accounted for from the common powers of nature. But philosophers, who carry their scrutiny a little farther, immediately perceive that, even, in the most familiar events, the energy of the cause is as unintelligible as in the most unusual, and that we only learn by experience the frequent *Conjunction* of objects, without being ever able to comprehend anything like *Connexion* between them. . . .

Part II

But to hasten a conclusion of this argument, which is already drawn out to too great a length: We have sought in vain for an idea of power or necessary connexion in all the sources from which we could suppose it to be derived. It appears that, in single instances of the operation of bodies, we never can, by our utmost scrutiny, discover any thing but one event following another, without being able to comprehend any force or power by which the cause operates, or any connexion between it and its supposed effect. The same difficulty occurs in contemplating the operations of mind on body—where we observe the motion of the latter to follow upon the volition of the former, but are not able to observe or conceive the tie which binds together the motion and volition, or the energy by which the mind produces this effect. The authority of the will over its own faculties and ideas is not a whit more comprehensible: So that, upon the whole, there appears not, throughout all nature, any one instance of connexion which is conceivable by us. All events seem entirely loose and separate. One event follows another; but we never can observe any tie between them. They seem *conjoined,* but never *connected.* And as we can have no idea of anything which never appeared to our outward sense or inward sentiment, the neces-sary conclusion *seems* to be that we have no idea of connexion or power at all, and that these words are absolutely without any meaning, when employed either in philosophical reasonings or common life.

But there still remains one method of avoiding this conclusion, and one source which we have not yet examined. When any natural object or event is presented, it is impossible for us, by any sagacity or penetration, to discover, or even conjecture, without experience, what event will result from it, or to carry our foresight beyond that object which is immediately present to the memory and senses. Even after one instance or experiment where we have observed a particular event to follow upon another, we are not entitled to form a general rule, or foretell what will happen in like cases; it being justly esteemed an unpardonable temerity to judge of the whole course of nature from one single experiment, however accurate or certain. But when one particular species of event has always, in all instances, been conjoined with another, we make no longer any scruple of foretelling one upon the appearance of the other, and of employing that reasoning, which can alone assure us of any matter of fact or existence. We then call the one object, *Cause;* the other, *Effect.* We suppose that there is some connexion between them; some power in the one, by which it infallibly produces the other, and operates with the greatest certainty and strongest necessity.

It appears, then, that this idea of a necessary connexion among events arises from a number of similar instances which occur of the constant conjunction of these events; nor can that idea ever be suggested by any one of these instances, surveyed in all possible lights and positions. But there is nothing in a number of instances, different from every single instance, which is supposed to be exactly similar; except only, that after a repetition of similar instances, the mind is carried by habit, upon the appearance of one event, to expect its usual attendant, and to believe that it will exist. This connexion, therefore, which we *feel* in the mind, this customary transition of the imagination from one object to its usual attendant, is the sentiment or impression from which we form the idea of power or necessary connexion. Nothing farther is in the case. Contemplate the subject on all sides; you will never find any other origin of that idea. This is the sole difference between one instance, from which we can never receive the idea of connexion, and a number of similar instances, by which it is suggested. The first time a man saw the communication of motion by impulse, as by the shock of two billiard balls, he could not pronounce that the one event was *connected:* but only that it was *conjoined* with the other. After he has observed several instances of this nature, he then pronounces them to be *connected.* What alteration has happened to give rise to this new idea of *connexion?* Nothing but that he now *feels* these events to be *connected* in his imagination, and can readily foretell the existence of one from the appearance of the other. When we say, therefore, that one object is connected with another, we mean only that they have acquired a connexion in our thought, and give rise to this inference, by which they become proofs of each other's existence: A conclusion which is somewhat extraordinary, but which seems founded on sufficient evidence. Nor will its evidence be weakened by any general diffidence of the understanding, or sceptical suspicion concerning every conclusion which is new and extraordinary. No conclusions can be more agreeable to scepticism than such as make discoveries concerning the weakness and narrow limits of human reason and capacity.

And what stronger instance can be produced of the surprising ignorance and weakness of the understanding than the present? For surely, if
there be any relation among objects which it imports to us to know perfectly, it is that of cause and effect. On this are founded all our reasonings
concerning matter of fact or existence. By means of it alone we attain any
assurance concerning objects which are removed from the present testimony of our memory and senses. The only immediate utility of all sciences,
is to teach us, how to control and regulate future events by their causes.
Our thoughts and enquiries are, therefore, every moment, employed about
this relation: Yet so imperfect are the ideas which we form concerning it,
that it is impossible to give any just definition of cause, except what is drawn
from something extraneous and foreign to it. Similar objects are always
conjoined with similar. Of this we have experience. Suitably to this experience, therefore, we may define a cause to be *an object, followed by another,*
and where all the objects similar to the first are followed by objects similar
to the second. Or in other words, *where, if the first object had not been, the*
second never had existed. The appearance of a cause always conveys the
mind, by a customary transition, to the idea of the effect. Of this also we
have experience. We may, therefore, suitably to this experience, form another definition of cause, and call it, *an object followed by another, and whose*
appearance always conveys the thought to that other. But though both these
definitions be drawn from circumstances foreign to the cause, we cannot
remedy this inconvenience, or attain any more perfect definition, which may
point out that circumstance in the cause, which gives it a connexion with
its effect. We have no idea of this connexion, nor even any distinct notion
what it is we desire to know, where we endeavour at a conception of it.
We say, for instance, that the vibration of this string is the cause of this
particular sound. But what do we mean by that affirmation? We either mean
that this vibration is followed by this sound, and that all similar vibrations
have been followed by similar sounds: Or, that this vibration is followed by
this sound, and that upon the appearance of one the mind anticipates the
senses, and forms immediately an idea of the other. We may consider the
relation of cause and effect in either of these two lights; but beyond these,
we have no idea of it.

To recapitulate, therefore, the reasonings of this section: Every idea
is copied from some preceding impression or sentiment; and where we
cannot find any impression, we may be certain that there is no idea. In all
single instances of the operation of bodies or minds, there is nothing that
produces any impression, nor consequently can suggest any idea of power
or necessary connexion. But when many uniform instances appear, and the
same object is always followed by the same event; we then begin to entertain
the notion of cause and connexion. We then *feel* a new sentiment or impres-

sion, to wit, a customary connexion in the thought or imagination between one object and its usual attendant; and this sentiment is the original of that idea which we seek for. For as this idea arises from a number of similar instances, and not from any single instance, it must arise from that circum-stance, in which the number of instances differ from every individual in-stance. But this customary connexion or transition of the imagination is the only circumstance in which they differ. In every other particular they are alike. The first instance which we saw of motion communicated by the shock of two billiard balls (to return to this obvious illustration) is exactly similar to any instance that may, at present, occur to us; except only, that we could not, at first, *infer* one event from the other; which we are enabled to do at present, after so long a course of uniform experience.

Custom, then, is the great guide of human life. It is that principle alone which renders our experience useful to us, and makes us expect, for the future, a similar train of events with those which have appeared in the past. Without the influence of custom, we should be entirely ignorant of every matter of fact beyond what is immediately present to the memory and senses. We should never know how to adjust means to ends, or to employ our natural powers in the production of any effect. There would be an end at once of all action, as well as of the chief part of speculation.

But here it may be proper to remark, that though our conclusions from experience carry us beyond our memory and senses, and assure us of mat-ters of fact which happened in the most distant places and most remote ages, yet some fact must always be present to the senses or memory, from which we may first proceed in drawing these conclusions. A man, who should find in a desert country the remains of pompous buildings, would conclude that the country had, in ancient times, been cultivated by civilized inhabitants; but did nothing of this nature occur to him, he could never form such an inference. We learn the events of former ages from history; but then we must peruse the volumes in which this instruction is contained, and thence carry up our inferences from one testimony to another, till we arrive at the eyewitnesses and spectators of these distant events. In a word, if we proceed not upon some fact, present to the memory or senses, our reasonings would be merely hypothetical; and however the particular links might be connected with each other, the whole chain of inferences would have nothing to support it, nor could we ever, by its means, arrive at the knowledge of any real existence. If I ask why you believe any particular matter of fact, which you relate, you must tell me some reason; and this reason will be some other fact, connected with it. But as you cannot proceed after this manner, *in infinitum,* you must at last terminate in some fact, which is present to your memory or senses; or must allow that your belief is entirely without foundation.

What, then, is the conclusion of the whole matter? A simple one; though, it must be confessed, pretty remote from the common theories of philosophy. All belief of matter of fact or real existence is derived merely from some object, present to the memory or senses, and a customary conjunction between that and some other object. Or in other words; having found, in many instances, that any two kinds of objects—flame and heat, snow and cold—have always been conjoined together; if flame or snow be presented anew to the senses, the mind is carried by custom to expect heat or cold, and to *believe* that such a quality does exist, and will discover itself upon a nearer approach. This belief is the necessary result of placing the mind in such circumstances. It is an operation of the soul, when we are so situated, as unavoidable as to feel the passion of love, when we receive benefits; or hatred, when we meet with injuries. All these operations are a species of natural instincts, which no reasoning or process of the thought and understanding is able either to produce or to prevent.

27

Cause Is More
than Regular Association

Alfred North Whitehead (1861–1947) was one of the most
eminent mathematicians and philosophers of our time. With
Bertrand Russell he wrote *Principia Mathematica* (1910–13),
a work which opened up vast new fields in mathematics.
His extensive contributions to philosophy are no less notable.

In contrast to Hume, Whitehead claims that we have many daily experiences in which we are directly aware of causal connection. He uses the
famous example of the reflex action in which an electric light is suddenly
turned on and a man's eyes blink. The man is directly aware that the
flash caused the blink. There is a necessary relationship between the light
and the blink. With such a doctrine Hume's influential theory of causation
is directly attacked.

─── TO STUDY

1. According to Whitehead, what is the primary fact of perception?
2. Give Hume's explanation of the example of the electric light and
   blinking.
3. Give Whitehead's explanation of the same example. What does
   Whitehead believe he has proven?

The discussion of the problem, constituted by the connection between causation and perception, has been conducted by the various schools of thought derived from Hume and Kant under the misapprehension generated by an inversion of the true constitution of experience. The inversion was explicit in the writings of Hume and of Kant: for both of them presentational immediacy was the primary fact of perception, and any apprehension of causation was, somehow or other, to be elicited from this primary fact. . . .

Owing to its long dominance, it has been usual to assume as an obvious fact the primacy of presentational immediacy. We open our eyes and our other sense-organs; we then survey the contemporary world decorated with sights, and sounds, and tastes; and then, by the sole aid of this information about the contemporary world, thus decorated, we draw what conclusions we can as to the actual world. No philosopher really holds that this is the sole source of information: Hume and his followers appeal vaguely to 'memory' and to 'practice,' in order to supplement their direct information; and Kant wrote other 'Critiques' in order to supplement his *Critique of Pure Reason*. But the general procedure of modern philosophical 'criticism' is to tie down opponents strictly to the front door of presentational immediacy as the sole source of information, while one's philosophy makes its escape by a back door veiled under the ordinary usages of language.

If this 'Humian' doctrine be true, certain conclusions as to 'behavior' ought to follow—conclusions which, in the most striking way, are not verified. It is almost indecent to draw the attention of philosophers to the minor transactions of daily life, away from the classic sources of philosophic knowledge; but, after all, it is the empiricists who began this appeal to Caesar.

According to Hume, our behaviour presupposing causation is due to the repetition of associated presentational experiences. Thus the vivid presentment of the antecedent percepts should vividly generate the behaviour, in action or thought, towards the associated consequent. The clear, distinct, overwhelming perception of the one is the overwhelming reason for the subjective transition to the other. For behaviour, interpretable as implying causation, is on this theory the subjective response to presentational immediacy. According to Hume this subjective response is the beginning and the end of all that there is to be said about causation. In Hume's theory the response is response to presentational immediacy, and to nothing else. Also the situation elicited in response is nothing but an immediate presentation, or the memory of one. Let us apply this explanation to reflex action:

in the dark, the electric light is suddenly turned on and the man's eyes blink. There is a simple physiological explanation of this trifling incident.

But this physiological explanation is couched wholly in terms of causal efficacy: it is the conjectural record of the travel of a spasm of excitement along nerves to some nodal centre, and of the return spasm of contraction back to the eyelids. The correct technical phraseology would not alter the fact that the explanation does not involve any appeal to presentational immediacy. . . . At the most there is a tacit supposition as to what a physiologist, who in fact was not there, might have seen if he had been there, and if he could have vivisected the man without affecting these occurrences, and if he could have observed with a microscope which also in fact was absent. Thus the physiological explanation remains from the point of view of Hume's philosophy, a tissue of irrelevancies. It presupposes a side of the universe about which, on Hume's theory, we must remain in blank ignorance.

Let us now dismiss physiology and turn to the private experience of the blinking man. The sequence of percepts, in the mode of presentational immediacy, are flash of light, feeling of eye-closure, instant of darkness. The three are practically simultaneous; though the flash maintains its priority over the other two, and these two latter percepts are indistinguishable as to priority. According to the philosophy of organism [i.e., Whitehead's philosophy], the man also experiences another percept in the mode of causal efficacy. He feels that the experiences of the *eye* in the matter of the flash are causal of the blink. The man himself will have no doubt of it. In fact, it is the feeling of causality which enables the man to distinguish the priority of the flash; and the inversion of the argument, whereby the temporal sequence 'flash to blink' is made the premise for the 'causality' belief, has its origin in pure theory. The man will explain his experience by saying, 'The flash made me blink'; and if his statement be doubted, he will reply, 'I know it, because I felt it.'

The philosophy of organism accepts the man's statement, that the flash *made* him blink. But Hume intervenes with another explanation. He first points out that in the mode of presentational immediacy there is no percept of the flash *making* the man blink. In this mode there are merely the two percepts—the flash and the blink—combining the two latter of the three percepts under the one term 'blink.' Hume refuses to admit the man's protestation, that the compulsion to blink is just what he did feel. The refusal is based on the dogma, that all percepts are in the mode of presentational immediacy—a dogma not to be upset by a mere appeal to direct experience. Besides Hume has another interpretation of the man's experience: what the man really felt was his *habit* of blinking after flashes. The word 'association' explains it all, according to Hume. But how can a 'habit' be felt, when a 'cause' cannot be felt? Is there any presentational immediacy in the feeling of a 'habit'? Hume by a sleight of hand confuses a 'habit of feeling blinks after flashes' with a *feeling of the habit* of feeling blinks after flashes.'

We have here a perfect example of the practice of applying the test of presentational immediacy to procure the critical rejection of some doctrines, and of allowing other doctrines to slip out by a back door, so as to evade the test. The notion of causation arose because mankind lives amid experiences in the mode of causal efficacy.

We will keep to the appeal to ordinary experience, and consider another situation, which Hume's philosophy is ill equipped to explain. The 'causal feeling' according to that doctrine arises from the long association of well-marked presentations of sensa, one precedent to the other. It would seem therefore that inhibitions of sensa, given in presentational immediacy, should be accompanied by a corresponding absence of 'causal feeling'; for the explanation of how there is 'causal feeling' presupposes the well-marked familiar sensa, in presentational immediacy. Unfortunately the contrary is the case. An inhibition of familiar sensa is very apt to leave us a prey to vague terrors respecting a circumambient world of causal operations. In the dark there are vague presences, doubtfully feared; in the silence, the irresistible causal efficacy of nature presses itself upon us; in the vagueness of the low hum of insects in an August woodland, the inflow into ourselves of feelings from enveloping nature overwhelms us; in the dim consciousness of half-sleep, the presentations of sense fade away, and we are left with the vague feeling of influences from vague things around us. It is quite untrue that the feelings of various types of influences are dependent upon the familiarity of well-marked sensa in immediate presentment. Every way of omitting the sensa still leaves us a prey to vague feelings of influence. Such feelings, divorced from immediate sensa, are pleasant, or unpleasant, according to mood; but they are always vague as to spatial and temporal definition, though their explicit dominance in experience may be heightened in the absence of sensa.

Further, our experience of our various bodily parts are primarily perceptions of them as *reasons* for 'projected' sensa: the hand is the *reason* for the projected touch-sensum, the *eye* is the *reason* for the projected sight-sensum. Our bodily experience is primarily an experience of the dependence of presentational immediacy upon causal efficacy. Hume's doctrine inverts this relationship by making causal efficacy, as an experience, dependent upon presentational immediacy. This doctrine, whatever be its merits, is not based upon any appeal to experience.

Readings

1. Broad, C. D. *The Mind and Its Place in Nature.* London; Kegan Paul Ltd., 1925, chap. 3.

2. Bunge, Mario. *Causality.* Cambridge: Peter Smith, 1959.

3. Ducasse, C. J. *Nature, Mind, and Death.* La Salle, Ill.: Open Court, 1951, Part II. Against Hume.

4. Hart, H. L. and A. Honore. *Causation and the Law.* Oxford: Oxford Univ. Press, 1958.

5. Laird, John. *Hume's Philosophy of Human Nature.* Conn.: The Shoe String Press, 1932.

6. Lowe, Victor. *Understanding Whitehead.* Baltimore: The Johns Hopkins Press, 1962

7. Nagel, Ernest. *The Structure of Science.* New York: Harcourt, Brace & World, 1961, chaps. 4, 10.

8. Parker, DeWitt. *Experience and Substance.* Ann Arbor: Univ. of Michigan Press, 1941, chaps. 12, 13, 14. Against Hume.

9. Taylor, Richard. "Causation," *Monist* (1963).

five

Can Causal Relations
Be Proven?

28

There Are No Possible Grounds For Induction

David Hume (1711–1776) is a British philosopher, historian, and essayist whose views on causality stimulated Kant to construct his "critical philosophy"; noted for his development of the empiricism of Locke and Berkeley and for his skepticism. He is the author of *Treatise on Human Nature*.

The problem of induction is related to and its consideration follows the consideration of causality. The problem of causality is the problem of definition of cause. The problem of induction is the determination of the presence of a causal relationship. One says that smoking causes cancer. The question here is: How does one know that smoking causes cancer? How can one prove it? Hume argues that one can never prove it. The question is: How do I know that in the future smoking will cause cancer? The usual argument is that smoking has caused cancer in the past and hence will cause it in the future. One presupposes that because smoking has been accompanied by cancer in the instances one has observed, then in the future smoking will be accompanied by cancer. One presupposes that *nature is uniform*. Hume says that there is no way of establishing the uniformity of nature and hence we can never justify the causal relationship between events. Such justification, according to Hume, is nothing but a *habit* of expecting what has happened in such-and-such circumstances to happen again in similar circumstances.

TO STUDY

1. Into what two kinds are all objects of human reason divided? How are they distinguished from one another?

2. What then is the subject into which Hume wishes to inquire?

3. Upon what are all reasonings concerning the matter of fact based?

4. What is the significance of the example of the two smooth pieces of marble?

5. Explain: "The mind can never possibly find the effect in the supposed cause."

6. Upon what is our belief in cause and effect relations based?

7. What is Hume's conclusion concerning the whole matter?

Section IV

Sceptical Doubts Concerning the Operations of the Understanding

Part I

All the objects of human reason or inquiry may naturally be divided into two kinds, to wit, *Relations of Ideas,* and *Matters of Fact.* Of the first kind are the sciences of Geometry, Algebra, and Arithmetic; and in short, every affirmation which is either intuitively or demonstratively certain. *That the square of the hypothenuse is equal to the square of the two sides,* is a proposition which expresses a relation between these figures. *That three times five is equal to the half of thirty,* expresses a relation between these numbers. Propositions of this kind are discoverable by the mere operation of thought, without dependence on what is anywhere existent in the universe. Though there never were a circle or triangle in nature, the truths demonstrated by Euclid would forever retain their certainty and evidence.

Matters of fact, which are the second objects of human reason, are not ascertained in the same manner; nor is our evidence of their truth, however great, of a like nature with the foregoing. The contrary of every matter of fact is still possible; because it can never imply a contradiction, and is conceived by the mind with the same facility and distinctness, as if ever so conformable to reality. *That the sun will not rise tomorrow* is no less intelligible a proposition, and implies no more contradiction than the affirmation *that it will rise.* We should in vain, therefore, attempt to demonstrate its falsehood. Were it demonstratively false, it would imply a contradiction

---

From *An Enquiry Concerning Human Understanding* (1748).

and could never be distinctly conceived by the mind.

It may, therefore, be a subject worthy of curiosity, to inquire what is the nature of that evidence which assures us of any real existence and matter of fact, beyond the present testimony of our senses, or the records of our memory. This part of philosophy, it is observable, has been little cultivated, either by the ancients or moderns; and, therefore, our doubts and errors, in the prosecution of so important an inquiry, may be the more excusable; while we march through such difficult paths without any guide or direction. They may even prove useful, by exciting curiosity, and destroying that implicit faith and security, which is the bane of all reasoning and free inquiry. The discovery of defects in the common philosophy, if any such there be, will not, I presume, be a discouragement, but rather an incitement, as is usual, to attempt something more full and satisfactory than has yet been proposed to the public.

All reasonings concerning matter of fact seem to be founded on the relation of *Cause and Effect.* By means of that relation alone we can go beyond the evidence of our memory and senses. If you were to ask a man why he believes any matter of fact which is absent; for instance, that his friend is in the country, or in France; he would give you a reason; and this reason would be some other fact; as a letter received from him, or the knowledge of his former resolutions and promises. A man finding a watch or any other machine in a desert island would conclude that there had once been men on that island. All our reasonings concerning fact are of the same nature. And here it is constantly supposed that there is a connection between the present fact and that which is inferred from it. Were there nothing to bind them together, the inference would be entirely precarious. The hearing of an articulate voice and rational discourse in the dark assures us of the presence of some person: Why? because these are the effects of the human make and fabric, and closely connected with it. If we anatomize all the other reasonings of this nature, we shall find that they are founded on the relation of cause and effect, and that this relation is either near or remote, direct or collateral. Heat and light are collateral effects of fire, and the one effect may justly be inferred from the other.

If we would satisfy ourselves, therefore, concerning the nature of that evidence, which assures us of matters of fact, we must inquire how we arrive at the knowledge of cause and effect.

I shall venture to affirm, as a general proposition, which admits of no exception, that the knowledge of this relation is not, in any instance, attained by reasonings *a priori;* but arises entirely from experience, when we find that any particular objects are constantly conjoined with each other. Let an object be presented to a man of ever so strong natural reason and abilities; if that object be entirely new to him, he will not be able, by the most accurate examination of its sensible qualities, to discover any of its causes or effects. Adam, though his rational faculties be supposed, at the very first, entirely perfect, could not have inferred from the fluidity and transparency of water that it would suffocate him, or from the light and warmth of fire that it would consume him. No object ever discovers, by the qualities which appear to the senses, either the causes which produced it, or the effects which will arise from it; nor can our reason, unassisted by experience, ever draw any inference concerning real existence and matter of fact.

This proposition, *that causes and effects are discoverable, not by reason but by experience,* will readily be admitted with regard to such objects as we remember to have once been altogether unknown to us, since we must be conscious of the utter inability, which we then lay under, of foretelling what would arise from them. Present two smooth pieces of marble to a man who has no tincture of natural philosophy; he will never discover that they will adhere together in such a manner as to require great force to separate them in a direct line, while they make so small a resistance to a lateral pressure. Such events, as bear little analogy to the common course of nature, are also readily confessed to be known only by experience; nor does any man imagine that the explosion of gun-powder, or the attraction of a loadstone, could ever be discovered by arguments *a priori.* In like manner, when an effect is supposed to depend upon an intricate machinery or secret structure of parts, we make no difficulty in attributing all our knowledge of it to experience. Who will assert that he can give the ultimate reason why milk or bread is proper nourishment for a man, not for a lion or a tiger?

But the same truth may not appear, at first sight, to have the same evidence with regard to events, which have become familiar to us from our first appearance in the world, which bear a close analogy to the whole course of nature, and which are supposed to depend on the simple qualities of objects, without any secret structure of parts. We are apt to imagine that we could discover these effects by the mere operation of our reason, without experience. We fancy, that were we brought on a sudden into this world, we could at first have inferred that one billiard ball would communicate motion to another upon impulse; and that we needed not to have waited for the event, in order to pronounce with certainty concerning it. Such is the influence of custom, that, where it is strongest, it not only covers our natural ignorance, but even conceals itself, and seems not to take place, merely because it is found in the highest degree.

But to convince us that all the laws of nature, and all the operations of bodies without exception, are known only by experience, the following reflections may, perhaps, suffice. Were any object presented to us, and were we required to pronounce concerning the effect which will result from it, without consulting past observation, after what manner, I beseech you, must the mind proceed in this operation? It must invent or imagine some event, which it ascribes to the object as its effect; and it is plain that this invention must be entirely arbitrary. The mind can never possibly find the effect in the supposed cause, by the most accurate scrutiny and examination. For the effect is totally different from the cause, and consequently can never be discovered in it. Motion in the second billiard ball is a quite distinct event from motion in the first; nor is there anything in the one to suggest the smallest hint of the other. A stone or piece of metal raised into the air, and left without any support, immediately falls: but to consider the matter *a priori,* is there anything we discover in this situation which can beget the idea of a downward, rather than an upward, or any other motion, in the stone or metal?

And as the first imagination or invention of a particular effect, in all natural operations, is arbitrary, where we consult not experience; so must we also esteem the supposed tie or connection between the cause and effect, which binds them together, and renders it impossible that any other effect could result from the operation of that cause. When I see, for instance, a billiard ball moving in a straight line towards another: even suppose motion in the second ball should by accident be suggested to me, as the result of their contact or impulse; may I not conceive, that a hundred different events might as well follow from that cause? May not both these balls remain at absolute rest? May not the first ball return in a straight line, or leap off from the second in any line or direction? All these suppositions are consistent and conceivable. Why then should we give preference to one, which is no more consistent or conceivable than the rest? All our reasonings *a priori* will never be able to show us any foundation for this preference.

In a word, then, every effect is a distinct event from its cause. It could not, therefore, be discovered in the cause, and the first invention or conception of it, *a priori,* must be entirely arbitrary. And even after it is suggested, the conjunction of it with the cause must appear equally arbitrary; since there are always many other effects, which, to reason, must seem fully as consistent and natural. In vain, therefore, should we pretend to determine any single event, or infer any cause or effect, without the assistance of observation and experience.

Hence, we may discover the reason why no philosopher, who is rational and modest, has ever pretended to assign the ultimate cause of any natural operation, or to show distinctly the action of that power, which produces any single effect in the universe. It is confessed that the utmost effort of human reason is to reduce the principles, productive of natural phenomena, to a greater simplicity, and to resolve the many particular effects into a few general causes by means of reasonings from analogy, experience, and observation. But as to the causes of these general causes, we should in vain attempt their discovery; nor shall we ever be able to satisfy ourselves by any particular explication of them. These ultimate springs and principles are totally shut up from human curiosity and inquiry. Elasticity, gravity, cohesion of parts, communication of motion by impulse—these are probably the ultimate causes and principles which we shall ever discover in nature; and we may esteem ourselves sufficiently happy, if, by accurate inquiry and reasoning, we can trace up the particular phenomena to, or neat to, these general principles. The most perfect philosophy of the natural kind only staves off our ignorance a little longer: as perhaps the most perfect philosophy of the moral or metaphysical kind serves only to discover larger portions of it. Thus the observation of human blindness and weakness is the result of all philosophy, and meets us at every turn, in spite of our endeavors to elude or avoid it.

Nor is geometry, when taken into the assistance of natural philosophy, ever able to remedy this defect, or lead us into the knowledge of ultimate causes, by all that accuracy of reasoning for which it is so justly celebrated. Every part of mixed mathematics proceeds upon the supposition that certain laws are established by nature in her operations; and abstract reasonings are employed, either to assist experience in the discovery of these laws, or to determine their influence in particular instances, where it depends upon any precise degree of distance and quantity. Thus, it is a law of motion, discovered by experience, that the moment or force of any body in motion is in the compound ratio or proportion of its solid contents and its velocity; and consequently, that a small force may remove the greatest obstacle or raise the greatest weight, if, by any contrivance or machinery, we can increase the velocity of that force, so as to make it an overmatch for its antagonist. Geometry assists us in the application of this law, by giving us the just dimensions of all the parts and figures which can enter into any species of machine; but still the discovery of the law itself is owing merely to experience, and all the abstract reasonings in the world could never lead us one step towards the knowledge of it. When we reason *a priori,* and consider merely any object or cause as it appears to the mind, independent of all observation, it never could suggest to us the notion of any distinct object, such as its effect; much less, show us the inseparable and inviolable connection between them. A man must be very sagacious who could discover by reasoning that crystal is the effect of heat, and ice of cold, without being previously acquainted with the operation of these qualities.

Part II

But we have not yet attained any tolerable satisfaction with regard to the question first proposed. Each solution still gives rise to a new question as difficult as the foregoing, and leads us on to farther inquiries. When it is asked, *What is the nature of all our reasonings concerning matter of fact?* the proper answer seems to be, that they are founded on the relation of cause and effect. When again it is asked, *What is the foundation of all our reasonings and conclusions concerning that relation?* it may be replied in one word, Experience. But if we still carry on our sifting humor, and ask, *What is the foundation of all conclusions from experience?* this implies a new question, which may be of more difficult solution and explication. Philosophers, that give themselves airs of superior wisdom and sufficiency, have a hard task when they encounter persons of inquisitive dispositions, who push them from every corner to which they retreat, and who are sure at last to bring them to some dangerous dilemma. The best expedient to prevent this confusion is to be modest in our pretensions; and even to discover the difficulty ourselves before it is objected to us. By this means, we may make a kind of merit of our very ignorance.

I shall content myself, in this section, with an easy task, and shall pretend only to give a negative answer to the question here proposed. I say then, that, even after we have experience of the operations of cause and effect, our conclusions from that experience are *not* founded on reasoning, or any process of the understanding. This answer we must endeavor both to explain and to defend.

It must certainly be allowed that nature has kept us at a great distance from all her secrets, and has afforded us only the knowledge of a few superficial qualities of objects, while she conceals from us those powers and principles on which the influence of those objects entirely depends. Our senses inform us of the color, weight, and consistence of bread; but neither sense nor reason can ever inform us of those qualities which fit it for the nourishment and support of a human body. Sight or feeling conveys an idea of the actual motion of bodies; but as to that wonderful force or power, which would carry on a moving body forever in a continued change of place, and which bodies never lose but by communicating it to others; of this we cannot form the most distant conception. But notwithstanding this ignorance of natural powers and principles, we always presume, when we see like sensible qualities, that they have like secret powers, and expect that effects, similar to those which we have experienced, will follow from them. If a body of like color and consistence with that bread, which we have formerly eaten, be presented to us, we make no scruple of repeating the experiment, and foresee, with certainty, like nourishment and support. Now this is a process of the mind or thought, of which I would willingly know the foundation. It is allowed on all hands that there is no known connection between the sensible qualities and the secret powers; and consequently, that the mind is, not led to form such a conclusion concerning their constant and regular conjunction, by anything which it knows of their nature. As to past *Experience,* it can be allowed to give *direct* and *certain* information of those precise objects only, and that precise period of time, which fell under its cognizance: but why this experience should be extended to future times, and to other objects, which for aught we know, may be only in appearance similar; this is the main question on which I would insist. The bread, which I formerly ate, nourished me; that is, a body of such sensible qualities was, at that time, endued with such secret powers: but does it follow, that other bread must also nourish me at another time, and that like sensible qualities must always be attended with like secret powers? The consequence seems nowise necessary. At least, it must be acknowledged that there is here a consequence drawn by the mind; that there is a certain step taken; a process of thought, and an inference, which wants to be explained. These two propositions are far from being the same; *I have found that such an object has always been attended with such an effect,* and *I foresee, that other objects, which are, in appearance, similar, will be attended with similar effects.* I shall allow, if you please, that the one proposition may justly be inferred from the other: I know, in fact, that it always is inferred. But if you insist that the inference is made by a chain of reasoning, I desire you to produce that reasoning. The connection between these propositions is not intuitive. There is required a medium, which may enable the mind to draw such an inference, if indeed it be drawn by reasoning and argument. What that medium is, I must confess, passes my comprehension; and it is incumbent on those to produce it, who assert that it really exists, and is the origin of all our conclusions concerning matter of fact.

This negative argument must certainly, in process of time, become altogether convincing, if many penetrating and able philosophers shall turn their inquiries this way and no one be ever able to discover any connecting proposition or intermediate step which supports the understanding in this conclusion. But as the question is yet new, every reader may not trust so far to his own penetration as to conclude, because an argument escapes his inquiry, that therefore it does not really exist. For this reason it may be requisite to venture upon a more difficult task; and, enumerating all the branches of human knowledge, endeavor to show that none of them can afford such an argument.

All reasonings may be divided into two kinds, namely, demonstrative reasoning, or that concerning relations of ideas, and moral reasoning, or that concerning matter of fact and existence. That there are no demonstrative arguments in the case seems evident; since it implies no contradiction that the course of nature may change, and that an object, seemingly like those which we have experienced, may be attended with different or contrary effects. May I not clearly and distinctly conceive that a body, falling from the clouds, and which, in all other respects, resembles snow, has yet the taste of salt or feeling of fire? Is there any more intelligible proposition than to affirm that all the trees will flourish in December and January, and decay in May and June? Now whatever is intelligible, and can be distinctly conceived, implies no contradiction, and can never be proved false by any demonstrative argument or abstract reasoning *a priori.*

If we be, therefore, engaged by arguments to put trust in past experience, and make it the standard of our future judgment, these arguments must be probable only, or such as regard matter of fact and real existence, according to the division above mentioned. But, that there is no argument of this kind, must appear, if our explication of that species of reasoning be admitted as solid and satisfactory. We have said that all arguments concerning existence are founded on the relation of cause and effect; that our knowledge of that relation is derived entirely from experience; and that all our experimental conclusions proceed upon the supposition that the future will be conformable to the past. To endeavor, therefore, the proof of this last supposition by probable arguments, or arguments regarding existence, must be evidently going in a circle, and taking that for granted which is the very point in question.

In reality, all arguments from experience are founded on the similarity which we discover among natural objects, and by which we are induced to expect effects similar to those which we have found to follow from such objects. And though none but a fool or madman will ever pretend to dispute the authority of experience, or to reject that great guide of human life, it may surely be allowed a philosopher to have so much curiosity at least as to examine the principle of human nature, which gives this mighty authority to experience, and makes us draw advantage from that similarity which nature has placed among different objects. From causes which appear *similar* we expect similar effects. This is the sum of all our experimental conclusions. Now it seems evident that if this conclusion were formed by reason, it would be as perfect at first, and upon one instance, as after ever so long a course of experience. But the case is far otherwise. Nothing so like as eggs; yet no one, on account of this appearing similarity, expects the same taste and relish in all of them. It is only after a long course of uniform experiments in any kind, that we attain a firm reliance and security with regard to a particular event. Now where is that process of reasoning which, from one instance, draws a conclusion so different from that which it infers from a hundred instances that are nowise different from that single one? This question I propose as much for the sake of information, as with an intention of raising difficulties. I cannot find, I cannot imagine any such reasoning. But I keep my mind still open to instruction, if anyone will vouchsafe to bestow it on me.

Should it be said that from a number of uniform experiments, we *infer* a connection between the sensible qualities and the secret powers; this, I must confess, seems the same difficulty, couched in different terms. The question still recurs, on what process of argument this *inference* is founded? Where is the medium, the interposing ideas, which join propositions so very wide of each other? It is confessed that the color, consistence, and other sensible qualities of bread appear not, of themselves, to have any connection with the secret powers of nourishment and support. For otherwise we could infer these secret powers from the first appearance of these sensible qualities, without the aid of experience; contrary to the sentiment of all philosophers, and contrary to plain matter of fact. Here, then, is our natural state of ignorance with regard to the powers and influence of all objects. How is this remedied by experience? It only shows us a number of uniform effects resulting from certain objects, and teaches us that those particular objects, at that particular time, were endowed with such powers and forces. When a new object, endowed with similar sensible qualities, is produced, we expect similar powers and forces, and look for a like effect. From a body of like color and consistence with bread we expect like nourishment and support. But this surely is a step or progress of the mind, which wants to be explained. When a man says, *I have found, in all past instances, such sensible qualities conjoined with such secret powers:* and when he says, *Similar sensible qualities will always be conjoined with similar secret powers,* he is not guilty of a tautology, nor are these propositions in any respect the same. You say that the one proposition is an inference from the other. But you must confess that the inference is not intuitive; neither is it demonstrative: of what nature is it, then? To say it is experimental, is begging the question. For all inferences from experience suppose, as their foundation, that the future will resemble the past, and that similar powers will be conjoined with similar sensible qualities. If there be any suspicion that the course of nature may change, and that the past may be no rule for the future, all experience becomes useless, and can give rise to no inference or conclusion. It is impossible, therefore, that any arguments from experience can prove this resemblance of the past to the future; since all these arguments are founded on the supposition of that resemblance. Let the course of things be allowed hitherto ever so regular; that alone, without some new argument or inference, proves not that, for the future, it will continue so. In vain do you pretend to have learned the nature of bodies from your past experience. Their secret nature, and consequently all their effects and influence, may change, without any change in their sensible qualities. This happens sometimes, and with regard to some objects: why may it not happen always, and with regard to all objects? What logic, what process of argument secures you against this supposition? My practice, you say, refutes my doubts. But you mistake the purport of my question. As an agent, I am quite satisfied in the point; but as a philosopher, who has some share of curiosity, I will not say scepticism, I want to learn the foundation of this inference. No reading, no inquiry has yet been able to remove my difficulty, or give me satisfaction in a matter of such importance. Can I do better than propose the difficulty to the public, even though, perhaps, I have small hopes of obtaining a solution? We shall at least, by this means, be sensible of our ignorance, if we do not augment our knowledge.

I must confess that a man is guilty of unpardonable arrogance who concludes, because an argument has escaped his own investigation, that, therefore, it does not really exist. I must also confess that, though all the learned, for several ages, should have employed themselves in fruitless search upon any subject, it may still, perhaps be rash to conclude positively that the subject must, therefore, pass all human comprehension. Even though we examine all the sources of our knowledge, and conclude them unfit for such a subject, there may still remain a suspicion that the enumeration is not complete, or the examination not accurate. But with regard to the present subject, there are some considerations which seem to remove all this accusation of arrogance or suspicion of mistake.

It is certain that the most ignorant and stupid peasants—nay, infants; nay, even brute beasts—improve by experience, and learn the qualities of natural objects, by observing the effects which result from them. When a child has felt the sensation of pain from touching the flame of a candle, he will be careful not to put his hand near any candle; but will expect a similar effect from a cause which is similar in its sensible qualities and appearance. If you assert, therefore, that the understanding of the child is led into this conclusion by any process of argument or ratiocination, I may justly require you to produce that argument; nor have you any pretense to refuse so equitable a demand. You cannot say that the argument is abstruse, and may possibly escape your inquiry; since you confess that it is obvious to the capacity of a mere infant. If you hesitate, therefore, a moment, or if, after reflection, you produce any intricate or profound argument, you, in a manner, give up the question, and confess that it is not reasoning which engages us to suppose the past resembling the future, and to expect similar effects from causes which are, to appearance, similar. This is the proposition which I intended to enforce in the present section. If I be right, I pretend not to have made any mighty discovery. And if I be wrong, I must acknowledge myself to be, indeed, a very backward scholar; since I cannot now discover an argument which, it seems, was perfectly familiar to me long before I was out of my cradle.

Section V

Sceptical Solution of These Doubts

Part I

The passion for philosophy, like that for religion, seems liable to this inconvenience, that, though it aims at the correction of our manners and extirpa-
tion of our vices, it may only serve, by imprudent management, to foster
a predominant inclination, and push the mind, with more determined resolution towards that side which already *draws* too much, by the bias and
propensity of the natural temper. It is certain that, while we aspire to the
magnanimous firmness of the philosophic sage, and endeavor to confine our
pleasures altogether within our own minds, we may, at last, render our
philosophy like that of Epictetus, and other *Stoics,* only a more refined
system of selfishness, and reason ourselves out of all virtue as well as social
enjoyment. While we study with attention the vanity of human life, and
turn all our thoughts toward the empty and transitory nature of riches and
honors, we are, perhaps, all the while flattering our natural indolence,
which, hating the bustle of the world and drudgery of business, seeks a
pretense of reason to give itself a full and uncontrolled indulgence. There
is, however, one species of philosophy which seems little liable to this
inconvenience, and that because it strikes in with no disorderly passion of
the human mind, nor can mingle itself with any natural affection or propensity; and that is the Academic or Sceptical philosophy. The academics
always talk of doubt and suspense of judgment, of danger in hasty determi-
nations, of confining to very narrow bounds the inquiries of the understanding, and of renouncing all speculations which lie not within the limits of
common life and practice. Nothing, therefore, can be more contrary than
such a philosophy to the supine indolence of the mind, its rash arrogance,
its lofty pretensions, and its supersitious credulity. Every passion is morti-
fied by it, except the love of truth; and that passion never is, nor can be,
carried to too high a degree. It is surprising, therefore, that this philosophy,
which, in almost every instance, must be harmless and innocent, should be
the subject of so much groundless reproach and obloquy. But, perhaps, the
very circumstance which renders it so innocent is what chiefly exposes it
to the public hatred and resentment. By flattering no irregular passion, it
gains few partisans: by opposing so many vices and follies, it raises to itself
abundance of enemies, who stigmatize it as libertine, profane, and irreligious.

Nor need we fear that this philosophy, while it endeavors to limit our
inquiries to common life, should ever undermine the reasonings of common
life, and carry its doubts so far as to destroy all action, as well as speculation.

Nature will always maintain her rights, and prevail in the end over any abstract reasoning whatsoever. Though we should conclude, for instance, as in the foregoing section, that, in all reasonings from experience, there is a step taken by the mind which is not supported by any argument or process of the understanding; there is no danger that these reasonings, on which almost all knowledge depends, will ever be affected by such a discovery. If the mind be not engaged by argument to make this step, it must be induced by some other principle of equal weight and authority; and that principle will preserve its influence as long as human nature remains the same. What that principle is may well be worth the pains of inquiry.

Suppose a person, though endowed with the strongest faculties of reason and reflection, to be brought on a sudden into this world; he would, indeed, immediately observe a continual succession of objects, and one event following another; but he would not be able to discover anything farther. He would not, at first, by any reasoning, be able to reach the idea of cause and effect; since the particular powers, by which all natural operations are performed, never appear to the senses, nor is it reasonable to conclude, merely because one event, in one instance, precedes another, that therefore the one is the cause, the other the effect. Their conjunction may be arbitrary and casual. There may be no reason to infer the existence of one from the appearance of the other. And in a word, such a person, without more experience, could never employ his conjecture or reasoning concerning any matter of fact, or be assured of anything beyond what was immediately present to his memory and senses.

Suppose, again, that he has acquired more experience, and has lived so long in the world as to have observed familiar objects or events to be constantly conjoined together; what is the consequence of this experience? He immediately infers the existence of the other. Yet he has not, by all his experience, acquired any idea or knowledge of the secret power by which the one object produces the other; nor is it, by any process of reasoning, he is engaged to draw this inference. But still he finds himself determined to draw it: and though he should be convinced that his understanding has no part in the operation, he would nevertheless continue in the same course of thinking. There is some other principle which determines him to form such a conclusion.

This principle is Custom or Habit. For wherever the repetition of any particular act or operation produces a propensity to renew the same act or operation, without being impelled by any reasoning or process of the understanding, we always say that this propensity is the effect of *Custom.* By employing that word, we pretend not to have given the ultimate reason of such a propensity. We only point out a principle of human nature, which is universally acknowledged, and which is well known by its effects. Perhaps we can push our inquiries no farther, or pretend to give the cause of this cause; but must rest contented with it as the ultimate principle, which we can assign, of all our conclusions from experience. It is sufficient satisfaction that we can go so far, without repining at the narrowness of our faculties because they will carry us no farther. And it is certain we here advance a very intelligible proposition at least, if not a true one, when we assert that, after the constant conjunction of two objects—heat and flame, for instance, weight and solidity—we are determined by custom alone to expect the one from the appearance of the other. This hypothesis seems even the only one which explains the difficulty, why we draw, from a thousand instances, an inference which we are not able to draw from one instance that is, in no respect, different from them. Reason is incapable of any such variation. The conclusions which it draws from considering one circle are the same which it would form upon surveying all the circles in the universe. But no man, having seen only one body move after being impelled by another, could infer that every other body will move after a like impulse. All inferences from experience, therefore, are effects of custom, not of reasoning.

Custom, then, is the great guide of human life. It is that principle alone which renders our experience useful to us, and makes us expect, for the future, a similar train of events with those which have appeared in the past. Without the influence of custom, we should be entirely ignorant of every matter of fact beyond what is immediately present to the memory and senses. We should never know how to adjust means to ends, or to employ our natural powers in the production of any effect. There would be an end at once of all action, as well as of the chief part of speculation.

But here it may be proper to remark that, though our conclusions from experience carry us beyond our memory and senses, and assure us of matters of fact which happened in the most distant places and most remote ages, yet some fact must always be present to the senses or memory, from which we may first proceed in drawing these conclusions. A man, who should find in a desert country the remains of pompous buildings, would conclude that the country had, in ancient times, been cultivated by civilized inhabitants; but did nothing of this nature occur to him, he could never form such an inference. We learn the events of former ages from history; but then we must peruse the volumes in which this instruction is contained, and thence carry up our inferences from one testimony to another, till we arrive at the eyewitnesses and spectators of these distant events. In a word, if we proceed not upon some fact, present to the memory or senses, our reasonings would be merely hypothetical; and however the particular links might be connected with each other, the whole chain of inferences would have nothing to support it, nor could we ever, by its means, arrive at the knowledge of any real existence. If I ask why you believe any particular matter of fact which you relate, you must tell me some reason; and this reason will be some other fact connected with it. But as you cannot proceed after this manner, *in infinitum,* you must at last terminate in some fact which is present to your memory or senses; or must allow that your belief is entirely without foundation.

What, then, is the conclusion of the whole matter? A simple one; though, it must be confessed, pretty remote from the common theories of philosophy. All belief of matter of fact or real existence is derived merely from some object, present to the memory or senses, and a customary conjunction between that and some other object. Or in other words; having found, in many instances, that any two kinds of objects—flame and heat, snow and cold—have always been conjoined together; if flame or snow be presented anew to the senses, the mind is carried by custom to expect heat or cold, and to *believe* that such a quality does exist and will discover itself upon a nearer approach. This belief is the necessary result of placing the mind in such circumstances. It is an operation of the soul, when we are so situated, as unavoidable as to feel the passion of love, when we receive benefits; or hatred, when we meet with injuries. All these operations are a species of natural instincts, which no reasoning or process of the thought and understanding is able either to produce or to prevent.

29

Induction Is Justified by Probability

Hans Reichenbach (1891–1953) was professor of philosophy at the University of California at Los Angeles. He is the
author of *The Philosophy of Space and Time* (1928); *Atom
and Cosmos* (1930); *The Theory of Probability* (1935);
Experience and Prediction (1938); *Philosophic Foundations
of Quantum Mechanics* (1944); *Elements of Symbolic Logic*
(1947); *The Rise of Scientific Philosophy* (1951).

In contrast to Hume, Reichenbach believes that it is possible to justify
induction on the basis of high probability. He argues that when we are
concerned with a certain type of event, such as smoking, if we arrive
at a constant percentage, our induction is justified. This constant percentage is referred to as "the limit of the frequency." Thus when the limit
of the frequency converges towards a constant percentage, we have proof
that a causal relation exists.

TO STUDY

1. How does Reichenbach define a posit? To what is positing applied?
   To what is it the key to understanding? Why did empiricism
   break down under Hume's criticism?

2. How are the manifold forms of induction exposed?

3. Define "induction by enumeration."

4. What is the "limit of the frequency"?

5. What is the justification of induction?

Suppose somebody casts a die and you are asked to predict whether or not face "six" will turn up. You will prefer to predict that face "six" will not turn up. Why? You do not know it for certain; but you have a greater probability, namely of ⁵/₆, for "nonsix" than for "six". You cannot claim that your prediction must come true; but it is advantageous for you to make this prediction rather than the contrary one, because you will be right in the greater number of cases.

A statement of this kind I have called a *posit*. A posit is a statement which we treat as true although we do not know whether it is so. We try to select our posits in such a way that they will be true as often as possible. The degree of probability supplies a *rating* of the posit; it tells us how good the posit is. Such is the only function of a probability. If we have the choice between a posit of the rating ⁵/₆ and one of the rating ²/₃, we shall prefer the first because this posit will be true more often. We see that the degree of probability has nothing to do with the truth of the individual statement, but that it functions as advice on how to select our posits.

The method of positing is applied to all kinds of probability statements. If we are told that the probability of a rain tomorrow is 80 per cent, we posit that it will rain, and act accordingly; for instance, we tell the gardener that he need not come tomorrow to water our garden. If we have information that the stock market will probably go down, we sell our stock. If the doctor tells us that smoking will probably shorten our lifetime, we stop smoking. If we are told that we shall probably get a job with higher pay by applying for a certain position, we make the application. Although all these statements about what will happen are only maintained as probable, we treat them as true and act accordingly; that is, we employ them in the sense of posits.

The concept of posit is the key to the understanding of predictive knowledge. A statement about the future cannot be uttered with the claim that it is true; we can always imagine that the contrary will happen, and we have no guarantee that future experience will not present to us as real what is imagination today. This very fact is the rock on which every rationalist interpretation of knowledge has been wrecked. A prediction of

From "The Pragmatic Justification of Induction" in *The Rise of Scientific Philosophy* by Hans Reichenbach (Berkeley: University of California Press, 1951), pp. 240–248. Reprinted by permission of the Regents of the University of California.

future experiences can be uttered only in the sense of a trial; we take its possible falsehood into account, and if the prediction turns out to be wrong, we are ready for another trial. The method of trial and error is the only existing instrument of prediction. A predictive statement is a posit; instead of knowing its truth we know only its rating, which is measured in terms of its probability.

The interpretation of predictive statements as posits solves the last problem that remains for an empiricist conception of knowledge: the problem of induction. Empiricism broke down under Hume's criticism of induction, because it had not freed itself from a fundamental rationalist postulate, the postulate that all knowledge must be demonstrable as true. For this conception the inductive method is unjustifiable, since there exists no proof that it will lead to true conclusions. It is different when the predictive conclusion is regarded as a posit. In this interpretation it does not require a proof that it is true; all that can be asked for is a proof that it is a good posit, or even the best posit available. Such a proof can be given, and the inductive problem can thus be solved.

The proof requires some further investigation; it cannot be given simply by showing that the inductive conclusion has a high probability. It requires an analysis of the methods of probability and must be based on considerations that are themselves independent of such methods. The justification of induction is to be given outside the theory of probability, because the theory of probability presupposes the use of induction. The meaning of this maxim will be made clear presently.

The proof is preceded by a mathematical investigation. The calculus of probability has been constructed in an axiomatic form, comparable to the geometry of Euclid; this construction shows that all the axioms of probability are purely mathematical theorems and thus analytic statements, if the frequency interpretation of probability is accepted. The only point where a non-analytic principle intervenes is the ascertainment of a degree of probability by means of an inductive inference. We find a certain relative frequency for a series of observed events and assume that the same frequency will hold approximately for further continuation of the series—that is the only synthetic principle on which the application of the calculus of probability is based.

This result is of greatest significance. The manifold forms of induction, including the hypothetico-deductive method, are expressible in terms of deductive methods, with the sole additon of induction by enumeration. The axiomatic method supplies the proof that all forms of induction are reducible to induction by enumeration: the mathematician of our time proves what Hume took for granted.

The result may appear surprising, because the method of constructing explanatory hypotheses, or of indirect evidence, looks so different from a simple induction by enumeration. But since it is possible to construe all forms of indirect evidence as inferences covered by the mathematical calculus of probability, these inferences are included in the result of the axiomatic investigation. By means of the power of deduction, the axiomatic system controls the most remote applications of probability inferences, like the engineer who controls a remote missile by radio waves; even involved inferential structures employed by the detective or by the scientist can be accounted for in terms of the axioms. These structures are superior to a simple induction by enumeration because they contain so much deductive logic—but their inductive content is exhaustively described as a network of inductions of the enumerative type.

I should like to illustrate how enumerative inductions can be combined into a network. For centuries Europeans had known white swans only, and they inferred that all swans in the world were white. One day black swans were discovered in Australia; so the inductive inference was shown to have led to a false conclusion. Would it have been possible to avoid the mistake? It is a matter of fact that other species of birds display a great variety of color among their individuals; so the logician should have objected to the inference by the argument that, if color varies among the individuals of other species, it may also vary among the swans. The example shows that one induction can be corrected by another induction. In fact, practically all inductive inferences are made, not in isolation, but within a network of many inductions.

When I say that all inductive inferences are reducible to induction by enumeration, I mean that they are expressible through a network of such simple inductions. The method by which these elementary inferences are combined can be of a much more complicated structure than the one employed in the preceding example.

Since all inductive inferences are reducible to induction by enumeration, all that is required for making inductive inferences legitimate is a justification of induction by enumeration. Such a justification is possible, when it is realized that inductive conclusions are not claimed to be true statements, but are uttered merely in the sense of posits.

When we count the relative frequency of an event, we find that the percentage found varies with the number of observed cases, but that the variations die down with increasing number. For instance, birth statistics show that of 1,000 births 49 per cent were boys; increasing the number of cases, we find 52 per cent boys among 5,000 births, 51 per cent boys among 10,000 births. Assume for a moment we know that going on we shall finally arrive at a constant percentage—the mathematician speaks of a limit of the frequency—what numerical value should we assume for this final percentage? The best we can do is to consider the last value found as the permanent one and to employ it as our posit. If the posit on further observation turns out to be false, we shall correct it; but if the series converges toward a final percentage, we must eventually arrive at values which are close to the final value. The inductive inference is thus shown to be the best instrument of finding the final percentage, or the probability of an event, if there is such a limiting percentage at all, that is, if the series converges toward a limit.

How do we know that there is a limit of the frequency? Of course, we have no proof for this assumption. But we know: if there is one, we shall find it by the inductive method. So if you want to find a limit of the frequency, use the inductive inference—it is the best instrument you have, because, if your aim can be reached, you will reach it that way. If it cannot be reached, your attempt was in vain; but then any other attempt must also break down.

The man who makes inductive inferences may be compared to a fisherman who casts a net into an unknown part of the ocean—he does not know whether he will catch fish, but he knows that if he wants to catch fish he has to cast his net. Every inductive prediction is like casting a net into the ocean of the happenings of nature; we do not know whether we shall have a good catch, but we try, at least, and try by the help of the best means available.

We try because we want to act—and he who wants to act cannot wait until the future has become observational knowledge. To control the future—to shape future happenings according to a plan—presupposes predictive knowledge of what will happen if certain conditions are realized; and if we do not know the truth about what will happen, we shall employ our best posits in the place of truth. Posits are the instruments of action where truth is not available; the justification of induction is that it is the best instrument of action known to us.

This justification of induction is very simple; it shows that induction is the best means to attain a certain aim. The aim is predicting the future—to formulate it as finding the limit of a frequency is but another version of the same aim. This formulation has the same meaning because predictive knowledge is probable knowledge and probability is the limit of a frequency. The probability theory of knowledge allows us to construct a justification of induction; it supplies a proof that induction is the best way of finding that kind of knowledge which is the only sort attainable. All knowledge is probable knowledge and can be asserted only in the sense of posits; and induction is the instrument of finding the best posits.

This solution of the problem of induction will be clarified if it is confronted with the rationalist theory of probability. The principle of indifference, which occupies a logical position similar to that of the principle of induction because it is used for the ascertainment of a degree of probability, is regarded by the rationalist as a self-evident principle of logic; he thus arrives at a *synthetic self-evidence*, at a synthetic a priori logic. Incidentally, the principle of induction by enumeration is often also regarded as a self-evident principle; this conception represents a second version of a synthetic a priori logic of probability. The empiricist conception of inductive logic is essentially different. The principle of induction by enumeration, which constitutes its only synthetic principle, is not regarded as self-evident, or as a postulate which logic could validate. What logic can prove is that the use of the principle is advisable if a certain aim is envisaged, the aim of predicting the future. This proof, the justification of induction, is constructed in terms of analytic considerations. The empiricist is allowed to use a synthetic principle, because he does not assert that the principle is true or must lead to true conclusions or to correct probabilities or to any kind of success; all he asserts is that employing the principle is the best he can do. This renunciation of any truth claim enables him to incorporate a synthetic principle in an analytic logic and to satisfy the condition that what he *asserts* on the basis of his logic is analytic truth only. He can do so because the conclusion of the inductive inference is not asserted by him, but only posited; what he asserts is that positing the conclusion is a means to his end. The empiricist principle that reason cannot make other than analytic contributions to knowledge, that there is no synthetic self-evidence, is thus fully carried through.

Readings

1. Ambrose, Alice. "The Problem of Justifying Inductive Inference," *Journal of Philosophy*, Vol. 44, no. 10 (May, 1947).

2. Barker, Stephen F. *Induction and Hypothesis.* Ithaca, N.Y.: Cornell Univ. Press, 1957, chapters 8 and 9.

3. Black, Max. *Language and Philosophy.* Ithaca, N.Y.: Cornell Univ. Press, 1949, chapter 3.

4. Braithwaite, R. B. *Scientific Explanation.* Cambridge: Cambridge Univ. Press, 1953, chapter 8.

5. Katz, Jerrold J. *The Problem of Induction and Its Solution.* Chicago: University of Chicago Press, 1962.

6. Keynes, J. M. A. *A Treatise on Probability.* London: Macmillan, 1921, Part 3.

7. Kneale, W. *Probability and Induction.* Oxford: Clarendon Press, 1949, pp. 234–237.

8. Madden, Edward H., ed. *The Structure of Scientific Thought.* Boston: Houghton-Mifflin, 1960, Part 6.

9. Russell, Bertrand. *Human Knowledge: Its Scope and Limits.* New York: Simon & Schuster, 1948, Part 5.

10. Salmon, Wesley C. *The Foundations of Scientific Inference.* Pittsburgh: University of Pittsburgh Press, 1967.

5

Metaphysics

one

Of What Does Reality Consist?

30

Reality Consists of Matter

Richard Taylor (1919–   ), professor of philosophy at the University of Rochester, has written highly acclaimed books and articles on a variety of philosophical problems.

Philosophers often occupy themselves with the question: What is the nature of the ultimate substance (or stuff or content) of which everything in the universe is composed? Of course, if they believe that there are two or more such ultimate substances, then they ask: What is the nature of each of them? Nearly every person believes he has both a body and a mind. Attempted proofs of this belief have been so strongly questioned that today only a few philosophers believe in the mind-body dualism. Richard Taylor believes there are no mental entities. He is a materialist.

Materialism, in its philosophical meaning, is the view that all that exists is material or is completely dependent upon matter for its existence. There are two aspects to this position: 1. there is only one basic kind of reality and that is material; 2. human beings are not entities composed of both a material body and an immaterial soul, but are fundamentally bodily in nature. The selection from Taylor represents the statement of an extreme materialist. It is important to be aware of the fact that materialists do not deny the existence of mind, but rather they deny that mind is a characteristic of an immaterial soul. The mind is matter just as everything is matter.

TO STUDY ──

1. On what basis does Taylor argue that there is no mind-body problem?

2. Why can't one provide a philosophical argument proving that something does or does not exist?

3. What is the grand presupposition of the mind-body problem?

4. What is the mentalistic thesis?

5. What is the materialistic thesis?

6. What is Taylor's refutation of the thesis that certain predicates cannot be applied to a man's body?

7. What is Taylor's argument against the thesis that there are unique acts which the body cannot do?

8. What is Taylor's refutation of the thesis that we directly know the existence of mental things?

9. What is the fourth argument and Taylor's reply?

10. Does matter think?

The mind-body problem, in all its variants, is a philosophical fabrication resting on no genuine data at all. It has arisen from certain presuppositions about matter and human nature familiar to philosophy from the time of the Pythagoreans, presuppositions which have persisted just to the extent that they have been left unexamined. And they have not been questioned very much simply because they are so familiar.

There are vexing, unsolved problems of psychology and problems of mental health, but there are no mind-body problems. And there are problems of "philosophical psychology," as they are sometimes called today—problems of perception, sensation, the analysis of deliberation, of purposeful behavior, and so on—but there are no mind-body problems.

The reason why there are no mind-body problems is the most straightforward imaginable: It is because there are no such things as *minds* in the first place. There being no minds, there are in strictness no mental states or events; there are only certain familiar states, capacities, and abilities which are conventionally but misleadingly called "mental." They are so-called, partly in deference to certain philosophical presuppositions,

From the *American Philosophical Quarterly*, vol. 6, no. 2 (April 1969). Reprinted with permission of the author and the *American Philosophical Quarterly*.

and partly as a reflection of our lack of understanding of them, that is of our ignorance.

Men and women are not minds, nor do they "have" minds. It is not merely that they do not "have" minds the way they have arms and legs; they do not have minds in any proper sense at all. And just as no man or woman has or ever has had any mind, so also are cats, dogs, frogs, vegetables, and the rest of living creation without minds—though philosophers of the highest rank, such as Aristotle, have felt driven to say that all living things, vegetables included, must have souls (else how could they be *living* things?) just as others of similar eminence, like Descartes, have thought that men must have minds, else how could they be *thinking* things? Today, when philosophers talk about mind-body problems, and advance various claims concerning the possible relationships between "mental" and "physical" states and events, they are, of course, talking about men. But they might as well be talking about frogs, because the presuppositions that give rise to these theories apply to other animals as well as to men.

I. Philosophical Arguments For the Existence or Nonexistence of Things

There cannot be any philosophical argument proving that something does or does not exist, so long as the description or definition of it is self-consistent. Thus there cannot be a philosophical argument proving that men do or do not, as some medieval thinkers believed, have an indestructible bone in their bodies. One can only say that such a bone has never been found (which is not a philosophical argument) and then exhibit the groundlessness or falsity of the presuppositions that gave rise to the belief in the first place. (In this case it was certain presuppositions concerning the requirements of the resurrection of the body.) Similarly, there can be no philosophical argument proving that men do or do not have souls, spirits, or minds, or that there are not *sui generis* mental states or events, assuming that these can be described in a self-consistent way. One can only note that such things have never been found in any man, living or dead, and then exhibit the arbitrariness and apparent falsity of the presuppositions that give rise to these opinions in the first place. Now of course, as far as *finding* them goes, many philosophers claim to find them all the time, *within themselves.* They are alleged to be *private* things, deeply hidden, discernible only by their possessors. All they really "find," however, are the most commonplace facts about themselves that are perfectly well known to anyone who knows anything at all—but of this, more later.

II. The Grand Presupposition of the Mind-Body Problem

What I must do now, then, is consider the presupposition that has given birth to the so-called "mind-body" problem, and show that there is nothing in it at all that anyone needs to believe; that, on the contrary, we have good evidence that it is false.

The presupposition can be tersely expressed by saying: *Matter cannot think.* That is the way a Cartesian would put it, but philosophers now spell it out a little better. Thus, we are apt to be told that thinking, choosing, deliberating, reasoning, perceiving, and even feeling, are not concepts of physics and chemistry, so that these terms have no application to bodies. Since, however, men do think, choose, deliberate, reason, perceive and feel, it follows that men are not "mere bodies." They are instead minds or souls or, as it is more common to say today "selves" or "persons," and such terms as "is thinking," "is choosing," "is perceiving," etc., are not physical or bodily but *personal* predications. A man may be in one clear sense a physical object, having arms and legs and so on, but a person is not just that visible and palpable object; there is more to a self or person than this. For it is the self or person that thinks, chooses, deliberates, feels, and so on, and not his body or some part of it.

Again—and this is really only another way of expressing the same presupposition—we are apt to be told that thoughts, choices, reasons, feelings, etc., are not physical things. It makes no sense to ask how large a thought is, whether it is soluble in alcohol, and so on. Yet these things do exist—any man can be aware of them, "within himself." Hence, that "self" within which such things occur must be something more than or other than the body. It might be just the totality of all those nonphysical ("mental") things, but in any case it is mental in nature, so a self or person is not the same thing as his body.

Or again, in case one boggles at calling thoughts, feelings, and the like, "things," at least (it is said) no one can deny that they are events or states. But they are not events or states that occur or obtain in the laboratories of physicists and chemists—except in the sense that they sometimes occur in physicists and chemists themselves, who sometimes happen to be in laboratories. No one could ever truly represent whatever might be happening in a test tube or vacuum tube as the transpiring of a thought or feeling. These things just do not—indeed, obviously could not—happen in test tubes or vacuum tubes, because they are not the *kind* of event involving changes of matter. They are a kind of "mental" event. And since these things do, obviously, happen in men, then things happen in men which are nonphysical, "mental," in nature. And so on.

III. "Selves" or "Persons" as Minds and Bodies

The word "self" and the plural "selves" are fairly common items of contemporary philosophical vocabulary. These words never occur outside of philosophy, except as suffixes to personal pronouns, but in philosophical contexts they are sometimes taken to denote rather extraordinary things. Selves are, indeed, about the strangest inhabitants of nature that one can imagine—except that, as sometimes described in philosophy, they are not even imaginable in the first place, being quite nonphysical. You cannot poke a self with a stick; the nearest you can come to that is to poke his body. The self that has that body is not supposed to be quite the same thing as his body—that is a (mere) physical object, a possible subject matter for physics and chemistry. *That* is not what thinks, reasons, deliberates, and so on; it is the self that does things like this.

At the same time, selves are never doubted to be the same things as *persons,* and persons are thought to be the same things as people, as men. And there is no doubt at all that men are visible, palpable objects, having arms and legs and so on: That they are in short, physical objects. So the thing becomes highly ambiguous. We do not, in contexts in which it would seem silly or embarrassing to do so, have to say that selves (men) are spirit beings (minds) which in some sense or other happen to "have" bodies. Clearly men are visible and palpable things, that is, are bodies. We can say that all right. But at the same time we need not say—indeed, *must* not say—that men are just (mere) bodies. There is, after all, a difference between a man's body, and that which thinks, perceives, feels, deliberates, and so on; and those are things that men (selves) do, not things that bodies do. Or again, there is, after all, a difference between bodily predicates (weighs 160 pounds, falls, is warm, etc.) and personal predicates (chooses, believes, loves his country, etc.). The former can be predicated of a man's body, just like any other body, but it would "make no sense" to predicate the latter of any (mere) body, and hence of any man's body. They are only predicated of persons. So even though selves are persons and persons are men and men are visible, palpable beings, we must not think that they are just nothing but physical beings. They are physical bodies with minds, or, as some would prefer, minds with physical bodies or, as most writers on this subject want to say, they are somehow *both.*

So the "mental" is discriminated from the (merely) "physical," and the mind-body problem emerges at once: What is the *connection* between them? What is the relationship between men's minds and their bodies? Or between mental and physical events? Or between personal and physical predicates? Anyone who raises this question—for these all amount to one and the same question—can see at once that it is going to be extremely difficult to answer. And this means that it is capable of nourishing a vast amount of philosophy. It has, in fact, kept philosophers on scattered continents busy for hundreds of years, and even today claims much of the time of philosophical faculties and their proteges. It seems a conceit to undertake to put an end to all this, but that is what I propose now to do.

IV. Mentalism And Materialism

Consider the following two theses:

> (I) A person is not something that has, possesses, utilizes, or contains a mind. That is, a person is not one thing and his mind another thing. A person or self and his mind are one and the same thing.

> (II) A person is not something that has, possesses, utilizes, or occupies a body. That is, a person is not one thing and his body another thing. A person or self and his body are one and the same thing.

We can call these two theses "mentalism" and "materialism" respectively, since the first asserts that men are minds and not bodies, and the second that they are bodies and not minds.

Now the first thing to note about these two rather crudely stated theses is that both of them cannot be true, since each asserts what the other denies. They could, of course, both be false, since a person might be identical neither with his body nor with his mind (though it is hard to think of any other candidate for the title of "person"), or a person might somehow be identical with the two of them at once. These two simple theses are, nevertheless, a good starting point for discussion, and I am going to maintain that (II), the materialist thesis, is absolutely true.

Philosophers have tended to regard (I), or some more sophisticated version of it, as correct, and to dismiss (II) as unworthy of consideration. In fact, however—and it is hard to see how this could have been so generally overlooked—*any* philosophical argument in favor of (I) against (II) is just as good an argument for (II) against (I). This I shall illustrate shortly.

In the meantime, let us give what is due to the humble fact that there are considerations drawn from common sense, indeed from the common knowledge of mankind, which favor, without proving (II). It is common knowledge that there are such things as human bodies, that there are men and women in the world. There is also one such body which everyone customarily, and without the least suggestion of absurdity, refers to as himself; he sees himself in the mirror, dresses himself, scratches himself, and so on. This is known, absolutely as well as anything can be known, and if any man were to profess doubt about it—if he doubted, for example, that there are such physical objects in the world as men and women, and therefore doubted the reality of his own body—then that man would have to be considered *totally* ignorant. For there is nothing more obvious than this. A man would be ignorant indeed if he did not know that there are such things as the sun, moon, earth, rivers, and lakes. I have never met anyone so ignorant as that. But a man who did not even know that there are men and women in the world, and that he—his body—was one of them, would be totally ignorant.

Now there is no such common knowledge of the existence of minds or souls. No one has ever found such a thing anywhere. Belief in such things rests either on religious persuasion or on philosophical arguments, sometimes on nothing but the connotations of familiar words. Such beliefs are opinions, easily doubted, and nothing that anyone knows. If a man denies that such things exist, as many have, then he exhibits no ignorance; he expresses only scepticism or doubt concerning certain religious or philosophical presuppositions or arguments.

If, accordingly, we are seeking some sort of thing with which to identify persons, then this is a *prima facie* consideration in favor of identifying them with their bodies, with things we know to be real, rather than with things postulated to suit the requirements of philosophical arguments or religious faith. This does not prove that men are nothing but bodies, of course, but it is enough to show that, since we know there are such things as persons, and we know there are such things as men (living human bodies), we had better regard these as the very same things *unless* there are some facts which would prohibit our doing so. And I shall maintain that there are no such facts. There are only philosophical arguments, not one of which proves anything.

The arguments for mentalism

I shall now consider the arguments I know, already adumbrated, in favor of what I have called mentalism. Of course not all philosophers who take seriously the mine-body problem subscribe to this simple thesis as I have formulated it, but the more sophisticated versions can be considered as we go along, and it will be seen that the arguments for these are equally inconclusive.

The first argument

There are certain predicates that undoubtedly apply to persons, but not to their bodies. Persons and their bodies cannot, therefore, be the same.

One can sometimes truly say of a person, for example, that he is intelligent, sentimental, that he loves his country, believes in God, holds strange theories on the doctrine of universals, and so on. But it would sound very odd—indeed, not even make sense—to assert any such things of any physical object whatever and hence of any man's body. It would at best be a confusion of categories to say that a certain man's *body* loves its country, for example.

Reply

If the foregoing is considered a good argument for the nonidentity of persons and bodies, then the following is obviously just as good an argument for not identifying them with their minds: There are certain predicates that undoubtedly apply to persons, but not to their minds. A person and his mind cannot, therefore, be the same. One can sometimes truly say of a person, for example, that he is walking, ran into a post, is feverish, or that he fell down. But it would sound very odd—indeed not even make sense—to assert such things of any mind whatever. It would at best be a confusion of categories to say, for instance, that a certain man's *mind* ran into a post.

Considerations such as these have led many philosophers to affirm that a person or the "true self" is neither a mind, nor a body. Hence, a person must be (a) something else altogether or, as some would prefer to say, the term "person" must express a "primitive" concept or (b) both mind and body; i.e., a person must be something having both mental and physical properties.

The former of these alternatives is simply evasive. Persons are real beings, so there must be existing things which are persons. If when we bump into a man we are not bumping into a person, and if at the same time we are not referring to a person when we say of someone that he is thinking, then it is quite impossible to see what is left to fill the role of a person. The word "person" may indeed be a primitive one, but this, I think, only means that such arguments as the two just cited are equally good and equally bad.

The second alternative that persons are beings having both mental and physical properties, is obviously only as good as the claim that there are such things as "mental properties" to begin with. Indeed, it is not even that good, for just as a physical property can be nothing but a property of a physical thing, i.e., a body, so also a mental property can be nothing but the property of a mental thing, i.e., a mind. For something to count as a physical property of something it is sufficient, and necessary, that the thing in question is a physical object. By the same token, for something to count as a mental property it is sufficient, and necessary, that it be the property that some mind possesses. Any property whatsoever that can be truly claimed to be the property of some body, animate or inanimate, is a physical property; the assertion that some body possesses a nonphysical property is simply a contradiction. This second alternative, that persons are beings possessing both physical and mental properties, therefore amounts to saying that a person is at one and the same time *two* utterly different things—a body with its physical properties and a mind with its mental properties. These are not supposed to be two things in the same sense that a family, for instance, is a plurality of beings consisting of husband, wife, and perhaps one or more children, but two wholly disparate kinds of beings having, as Descartes put it, nothing in common. Now this is no resolution of the antithesis between what I have called mentalism and materialism. It is only a reformulation of that issue. For now we can surely ask: Which of these two is the person, the true self? The body which has a mind, or the mind which has a body? And we are then back where we started.

The second argument

This argument consists of pointing out the rather remarkable things that a person can do but which, it is alleged, no physical object, of whatever complexity, can do, from which it of course follows that a person is not a physical object and hence not identical with his own body. A person, for example, can reason, deliberate about ends and means, plan for the future, draw inferences from evidence, speculate, and so on. No physical objects do such things, and even complicated machines can at best only simulate these activities. Indeed, it would not even make sense to say that a man's body was, for example, speculating on the outcome of an election, though this would not be an absurd description of some person. A person, therefore, is not the same thing as his body, and can only be described in terms of certain concepts of mind.

Reply

This argument is not very different from the first; it only substitutes activities for properties which are baptized "mental." And one reply to it is the same as to the first argument; namely, that since persons often do things that no mind could do—for instance, they run races, go fishing, raise families, and so on—then it follows that persons are not minds.

A far better reply, however, and one that is not so question-begging as it looks, is to note that since men do reason, deliberate, plan, speculate, draw inferences, run races, go fishing, raise families, and so on, and since the men that do all such things are the visible, palpable beings that we see around us all the time, then it follows that *some* physical objects—namely, men—do all these things. All are, accordingly, the activities of physical objects; they are not activities divided between a physical object, the visible man, on the one hand, and some invisible thing, his mind, on the other.

Consider the statement: "I saw George yesterday; he was trying to figure out the best way to get from Albany to Montpelier." Now this statement obviously refers, in a normal context, to a person, and it is perfectly clear that the name "George" and the pronoun "he" refer to *one and the same* being, that person. And what they both refer to is something that was seen, a certain man's body; they do not refer to some unseen thing, of which that body is some sort of visible manifestation. If that were so, then the statement would not really be true. And in any case, it would be embarrassingly silly to suppose that a more accurate rendition of the thought expressed in this statement might be: "I saw George's body yesterday. His mind was trying to figure out how to get (how to get what?) from Albany to Montpelier." It is, accordingly, one and the same thing which (*a*) is seen, and (*b*) figures and plans, and that thing is undoubtedly the physical object George. Now if conventions incline us to describe figuring out something as a "mental" activity, then we shall have to say that some purely physical objects—namely, living men—engage in mental activities. But this is simply misleading, if not contradictory, for it suggests that we are ascribing to a physical object an activity of something that is not physical, but mental. It would, therefore, be far better to say that some physical objects, namely, men or persons, sometimes perform physical activities such as figuring and planning which are quite unlike those we are accustomed to finding in certain other physical objects such as machines and the like.

The third argument

This argument, the commonest of all, is to the effect that while there may or may not be such things as "minds" (whatever that might mean), there are indisputably certain nonphysical things which are quite properly called "mental," as anyone can verify within himself. Indeed, it is sometimes claimed that nothing, not even the reality of our own bodies, is as certain as the existence of these mental things, which are perceived "directly."

Reply

What are here referred to as mental entities are, of course, such things as thoughts, mental images, after-images, sensations, feelings, and so on. Pains are frequently mentioned in this context, being, presumably, things whose existence no one would question. Having got to this point then the next step, of course, is to speculate on the connection between these mental things and certain "physical" states of the body. They evidently are not the same, and yet it is hard to see what the connection could be. Speculation also extends to such questions as whether two or more men might have "the same" pain, or why it is impossible that they should in view of the fact that they can hold common possession of ordinary "physical" things like clocks and books. Again, curiosity is aroused by the fact that a mental image, for instance, seems to have color, and yet it somehow can be perceived only by one person, its owner. Again, images sometimes seem to have shape—enough so that a perceiver can distinguish one from another, for instance—and yet no assignable size. Here, really, is a gold mine for philosophical speculation, and such speculations have filled, as they still fill, volumes.

Now surely there is a *better* way to express all that is known to be true in all this, and it is a way that does not even permit these odd theories to get started. What we know is true, and all we know is true, is that men think, sense, imagine, feel, etc. It is sheer redundancy to say that men think things called "thoughts," sense things called "sensations," imagine "images," and feel "feelings." There are no such things. And to say there are no such things is *not* to deny that men think, sense, imagine, and feel.

What, for instance, does it mean to say a man feels a pain in his foot? Absolutely nothing, except that his foot hurts. But this hurting, what sort of thing is it? It is not a thing at all; not a thing felt, and certainly not a mental thing that is felt *in his foot.* It is a state, and in no sense a state of his mind, but a straightforward state of his foot. But can that be a *physical* state? Well, it is assuredly a state of his foot, and that is a physical object; there is nothing else—no spirit foot, no spirit being, no spirit mind—that it can be a state of. Why, then, cannot other people have that same state? Why cannot other people feel the same pain I feel in my foot? And if it is a physical state, why cannot we open the foot and *see* it there? Or make some straightforward test of its presence in another man's foot?

To ask questions like these is just not to understand what is meant by describing an object as being in a certain state. Consider a piece of molten lead. Now this molten state, what sort of thing is it? The answer is that it is not a thing at all; it is a state or condition of a thing. Is it a physical state? Well, it is a state of the lead, and that is a physical object; there is nothing else for it to be a state of. Why, then, cannot another piece of lead have that same state? Why cannot something else have the molten state of this piece of lead? Of course something else can, in the only meaningful sense that can be attached to such a question; that is, another piece of lead, or some things which are not lead can melt the same way this piece of lead melted. To ask why another piece of lead cannot have the molten state of this piece of lead is, of course, unintelligible, unless it is interpreted the way just suggested, in which case the answer is that it can. But similarly, to ask why another man cannot have the pain that this man is feeling is also unintelligible, unless construed as the question why other men cannot suffer pain, in which case its presupposition is wrong—they can. And if the piece of lead's being melted is a "physical" state, why can we not separate the lead into drops and see that state? Simply because it is a state of the lead, and not some other thing contained in the lead. Indeed, to separate it into drops *is* to see, not its meltedness (there is no such thing), but that it is melted—that is just the test. We do not have to *ask* the lead whether it is melted, and rely upon its testimony; we can tell by its behavior. And in the same way we can sometimes—admittedly not always—see that a man is suffering, without having to ask him. That we sometimes go wrong here does not result from the fact that his suffering is something quite hidden within him, which he alone can find and then report; there is nothing hidden, and nothing for him to find. Still, there is a straightforward way of testing whether a piece of lead is melted, and there is no similarly straightforward way of testing whether a man's foot hurts— he may only be pretending it does. Does this indicate that there might be a pain, which he has found in his foot but might conceal, as he might conceal the contents of his wallet? Surely not; it shows only that men, unlike pieces of lead, are capable of dissimulating. No philosophy was needed to unearth that commonplace fact. It is easier to test for the presence of some states of properties than others, and this is true not only of the states of men's bodies, but of everything under the sun. But things that are hard to establish do not, just by virtue of that, warrant the title of "mental."

Similar remarks can be made about images, which are frequent candidates for the role of mental entities. When queried about their mental imagery, people often will describe it in colorful detail and even with pride, not unlike the regard one might have for a precious gem accessible only to himself. It turns out, though, that all one thereby describes is his power of imagination, which is, of course, sometimes quite great. To say that one has a lively imagination, even great powers of imagination, does not mean that he can create within his mind, *ex nihilo,* things called "images" and composed of some mental, nonphysical, spiritual material.

There is no material that is nonmaterial, and there are no images composed of this or anything else—except, of course, those physical objects (pictures, etc.) visible to anyone who can see, which are rightly called images of things. When someone *sees* something, there is (*i*) the man who sees, and (*ii*) the thing seen; for instance, some building or scene. There is not, between these, a third thing called the appearance of what is seen; philosophers are pretty much agreed on this. But similarly, when someone *imagines* something or, as it is misleadingly put, "forms an image" of it, there is (*i*) the man who imagines, and (*ii*) sometimes, but not always, something that he imagines; for instance, some building or scene, which might or might not be real. There is not, between these, a third thing called the image of what is imagined. There is just the imagining of the thing in question. And to say that a man is imagining something is to say what he is doing, or perhaps to refer to some state he is in; it is not to refer to some inner thing that he creates and, while it lasts, exclusively possesses.

It is enough, it seems to me, to point this out; that is, to point out that we can say all we want to say about men's powers of imagination without ever introducing the substantive "an image." Philosophy is robbed of nothing by the disposal of these, and there is absolutely no fact about human nature which requires us to affirm their existence. But if one does insist upon the reality of mental images, and professes, for instance, to find them right in his own mind by introspecting—and it is astonishing how eager students of philosophy seem to be to make this claim—then we can ask some very embarrassing questions. Suppose, for instance, one professes to be able to form a very clear image of, say, the campus library—he can bring it before his mind, hold it there, perhaps even turn it bottom side up, and banish it at will. We ask him, then, to hold it before his mind and count the number of steps in the image, the number of windows, the number and disposition of pigeons on the roof, and so on. He could do these things if he had a photograph of the thing before him. But he cannot do them with the image, in spite of the fact that it is supposed to be right there "before his mind," easily and "directly" inspectable. He can tell how many steps there are only if he has sometime counted the steps on the building itself (or in a photograph of it) and now *remembers*—but that is not counting the steps in the image. Or he can *imagine* that it has, say, 30 steps, and then *say* "30"—but that is not counting anything either; it is only a performance. The image he professes to "have" there, so clearly and with such detail, does not even exist. He claims to have produced in his mind an image of the library; but all he has actually done is imagine the library.

What, then, is imagining something? Is it an activity, a state, or what? It does not really matter here how we answer that; it is only *not* the producing of an entity called a "mental image." Let us suppose for this context, then, that to be imagining something is to be in a certain *state*. Is it, then, a *physical* state? Well, it is a state of a man, just as drunkenness, sleep, perspiration, obesity, etc., are sometimes states of this man or that. What is meant by asking whether these are "physical" states, other than asking whether they are states of a physical object? What shall we say of being in a state of sleep, for instance? It is the state of a man, and a man is a physical—that is, a visible and palpable—being. You cannot poke a man's state of imagining something with a stick; all you can do is poke him. That is true. But you cannot poke his somnolence with a stick either. There is nothing to poke; there is only the man sleeping, or the man imagining, or the man becoming drunk, or whatever.

How then can a man, if he is nothing but a (mere) physical object, be in such a state as this, that is, of imagining something? If he is only a body and can do this, why cannot sticks and stones be in such a state, for are they not bodies too? The answer is: For just the same reason that sticks and stones cannot be drunken, asleep, perspiring, obese, or hungry; namely, that they are sticks and stones and not men. The reason is not that they lack minds. Even if they had them, they still could not be drunken, asleep, perspiring, obese or hungry, for they would still be sticks and stones and not men.

The fourth (and last) argument

It is fairly common for people, including philosophers, to say that they can perfectly well imagine surviving the death of their bodies, which would be quite impossible for anyone who supposed that he and his body were one and the same thing. Admittedly no one knows whether there is any survival of death, but it is at least not necessarily false. The doctrine of metempsychosis,[1] for example, though there may be no reason for believing it, cannot be shown to be impossible just on philosophical grounds. It would be impossible, however, if a person and his body were identical, and so would any other form of survival. We know the fate of the body: dust. If I am the same as my body, then it is logically impossible that I should not share that fate.

Reply

All this argument shows is that not everyone, perhaps even no one, *knows* that he and his body are one and the same thing. It does not in the

---

[1] The passing of the soul at death into another body. [Ed.]

least show that, in fact, they are not. Some things, like the Evening Star and the Morning Star, which some are accustomed to thinking of and describing as different things, nevertheless do turn out to be the same.

Suppose a god were to promise me a life after death—promising, perhaps, to have me (the very person that I am) reborn elsewhere with a different body. Now such a promise might quicken a real hope in me, provided I am capable (as everyone is) of thinking of myself as being something different from my body. But the fact that I can think such a distinction does not show that there is one, and in case there is not—in case I happen to be identical with my body—then of course no god could fulfill such a promise. Consider this analogy: If an enemy of our country did not know that Albany is (the same thing as) the capital of New York, then he might be very interested in a proposal to bomb the one but to spare the other. It would nevertheless be a proposal that no one could carry out. The fact that someone who is ignorant of this identity can entertain the possibility of its being carried out does not show that it is possible; it shows only that he does not know that it is not.

V. The Soul as Life and the Soul as Thought

It is useful in concluding, I think, to compare the philosophical conception of the mind with what was once the philosophical conception of life. It was once pretty much taken for granted that men and other animals *possess* something which inanimate things lack, namely, life and that it is *because* they possess this that they can do all sorts of things that inanimate things cannot do, such as move themselves, assimilate nourishment, reproduce their kind, and so on. Aristotle classified the souls of living things according to the abilities they imparted to their owners, and thought that even vegetables had souls. Indeed, an animal's *life* and *soul* were generally thought to be one and the same thing. The very word "animal" has its origin in this belief. Socrates, according to Plato, was even able to convince himself of his own immortality on the basis of this notion for, he thought, if it is only because he has a life or soul to begin with that he is a living man, then it is idle to fear the death of that very soul. Life seemed to him identical with his soul, but accidental to his body, indeed even foreign to such a thing of clay. A similar model was at work in Descartes' philosophy when he declared that the soul could never stop thinking. Thought seemed to him identical with his soul, but positively foreign to his body.

Now of course we still talk of life that way, but we no longer take such common modes of speech as descriptive of any reality. We speak of a man "losing" his life, of a man "taking" another's life, of the "gift" of life, and even of the "breath" of life which God is supposed to infuse into an otherwise *lifeless* body. But these are plainly metaphors. No one supposes that a man or animal moves, assimilates nourishment, reproduces, and so on *because* it is possessed of life. We no longer think of life as something added to an animal body, some separable thing that quickens matter. To distinguish something as a living animal is only to call attention to the very complicated way the matter of its body is organized and to a large class of capacities which result from such organization. A living body is simply one in which certain processes, some of them frightfully complex and ill understood, take place. A living body, in short, differs from a nonliving one, not in what it possesses, but in what it does, and these are facts about it that can be verified in a straightforward way.

I have been urging a similar way of speaking of the mind; not as something mysteriously *embodied* here and there, and something that is supposed to *account* for the more or less intelligent behavior of certain beings. A being capable of more or less intelligent thought and action differs from one lacking such capacities, not in something it possesses, but precisely in what it does. And this, incidentally, explains why a man tends to regard it as a deep insult to be told that he has no mind. It is not because he is thus divested in our eyes of some possession dearly prized, but rather, because such a remark is quite rightly taken to mean that he lacks certain important and distinctively human abilities and capacities. If a man is assured that his possession of certain more or less intellectual abilities is in no way in question, he feels divested of nothing upon learning that among his parts or possessions there is none that is properly denoted "a mind."

VI. Does Matter Think?

Probably every philosopher has felt more or less acutely at one time or another a profound puzzlement in the idea of (mere) matter doing those various things rightly ascribable only to persons. How, it is wondered, can a body think, deliberate, imagine things, figure and plan, and so on?

This is really no proper source of bafflement, however. No one can say, *a priori,* what the highly organized material systems of one's body are or are not capable of. It was once thought incredible that matter, unquickened by any soul, could be alive, for matter seemed to inquirers to be inert or lifeless by its very nature. Yet we see around us all the time specimens of living matter—in the merest insects, for instance—so philosophical prejudice has had to yield to the fact. Similarly, I submit, we see around us all the time specimens of thinking matter; that is, material beings which deliberate, imagine, plan, and so on. For men do in fact do these things, and when we see a man, we are seeing a material being—a dreadfully complex and highly organized one, to be sure, but no less a visible and palpable object for that. In any case, the seeming mystery or incredibility that may attach to the idea of matter exercising intellectual capacities is hardly dissolved by postulating something *else* to exercise those capacities. If there is a difficulty in comprehending how a body can do such things, there is surely no less difficulty in seeing how something which is not a bòdy can do them any better.

THINK ABOUT

1. "The universe is not to be narrowed down to the limits of the Understanding—but the Understanding must be stretched and enlarged to take in the image of the Universe as it is discovered."

    Francis Bacon

2. "In trying to distinguish appearance from reality and lay bare the fundamental structure of the universe, science has had to transcend the 'rabble of the senses.' "

    Lincoln Barnett

3. "Wherein, he resembled my Right Reverend friend, Bishop Berkeley (who was) extremely matter-of-fact in all matters touching matter itself. Besides being pervious to the points of pins, and possessing a palate capable of appreciating plum-puddings."

    Herman Melville

4. "It was brilliant of Berkeley to get rid of all materialism with one strategic blow simply by proving that matter does not exist; it was a towering masterpiece of logical prestidigitation, and gives us fair warning that persons studying philosophy should keep both eyes on the philosopher. But it was a trifle dishonest; even a bishop might have hesitated at such a pious fraud."

    Will Durant

5. "Your mind is a jail; it can never know how much of the object it knows is in the object, or in the mind that 'knows.' Such are the sensations whose verdict gives you 'truth.' "

    Will Durant

6. "Lord Russell tells us that he once received a letter from a well-

known logician, a Mrs. Franklin, admitting that she was herself a solipsist and was surprised that no one else was. Russell comments: 'Coming from a logician, this surprise surprised me.' "

7. The statement is sometimes made that George Berkeley denied the existence of the real world of nature. Discuss this statement, indicating (a) in what sense it is true or false, and (b) some of the possible meanings of the term *real* as it is used by philosophers.

31

Reality Consists of
Ideas

George Berkeley (1685–1753) was an Anglican minister and one of the most acute of British philosophers. Before he was twenty, the main principles of his pluralistic idealism were fully formed. His major works, *A Treatise on the Principles of Human Knowledge* and *Three Dialogues Between Hylas and Philonous,* were published in 1710 and 1713. The analysis of knowledge which they contain has had great influence on all subsequent philosophy.

Idealism, in contrast to materialism, argues that reality is basically spiritual. There is no matter; all is mental. This use of idealism should be contrasted with the way it is ordinarily used, when it generally refers to high moral aims. Idealism in this sense originated with the philosophy of Berkeley. He argues in the selection that the existence of physical objects is to be perceived. These objects are only ideas. He argues for this thesis according to the following syllogism:

A thing is a group of ideas (of sensation).
A group of ideas (of sensation) can exist only in a mind.
Therefore, a thing can exist only in a mind.

The first premise states that a thing consists only of ideas. The second that ideas or qualities cannot exist independently of the mind. Do you agree with both?

TO STUDY

1. I perceive an apple and eat it. Do I eat my ideas if the apple I perceive is a collection of ideas? Is an apple really a collection of ideas as enumerated by Berkeley and nothing more?

2. In paragraph 4 he uses the first person plural pronouns "we" and "our own," substituting these for the first person singular "I," which is ordinarily used in his arguments. Is this substitution philosophically legitimate?

3. Berkeley understands the relationship between ideas and things as "resemblance." Is this the only possible relationship conceivable between them? Can his interpretation be justified?

4. Why does Berkeley believe the concept of matter contradictory?

5. What is the role of God in Berkeley's theory?

6. What is the difference between the real and the imaginary?

It is evident to any one who takes a survey of the *objects of human knowledge*, that they are either *ideas* actually imprinted on the senses; or else such as are perceived by attending to the passions and operations of the mind; or lastly, *ideas* formed by help of memory and imagination—either compounding, dividing, or barely representing those originally perceived in the aforesaid ways. By sight I have the ideas of light and colours, with their several degrees and variations. By touch I perceive hard and soft, heat and cold, motion and resistance; and of all these more and less either as to quantity or degree. Smelling furnishes me with odours; the palate with tastes; and hearing conveys sounds to the mind in all their variety of tone and composition.

And as several of these are observed to accompany each other, they come to be marked by one name, and so to be reputed as one *thing*. Thus, for example, a certain colour, taste, smell, figure and consistence having been observed to go together, are accounted one distinct thing, signified by the name apple; other collections of ideas constitute a stone, a tree, a book, and the like sensible things; which as they are pleasing or disagreeable excite the passions of love, hatred, joy, grief, and so forth. . . .

2. But, besides all that endless variety of ideas or objects of knowledge,

From Berkeley: A *Treatise Concerning the Principles of Human Knowledge* (1710). [Note: The following selections are all from Part I and are given in the following order. The Unreality of a Material World: paragraphs 1, 3, 8–11, 14–15, 18–20, 23, 34, 37–38, 40–45; The True Nature of the World: paragraphs 2, 25–27, 136–139, 28–31, 145–149.]

there is likewise something which knows or perceives them, and exercises divers operations, as willing, imagining, remembering, about them. This perceiving, active being is what I call *mind, spirit, soul,* or *myself.* By which words I do not denote any one of my ideas, but a thing entirely distinct from them, wherein they exist, or, which is the same thing, whereby they are perceived—for the existence of an idea consists in being perceived.

3. That neither our thoughts, nor passions, nor ideas formed by the imagination, exist without the mind, is what everybody will allow. And to me it is no less evident that the various sensations or ideas imprinted on the sense, however blended or combined together (that is, whatever objects they compose), cannot exist otherwise than in a mind perceiving them.—I think an intuitive knowledge may be obtained of this by any one that shall attend to what is meant by the term *exist* when applied to sensible things. The table I write on I say exists, that is, I see and feel it; and if I were out of my study I should say it existed—meaning thereby that if I was in my study I might perceive it, or that some other spirit actually does perceive it. There was an odour, that is, it was smelt; there was a sound, that is, it was heard; a colour or figure, and it was perceived by sight or touch. This is all that I can understand by these and the like expressions. For as to what is said of the absolute existence of unthinking things without any relation to their being perceived, that is to me perfectly unintelligible. Their *esse* is *percipi,* nor is it possible they should have any existence out of the minds or thinking things which perceive them.

4. It is indeed an opinion strangely prevailing amongst men, that houses, mountains, rivers, and in a word all sensible objects, have an existence, natural or real, distinct from their being perceived by the understanding. But, with how great an assurance and acquiescence soever this principle may be entertained in the world, yet whoever shall find in his heart to call it in question may, if I mistake not, perceive it to involve a manifest contradiction. For, what are the forementioned objects but the things we perceive by sense? and what do we perceive besides our own ideas or sensations? and is it not plainly repugnant that any one of these, or any combination of them, should exist unperceived?

5. If we thoroughly examine this tenet it will, perhaps, be found at bottom to depend on the doctrine of *abstract ideas.* For can there be a nicer strain of abstraction than to distinguish the existence of sensible objects from their being perceived, so as to conceive them existing unperceived? Light and colours, heat and cold, extension and figures—in a word the things we see and feel—what are they but so many sensations, notions, ideas, or impressions on the sense? and is it possible to separate, even in thought, any of these from perception? For my part, I might as easily divide a thing from itself. I may, indeed, divide in my thoughts, or conceive apart

from each other, those things which, perhaps, I never perceived by sense so divided. Thus, I imagine the trunk of a human body without the limbs, or conceive the smell of a rose without thinking on the rose itself. So far, I will not deny, I can abstract—if that may properly be called *abstraction* which extends only to the conceiving separately such objects as it is possible may really exist or be actually perceived asunder. But my conceiving or imagining power does not extend beyond the possibility of real existence or perception. Hence, as it is impossible for me to see or feel anything without an actual sensation of that thing, so is it impossible for me to conceive in my thoughts any sensible thing or object distinct from the sensation or perception of it. [In truth, the object and the sensation are the same thing, and cannot therefore be abstracted from each other.]

6. Some truths there are so near and obvious to the mind that a man need only open his eyes to see them. Such I take this important one to be, viz. that all the choir of heaven and furniture of the earth, in a word all those bodies which compose the mighty frame of the world, have not any subsistence without a mind, that their *being* is to be perceived or known; that consequently, so long as they are not actually perceived by me, or do not exist in my mind or that of any other created spirit, they must either have no existence at all, or else subsist in the mind of some Eternal Spirit—it being perfectly unintelligible, and involving all the absurdity of abstraction, to attribute to any single part of them an existence independent of a spirit. [To be convinced of which, the reader need only reflect, and try to separate in his own thoughts the *being* of a sensible thing from its *being perceived.*]

7. From what has been said it is evident there is not any other Substance than *Spirit,* or that which perceives. But, for the fuller demonstration of this point, let it be considered the sensible qualities are colour, figure, motion, smell, taste, &c., *i.e.,* the ideas perceived by sense. Now, for an idea to exist in an unperceiving thing is a manifest contradiction, for to have an idea is all one as to perceive; that therefore wherein colour, figure, &c., exist must perceive them; hence it is clear there can be no unthinking substance or *substratum* of those ideas.

8. But, say you, though the ideas themselves do not exist without the mind, yet there may be things like them, whereof they are copies or resemblances, which things exist without the mind in an unthinking substance. I answer, an idea can be like nothing but an idea; a colour or figure can be like nothing but another colour or figure. If we look but never so little into our thoughts, we shall find it impossible for us to conceive a likeness except only between our ideas. Again, I ask whether those supposed originals or external things, of which our ideas are the pictures or representations, be themselves perceivable or no? If they are, then they are ideas and

we have gained our point; but if you say they are not, I appeal to any one whether it be sense to assert a colour is like something which is invisible; hard or soft, like something which is intangible; and so of the rest.

9. Some there are who make a distinction betwixt *primary* and *secondary* qualities. By the former they mean extension, figure, motion, rest, solidity or impenetrability, and number; by the latter they denote all other sensible qualities, as colours, sounds, tastes, and so forth. The ideas we have of these they acknowledge not to be the resemblances of anything existing without the mind, or unperceived, but they will have our ideas of the primary qualities to be patterns or images of things which exist without the mind, in an unthinking substance which they call Matter. By Matter, therefore, we are to understand an inert, senseless substance, in which extension, figure, and motion do actually subsist. But it is evident, from what we have already shewn, that extension, figure, and motion are only ideas existing in the mind, and that an idea can be like nothing but another idea, and that consequently neither they nor their archetypes can exist in an unperceiving substance. Hence, it is plain that the very notion of what is called *Matter or corporeal substance,* involves a contradiction in it.

25. All our ideas, sensations, notions, or the things which we perceive, by whatsoever names they may be distinguished, are visibly inactive—there is nothing of power or agency included in them. So that one idea or object of thought cannot produce or make any alteration in another. To be satisfied of the truth of this, there is nothing else requisite but a bare observation of our ideas. For, since they and every part of them exist only in the mind, it follows that there is nothing in them but what is perceived: but whoever shall attend to his ideas, whether of sense or reflection, will not perceive in them any power or activity; there is, therefore, no such thing contained in them. A little attention will discover to us that the very being of an idea implies passiveness and inertness in it, insomuch that it is impossible for an idea to do anything, or, strictly speaking, to be the cause of anything: neither can it be the resemblance or pattern of any active being, as is evident from sect. 8. Whence it plainly follows that extension, figure, and motion cannot be the cause of our sensations. To say, therefore, that these are the effects of powers resulting from the configuration, number, motion, and size of corpuscles, must certainly be false.

26. We perceive a continual succession of ideas, some are anew excited, others are changed or totally disappear. There is therefore some cause of these ideas, whereon they depend, and which produces and changes them. That this cause cannot be any quality or idea or combination of ideas, is clear from the preceding section. It must therefore be a substance; but it has been shewn that there is no corporeal or material substance: it remains

therefore that the cause of ideas is an incorporeal active substance or Spirit.

27. A Spirit is one simple, undivided, active being—as it perceives ideas it is called the *understanding,* and as it produces or otherwise operates about them it is called the *will.* Hence there can be no *idea* formed of a soul or spirit; for all ideas whatever, being passive and inert (vid. sec. 25), they cannot represent unto us, by way of image or likeness, that which acts. A little attention will make it plain to any one that to have an idea which shall be like that active principle of motion and change of ideas is absolutely impossible. Such is the nature of *spirit,* or that which acts, that it cannot be of itself perceived, but only by the effects which it produceth. If any man shall doubt of the truth of what is here delivered, let him but reflect and try if he can frame the idea of any power or active being; and whether he has ideas of two principal powers, marked by the names *will* and *understanding,* distinct from each other as well as from a third idea of Substance or Being in general, with a relative notion of its supporting or being the subject of the aforesaid powers—which is signified by the name *soul* or *spirit.* This is what some hold; but, so far as I can see, the words *will,* [*understanding, mind,*] *soul, spirit,* do not stand for different ideas, or, in truth, for any idea at all, but for something which is very different from ideas, and which, being an agent, cannot be like unto, or represented by, any idea whatsoever. [Though it must be owned at the same time that we have some *notion* of soul, spirit, and the operations of the mind; such as willing, loving, hating—inasmuch as we know or understand the meaning of these words.]

28. I find I can excite ideas in my mind at pleasure, and vary and shift the scene as oft as I think fit. It is no more than willing, and straightway this or that idea arises in my fancy; and by the same power it is obliterated and makes way for another. This making and unmaking of ideas doth very properly denominate the mind active. Thus much is certain and grounded on experience: but when we talk of unthinking agents, or of exciting ideas exclusive of volition, we only amuse ourselves with words.

29. But, whatever power I may have over my own thoughts, I find the ideas actually perceived by Sense have not a like dependence on my will. When in broad daylight I open my eyes, it is not in my power to choose whether I shall see or no, or to determine what particular objects shall present themselves to my view; and so likewise as to the hearing and other senses, the ideas imprinted on them are not creatures of my will. There is therefore some *other* Will or Spirit that produces them.

30. The ideas of Sense are more strong, lively, and distinct than those of the imagination; they have likewise a steadiness, order, and coherence, and are not excited at random, as those which are the effects of human wills often are, but in a regular train or series—the admirable connexion whereof

sufficiently testifies the wisdom and benevolence of its Author. Now the set rules or established methods wherein the Mind we depend on excites in us the ideas of sense, are called the *laws of nature;* and these we learn by experience, which teaches us that such and such ideas are attended with such and such other ideas, in the ordinary course of things.

31. This gives us a sort of foresight which enables us to regulate our actions for the benefit of life. And without this we should be eternally at a loss; we could not know how to act anything that might procure us the least pleasure, or remove the least pain of sense. That food nourishes, sleep refreshes, and fire warms us; that to sow in the seed-time is the way to reap in the harvest; and in general that to obtain such or such ends, such or such means are conducive—all this we know, not by discovering any necessary connexion between our ideas, but only by the observation of the settled laws of nature, without which we should be all in uncertainty and confusion, and a grown man no more know how to manage himself in the affairs of life than an infant just born.

32. And yet this consistent uniform working, which so evidently displays the goodness and wisdom of that Governing Spirit whose Will constitutes the laws of nature, is so far from leading our thoughts to Him, that it rather sends them wandering after second causes. For, when we perceive certain ideas of Sense constantly followed by other ideas, and we know this is not of our own doing, we forthwith attribute power and agency to the ideas themselves, and make one the cause of another, than which nothing can be more absurd and unintelligible. Thus, for example, having observed that when we perceive by sight a certain round luminous figure we at the same time perceive by touch the idea or sensation called heat, we do from thence conclude the sun to be the cause of heat. And in like manner perceiving the motion and collision of bodies to be attended with sound, we are inclined to think the latter the effect of the former.

33. The ideas imprinted on the Senses by the Author of nature are called *real things:* and those excited in the imagination being less regular, vivid, and constant, are more properly termed *ideas,* or *images of things,* which they copy and represent. But then our sensations, be they never so vivid and distinct, are nevertheless ideas, that is, they exist in the mind, or are perceived by it, as truly as the ideas of its own framing. The ideas of Sense are allowed to have more reality in them, that is, to be more strong, orderly, and coherent than the creatures of the mind; but this is no argument that they exist without the mind. They are also less dependent on the spirit, or thinking substance which perceives them, in that they are excited by the will of another and more powerful spirit; yet still they are *ideas,* and certainly no idea, whether faint or strong, can exist otherwise than in a mind perceiving it.

Readings

1. Lange, F. A. *The History of Materialism.* New York: Humanities, 1957. Classic history of materialism.
2. Ritchie, A. D. *George Berkeley.* New York: Barnes & Noble, 1967. A re-look at Berkeley.
3. Sellars, R. W., ed. *Philosophy for the Future.* New York: Harper and Row, 1949. An anthology about contemporary materialism.
4. Steinkraus, Warren, ed. *New Studies in Berkeley's Philosophy.* New York: Holt, Rinehart and Winston, 1966. Anthology on Berkeley.
5. Warnock, G. J. *Berkeley.* London: Penguin Books, 1953. A good paperback on Berkeley.

two

Can Other Minds
Be Proven To Exist?

32

Yes, by the Analogical Argument

Bertrand Russell (1872–1970), the grandson of Lord John Russell, a prime minister under Queen Victoria, was born in Wales. He studied mathematics and philosophy at Trinity College, Cambridge from 1890 to 1894. He was a fellow at Trinity from 1895 to 1901, and a lecturer in philosophy there from 1910 to 1916. In 1916, Russell was dismissed from his position because of his pacifist activities. Then, in 1918, he was sentenced to six months in prison because of an allegedly libelous article in which he expressed his opposition to World War I and his desire for peace. Russell was a fellow of the Royal Society, an honorary fellow of the British Academy, and a recipient of the Order of Merit. He was awarded the Nobel Prize for literature in 1950.

We all believe that people other than ourselves exist and have minds. We believe this almost as strongly as we believe anything. But when the question arises as to how we can prove the existence of other minds, it is found to be a difficult problem.

Russell proves the existence of other minds by the most common method, namely, the method of analogy. To say that other minds exist is to say in part that other people have ideas and emotions. Hence, we come to know when others are in pain by means of an analogical inference based on their behavior (on occasion) and our own behavior when we are in pain. This is the most common argument used by Russell and by others.

─────────────────────────────────────**TO STUDY**

1. On what logical grounds does Russell believe that we can establish the existence of other people?
2. State the abstract schema of the argument.
3. State the argument formally.
4. What is Russell's postulate?

The postulates hitherto considered have been such as are required for knowledge of the physical world. Broadly speaking, they have led us to admit a certain degree of knowledge as to the space-time structure of the physical world, while leaving us completely agnostic as regards its qualitative character. But where other human beings are concerned, we feel that we know more than this; we are convinced that other people have thoughts and feelings that are qualitatively fairly similar to our own. We are not content to think that we know only the space-time structure of our friends' minds, or their capacity for initiating causal chains that end in sensations of our own. A philosopher might pretend to think that he knew only this, but let him get cross with his wife and you will see that he does not regard her as a mere spatio-temporal edifice of which he knows the logical properties but not a glimmer of the intrinsic character. We are therefore justified in inferring that his skepticism is professional rather than sincere.

The problem with which we are concerned is the following. We observe in ourselves such occurrences as remembering, reasoning, feeling pleasure, and feeling pain. We think that sticks and stones do not have these experiences, but that other people do. Most of us have no doubt that the higher animals feel pleasure and pain, though I was once assured by a fisherman that "Fish have no sense nor feeling." I failed to find out how he had acquired this knowledge. Most people would disagree with him, but would be doubtful about oysters and starfish. However this may be, common sense admits an increasing doubtfulness as we descend in the animal kingdom, but as regards human beings it admits no doubt.

It is clear that belief in the minds of others requires some postulate that is not required in physics, since physics can be content with a knowledge of structure. My present purpose is to suggest what this further postulate may be.

It is clear that we must appeal to something that may be vaguely called "analogy." The behavior of other people is in many ways analogous to our own, and we suppose that it must have analogous causes. What people say is what we should say if we had certain thoughts, and so we infer that they probably have these thoughts. They give us information which we can sometimes subsequently verify. They behave in ways in which we behave when we are pleased (or displeased) in circumstances in which we should be pleased (or displeased). We may talk over with a friend some incident which we have both experienced, and find that his reminiscences dovetail with our own; this is particularly convincing when he remembers something that we have forgotten but that he recalls to our thoughts. Or again: you set your boy a problem in arithmetic, and with luck he gets the right answer; this persuades you that he is capable of arithmetical reasoning. There are, in short, very many ways in which my responses to stimuli differ from those of "dead" matter, and in all these ways other people resemble me. As it is clear to me that the causal laws governing my behavior have to do with "thoughts," it is natural to infer that the same is true of the analogous behavior of my friends.

The inference with which we are at present concerned is not merely that which takes us beyond solipsism, by maintaining that sensations have causes about which *something* can be known. This kind of inference, which suffices for physics, has already been considered. We are concerned now with a much more specific kind of inference, the kind that is involved in our knowledge of the thoughts and feelings of others—assuming that we have such knowledge. It is of course obvious that such knowledge is more or less doubtful. There is not only the general argument that we may be dreaming; there is also the possibility of ingenious automata. There are calculating machines that do sums much better than our schoolboy sons; there are gramophone records that remember impeccably what So-and-so said on such-and-such an occasion; there are people in the cinema who, though copies of real people, are not themselves alive. There is no theoretical limit to what ingenuity could achieve in the way of producing the illusion of life where in fact life is absent.

But, you will say, in all such cases it was the thoughts of human beings that produced the ingenious mechanism. Yes, but how do you know this? And how do you know that the gramophone does *not* "think"?

There is, in the first place, a difference in the causal laws of observable behavior. If I say to a student, "Write me a paper on Descartes' reasons for believing in the existence of matter," I shall, if he is industrious, cause a certain response. A gramophone record might be so constructed as to respond to this stimulus, perhaps better than the student, but if so it would be incapable of telling me anything about any other philosopher, even if

I threatened to refuse to give it a degree. One of the most notable peculiarities of human behavior is change of response to a given stimulus. An ingenious person could construct an automaton which would always laugh at his jokes, however often it heard them; but a human being, after laughing a few times, will yawn, and end by saying, "How I laughed the first time I heard that joke."

But the differences in observable behavior between living and dead matter do not suffice to prove that there are "thoughts" connected with living bodies other than my own. It is probably possible theoretically to account for the behavior of living bodies by purely physical causal laws, and it is probably impossible to refute materialism by external observation alone. If we are to believe that there are thoughts and feelings other than our own, that must be in virtue of some inference in which our own thoughts and feelings are relevant, and such an inference must go beyond what is needed in physics.

I am, of course, not discussing the history of how we come to believe in other minds. We find ourselves believing in them when we first begin to reflect; the thought that Mother may be angry or pleased is one which arises in early infancy. What I am discussing is the possibility of a postulate which shall establish a rational connection between this belief and data, e.g., between the belief "Mother is angry" and the hearing of a loud voice.

The abstract schema seems to be as follows. We know, from observation of ourselves, a causal law of the form "A causes B," where A is a "thought" and B a physical occurrence. We sometimes observe a B when we cannot observe any A; we then infer an unobserved A. For example: I know that when I say, "I'm thirsty," I say so, usually because I am thirsty, and therefore, when I hear the sentence "I'm thirsty" at a time when I am not thirsty, I assume that someone else is thirsty. I assume this the more readily if I see before me a hot, drooping body which goes on to say, "I have walked twenty desert miles in this heat with never a drop to drink." It is evident that my confidence in the "inference" is increased by increased complexity in the datum and also by increased certainty of the causal law derived from subjective observation, provided the causal law is such as to account for the complexities of the datum.

It is clear that in so far as plurality of causes is to be suspected, the kind of inference we have been considering is not valid. We are supposed to know "A causes B," and also to know that B has occurred; if this is to justify us in inferring A, we must know that *only* A causes B. Or, if we are content to infer that A is probable, it will suffice if we can know that in most cases it is A that causes B. If you hear thunder without having seen lightning, you confidently infer that there was lightning, because you are convinced that the sort of noise you heard is seldom caused by anything except lightning. As this example shows, our principle is not only employed to establish the existence of other minds but is habitually assumed, though in a less concrete form, in physics. I say "a less concrete form" because unseen lightning is only abstractly similar to seen lightning, whereas we suppose the similarity of other minds to our own to be by no means purely abstract.

Complexity in the observed behavior of another person, when this can all be accounted for by a simple cause such as thirst, increases the probability of the inference by diminishing the probability of some other cause. I think that in ideally favorable circumstances the argument would be formally as follows:

From subjective observation I know that A, which is a thought or feeling, causes B, which is a bodily act, e.g., a statement. I know also that, whenever B is an act of my own body, A is its cause. I now observe an act of the kind B in a body not my own, and I am having no thought or feeling of the kind A. But I still believe, on the basis of self-observation, that only A can cause B; I therefore infer that there was an A which caused B, though it was not an A that I could observe. On this ground I infer that other people's bodies are associated with minds, which resemble mine in proportion as their bodily behavior resembles my own.

In practice, the exactness and certainty of the above statement must be softened. We cannot be sure that, in our subjective experience, A is the only cause of B. And even if A is the only cause of B in our experience, how can we know that this holds outside our experience? It is not necessary that we should know this with any certainty; it is enough if it is highly probable. It is the assumption of probability in such cases that is our postulate. The postulate may therefore be stated as follows:

If, whenever we can observe whether A and B are present or absent, we find that every case of B has an A as a causal antecedent, then it is probable that most B's have A's as causal antecedents, even in cases where observation does not enable us to know whether A is present or not.

This postulate, if accepted, justifies the inference to other minds, as well as many other inferences that are made unreflectingly by common sense.

33

Not by the Argument from Analogy

Norman Malcolm (1911–   ) is a professor of philosophy at Cornell University. He is the author of *Ludwig Wittgenstein: A Memoir* (1958), *Dreaming* (1959), and *Knowledge and Certainty* (1963).

Malcolm argues that the analogical argument is not satisfactory. He argues that it involves a mistaken assumption; namely, that a person learns from his own case what thinking, feeling, and sensation are.

─── TO STUDY

1. Why does Malcolm believe Mill's argument by analogy to be weak?

2. Explain: Mill has no *criterion* for determining whether another has thoughts and feelings.

3. What dilemma does Malcolm believe all "analogical philosophers" face?

4. What is Hampshire's analogical argument? What is Malcolm's argument against Hampshire?

5. What is Price's analogical argument? What is Malcolm's argument against Price?

6. What is "the most fundamental error of the argument from analogy"?

7. Explain: The destruction of the argument from analogy also destroys the problem for which it was supposed to provide a solution.

8. Explain Wittgenstein's suggestion for conceiving first person psychological sentences.

I

I believe that the argument from analogy for the existence of other minds still enjoys more credit than it deserves, and my first aim will be to show that it leads nowhere. J. S. Mill is one of many who have accepted the argument and I take his statement of it as representative. He puts to himself the question, "By what evidence do I know, or by what considerations am I led to believe, that there exist other sentient creatures, that the walking and speaking figures which I see and hear, have sensations and thoughts, or in other words, possess Minds?" His answer is the following:

> I conclude that other human beings have feelings like me, because, first, they have bodies like me, which I know, in my own case, to be the antecedent condition of feelings; and because, secondly, they exhibit the acts, and other outward signs, which in my own case I know by experience to be caused by feelings. I am conscious in myself of a series of facts connected by an uniform sequence, of which the beginning is modifications of my body, the middle is feelings, the end is outward demeanor. In the case of other human beings I have the evidence of my senses for the first and last links of the series, but not for the intermediate link. I find, however, that the sequence between the first and last is as regular and constant in those other cases as it is in mine. In my own case I know that the first link produces the last through the intermediate link, and could not produce it without. Experience, therefore, obliges me to conclude that there must be an intermediate link; which must either be the same in others as in myself, or a different one: I must either believe them to be alive, or to be automatons: and by believing them to be alive, that is, by supposing the link to be of the same nature as in the case of which I have experience, and which is in all other respects similar, I bring other human beings, as phenomena, under the same generalizations which I know by experience to be the true theory of my own existence.[1]

I shall pass by the possible objection that this would be very *weak* inductive reasoning, based as it is on the observation of a single instance. More

---

From "Knowledge of Other Minds" by Norman Malcolm, *The Journal of Philosophy*, LV (November 6, 1958), 969–978. Reprinted by permission of the publisher and author.

[1] J. S. Mill, *An Examination of Sir William Hamilton's Philosophy*, 6th ed. (New York: Longmans, Green & Co., Inc., 1889), pp. 243–244.

interesting is the following point: Suppose this reasoning could yield a conclusion of the sort "It is probable that that human figure" (pointing at some person other than oneself) "has thoughts and feelings." Then there is a question as to whether this conclusion can *mean* anything to the philosopher who draws it, because there is a question as to whether the sentence "That human figure has thoughts and feelings" can mean anything to him. Why should this be a question? Because the assumption from which Mill starts is that he has *no criterion* for determining whether another "walking and speaking figure" does or does not have thoughts and feelings. If he had a criterion he could apply it, establishing with certainty that this or that human figure does or does not have feelings (for the only plausible criterion would lie in behavior and circumstances that are open to view), and there would be no call to resort to tenuous analogical reasoning that yields at best a probability. If Mill has no criterion for the existence of feelings other than his own then in that sense he does not understand the sentence "That human figure has feelings" and therefore does not understand the sentence "It is *probable* that that human figure has feelings."

There is a familiar inclination to make the following reply: "Although I have no criterion of verification still I *understand,* for example, the sentence 'He has a pain.' For I understand the meaning of 'I have a pain,' and 'He has a pain' means that he has the *same* thing I have when I have a pain." But this is a fruitless maneuver. If I do not know how to establish that someone has a pain then I do not know how to establish that he has the *same* as I have when I have a pain.[2] You cannot improve my understanding of "He has a pain" by this recourse to the notion of "the same," unless you give me a criterion for saying that someone *has* the same as I have. If you can do this you will have no use for the argument from analogy: and if you cannot then you do not understand the supposed conclusion of that argument. A philosopher who purports to rely on the analogical argument cannot, I think, escape this dilemma.

There have been various attempts to repair the argument from analogy. Mr. Stuart Hampshire has argued[3] that its validity as a method of inference can be established in the following way: Others sometimes infer that I am feeling giddy from my behavior. Now I have direct, non-inferential knowledge, says Hampshire, of my own feelings. So I can check inferences made

---

[2] "It is no explanation to say: the supposition that he has a pain is simply the supposition that he has the same as I. For *that* part of the grammar is quite clear to me: that is, that one will say that the stove has the same experience as I, *if* one says: it is in pain and I am in pain" (Ludwig Wittgenstein, *Philosophical Investigations* (New York: The Macmillan Company, 1953), sec. 350).

[3] "The Analogy of Feeling," *Mind,* January 1952, pp. 1–12.

about me against the facts, checking thereby the accuracy of the "methods" of inference.

> All that is required for testing the validity of any method of factual inference is that each one of us should sometimes be in a position to confront the conclusions of the doubtful method of inference with what is known by him to be true independently of the method of inference in question. Each one of us is certainly in this position in respect of our common methods of inference about the feelings of persons other than ourselves, in virtue of the fact that each one of us is constantly able to compare the results of this type of inference with what he knows to be true directly and non-inferentially; each one of us is in the position to make this testing comparison, whenever he is the designated subject of a statement about feelings and sensations. I, Hampshire, know by what sort of signs I may be misled in inferring Jones's and Smith's feelings, because I have implicitly noticed (though probably not formulated) where Jones, Smith and others generally go wrong in inferring my feelings (op. cit., pp. 4–5).

Presumably I can also note when the inferences of others about my feelings do not go wrong. Having ascertained the reliability of some inference-procedures I can use them myself, in a guarded way, to draw conclusions about the feelings of others, with a modest but justified confidence in the truth of those conclusions.

My first comment is that Hampshire has apparently forgotten the purpose of the argument from analogy, which is to provide some probability that "the walking and speaking figures which I see and hear, have sensations and thoughts" (Mill). For the reasoning that he describes involves the assumption that other human figures *do* have thoughts and sensations: for they are assumed to *make inferences* about me from *observations* of my behavior. But the philosophical problem of the existence of other minds *is* the problem of whether human figures other than oneself do, among other things, make observations, inferences, and assertions. Hampshire's supposed defense of the argument from analogy is an *ignoratio elenchi* [failure to appreciate what needs to be proved].

If we struck from the reasoning described by Hampshire all assumption of thoughts and sensations in others we should be left with something roughly like this: "When my behavior is such and such there come from nearby human figures the sounds 'He feels giddy.' And generally I do feel giddy at the time. Therefore when another human figure exhibits the same behavior and I say 'He feels giddy,' it is probable that he does feel giddy." But the reference here to the sentence-like sounds coming from other human bodies is irrelevant, since I must not assume that those sounds express inferences. Thus the reasoning becomes simply the classical argument from analogy: "When my behavior is such and such I feel giddy; so probably when another human figure behaves the same way he feels the same way." This argument, again, is caught in the dilemma about the criterion of the *same.*

The version of analogical reasoning offered by Professor H. H. Price[4] is more interesting. He suggests that "one's evidence for the existence of other minds is derived primarily from the understanding of language" (p. 429). His idea is that if another body gives forth noises one understands, like "There's the bus," and if these noises give one new information, this "provides some evidence that the foreign body which uttered the noises is animated by a mind like one's own. . . . Suppose I am often in its neighborhood, and it repeatedly produces utterances which I can understand, and which I then proceed to verify for myself. And suppose that this happens in many different kinds of situations. I think that my evidence for believing that this body is animated by a mind like my own would then become very strong" (p. 430). The body from which these informative sounds proceed need not be a human body. "If the rustling of the leaves of an oak formed intelligible words conveying new information to me, and if gorse-bushes made intelligible gestures, I should have evidence that the oak or the gorse-bush was animated by an intelligence like my own" (p. 436). Even if the intelligible and informative sounds did not proceed from a body they would provide evidence for the existence of a (disembodied) mind (p. 435).

Although differing sharply from the classical analogical argument, the reasoning presented by Price is still analogical in form: I know by introspection that when certain combinations of sounds come from me they are "symbols in acts of spontaneous thinking"; therefore similar combinations of sounds, not produced by me, "probably function as instruments to an act of spontaneous thinking, which in this case is not my own" (p. 446). Price says that the reasoning also provides an *explanation* of the otherwise mysterious occurrence of sounds which I understand but did not produce. He anticipates the objection that the hypothesis is nonsensical because unverifiable. "The hypothesis is a perfectly conceivable one," he says, "in the sense that I know very well what the world would have to be like if the hypothesis were true—what sorts of entities there must be in it, and what sorts of events must occur in them. I know from introspection what acts of thinking and perceiving are, and I know what it is for such acts to be combined into the unity of a single mind . . ." (pp. 446–447).

I wish to argue against Price that no amount of intelligible sounds coming from an oak tree or a kitchen table could create any probability that it has sensations and thoughts. The question to be asked is: What would

---

[4] "Our Evidence for the Existence of Other Minds," *Philosophy,* XIII (1938), 425–456.

show that a tree or table *understands* the sounds that come from it? We can imagine that useful warnings, true descriptions and predictions, even "replies" to questions, should emanate from a tree, so that it came to be of enormous value to its owner. How should we establish that it understood those sentences? Should we "question" it? Suppose that the tree "said" that there was a vixen in the neighborhood, and we "asked" it "What is a vixen?," and it "replied," "A vixen is a female fox." It might go on to do as well for "female" and "fox." This performance might incline us to say that the tree understood the words, in contrast to the possible case in which it answered "I don't know" or did not answer at all. But would it show that the tree understood the words in the same sense that a person could understand them? With a person such a performance would create a presumption that he could make correct *applications* of the word in question; but not so with a tree. To see this point think of the normal teaching of words (e.g., "spoon," "dog," "red") to a child and how one decides whether he understands them. At a primitive stage of teaching one does not require or expect definitions, but rather that the child should *pick out* reds from blues, dogs from cats, spoons from forks. This involves his looking, pointing, reaching for and going to the right things and not the wrong ones. That a child says "red" when a red thing and "blue" when a blue thing is put before him is indicative of a mastery of those words *only* in conjunction with the other activities of looking, pointing, trying to get, fetching, and carrying. Try to suppose that he says the right words but looks at and reaches for the wrong things. Should we be tempted to say that he has mastered the use of those words? No, indeed. The disparity between words and behavior would make us say that he does not understand the words. In the case of a tree there could be no disparity between its words and its "behavior" because it is logically incapable of behavior of the relevant kind.

Since it has nothing like the human face and body it makes no sense to say of a tree, or an electronic computer, that it is looking or pointing at or fetching something. (Of course one can always *invent* a sense for these expressions.) Therefore it would make no sense to say that it did or did not understand the above words. Trees and computers cannot either pass or fail the tests that a child is put through. They cannot take them. That an object was a source of intelligible sounds or other signs (no matter how sequential) would not be enough by itself to establish that it had thoughts or sensations. How informative sentences and valuable predictions could emanate from a gorse-bush might be a grave scientific problem, but the explanation could never be that the gorse-bush had a mind. Better no explanation than nonsense!

It might be thought that the above difficulty holds only for words whose meaning has a "perceptual content" and that if we imagined, for example, that our gorse-bush produced nothing but pure mathematical propositions we should be justified in attributing thought to it, although not sensation. But suppose there was a remarkable "calculating boy" who could give right answers to arithmetical problems but could not apply numerals to reality in empirical propositions, e.g., he could not *count* any objects. I believe that everyone would be reluctant to say that he *understood* the mathematical signs and truths that he produced. If he could count in the normal way there would not be this reluctance. And "counting in the normal way" involves looking, pointing, reaching, fetching, and so on. That is, it requires the human face and body, and human behavior—or something similar. Things which do not have the human form, or anything like it, not merely do not but *cannot* satisfy the criteria for thinking. I am trying to bring out part of what Wittgenstein meant when he said, "We only say of a human being and what is like one that it thinks" (*Investigations,* sec. 360), and "The human body is the best picture of the human soul" (*ibid.,* p. 178).

I have not yet gone into the most fundamental error of the argument from analogy. It is present whether the argument is the classical one (the analogy between my body and other bodies) or Price's version (the analogy between my language and the noises and signs produced by other things). It is the mistaken assumption that *one learns from one's own case* what thinking, feeling, sensation are. Price gives expression to this assumption when he says: "I know from introspection what acts of thinking and perceiving are . . ." (*op. cit.,* p. 447). It is the most natural assumption for a philosopher to make and indeed seems at first to be the only possibility. Yet Wittgenstein has made us see that it leads first to solipsism and then to nonsense. I shall try to state as briefly as possible how it produces those results.

A philosopher who believes that one must learn what thinking, fear, or pain is "from one's own case," does not believe that the thing to be observed is one's behavior, but rather something "inward." He considers behavior to be related to the inward states and occurrences merely as an accompaniment or possibly an effect. He cannot regard behavior as a *criterion* of psychological phenomena: for if he did he would have no use for the analogical argument (as was said before) and also the priority given to "one's own case" would be pointless. He believes that he notes something in himself that he calls "thinking" or "fear" or "pain," and then he tries to infer the presence of the *same* in others. He should then deal with the question of what his criterion of the *same* in others is. This he cannot do because it is of the essence of his viewpoint to reject circumstances and behavior as a criterion of mental phenomena in others. And what else could serve as a criterion? He ought, therefore, to draw the conclusion that the notion of thinking, fear, or pain in others is in an important sense meaningless. He has no idea of what would count for or against it.⁵ "That there should be thinking or pain other than my own is unintelligible," he ought to hold. This would be a rigorous solipsism, and a correct outcome of the assumption that one can know only from one's own case what the mental phenomena are. An equivalent way of putting it would be: "When I say 'I am in pain,' by 'pain' I mean a certain inward state. When I say '*He* is in pain,' by 'pain' I mean *behavior*. I cannot attribute pain to others *in the same sense* that I attribute it to myself."

Some philosophers before Wittgenstein may have seen the solipsistic result of starting from "one's own case." But I believe he is the first to have shown how that starting point destroys itself. This may be presented as follows: One supposes that one inwardly picks out something as thinking or pain and thereafter identifies it whenever it presents itself in the soul. But the question to be pressed is, Does one make *correct* identifications? The proponent of these "private" identifications has nothing to say here. He feels sure that he identifies correctly the occurrences in his soul; but feeling sure is no guarantee of being right. Indeed he has no idea of what being *right* could mean. He does not know how to distinguish between actually making correct identifications and being under the impression that he does. (See *Investigations,* secs. 258–9.) Suppose that he identified the emotion of anxiety as the sensation of pain? Neither he nor anyone else could know about this "mistake." Perhaps he makes a mistake *every* time! Perhaps all of us do! We ought to see now that we are talking nonsense. We do not know what a *mistake* would be. We have no standard, no examples, no customary practice, with which to compare our inner recognitions. The inward identification cannot hit the bull's-eye, or miss it either, because there is no bull's-eye. When we see that the ideas of correct and incorrect have no application to the supposed inner identification, the latter notion loses its appearance of sense. Its collapse brings down both solipsism and the argument from analogy.

II

The destruction of the argument from analogy also destroys the *problem* for which it was supposed to provide a solution. A philosopher feels himself in a difficulty about other minds because he assumes that first of all he is acquainted with mental phenomena "from his own case." What troubles him is how to make the transition from his own case to the case of others. When his thinking is freed of the illusion of the priority of his own case,

---

⁵ One reason why philosophers have not commonly drawn this conclusion may be, as Wittgenstein acutely suggests, that they assume that they have "an infallible paradigm of identity in the identity of a thing with itself" (*Investigations,* sec. 215).

then he is able to look at the familiar facts and to acknowledge that the circumstances, behavior, and utterances of others actually are his *criteria* (not merely his evidence) for the existence of their mental states. Previously this had seemed impossible.

But now he is in danger of flying to the opposite extreme of behaviorism, which errs by believing that through observation of one's own circumstances, behavior, and utterances one can find out that one is thinking or angry. The philosophy of "from one's own case" and behaviorism, though in a sense opposites, make the common assumption that the first-person, present-tense psychological statements are verified by self-observation. According to the "one's own case" philosophy the self-observation cannot be checked by others; according to behaviorism the self-observation would be by means of outward criteria that are available to all. The first position becomes unintelligible; the second is false for at least many kinds of psychological statements. We are forced to conclude that the first-person psychological statements are not (or hardly ever) verified by self-observation. It follows that they have no verification at all; for if they had a verification it would have to be by self-observation.

But if sentences like "My head aches" or "I wonder where she is" do not express observations then what do they do? What is the relation between my declaration that my head aches and the fact that my head aches, if the former is not the report of an observation? The perplexity about the existence of *other* minds has, as the result of criticism, turned into a perplexity about the meaning of one's own psychological sentences about oneself. At our starting point it was the sentence *"His* head aches" that posed a problem; but now it is the sentence *"My* head aches" that puzzles us.

One way in which this problem can be put is by the question, "How does *one know when to say* the words 'My head aches'?" The inclination to ask this question can be made acute by imagining a fantastic but not impossible case of a person who has survived to adult years without ever experiencing pain. He is given various sorts of injections to correct this condition, and on receiving one of these one day, he jumps and exclaims, "Now I feel pain!" One wants to ask, "How did he *recognize* the new sensation as a *pain?"*

Let us note that if the man gives an answer (e.g., "I knew it must be pain because of the way I jumped") then he proves by that very fact that he has not mastered the correct use of the words "I feel pain." They cannot be used to state a *conclusion.* In telling us *how* he did it he will convict himself of a misuse. Therefore the question "How did he recognize his sensation?" requests the impossible. The inclination to ask it is evidence of our inability to grasp the fact that the use of this psychological sentence has nothing to do with recognizing or identifying or observing a state of oneself.

The fact that this imagined case produces an especially strong tempta-tion to ask the "How?" question shows that we have the idea that it must be more difficult to give the right name of one's sensation *the first time*. The implication would be that it is not so difficult *after* the first time. Why should this be? Are we thinking that then the man would have a paradigm of pain with which he could compare his sensations and so be in a position to know right off whether a certain sensation was or was not a pain? But the paradigm would be either something "outer" (behavior) or something "inner" (perhaps a memory impression of the sensation). If the former then he is misusing the first-person sentence. If the latter then the question of whether he compared *correctly* the present sensation with the inner para-digm of pain would be without sense. Thus the idea that the use of the first-person sentences can be governed by paradigms must be abandoned. It is another form of our insistent misconception of the first-person sen-tence as resting somehow on the identification of a psychological state.

These absurdities prove that we must conceive of the first-person psy-chological sentences in some entirely different light. Wittgenstein presents us with the suggestion that the first-person sentences are to be thought of as similar to the natural nonverbal, behavioral expressions of psychological states. "My leg hurts," for example, is to be assimilated to crying, limping, holding one's leg. This is a bewildering comparison and one's first thought is that two sorts of things could not be more unlike. By saying the sentence one can make a *statement;* it has a *contradictory;* it is *true* or *false;* in saying it one *lies* or *tells the truth;* and so on. None of these things, exactly, can be said of crying, limping, holding one's leg. So how can there be any resemblance? But Wittgenstein knew this when he deliberately likened such a sentence to "the primitive, the natural, expressions" of pain, and said that it is "new pain-behavior" (*ibid.,* sec. 244). This analogy has at least two important merits: first, it breaks the hold on us of the question "How does one *know when to say* 'My leg hurts'?", for in the light of the analogy this will be as nonsensical as the question "How does one know when to cry, limp, or hold one's leg?"; second, it explains how the utterance of a first-person psychological sentence by another person can have *importance* for us, although not as an identification—for in the light of the analogy it will have the same importance as the natural behavior which serves as our preverbal criterion of the psychological states of others.

Readings

1. Ayer, A. J. *The Problem of Knowledge.* London: St. Martin's Press, 1956, chap. 5.

2. Broad, C. D. *Mind and Its Place in Nature.* New Jersey: Littlefield, 1960, chap. 7.

3. Jones, J. R. "Our Knowledge of Other Persons," *Philosophy,* Vol. 25 (1950).

4. Thomson, James. "The Argument From Analogy and Our Knowledge of Other Minds," *Mind,* Vol. 60 (1951).

5. Wisdom, John. *Other Minds.* Oxford: Oxford Univ. Press, 1956.

three

Is Reality General or Particular?

34

Universals
Are Real

Plato (427/8–374/8 B.C.), one of the great Greek philosophers, has exerted more influence upon the development of
Western philosophy than any other writer with the possible
exception of his student, Aristotle. He established the Academy in Athens, the first of the major schools of ancient Greece.
His works, written in dialogue form and featuring his teacher
Socrates as the principal figure, have continued to be widely
read not only for their intellectual content but also for their
literary merit.

Of all the words we use, hardly any of them with the exception of those
called proper names stand for particular things. We use words such as
"table," "red," "greater," "strike," etc. These words stand for types of
things, or for qualities, relations or actions, which do not exist by themselves
at all. One observes particular tables, or particular reds, but one never
observes a table in general or a red in general. *For what, then, do such
universal terms stand?* This is the problem of universals.

Plato, a realist concerning universals, says that these terms stand
for what a number of particular things have in common, and it is this
common element which is referred to as a universal. Unlike some realists,
Plato believes that these universals exist eternally in a non-temporal, non-
spatial realm quite independent of our space-time world. He argues for the
unique existence of these universals, or Ideas, in the following way. We have
knowledge of objects such as perfect circles which cannot be based on
anything we have sensed. Knowledge must have an object. Therefore there

must exist some other entities (the Ideas) distinct from those of the senses.

Plato expressed these thoughts in two famous passages: "The Divided Line" and the "Allegory of the Cave." His epistemological system is divided into four types: conjecture, practical belief, reasoning, and dialectic. This system corresponds to four degrees of reality: images, physical objects, mathematical objects, and the forms. The famous allegory of the cave has four corresponding aspects:

Comparison of Analogy of "The Divided Line"
with the "Allegory of the Cave"

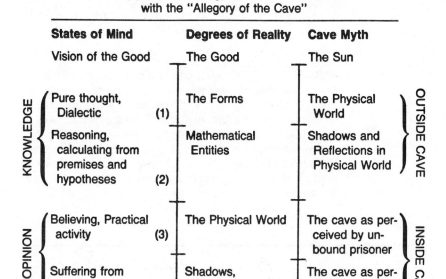

States of Mind		Degrees of Reality	Cave Myth
Vision of the Good		The Good	The Sun
KNOWLEDGE Pure thought, Dialectic	(1)	The Forms	The Physical World
Reasoning, calculating from premises and hypotheses	(2)	Mathematical Entities	Shadows and Reflections in Physical World
OPINION Believing, Practical activity	(3)	The Physical World	The cave as perceived by unbound prisoner
Suffering from illusions	(4)	Shadows, Reflections	The cave as perceived by bound prisoner

OUTSIDE CAVE

INSIDE CAVE

TO STUDY

1. Describe the nature of the Forms.
2. What is the relation between the Good and the Sun? What is the analogy between the Sun and the Good?
3. What are the four levels of reality and "knowledge"? Give examples.
4. Draw a sketch of the Cave allegory.

The Objects of Knowledge

. . . Let me remind you of the distinction we drew earlier and have often drawn on other occasions, between the multiplicity of things that we call good or beautiful or whatever it may be and, on the other hand, Goodness itself or Beauty itself and so on. Corresponding to each of these sets of many things, we postulate a single Form or real essence, as we call it.*

Yes, that is so.

Further, the many things, we say, can be seen, but are not objects of rational thought; whereas the Forms are objects of thought, but invisible.

Yes, certainly.

And we see things with our eyesight, just as we hear sounds with our ears and, to speak generally, perceive any sensible thing with our sense-faculties.

Of course.

Have you noticed, then, that the artificer who designed the senses has been exceptionally lavish of his materials in making the eyes able to see and their objects visible?

That never occurred to me.

Well, look at it in this way. Hearing and sound do not stand in need of any third thing, without which the ear will not hear nor sound be heard,[1] and I think the same is true of most, not to say all, of the other senses. Can you think of one that does require anything of the sort?

No, I cannot.

But there is this need in the case of sight and its objects. You may have the power of vision in your eyes and try to use it, and color may be there in the objects; but sight will see nothing and the colors will remain invisible in the absence of a third thing peculiarly constituted to serve this very purpose.

By which you mean—?

Naturally I mean what you call light; and if light is a thing of value, the sense of sight and the power of being visible are linked together by a very precious bond, such as unites no other sense with its object.

[This portion of Plato's *The Republic* is from pages 213–228 of the translation by F. M. Cornford, published in 1941 by the Oxford University Press, and reprinted here with the permission of Clarendon Press of Oxford, England.]

* Socrates is speaking to a group of people, and Glaucon is his interlocutor.

[1] Plato held that the hearing of sound is caused by blows inflicted by the air (*Timaeus* 67 B, 80 A); but the air is hardly analogous to light.

No one could say that light is not a precious thing.

And of all the divinities in the skies[2] is there one whose light, above all the rest, is responsible for making our eyes see perfectly and making objects perfectly visible?

There can be no two opinions: of course you mean the Sun.

And how is sight related to this deity? Neither sight nor the eye which contains it is the sun, but of all the sense-organs it is the most sun-like; and further, the power it possesses is dispensed by the Sun, like a stream flooding the eye. And again, the Sun is not vision, but it is the cause of vision and also is seen by the vision it causes.

Yes.

It was the Sun, then, that I meant when I spoke of that offspring which the Good has created in the visible world, to stand there in the same relation to vision and visible things as that which the Good itself bears in the intelligible world to intelligence and to intelligible objects.

How is that? You must explain further.

You know what happens when the colors of things are no longer irradiated by the daylight, but only by the fainter luminaries[3] of the night: when you look at them, the eyes are dim and seem almost blind, as if there were no unclouded vision in them. But when you look at things on which the Sun is shining, the same eyes see distinctly and it becomes evident that they do contain the power of vision.

Certainly.

Apply this comparison, then, to the soul. When its gaze is fixed upon an object irradiated by truth and reality, the soul gains understanding and knowledge and is manifestly in possession of intelligence. But when it looks towards that twilight world of things that come into existence and pass away, its sight is dim and it has only opinions and beliefs which shift to and fro, and it seems like a thing that has no intelligence.

That is true.

This, then, which gives to the objects of knowledge their truth and to him who knows them his power of knowing, is the Form or essential nature of Goodness. It is the cause of knowledge and truth; and so, while you may think of it as an object of knowledge, you will do well to regard it as something beyond truth and knowledge and, precious as these both are, of still higher worth. And, just as in our analogy light and vision were to be thought of as like the Sun, but not identical with it, so here both knowledge and truth are to be regarded as like the Good,

---

[2] Plato held that the heavenly bodies are immortal living creatures, i.e. gods.

[3] *Luminaries:* planets and stars.

but to identify either with the Good is wrong. The Good must hold a yet higher place of honor.

You are giving it a position of extraordinary splendour, if it is the source of knowledge and truth and itself surpasses them in worth. You surely cannot mean that it is pleasure.

Heaven forbid, I exclaimed. But I want to follow up our analogy still further. You will agree that the Sun not only makes the things we see visible, but also brings them into existence and gives them growth and nourishment; yet he is not the same thing as existence. And so with the objects of knowledge: these derive from the Good not only their power of being known, but their very being and reality; and Goodness is not the same thing as being, but even beyond being, surpassing it in dignity and power.

Glaucon exclaimed with some amusement at my exalting Goodness in such extravagant terms.

It is your fault, I replied; you forced me to say what I think.

Yes, and you must stop there. At any rate, complete your comparison with the Sun, if there is any more to be said.

There is a great deal more, I answered.

Let us hear it, then; don't leave anything out.

I am afraid much must be left unspoken. However, I will not, if I can help it, leave anything that can be said on this occasion.

Please do not.

Four Stages of Cognition. The Line

Conceive, then, that there are these two powers I speak of, the Good reigning over the domain of all that is intelligible, the Sun over the visible world—or the heaven as I might call it; only you would think I was showing off my skill in etymology. At any rate have you these two orders of things clearly before your mind: the visible and the intelligible?

I have.

Now take a line divided into two unequal parts, one to represent the visible order, the other the intelligible; and divide each part again in the same proportion, symbolizing degrees of comparative clearness or obscurity. Then (A) one of the two sections in the visible world will stand for images. By images I mean first shadows, and then reflections in water or in close-grained, polished surfaces, and everything of that kind, if you understand.

Yes, I understand.

Let the second section (B) stand for the actual things of which the first are likenesses, the living creatures about us and all the works of nature or of human hands.

So be it.

Will you also take the proportion in which the visible world has been divided as corresponding to degrees of reality and truth, so that the likeness shall stand to the original in the same ratio as the sphere of appearances and belief to the sphere of knowledge?

Certainly.

Now consider how we are to divide the part which stands for the intelligible world. There are two sections. In the first (C) the mind uses as images those actual things which themselves had images in the visible world; and it is compelled to pursue its inquiry by starting from assumptions and travelling, not up to a principle, but down to a conclusion. In the second (D) the mind moves in the other direction, from an assumption up towards a principle which is not hypothetical; and it makes no use of the images employed in the other section, but only of Forms, and conducts its inquiry solely by their means.

I don't quite understand what you mean.

Then we will try again; what I have just said will help you to understand. (C) You know, of course, how students of subjects like geometry and arithmetic begin by postulating odd and even numbers, or the various figures and the three kinds of angle, and other such data in each subject. These data they take as known; and, having adopted them as assumptions, they do not feel called upon to give any account of them to themselves or to anyone else, but treat them as self-evident. Then, starting from these assumptions, they go on until they arrive, by a series of consistent steps, at all the conclusions they set out to investigate.

Yes, I know that.

You also know how they make use of visible figures and discourse about them, though what they really have in mind is the originals of which these figures are images: they are not reasoning, for instance, about this particular square and diagonal which they have drawn, but about *the* Square and *the* Diagonal; and so in all cases. The diagrams they draw and the models they make are actual things, which may have their shadows or images in water; but now they serve in their turn as images, while the student is seeking to behold those realities which only thought can apprehend.[4]

---

[4] Conversely, the fact that the mathematician can use visible objects as illustrations indicates that the realities and truths of mathematics are embodied, though imperfectly, in the world of visible and tangible things; whereas the counterparts of the moral Forms can only be beheld by thought.

True.

This, then, is the class of things that I spoke of as intelligible, but with two qualifications: first, that the mind, in studying them, is compelled to employ assumptions, and, because it cannot rise above these, does not travel upwards to a first principle; and second, that it uses as images those actual things which have images of their own in the section below them and which, in comparison with those shadows and reflections, are reputed to be more palpable and valued accordingly.

I understand: you mean the procedure of geometry and of the kindred arts.

(D) Then by the second section of the intelligible world you may understand me to mean all that unaided reasoning apprehends by the power of dialectic, when it treats its assumptions, not as first principles, but as *hypotheses* in the literal sense, things 'laid down' like a flight of steps up which it may mount all the way to something that is not hypothetical, the first principle of all; and having grasped this, may turn back and, holding on to the consequences which depend upon it, descend at last to a conclusion, never making use of any sensible object, but only of Forms, moving through Forms from one to another and ending with Forms.

I understand, he said, though not perfectly; for the procedure you describe sounds like an enormous undertaking. But I see that you mean to distinguish the field of intelligible reality studied by dialectic as having a greater certainty and truth than the subject-matter of the 'arts', as they are called, which treat their assumptions as first principles. The students of these arts are, it is true, compelled to exercise thought in contemplating objects which the senses cannot perceive; but because they start from assumptions without going back to a first principle, you do not regard them as gaining true understanding about those objects, although the objects themselves, when connected with a first principle, are intelligible. And I think you would call the state of mind of the students of geometry and other such arts, not intelligence, but thinking, as being something between intelligence and mere acceptance of appearances.

You have understood me quite well enough, I replied. And now you may take, as corresponding to the four sections, these four states of mind: *intelligence* for the highest, *thinking* for the second, *belief* for the third, and for the last *imagining*. These you may arrange as the terms in a proportion, assigning to each a degree of clearness and certainty

---

Palpable: clearly discernible.
Dialectic: here, logic, formal thought.

corresponding to the measure in which their objects possess truth and reality.

I understand and agree with you. I will arrange them as you say.

The Allegory of the Cave

Next, said I, here is a parable to illustrate the degrees in which our nature may be enlightened or unenlightened. Imagine the condition of men living in a sort of cavernous chamber underground, with an entrance open to the light and a long passage all down the cave. Here they have been from childhood, chained by the leg and also by the neck, so that they cannot move and can see only what is in front of them, because the chains will not let them turn their heads. At some distance higher up is the light of a fire burning behind them; and between the prisoners and the fire is a track with a parapet built along it, like the screen at a puppet-show, which hides the performers while they show their puppets over the top.

I see, said he.

Now behind this parapet imagine persons carrying along various artificial objects, including figures of men and animals in wood or stone or other materials, which project above the parapet. Naturally, some of these persons will be talking, others silent.

It is a strange picture, he said, and a strange sort of prisoners.

Like ourselves, I replied; for in the first place prisoners so confined would have seen nothing of themselves or of one another, except the shadows thrown by the fire-light on the wall of the Cave facing them, would they?

Not if all their lives they had been prevented from moving their heads.

And they would have seen as little of the objects carried past.

Of course.

Now, if they could talk to one another, would they not suppose that their words referred only to those passing shadows which they saw?

Necessarily.

And suppose their prison had an echo from the wall facing them? When one of the people crossing behind them spoke, they could only suppose that the sound came from the shadow passing before their eyes.

No doubt.

In every way, then, such prisoners would recognize as reality nothing but the shadows of those artificial objects.

Inevitably.

Now consider what would happen if their release from the chains and the healing of their unwisdom should come about in this way. Suppose one of them set free and forced suddenly to stand up, turn his head, and walk with eyes lifted to the light; all these movements would be painful, and he would be too dazzled to make out the objects whose shadows he had been used to see. What do you think he would say, if someone told him that what he had formerly seen was meaningless illusion, but now, being somewhat nearer to reality and turned towards more real objects, he was getting a truer view? Suppose further that he were shown the various objects being carried by and were made to say, in reply to questions, what each of them was. Would he not be perplexed and believe the objects now shown him to be not so real as what he formerly saw?

Yes, not nearly so real.

And if he were forced to look at the fire-light itself, would not his eyes ache, so that he would try to escape and turn back to the things which he could see distinctly, convinced that they really were clearer than these other objects now being shown to him?

Yes.

And suppose someone were to drag him away forcibly up the steep and rugged ascent and not let him go until he had hauled him out into the sunlight, would he not suffer pain and vexation at such treatment, and, when he had come out into the light, find his eyes so full of its radiance that he could not see a single one of the things that he was now told were real?

Certainly he would not see them all at once.

He would need, then, to grow accustomed before he could see things in that upper world. At first it would be easiest to make out shadows, and then the images of men and things reflected in water, and later on the things themselves. After that, it would be easier to watch the heavenly bodies and the sky itself by night, looking at the light of the moon and stars rather than the Sun and the Sun's light in the day-time.

Yes, surely.

Last of all, he would be able to look at the Sun and contemplate its nature, not as it appears when reflected in water or any alien medium, but as it is in itself in its own domain.

No doubt.

And now he would begin to draw the conclusion that it is the Sun that produces the seasons and the course of the year and controls everything in the visible world, and moreover is in a way the cause of all that he and his companions used to see.

Clearly he would come at last to that conclusion.

Then if he called to mind his fellow prisoners and what passed for wisdom in his former dwelling-place, he would surely think himself happy in the change and be sorry for them. They may have had a practice of honoring and commending one another, with prizes for the man who had the keenest eye for the passing shadows and the best memory for the order in which they followed or accompanied one another, so that he could make a good guess as to which was going to come next. Would our released prisoner be likely to covet those prizes or to envy the men exalted to honor and power in the Cave? . . .

Yes, he would prefer any fate to such a life.

Now imagine what would happen if he went down again to take his former seat in the Cave. Coming suddenly out of the sunlight, his eyes would be filled with darkness. He might be required once more to deliver his opinion on those shadows, in competition with the prisoners who had never been released, while his eyesight was still dim and unsteady; and it might take sometime to become used to the darkness. They would laugh at him and say that he had gone up only to come back with his sight ruined; it was worth no one's while even to attempt the ascent. If they could lay hands on the man who was trying to set them free and lead them up, they would kill him.

Yes, they would.

Every feature in this parable, my dear Glaucon, is meant to fit our earlier analysis. The prison dwelling corresponds to the region revealed to us through the sense of sight, and the fire-light within it to the power of the Sun. The ascent to see the things in the upper world you may take as standing for the upward journey of the soul into the region of the intelligible; then you will be in possession of what I surmise, since that is what you wish to be told. Heaven knows whether it is true; but this, at any rate, is how it appears to me. In the world of knowledge, the last thing to be perceived and only with great difficulty is the essential Form of Goodness. Once it is perceived, the conclusion must follow that, for all things, this is the cause of whatever is right and good; in the visible world it gives birth to light and to the lord of light, while it is itself sovereign in the intelligible world and the parent of intelligence and truth. Without having had a vision of this Form no one can act with wisdom, either in his own life or in matters of state.

So far as I can understand, I share your belief.

Then you may also agree that it is no wonder if those who have reached this height are reluctant to manage the affairs of men. Their souls long to spend all their time in that upper world—naturally enough, if here once more our parable holds true. Nor, again, is it at all strange that one who comes from the comtemplation of divine things to the miseries of human life should appear awkward and ridiculous when, with eyes still dazed and not yet accustomed to the darkness, he is compelled, in a law-court or elsewhere, to dispute about the shadows of justice or the images that cast those shadows, and to wrangle over the notions of what is right in the minds of men who have never beheld Justice itself.

It is not at all strange.

No; a sensible man will remember that the eyes may be confused in two ways—by a change from light to darkness or from darkness to light; and he will recognize that the same thing happens to the soul. When he sees it troubled and unable to discern anything clearly, instead of laughing thoughtlessly, he will ask whether, coming from a brighter existence, its unaccustomed vision is obscured by the darkness, in which case he will think its condition enviable and its life a happy one; or whether, emerging from the depths of ignorance, it is dazzled by excess of light. If so, he will rather feel sorry for it; or, if he were inclined to laugh, that would be less ridiculous than to laugh at the soul which has come down from the light.

That is a fair statement.

If this is true, then, we must conclude that education is not what it is said to be by some, who profess to put knowledge into a soul which does not possess it, as if they could put sight into blind eyes. On the contrary, our own account signifies that the soul of every man does possess the power of learning the truth and the organ to see it with; and that, just as one might have to turn the whole body round in order that the eye should see light instead of darkness, so the entire soul must be turned away from this changing world, until its eye can bear to contemplate reality and that supreme splendor which we have called the Good. Hence there may well be an art whose aim would be to effect this very thing, the conversion of the soul, in the readiest way; not to put the power of sight into the soul's eye, which already has it, but to ensure that, instead of looking in the wrong direction, it is turned the way it ought to be.

Yes it may well be so.

It looks, then, as though wisdom were different from those ordinary virtues, as they are called, which are not far removed from bodily qualities, in that they can be produced by habituation and exercise in a soul which has not possessed them from the first. Wisdom, it seems, is certainly the virtue of some diviner faculty, which never loses its power, though its use for good or harm depends on the direction towards which it is turned. You must have noticed in dishonest men with a reputation for sagacity the shrewd glance of a narrow intelligence piercing the objects to which it is directed. There is nothing wrong with their power of vision, but it has been forced into the service of evil, so that the keener its sight, the more harm it works.

35

Particulars
Are Real

David Hume (1711–1776), an outstanding British empiricist, wrote not only upon philosophical subjects, but also became famous as a historian. Among his major works are *A Treatise of Human Nature* (1739–40), *Essays, Moral and Political* (1741–42), and *The History of England* (1754–62).

Hume, a nominalist regarding universals, argues that all of our ideas are ideas of particular entities, qualities, or relations. We do not sense tables in general, but only particular tables. Nominalists such as Hume contend that there is nothing universal in the world, but only in the language we use to describe the world. They say that many particulars resemble each other and hence for the sake of convenience we give the same name to these resembling objects.

─TO STUDY

1. What is Berkeley's view as to the nature of general ideas?
2. According to Hume, how do we form most of our general ideas?
3. What is Hume's argument refuting the view that abstract ideas have no particular degree of quantity or quality?
4. What purposes of life are served by applying the same treatment to resembling ideas? Explain Hume's example of the triangle.
5. Explain: "Some ideas are particular in their nature, but general in their representation."

6. Explain Hume's basic principle that "All ideas, which are different, are separable."

A very material question has been started concerning *abstract* or *general* ideas, *whether they be general or particular in the mind's conception of them.* A great philosopher[1] has disputed the received opinion in this particular, and has asserted, that all general ideas are nothing but particular ones, annexed to a certain term, which gives them a more extensive signification, and makes them recall upon occasion other individuals, which are similar to them. As I look upon this to be one of the greatest and most valuable discoveries that has been made of late years in the republic of letters, I shall here endeavor to confirm it by some arguments, which I hope will put it beyond all doubt and controversy.

'Tis evident, that in forming most of our general ideas, if not all of them, we abstract from every particular degree of quantity and quality, and that an object ceases not to be of any particular species on account of every small alteration in its extension, duration, and other properties. It may therefore be thought, that here is a plain dilemma, that decides concerning the nature of those abstract ideas, which have afforded so much speculation to philosophers. The abstract idea of a man represents men of all sizes and all qualities; which 'tis concluded it cannot do, but either by representing at once all possible sizes and all possible qualities, or by representing no particular one at all. Now it having been esteemed absurd to defend the former proposition, as implying an infinite capacity in the mind, it has been commonly inferred in favor of the latter; and our abstract ideas have been supposed to represent no particular degree either of quantity or quality. But that this inference is erroneous, I shall endeavor to make appear, *first,* by proving, that 'tis utterly impossible to conceive any quantity or quality, without forming a precise notion of its degrees; and *secondly* by showing, that though the capacity of the mind be not infinite, yet we can at once form a notion of all possible degrees of quantity and quality, in such a manner at least, as, however imperfect, may serve all the purposes of reflection and conversation.

To begin with the first proposition, *that the mind cannot form any notion of quantity or quality without forming a precise notion of degrees of each;* we may prove this by the three following arguments. First, we have observed, that whatever objects are different are distinguishable, and that whatever objects are distinguishable are separable by the thought and imag-

---

[1] Dr. Berkeley. [Cf. George Berkeley, *A Treatise Concerning the Principles of Human Knowledge,* Introduction, Secs. 18ff.]

ination. And we may here add, that these propositions are equally true in the *inverse,* and that whatever objects are separable are also distinguishable, and that whatever objects are distinguishable are also different. For how is it possible we can separate what is not distinguishable, or distinguish what is not different? In order therefore to know whether abstraction implies a separation, we need only consider it in this view, and examine whether all the circumstances, which we abstract from in our general ideas, be such as are distinguishable and different from those, which we retain as essential parts of them. But 'tis evident at first sight, that the precise length of a line is not different nor distinguishable from the line itself; nor the precise degree of any quality from the quality. These ideas, therefore, admit no more of separation than they do of distinction and difference. They are consequently conjoined with each other in the conception; and the general idea of a line, notwithstanding all our abstractions and refinements, has in its appearance in the mind a precise degree of quantity and quality; however it may be made to represent others, which have different degrees of both.

Secondly, 'tis confessed, that no object can appear to the senses; or in other words, that no impression can become present to the mind, without being determined in its degrees both of quantity and quality. The confusion, in which impressions are sometimes involved, proceeds only from their faintness and unsteadiness, not from any capacity in the mind to receive any impression, which in its real existence has no particular degree nor proportion. That is a contradiction in terms; and even implies the flattest of all contradictions, viz., that 'tis possible for the same thing both to be and not to be.

Now since all ideas are derived from impressions, and are nothing but copies and representations of them, whatever is true of the one must be acknowledged concerning the other. Impressions and ideas differ only in their strength and vivacity. The foregoing conclusion is not founded on any particular degree of vivacity. It cannot therefore be affected by any variation in that particular. An idea is a weaker impression; and as strong impression must necessarily have a determinate quantity and quality, the case must be the same with its copy or representative.

Thirdly, 'tis a principle generally received in philosophy that everything in nature is individual, and that 'tis utterly absurd to suppose a triangle really existent, which has no precise proportion of sides and angles. If this therefore be absurd in *fact and reality,* it must also be absurd in *idea;* since nothing of which we can form a clear and distinct idea is absurd and impossible. but to form the idea of an object, and to form an idea simply, is the same thing; the reference of the idea to an object being an extraneous denomination, of which in itself it bears no mark or character. Now as 'tis impossible to form an idea of an object, that is possessed of quantity and quality, and yet is possessed of no precise degree of either; it follows that there is an equal impossibility of forming an idea, that is not limited and confined in both these particulars. Abstract ideas are therefore in themselves individual, however they may become general in their representation. The image in the mind is only that of a particular object, though the application of it in our reasoning be the same, as if it were universal.

This application of ideas beyond their nature proceeds from our collecting all their possible degrees of quantity and quality in such an imperfect manner as may serve the purposes of life, which is the second proposition I proposed to explain. When we have found a resemblance among several objects, that often occur to us, we apply the same name to all of them, whatever differences we may observe in the degrees of their quantity and quality, and whatever other differences may appear among them. After we have acquired a custom of this kind, the hearing of that name revives the idea of one of these objects, and makes the imagination conceive it with all its particular circumstances and proportions. But as the same word is supposed to have been frequently applied to other individuals, that are different in many respects from that idea, which is immediately present to the mind; the word not being able to revive the idea of all these individuals, but only touches the soul, if I may be allowed so to speak, and revives that custom, which we have acquired by surveying them. They are not really and in fact present to the mind, but only in power; nor do we draw them all out distinctly in the imagination, but keep ourselves in a readiness to survey any of them, as we may be prompted by a present design or necessity. The word raises up an individual idea, along with a certain custom; and that custom produces any other individual one, for which we may have occasion. But as the production of all the ideas, to which the name may be applied, is in most cases impossible, we abridge that work by a more partial consideration, and find but few inconveniences to arise in our reasoning from that abridgment.

For this is one of the most extraordinary circumstances in the present affair, that after the mind has produced an individual idea, upon which we reason, the attendant custom, revived by the general or abstract term, readily suggests any other individual, if by chance we form any reasoning, that agrees not with it. Thus should we mention the word *triangle,* and form the idea of a particular equilateral one to correspond to it, and should we afterwards assert, *that the three angles of a triangle are equal to each other,* the other individuals of a scalenum and isosceles, which we overlooked at first, immediately crowd in upon us, and make us perceive the falsehood of this proposition, though it be true with relation to that idea, which we had formed. If the mind suggests not always these ideas upon occasion, it proceeds from some imperfection in its faculties; and such a one as is often the source of false reasoning and sophistry. But this is principally the case with those ideas which are abstruse and compounded. On other occasions the custom is more entire, and 'tis seldom we run into such errors.

Nay so entire is the custom, that the very same idea may be annexed to several different words, and may be employed in different reasonings, without any danger of mistake. Thus the idea of an equilateral triangle of an inch perpendicular may serve us in talking of a figure, or a rectilineal figure, of a regular figure, of a triangle, and of an equilateral triangle. All these terms, therefore, are in this case attended with the same idea; but as they are wont to be applied in a greater or lesser compass, they excite their particular habits, and thereby keep the mind in a readiness to observe, that no conclusion be formed contrary to any ideas, which are usually comprised under them.

Before those habits have become entirely perfect, perhaps the mind may not be content with forming the idea of only one individual, but may run over several, in order to make itself comprehend its own meaning, and the compass of that collection, which it intends to express by the general term. That we may fix the meaning of the word *figure*, we may revolve in our mind the ideas of circles, squares, parallelograms, triangles of different sizes and proportions, and may not rest on one image or idea. However this may be, 'tis certain *that* we form the idea of individuals, whenever we use any general term; *that* we seldom or never can exhaust these individuals; and *that* those, which remain, are only represented by means of that habit, by which we recall them, whenever any present occasion requires it. This then is the nature of our abstract ideas and general terms; and 'tis after this manner we account for the foregoing paradox, *that some ideas are particular in their nature, but general in their representation.* A particular idea becomes general by being annexed to a general term; that is, to a term, which from a customary conjunction has a relation to many other particular ideas, and readily recalls them in the imagination.

Before I leave this subject I shall employ the same principles to explain that *distinction of reason,* which is so much talked of, and is so little understood, in the schools. Of this kind is the distinction betwixt figure and the body figured; motion and the body moved. The difficulty of explaining this distinction arises from the principle above explained, *that all ideas, which are different, are separable.* For it follows from thence, that if the figure be different from the body, their ideas must be separable as well as distinguishable; if they be not different, their ideas can neither be separable nor distinguishable. What then is meant by a distinction of reason, since it implies neither a difference nor separation.

To remove this difficulty we must have recourse to the foregoing explication of abstract ideas. 'Tis certain that the mind would never have dreamed of distinguishing a figure from the body figured, as being in reality neither distinguishable, nor different, nor separable; did it not observe, that even in this simplicity there might be contained many different resemblances and relations. Thus when a globe of white marble is presented, we receive only the impression of a white color disposed in a certain form, nor are we able to separate and distinguish the color from the form. But observing afterwards a globe of black marble and a cube of white, and comparing them with our former object, we find two separate resemblances, in what formerly seemed, and really is, perfectly inseparable. After a little more practice of this kind, we begin to distinguish the figure from the color by a *distinction of reason;* that is, we consider the figure and color together, since they are in effect the same and undistinguishable; but still view them in different aspects, according to the resemblances, of which they are susceptible. When we would consider only the figure of the globe of white marble, we form in reality an idea both of the figure and color, but tacitly carry our eye to its resemblance with the globe of black marble. And in the same manner, when we would consider its color only, we turn our view to its resemblance with the cube of white marble. By this means we accompany our ideas with a kind of reflection, of which custom renders us, in a great measure, insensible. A person, who desires us to consider the figure of a globe of white marble without thinking on its color, desires an impossibility; but his meaning is, that we should consider the figure and color together, but still keep in our eye the resemblance to the globe of black marble, or that to any other globe of whatever color or substance.

Readings

1. Aaron, R. I. *The Theory of Universals.* Oxford: Oxford Univ. Press, 1952.
2. Ayer, A. J. "Particulars and Universals," *Proceedings of the Aristotelian Society* (1933–34).
3. Pears, D. F. "Universals," *Philosophical Quarterly* (1950–51).
4. Woozley, A. D. *Theory of Knowledge.* London: Hutchinson, 1949.

6

Philosophy of Religion

one

How Can God Be
Proven to Exist?

36

The Ontological Argument

St. Anselm of Canterbury was born in Aosta in 1033. In 1093 he was made Archbishop of Canterbury. During his years in the abbey he wrote the two works for which he is best known, *The Monologium* and *The Proslogium*. Anselm's name will forever be associated with the ontological argument for the existence of God.

Most men believe that God exists and many men attempt to give reasons or proofs for His existence. Kant said that there are only three possible bases upon which one can prove God's existence: no experience, one experience, and many experiences. Arguing from the nature of God Himself, that is, independent of experience, is referred to as the *ontological argument*. This proof was first given by St. Anselm. It is claimed that once we understand the nature of God we realize that it implies His existence. One might argue that God is a perfect Being, and it is an imperfection not to exist. God, however, is perfect. Hence, since He is perfect, He must exist.

―TO STUDY

1. What is St. Anselm's conception of God?
2. What argument does St. Anselm offer as proof that this God exists?
3. According to St. Anselm, in what way may God be conceived not to exist?

. . . Lord, I acknowledge and I thank thee that thou hast created me in this thine image, in order that I may be mindful of thee, may conceive of thee, and love thee; but that image has been so consumed and wasted away by vices, and obscured by the smoke of wrong-doing, that it cannot achieve that for which it was made, except thou renew it, and create it anew. I do not endeavor, O Lord, to penetrate thy sublimity, for in no wise do I compare my understanding with that; but I long to understand in some degree thy truth, which my heart believes and loves. For I do not seek to understand that I may believe, but I believe in order to understand. For this also I believe,—that unless I believed, I should not understand. . . .

And so, Lord, do thou, who dost give understanding to faith, give me, so far as thou knowest it to be profitable, to understand that thou art as we believe; and that thou art that which we believe. And, indeed, we believe that thou art a being than which nothing greater can be conceived. Or is there no such nature, since the fool hath said in his heart, there is no God? . . . But, at any rate, this very fool, when he hears of this being of which I speak—a being than which nothing greater can be conceived—understands what he hears, and what he understands is in his understanding; although he does not understand it to exist.

For, it is one thing for an object to be in the understanding, and another to understand that the object exists. When a painter first conceives of what he will afterwards perform, he has it in his understanding, but he does not yet understand it to be, because he has not yet performed it. But after he has made the painting, he both has it in his understanding, and he understands that it exists, because he has made it.

Hence, even the fool is convinced that something exists in the understanding, at least, than which nothing greater can be conceived. For, when he hears of this, he understands it. And whatever is understood, exists in the understanding. And assuredly that, than which nothing greater can be conceived, cannot exist in the understanding alone. For, suppose it exists in the understanding alone: then it can be conceived to exist in reality; which is greater.

Therefore, if that, than which nothing greater can be conceived, exists in the understanding alone, the very being, than which nothing greater can be conceived, is one, than which a greater can be conceived. But obviously this is impossible. Hence, there is no doubt that there exists a being, than which nothing greater can be conceived, and it exists both in the understanding and in reality. . . .

And it assuredly exists so truly, that it cannot be conceived not to exist.

From part of Chap. 1, and Chaps. 2 through 4 of the *Proslogium*, translated from the Latin by Sidney Norton Deane, Open Court Publishing Co., 1903.

For, it is possible to conceive of a being which cannot be conceived not to exist; and this is greater than one which can be conceived not to exist. Hence, if that, than which nothing greater can be conceived, can be conceived not to exist, it is not that, than which nothing greater can be conceived. But this is an irreconcilable contradiction. There is, then, so truly a being than which nothing greater can be conceived to exist, that it cannot even be conceived not to exist; and this being thou art, O Lord, our God.

So truly, therefore, dost thou exist, O Lord, my God, that thou canst not be conceived not to exist; and rightly. For, if a mind could conceive of a being better than thee, the creature would rise above the Creator; and this is most absurd. And, indeed, whatever else there is, except thee alone, can be conceived not to exist. To thee alone, therefore, it belongs to exist more truly than all other beings, and hence in a higher degree than all others. For, whatever else exists does not exist so truly, and hence in a less degree it belongs to it to exist. Why, then, has the fool said in his heart, there is no God . . . since it is so evident, to a rational mind, that thou dost exist in the highest degree of all? Why, except that he is dull and a fool? . . .

But how has the fool said in his heart what he could not conceive; or how is it that he could not conceive what he said in his heart? Since it is the same to say in the heart, and to conceive.

But, if really, nay, since really, he both conceived, because he said in his heart; and did not say in his heart, because he could not conceive; there is more than one way in which a thing is said in the heart or conceived. For, in one sense, an object is conceived, when the word signifying it is conceived; and in another, when the very entity, which the object is, is understood.

In the former sense, then, God can be conceived not to exist; but in the latter, not at all. For no one who understands what fire and water are can conceive fire to be water, in accordance with the nature of the facts themselves, although this is possible according to the words. So, then, no one who understands what God is can conceive that God does not exist; although he says these words in his heart, either without any, or with some foreign, signification. For, God is that than which a greater cannot be conceived. And he who thoroughly understands this, assuredly understands that this being so truly exists, that not even in concept can it be non-existent. Therefore, he who understands that God so exists, cannot conceive that he does not exist.

I thank thee, gracious Lord, I thank thee; because what I formerly believed by thy bounty, I now so understand by thine illumination, that if I were unwilling to believe that thou dost exist, I should not be able not to understand this to be true.

THINK ABOUT

1. "If God did not exist it would be necessary to invent him."

   Voltaire

2. "It seems as though the conception of a human soul . . . served as a type or model on which (human being) framed not only his ideas of other souls of lower grade, but also his ideas of spiritual beings in general, from the tiniest elf that sports in the long grass up to the heavenly Creator and Ruler of the world, the Great Spirit."

   E. B. Tylor

3. "One who has experienced this will understand something of it; it cannot be more clearly expressed, since all that comes to pass in this state is so obscure. I can only say that the soul feels close to God and that there abides within it such a certainty that it cannot possibly do other than believe."

   St. Theresa of Avila

4. "Faith is a species of belief, and belief is defined 'an assent to a proposition upon rational grounds.' Without rational grounds there is no belief, and consequently no faith."

   John Wesley

5. Saint Augustine was asked by a scoffer what God was doing before He created the world. Replied the great theologian: "He was busy creating hell for people who ask foolish questions."

6. "Most intellectual people do not believe in God, but they fear him just the same."

   Wilhelm Reich

7. "The rash assertion that 'God made man in His own image' is ticking like a time bomb at the foundations of many faiths, and as the hierarchy of the universe is disclosed to us, we may have to recognize this chilling truth: if there are any gods whose chief concern is man, they cannot be very important gods."

   Arthur C. Clarke

8. "To be man is to strive to be God."

   Jean-Paul Sartre

37

The Cosmological Argument

St. Thomas Aquinas (1225–1274), born in Roccasicca (lower Italy), received his education at the Monte Cassino Abbey and in Naples, Cologne, and Paris; taught theology in Paris (1256–72) and several years in Rome and other cities. He is generally regarded as the greatest of the Scholastic theologians. His two major works are *Summa Theologica* and *Summa Contra Gentiles,* which respectively synthesized Aristotelian and Christian doctrines, and attempted to answer the objections against Catholicism.

The proof of God's existence which argues on the basis of many experiences is called the cosmological or first cause argument. This argues that the things of the world all must have had a cause, and since there can't be an infinity of causes, there must be a first cause, which is God. St. Thomas is most famous for arguing in this manner. His various proofs given in the article in this section are quite sophisticated and the student must carefully state them before attempting any critical analysis.

─TO STUDY

What are the five ways in which Aquinas claims that the existence of God can be proven? Construct three of the arguments in logical form.

Objection 1. It seems that God does not exist; because if one of two contraries be infinite, the other would be altogether destroyed. But the name *God* means that He is infinite goodness. If, therefore, God existed, there would be no evil discoverable; but there is evil in the world. Therefore God does not exist.

Obj. 2. Further, it is superfluous to suppose that what can be accounted for by a few principles has been produced by many. But it seems that everything we see in the world can be accounted for by other principles, supposing God did not exist. For all natural things can be reduced to one principle, which is nature; and all voluntary things can be reduced to one principle, which is human reason, or will. Therefore there is no need to suppose God's existence.

On the Contrary, It is said in the person of God: *I am Who am* (Exod. iii. 14).

I answer that, The existence of God can be proved in five ways.

The first and more manifest way is the argument from motion. It is certain, and evident to our senses, that in the world some things are in motion. Now whatever is moved is moved by another, for nothing can be moved except it is in potentiality to that towards which it is moved; whereas a thing moves inasmuch as it is in act. For motion is nothing else than the reduction of something from potentiality to actuality. But nothing can be reduced from potentiality to actuality, except by something in a state of actuality. Thus that which is actually hot, as fire, makes wood, which is potentially hot, to be actually hot, and thereby moves and changes it. Now it is not possible that the same thing should be at once in actuality and potentiality in the same respect, but only in different respects. For what is actually hot cannot simultaneously be potentially hot; but it is simultaneously potentially cold. It is therefore impossible that in the same respect and in the same way a thing should be both mover and moved, *i.e.,* that it should move itself. Therefore, whatever is moved must be moved by another. If that by which it is moved be itself moved, then this also must needs be moved by another, and that by another again. But this cannot go on to infinity, because then there would be no first mover, and, consequently, no other mover, seeing that subsequent movers move only inasmuch as they are moved by the first mover; as the staff moves only because it is moved by the hand. Therefore it is necessary to arrive at a first mover, moved by no other; and this everyone understands to be God.

The second way is from the nature of efficient cause. In the world of sensible things we find there is an order of efficient causes. There is no case known (neither is it, indeed, possible) in which a thing is found to be the efficient cause of itself; for so it would be prior to itself, which is impossible. Now in efficient causes it is not possible to go on to infinity, because in all efficient causes following in order, the first is the cause of the intermediate cause, and the intermediate is the cause of the ultimate cause, whether the intermediate cause be several, or one only. Now to take away the cause is to take away the effect. Therefore, if there be no first cause among efficient causes, there will be no ultimate, nor any intermediate, cause. But if in efficient causes it is possible to go on to infinity, there will be no first efficient cause, neither will there be an ultimate effect, nor any intermediate efficient causes; all of which is plainly false. Therefore it is necessary to admit a first efficient cause, to which everyone gives the name of God.

The third way is taken from possibility and necessity, and runs thus. We find in nature things that are possible to be and not to be, since they are found to be generated, and to be corrupted, and consequently, it is possible for them to be and not to be. But it is impossible for these always to exist, for that which cannot-be at some time is not. Therefore, if everything cannot-be, then at one time there was nothing in existence. Now if this were true, even now there would be nothing in existence, because that which does not exist begins to exist only through something already existing. Therefore, if at one time nothing was in existence, it would have been impossible for anything to have begun to exist; and thus even now nothing would be in existence—which is absurd. Therefore, not all beings are merely possible, but there must exist something the existence of which is necessary. But every necessary thing either has its necessity caused by another, or not. Now it is impossible to go on to infinity in necessary things which have their necessity caused by another, as has been already proved in regard to efficient causes. Therefore we cannot but admit the existence of some being having of itself its own necessity, and not receiving it from another, but rather causing in others their necessity. This all men speak of as God.

The fourth way is taken from the gradation to be found in things. Among beings there are some more and some less good, true, noble, and the like. But *more* and *less* are predicated of different things according as they resemble in their different ways something which is the maximum, as a thing is said to be hotter according as it more nearly resembles that which is hottest; so that there is something which is truest, something best, something noblest, and, consequently, something which is most being, for those things that are greatest in truth are greatest in being, as it is written in [Aristotle's] *Metaphysics* ii. Now the maximum in any genus is the cause of all in that genus, as fire, which is the maximum of heat, is the cause of all hot things, as is said in the same book. Therefore there must also be something which is to all beings the cause of their being, goodness, and every other perfection; and this we call God.

The fifth way is taken from the governance of the world. We see that things which lack knowledge, such as natural bodies, act for an end, and this is evident from their acting always, or nearly always, in the same way, so as to obtain the best result. Hence it is plain that they achieve their end, not fortuitously, but designedly. Now whatever lacks knowledge cannot move towards an end, unless it be directed by some being endowed with knowledge and intelligence; as the arrow is directed by the archer. Therefore some intelligent being exists by whom all natural things are directed to their end: and this being we call God.

Reply Obj. 1. As Augustine says: *Since God is the highest good, He would not allow any evil to exist in His works; unless His omnipotence and goodness were such as to bring good even out of evil.* This is part of the infinite goodness of God, that He should allow evil to exist, and out of it produce good.

Reply Obj. 2. Since nature works for a determinate end under the direction of a higher agent, whatever is done by nature must be traced back to God as to its first cause. So likewise whatever is done voluntarily must be traced back to some higher cause other than human reason and will, since these can change and fail; for all things that are changeable and capable of defect must be traced back to an immovable and self-necessary first principle as has been shown.

38

argument from design

The Teleological Argument

William Paley (1743–1805), Archdeacon of Carlisle, wrote a number of apologetic works, of which the two most famous are his *Evidences of Christianity* (1794) and his *Natural Theology, or Evidences of the Existences and Attributes of the Deity collected from the Appearances of Nature* (1802).

The proof of God's existence which argues from a single experience is called the *teleological* or *design argument*. Such a proof is by analogy and is meant to show that there is a resemblance between the world and machines, and that just as machines have makers so the world must have a designer who is God. Paley's article is famous for presenting this argument on the basis of the analogy between a watch and the world. After reformulating these arguments, the student should not only examine their soundness, but ask also whether they prove the type of God which has been the intent of the author to prove.

────────────TO STUDY

1. What is the analogical argument stated by Paley? Structure the argument carefully.

2. According to Paley's teleological argument, why is it not necessary that the universe (the machine) be perfect?

3. Why does Paley believe the watch could not be structured by chance? Why couldn't the watch simply be the result of laws of metallic nature?

Statement of the Argument

In crossing a heath, suppose I pitched my foot against a *stone,* and were asked how the stone came to be there, I might possibly answer, that, for anything I knew to the contrary, it had lain there for ever; nor would it, perhaps, be very easy to show the absurdity of this answer. But suppose I found a *watch* upon the ground, and it should be inquired how the watch happened to be in that place, I should hardly think of the answer which I had before given—that, for anything I knew, the watch might have always been there. Yet why should not this answer serve for the watch as well as for the stone? why is it not as admissible in the second case as in the first? For this reason, and for no other, viz., that, when we come to inspect the watch, we perceive (what we could not discover in the stone) that its several parts are framed and put together for a purpose, e.g., that they are so formed and adjusted as to produce motion, and that motion so regulated as to point out the hour of the day; that, if the different parts had been differently shaped from what they are, if a different size from what they are, or placed after any other manner, or in any other order than that in which they are placed, either no motion at all would have been carried on in the machine, or none which would have answered the use that is now served by it. To reckon up a few of the plainest of these parts, and of their offices, all tending to one result:—We see a cylindrical box containing a coiled elastic spring, which, by its endeavor to relax itself, turns round the box. We next observe a flexible chain (artificially wrought for the sake of flexure) communicating the action of the spring from the box to the fusee. We then find a series of wheels, the teeth of which catch in, and apply to, each other, conducting the motion from the fusee to the balance, and from the balance to the pointer, and, at the same time, by the size and shape of those wheels, so regulating that motion as to terminate in causing an index, by an equable and measured progression, to pass over a given space in a given time. We take notice that the wheels are made of brass, in order to keep them from rust; the springs of steel, no other metal being so elastic; that over the face of the watch there is placed a glass, a material employed in no other part of the work, but in the room of which, if there had been any other than a transparent substance, the hour could not be seen without opening the case. This mechanism being observed (it requires indeed an examination of the instrument, and perhaps some previous knowledge of the subject, to perceive and understand it; but being once, as we have said, observed and understood), the inference, we think, is inevitable, that the watch must have had a maker; that there must have existed, at some place or other,

From *Natural Theology* (1802) by William Paley.

an artificer or artificers who formed it for the purpose which we find it actually to answer; who comprehended its construction, and designed its use.

I. Nor would it, I apprehend, weaken the conclusion, that we had never seen a watch made; that we had never known an artist capable of making one; that we were altogether incapable of executing such a piece of workmanship ourselves, or of understanding in what manner it was performed; all this being no more than what is true of some exquisite remains of ancient art, of some lost arts, and, to the generality of mankind, of the more curious productions of modern manufacture. Does one man in a million know how oval frames are turned? Ignorance of this kind exalts our opinion of the unseen and unknown artist's skill, if he be unseen and unknown, but raises no doubt in our minds of the existence and agency of such an artist, at some former time, and in some place or other. Nor can I perceive that it varies at all the inference, whether the question arise concerning a human agent, or concerning an agent of a different species, or an agent possessing, in some respect, a different nature.

II. Neither, secondly, would it invalidate our conclusion, that the watch sometimes went wrong, or that it seldom went exactly right. The purpose of the machinery, the design, and the designer, might be evident, and, in the case supposed, would be evident, in whatever way we accounted for the irregularity of the movement, or whether we could account for it or not. It is not necessary that a machine be perfect, in order to show with what design it was made; still less necessary, where the only question is, whether it were made with any design at all.

III. Nor, thirdly, would it bring any uncertainty into the argument, if there were a few parts of the watch, concerning which we could not discover, or had not yet discovered, in what manner they conduced to the general effect; or even some parts, concerning which we could not ascertain whether they conduced to that effect in any manner whatever. For, as to the first branch of the case, if by the loss, or disorder, or decay of the parts in question, the movement of the watch were found in fact to be stopped, or disturbed, or retarded, no doubt would remain in our minds as to the utility or intention of these parts, although we should be unable to investigate the manner according to which, or the connection by which, the ultimate effect depended upon their action or assistance; and the more complex is the machine, the more likely is this obscurity to arise. Then, as to the second thing supposed, namely, that there were parts which might be spared without prejudice to the movement of the watch, and that he had proved this by experiment, these superfluous parts, even if we were completely assured that they were such, would not vacate the reasoning which we had instituted concerning other parts. The indication of contrivance remained, with respect to them, nearly as it was before.

IV. Nor, fourthly, would any man in his senses think the existence of the watch, with its various machinery, accounted for, by being told that it was one out of possible combinations of material forms; that whatever he had found in the place where he found the watch, must have contained some internal configuration or other; and that this configuration might be the structure now exhibited, viz., of the works of a watch, as well as a different structure.

V. Nor, fifthly, would it yield his inquiry more satisfaction, to be answered, that there existed in things a principle of order, which had disposed the parts of the watch into their present form and situation. He never knew a watch made by the principle of order; nor can he even form to himself an idea of what is meant by a principle of order, distinct from the intelligence of the watchmaker.

VI. Sixthly, he would be surprised to hear that the mechanism of the watch was no proof of contrivance, only a motion to induce the mind to think so:

VII. And not less surprised to be informed, that the watch in his hand was nothing more than the result of the laws of *metallic* nature. It is a perversion of language to assign any law as the efficient, operative cause of anything. A law presupposes an agent; for it is only the mode according to which an agent proceeds; it implies a power; for it is the order according to which that power acts. Without this agent, without this power, which are both distinct from itself the *law* does nothing, is nothing. The expression, "the law of metallic nature," may sound strange and harsh to a philosophic ear; but it seems quite as justifiable as some others which are more familiar to him such as "the law of vegetable nature," "the law of animal nature," or, indeed, as "the law of nature" in general, when assigned as the cause of phenomena in exclusion of agency and power, or when it is substituted into the place of these.

VIII. Neither, lastly, would our observer be driven out of his conclusion, or from his confidence in its truth, by being told that he knew nothing at all about the matter. He knows enough for his argument: he knows the utility of the end: he knows the subserviency and adaptation of the means to the end. These points being known, his ignorance of other points, his doubts concerning other points, affect not the certainty of his reasoning. The consciousness of knowing little need not beget a distrust of that which he does know. . . .

Application of the Argument

Every indication of contrivance, every manifestation of design, which existed in the watch, exists in the works of nature; with the difference, on the side of nature, of being greater and more, and that in a degree which exceeds all computation. I mean that the contrivances of nature surpass the contrivances of art, in the complexity, subtlety, and curiosity of the mechanism; and still more, if possible, do they go beyond them in number and variety; yet in a multitude of cases, are not less evidently mechanical, not less evidently contrivances, not less evidently accommodated to their end, or suited to their office, than are the most perfect productions of human ingenuity. . . .

39

The Existence of God
Is a Good Bet

Blaise Pascal (1623–1662), philosopher, scientist and mystic, was already making important contributions to mathematics and physics by the time of his conversion to Jansenist Christianity in 1653. He is regarded as the founder of modern probability theory and he significantly advanced the study of differential calculus. His religious writings were published posthumously in 1670 under the title *Pensées de M. Pascal sur la religion et sur quelques autres subjets.*

Pascal, unlike the three previous philosophers, states that there is no rational proof for or against God's existence. Nonetheless, you must choose to believe or not. Hence, why not wager on that belief which will bring you the most happiness. The choice is obvious, for through believing in God, we can not only gain infinite happiness and immortality, but we have nothing to lose in so doing.

TO STUDY

1. Upon what basis does Pascal argue that we can't know God's existence?
2. State Pascal's wager.
3. For what reasons does Pascal think we must bet on the existence of God?

Let us now speak according to natural lights.

If there is a God, He is infinitely incomprehensible, since, having neither parts nor limits, He has no affinity to us. We are then incapable of knowing either what He is or if He is. This being so, who will dare to undertake the decision of the question? Not we, who have no affinity to Him.

Who then will blame Christians for not being able to give a reason for their belief, since they profess a religion for which they cannot give a reason? They declare, in expounding it to the world, that it is a foolishness, *stultitiam;* and then you complain that they do not prove it! If they proved it, they would not keep their word; it is in lacking proofs, that they are not lacking in sense. "Yes, but although this excuses those who offer it as such, and takes away from them the blame of putting it forward without reason, it does not excuse those who receive it." Let us then examine this point, and say, "God is, or He is not." But to which side shall we incline? Reason can decide nothing here. There is an infinite chaos which separated us. A game is being played at the extremity of this infinite distance where heads or tails will turn up. What will you wager? According to reason, you can do neither the one thing nor the other; according to reason, you can defend neither of the propositions.

Do not then reprove for error those who have made a choice; for you know nothing about it. "No, but I blame them for having made, not this choice, but a choice; for again both he who chooses heads and he who chooses tails are equally at fault, they are both in the wrong. The true course is not to wager at all."

Yes; but you must wager. It is not optional. You are embarked. Which will you choose then? Let us see. Since you must choose, let us see which interests you least. You have two things to lose, the true and the good; and two things to stake, your reason and your will, your knowledge and your happiness; and your nature has two things to shun, error and misery. Your reason is no more shocked in choosing one rather than the other, since you must of necessity choose. This is one point settled. But your happiness? Let us weigh the gain and the loss in wagering that God is. Let us estimate these two chances. If you gain, you gain all; if you lose, you lose nothing. Wager, then, without hesitation that He is.—"That is very fine. Yes, I must wager; but I may perhaps wager too much."—Let us see. Since there is an equal risk of gain and of loss, if you had only to gain two lives, instead of one, you might still wager. But if there were three lives to gain, you would have to play (since you are under the necessity of playing), and you would be imprudent, when you are forced to play, not to change your life to gain three at a game where there is an equal risk of loss and gain. But there is an eternity of life and happiness. And this being so, if there were an infinity of chances, of which one only would be for you, you would still be right in wagering one to win two, and you would act stupidly, being obliged to play, by refusing to stake one life against three at a game in which out of an infinity of chances there is one for you, if there were an infinity of an infinitely happy life to gain. But there is here an infinity of an infinitely happy life to gain, a chance of gain against a finite number of chances of loss, and what you stake is finite. It is all divided; wherever the infinite is and there is not an infinity of chances of loss against that of gain, there is no time to hesitate, you must give all. And thus, when one is forced to play, he must renounce reason to preserve his life, rather than risk it for infinite gain, as likely to happen as the loss of nothingness.

For it is no use to say it is uncertain if we will gain, and it is certain that we risk, and that the infinite distance between the *certainty* of what is staked and the *uncertainty* of what will be gained, equals the finite good which is certainly staked against the uncertain infinite. It is not so, as every player stakes a certainty to gain an uncertainty, and yet he stakes a finite certainty to gain a finite uncertainty, without transgressing against reason. There is not an infinite distance between the certainty staked and the uncertainty of the gain; that is untrue. In truth, there is an infinity between the certainty of gain and the certainty of loss. But the uncertainty of the gain is proportioned to the certainty of the stake according to the proportion of the chances of gain and loss. Hence it comes that, if there are as many risks on one side as on the other, the course is to play even; and then the certainty of the stake is equal to the uncertainty of the gain, so far is it from fact that there is an infinite distance between them. And so our proposition is of infinite force, when there is the finite to stake in a game where there are equal risks of gain and of loss, and the infinite to gain. This is demonstrable; and if men are capable of any truths, this is one.

"I confess it, I admit it. But, still, is there no means of seeing the faces of the cards?"—Yes, Scripture and the rest, etc. "Yes, but I have my hands tied and my mouth closed; I am forced to wager, and am not free. I am not released, and am so made that I cannot believe. What, then, would you have me do?"

True. But at least learn your inability to believe, since reason brings you to this, and yet you cannot believe. Endeavour then to convince yourself, not by increase of proofs of God, but by the abatement of your passions. You would like to attain faith, and do not know the way; you would like to cure yourself of unbelief, and ask the remedy for it. Learn of those who have been bound like you, and who now stake all their possessions. These are people who know the way which you would follow, and who are cured of all ill of which you would be cured. Follow the way by which they began; by acting as if they believed, taking the holy water, having masses said, etc. Even this will naturally make you believe, and deaden your acuteness.—"But this is what I am afraid of."—And why? What have you to lose?

But to show you that this leads you there, it is this which will lessen the passions, which are your stumbling-blocks.

The end of this discourse.—Now, what harm will befall you in taking this side? You will be faithful, honest, humble, grateful, generous, a sincere friend, truthful. Certainly you will not have those poisonous pleasures, glory and luxury; but will you not have others? I will tell you that you will thereby gain in this life, and that, at each step you take on this road, you will see so great certainty of gain, so much nothingness in what you risk, that you will at last recognise that you have wagered for something certain and infinite, for which you have given nothing.

"Ah! This discourse transports me, charms me," etc.

If this discourse pleases you and seems impressive, know that it is made by a man who has knelt, both before and after it, in prayer to that Being, infinite and without parts, before whom he lays all he has, for you also to lay before Him all you have for your own good and for His glory, that so strength may be given to lowliness.

234

If we must not act save on a certainty, we ought not to act on religion, for it is not certain. But how many things we do on an uncertainty, sea voyages, battles! I say then we must do nothing at all, for nothing is certain, and that there is more certainty in religion than there is as to whether we may see to-morrow; for it is not certain that we may see to-morrow, and it is certainly possible that we may not see it. We cannot say as much about religion. It is not certain that it is; but who will venture to say that it is certainly possible that it is not? Now when we work for to-morrow, and so on an uncertainty, we act reasonably; for we ought to work for an uncertainty according to the doctrine of chance which was demonstrated above.

Saint Augustine has seen that we work for an uncertainty, on sea, in battle, etc. But he has not seen the doctrine of chance which proves that we should do so. Montaigne has seen that we are shocked at a fool, and that habit is all-powerful; but he has not seen the reason of this effect.

All these persons have seen the effects, but they have not seen the causes. They are, in comparison with those who have discovered the causes, as those who have only eyes are in comparison with those who have intellect. For the effects are perceptible by sense, and the causes are visible only to the intellect. And although these effects are seen by the mind, this mind is, in comparison with the mind which sees the causes, as the bodily senses are in comparison with the intellect.

40

God Can't Be Proven to Exist

Søren Kierkegaard (1813–1855), the father of modern existentialism, has also had a deep influence upon the widespread twentieth-century theological movement associated with the name of Karl Barth. In his *Philosophical Fragments* (1936) and *Concluding Unscientific Postscript* (1942) Kierkegaard attacked the rationalist desire for proofs as an evasion of the claim of revelation.

In contrast to these attempts to prove God's existence from reason and experience, Søren Kierkegaard believes this endeavor impossible. He argues that in these proofs one doesn't prove existence but at most a conception. He asks that if we attempt to prove God's existence, then which facts of the world do we use for this proof? Might not a fact appear which would destroy our belief in the proof? Without the proof, he says, existence is still there, and what do we have with the proof? What is this unknown which we seek to prove? Is it any more than the limit of Reason itself? Reason deceives because Reason cannot bring God to men.

-------TO STUDY

1. Is the dilemma Kierkegaard states relating God's existence to proof a sound argument?
2. Explain: "I reason from existence, not towards existence." Is the example of Napoleon and his deeds a good one?

3. According to Kierkegaard, where are the works of God?
4. Why doesn't the existence of God come out of proof?
5. With what does reason come rapidly into collision? What is its nature?

But what is this unknown something with which the Reason collides when inspired by its paradoxical passion, with the result of unsettling even man's knowledge of himself? It is the Unknown. It is not a human being, insofar as we know what man is; nor is it any other known thing. So let us call this unknown something: *God*. It is nothing more than a name we assign to it. The idea of demonstrating that this unknown something (God) exists could scarcely suggest itself to the Reason. For if God does not exist it would of course be impossible to prove it; and if he does exist it would be folly to attempt it. For at the very outset, in beginning my proof, I will have presupposed it, not as doubtful but as certain (a presupposition is never doubtful, for the very reason that it is a presupposition), since otherwise I would not begin, readily understanding that the whole would be impossible if he did not exist. But if when I speak of proving God's existence I mean that I propose to prove that the Unknown, which exists, is God, then I express myself unfortunately. For in that case I do not prove anything, least of all an existence, but merely develop the content of a conception. Generally speaking, it is a difficult matter to prove that anything exists; and what is still worse for the intrepid souls who undertake the venture, the difficulty is such that fame scarcely awaits those who concern themselves with it. The entire demonstration always turns into something very different from what it assumes to be, and becomes an additional development of the consequences that flow from [our] having assumed that the object in question exists. Thus I always reason from existence, not toward existence, whether I move in the sphere of palpable sensible fact or in the realm of thought. I do not, for example, prove that a stone exists, but that some existing thing is a stone. The procedure in a court of justice does not prove that a criminal exists, but that the accused, whose existence is given, is a criminal. Whether we call existence an *accessorium* or the eternal *prius*, it is never subject to demonstration. Let us take ample time for consideration. We have no such reason for haste as have those who from concern for themselves or for God or for some other thing, must make haste to get its

From *Philosophical Fragments* by Søren Kierkegaard, orig. trans. David F. Swenson. New intro. and commentary by Neils Thulstrup. Translation revised and commentary translated by Howard V. Hong (copyright © 1936, 1962 by Princeton University Press; Princeton Paperpack, 1967), pp. 31–36. Reprinted by permission of Princeton University Press.

existence demonstrated. Under such circumstances there may indeed be need for haste, especially if the prover sincerely seeks to appreciate the danger that he himself, or the thing in question, may be non-existent unless the proof is finished; and does not surreptitiously entertain the thought that it exists whether he succeeds in proving it or not.

If it were proposed to prove Napoleon's existence from Napoleon's deeds, would it not be a most curious proceeding? His existence does indeed explain his deeds, but the deeds do not prove his existence, unless I have already understood the word "his" so as thereby to have assumed his existence. But Napoleon is only an individual, and insofar there exists no absolute relationship between him and his deeds; some other person might have performed the same deeds. Perhaps this is the reason why I cannot pass from the deeds to existence. If I call these deeds the deeds of Napoleon, the proof becomes superfluous, since I have already named him; if I ignore this, I can never prove from the deeds that they are Napoleon's, but only in a purely ideal manner that such deeds are the deeds of a great general, and so forth. But between God and his works there exists an absolute relationship; God is not a name but a concept. Is this perhaps the reason that his *essentia involvit existentiam* [essence involves existence]? The works of God are such that only God can perform them. Just so, but where then are the works of God? The works from which I would deduce his existence are not immediately given. The wisdom of God in nature, his goodness, his wisdom in the governance of the world—are all these manifest, perhaps, upon the very face of things? Are we not here con-fronted with the most terrible temptations to doubt, and is it not impossible finally to dispose of all these doubts? But from such an order of things I will surely not attempt to prove God's existence; and even if I began I would never finish, and would in addition have to live constantly in suspense, lest something so terrible should suddenly happen that my bit of proof would be demolished. From what works then do I propose to derive the proof? From the works as apprehended through an ideal inter-pretation, i.e., such as they do not immediately reveal themselves. But in that case it is not from the works that I prove God's existence. I merely develop the ideality I have presupposed, and because of my confi-dence in *this* I make so bold as to defy all objections, even those that have not yet been made. In beginning my proof I presuppose the ideal interpretation, and also that I will be successful in carrying it through; but what else is this but to presuppose that God exists, so that I really begin by virtue of confidence in him?

And how does God's existence emerge from the proof? Does it follow straightway, without any breach of continuity? Or have we not here an analogy to the behaviour of these toys, the little Cartesian dolls? As soon as I let go of the doll it stands on its head. As soon as I let it go—I must therefore let it go. So also with the proof for God's existence. As long as I keep my hold on the proof, i.e., continue to demonstrate, the existence does not come out, if for no other reason than that I am engaged in proving it; but when I let the proof go, the existence is there. But this act of letting go is surely also something; it is indeed a contribution of mine. Must not this also be taken into the account, this little moment, brief as it may be—it need not be long, for it is a *leap*. However brief this moment, if only an instantaneous now, this "now" must be included in the reckoning. If anyone wishes to have it ignored, I will use it to tell a little anecdote, in order to show that it really does exist. Chrysippus was experimenting with a sorites to see if he could not bring about a break in its quality, either progressively or retrogressively. But Carneades could not get it in his head when the new quality actually emerged. Then Chrysippus told him to try making a little pause in the reckoning, and so—so it would be easier to understand. Carneades replied: "With the greatest pleasure, please do not hesitate on my account; you may not only pause, but even lie down to sleep, and it will help you just as little; for when you awake we will begin again where you left off. Just so; it boots as little to try to get rid of something by sleeping as to try to come into the possession of something in the same manner."

Whoever therefore attempts to demonstrate the existence of God (except in the sense of clarifying the concept, and without the *reservatio finalis* noted above, that the existence emerges from the demonstration by a leap) proves in lieu thereof something else, something which at times perhaps does not need a proof, and in any case needs none better; for the fool says in his heart that there is no God, but whoever says in his heart or to men: "Wait just a little and I will prove it"—what a rare man of wisdom is he![1] If in the moment of beginning his proof it is not absolutely undetermined whether God exists or not, he does not prove it; and if it is thus undetermined in the beginning he will never come to begin, partly from fear of failure, since God perhaps does not exist, and partly because he has nothing with which to begin. A project of this kind would scarcely have been undertaken by the ancients. Socrates at least, who is credited with having put forth the physico-teleological proof for God's existence, did not go about it in any such manner. He always presupposes God's existence, and under this presupposition seeks to interpenetrate nature with the idea of purpose. Had he been asked why he pursued this method, he would doubtless have explained that he lacked the courage to venture out upon so perilous a voyage of discovery without having made sure of God's existence

---

[1] What an excellent subject for a comedy of the higher lunacy!

behind him. At the word of God he casts his net as if to catch the idea of purpose; for nature herself finds many means of frightening the inquirer, and distracts him by many a digression.

The paradoxical passion of the Reason thus comes repeatedly into collision with the Unknown, which does indeed exist, but is unknown, and insofar does not exist. The Reason cannot advance beyond this point, and yet it cannot refrain in its paradoxicalness from arriving at this limit and occupying itself therewith. It will not serve to dismiss its relation to it simply by asserting that the Unknown does not exist, since this itself involves a relationship. But what then is the Unknown, since the designation of it as God merely signifies for us that it is unknown? To say that it is the Unknown because it cannot be known, and even if it were capable of being known, it could not be expressed, does not satisfy the demands of passion, though it correctly interprets the Unknown as a limit; but a limit is precisely a torment for passion, though it also serves as an incitement. And yet the Reason can come no further, whether it risks an issue *via negationis* or *via eminentia.*[2]

What then is the Unknown? It is the limit to which the Reason repeatedly comes, and insofar, substituting a static form of conception for the dynamic, it is the different, the absolutely different. But because it is absolutely different, there is no mark by which it could be distinguished. When qualified as absolutely different it seems on the verge of disclosure, but this is not the case; for the Reason cannot even conceive an absolute unlikeness. The Reason cannot negate itself absolutely, but uses itself for the purpose, and thus conceives only such an unlikeness within itself as it can conceive by means of itself; it cannot absolutely transcend itself, and hence conceives only such a superiority over itself as it can conceive by means of itself. Unless the Unknown (God) remains a mere limiting conception, the single idea of difference will be thrown into a state of confusion, and become many ideas of many differences. The Unknown is then in a condition of dispersion διασπορά and the Reason may choose at pleasure from what is at hand and the imagination may suggest (the monstrous, the ludicrous, etc.).

But it is impossible to hold fast to a difference of this nature. Every time this is done it is essentially an arbitrary act, and deepest down in the heart of piety lurks the mad caprice which knows that it has itself produced its God. If no specific determination of difference can be held fast, because there is no distinguishing mark, like and unlike finally become identified with one another, thus sharing the fate of all such dialectical opposites. The unlikeness clings to the Reason and confounds it, so that the Reason no

---

[2] I.e., by the method of making negative statements about God or by the method of attributing known qualities to God in a higher degree (ED.).

longer knows itself and quite consistently confuses itself with the unlikeness. On this point paganism has been sufficiently prolific in fantastic inventions. As for the last-named supposition, the self-irony of the Reason, I shall attempt to delineate it merely by a stroke or two, without raising any question of its being historical. There lives an individual whose appearance is precisely like that of other men; he grows up to manhood like others, he marries, he has an occupation by which he earns his livelihood, and he makes provision for the future as befits a man. For though it may be beautiful to live like the birds of the air, it is not lawful, and may lead to the sorriest of consequences: either starvation if one has enough persistence, or dependence on the bounty of others. This man is also God. How do I know? I cannot know it, for in order to know it I would have to know God, and the nature of the difference between God and man; and this I cannot know, because the Reason has reduced it to likeness with that from which it was unlike. Thus God becomes the most terrible of deceivers, because the Reason has deceived itself. The Reason has brought God as near as possible, and yet he is as far away as ever.

Readings

1. Bertocci, Peter A. *Introduction to the Philosophy of Religion.* Englewood Cliffs, N.J.: Prentice-Hall, 1951. See especially Chapters XI–XVIII which are a discussion of arguments for the existence of God and a restatement of the teleological argument by an American proponent of personal idealism.

2. Burrill, Donald, ed. *The Cosmological Arguments.* New York: Doubleday, 1967. An anthology of supporters and critics.

3. Platinga, Alvin. *The Ontological Arguments.* New York: Doubleday, 1961. An anthology of supporters and critics.

4. Taylor, Richard. *Metaphysics.* Englewood Cliffs, N.J.: Prentice-Hall, 1963. Chapter 7 contains an able restatement of the cosmological argument for God's existence.

two

Does the Idea of A Good God Exclude Evil?

41

Yes, a Good God Doesn't Permit Suffering

Fyodor Dostoevsky (1822–1881) was one of the two or three greatest Russian novelists. Some of his famous novels are *Crime and Punishment* (1866), *The Idiot* (1868), and *The Brothers Karamazov* (1880).

Before, since, and after the time of Job, men have speculated about the existence of evil and the presence of God. They have asked how it is possible for an all-powerful, all-good God to permit suffering in the world. This problem has traditionally been formulated as a dilemma:

> If God is omnipotent, He can prevent all evil;
> If He is perfectly good, He must want to prevent all evil;
> But evil exists, so God is either not omnipotent or not perfectly good.

If one chooses either one of these alternatives, then one gives up traditional Hebrew-Christian monotheism.

In the selection from *The Brothers Karamazov*, Dostoevsky touches on many of the arguments for the necessity of evil. He argues against the necessity of evil for the total harmony of the world, he argues against the view that others must pay for their fathers' sins, and finally he argues that the suffering of innocent children is the ultimate test which any theory that attempts to solve the problem of evil must answer.

TO STUDY

1. Essentially what argument does Ivan use to challenge the existence of a good and omnipotent God?

2. Does Ivan believe in God? If so, why?

3. What examples does Ivan use to illustrate his point that there is unjustified evil in the world? State as many of his arguments as you can find.

"Well, tell me where to begin, give your orders. The existence of God, eh?"

"Begin where you like. You declared yesterday at father's that there was no God." Alyosha looked searchingly at his brother.

"I said that yesterday at dinner on purpose to tease you and I saw your eyes glow. But now I've no objection to discussing with you, and I say so very seriously. I want to be friends with you, Alyosha, for I have no friends and want to try it. Well, only fancy, perhaps I too accept God," laughed Ivan, "that's a surprise for you, isn't it?"

"Yes of course, if you are not joking now."

"Joking? I was told at the elder's yesterday that I was joking. You know, dear boy, there was an old sinner in the eighteenth century who declared that, if there were no God, he would have to be invented. *S'il n'existait pas Dieu, il faudrait l'inventer.* And man has actually invented God. And what's strange, what would be marvelous, is not that God should really exist; the marvel is that such an idea, the idea of the necessity of God, could enter the head of such a savage, vicious beast as man. So holy it is, so touching, so wise and so great a credit it does to man. As for me, I've long resolved not to think whether man created God or God man. And I won't go through all the axioms laid down by Russian boys on that subject, all derived from European hypotheses; for what's a hypothesis there, is an axiom with the Russian boy, and not only with the boys but with their teachers too, for our Russian professors are often just the same boys themselves. And so I omit all the hypotheses. For what are we aiming at now? I am trying to explain as quickly as possible my essential nature, that is what manner of man I am, what I believe in, and for what I hope, that's it, isn't it? And therefore I tell you that I accept God simply. But you must note this: if God exists and if He really did create the world, then, as we all know, He created it according to the geometry of Euclid and the human mind with the conception of only three dimensions in space. Yet there have been and still are geometricians and philosophers, and even some

From *The Brothers Karamazov,* trans. by Constance Garnett.

of the most distinguished, who doubt whether the whole universe, or to speak more widely the whole of being, was only created in Euclid's geometry; they even dare to dream that two parallel lines, which according to Euclid can never meet on earth, may meet somewhere in infinity. I have come to the conclusion that, since I can't understand even that, I can't expect to understand about God. I acknowledge humbly that I have no faculty for settling such questions, I have a Euclidian earthly mind, and how could I solve problems that are not of this world? And I advise you never to think about it either, my dear Alyosha, especially about God, whether He exists or not. All such questions are utterly inappropriate for a mind created with an idea of only three dimensions. And so I accept God and am glad to, and what's more I accept His wisdom, His purpose—which are utterly beyond our ken; I believe in the underlying order and the meaning of life; I believe in the eternal harmony in which they say we shall one day be blended. I believe in the Word to Which the universe is striving, and Which Itself was 'with God,' and Which Itself is God and so on, and so on, to infinity. There are all sorts of phrases for it. I seem to be on the right path, don't I? Yet would you believe it, in the final result I don't accept this world of God's, and, although I know it exists, I don't accept it at all. It's not that I don't accept God, you must understand, it's the world created by Him I don't and cannot accept. Let me make it plain. I believe like a child that suffering will be healed and made up for, that all the humiliating absurdity of human contradictions will vanish like a pitiful mirage, like the despicable fabrication of the impotent and infinitely small Euclidian mind of man, that in the world's finale, at the moment of eternal harmony, something so precious will come to pass that it will suffice for all hearts, for the comforting of all resentments, for the atonement of all the crimes of humanity, of all the blood they've shed; that it will make it not only possible to forgive but to justify all that has happened with men—but though all that may come to pass, I don't accept it. I won't accept it. Even if parallel lines do meet and I see it myself, I shall see it and say that they've met, but still I won't accept it. That's what's at the root of me, Alyosha; that's my creed.

   ". . . Do you understand why this infamy must be and is permitted? Without it, I am told, man could not have known good and evil. Why should he know that diabolical good and evil when it costs so much? Why, the whole world of knowledge is not worth that child's prayer to 'dear, Kind God'! I say nothing of the sufferings of grown-up people, they have eaten the apple, damn them, and the devil take them all! But these little ones! I am making you suffer, Alyosha, you are not yourself. I'll leave off if you like."

   "Never mind. I want to suffer too," muttered Alyosha.

"One picture, only one more, because it's so curious, so characteristic, and I have only just read it in some collection of Russian antiquities. I've forgotten the name. I must look it up. It was in the darkest days of serfdom at the beginning of the century, and long live the Liberator of the People! There was in those days a general of aristocratic connections, the owner of great estates, one of these men—somewhat exceptional, I believe, even then—who, retiring from the service into a life of leisure, are convinced that they've earned absolute power over the lives of their subjects. There were such men then. So our general, settled on his property of two thousand souls, lives in pomp and domineers over his poor neighbors as though they were dependents and buffoons. He has kennels of hundreds of hounds and nearly a hundred dog-boys—all mounted, and in uniform. One day a serf boy, a little child of eight, threw a stone in play and hurt the paw of the general's favorite hound. 'Why is my favorite dog lame?' He is told that the boy threw a stone that hurt the dog's paw. 'So you did it.' The general looked the child up and down. 'Take him.' He was taken—taken from his mother and kept shut up all night. Early that morning the general comes out on horseback, with the hounds, his dependents, dog-boys, and huntsmen, all mounted around him in full hunting parade. The servants are summoned for their edification, and in front of them all stands the mother of the child. The child is brought from the lock-up. It's a gloomy, cold, foggy autumn day, a capital day for hunting. The general orders the child to be undressed; the child is stripped naked. He shivers, numb with terror not daring to cry. . . . 'Make him run,' commands the general. 'Run! run!' shout the dog-boys. The boy runs. . . . 'At him!' yells the general, and he sets the whole pack of hounds on the child. The hounds catch him, and tear him to pieces before his mother's eyes! . . . I believe the general was afterwards declared incapable of administering his estates. Well—what did he deserve? To be shot? to be shot for the satisfaction of our moral feelings? Speak, Alyosha!"

"To be shot," murmured Alyosha, lifting his eyes to Ivan with a pale twisted smile.

"Bravo!" cried Ivan delighted. "If even you say so . . . You're a pretty monk! So there is a little devil sitting in your heart, Alyosha Karamazov!"

"What I said was absurd, but—"

"That's just the point that 'but'!" cried Ivan. "Let me tell you, novice, that the absurd is only too necessary on earth. The world stands on absurdities, and perhaps nothing would have come to pass in it without them. We know what we know!"

"What do you know?"

"I understand nothing," Ivan went on, as though in delirium. "I don't want to understand anything now. I want to stick to the fact. I made up my mind long ago not to understand. If I try to understand anything, I shall be false to the fact and I have determined to stick to the fact."

"Why are you trying me?" Alyosha cried, with sudden distress. "Will you say what you mean at last?"

"Of course, I will; that's what I've been leading up to. You are dear to me, I don't want to let you go, and I won't give you up to your Zossima."

Ivan for a minute was silent, his face became all at once very sad.

"Listen! I took the case of the children only to make my case clearer. Of the other tears of humanity with which the earth is soaked from its crust to its center, I will say nothing. I have narrowed my subject on purpose. I am a bug, and I recognize in all humility that I cannot understand why the world is arranged as it is. Men are themselves to blame, I suppose; they were given paradise, they wanted freedom, and stole fire from heaven, though they knew they would become unhappy, so there is no need to pity them. With my pitiful, earthly, Euclidian understanding, all I know is that there is suffering and that there are none guilty; that cause follows effect, simply and directly; that everything flows and finds its level—but that's only Euclidian nonsense, I know that, and I can't consent to live by it! What comfort is it to me that there are none guilty and that cause follows effect simply and directly, and that I know it—I must have justice, or I will destroy myself. And not justice in some remote infinite time and space, but here on earth, and that I could see myself. I have believed in it. I want to see it, and if I am dead by then, let me rise again, for if it all happens without me, it will be too unfair. Surely I haven't suffered, simply that I, my crimes and my sufferings, may manure the soil of the future harmony for somebody else. I want to see with my own eyes the hind lie down with the lion and the victim rise up and embrace his murderer. I want to be there when every one suddenly understands what it has all been for. All the religions of the world are built on this longing, and I am a believer. But then there are the children, and what am I to do about them? That's a question I can't answer. For the hundredth time I repeat, there are numbers of questions, but I've only taken the children, because in their case what I mean is so unanswerably clear. Listen! If all must suffer to pay for the eternal harmony, what have children to do with it, tell me, please? It's beyond all comprehension why they should suffer, and why they should pay for the harmony. Why should they, too, furnish material to enrich the soil for the harmony of the future? I understand solidarity in sin among men. I understand solidarity in retribution, too; but there can be no such solidarity with children. And if it is really true that they must share responsibility for all their fathers' crimes, such a truth is not of this world and is beyond my comprehension. Some jester will say, perhaps, that the child would have grown up and have sinned, but you see he didn't grow up, he was torn to pieces by the dogs, at eight years old. Oh, Alyosha, I am not blaspheming! I understand, of course, what an upheaval of the universe it will be, when everything in heaven and earth blends in one hymn of praise and everything that lives and has lived cries aloud: 'Thou art just, O Lord, for Thy ways are revealed,' when the mother embraces the fiend who threw her child to the dogs, and all three cry aloud with tears, 'Thou are just, O Lord!' then, of course, the crown of knowledge will be reached and all will be made clear. But what pulls me up here is that I can't accept that harmony. And while I am on earth, I make haste to take my own measures. You see, Alyosha, perhaps it really may happen that if I live to that moment, or rise again to see it, I, too, perhaps, may cry aloud with the rest, looking at the mother embracing the child's torturer, 'Thou art just, O Lord!' but I don't want to cry aloud then. While there is still time, I hasten to protect myself and so I renounce the higher harmony altogether. It's not worth the tears of that one tortured child who beat itself on the breast with its little fist and prayed in its stinking outhouse, with its unexpiated tears to 'dear, kind God'! It's not worth it, because those tears are unatoned for. They must be atoned for, or there can be no harmony. But how? How are you going to atone for them? Is it possible? By their being avenged? But what do I care for avenging them? What do I care for a hell for oppressors? What good can hell do, since those children have already been tortured? And what becomes of harmony, if there is hell? I want to forgive. I want to embrace. I don't want more suffering. And if the sufferings of children go to swell the sum of sufferings which was necessary to pay for truth, then I protest that the truth is not worth such a price. I don't want the mother to embrace the oppressor who threw her son to the dogs! She dare not forgive him! Let her forgive him for herself, if she will, let her forgive the torturer for the immeasurable suffering of her mother's heart. But the sufferings of her tortured child she has no right to forgive; she dare not forgive the torturer, even if the child were to forgive him! And if that is so, if they dare not forgive, what becomes of harmony? Is there in the whole world a being who would have the right to forgive and could forgive? I don't want harmony. From love for humanity I don't want it. I would rather be left with the unavenged suffering. I would rather remain with my unavenged suffering and unsatisfied indignation, *even if I were wrong.* Besides, too high a price is asked for harmony; it's beyond our means to pay so much to enter on it. And so I hasten to give back my entrance ticket, and if I am an honest man I am bound to give it back as soon as possible. And that I am doing. It's not God that I don't accept, Alyosha, only I most respectfully return Him the ticket."

"That's rebellion," murmured Alyosha, looking down.

"Rebellion? I am sorry you call it that," said Ivan earnestly. "One can hardly live in rebellion, and I want to live. Tell me yourself, I challenge you—answer. Imagine that you are creating a fabric of human destiny with the object of making men happy in the end, giving them peace and rest at last, but that it was essential and inevitable to torture to death only one tiny creature—that baby beating its breast with its fist, for instance—and to found that edifice on its unavenged tears, would you consent to be the architect on those conditions? Tell me, and tell the truth."

"No, I wouldn't consent," said Alyosha softly.

"And can you admit the idea that men for whom you are building it would agree to accept their happiness on the foundation of the unexpiated blood of a little victim? And accepting it would remain happy for ever?"

"No, I can't admit it. . . ."

THINK ABOUT

1. "The world is now without mysteries."

   Pierre Berthelot (1885)

2. Look round this universe. What an immense profusion of beings, animated and organized, sensible and active! You admire this prodigious variety and fecundity. But inspect a little more narrowly these living existences, the only beings worth regarding. How hostile and destructive to each other! How insufficient all of them for their own happiness! How contemptible or odious to the spectator! The whole presents nothing but the idea of a blind nature, impregnated by a great vivifying principle, and pouring forth from her lap, without discernment or parental care, her maimed and abortive children!

3. Whoever can prevent the sin of another and does not do so, but rather contributes to it although he is well informed of it, is accessory to it. God can prevent the sin of intelligent creatures; but he does not do so, and rather contributes to it by his concurrence and by the opportunities which he brings about, although he has a perfect knowledge of it.

4. Whoever punishes those who have done as well as it was in their power to do, is unjust.

42

No, God Can
Allow Some Evil

John Hick (1922–   ), lecturer in Divinity at Cambridge University, was formerly Stuart Professor of Christian Philosophy at Princeton Theological Seminary. He received his M.A. degree from the University of Edinburgh and his D.Phil. from Oxford University. Dr. Hick is the author of *Faith and Knowledge* (1966) and *Philosophy of Religion* (1963), and the editor of *The Existence of God* (1964) and *Faith and the Philosophers* (1964).

Hick suggests various Christian solutions to the problem of evil and indeed raises the point of how unsatisfactory the world would be if it were free of suffering.

──────────────────────────────────────TO STUDY

1. According to Hick, what is the most powerful positive objection to the belief in God?

2. On what ground does he refute the Christian Science solution to the problem of evil?

2. On what ground the personalist school?

4. On what ground the Augustinian solution?

5. What objection has been raised to the traditional Christian position concerning moral evil?

6. What objection has been raised to the traditional Christian position concerning non-moral evil? What is Hick's reply?

To many, the most powerful positive objection to belief in God is the fact of evil. Probably for most agnostics it is the appalling depth and extent of human suffering, more than anything else, that makes the idea of a loving Creator seem so implausible and disposes them toward one or another of the various naturalistic theories of religion.

As a challenge to theism, the problem of evil has traditionally been posed in the form of a dilemma: if God is perfectly loving, he must wish to abolish evil; and if he is all-powerful, he must be able to abolish evil. But evil exists; therefore God cannot be both omnipotent and perfectly loving.

Certain solutions, which at once suggest themselves, have to be ruled out so far as the Judaic-Christian faith is concerned.

To say, for example (with contemporary Christian Science), that evil is an illusion of the human mind, is impossible within a religion based upon the stark realism of the Bible. Its pages faithfully reflect the characteristic mixture of good and evil in human experience. They record every kind of sorrow and suffering, every mode of man's inhumanity to man and of his painfully insecure existence in the world. There is no attempt to regard evil as anything but dark, menacingly ugly, heart-rending, and crushing. In the Christian scriptures, the climax of this history of evil is the crucifixion of Jesus, which is presented not only as a case of utterly unjust suffering, but as the violent and murderous rejection of God's Messiah. There can be no doubt, then, that for biblical faith, evil is unambiguously evil, and stands in direct opposition to God's will.

Again, to solve the problem of evil by means of the theory (sponsored, for example, by the Boston "Personalist" School)[1] of a finite deity who does the best he can with a material, intractable and co-eternal with himself, is to have abandoned the basic premise of Hebrew-Christian monotheism; for the theory amounts to rejecting belief in the infinity and sovereignty of God.

Indeed, any theory which would avoid the problem of the origin of evil by depicting it as an ultimate constituent of the universe, coordinate with good, has been repudiated in advance by the classic Christian teaching, first developed by Augustine, that evil represents the going wrong of something which in itself is good.[2] Augustine holds firmly to the Hebrew-Christian conviction that the universe is *good*—that is to say, it is the creation of a good God for a good purpose. He completely rejects the ancient

---

From *Philosophy of Religion* by John Hick (Englewood Cliffs, N.J.: Prentice-Hall, Inc., 1963), pp. 40–47. Copyright 1963. Reprinted by permission of Prentice-Hall, Inc.
[1] Edgar Brightman's *A Philosophy of Religion* (Englewood Cliffs, N.J.: Prentice-Hall, Inc., 1940), Chaps. 8–10, is a classic exposition of one form of this view.
[2] See Augustine's *Confessions,* Book VII, Chap. 12; *City of God,* Book XII, Chap. 3; *Enchiridion,* Chap. 4.

prejudice, widespread in his day, that matter is evil. There are, according to Augustine, higher and lower, greater and lesser goods in immense abundance and variety; but everything which has being is good in its own way and degree, except in so far as it may have become spoiled or corrupted. Evil—whether it be an evil will, an instance of pain, or some disorder or decay in nature—has not been set there by God, but represents the distortion of something that is inherently valuable. Whatever exists is, as such, and in its proper place, good; evil is essentially parasitic upon good, being disorder and perversion in a fundamentally good creation. This understanding of evil as something negative means that it is not willed and created by God; but it does not mean (as some have supposed) that evil is unreal and can be disregarded. Clearly, the first effect of this doctrine is to accentuate even more the question of the origin of evil.

Theodicy,[3] as many modern Christian thinkers see it, is a modest enterprise, negative rather than positive in its conclusions. It does not claim to explain, nor to explain away, every instance of evil in human experience, but only to point to certain considerations which prevent the fact of evil (largely incomprehensible though it remains) from constituting a final and insuperable bar to rational belief in God.

In indicating these considerations it will be useful to follow the traditional division of the subject. There is the problem of *moral evil* or wickedness: why does an all-good and all-powerful God permit this? And there is the problem of the *non-moral evil* of suffering or pain, both physical and mental: why has an all-good and all-powerful God created a world in which this occurs?

Christian thought has always considered moral evil in its relation to human freedom and responsibility. To be a person is to be a finite center of freedom, a (relatively) free and self-directing agent responsible for one's own decisions. This involves being free to act wrongly as well as to act rightly. The idea of a person who can be infallibly guaranteed always to act rightly is self-contradictory. There can be no guarantee in advance that a genuinely free moral agent will never choose amiss. Consequently, the possibility of wrongdoing or sin is logically inseparable from the creation of finite persons, and to say that God should not have created beings who might sin amounts to saying that he should not have created people.

This thesis has been challenged in some recent philosophical discussions of the problem of evil, in which it is claimed that no contradiction is involved in saying that God might have made people who would be

---

[3] The word "theodicy" from the Greek *theos* (God) and *dike* (righteous) means the justification of God's goodness in face of the fact of evil.

genuinely free and who could yet be guaranteed always to act rightly. A quotation from one of these discussions follows:

> If there is no logical impossibility in a man's freely choosing the good on one, or on several occasions, there cannot be a logical impossibility in his freely choosing the good on every occasion. God was not, then, faced with a choice between making innocent automata and making beings who, in acting freely, would sometimes go wrong: there was open to him the obviously better possibility of making beings who would act freely but always go right. Clearly, his failure to avail himself of this possibility is inconsistent with his being both omnipotent and wholly good.[4]

A reply to this argument is suggested in another recent contribution to the discussion.[5] If by a free action we mean an action which is not externally compelled but which flows from the nature of the agent as he reacts to the circumstances in which he finds himself, there is, indeed, no contradiction between our being free and our actions being "caused" (by our own nature) and therefore being in principle predictable. There is a contradiction, however, in saying that God is the cause of our acting as we do but that we are free beings in relation to God. There is, in other words, a contradiction in saying that God has made us so that we shall of necessity act in a certain way, and that we are genuinely independent persons in relation to him. If all our thoughts and actions are divinely predestined, however free and morally responsible we may seem to be to ourselves, we cannot be free and morally responsible in the sight of God, but must instead be his helpless puppets. Such "freedom" is like that of a patient acting out a series of posthypnotic suggestions: he appears, even to himself, to be free, but his volitions have actually been predetermined by another will, that of the hypnotist, in relation to whom the patient is not a free agent.

A different objector might raise the question of whether or not we deny God's omnipotence if we admit that he is unable to create persons who are free from the risks inherent in personal freedom. The answer that has always been given is that to create such beings is logically impossible. It is no limitation upon God's power that he cannot accomplish the logically impossible, since there is nothing here to accomplish, but only a meaningless conjunction of words[6]—in this case "person who is not a person." God

---

[4] J. L. Mackie, "Evil and Omnipotence," *Mind* (April, 1955), p. 209. A similar point is made by Antony Flew in "Divine Omnipotence and Human Freedom," *New Essays in Philosophical Theology*. An important critical comment on these arguments is offered by Ninian Smart in "Omnipotence, Evil and Supermen," *Philosophy* (April, 1961), with replies by Flew (January, 1962) and Mackie (April, 1962).

[5] Flew, in *New Essays in Philosophical Theology*.

[6] As Aquinas said, ". . . nothing that implies a contradiction falls under the scope of God's omnipotence." *Summa Theologica,* Part I, Question 25, article 4.

is able to create beings of any and every conceivable kind; but creatures who lack moral freedom, however superior they might be to human beings in other respects, would not be what we mean by persons. They would constitute a different form of life which God might have brought into existence instead of persons. When we ask why God did not create such beings in place of persons, the traditional answer is that only persons could, in any meaningful sense, become "children of God," capable of entering into a personal relationship with their Creator by a free and uncompelled response to his love.

When we turn from the possibility of moral evil as a correlate of man's personal freedom to its actuality, we face something which must remain inexplicable even when it can be seen to be possible. For we can never provide a complete causal explanation of a free act; if we could, it would not be a free act. The origin of moral evil lies forever concealed within the mystery of human freedom.

The necessary connection between moral freedom and the possibility, now actualized, of sin throws light upon a great deal of the suffering which afflicts mankind. For an enormous amount of human pain arises either from the inhumanity or the culpable incompetence of mankind. This includes such major scourges as poverty, oppression and persecution, war, and all the injustice, indignity, and inequity which occur even in the most advanced societies. These evils are manifestations of human sin. Even disease is fostered to an extent, the limits of which have not yet been determined by psychosomatic medicine, by moral and emotional factors seated both in the individual and in his social environment. To the extent that all of these evils stem from human failures and wrong decisions, their possibility is inherent in the creation of free persons inhabiting a world which presents them with real choices which are followed by real consequences.

We may now turn more directly to the problem of suffering. Even though the major bulk of actual human pain is traceable to man's misused freedom as a sole or part cause, there remain other sources of pain which are entirely independent of the human will, for example, earthquake, hurricane, storm, flood, drought, and blight. In practice, it is often impossible to trace a boundary between the suffering which results from human wickedness and folly and that which falls upon mankind from without. Both kinds of suffering are inextricably mingled together in human experience. For our present purpose, however, it is important to note that the latter category does exist and that it seems to be built into the very structure of our world. In response to it, theodicy, if it is wisely conducted, follows a negative path. It is not possible to show positively that each item of human pain serves the divine purpose of good; but, on the other hand, it does seem possible to show that the divine purpose as it is understood in Judaism and

Christianity could not be forwarded in a world which was designed as a permanent hedonistic paradise.

An essential premise of this argument concerns the nature of the divine purpose in creating the world. The skeptic's assumption is that man is to be viewed as a completed creation and that God's purpose in making the world was to provide a suitable dwelling-place for this fully-formed creature. Since God is good and loving, the environment which he has created for human life to inhabit is naturally as pleasant and comfortable as possible. The problem is essentially similar to that of a man who builds a cage for some pet animal. Since our world, in fact, contains sources of hardship, inconvenience, and danger of innumerable kinds, the conclusion follows that this world cannot have been created by a perfectly benevolent and all-powerful deity.[7]

Christianity, however, has never supposed that God's purpose in the creation of the world was to construct a paradise whose inhabitants would experience a maximum of pleasure and a minimum of pain. The world is seen, instead, as a place of "soul-making" in which free beings grappling with the tasks and challenges of their existence in a common environment, may become "children of God" and "heirs of eternal life." A way of thinking theologically of God's continuing creative purpose for man was suggested by some of the early Hellenistic Fathers of the Christian Church, especially Irenaeus. Following hints from St. Paul, Irenaeus taught that man has been made as a person in the image of God but has not yet been brought as a free and responsible agent into the finite likeness of God, which is revealed in Christ.[8] Our world, with all its rough edges, is the sphere in which this second and harder stage of the creative process is taking place.

This conception of the world (whether or not set in Irenaeus' theological framework) can be supported by the method of negative theodicy. Suppose, contrary to fact, that this world were a paradise from which all possibility of pain and suffering were excluded. The consequences would be very far-reaching. For example, no one could ever injure anyone else: the murderer's knife would turn to paper or his bullets to thin air; the bank safe, robbed of a million dollars, would miraculously become filled with another million dollars (without this device, on however large a scale, proving inflationary); fraud, deceit, conspiracy, and treason would somehow always leave the fabric of society undamaged. Again, no one would

---

[7] This is the nature of David Hume's argument in his discussion of the problem of evil in his *Dialogues*, Part XI (reprinted in the present volume, see Selection 41, pp. 439ff. above).
[8] See Irenaeus' *Against Heresies*, Book IV, Chaps. 37 and 38.

ever be injured by accident: the mountain-climber, steeplejack, or playing child falling from a height would float unharmed to the ground; the reckless driver would never meet with disaster. There would be no need to work, since no harm could result from avoiding work; there would be no call to be concerned for others in time of need or danger, for in such a world there could be no real needs or dangers.

To make possible this continual series of individual adjustments, nature would have to work by "special providences" instead of running according to general laws which men must learn to respect on penalty of pain or death. The laws of nature would have to be extremely flexible: sometimes gravity would operate, sometimes not; sometimes an object would be hard and solid, sometimes soft. There could be no sciences, for there would be no enduring world structure to investigate. In eliminating the problems and hardships of an objective environment, with its own laws, life would become like a dream in which, delightfully but aimlessly, we would float and drift at ease.

One can at least begin to imagine such a world. It is evident that our present ethical concepts would have no meaning in it. If, for example, the notion of harming someone is an essential element in the concept of a wrong action, in our hedonistic paradise there could be no wrong actions—nor any right actions in distinction from wrong. Courage and fortitude would have no point in an environment in which there is, by definition, no danger or difficulty. Generosity, kindness, the *agape* aspect of love, prudence, unselfishness, and all other ethical notions which presuppose life in a stable environment, could not even be formed. Consequently, such a world, however well it might promote pleasure, would be very ill adapted for the development of the moral qualities of human personality. In relation to this purpose it would be the worst of all possible worlds.

It would seem, then, that an environment intended to make possible the growth in free beings of the finest characteristics of personal life, must have a good deal in common with our present world. It must operate according to general and dependable laws; and it must involve real dangers, difficulties, problems, obstacles, and possibilities of pain, failure, sorrow, frustration, and defeat. If it did not contain the particular trials and perils which—subtracting man's own very considerable contribution—our world contains, it would have to contain others instead.

To realize this is not, by any means, to be in possession of a detailed theodicy. It is to understand that this world, with all its "heartaches and the thousand natural shocks that flesh is heir to," an environment so manifestly not designed for the maximization of human pleasure and the minimization of human pain, may be rather well adapted to the quite different purpose of "soul-making."[9]

These considerations are related to theism as such. Specifically, Christian theism goes further in the light of the death of Christ, which is seen paradoxically both (as the murder of the divine Son) as the worst thing that has ever happened and (as the occasion of Man's salvation) as the best thing that has ever happened. As the supreme evil turned to supreme good, it provides the paradigm for the distinctively Christian reaction to evil. Viewed from the standpoint of Christian faith, evils do not cease to be evils; and certainly, in view of Christ's healing work, they cannot be said to have been sent by God. Yet, it has been the persistent claim of those seriously and wholeheartedly committed to Christian discipleship that tragedy, though truly tragic, may nevertheless be turned, through a man's reaction to it, from a cause of despair and alienation from God to a stage in the fulfillment of God's loving purpose for that individual. As the greatest of all evils, the crucifixion of Christ, was made the occasion of man's redemption, so good can be won from other evils. As Jesus saw his execution by the Romans as an experience which God desired him to accept, an experience which was to be brought within the sphere of the divine purpose and made to serve the divine ends, so the Christian response to calamity is to accept the adversities, pains, and afflictions which life brings, in order that they can be turned to a positive spiritual use.[10]

At this point, theodicy points forward in two ways to the subject of life after death.

First, although there are many striking instances of good being triumphantly brought out of evil through a man's or a woman's reaction to it, there are many other cases in which the opposite has happened. Sometimes obstacles breed strength of character, dangers evoke courage and unselfishness, and calamities produce patience and moral steadfastness. But sometimes they lead, instead, to resentment, fear, grasping selfishness, and disintegration of character. Therefore, it would seem that any divine purpose of soul-making which is at work in earthly history must continue beyond this life if it is ever to achieve more than a very partial and fragmentary success.

---

[9] This brief discussion has been confined to the problem of human suffering. The large and intractable problem of animal pain is not taken up here. For a discussion of it, see, for example, Nels Ferré, *Evil and the Christian Faith* (New York: Harper & Row, Publishers, Inc., 1947), Chap. 7; and Austin Farrer, *Love Almighty and Ills Unlimited* (New York: Doubleday & Company, Inc., 1961), Chap. 5.

[10] This conception of providence is stated more fully in John Hick, *Faith and Knowledge* (Ithaca: Cornell University Press, 1957), Chap. 7, from which some sentences are incorporated in this paragraph.

Second, if we ask whether the business of soul-making is worth all the toil and sorrow of human life, the Christian answer must be in terms of a future good which is great enough to justify all that has happened on the way to it.

Readings

1. *The Bible.* "Job." A dramatic presentation which deals with the problem of evil and the omnipotence of God.

2. Hick, John. *Evil and the God of Love.* New York: Harper & Row, 1966. A careful analysis of the problem of pain and of moral evil.

3. Lewis, Edwin. *The Creator and the Adversary.* New York: Abingdon-Cokesbury Press, 1948. A good exposition of the relation of evil to belief in God from the perspective of a Protestant theologian who struggles with the question of a limited God.

4. Pike, Nelson. *God and Evil.* Englewood Cliffs, N.J.: Prentice-Hall, 1964. An anthology of Hume and recent writers.

three

Are Religious Ethics
Adequate?

＞

43

Yes, Via Judeo-
Christian Ideals

Philosophers do not give as much attention to religious ethics as they should. Religion provides ethical principles and attitudes for the majority of the population. Whether or not the populus adheres to these principles is another question. Most people believe religious ethical doctrines are important and effective. Hence, philosophers should have given them more attention.

The Judeo-Christian Ethical Ideals come from both the Old and New Testaments. They contain most of the ethical religious principles of these religions. The student must ask himself whether or not these are the central principles, whether there are any conflicting principles, and finally, how complete an ethical system is represented.

────────── TO STUDY

1. What are the central ethical tenets of The Old Testament as stated in these selections?
2. What are the central ethical tenets of The New Testament as stated in these selections?

The Ten Commandments
Exodus 20: 1-17

And God spoke all these words, saying,

"I am the LORD your God, who brought you out of the land of Egypt, out of the house of bondage.

"You shall have no other gods before me.

"You shall not make yourself a graven image, or any likeness of anything that is in heaven above, or that is in the earth beneath, or that is in the water under the earth; you shall not bow down to them or serve them; for I the LORD your God am a jealous God, visiting the iniquity of the fathers upon the children to the third and the fourth generation of those who hate me, but showing steadfast love to thousands of those who love me and keep my commandments.

"You shall not take the name of the LORD your God in vain; for the LORD will not hold him guiltless who takes his name in vain.

"Remember the sabbath day, to keep it holy. Six days you shall labor, and do all your work; but the seventh day is a sabbath to the LORD your God; in it you shall not do any work, you, or your son, or your daughter, your manservant, or your maidservant, or your cattle, or the sojourner who is within your gates; for in six days the LORD made heaven and earth, the sea, and all that is in them, and rested the seventh day; therefore the LORD blessed the sabbath day and hallowed it.

"Honor your father and your mother, that your days may be long in the land which the LORD your God gives you.

"You shall not kill.

"You shall not commit adultery.

"You shall not steal.

"You shall not bear false witness against your neighbor.

"You shall not covet your neighbor's house, you shall not covet your neighbor's wife, or his manservant, or his maidservant, or his ox, or his ass, or anything that is your neighbor's."

The Man Who Walks Uprightly
Psalm 15
A Psalm of David

O LORD, who shall sojourn in thy tent?
Who shall dwell on thy holy hill?

He who walks blamelessly, and does what is right,
   and speaks truth from his heart;
who does not slander with his tongue,
   and does no evil to his friend,
   nor takes up a reproach against his neighbor;
in whose eyes a reprobate is despised,
   but who honors those who fear the LORD;
who swears to his own hurt and does not change;
   who does not put out his money at interest,
   and does not take a bribe against the innocent.

He who does these things shall never be moved.

Prophets of Righteousness and Justice

He who walks righteously and speaks uprightly;
   he who despises the gain of oppressions,
   who shakes his hands, lest they hold a bribe,
   who stops his ears from hearing of bloodshed,
   and shuts his eyes from looking upon evil.
He will dwell on the heights; his place of defense
   will be the fortresses of rocks; his bread will be
   given him, his water will be sure.   *Isaiah 33: 15–16*

Thus says the Lord:
   Keep justice, and do righteousness, for soon my
   salvation will come, and my deliverance be revealed.
                                           Isaiah 56:1
For thus says the Lord to the house of Israel:
"Seek me and live; . . . *Amos 5:4*

"I hate, I despise your feasts,
   and I take no delight in your solemn assemblies.
Even though you offer me your burnt offerings and
      cereal offerings,
   I will not accept them,
and the peace offerings of your fatted beasts
   I will not look upon.
Take away from me the noise of your songs;
   to the melody of your harps I will not listen.
But let justice roll down like waters,

and righteousness like an everflowing stream.

Amos 5: 21–24

Woe to those who lie upon beds of ivory,
  and stretch themselves upon their couches,
  and eat lambs from the flock,
  and calves from the midst of the stall;
who sing idle songs to the sound of the harp,
  and like David invent for themselves instruments
    of music;
who drink wine in bowls,
  and anoint themselves with the finest oils,
  but are not grieved over the ruin of Joseph!
Therefore they shall now be the first of those to go into exile,
  and the revelry of those who stretch themselves shall
    pass away." *Amos 6: 4–7*

He has showed you, O man, what is good; and what does
  the Lord require of you but to do justice, and to
  love kindness, and to walk humbly with your God.

Micah 6: 8

The Sermon on The Mount
Matthew 5

Seeing the crowds, he went up on the mountain, and when he sat down his disciples came to him.

And he opened his mouth and taught them, saying:

"Blessed are the poor in spirit, for theirs is the kingdom of heaven.

"Blessed are those who mourn, for they shall be comforted.

"Blessed are the meek, for they shall inherit the earth.

"Blessed are those who hunger and thirst for righteousness, for they shall be satisfied.

"Blessed are the merciful, for they shall obtain mercy.

"Blessed are the pure in heart, for they shall see God.

"Blessed are the peacemakers, for they shall be called sons of God.

"Blessed are those who are persecuted for righteousness' sake, for theirs is the kingdom of heaven.

"Blessed are you when men revile you and persecute you and utter all kinds of evil against you falsely on my account. Rejoice and be glad, for your reward is great in heaven, for so men persecuted the prophets who were before you.

"You are the salt of the earth; but if salt has lost its taste, how shall its saltness be restored? It is no longer good for anything except to be thrown out and trodden under foot by men.

"You are the light of the world. A city set on a hill cannot be hid. Nor do men light a lamp and put it under a bushel, but on a stand, and it gives light to all in the house. Let your light so shine before men, that they may see your good works and give glory to your Father who is in heaven.

"Think not that I have come to abolish the law and the prophets; I have come not to abolish them but to fulfil them. For truly, I say to you, till heaven and earth pass away, not an iota, not a dot, will pass from the law until all is accomplished. Whoever then relaxes one of the least of these commandments and teaches men so, shall be called least in the kingdom of heaven; but he who does them and teaches them shall be called great in the kingdom of heaven. For I tell you, unless your righteousness exceeds that of the scribes and Pharisees, you will never enter the kingdom of heaven.

"You have heard that it was said to the men of old, 'You shall not kill; and whoever kills shall be liable to judgment.' But I say to you that every one who is angry with his brother shall be liable to judgment; whoever insults his brother shall be liable to the council, and whoever says, 'You fool!' shall be liable to the hell of fire. So if you are offering your gift at the altar, and there remember that your brother has something against you, leave your gift there before the altar and go; first be reconciled to your brother, and then come and offer your gift. Make friends quickly with your accuser, while you are going with him to court, lest your accuser hand you over to the judge, and the judge to the guard, and you be put in prison; truly, I say to you, you will never get out till you have paid the last penny.

"You have heard that it was said, 'You shall not commit adultery.' But I say to you that every one who looks at a woman lustfully has already committed adultery with her in his heart. If your right eye causes you to sin, pluck it out and throw it away; it is better that you lose one of your members than that your whole body be thrown into hell. And if your right hand causes you to sin, cut if off and throw it away; it is better that you lose one of your members than that your whole body go into hell.

"It was also said, 'Whoever divorces his wife, let him give her a certificate of divorce.' But I say to you that every one who divorces his wife, except on the ground of unchastity, makes her an adulteress; and whoever marries a divorced woman commits adultery.

"Again you have heard that it was said to the men of old, 'You shall not swear falsely, but shall perform to the Lord what you have sworn.' But I say to you, Do not swear at all, either by heaven, for it is the throne of God, or by the earth, for it is his footstool, or by Jerusalem, for it is the city of the great King. And do not swear by your head, for you cannot make one hair white or black. Let what you say be simply 'Yes' or 'No'; anything more than this comes from evil.

"You have heard that it was said, 'An eye for an eye and a tooth for a tooth.' But I say to you, Do not resist one who is evil. But if any one strikes you on the right cheek, turn to him the other also; and if any one would sue you and take your coat, let him have your cloak as well; and if any one forces you to go one mile, go with him two miles. Give to him who begs from you, and do not refuse him who would borrow from you.

"You have heard that it was said, 'You shall love your neighbor and hate your enemy.' But I say to you, Love your enemies and pray for those who persecute you, so that you may be sons of your Father who is in heaven; for he makes his sun rise on the evil and on the good, and sends rain on the just and on the unjust. For if you love those who love you, what reward have you? Do not even the tax collectors do the same? And if you salute only your brethren, what more are you doing than others? Do not even the Gentiles do the same? You, therefore, must be perfect, as your heavenly Father is perfect."

The Great Commandments
Matthew 22: 34-40

But when the Pharisees heard that he had silenced the Sadducees, they came together. And one of them, a lawyer, asked him a question, to test him. "Teacher, which is the great commandment in the law?" And he said to him, "You shall love the Lord your God with all your heart, and with all your soul, and with all your mind. This is the great and first commandment. And a second is like it, You shall love your neighbor as yourself. On these two commandments depend all the law and the prophets."

The Parable of The Last Judgment
Matthew 25: 31-46

When the Son of man comes in his glory, and all the angels with him, then he will sit on his glorious throne. Before him will be gathered all the nations, and he will separate them one from another as a shepherd separates the sheep from the goats, and he will place the sheep at his right hand, but the goats at the left. Then the King will say to those at his right hand, "Come, O blessed of my Father, inherit the kingdom prepared for you from the foundation of the world; for I was hungry and you gave me food, I was thirsty and you gave me drink, I was a stranger and you welcomed me, I was naked and you clothed me, I was sick and you visited me, I was in prison and you came to me." Then the righteous will answer him, "Lord, when did we see thee hungry and feed thee, or thirsty and give thee drink? And when did we see thee a stranger and welcome thee, or naked and clothe thee? And when did we see thee sick or in prison and visit thee?" And the King will answer them, "Truly, I say to you, as you did it to one of the least of these my brethren, you did it to me." Then he will say to those at his left hand, "Depart from me, you cursed, into the eternal fire prepared for the devil and his angels; for I was hungry and you gave me no food, I was thirsty and you gave me no drink, I was a stranger and you did not welcome me, naked and you did not clothe me, sick and in prison and you did not visit me."

Then they also will answer, "Lord, when did we see thee hungry or thirsty or a stranger or naked or sick or in prison, and did not minister to thee?" Then he will answer them, "Truly, I say to you, as you did it not to one of the least of these, you did it not to me." And they will go away into eternal punishment, but the righteous into eternal life.

From the Epistles of Paul

If I speak in the tongues of men and of angels, but have not love, I am a noisy gong or a clanging cymbal. And if I have prophetic powers, and understand all mysteries and all knowledge, and if I have all faith, so as to remove mountains, but have not love, I am nothing. If I give away all I have, and if I deliver my body to be burned, but have not love, I gain nothing.

Love is patient and kind; love is not jealous or boastful; it is not arrogant or rude. Love does not insist on its own way; it is not irritable or resentful; it does not rejoice at wrong, but rejoices in the right. Love bears all things, believes all things, hopes all things, endures all things.

Love never ends; as for prophecy, it will pass away; as for tongues, they will cease; as for knowledge, it will pass away. For our knowledge is imperfect and our prophecy is imperfect; but when the perfect comes, the imperfect will pass away.

When I was a child, I spoke like a child, I thought like a child, I reasoned like a child; when I became a man, I gave up childish ways. For now we see in a mirror dimly, but then face to face. Now I know in part; then I shall understand fully, even as I have been fully understood. So faith, hope, love abide, these three; but the greatest of these is love. *I Corinthians 13*

Let love be genuine; hate what is evil, hold fast to what is good; love one another with brotherly affection; outdo one another in showing honor.

Never flag in zeal, be aglow with the Spirit, serve the Lord. Rejoice in your hope, be patient in tribulation, be constant in prayer. Contribute to the needs of the saints, practice hospitality.

Bless those who persecute you; bless and do not curse them. Rejoice with those who rejoice, weep with those who weep. Live in harmony with one another; do not be haughty, but associate with the lowly; never be conceited. Repay no one evil for evil, but take thought for what is noble in the sight of all. Beloved, never avenge yourselves, but leave it to the wrath of God; for it is written, "Vengeance is mine, I will repay, says the Lord." No, "if your enemy is hungry, feed him; if he is thirsty, give him drink; for by so doing you will heap burning coals upon his head." Do not be overcome by evil, but overcome evil with good.   *Romans 12: 9–21*

Brethren, if a man is overtaken in any trespass, you who are spiritual should restore him in a spirit of gentleness. Look to yourself, lest you too be tempted. Bear one another's burdens, and so fulfil the law of Christ. For if any one thinks he is something, when he is nothing, he deceives himself. But let each one test his own work, and then his reason to boast will be in himself alone and not in his neighbor. For each man will have to bear his own load. . . .

And let us not grow weary in well-doing, for in due season we shall reap, if we do not lose heart. So then, as we have opportunity, let us do good to all men, and especially to those who are of the household of faith. . . .   *Galatians 6: 1–5; 9–10*

But be doers of the word, and not hearers only, deceiving yourselves. For if any one is a hearer of the word and not a doer, he is like a man who observes his natural face in a mirror; for he observes himself and goes away and at once forgets what he was like. But he who looks into the perfect law, the law of liberty, and perseveres, being no hearer that forgets but a doer that acts, he shall be blessed in his doing.

If any one thinks he is religious, and does not bridle his tongue but deceives his heart, this man's religion is vain. Religion that is pure and undefiled before God and the Father is this: to visit orphans and widows in their affliction, and to keep oneself unstained from the world.   *James 1: 22–27*

THINK ABOUT

1. "Out here it doesn't matter whether you're Catholic, Protestant or Jewish. I'll decide when I get home."
2. "In the long run men give their supreme loyalties to overall pat-

terns of life, to those ideas and attitudes concerning the nature of the world and of life, which provide them with incentive and direction for living. These patterns of thought and action commonly have gone by the name of religion. Their importance is evidenced by the fact that no human society of any size is long without them, and by the fact that they outlive nations and governments."

Arthur E. Morgan

3. "The Law of God, which we call the moral law, must alone be the scope, and rule, and end of all laws."

John Calvin

4. "All of the significant issues regarding life and death are brought into focus by the question of life's meaning. But how we look at life is in large measure shaped by our perspective on death."

Richard Doss

5. "The great difficulty of the moral life is that our knowledge of right conduct, as embodied in the Decalogue, the Sermon on the Mount, or the Analects of Confucius, is abstract—like the articles of a constitution. The concrete application of the rules cannot help being difficult because we find ourselves in complex situations in which we usually are required to act on the spur of the moment. The Constitution states that a man may not be deprived of property without due process of law. What is 'due process'? To answer this there are millions of words defining circumstances which the courts have studied at leisure. A comparable question in ethics cannot be similarly studied and defined to fit every case. For example: should one tell the truth, regardless of consequences? Ask any intelligent, responsible person you know and he or she will say: 'It depends. Some consequences should be disregarded. Others not.' Just so."

Jacques Barzun

6. "It will be agreed on all hands that no number of moral rules will save us from exercising intuition; for a rule can only be general, but an act must be particular, so it will always be necessary to satisfy ourselves that an act comes under the rule, and for this no rule can be given."

E. F. Carritt

44

No, Christian Ethics
Are Inadequate

Bertrand Russell (1872–1970), the grandson of Lord John Russell, a prime minister under Queen Victoria, was born in Wales. He studied mathematics and philosophy at Trinity College, Cambridge from 1890 to 1894. He was a fellow at Trinity from 1895 to 1901, and a lecturer in philosophy there from 1910 to 1916. In 1916, Russell was dismissed from his position because of his pacifist activities. Then, in 1918, he was sentenced to six months in prison because of an allegedly libelous article in which he expressed his opposition to World War I and his desire for peace. Russell was a fellow of the Royal Society, an honorary fellow of the British Academy, and a recipient of the Order of Merit. He was awarded the Nobel Prize for literature in 1950.

Bertrand Russell is highly critical of Christian ethics. He questions whether the character of Christ is as perfect as has been claimed; he questions some of the principles, and whether Christianity has retarded moral progress.

TO STUDY

1. What is Bertrand Russell's definition of a Christian? Why is Russell not a Christian?

2. What value does Russell find in the various maxims of Christ? Discuss specific maxims.

3. What effects does Russell see in Christ's teachings?
4. What defects does Russell see in Christ's character?
5. According to Russell, what is the relationship between morality and religion?
6. In what way does Russell believe the churches have retarded progress?
7. On what does Russell believe religion is mainly founded?
8. What does Russell believe we must do?
9. Evaluate his Ten Commandments. Are they sufficient? Are they biased?

As your Chairman has told you, the subject about which I am going to speak to you tonight is "Why I Am Not a Christian." Perhaps it would be as well, first of all, to try to make out what one means by the word *Christian*. It is used these days in a very loose sense by a great many people. Some people mean no more by it than a person who attempts to live a good life. In that sense I suppose there would be Christians in all sects and creeds; but I do not think that that is the proper sense of the word, if only because it would imply that all the people who are not Christians—all the Buddhists, Confucians, Mohammedans, and so on—are not trying to live a good life. I do not mean by a Christian any person who tries to live decently according to his lights. I think that you must have a certain amount of definite belief before you have a right to call yourself a Christian. The word does not have quite such a full-blooded meaning now as it had in the times of St. Augustine and St. Thomas Aquinas. In those days, if a man said that he was a Christian it was known what he meant. You accepted a whole collection of creeds which were set out with great precisions, and every single syllable of those creeds you believed with the whole strength of your convictions.

What Is a Christian?

Nowadays it is not quite that. We have to be a little more vague in our meaning of Christianity. I think, however, that there are two different items which are quite essential to anybody calling himself a Christian. The first is one of a dogmatic nature—namely, that you must believe in God and

From *Why I Am Not a Christian* by Bertrand Russell (London and New York, 1957), pp. 3–5; 14–23. Copyright © 1957 by Allen & Unwin. Reprinted by permission of Simon & Schuster.

immortality. If you do not believe in those two things, I do not think that you can properly call yourself a Christian. Then, further than that, as the name implies, you must have some kind of belief about Christ. The Mohammedans, for instance, also believe in God and in immortality, and yet they would not call themselves Christians. I think you must have at the very lowest the belief that Christ was, if not divine, at least the best and wisest of men. If you are not going to believe that much about Christ, I do not think you have any right to call yourself a Christian. Of course, there is another sense, which you find in *Whitaker's Almanack* and in geography books, where the population of the world is said to be divided into Christians, Mohammedans, Buddhists, fetish worshipers, and so on; and in that sense we are all Christians. The geography books count us all in, but that is a purely geographical sense, which I suppose we can ignore. Therefore I take it that when I tell you why I am not a Christian I have to tell you two different things: first, why I do not believe in God and in immortality; and, secondly, why I do not think that Christ was the best and wisest of men, although I grant him a very high degree of moral goodness.

But for the successful efforts of unbelievers in the past, I could not take so elastic a definition of Christianity as that. As I said before, in olden days it had a much more full-blooded sense. For instance, it included the belief in hell. Belief in eternal hell-fire was an essential item of Christian belief until pretty recent times. In this country, as you know, it ceased to be an essential item because of a decision of the Privy Council, and from that decision the Archbishop of Canterbury and the Archbishop of York dissented; but in this country our religion is settled by Act of Parliament, and therefore the Privy Council was able to override their Graces and hell was no longer necessary to a Christian. Consequently I shall not insist that a Christian must believe in hell. . . .

The Character Of Christ

I now want to say a few words upon a topic which I often think is not quite sufficiently dealt with by Rationalists, and that is the question whether Christ was the best and the wisest of men. It is generally taken for granted that we should all agree that that was so. I do not myself. I think that there are a good many points upon which I agree with Christ a great deal more than the professing Christians do. I do not know that I could go with Him all the way, but I could go with Him much further than most professing Christians can. You will remember that He said, "Resist not evil: but whosoever shall smite thee on thy right cheek, turn to him the other also." That is not a new precept or a new principle. It was used by Lao-tse and Buddha some 500 or 600 years before Christ, but it is not a principle which as a matter of fact Christians accept. I have no doubt that the present Prime Minister,* for instance, is a most sincere Christian, but I should not advise any of you to go and smite him on one cheek. I think you might find that he thought this text was intended in a figurative sense.

Then there is another point which I consider excellent. You will remember that Christ said, "Judge not lest ye be judged." That principle I do not think you would find was popular in the law courts of Christian countries. I have known in my time quite a number of judges who were very earnest Christians, and none of them felt that they were acting contrary to Christian principles in what they did. Then Christ says, "Give to him that asketh of thee, and from him that would borrow of thee turn not thou away." That is a very good principle. Your Chairman has reminded you that we are not here to talk politics, but I cannot help observing that the last general election was fought on the question of how desirable it was to turn away from him that would borrow of thee, so that one must assume that the Liberals and Conservatives of this country are composed of people who do not agree with the teaching of Christ, because they certainly did very emphatically turn away on that occasion.

Then there is one other maxim of Christ which I think has a great deal in it, but I do not find that it is very popular among some of our Christian friends. He says, "If thou wilt be perfect, go and sell that which thou hast, and give to the poor." That is a very excellent maxim, but, as I say, it is not much practiced. All these, I think, are good maxims, although they are a little difficult to live up to. I do not profess to live up to them myself; but then, after all, it is not quite the same thing as for a Christian.

Defects in Christ's Teaching

Having granted the excellence of these maxims, I come to certain points in which I do not believe that one can grant either the superlative wisdom or the superlative goodness of Christ as depicted in the gospels; and here I may say that one is not concerned with the historical question. Historically it is quite doubtful whether Christ ever existed at all, and if He did we do not know anything about Him, so that I am not concerned with the historical question, which is a very difficult one. I am concerned with Christ as He appears in the Gospels, taking the Gospel narrative as it stands, and there one does find some things that do not seem to be very wise. For one thing, He certainly thought that His second coming would occur in clouds of glory before the death of all the people who were living at that time. There are a great many texts that prove that. He says, for instance, "Ye

---

* Stanley Baldwin.

466 Philosophy of Religion

shall not have gone over the cities of Israel till the Son of Man be come."
Then He says, "There are some standing here which shall not taste death
till the Son of Man comes into His kingdom"; and there are a lot of places
where it is quite clear that He believed that His second coming would
happen during the lifetime of many then living. That was the belief of His
earlier followers, and it was the basis of a good deal of His moral teaching.
When He said, "Take no thought for the morrow," and things of that sort,
it was very largely because He thought that the second coming was going
to be very soon, and that all ordinary mundane affairs did not count. I have,
as a matter of fact, known some Christians who did believe that the second
coming was imminent. I knew a parson who frightened his congregation
terribly by telling them that the second coming was very imminent indeed,
but they were much consoled when they found that he was planting trees
in his garden. The early Christians did really believe it, and they did abstain
from such things as planting trees in their gardens, because they did accept
from Christ the belief that the second coming was imminent. In that respect,
clearly He was not so wise as some other people have been, and He was
certainly not superlatively wise.

The Moral Problem

Then you come to moral questions. There is one very serious defect to my
mind in Christ's moral character, and that is that He believed in hell. I do
not myself feel that any person who is really profoundly humane can believe
in everlasting punishment. Christ certainly as depicted in the Gospels did
believe in everlasting punishment, and one does find repeatedly a vindictive
fury against those people who would not listen to His preaching—an attitude which is not uncommon with preachers, but which does somewhat
detract from superlative excellence. You do not, for instance find that
attitude in Socrates. You find him quite bland and urbane toward the people
who would not listen to him; and it is, to my mind, far more worthy of
a sage to take that line than to take the line of indignation. You probably
all remember the sort of things that Socrates was saying when he was dying,
and the sort of things that he generally did say to people who did not agree
with him.

You will find that in the Gospels Christ said, "Ye serpents, ye generation of vipers, how can ye escape the damnation of hell." That was said
to people who did not like His preaching. It is not really to my mind quite
the best tone, and there are a great many of these things about hell. There
is, of course, the familiar text about the sin against the Holy Ghost:
"Whosoever speaketh against the Holy Ghost it shall not be forgiven him
neither in this World nor in the world to come." That text has caused an

unspeakable amount of misery in the world, for all sorts of people have imagined that they have committed the sin against the Holy Ghost, and thought that it would not be forgiven them either in this world or in the world to come. I really do not think that a person with a proper degree of kindliness in his nature would have put fears and terrors of that sort into the world.

Then Christ says, "The Son of Man shall send forth His angels, and they shall gather out of His kingdom all things that offend, and them which do iniquity, and shall cast them into a furnace of fire; there shall be wailing and gnashing of teeth"; and He goes on about the wailing and gnashing of teeth. It comes in one verse after another, and it is quite manifest to the reader that there is a certain pleasure in contemplating wailing and gnashing of teeth, or else it would not occur so often. Then you all, of course, remember about the sheep and the goats; how at the second coming He is going to divide the sheep from the goats, and He is going to say to the goats, "Depart from me, ye cursed, into everlasting fire." He continues, "And these shall go away into everlasting fire." Then He says again, "If thy hand offend thee, cut it off; it is better for thee to enter into life maimed, than having two hands to go into hell, into the fire that never shall be quenched; where the worm dieth not and the fire is not quenched." He repeats that again and again also. I must say that I think all this doctrine, that hell-fire is a punishment for sin, is a doctrine of cruelty. It is a doctrine that put cruelty into the world and gave the world generations of cruel torture; and the Christ of the Gospels, if you could take Him as His chroniclers represent Him, would certainly have to be considered partly responsible for that.

There are other things of less importance. There is the instance of the Gadarene swine, where it certainly was not very kind to the pigs to put the devils into them and make them rush down the hill to the sea. You must remember that He was omnipotent, and He could have made the devils simply go away; but He chose to send them into the pigs. Then there is the curious story of the fig tree, which always rather puzzled me. You remember what happeneed about the fig tree. "He was hungry; and seeing a fig tree afar off having leaves, He came if haply He might find anything thereon; and when He came to it He found nothing but leaves, for the time of figs was not yet. And Jesus answered and said unto it: 'No man eat fruit of thee hereafter for ever'. . . and Peter . . . saith unto Him: 'Master, behold the fig tree which thou cursedst is withered away.' " This is a very curious story, because it was not the right time of year for figs, and you really could not blame the tree. I cannot myself feel that either in the matter of wisdom or in the matter of virtue Christ stands quite as high as some other people known to history. I think I should put Buddha and Socrates above Him in those respects.

The Emotional Factor

As I said before, I do not think that the real reason why people accept religion has anything to do with argumentation. They accept religion on emotional grounds. One is often told that it is a very wrong thing to attack religion, because religion makes men virtuous. So I am told; I have not noticed it. You know, of course, the parody of that argument in Samuel Butler's book, *Erewhon Revisited.* You will remember that in *Erewhon* there is a certain Higgs who arrives in a remote country, and after spending some time there he escapes from that country in a balloon. Twenty years later he comes back to that country and finds a new religion in which he is worshiped under the name of the "Sun Child," and it is said that he ascended into heaven. He finds that the Feast of the Ascension is about to be celebrated, and he hears Professors Hanky and Panky say to each other that they never set eyes on the man Higgs, and they hope they never will; but they are the high priests of the religion of the Sun Child. He is very indignant, and he comes up to them, and he says, "I am going to expose all this humbug and tell the people of Erewhon that it was only I, the man Higgs, and I went up in a balloon." He was told, "You must not do that, because all the morals of this country are bound round this myth, and if they once know that you did not ascend into heaven they will all become wicked"; and so he is persuaded of that and he goes quietly away.

That is the idea—that we should all be wicked if we did not hold to the Christian religion. It seems to me that the people who have held to it have been for the most part extremely wicked. You find this curious fact, that the more intense has been the religion of any period and the more profound has been the dogmatic belief, the greater has been the cruelty and the worse has been the state of affairs. In the so-called ages of faith, when men really did believe the Chrisian religion in all its completeness, there was the Inquisition, with its tortures; there were millions of unfortunate women burned as witches; and there was every kind of cruelty practiced upon all sorts of people in the name of religion.

You find as you look around the world that every single bit of progress in humane feeling, every improvement in the criminal law, every step toward the diminution of war, every step toward better treatment of the colored races, or every mitigation of slavery, every moral progress that there has been in the world, has been consistently opposed by the organized churches of the world. I say quite deliberately that the Christian religion, as organized in its churches, has been and still is the principal enemy of moral progress in the world.

How the Churches Have Retarded Progress

You may think that I am going too far when I say that that is still so. I do not think that I am. Take one fact. You will bear with me if I mention it. It is not a pleasant fact, but the churches compel one to mention facts that are not pleasant. Supposing that in this world that we live in today an inexperienced girl is married to a syphilitic man; in that case the Catholic Church says, "This is an indissoluble sacrament. You must endure celibacy or stay together. And if you stay together, you must not use birth control to prevent the birth of syphilitic children." Nobody whose natural sympathies have not been warped by dogma, or whose moral nature was not absolutely dead to all sense of suffering, could maintain that it is right and proper that that state of things should continue.

That is only an example. There are a great many ways in which, at the present moment, the church, by its insistence upon what it chooses to call morality, inflicts upon all sorts of people undeserved and unnecessary suffering. And of course, as we know, it is in its major part an opponent still of progress and of improvement in all the ways that diminish suffering in the world, because it has chosen to label as morality a certain narrow set of rules of conduct which have nothing to do with human happiness; and when you say that this or that ought to be done because it would make for human happiness, they think that has nothing to do with the matter at all. "What has human happiness to do with morals? The object of morals is not to make people happy."

Fear, the Foundation of Religion

Religion is based, I think, primarily and mainly upon fear. It is partly the terror of the unknown and partly, as I have said, the wish to feel that you have a kind of elder brother who will stand by you in all your troubles and disputes. Fear is the basis of the whole thing—fear of the mysterious, fear of defeat, fear of death. Fear is the parent of cruelty, and therefore it is no wonder if cruelty and religion have gone hand in hand. It is because fear is at the basis of those two things. In this world we can now begin a little to understand things, and a little to master them by help of science, which has forced its way step by step against the Christian religion, against the churches, and against the opposition of all the old precepts. Science can help us to get over this craven fear in which mankind has lived for so many generations. Science can teach us, and I think our own hearts can teach us, no longer to look around for imaginary supports, no longer to invent allies in the sky, but rather to look to our own efforts here below to make this world a fit place to live in, instead of the sort of place that the churches in all these centuries have made it.

What We Must Do

We want to stand upon our own feet and look fair and square at the world—its good facts, its bad facts, its beauties, and its ugliness; see the world as it is and be not afraid of it. Conquer the world by intelligence and not merely by being slavishly subdued by the terror that comes from it. The whole conception of God is a conception derived from the ancient Oriental despotisms. It is a conception quite unworthy of free men. When you hear people in church debasing themselves and saying that they are miserable sinners, and all the rest of it, it seems contemptible and not worthy of self-respecting human beings. We ought to stand up and look the world frankly in the face. We ought to make the best we can of the world, and if it is not so good as we wish, after all it will still be better than what these others have made of it in all these ages. A good world needs knowledge, kindliness, and courage; it does not need a regretful hankering after the past or a fettering of the free intelligence by the words uttered long ago by ignorant men. It needs a fearless outlook and a free intelligence. It needs hope for the future, not looking back all the time toward a past that is dead, which we trust will be far surpassed by the future that our intelligence can create.

The Ten Commandments*

1. Do not feel certain of anything.
2. Do not think it worthwhile to produce belief by concealing evidence, for the evidence is sure to come to light.
3. Never try to discourage thinking, for you are sure to succeed.
4. When met with opposition, even if it should be from your husband or your children, endeavour to overcome it by argument and not by authority, for a victory dependent upon authority is unreal and illusory.
5. Have no respect for the authority of others, for there are always contrary authorities to be found.
6. Do not use power to suppress opinions you think pernicious, for if you do the opinions will suppress you.
7. Do not fear to be eccentric in opinion, for every opinion now accepted was once eccentric.
8. Find more pleasure in intelligent dissents than in passive agreement, for, if you value intelligence as you should, the former implies a deeper agreement than the latter.

---

* *The Independent,* June, 1965, p. 4.

9. Be scrupulously truthful, even when truth is inconvenient, for it is more inconvenient when you try to conceal it.
10. Do not feel envious of the happiness of those who live in a fool's paradise, for only a fool will think that it is happiness.

Readings

1. Ewing, A. C. *The Definition of Good.* New York: Humanities Press, 1947, pp. 106–9. Good criticism.
2. Frankena, W. "Love and Principle in Christian Ethics," in *Christian Morals Today,* 1964. Good defense.
3. Gould, James. "The Not-So-Golden Rule," *Southern Journal of Philosophy* (1963). Excellent criticism.
4. Johnson, Ernest F., ed. *Patterns of Ethics in America Today,* Chap. 1, "Ethics of Judaism"; Chap. 2, "Ethics of Roman Catholicism"; Chap. 3, "Ethics of Protestantism." New York: Collier Books, 1962.
5. Ramsey, Paul. *Basic Christian Ethics.* New York: Scribners, 1950. A defense.

7

Political Philosophy

one

What Is Freedom?

45

Freedom Is Authority

Fyodor Dostoevsky (1822–1881) was one of the two or three greatest Russian novelists. Some of his famous novels are *Crime and Punishment* (1866), *The Idiot* (1868), and *The Brothers Karamazov* (1880).

The subject of human freedom is one which raises fundamental issues about the nature of man and his goals. Do men really wish to have a wide measure of freedom to choose and to determine their own lives? Would they not be happier without the burdens of such freedom? Can they be trusted to use such freedom wisely?

In the literature of Western civilization, Fyodor Dostoevsky has provided one of the most famous discussions of these basic questions. In a chapter of his novel *The Brothers Karamazov,* Dostoevsky narrates a conversation between two of the central characters, Ivan Karamazov and his younger brother Alyosha. For the novel as a whole, Ivan and Alyosha represent contrasting types. Ivan is primarily an intellectual who portrays the problems of one who has become skeptical of traditional beliefs and faiths, whereas Alyosha is primarily a man of faith, training for a future career as a Christian priest. At the point in the novel from which the reading selection is taken, Ivan has written a story about the Grand Inquisitor and he proceeds to tell it to Alyosha.

Ivan sets the scene of his tale in Spain of the sixteenth century. He imagines Christ returning to earth and meeting a cardinal of the church, the Grand Inquisitor, who has been responsible for burning a hundred heretics the day before. The Grand Inquisitor recognizes Christ, imprisons him, and then explains why Christ must also be sentenced to death by fire.

In the eyes of the Grand Inquisitor, Christ's heresy consists of the value which he placed upon man's freedom of choice and conscience. The Grand Inquisitor reviews Christ's three temptations and notes that in each case Christ could have chosen to enslave men and thereby make them happy but did not do so for the sake of leaving them free. When Christ, in the first temptation, would not turn stones into bread, he thwarted the desire of men to have someone to worship. When Christ next refused to prove he was the son of God by flinging himself from the top of a temple and being saved by angels, he rejected the needs of men for "miracle, mystery, and authority." Finally, when Christ would not take the kingdoms of the world, he turned down the opportunity to give men unity and peace on earth. For the Grand Inquisitor, men are weak by nature and the true lover of humanity must correct Christ's work by removing their freedom and giving them "all that man seeks on earth—that is, some one to worship, some one to keep his conscience, and some means of uniting all in one unanimous and harmonious ant-heap."

The freedom Christ championed was different from the negative freedom from constraint. It was the freedom experienced through living by religious ideals. We would all say that Christ was in some sense a relatively free man. He certainly was not politically free. He certainly was not economically free. The Christian moral ideal contains the Ten Commandments, the Golden Rule, etc. This was Christ's freedom, i.e., living by His ideal. It may not be the best ideal, but it is a significant one. Thus, Christ's freedom was His acquired freedom, the kind achieved by the man who lives by a significant moral ideal.

TO STUDY

1. On what grounds can The Grand Inquisitor say to Christ, "Thou hast no right to add anything to what Thou has said of old"?

2. What does The Grand Inquisitor mean when he says Christ cannot take from man the freedom He had exalted? What freedom have the people given to the church?

3. What is meant when it is said "Freedom and bread enough for all are inconceivable together"?

4. What freedom is the church ready to endure which the people have found so dreadful?

5. What is meant when The Grand Inquisitor says, "Instead of taking possession of men's freedom, Thou didst increase it"? Again, what

is meant by "We have been on his side and not on Thine"? Again, "They will only become free when they renounce their freedom to us and submit to us"?

"My story is laid in Spain, in Seville, in the most terrible time of the Inquisition, when fires were lighted every day to the glory of God, and 'in the splendid *auto da fé* the wicked heretics were burnt.' Oh, of course, this was not the coming in which He will appear according to His promise at the end of time in all His heavenly glory, and which will be sudden 'as lightning flashing from east to west.' No, He visited His children only for a moment, and there where the flames were crackling round the heretics. In His infinite mercy He came once more among men in that human shape in which He walked among men for three years fifteen centuries ago. He came down to the 'hot pavement' of the southern town in which on the day before almost a hundred heretics had, *ad majorem Dei,* been burnt by the cardinal, the Grand Inquisitor, in a magnificent *auto da fé,* in the presence of the king, the court, the knights, the cardinals, the most charming ladies of the court, and the whole population of Seville.

"He came softly, unobserved, and yet, strange to say, every one recognized Him. That might be one of the best passages in the poem. I mean, why they recognized Him. The people are irresistibly drawn to Him, they surround Him, they flock about Him, follow Him. He moves silently in their midst with a gentle smile of infinite compassion. The sun of love burns in His heart, light and power shine from His eyes, and their radiance, shed on the people, stirs their hearts with responsive love. He holds out His hands to them, blesses them, and a healing virtue comes from contact with Him, even with His garments. An old man in the crowd, blind from childhood, cries out, 'O Lord, heal me and I shall see Thee!' and, as it were, scales fall from his eyes and the blind man sees Him. The crowd weeps and kisses the earth under His feet. Children throw flowers before Him, sing, and cry hosannah. 'It is He—it is He!' all repeat. 'It must be He, it can be no one but Him!' He stops at the steps of the Seville cathedral at the moment when the weeping mourners are bringing in a little open white coffin. In it lies a child of seven, the only daughter of a prominent citizen. The dead child lies hidden in flowers. 'He will raise your child,' the crowd shouts to the weeping mother. The priest, coming to meet the coffin, looks perplexed, and frowns, but the mother of the dead child throws herself at His feet with a wail. 'If it is Thou, raise my child!' she cries, holding out her hands to

From *The Brothers Karamazov,* trans. by Constance Garnett.

Him. The procession halts, the coffin is laid on the steps at His feet. He looks with compassion, and His lips once more softly pronounce, 'Maiden, arise!' and the maiden arises. The little girl sits up in the coffin and looks around, smiling with wide-open wondering eyes, holding a bunch of white roses they had put in her hand.

"There are cries, sobs, confusion among the people, and at that moment the cardinal himself, the Grand Inquisitor, passes by the cathedral. He is an old man, almost ninety, tall and erect, with a withered face and sunken eyes, in which there is still a gleam of light. He is not dressed in his gorgeous cardinal's robes, as he was the day before, when he was burning the enemies of the Roman Church—at that moment he was wearing his coarse, old, monk's cassock. At a distance behind him come his gloomy assistants and slaves and the 'holy guard.' He stops at the sight of the crowd and watches it from a distance. He sees everything; he sees them set the coffin down at His feet, sees the child rise up, and his face darkens. He knits his thick grey brows and his eyes gleam with a sinister fire. He holds out his finger and bids the guards take Him. And such is his power, so completely are the people cowed into submission and trembling obedience to him, that the crowd immediately make way for the guards, and in the midst of deathlike silence they lay hands on Him and lead Him away. The crowd instantly bows down to the earth, like one man, before the old inquisitor. He blesses the people in silence and passes on. The guards lead their prisoner to the close, gloomy vaulted prison in the ancient palace of the Holy Inquisition and shut Him in it. The day passes and is followed by the dark, burning 'breathless' night of Seville. The air is 'fragrant with laurel and lemon.' In the pitch darkness the iron door of the prison is suddenly open and the Grand Inquisitor himself comes in with a light in his hand. He is alone; the door is closed at once behind him. He stands in the doorway and for a minute or two gazes into His face. At last he goes up slowly, sets the light on the table and speaks.

" 'Is it Thou? Thou?' but receiving no answer, he adds at once, 'Don't answer, be silent. What canst Thou say, indeed? I know too well what Thou wouldst say. And Thou hast no right to add anything to what Thou hadst said of old. Why, then, art Thou come to hinder us? For Thou hast come to hinder us, and Thou knowest that. But dost Thou know what will be tomorrow? I know not who Thou art and care not to know whether it is Thou or only a semblance of Him, but tomorrow I shall condemn Thee and burn Thee at the stake as the worst of heretics. And the very people who have today kissed Thy feet, tomorrow at the faintest sign from me will rush to heap up the embers of Thy fire. Knowest Thou that? Yes, maybe Thou knowest it,' he added with thoughtful penetration, never for a moment taking his eyes off the Prisoner."

"I don't quite understand, Ivan. What does it mean?" Alyosha, who has been listening in silence, said with a smile. "Is it simply a wild fantasy, or a mistake on the part of the old man—some impossible *quiproquo?*"

"Take it as the last," said Ivan, laughing, "if you are so corrupted by modern realism and can't stand anything fantastic. If you like it to be a case of mistaken identity, let it be so. It is true," he went on, laughing, "the old man was ninety; and he might well be crazy over his set idea. He might have been struck by the appearance of the Prisoner. It might, in fact, be simply his ravings, the delusion of an old man of ninety, over-excited by the *auto de fé* of a hundred heretics the day before. But does it matter to us after all whether it was a mistake of identity or a wild fantasy? All that matters is that the old man should speak out, should speak openly of what he has thought in silence for ninety years."

"And the Prisoner too is silent? Does He look at him and not say a word?"

"That's inevitable in any case," Ivan laughed again. "The old man has told Him He hasn't the right to add anything to what He has said of old. One may say it is the most fundamental feature of Roman Catholicism, in my opinion at least. 'All has been given by Thee to the Pope,' they say, 'and all, therefore, is still in the Pope's hands, and there is no need for Thee to come now at all. Thou must not meddle for the time, at least.' That's how they speak and write too—the Jesuits, at any rate. I have read it myself in the works of their theologians. 'Hast Thou the right to reveal to us one of the mysteries of that world from which thou hast come?' my old man asks Him, and answers the question for Him. 'No, Thou hast not: that Thou mayest not add to what has been said of old, and mayest not take from men the freedom which Thou didst exalt when Thou wast on earth. Whatsoever thou revealest anew will encroach on men's freedom of faith; for it will be manifest as a miracle, and the freedom of their faith was dearer to Thee than anything in those days fifteen hundred years ago. Didst Thou not often say then, "I will make you free"? But now Thou hast seen these "free" men,' the old man adds suddenly, with a pensive smile. 'Yes, we've paid dearly for it,' he goes on, looking sternly at Him, 'but at last we have completed that work in Thy name. For fifteen centuries we have been wrestling with Thy freedom, but now it is ended and over for good. Dost Thou not believe that it's over for good? Thou lookest meekly at me and deignest not even to be wroth with me. But let me tell Thee that now, today, people are more persuaded than ever that they have perfect freedom, yet they have brought their freedom to us and laid it humbly at our feet. But that has been our doing. Was this what Thou didst? Was this Thy freedom?' "

"I don't understand again," Alyosha broke in. "Is he ironical, is he jesting?"

"Not a bit of it! He claims it as a merit for himself and his Church that at last they have vanquished freedom and have done so to make men happy. 'For now' (he is speaking of the Inquisition, of course) 'for the first time it has become possible to think of the happiness of men. Man was created a rebel; and how can rebels be happy? Thou wast warned,' he says to Him. 'Thou has had no lack of admonitions and warnings, but Thou didst not listen to those warnings: Thou didst reject the only way by which men might be made happy. But, fortunately, departing Thou didst hand on the work to us. Thou hast promised, Thou has established by Thy word. Thou hast given to us the right to bind and to unbind, and now, of course, Thou canst not think of taking it away. Why, then, hast Thou come to hinder us?"_ *Happiness & freedom are incompatible —*

"And what's the meaning of 'no lack of admonitions and warnings'?" asked Alyosha.

"Why, that's the chief part of what the old man must say."

" 'The wise and dread spirit, the spirit of self-destruction and non-existence,' the old man goes on, 'the great spirit talked with Thee in the wilderness, and we are told in the books that he "tempted" Thee. Is that so? And could anything truer be said than what he revealed to Thee in three questions and what Thou didst reject, and what in the books is called "the temptation"? And yet if there has ever been on earth a real stupendous miracle, it took place on that day, on the day of the three temptations. The statement of those three questions was itself the miracle. If it were possible to imagine simply for the sake of argument that those three questions of the dread spirit has perished utterly from the books, and that we had to restore them and to invent them anew, and to do so had gathered together all the wise men of the earth—rulers, chief priests, learned men, philosophers, poets—and had set them the task to invent three questions, such as would not only fit the occasion, but express in three words, three human phrases, the whole future history of the world and of humanity—dost Thou believe that all the wisdom of the earth united could have invented anything in depth and force equal to the three questions which were actually put to Thee then by the wise and mighty spirit in the wilderness? From those questions alone, from the miracle of their statement, we can see that we have here to do not with the fleeting human intelligence, but with the absolute and eternal. For in those three questions the whole subsequent history of mankind is, as it were, brought together into one whole, and foretold, and in them are united all the unsolved historical contradictions of human nature. At the time it could not be so clear, since the future was unknown; but now that fifteen hundred years have passed, we see that everything in those three questions was so justly divined and foretold, and has been so truly fulfilled, that nothing can be added to them or taken from them.

" 'Judge Thyself who was right—Thou or he who questioned Thee then? Remember the first question; its meaning, in other words, was this: "Thou wouldst go into the world, and art going with empty hands, with some promise of freedom which men in their simplicity and their natural unruliness cannot even understand, which they fear and dread—for nothing has ever been more insupportable for a man and a human society than freedom. But seest Thou these stones in this parched and barren wilderness? Turn them into bread, and mankind will run after Thee like a flock of sheep, grateful and obedient, though for ever trembling, lest Thou withdraw Thy hand and deny them Thy bread." But Thou wouldst not deprive man of freedom and didst reject the offer, thinking, what is that freedom worth, if obedience is bought with bread? Thou didst reply that man lives not by bread alone. But dost Thou know that for the sake of that earthly bread the spirit of the earth will rise up against Thee and will strive with Thee and overcome Thee and all will follow him, crying, "Who can compare with this beast? He has given us fire from heaven!" Dost Thou know that the ages will pass, and humanity will proclaim by the lips of their sages that there is no crime, and therefore no sin; there is only hunger? "Feed men, and then ask of them virtue!" that's what they'll write on the banner, which they will raise against Thee, and with which they will destroy Thy temple. Where Thy temple stood will rise a new building; the terrible tower of Babel will be built again, and though, like the one of old, it will not be finished, yet Thou mightest have prevented that new tower and have cut short the sufferings of men for a thousand years; for they will come back to us after a thousand years of agony with their tower. They will seek us again, hidden underground in the catacombs, for we shall be again persecuted and tortured. They will find us and cry to us, "Feed us, for those who have promised us fire from heaven haven't given it!" And then we shall finish building their tower, for he finishes the building who feeds them. And we alone shall feed them in Thy name, declaring falsely that it is in Thy name. Oh, never, never can they feed themselves without us! No science will give them bread so long as they remain free. In the end they will lay their freedom at our feet, and say to us, "Make us your slaves, but feed us." They will understand themselves, at last, that freedom and bread enough for all are inconceivable together, for never, never will they be able to share between them! They will be convinced, too, that they can never be free, for they are weak, vicious, worthless and rebellious. Thou didst promise them the bread of Heaven, but, I repeat again, can it compare with earthly bread in the eye of the weak, ever sinful and ignoble race of men? And if for the sake of the bread of Heaven thousands and tens of thousands shall follow

Thee, what is to become of the millions and tens of thousands of millions of creatures who will not have the strength to forego the earthly bread for the sake of the heavenly? Or dost Thou care only for the tens of thousands of the great and strong, while the millions, numerous as the sands of the sea, who are weak but love Thee, must exist only for the sake of the great and strong? No, we care for the weak too. They are sinful and rebellious, but in the end they too will become obedient. They will marvel at us and look on us as gods, because we are ready to endure the freedom which they have found so dreadful and to rule over them—so awful it will seem to them to be free. But we shall tell them that we are Thy servants and rule them in Thy name. We shall deceive them again, for we will not let Thee come to us again. That deception will be our suffering for we shall be forced to lie.

" 'This is the significance of the first question in the wilderness, and this is what Thou has rejected for the sake of that freedom which Thou hast exalted above everything. Yet in this question lies hid the great secret of this world. Choosing "bread," Thou wouldst have satisfied the universal and everlasting craving of humanity—to find some one to worship. So long as man remains free he strives for nothing so incessantly and so painfully as to find some one to worship. But man seeks to worship what is established beyond dispute, so that all men would agree at once to worship it. For these pitiful creatures are concerned not only to find what one or the other can worship, but to find something that all would believe in and worship; what is essential is that all may be *together* in it. This craving for *community* of worship is the chief misery of every man individually and of all humanity from the beginning of time. For the sake of common worship they've slain each other with the sword. They have set up gods and challenged one another, "Put away your gods and come and worship ours, or we will kill you and your gods!" And so it will be to the end of the world, even when gods disappear from the earth; they will fall down before idols just the same. Thou didst know, Thou couldst not but have known, this fundamental secret of human nature, but Thou didst reject the one infallible banner which was offered Thee to make all men bow down to Thee alone—the banner of earthly bread; and Thou hast rejected it for the sake of freedom and the bread of Heaven. Behold what Thou didst further. And all again in the name of Freedom! I tell Thee that man is tormented by no greater anxiety than to find some one quickly to whom he can hand over that gift of freedom with which the ill-fated creature is born. But only one who can appease their conscience can take over their freedom. In bread there was offered Thee an invincible banner; give bread, and man will worship Thee, for nothing is more certain than bread. But if some one else gains possession of his conscience—oh! then he will cast away Thy bread and follow after him who has ensnared his conscience. In that Thou wast right. For the secret of man's being is not only to live but to have something to live for. Without a stable conception of the object of life, man would not consent to go on living, and would rather destroy himself than remain on earth, though he had bread in abundance. That is true. But what happened? Instead of taking men's freedom from them, Thou didst make it greater than ever! Didst Thou forget that man prefers peace, and even death, to freedom of choice in the knowledge of good and evil? Nothing is more seductive for man than his freedom of conscience, but nothing is a greater cause of suffering. And behold, instead of giving a firm foundation for setting the conscience of man at rest for ever, Thou didst choose all that is exceptional, vague and enigmatic; Thou didst choose what was utterly beyond the strength of men, acting as though Thou didst not love them at all—Thou who didst come to give Thy life for them! Instead of taking possession of men's freedom, Thou didst increase it, and burdened the spiritual kingdom of mankind with its sufferings for ever. Thou didst desire man's free love, that he should follow Thee freely, enticed and taken captive by Thee. In place of the rigid ancient law, man must hereafter with free heart decide for himself what is good and what is evil, having only Thy image before him as his guide. But didst Thou not know he would at last reject even Thy image and Thy truth, if he is weighed down with the fearful burden of free choice? They will cry aloud at last that the truth is not in Thee, for they could not have been left in greater confusion and suffering than Thou hast caused, laying upon them so many cares and unanswerable problems.

" 'So that, in truth, Thou didst Thyself lay the foundation for the destruction of Thy kingdom, and no one is more to blame for it. Yet what was offered Thee? There are three powers, three powers alone, able to conquer and to hold captive for ever the conscience of these impotent rebels for their happiness—those forces are miracle, mystery and authority. Thou hast rejected all three and hast set the example for doing so. When the wise and dread spirit set Thee on the pinnacle of the temple and said to Thee, "If Thou wouldst know whether Thou art the Son of God then cast Thyself down, for it is written: the angels shall hold him up lest he fall and bruise himself, and Thou shalt know then whether Thou art the Son of God and shalt prove then how great is Thy faith in Thy Father." But Thou didst refuse and wouldst not cast Thyself down. Oh! of course, Thou didst proudly and well, like God; but the weak, unruly race of men, are they gods? Oh, Thou didst know then that in taking one step, in making one movement to cast Thyself down, Thou wouldst be tempting God and have lost all Thy faith in Him, and wouldst have been dashed to pieces against that earth which Thou didst come to save. And the wise spirit that tempted Thee would have rejoiced. But I ask again, are there many like Thee? And couldst Thou believe for one moment that men, too, could face such a temptation? Is the nature of men such, that they can reject miracle, and at the great moments of their life, moments of their deepest, most agonising spiritual difficulties, cling only to the free verdict of the heart? Oh, Thou didst know that Thy deed would be recorded in books, would be handed down to remote times and the utmost ends of the earth, and Thou didst hope that man, following Thee, would cling to God and not ask for a miracle. But Thou didst not know that when man rejects miracle he rejects God too; for man seeks not so much God as the miraculous. And as man cannot bear to be without the miraculous, he will create new miracles of his own for himself, and will worship deeds of sorcery and witchcraft, though he might be a hundred times over a rebel, heretic and infidel. Thou didst not come down from the Cross when they shouted to Thee, mocking and reviling Thee, "Come down from the cross and we will believe that Thou art He." Thou didst not come down, for again Thou wouldst not enslave man by a miracle, and didst crave faith given freely, not based on miracle. Thou didst crave for free love and not the base raptures of the slave before the might that has overawed him for ever. But Thou didst think too highly of men therein, for they are slaves, of course, though rebellious by nature. Look round and judge; fifteen centuries have passed, look upon them. Whom hast Thou raised up to Thyself? I swear, man is weaker and baser by nature than Thou hast believed him! Can he, can he do what Thou didst? By showing him so much respect, Thou didst, as it were, cease to feel for him, for Thou didst ask far too much from him—Thou who hast loved him more than Thyself! Respecting him less, Thou wouldst have asked less of him. That would have been more like love, for his burden would have been lighter. He is weak and vile. What though he is everywhere now rebelling against our power, and proud of his rebellion? It is the pride of a child and a schoolboy. They are little children rioting and barring out the teacher at school. But their childish delight will end; it will cost them dear. They will cast down temples and drench the earth with blood. But they will see at last, the foolish children, that, though they are rebels, they are impotent rebels, unable to keep up their own rebellion. Bathed in their foolish tears, they will recognise at last that He who created them rebels must have meant to mock at them. They will say this in despair, and their utterance will be a blasphemy which will make them more unhappy still, for man's nature cannot bear blasphemy, and in the end always avenges it on itself. And so unrest, confusion and unhappiness—that is the present lot of man after Thou didst bear so much for their freedom! Thy great prophet tells in vision and in image, that he saw all those who took part in the first resurrection and that there were of each tribe twelve thousand. But if there were so many of them, they must have been not men but gods. They had borne Thy cross, they had endured scores of years in the barren, hungry wilderness, living upon locusts roots—and Thou mayest indeed point with pride at those children of freedom, of free love, of free and splendid sacrifice for Thy name. But remember that they were only some thousands; and what of the rest? And how are the other weak ones to blame, because they could not endure what the strong have endured? How is the weak soul to blame that it is unable to receive such terrible gifts? Canst Thou have simply come to the elect and for the elect? But if so, it is a mystery and we cannot understand it. And if it is a mystery, we too have a right to preach a mystery, and to teach them that it's not the free judgment of their hearts, not love that matters, but a mystery which they must follow blindly, even against their conscience. So we have done. We have corrected Thy work and have founded it upon *miracle, mystery* and *authority*. And men rejoiced that they were again led like sheep, and that the terrible gift that had brought them such suffering, was, at last, lifted from their hearts. Were we right teaching them this? Speak! Did we not love mankind, so meekly acknowledging their feebleness, lovingly lightening their burden, and permitting their weak nature even sin with our sanction? Why hast Thou come now to hinder us? And why dost Thou look silently and searchingly at me with Thy mild eyes? Be angry. I don't want Thy love, for I love Thee not. And what use is it for me to hide anything from Thee? Don't I know to Whom I am speaking? All that I can say is known to Thee already. And is it for me to conceal from Thee our mystery? Perhaps it is Thy will to hear it from my lips. Listen, then. We are not working with Thee, but with *him*—that is our mystery. It's long—eight centuries—since we have been on *his* side and not on Thine. Just eight centuries ago, we took from him what Thou didst reject with scorn, that last gift he offered Thee, showing Thee all the kingdoms of the earth. We took from him Rome and the sword of Caesar, and proclaimed ourselves sole rulers of the earth, though hitherto we have not been able to complete our work. But whose fault is that? Oh, the work is only beginning, but it has begun. It has long to await completion and the earth has yet much to suffer, but we shall triumph and shall be Caesars, and then we shall plan the universal happiness of man. But Thou mightest have taken even then the sword of Caesar. Why didst thou reject that last gift? Hadst Thou accepted that last counsel of the mighty spirit, Thou wouldst have accomplished all that man seeks on earth—that is, some one to worship, some one to keep his conscience, and some means of uniting all in one unanimous and harmonious ant-heap, for the craving for universal unity is the third and last anguish of men. Mankind as a whole has always striven to organise a universal state. There have been many great nations with great histories, but the more highly they were developed the more unhappy they were, for they felt more acutely than other people the craving for worldwide union. The great conquerors, Timours and Ghenghis-Khans, whirled like hurricanes over the face of the earth striving to subdue its people, and they too were but the unconscious expression of the same craving for universal unity. Hadst Thou taken the world and Caesar's purple, Thou wouldst have founded the universal state and have given universal peace. For who can rule men if not he who holds their conscience and their bread in his hands? We have taken the sword of Caesar, and in taking it, of course, have rejected Thee and followed *him*. Oh, ages are yet to come of the confusion of free thought, of their science and cannibalism. For having begun to build their tower of Babel without us, they will end, of course, with cannibalism. But then the beast will crawl to us and lick our feet and spatter them with tears of blood. And we shall sit upon the beast and raise the cup, and on it will be written, "Mystery." But then, and only then, the reign of peace and happiness will come for men. Thou art proud of Thine elect, but Thou hast only the elect, while we give rest to all. And besides, how many of those elect, those mighty ones who could become elect, have grown weary waiting for Thee, and have transferred and will transfer the powers of their spirit and the warmth of their heart to the other camp, and end by raising their *free* banner against Thee. Thou didst Thyself lift up that banner. But with us all will be happy and will no more rebel nor destroy one another as under Thy freedom. Oh, we shall persuade them that they will only become free when they renounce their freedom to us and submit to us. And shall we be right or shall we be lying? They will be convinced that we are right, for they will remember the horrors of slavery and confusion to which Thy freedom brought them. Freedom, free thought and science, will lead them into such straits and will bring them face to face with such marvels and insoluble mysteries, that some of them, the fierce and rebellious, will destroy themselves, others, rebellious but weak, will destroy one another, while the rest, weak and unhappy, will crawl fawning to our feet and whine to us: "Yes, you were right, you alone possess His mystery, and we come back to you, save us from ourselves!"

" 'Receiving bread from us, they will see clearly that we take the bread made by their hands from them, to give it to them, without any miracle. They will see that we do not change the stones to bread, but in truth they will be more thankful for taking it from our hands than for the bread itself! For they will remember only too well that in old days, without our help, even the bread they made turned to stones in their hands, while since they have come back to us, the very stones have turned to bread in their hands. Too, too well they know the value of complete submission! And until men know that, they will be unhappy. Who is most to blame for their not knowing it, speak? Who scattered the flock and sent it astray on unknown paths? But the flock will come together again and will submit once more, and then it will be once for all. Then we shall give them the quiet humble happiness of weak creatures such as they are by nature. Oh, we shall persuade them at last not to be proud, for Thou didst lift them up and thereby taught them to be proud. We shall show them that they are weak, that they are only pitiful children, but that childlike happiness is the sweetest of all. They will become timid and will look to us and huddle close to us in fear, as chicks to the hen. They will marvel at us and will be awestricken before us, and will be proud at our being so powerful and clever, that we have been able to subdue such a turbulent flock of thousands of millions. They will tremble impotently before our wrath, their minds will grow fearful, they will be quick to shed tears like women and children, but they will be just as ready at a sign from us to pass to laughter and rejoicing, to happy mirth and childish song. Yes, we shall set them to work, but in their leisure hours we shall make their life like a child's game, with children's songs and innocent dance. Oh, we shall allow them even sin, they are weak and helpless, and they will love us like children because we allow them to sin. We shall tell them that every sin will be expiated, if it is done with our permission, that we allow them to sin because we love them, and the punishment for these sins we take upon ourselves. And we shall take it upon ourselves, and they will adore us as their saviours, who have taken on themselves their sins before God. And they will have no secrets from us. We shall allow or forbid them to live with their wives and mistresses, to have or not to have children—according to whether they have been obedient or disobedient—and they will submit to us gladly and cheerfully. The most painful secrets of their conscience, all, all they will bring to us, and we shall have an answer for all. And they will be glad to believe our answer, for it will save them from the great anxiety and terrible agony they endure at present in making a free decision for themselves. And all will be happy, all the millions of creatures except the hundred thousand who rule over them. For only we, we who guard the mystery, shall be unhappy. There will be thousands of millions of happy babes, and a hundred thousand sufferers who have taken upon themselves the curse of the knowledge of good and evil. Peacefully they will die, peacefully they will expire in Thy name, and beyond the grave they will find nothing but death. But we shall keep the secret, and for our happiness we shall allure them with the reward of heaven and eternity. Though if there were anything in the other world, it certainly would not be for such as they. It is prophesied that Thou wilt come again in victory, Thou wilt come with Thy chosen, the proud and strong, but we will say that they have only saved themselves, but we have saved all. We are told that the harlot who sits upon the beast, and holds in her hands the *mystery*, shall be put to shame, that the weak will rise up again, and will rend her royal purple and will strip naked her loathsome body. But then I will stand up and point out to Thee the thousand millions of happy children who have known no sin. And we who have taken their sins upon us for their happiness will stand up before Thee and say: "Judge us if Thou canst and darest." Know that I fear Thee not, Know that I too have been in the wilderness, I too have lived on roots and locusts, I too prized the freedom with which Thou has blessed men, and I too was striving to stand among Thy elect, among the strong and powerful, thirsting "to make up the number." But I awakened and would not serve madness. I turned back and joined the ranks of those *who have corrected Thy work.* I left the proud and went back to the humble, for the happiness of the humble. What I say to Thee will come to pass, and our dominion will be built up. I repeat, tomorrow Thou shalt see that obedient flock who at a sign from me will hasten to heap up the hot cinders about the pile on which I shall burn Thee for coming to hinder us. For if any one has ever deserved our fires, it is Thou. Tomorrow I shall burn Thee. Dixi.'

". . . When the Inquisitor ceased speaking, he waited some time for his prisoner to answer him. His silence weighed down upon him. He saw that the prisoner had listened intently all the time, looking gently in his face and evidently not wishing to reply. The old man longed for Him to say something, however bitter and terrible. But he suddenly approached the old man in silence and softly kissed him on his bloodless aged lips. That was all his answer. The old man shuddered. His lips moved. He went to the door, opened it, and said to Him: 'Go, and come no more. . . come not at all, never, never!' And he let Him out into the dark alleys of the town. The prisoner went away."

"And the old man?"

"The kiss glows in his heart, but the old man adheres to his idea."

"And you with him, you too?" cried Alyosha, mournfully

Ivan laughed.

"Why, it's all nonsense, Alyosha. It's only a senseless poem of a senseless student, who could never write two lines of verse. Why do you take it so seriously? . . ."

THINK ABOUT

1. "Somehow, our sense of justice never turns in its sleep till long after the sense of injustice in others has been thoroughly aroused; nor is it ever up and doing till those others have begun to make themselves thoroughly disagreeable, and not even then will it be up and doing more than is urgently required of it by our convenience at the moment." Max Beerbohm (1921)

2. "The justice of the punishment depends on the justice of the general system of rights; not merely on the propriety with reference to social well-being of maintaining this or that particular right which the crime punished violates, but on the question whether the social organisation in which a criminal has lived and acted is one that has given him a fair chance of not being a criminal."

T. H. Green (1882)

3. "The idea of liberty appeared in Greece, and its *first* meaning was purely political and social. Understood thus, it designates that complex of attributes included in the epithet 'liberal.' During the period of political decadence which followed the reign of Alexander, liberty acquired an inner and spiritual meaning. It signified the liberation from the passions and the emotions. It described the independence of the wise man. Christianity brought an entirely different meaning, namely, *free will*, i.e., the liberty to choose between good and evil. This idea allows acts to be imputed to agents and makes men responsible individually."

M. Emile Brehier

4. The biggest problem confronting the UNESCO committee was the relation between the traditional democratic rights and the social and economic rights newly proclaimed in the XIXth and the XXth century. The list of rights is split into two rigorously distinct parts: on the one hand such rights as freedom of religion and freedom of speech which guarantee the individuals' independence, and on the other such rights as liberation from poverty and fear, which require the active participation of other human beings and depend, in the long run upon a world organization . . .

5. Fear of serious injury cannot alone justify suppression of free speech and assembly. Men feared witches and burnt women.

6. So regarded, two things are clear about liberty. While its large outlines may have a fairly permanent character, its particular content is always changing with the conditions of time and place. To one age the demand for liberty may express itself in an insistence upon religious toleration; to another political enfranchisement may be its essential expression. This serves to remind us that liberty is always inherent in a social process and is unintelligible apart from it.

46

Freedom Is Natural, Acquired, And Circumstantial

Herbert Joseph Muller (1905–   ) is Distinguished Service
Professor at Indiana University. Among other major works,
he has written a trilogy on the history of freedom in Western
civilization: *Freedom in the Ancient World* (1961), *Freedom
in the Western World* (1963), and *Freedom in the Modern
World* (1966).

Writing from the point of view of a historian who has devoted much
of his life to research on the development of freedom in Western civilization, Herbert J. Muller also finds that there is a relatively neutral, objective
definition of freedom which provides a unity of conception to the many
concrete freedoms discussed and sought by men. For him, freedom means
"the condition of being able to choose and to carry out purposes." This
definition implies three fundamental kinds of freedom. First, is *circumstantial,* which itself has three aspects: political, economic and social.
Second, there is *natural* freedom or free will. Man may or may not have
it, but if he does, it is a kind of freedom. Third, there is the freedom
of the free personality, which is an *acquired* freedom achieved through
living via chosen good ideals. Muller believes any adequate discussion
of freedom must concern itself with all of these aspects.

TO STUDY

1. Give an example of each of Muller's three aspects of freedom.
2. Why isn't the person with a "total absence of obstacles" a free
   person?

3. Explain: "If he is a Shakespeare . . . , he may know a god-like freedom."

4. Give examples of the difference between *feeling* free and *being* free.

5. Differentiate *rational* freedom from *spiritual* freedom using examples.

6. What is "positive" freedom?

7. What is "natural" freedom?

8. What is "acquired" freedom?

To the ordinary man, freedom means the feeling of being able to do as he likes, act at his own sweet pleasure. We all know and like this feeling; it always enters consciousness as "Free, hurrah!" But we also know that the good feeling never lasts. Presently, restless or discontent, we realize the truism that man never is free to do just what he pleases or only what he pleases. Then we may ask what freedom "really" means—only to get really confused. As a hurrah word, it has meant different things to different men, the more because of its liaisons with other good feelings. Mortimer Adler and a team of scholars spent several years analyzing the meanings it has had for Western thinkers, and the ordinary man might be dismayed by the report of their findings in *The Idea of Freedom*, a digest that takes up more than six hundred pages. Here it appears that philosophers have usually meant by freedom the very opposite of our sweet pleasure. "True freedom," most of them have agreed, consists in doing one's duty, being virtuous and wise, being one's "true self." They thereby confirm the popular idea that freedom is a good thing, but they do not clear up the confusion. They have never agreed on what duty and wisdom consist in or on how to recognize one's true self, tell whether it is the inner voice that cries no or the voice that cries yes. They too are talking about different things.

Common sense may now rebel, declaring that these are only verbal complications—we all know what freedom really is even if we can't put it into words. But then let us ask a natural, sensible question. America has been known all over the world as a free country, though recently some people have had doubts; and are Americans today more free or less free than they were a generation ago, before the New Deal? Or than their ancestors were a century ago on the frontier, in their rude cabins? Or than the ancient Athenians were, in a society without time clocks and stop signals? The most sensible answer might seem to be another question: Who can say?

Now, I do not assume that the confusion can be dispelled by logical or semantic rigor. We cannot give an utterly precise meaning to so broad and rich a concept as freedom, at least without arbitrarily excluding a great deal of its vital historical meaning. Neither can we hope to sterilize it, stop it from touching off hurrahs. Yet we must be able to give meaningful answers to such pertinent questions about the state of freedom if we are going to talk about the subject at all. Short of exactitude, we can aim at a relatively neutral, objective, operational definition: one that refers to roughly observable conditions, permits roughly verifiable statements about them, and so makes theoretically possible a rough agreement. In giving us pause, the questions also give us cues. They make plain that *freedom* means concretely *freedoms*, of various kinds. We cannot make out any such thing as "true" freedom in the abstract, but we can distinguish some common garden varieties, can specify in what respects some men are more or less free than others.

As the only true meanings of a word, strictly speaking, are dictionary meanings, we might at least begin by accepting common usage, based on common experience. It is remarkable, indeed, how much confusion we can avoid by clinging to the simple idea that freedom means first of all being *free* in the ordinary sense—unconfined, unfettered, unconstrained—and not necessarily dutiful, virtuous, or wise. We can never positively demonstrate that Americans are better or worse men than they used to be, but we can point to positive ways in which they are more or less confined and constrained. Then we might hope to discuss more profitably the further question of the uses and abuses of freedom, its relation to other goods.

In formal terms, *freedom* in this work will mean "the condition of being able to choose and to carry out purposes." This definition has three immediate implications: (1) the primary dictionary meaning—the absence of external constraints; (2) practicable purposes, or an actual ability with available means; and (3) a power of conscious choice, between significant, known alternatives. It accordingly involves the common ideas of freedom *from,* freedom *to,* and freedom *of,* but it leaves open the question of freedom *for* what. In simple words, a man is free in so far as he can do something or choose not to do it, can make up his own mind, can say yes or no to any given question or command, can decide for himself the matter of duty or *for* what. He is not free in so far as he is prohibited from following his inclinations or is obliged to do something against his own volition, whether by direct coercion or by fear of consequences, even though it might be better for him than his heart's desire. Granted that such statements may ring bells, they are none the less meaningful and refer objectively to a recognizable condition—a condition that feels good but may not produce further good, may lead to folly, sin, or unhappiness.

All these statements must of course be qualified. Man is always constrained by physical necessities, subject to natural law, and as he lives with his fellows he must always submit to further social constraints. Freedom is restricted only when the constraints appear to be arbitrary—unaccustomed, unnecessary, unreasonable, or unjust. The primary historical source of such restriction has been political power, the subjection of most men to the will of one or a few. Since these subjects have generally accepted as natural what seems to us arbitrary rule, we cannot readily set up a universal criterion for deciding what constraints are unreasonable or unjust. But we can begin by determining the actual constraints, by whom and on whom. We can state it as a fact that freedom is broadened in so far as arbitrary power is limited, rule is constrained by the recognition of rights, and rights are extended to all members of a society, guaranteed by law.[1] In this respect Americans today are certainly freer than the overwhelming majority of men ever were in the past, or than Germans were under Hitler. In recent years they have as certainly been subjected to unaccustomed constraints by security regulations and peacetime draft; though most of them have accepted these as reasonable.

The absence of external constraints has little meaning, however, until it is coupled with the positive idea of "actual ability with available means." A child dropped in the middle of a desert is freed from constraints—he no longer has to go to school, eat spinach, do chores; but he is free only to starve. As nominal was the freedom of many children who once had only a choice of factories in which to work twelve hours a day, or of the many poor who were "just as free as the rich to sleep under bridges." Effective freedom requires opportunities as well as rights. From this point of view, the major historical barrier has been not merely political oppression but poverty and ignorance. All other things equal, a man with money is freer than a man without it, an educated man freer than an illiterate. In this respect too Americans have plainly been much freer in their land of opportunity than were the masses of the past, including ordinary Athenians, and today are on the whole better off than their

---

[1] In the form of civil liberties, such rights have led some thinkers to make fine distinctions between *freedom* and *liberty,* but in common usage the terms are virtually interchangeable. The French have got along with only one word, *liberté.* While making no real distinction, I have preferred *freedom* because it has an adjective to go with it, as *liberty* does not. *Liberal* has a specialized meaning, and may further confuse the issues because to many Americans it is a bad word.

ancestors. They have been made so by free public education, more recently by social security and unemployment relief—by measures that have created new problems, involving threats to freedom, but that have nevertheless given most Americans more opportunity, more power to carry out their purposes.

Most important—and most troublesome—is the intimately related power of conscious choice, through intelligence and knowledge. Other animals are able to carry out their instinctive purposes, and may seem so unhampered that men sometimes envy them, saying that they would like to be free as birds. Actually, of course, birds are not simply free to fly and sing—they *have* to fly and sing. Man also has to go through many motions in order to go on living, but he is the only animal that can deliberately choose and change his purposes, even to deciding not to go on living. Over the last five thousand years of his history he has enormously widened the range of his choices. In this view, freedom has been limited by stupidity and ignorance but more specifically by social constraints, the power of custom and convention. These induce *internal* constraints, which may appear as dutifulness or reverence, but may owe chiefly to inertia, superstition, insecurity, anxiety, or dread. We must therefore qualify the apparent freedom of primitive societies, which civilized men are also wont to envy in their harried or sentimental moods. The most easygoing primitives (such as the Stone Age Eskimos described by Stefansson) are free to consider relatively few possibilities and do relatively few things, but the great majority are hidebound by tribal custom. All have a severely limited range of self-determination, or power to decide for themselves what kind of selves they would like to be or become.

An immediate difficulty here is that internal constraints, as states of mind, are more intangible, elusive, and ambiguous than external constraints or positive abilities. To minimize this difficulty, some social analysts prefer Bertrand Russell's negative definition of freedom as "the absence of obstacles to the realization of desires," ruling out consideration of the nature of these desires. I am assuming that we may waive for the time being the question of the property or wisdom of the desires, but that we should take into consideration the range and openness of choice, the awareness of different possibilities, the desire to make choices— the *presence* of conditions helping to refine, extend, and enrich consciousness—as essential to the distinctive freedom that man is capable of, even though this gets him (and the analyst) into more trouble. Considering only "the absence of obstacles," no creature is freer than a well-fed, castrated household cat, and the freest man is the perfectly conditioned inhabitant of Huxley's Brave New World. A civilized man is conscious of richer possibilities than a South Seas islander, and as he seeks them is bound to face more obstacles; yet he alone is able to make his desires and his choices really his own. If he is a Shakespeare or a Beethoven, he may become aware of still more obstacles, lay himself wide open to frustration, but in his creativity he may know a godlike freedom. And for ordinary mortals this matter of the power and the range of conscious choice becomes more important as we approach our own society. An immense increase in power over the natural environment has created a multiplicity of choices, a wealth of means and opportunities for the realiza- tion of desire—and as many more potential obstacles, opportunities for waste, blunder, and frustration.

On this count ordinary Americans are again much freer than the masses of men throughout history, and potentially freer than ordinary Athenians in ancient Greece, than their ancestors on the rude frontier, or than their fathers in the strait-laced small town. But here we may not be at all sure. One reason is the growing conformism, the popular ideal of being "well adjusted" at any cost, with little idea of the possible costs. The conformism is due immediately to the constraints upon those seeking economic and social success, but it is due as well to consensus, a willing acceptance of such constraints. In their prosperity, many Ameri- cans seem content to think and to want what others tell them to. They display little desire to realize their own purposes, make individual choices beyond choices in the latest models. In the absence of serious obstacles to the realization of paltry desires, they may feel free because they feel complacent.

They bring up another complication—the basic distinction between subjective and objective freedom, or between *feeling* free and *being* free. It is not an absolute distinction. One who does not feel free is liable to impotence, however great his latent abilities and wide his actual opportuni- ties; one who does feel free may exercise his powers more fully and effec- tively, however limited they be. Feelings are no less real for being subjec- tive or scientifically disreputable, and they cannot be simply disregarded, since they influence the capacity to choose and carry out purposes. They are among the chief threats to freedom in the modern world, in which a vast collective power and mass have dwarfed the individual, and ever bigger organizations make men feel ever smaller.

Nevertheless I assume that we should look first to objective free- dom—to the roughly observable conditions and powers rather than the infinite subjective experiences that flow from them. We can hope to answer with some assurance the question how free peoples actually were in the past. We might find it very hard to say how free they felt. And in any case feelings are not a trustworthy index to the state of freedom as I define it. Primitives may consider themselves free, or more precisely not feel unfree, because they are unconscious of the constraints we perceive. Although we cannot be sure of the state of mind of the illiterate peasant masses throughout history, their usual passivity suggests that they generally took their subjection for granted and did not feel deprived of the freedoms we take for granted; folklore gives little indication of a yearning for such freedom. When feelings are written into the record by civilized peoples, they as often lend themselves to an ironic as to a compassionate contemplation. Scribes proclaim the deathless glory and felicity of rotten empires on the verge of collapse. Priests give thanks to false gods for blessings won by human effort. Today the many Americans who get red in the face over the "creeping socialism that is destroying our freedom" remain as free as ever to voice their complaints, to vote the rascals out, to go about their increasingly profitable business, and to enjoy the highest standard of living in all history; while in pursuing success they may look to outsiders like the veriest slaves to business, and in enjoying it may respond like puppets to advertisers and publicity men.

Such ambiguities accentuate the complexity of the social condition, the tangle of variable, immeasurable factors that make it impossible to specify with precision the kinds and degrees of freedom. The awareness of such ambiguities also indicates the possibility of at least a partial detachment, a reasonably objective view of the conditions that make men feel as they do, and make it necessary to discount and supplement their feelings. And immediately it spots a primary source of confusion—the inveterate tendency to identify freedom with other goods. One seeking to adhere to a neutral, operational definition is obliged to spell out what he does *not* mean by freedom.

Dreaming of his beloved, the imprisoned poet sang:

> Stone walls do not a prison make,
> Nor iron bars a cage.

We may rejoice that he felt so; but then we must add prosaically that iron bars do make a cage, that only a poet who had known freedom could write this, and that he will be freer when he is outside the stone walls. As an ardent lover, he might then run afoul of John Milton:

> License they mean when they cry liberty,
> For who loves that must first be good and wise.

Prizing liberty, we may relish this lofty sentiment too; but again we must first acknowledge that liberty can be loved by sinners and fools, can run into "license." We must face up to such historical actualities as republican Florence in the Renaissance—the freest, most brilliantly creative city of the age, and one of the most licentious. To identify freedom and virtue promotes the understanding of neither.

As high-minded, and often as arbitrary, is the concept of "rational freedom" that philosophers have been fond of. "A free man," wrote Spinoza out of a tradition dating back to Plato, "is one who lives according to the dictate of reason alone." Human freedom does require a measure of rationality; a man governed by impulse or passion is obviously limited in his ability to choose his purposes; and it may be argued that no kind of freedom is more important than freedom from bondage to unconscious or irrational desire. Yet Spinoza was strictly defining a *wise* man—or more strictly a monster. Free men and free countries have never been governed by the dictate of reason alone. Philosophers have never agreed on the content of this dictate. Spinoza himself might be called a slave to his passion for utter rationality. The endless disagreement among the wise men may not clinch the right to be wrong, but at least it gives good reason to question any prescribed form of rationality. "If only rational freedom be allowed," Edgar Sheffield Brightman observed, "freedom ceases to be free and rationality ceases to be rational."

Another practical objection to such definitions is that they have commonly encouraged an indifference to seemingly unreasonable external constraints, in particular the condition of the masses of men. The last word in "rational freedom" is the Stoic ideal of freedom from all desire. "If once you swerve from this course," Epictetus warned, "you are a slave, you are a subject, you have become liable to hindrance and to compulsion." So indeed you have—freedom is always a risky business. The way of the Stoics could afford more tranquillity, to men in any condition of life; it was a "freedom" that even slaves could enjoy. But this is precisely the objection to it. A slave is not actually free, no matter how indifferent he may be to his chains. In spite of their ideal of universal brotherhood, most Stoics were content to accept the institution of slavery, though most slaves were not. Prizing above all the power to accept any lot, to "choose" whatever happened, the Stoics could ignore all constraints except desire itself, or their own desire to be imperturbable at any cost.

For similar reasons one may question the more common and attractive idea of "spiritual freedom," or specifically the Christian teaching, "In God's service is perfect freedom." This service can promote freedom in the ordinary sense of the word—*if* it is a free, conscious choice, and service of a God who encourages purposeful activity on earth, including free inquiry into his own purposes. Historically, however, the service of God has not always made for such freedom. Most men have served him out of unthinking habit, when not compulsion or fear. Those who seemed to be most intimately acquainted with his will gave different accounts of it, but typically they permitted men little latitude in choice. Martin Luther, who preached so eloquently the "spiritual liberty" of Christians, was as fiercely hostile to religious, intellectual, or political freedom. Only in recent centuries has God blessed the idea of political freedom, and more doubtfully of intellectual freedom. At its best, "spiritual freedom" is essentially subjective, the feeling of emancipation that may come through religious experience. A more precise word for it is peace of mind. If it brings freedom from anxiety, its essence is still service: obedience, submission, renunciation—"Not mine but Thy will be done." Such holiness may not be wholesome, but may come down to a surrender of human powers and purposes for the sake of freedom *from* freedom.

In general, the proponents of both rational and spiritual freedom have been inclined to agree that it means only the freedom to do what is right and good, by their own standards. What I mean by it is a state in which the individual may decide for himself what is right and good. It includes freedom of conscience, a kind of freedom that appeared late and intermittently in history, and that Lord Acton (himself a devout Catholic) made the very essence of freedom: "the assurance that every man shall be protected in doing what he believes to be his duty against the influence of authority and majorities, custom and opinion." And I have been stressing these objections to "true freedom" because those who know what it is naturally assume that all other good men will think and feel as they do, want the same good that they call freedom. At best, they confuse the actual social problem, which arises from the different kinds of freedom desired by different men, and the need of accommodating and adjusting these different desires. At worst, they tend to impose their standards of the right and good, and so to deny men actual freedom in thought and deed.

Western history is an endless illustration of such confusion and coercion. In Western thought a celebrated example is Hegel's pronouncement that "positive freedom" is achieved by an "utter obedience or complete abnegation of one's own opinion and reasonings," which meant specifically an utter obedience to the Prussian state. Only in being what the state wills us to be, added his English disciple Bosanquet, can we find freedom; and he concluded, "Thus it is that we can speak, without a contradiction, of being forced to be free." It is gratifying to a dialectician to be able to speak so, but it therefore becomes necessary to insist that this *is* a contradiction, compulsion is *not* freedom. For such philosophical double talk comes down to a hoary linguistic trick that today is a means of systematic, high-powered fraud—the trick of exploiting the emotional value of a word in order to sell some other idea. Insensibly it leads to the "Newspeak" of George Orwell: "Freedom is slavery."

All this is by no means to deny the intimate connection of freedom with questions of what is right and good. The power to choose one's own purposes leads naturally to the ideal of sovereignty over oneself, mastery of mean, irrational, self-defeating desires. When men claim the *right* to freedom, moreover, they must logically assume the moral obligation to respect the rights of others and the claims of the whole community, else there can be no effective freedom. They become more deeply indebted to the many other men, living and dead, who have upheld the ideal of freedom as an ethical principle. The very growth of freedom forces the questions of what is right and good, which ordinarily do not trouble primitive societies or most men in closed societies. Hence no student of freedom can ignore these questions, no matter how conscientiously he tries to refrain from moral judgment. He is obliged to consider its relation to such social needs as order and security, to such social ideals as justice and equality, to cultural or spiritual values in general. In the modern democracies, where common men have been freer to do as they please, he has to consider the questions raised by what they please to do; for the popular ends of freedom react upon the institutional means, and may confuse or obstruct the processes of democracy. I am merely assuming, once more, that one may hope to get a clearer view of such problems if one keeps one's eye on objective freedom, in the relatively neutral sense of my definition, and distinguishes the question of its nature from the question of its proper uses or ends.

Lest this definition seem arbitrary, I conclude with a restatement in terms of the categories made out by Mortimer Adler and his associates, from their exhaustive analysis of twenty-five centuries of thought on the idea of freedom. They found that all conceptions of it came down to variants on three basic definitions: *circumstantial* freedom of self-realization, or the ability of a man under favorable circumstances to act as he wishes for his own good as he sees it; *acquired* freedom of self-perfection, or the ability of a man through acquired virtue or wisdom to will or live as he ought in conformity to the moral law or an ideal befitting human nature; and *natural* freedom of self-determination, or the ability of a man to change his own character creatively by deciding for himself what he shall do or become. (The wording is Adler's.) Common to all the definitions are the idea of a positive ability and the idea of the "self" contrasted with some other, exempt from the power of others. Adler summarizes the underlying agreement as follows: "A man is free who has in himself the ability or power whereby he can make what he does his own action and what he achieves his own property."

Now I have emphasized this ability or power as distinctive of human freedom, beyond the ability of animals to carry out their instinctive purposes. My definition accordingly includes the idea of "natural" freedom, latent in all men by virtue of their powers of mind; but unlike many thinkers who have regarded such freedom as primary, I hold that the realization of the power of self-determination depends on circumstance or culture. My definition also includes the concept of "acquired" freedom, though in a broader sense and with important qualifications; for in most definitions this is the "rational" or "spiritual" freedom popular with philosophers. I believe it essential to conceive freedom as something that has been achieved and that can be increased, diminished, or lost. For similar reasons I object to definitions that limit it to a particular mode of self-perfection, and that slight when they do not exclude the common garden varieties of freedom. As Adler makes clear, most proponents of "acquired" freedom have held that it could be acquired only by a superior few. As he perhaps does not make clear enough, most have been indifferent to social and political conditions that made it difficult or impossible for ordinary men to become masters of their faculties, to make their actions their own, or to achieve any perfection beyond complete obedience.

For a historian, the most important freedom is "circumstantial." It forces attention to the whole culture by which the self is molded, and thought about freedom is conditioned. One variant of it is political freedom, a major theme in Western history. Allied with this was the characteristic Western effort at social reform, the deliberate alteration of circumstance. But apart from such efforts I assume that for a society at large "circumstantial" freedom is essential to the other freedoms. However "natural," the freedom of self-determination has been rare or negligible in primitive societies, and among the illiterate masses of most civilized societies. If the "acquired" freedom of self-perfection may make a man superior to circumstance, its attainment initially requires the favorable circumstance of a high level of culture. The philosophers and saints who have preached such freedom had to preach it because it was beyond the ken of most men. The circumstances of civilization made possible their lofty ideal, and in most societies also made it attractive because there was little if any hope of more "circumstantial" freedom.[2]

And so I think it may be well to stress at the end that the noble ideal of freedom involves the possibly ignoble idea of doing as one pleases, the irresponsible idea of doing things just for fun. As the old ex-slave said, he liked freedom because "there's a kind of looseness about it."

---

[2] Adler has confined his study to Western thought, for reasons possibly parochial but still legitimate. In Eastern thought, from ancient Egypt to India and China, there has been little specific concern with freedom or effort to define it. Many of the wise and holy men never used the word. But Adler could find a great deal of Eastern thought to illustrate the concept of acquired freedom of self-perfection.

Most of us cherish this looseness. As we acknowledge our obligations and our immense indebtedness to our fellows, recognize that "no man is an island," we still want an island of privacy, where we can sprawl and indulge our own sweet pleasure. If we are depressed by the growing conformism, we might cherish as well the stubbornness, even the cussedness of the ordinary man in resisting his superiors who are so sure that they know better than he what is good for him. "It is man's inherent willfulness that I would preserve," Learned Hand declared, "and in which I wish to set the stronghold of that Liberty I prize; that stone which social reformers have always rejected I would make the head of the corner." This willfulness can be very dangerous, needless to add. Still, it is in fact of the essence of human freedom. If it is ever extinguished in man, he may at last become a contented, well-behaved animal; but he will no longer be a free one.

two

What Are the Limits of Free Speech?

47

Freedom Is Democracy and Free Speech Should Be Unlimited

John Stuart Mill (1806–73) was the most influential British philosopher in the nineteenth century. His major works include *On Liberty* (1859), *Considerations on Representative Government* (1861), *Utilitarianism* (1863), and *The Subjection of Women* (1869).

John Stuart Mill published his famous essay *On Liberty* in 1859. Mill's classic presentation of the arguments for freedom for all individual thought and discussion, no matter how completely false or true or partially false and true the opinions in question are, is especially relevant today when authoritarian elements abroad and in our own midst threaten to stifle any hope of realizing a democratic civilization for mankind.

In arguing against the repression of any opinion, Mill sets forth the following dilemma: If an opinion is suppressed, and it is true, then we lose the opportunity of exchanging truth for falsehood. If an opinion is suppressed, and the opinion is false, then we lose the opportunity of obtaining a clearer conception of our own position. Hence there shouldn't be any censorship of political speech.

Mill's essay, however, also raises another important problem for our own age, the problem of the tyranny of the majority. This is the tyranny of those who hold the prevailing feeling and opinion towards those who dissent from them, the tyrannical tendency of society to impose its own ideas and practices as rules of conduct on those who dissent from them. One wonders if the tyranny of the majority is an inseparable evil of democracy.

TO STUDY

1. What is the subject of Mill's essay?
2. In what two ways have the patriots set limits on the power of the ruler?
3. Explain: "the tyranny of the majority" and its dangers.
4. According to Mill, what is the relation between intolerance and religion?
5. What is the simple principle asserted in this essay? Explain as fully as possible.
6. Discuss Mill's position regarding true speech. Should it be limited?

The subject of this Essay is not the so-called Liberty of the Will, so unfortunately opposed to the misnamed doctrine of Philosophical Necessity; but Civil, or Social Liberty: the nature and limits of the power which can be legitimately exercised by society over the individual. A question seldom stated, and hardly ever discussed, in general terms, but which profoundly influences the practical controversies of the age by its latent presence, and is likely soon to make itself recognized as the vital question of the future. It is so far from being new, that, in a certain sense, it has divided mankind, almost from the remotest ages, but in the stage of progress into which the more civilized portions of the species have now entered, it presents itself under new conditions, and requires a different and more fundamental treatment.

The struggle between Liberty and Authority is the most conspicuous feature in the portions of history with which we are earliest familiar, particularly in that of Greece, Rome, and England. But in old times this contest was between subjects, or some classes of subjects, and the government. By liberty, was meant protection against the tyranny of the political rulers. The rulers were conceived (except in some of the popular governments of Greece) as in a necessarily antagonistic position to the people whom they ruled. They consisted of a governing One, or a governing tribe or caste, who derived their authority from inheritance or conquest; who, at all events, did not hold it at the pleasure of the governed, and whose supremacy men did not venture, perhaps did not desire, to contest, whatever precautions might be taken against its oppressive exercise. Their power was regarded as necessary, but also as highly dangerous; as a weapon which they would attempt to use against their subjects, no less than against external enemies. To

From *On Liberty*, 1859.

prevent the weaker members of the community from being preyed upon by innumerable vultures, it was needful that there should be an animal of prey stronger than the rest, commissioned to keep them down. But as the king of the vultures would be no less bent upon preying on the flock than any of the minor harpies, it was indispensable to be in a perpetual attitude of defence against his beak and claws. The aim, therefore, of patriots, was to set limits to the power which the ruler should be suffered to exercise over the community; and this limitation was what they meant by liberty. It was attempted in two ways. First, by obtaining a recognition of certain immunities, called political liberties or rights, which it was to be regarded as a breach of duty in the ruler to infringe, and which, if he did infringe, specific resistance, or general rebellion, was held to be justifiable. A second, and generally a later expedient, was the establishment of constitutional checks; by which the consent of the community, or of a body of some sort supposed to represent its interests, was made a necessary condition to some of the more important acts of the governing power. To the first of these modes of limitation, the ruling power, in most European countries, was compelled, more or less, to submit. It was not so with the second; and to attain this, or when already in some degree possessed, to attain it more completely, became everywhere the principal object of the lovers of liberty. And so long as mankind were content to combat one enemy by another, and to be ruled by a master, on condition of being guaranteed more or less efficaciously against his tyranny, they did not carry their aspirations beyond this point.

A time, however, came, in the progress of human affairs, when men ceased to think it a necessity of nature that their governors should be an independent power, opposed in interest to themselves. It appeared to them much better that the various magistrates of the State should be their tenants or delegates, revocable at their pleasure. In that way alone, it seemed, could they have complete security that the powers of government would never be abused to their disadvantage. By degrees, this new demand for elective and temporary rulers became the prominent object of the exertions of the popular party, wherever any such party existed; and superseded, to a considerable extent, the previous efforts to limit the power of rulers. As the struggle proceeded for making the ruling power emanate from the periodical choice of the ruled, some persons began to think that too much importance had been attached to the limitation of the power itself. *That* (it might seem) was a resource against rulers whose interests were habitually opposed to those of the people. What was now wanted was, that the rulers should be identified with the people; that their interest and will should be the interest and will of the nation. The nation did not need to be protected against its own will. There was no fear of its tyrannizing over itself. Let the rulers be effectually responsible to it, promptly removable by it, and could afford to trust them with power of which it could itself dictate the use to be made. Their power was but the nation's own power, concentrated, and in a form convenient for exercise. This mode of thought, or rather perhaps of feeling, was common among the last generation of European liberalism, in the Continental section of which, it still apparently predominates. Those who admit any limit to what a government may do, except in the case of such governments as they think ought not to exist, stand out as brilliant exceptions among the political thinkers of the Continent. A similar tone of sentiment might by this time have been prevalent in our own country, if the circumstances which for a time encouraged it had continued unaltered.

But, in political and philosophical theories, as well as in persons, success discloses faults and infirmities which failure might have concealed from observation. The notion, that the people have no need to limit their power over themselves, might seem axiomatic, when popular government was a thing only dreamed about, or read of as having existed at some distant period of the past. Neither was that notion necessarily disturbed by such temporary aberrations as those of the French Revolution, the worst of which were the work of an usurping few, and which, in any case, belonged, not to the permanent working of popular institutions, but to a sudden and convulsive outbreak against monarchical and aristocratic despotism. In time, however, a democratic republic came to occupy a large portion of the earth's surface, and made itself felt as one of the most powerful members of the community of nations; and elective and responsible government became subject to the observations and criticisms which wait upon a great existing fact. It was now perceived that such phrases as "self-government," and "the power of the people over themselves," do not express the true state of the case. The "people" who exercise the power, are not always the same people with those over whom it is exercised, and the "self-government" spoken of, is not the government of each by himself, but of each by all the rest. The will of the people, moreover, practically means, the will of the most numerous or the most active *part* of the people; the majority, or those who succeed in making themselves accepted as the majority: the people, consequently, *may* desire to oppress a part of their number: and precautions are as much needed against this, as against any other abuse of power. The limitation, therefore, of the power of government over individuals, loses none of its importance when the holders of power are regularly accountable to the community, that is, to the strongest party therein. This view of things, recommending itself equally to the intelligence of thinkers and to the inclination of those important classes in European society to whose real or supposed interests democracy is adverse, has had no difficulty in establishing itself; and in political speculations "the tyranny of the majority" is now generally included among the evils against which society requires to be on its guard.

Like other tyrannies, the tyranny of the majority was at first, and is still vulgarly, held in dread, chiefly as operating through the acts of the public authorities. But reflecting persons perceived that when society is itself the tyrant—society collectively, over the separate individuals who compose it—its means of tyrannizing are not restricted to the acts which it may do by the hands of its political functionaries. Society can and does execute its own mandates: and if it issues wrong mandates instead of right, or any mandates at all in things with which it ought not to meddle, it practises a social tyranny more formidable than many kinds of political oppression, since, though not usually upheld by such extreme penalties, it leaves fewer means of escape, penetrating much more deeply into the details of life, and enslaving the soul itself. Protection, therefore, against the tyranny of the magistrate is not enough; there needs protection also against the tyranny of the prevailing opinion and feeling; against the tendency of society to impose, by other means than civil penalties, its own ideas and practices as rules of conduct on those who dissent from them; to fetter the development, and, if possible, prevent the formation, of any individuality not in harmony with its ways, and compel all characters to fashion themselves upon the model of its own. There is a limit to the legitimate interference of collective opinion with individual independence; and to find that limit, and maintain it against encroachment, is as indispensable to a good condition of human affairs, as protection against political despotism.

But though this proposition is not likely to be contested in general terms, the practical question, where to place the limit—how to make the fitting adjustment between individual independence and social control—is a subject on which nearly everything remains to be done. All that makes existence valuable to any one, depends on the enforcements of restraints upon the actions of other people. Some rules of conduct, therefore, must be imposed, by law in the first place, and by opinion on many things which are not fit subjects for the operation of law. What these rules should be, is the principal question in human affairs; but if we except a few of the most obvious cases, it is one of those which least progress has been made in resolving. No two ages, and scarcely any two countries, have decided it alike; and the decision of one age or country is a wonder to another. Yet the people of any given age and country no more suspect any difficulty in it, than if it were a subject on which mankind had always been agreed. The rules which obtain among themselves appear to them self-evident and self-justifying. This all but universal illusion is one of the examples of the magical influence of custom, which is not only, as the proverb says, a second nature, but is continually mistaken for the first. The effect of custom, in preventing any misgiving respecting the rules of conduct which mankind impose on one another, is all the more complete because the subject is one on which it is not generally considered necessary that reasons should be given, either by one person to others, or by each to himself. People are accustomed to believe, and have been encouraged in the belief by some who aspire to the character of philosophers, that their feelings, on subjects of this nature, are better than reasons, and render reasons unnecessary. The practical principle which guides them to their opinions on the regulation of human conduct, is the feeling in each person's mind that everybody should be required to act as he, and those with whom he sympathizes, would like them to act. No one, indeed, acknowledges to himself that his standard of judgment is his own liking; but an opinion on a point of conduct, not supported by reasons, can only count as one person's prefence; and if the reasons, when given, are a mere appeal to a similar preference felt by other people, it is still only many people's liking instead of one. To an ordinary man, however, his own preference, thus supported, is not only a perfectly satisfactory reason, but the only one he generally has for any of his notions of morality, taste, or propriety, which are not expressly written in his religious creed; and his chief guide in the interpretation even of that. Men's opinions, accordingly, on what is laudable or blameable, are affected by all the multifarious causes which influence their wishes in regard to the conduct of others, and which are as numerous as those which determine their wishes on any other subject. Sometimes their reason—at other times their prejudices or superstitions: often their social affections, not seldom their antisocial ones, their envy or jealousy, their arrogance or contemptuousness: but most commonly, their desires or fears for themselves—their legitimate or illegitimate self-interest. Wherever there is an ascendant class, a large portion of the morality of the country emanates from its class interests, and its feelings of class superiority. The morality between Spartans and Helots, between planters and negroes, between princes and subjects, between nobles and roturiers, between men and women, has been for the most part the creation of these class interests and feelings: and the sentiments thus generated, react in turn upon the moral feelings of the members of the ascendant class, in their relations among themselves. Where, on the other hand, a class, formerly ascendant, has lost its ascendency, or where its ascendency is unpopular, the prevailing moral sentiments frequently bear the impress of an impatient dislike of superiority. Another grand determining principle of the rules of conduct, both in act and forbearance which have been enforced by law or opinion, has been the servility of mankind towards the supposed preferences or aversions of their temporal masters, or of their gods. This servility, though essentially selfish, is not hypocrisy; it gives rise to perfectly genuine sentiments of abhorrence; it made men burn magicians and heretics. Among so many baser influences, the general and obvious interests of society have of course had a share, and a large one, in the direction of the moral sentiments: less, however, as a matter of reason, and on their own account, than as a consequence of the sympathies and antipathies which grew out of them: and sympathies and antipathies which had little or nothing to do with the interests of society, have made themselves felt in the establishment of moralities with quite as great force.

The likings and dislikings of society, or of some powerful portion of it, are thus the main thing which has practically determined the rules laid down for general observance, under the penalties of law or opinion. And in general, those who have been in advance of society in thought and feeling, have left this condition of things unassailed in principle, however they may have come into conflict with it in some of its details. They have occupied themselves rather in inquiring what things society ought to like or dislike, than in questioning whether its likings or dislikings should be a law to individuals. They preferred endeavoring to alter the feelings of mankind on the particular points on which they were themselves heretical, rather than make common cause in defence of freedom, with heretics generally The only case in which the higher ground has been taken on principle and maintained with consistency, by any but an individual here and there, is that of religious belief: a case instructive in many ways, and not least so as forming a most striking instance of the fallibility of what is called the moral sense: for the *odium theologicum,* in a sincere bigot, is one of the most unequivocal cases of moral feeling. Those who first broke the yoke of what called itself the Universal Church, were in general as little willing to permit difference of religious opinion as that church itself. But when the heat of the conflict was over, without giving a complete victory to any party, and each church or sect was reduced to limit its hopes to retaining possession of the ground it already occupied; minorities, seeing that they had no chance of becoming majorities, were under the necessity of pleading to those whom they could not convert, for permission to differ. It is accordingly on this battle-field, almost solely, that the right of the individual against society have been asserted on broad grounds of principle, and the claim of society to exercise authority over dissentients openly controverted. The great writers to whom the world owes what religious liberty it possesses, have mostly asserted freedom of conscience as an indefeasible right, and denied absolutely that a human being is accountable to others for his religious belief. Yet so natural to mankind is intolerance in whatever they really care about, that religious freedom has hardly anywhere been practically realized, except where religious indifference, which dislikes to have its peace disturbed by theological quarrels, has added its weight to the scale. In the minds of almost all religious persons, even in the most tolerant countries, the duty of toleration is admitted with tacit reserves. One person will bear with dissent in matters of church government, but not a dogma; another can tolerate everybody, short of a Papist or an Unitarian; another, every one who believes in revealed religion; a few extend their charity a little further, but stop at the belief in a God and in a future state. Wherever the sentiment of the majority is still genuine and intense, it is found to have abated little of its claim to be obeyed.

In England, from the peculiar circumstances of our political history, though the yoke of opinion is perhaps heavier, that of law is lighter, than in most other countries of Europe; and there is considerable jealousy of direct interference, by the legislative or the executive power with private conduct; not so much from any just regard for the independence of the individual, as from the still subsisting habit of looking on the government as representing an opposite interest to the public. The majority have not yet learnt to feel the power of the government their power, or its opinions their opinions. When they do so, individual liberty will probably be as much exposed to invasion from the government, as it already is from public opinion. But, as yet, there is a considerable amount of feeling ready to be called forth against any attempt of the law to control individuals in things in which they have not hitherto been accustomed to be controlled by it; and this with very little discrimination as to whether the matter is, or is not, within the legitimate sphere of legal control; insomuch that the feeling, highly salutary on the whole, is perhaps quite as often misplaced as well grounded in the particular instances of its application. There is, in fact, no recognized principle by which the propriety or impropriety of government interference is customarily tested. People decide according to their personal preferences. Some, whenever they see any good to be done, or evil to be remedied, would willingly instigate the government to undertake the business; while others prefer to bear almost any amount of social evil, rather than add one to the departments of human interests amenable to governmental control. And men range themselves on one or the other side in any particular case, according to this general direction of their sentiments; or according to the degree of interest which they feel in the particular thing which it is proposed that the government should do; or according to the belief they entertain that the government would, or would not, do it in the manner they prefer; but very rarely on account of any opinion to which they consistently adhere, as to what things are fit to be done by a government. And it seems to me that, in consequence of this absence of rule or principle, one side is at present as often wrong as the other; the interference of government is, with about equal frequency, improperly invoked and improperly condemned.

The object of this Essay is to assert one very simple principle, as entitled to govern absolutely the dealings of society with the individual in the way of compulsion and control, whether the means used by physical force in the form of legal penalties, or the moral coercion of public opinion. That principle is, that the sole end for which mankind are warranted, individually or collectively, in interfering with the liberty of action of any of their number, is self-protection. That the only purpose for which power can be rightfully exercised over any member of a civilized community, against his will, is to prevent harm to others. His own good, either physical or moral, is not a sufficient warrant. He cannot rightfully be compelled to do or forbear because it will be better for him to do so, because it will make him happier, because, in the opinions of others, to do so would be wise, or even right. There are good reasons for remonstrating with him, or reasoning with him, or persuading him, or entreating him, but not for compelling him, or visiting him with any evil, in case he do otherwise. To justify that, the conduct from which it is desired to deter him must be calculated to produce evil to some one else. The only part of the conduct of any one, for which he is amenable to society, is that which concerns others. In the part which merely concerns himself, his independence is, of right, absolute. Over himself, over his own body and mind, the individual is sovereign.

It is, perhaps, hardly necessary to say that this doctrine is meant to apply only to human beings in the maturity of their faculties. We are not speaking of children, or of young persons below the age which the law may fix as that of manhood or womanhood. Those who are still in a state to require being taken care of by others, must be protected against their own actions as well as against external injury. For the same reason, we may leave out of consideration those backward states of society in which the race itself may be considered as in its nonage. The early difficulties in the way of spontaneous progress are so great, that there is seldom any choice of means for overcoming them; and a ruler full of the spirit of improvement is warranted in the use of any expedients that will attain an end, perhaps otherwise unattainable. Despotism is a legitimate mode of government in dealing with barbarians, provided the end be their improvement, and the means justified by actually effecting that end. Liberty, as a principle, has no application to any state of things anterior to the time when mankind have become capable of being improved by free and equal discussion. Until then, there is nothing for them but implicit obedience to an Akbar or a Charlemagne, if they are so fortunate as to find one. But as soon as mankind have attained the capacity of being guided to their own improvement by conviction or persuasion (a period long since reached in all nations with whom we need here concern ourselves), compulsion, either in the direct form or in that of pains and penalties for non-compliance, is no longer admissible as a means to their own good, and justifiable only for the security of others.

It is proper to state that I forego any advantage which could be derived to my argument from the idea of abstract right, as a thing independent of utility. I regard utility as the ultimate appeal on all ethical questions; but it must be untility in the largest sense, grounded on the permanent interests of man as a progressive being. Those interests, I contend, authorize the subjection of individual spontaneity to external control, only in respect to those actions of each, which concern the interest of other people. If any one does an act hurtful to others, there is a *primâ facie* case for punishing him, by law, or, where legal penalties are not safely applicable, by general disapprobation. There are also many positive acts for the benefit of others, which he may rightfully be compelled to perform; such as, to give evidence in a court of justice; to bear his fair share in the common defence, or in any other joint work necessary to the interest of the society of which he enjoys the protection; and to perform certain acts of individual beneficence, such as saving a fellow creature's life, or interposing to protect the defence-less against ill-usage, things which whenever it is obviously a man's duty to do, he may rightfully be made responsible to society for not doing. A person may cause evil to others not only by his actions but by his inaction, and in either case he is justly accountable to them for the injury. The latter case, it is true, requires a much more cautious exercise of compulsion than the former. To make any one answerable for doing evil to others, is the rule; to make him answerable for not preventing evil, is, comparatively speaking, the exception. Yet there are many cases clear enough and grave enough to justify that exception. In all things which regard the external relations of the individual, he is *de jure* amenable to those whose interests are concerned, and if need be, to society as their protector. There are often good reasons for not holding him to the responsibility; but these reasons must arise from the special expediencies of the case: either because it is a kind of case in which he is on the whole likely to act better, when left to his own discretion, than when controlled in any way in which society have it in their power to control him; or because the attempt to exercise control would produce other evils, greater than those which it would prevent. When such reasons as these preclude the enforcement of responsibility, the conscience of the agent himself should step into the vacant judgment-seat, and protect those interests of others which have no external protection; judging himself all the more rigidly, because the case does not admit of his being made accountable to the judgment of his fellow-creatures.

But there is a sphere of action in which society, as distinguished from the individual, has, if any, only an indirect interest; comprehending all that portion of a person's life and conduct which affects only himself, or, if it also affects others, only with their free, voluntary, and undeceived consent and participation. When I say only himself, I mean directly, and in the first instance: for whatever affects himself, may affect others *through* himself; and the objection which may be grounded on this contingency, will receive consideration in the sequel. This, then, is the appropriate region of human liberty. It comprises, first, the inward domain of consciousness; demanding liberty of conscience, in the most comprehensive sense; liberty of thought and feeling; absolute freedom of opinion and sentiment on all subjects, practical or speculative, scientific, moral, or theological. The liberty of expressing and publishing opinions may seem to fall under a different principle, since it belongs to that part of the conduct of an individual which concerns other people; but, being almost of as much importance as the liberty of thought itself, and resting in great part on the same reasons, is practically inseparable from it. Secondly, the principle requires liberty of tastes and pursuits; of framing the plan of our life to suit our own character; of doing as we like, subject to such consequences as may follow; without impediment from our fellow-creatures, so long as what we do does not harm them, even though they should think our conduct foolish, perverse, or wrong. Thirdly, from this liberty of each individual, follows the liberty, within the same limits, of combination among individuals; freedom to unite, for any purpose not involving harm to others: the persons combining being supposed to be of full age, and not forced or deceived.

No society in which these liberties are not, on the whole, respected, is free, whatever may be its form of government; and none is completely free in which they do not exist absolute and unqualified. The only freedom which deserves the name, is that of pursuing our own good in our own way, so long as we do not attempt to deprive others of theirs, or impede their efforts to obtain it. Each is the proper guardian of his own health, whether bodily, or mental and spiritual. Mankind are greater gainers by suffering each other to live as seems good to themselves, than by compelling each to live as seems good to the rest.

Though this doctrine is anything but new, and, to some persons, may have the air of a truism, there is no doctrine which stands more directly opposed to the general tendency of existing opinion and practice. Society has expended fully as much effort in the attempt (according to its lights) to compel people to conform to its notions of personal, as of social excellence. The ancient commonwealths thought themselves entitled to practise, and the ancient philosophers countenanced, the regulation of every part of private conduct by public authority, on the ground that the State had a deep interest in the whole bodily and mental discipline of every one of its citizens; a mode of thinking which may have been admissible in small republics surrounded by powerful enemies, in constant peril of being subverted by foreign attack or internal commotion, and to which even a short interval of relaxed energy and self-command might so easily be fatal, that they could not afford to wait for the salutary permanent effects of freedom. In the modern world, the greater size of political communities, and above all, the separation between the spiritual and temporal authority (which placed the direction of men's consciences in other hands than those which controlled their worldly affairs), prevented so great an interference by law in the details of private life; but the engines of moral repression have been wielded more strenuously against divergence from the reigning opinion in self-regarding, than even in social matters; religion, the most powerful of the elements which have entered into the formation of moral feeling, having almost always been governed either by the ambition of a hierarchy, seeking control over every department of human conduct, or by the spirit of Puritanism. And some of those modern reformers who have placed themselves in strongest opposition to the religions of the past, have been noway behind either churches or sects in their assertion of the right of spiritual domination: M. Comte, in particular, whose social system, as unfolded in his *Traité de Politique Positive,* aims at establishing (though by moral more than by legal appliances) a despotism of society over the individual, surpassing anything contemplated in the political ideal of the most rigid disciplinarian among the ancient philosophers.

Apart from the peculiar tenets of individual thinkers, there is also in the world at large an increasing inclination to stretch unduly the powers of society over the individual, both by the force of opinion and even by that of legislation: and as the tendency of all the changes taking place in the world is to strengthen society, and diminish the power of the individual, this encroachment is not one of the evils which tend spontaneously to disappear, but, on the contrary, to grow more and more formidable. The disposition of mankind, whether as rulers or as fellow-citizens, to impose their own opinions and inclinations as a rule of conduct on others, is so energetically supported by some of the best and by some of the worst feelings incident to human nature, that it is hardly ever kept under restraint by anything but want of power; and as the power is not declining, but growing, unless a strong barrier of moral conviction can be raised against the mischief, we must expect, in the present circumstances of the world, to see it increase.

We have now recognized the necessity to the mental well-being of mankind (on which all their other well-being depends) of freedom of opinion, and freedom of the expression of opinion, on four distinct grounds; which we will now briefly recapitulate.

First, if any opinion is compelled to silence, that opinion may, for aught we can certainly know, be true. To deny this is to assume our own infallibility.

Secondly, though the silenced opinion be an error, it may, and very commonly does, contain a portion of truth; and since the general or prevailing opinion on any subject is rarely or never the whole truth, it is only by the collision of adverse opinions that the remainder of the truth has any chance of being supplied.

Thirdly, even if the received opinion be not only true, but the whole truth; unless it is suffered to be, and actually is, vigorously and earnestly contested, it will, by most of those who receive it, be held in the manner of a prejudice, with little comprehension or feeling of its rational grounds. And not only this, but, fourthly, the meaning of the doctrine itself will be in danger of being lost, or enfeebled, and deprived of its vital effect on the character and conduct: the dogma becoming a mere formal profession, inefficacious for good, but cumbering the ground, and preventing the growth of any real and heartfelt conviction, from reason or personal experience.

48

Free Speech Should Be Limited

James Gould (1922–   ) is the author of *Readings on Logic* (1964), *Freedom* (1970), and *Philosophy for a New Generation* (1970).

In contrast to Mill, Gould argues that a line should be drawn between permitted and non-permitted political speech according to the famous dictum of Holmes: Political speech should be suppressed if it represents a "clear and present danger." On the other hand, Gould argues against the view that one must balance the interest of free speech against the possibility of speech creating undesirable evils such as endangering the security of a nation.

TO STUDY

1. What reasons does Gould give for the necessity of free speech?

2. What is a major difference to be noted in determining whether or not a person has violated a free speech law as opposed to other breaches of the law?

3. What does Gould cite as an example supporting the necessity for having some form of speech abridgment?

4. What are the two rules which Gould cites which are possible criteria for determining whether or not a breach of the right of free speech has been made? Explain each. Which is the more flexible and which could more easily be misapplied? Which is best?

Eldridge Cleaver is back in the United States. There is a good deal of talk that he ought to be put in jail for the speeches he has made in Cuba, Sweden, France, etc. Should he be? What's your opinion? How consistent is your opinion with your belief in free speech? How does it square with the belief that the United States is the great bastion of free speech in the World? We believe that we have more political free speech than any other country in the World; this is our proud heritage.

Free speech is important: First, it enables us to get at the truth of a matter by allowing all possible positions to be presented and thereby a choice can be made. Second, it allows an individual to participate in his government and thereby enable the necessary orderly changes to occur in society. The general populace may not be aware of dangers, faults, or injustices which happen to exist at a given moment. As an example one can cite the fact that the possible danger from radioactive fallout has made us conscious of the ultimate need for disarmament. Yet until recently anyone who advocated thorough disarmament was suspect. Again, the elderly people of our society have clearly made known their strong need for medical care, and have caused bills to be passed, even by conservatives, on behalf of the aged. These people long have needed medical aid, but until recently anyone who advocated it was a suspect socialist. Still again, at times in our history talk about limiting the power of labor has been suspect and groups have feared to speak forcefully on this issue. Thus, from these examples, it can be realized that problems which need to be discussed often aren't, because the people who would like to speak out could be politically, economically, or socially harmed.

Hence, free speech is very important to a nation. Those nations that have it progress; those that don't are held back. We have it, Sweden has it, England has it; while Russia, China, and Spain don't have it. And in areas where they lack it, they don't make progress. But don't rely on the courts to provide the bulwark for free speech, for the strongest force for the protection of free speech is in the attitude of the general populace itself. When there is a strong, almost universal attitude, which holds that everyone has a right to speak and believe as he wishes, then such a nation will be free.

If it is true that we are the World's freest country and if free speech is important, then why do so many want to put Eldridge Cleaver in jail for his speeches? Notice a couple of points. First, the advocates of jailing Cleaver aren't claiming that he has done any overt acts violating the laws of the United States; but rather, his jailing should be a consequence of his speeches. The first point is that issues about free speech concern speech only and not overt acts. Illegal overt acts are punishable by various laws. Free speech is always a matter of words used. The fact that some individuals ought to be punished for the words they use brings out the second point I wish to stress here. In spite of the fact that everyone believes that people should speak out as they wish (in a responsible manner), nearly everyone agrees that there must be some limit to free speech. There must be a line drawn between permissible and non-permissible speech. The problem is where to draw the line. We may see the problem of drawing the line as the claim of civil liberties to absolute respect against the counter-claim of the security of the political state. But drawing the line, difficult as it may in practice be, is an absolute necessity. The necessity and problem of drawing the line can be illustrated by the fact that a state cannot, under most circumstances, allow a person to advocate the enemies' causes during wartime (*e.g.,* at a time of possible invasion) or, by the famous illustration of Holmes, that falsely shouting "fire!" in a crowded theatre cannot be permitted. To permit these cases would be to draw the line too close to endangering the state—as a whole in the first case, or a part of its members in the second. On the other hand, to suppress the ideas of the fascist or the socialist is to draw the line too close to endangering the claims of civil liberties. Should the line be drawn in such a way as to punish all people like Carmichael? Who else, then, should be punished? Rapp Brown? Leaders of the Ku Klux Klan? Certain Southern governors? Black Muslims? The John Birchers? The Trotskyite Labor Party? The Hippies advocating drugs? Draft Card burners and other anti-war protesters? Senator Eugene McCarthy? Senator Joseph McCarthy? Probably no one would want to punish all of the above, and probably all would claim that at least some of these have violated a good, proper free speech rule.

Until recently, the rule (which drew the line) that was followed in the United States was the "clear and present danger" doctrine which Justice Holmes set down in 1919: "The question in every case is whether the words used are used in such circumstances and are of such a nature as to create *a clear and present danger* that they will bring about the substantive evils that Congress has a right to prevent." This means that no one should be punished for speaking unless their speech will immediately lead to a definite dangerous act. If a man argues and incites people to grow their hair long, not wear lipstick, not salute the Flag, then there is no dangerous degree of evil advocated such that it must be stopped immediately. If he advocates doing away with the Klan, the Trotskyites, labor unions, National Association of Manufacturers, in some distant future, then Holmes would say he shouldn't be punished. A man should only be punished, according to Holmes, if his speech creates a clear and present danger.

In 1952 the Vinson court drew a different line: "In each case we must ask whether the gravity of the evil discounted by its improbability justified such invasion of free speech as is necessary to avoid danger." In this case both the concepts of time and substantial evil have a different meaning from that of Holmes' rule. The factor of time as immediate has been radically changed. The Vinson position maintains that the more serious the substantial evil, the less serious the factor of time. In fact, the factor of time is in some cases nearly disregarded, *i.e.,* if the evil is believed to be very serious. More precisely, time and substantial evil are functionally related: If the evil is small but quite imminently probable, then the speech is to be prohibited —as a man who through his speech incites people in such a manner that they begin to throw rocks. On the other hand, if the evil is very great and held to be probable, then although the event is forecast to occur in the very indefinite future, this speech is to be punished or prohibited. Concerning the other factor, the substantial evil, Vinson contends that advocating harm such as revolution in a party platform is such a significant evil. Hence it follows from this drawing of the line that a given judge may punish those groups whom he predicts will in the indefinite future represent a substantial evil to the country. This is referred to as "the balancing theory of free speech" in which the court balances the benefits of free speech against the possibility of the speech creating undesirable evils such as endangering the security of the nation. Its advocates claim that the First Amendment ("There shall be no abridgement of free speech") is not absolute, for this would wipe out the laws on libel, fraud, etc. Even Holmes does not treat it as absolute. There are, however, many critics of the balancing theory who say that with this approach there is no floor beneath which freedom of speech may not be allowed to sink. Furthermore, they argue that, not only does the balancing theory give no encouragement to free speech, but it assures us little, if any more, freedom of speech than we should have had if the First Amendment had never been adopted. These, then, are the two main theories of free speech which have been argued for in the United States. Which one do you favor? Clearly, it is the "clear and present danger" doctrine which is preferable, for the Vinson rule can lead to the prohibition of any given political speech. It is important, then, for each of us to make our communities know what is a good free speech rule.

three

Are Women Free?

49

Women Are Not Free

Kate Millet (1934–   ) is a professor, author, and feminist leader and is generally known as the "principal theoretician" of the women's liberation movement. She wrote *Sexual Politics* (1970).

Most people conceive politics to be events that occur in and among governments. Kate Millet argues that politics is really little else except *power* relationships, and hence the relation between men and women is a political one. Men rule women. Sometimes they rule by force, but as men have been in power since time began the belief that men should rule has been internalized in the female. One speaks of this as "the interiorization of patriarchal ideology."

─────────────────────────────────────── TO STUDY

1. Explain Millet's thesis that some relations between men and women are basically political in nature.

2. According to Millet, how does sexual politics obtain consent? Explain.

3. According to Millet, what is the relation between romantic love and the social status of women?

4. Explain patriarchy and its relation to women. Explain the phrase "the interiorization of patriarchal ideology." What is the greatest psychological weapon?

5. Discuss Millet's interpretation of the tale of Adam and Eve.

In introducing the term "sexual politics," one must first answer the inevitable question "Can the relationship between the sexes be viewed in a political light at all?" The answer depends on how one defines politics.[1] This essay does not define the political as that relatively narrow and exclusive world of meetings, chairmen, and parties. The term "politics" shall refer to power-structured relationships, arrangements whereby one group of persons is controlled by another. By way of parenthesis one might add that although an ideal politics might simply be conceived of as the arrangement of human life on agreeable and rational principles from whence the entire notion of power *over* others should be banished, one must confess that this is not what constitutes the political as we know it, and it is to this that we must address ourselves.

The following sketch, which might be described as "notes toward a theory of patriarchy," will attempt to prove that sex is a status category with political implications. Something of a pioneering effort, it must perforce be both tentative and imperfect. Because the intention is to provide an overall description, statements must be generalized, exceptions neglected. and subheadings overlapping and, to some degree, arbitrary as well

The word "politics" is enlisted here when speaking of the sexes primarily because such a word is eminently useful in outlining the real nature of their relative status, historically and at the present. It is opportune, perhaps today even mandatory, that we develop a more relevant psychology and philosophy of power relationships beyond the simple conceptual framework provided by our traditional formal politics. Indeed, it may be imperative that we give some attention to defining a theory of politics which treats of power relationships on grounds less conventional than those to which we are accustomed.[2] I have therefore found it pertinent to define them on grounds of personal contact and interaction between members of well-defined and coherent groups: races, castes, classes, and sexes. For it is precisely because certain groups have no representation in

Excerpts from *Sexual Politics* by Kate Millett (New York: Doubleday, 1969–1970), Ch. 2. Copyright © 1969, 1970 by Kate Millet. Reprinted by permission of Doubleday & Company, Inc.

[1] The American Heritage Dictionary's fourth definition is fairly approximate: "methods or tactics involved in managing a state or government." *American Heritage Dictionary* (New York: American Heritage and Houghton Mifflin, 1969). One might expand this to a set of stratagems designed to maintain a system. If one understands patriarchy to be an instituition perpetuated by such techniques of control, one has a working definition of how politics is conceived in this essay.

[2] I am indebted here to Ronald V. Samson's *The Psychology of Power* (New York: Random House, 1968) for his intelligent investigation of the connection between formal power structures and the family and for his analysis of how power corrupts basic human relationships.

a number of recognized political structures that their position tends to be so stable, their oppression so continuous.

In America, recent events have forced us to acknowledge at last that the relationship between the races is indeed a political one which involves the general control of one collectivity, defined by birth, over another collectivity, also defined by birth. Groups who rule by birthright are fast disappearing, yet there remains one ancient and universal scheme for the domination of one birth group by another—the scheme that prevails in the area of sex. The study of racism has convinced us that a truly political state of affairs operates between the races to perpetuate a series of oppressive circumstances. The subordinated group has inadequate redress through existing political institutions, and is deterred thereby from organizing into conventional political struggle and opposition.

Quite in the same manner, a disinterested examination of our system of sexual relationship must point out that the situation between the sexes now, and throughout history, is a case of that phenomenon Max Weber defined as *herrschaft*, a relationship of dominance and subordinance.[3] What goes largely unexamined, often even unacknowledged (yet is institutionalized nonetheless) in our social order, is the birthright priority whereby males rule females. Through this system a most ingenious form of "interior colonization" has been achieved. It is one which tends moreover to be sturdier than any form of segregation, and more rigorous than class stratification, more uniform, certainly more enduring. However muted its present appearance may be, sexual dominion obtains nevertheless as perhaps the most pervasive ideology of our culture and provides its most fundamental concept of power.

This is so because our society, like all other historical civilizations, is a patriarchy.[4] The fact is evident at once if one recalls that the military, industry, technology, universities, science, political office, and finance—in short, every avenue of power within the society, including the coercive force of the police, is entirely in male hands. As the essence of politics is power,

---

[3] "Domination in the quite general sense of power, i.e. the possibility of imposing one's will upon the behavior of other persons, can emerge in the most diverse forms." In this central passage of *Wirtschaft und Gesellschaft* Weber is particularly interested in two such forms: control through social authority ("patriarchal, magisterial, or princely") and control through economic force. In patriarchy as in other forms of domination "that control over economic goods, i.e. economic power, is a frequent, often purposively willed, consequence of domination as well as one of its most important instruments." Quoted from Max Rheinstein's and Edward Shil's translation of portions of *Wirtschaft und Gesellschaft* entitled *Max Weber on Law in Economy and Society* (New York: Simon and Schuster, 1967), pp. 323–24.

[4] No matriarchal societies are known to exist at present. Matrilineality, which may be, as some anthropologists have held, a residue or a transitional stage of matriarchy, does not constitute an exception to patriarchal rule, it simply channels the power held by males through female descent—, e.g. the Avunculate.

such realization cannot fail to carry impact. What lingers of supernatural authority, the Deity, "His" ministry, together with the ethics and values, the philosophy and art of our culture—its very civilization—as T. S. Eliot once observed, is of male manufacture.

If one takes patriarchal government to be the institution whereby that half of the populace which is female is controlled by that half which is male, the principles of patriarchy appear to be two fold: male shall dominate female, elder male shall dominate younger. However, just as with any human institution, there is frequently a distance between the real and the ideal; contradictions and exceptions do exist within the system. While patriarchy as an institution is a social constant so deeply entrenched as to run through all other political, social, or economic forms, whether of caste or class, feudality or bureaucracy, just as it pervades all major religions, it also exhibits great variety in history and locale. In democracies,[5] for example, females have often held no office or do so (as now) in such minuscule numbers as to be below even token representation. Aristocracy, on the other hand, with its emphasis upon the magic and dynastic properties of blood, may at times permit women to hold power. The principle of rule by elder males is violated even more frequently. Bearing in mind the variation and degree in patriarchy—as say between Saudi Arabia and Sweden, Indonesia and Red China—we also recognize our own form in the U.S. and Europe to be much altered and attenuated by the reforms described in the next chapter.

I. Ideological

Hannah Arendt[6] has observed that government is upheld by power supported either through consent or imposed through violence. Conditioning to an ideology amounts to the former. Sexual politics obtains consent through the "socialization" of both sexes to basic patriarchal polities with regard to temperament, role, and status. As to status, a pervasive assent to the prejudice of male superiority guarantees superior status in the male, inferior in the female. The first item, temperament, involves the formation of human personality along stereotyped lines of sex category ("masculine" and "feminine"), based on the needs and values of the dominant group and dictated by what its members cherish in themselves and find convenient in subordinates; aggression, intelligence, force, and efficacy in the male; passivity, ignorance, docility, "virtue," and ineffectuality in the female This is

---

[5] Radical democracy would, of course, preclude patriarchy. One might find evidence of a general satisfaction with a less than perfect democracy in the fact that women have so rarely held power within modern "democracies."

[6] Hannah Arendt, "Speculations on Violence," *The New York Review of Books*, Vol. XII No. 4, February 27, 1969, p. 24.

complemented by a second factor, sex role, which decrees a consonant and highly elaborate code of conduct, gesture and attitude for each sex. In terms of activity, sex role assigns domestic service and attendance upon infants to the female, the rest of human achievement, interest, and ambition to the male. The limited role allotted the female tends to arrest her at the level of biological experience. Therefore, nearly all that can be described as distinctly human rather than animal activity (in their own way animals also give birth and care for their young) is largely reserved for the male. Of course, status again follows from such an assignment. Were one to analyze the three categories one might designate status as the political component, role as the sociological, and temperament as the psychological—yet their interdependence is unquestionable and they form a chain. Those awarded higher status tend to adopt roles of mastery, largely because they are first encouraged to develop temperaments of dominance. That this is true of caste and class as well is self-evident.

II. Biological

Patriarchal religion, popular attitude, and to some degree, science as well[7] assumes these psycho-social distinctions to rest upon biological differences between the sexes, so that where culture is acknowledged as shaping behavior, it is said to do no more than cooperate with nature. Yet the temperamental distinctions created in patriarchy ("masculine" and "feminine" personality traits) do not appear to originate in human nature, those of role and status still less.

Not only is there insufficient evidence for the thesis that the present social distinctions of patriarchy (status, role, temperament) are physical in origin, but we are hardly in a position to assess the existing differentiations, since distinctions which we know to be culturally induced at present so outweigh them. Whatever the "real" differences between the sexes may be, we are not likely to know them until the sexes are treated differently, that is alike. And this is very far from being the case at present. Important new research not only suggests that the possibilities of innate temperamental differences seem more remote than ever, but even raises questions as to the validity and permanence of psycho-sexual identity. In doing so it gives fairly concrete positive evidence of the overwhelmingly *cultural* character of gender, i.e. personality structure in terms of sexual category.

What Stoller and other experts define as "core gender identity" is now

---

[7] The social, rather than the physical sciences are referred to here. Traditionally, medical science had often subscribed to such beliefs. This is no longer the case today, when the best medical research points to the conclusion that sexual stereotypes have no bases in biology.

thought to be established in the young by the age of eighteen months. This is how Stoller differentiates between sex and gender:

> Dictionaries stress that the major connotation of sex is a biological one, as for example, in the phrases *sexual relations* or *the male sex.* In agreement with this, the word *sex,* in this work will refer to the male or female sex and the component biological parts that determine whether one is a male or a female; the word *sexual* will have connotations of anatomy and physiology. This obviously leaves tremendous areas of behavior, feelings, thoughts and fantasies that are related to the sexes and yet do not have primarily biological connotations. It is for some of these psychological phenomena that the term gender will be used: one can speak of the male sex or the female sex, but one can also talk about masculinity and femininity and not necessarily be implying anything about anatomy or physiology. Thus, while *sex* and *gender* seem to common sense inextricably bound together, one purpose of this study will be to confirm the fact that the two realms (sex and gender) are not inevitably bound in anything like a one-to-one relationship, but each may go into quite independent ways.[8]

In cases of genital malformation and consequent erroneous gender assignment at birth, studied at the California Gender Identity Center, the discovery was made that it is easier to change the sex of an adolescent male, whose biological identity turns out to be contrary to his gender assignment and conditioning—through surgery—than to undo the educational consequences of years, which have succeeded in making the subject temperamentally feminine in gesture, sense of self, personality and interests. Studies done in California under Stoller's direction offer proof that gender identity (I am a girl, I am a boy) is the primary identity any human being holds—the first as well as the most permanent and far-reaching. Stoller later makes emphatic the distinction that sex is biological, gender psychological, and therefore cultural: *"Gender* is a term that has psychological or cultural rather than biological connotations. If the proper terms for sex are "male" and "female," the corresponding terms for gender are "masculine" and "feminine"; these latter may be quite independent of (biological) sex."[9] Indeed, so arbitrary is gender, that it may even be contrary to physiology: ". . . although the external genitalia (penis, testes, scrotum) contribute to the sense of maleness, no one of them is essential for it, not even all of them together. In the absence of complete evidence, I agree in general with Money, and the Hampsons who show in their large series of intersexed patients that gender role is determined by postnatal forces, regardless of the anatomy and physiology of the external genitalia."[10]

---

[8] Robert J. Stoller, *Sex and Gender* (New York: Science House, 1968), from the preface, pp. viii–ix.
[9] *Ibid.,* p. 9.
[10] *Ibid.,* p. 48.

III. Sociological

Patriarchy's chief institution is the family. It is both a mirror of and a connection with the larger society; a patriarchal unit within a patriarchal whole. Mediating between the individual and the social structure, the family effects control and conformity where political and other authorities are insufficient.[11] As the fundamental instrument and the foundation unit of patriarchal society the family and its roles are prototypical. Serving as an agent of the larger society, the family not only encourages its own members to adjust and conform, but acts as a unit in the government of the patriarchal state which rules its citizens through its family heads. Even in patriarchal societies where they are granted legal citizenship, women tend to be ruled through the family alone and have little or no formal relation to the state.[12]

As co-operation between the family and the larger society is essential, else both would fall apart, the fate of three patriarchal institutions, the family, society, and the state are interrelated. In most forms of patriarchy this has generally led to the granting of religious support in statements such as the Catholic precept that "the father is head of the family," or Judaism's delegation of quasi-priestly authority to the male parent. Secular governments today also confirm this, as in census practices of designating the male as head of household, taxation, passports, etc. Female heads of household tend to be regarded as undesirable; the phenomenon is a trait of poverty or misfortune. The Confucian prescription that the relationship between ruler and subject is parallel to that of father and children points to the essentially feudal character of the patriarchal family (and conversely, the familial character of feudalism) even in modern democracies.[13]

IV. Class

It is in the area of class that the castelike status of the female within patriarchy is most liable to confusion, for sexual status often operates in a superficially confusing way within the variable of class. In a society where status is dependent upon the economic, social, and educational circum-

[11] In some of my remarks on the family I am indebted to Goode's short and concise analysis. See William J. Goode, *The Family* (Englewood Cliffs, New Jersey: Prentice-Hall, 1964).
[12] Family, society, and state are three separate but connected entities: women have a decreasing importance as one goes from the first to the third category. But as each of the three categories exists within or is influenced by the overall institution of patriarchy, I am concerned here less with differentiation than with pointing out a general similarity.
[13] J. K. Folsom makes a convincing argument as to the anomalous character of patriarchal family systems within democratic society. See Joseph K. Folsom *The Family and Democratic Society* (New York: John Wiley, 1934, 1943).

stances of class, it is possible for certain females to appear to stand higher than some males. Yet not when one looks more closely at the subject. This is perhaps easier to see by means of analogy: a black doctor or lawyer has higher social status than a poor white sharecropper. But race, itself a caste system which subsumes class, persuades the latter citizen that he belongs to a higher order of life, just as it oppresses the black professional in spirit, whatever his material success may be. In much the same manner, a truck driver or butcher has always his "manhood" to fall back upon. Should this final vanity be offended, he may contemplate more violent methods. The literature of the past thirty years provides a staggering number of incidents in which the caste of virility triumphs over the social status of wealthy or even educated women. In literary contexts one has to deal here with wish-fulfillment. Incidents from life (bullying, obscene, or hostile remarks) are probably another sort of psychological gesture of ascendancy. Both convey more hope than reality, for class divisions are generally quite impervious to the hostility of individuals. And yet while the existence of class division is not seriously threatened by such expressions of enmity, the existence of sexual hierarchy has been re-affirmed and mobilized to "punish" the female quite effectively.

The function of class or ethnic mores in patriarchy is largely a matter of how overtly displayed or how loudly enunciated the general ethic of masculine supremacy allows itself to become. Here one is confronted by what appears to be a paradox: while in the lower social strata, the male is more likely to claim authority on the strength of his sex rank alone, he is actually obliged more often to share power with the women of his class who are economically productive; whereas in the middle and upper classes, there is less tendency to assert a blunt patriarchal dominance, as men who enjoy such status have more power in any case.[14]

It is generally accepted that Western patriarchy has been much softened by the concepts of courtly and romantic love. While this is certainly true, such influence has also been vastly overestimated. In comparison with the candor of "machismo" or oriental behavior, one realizes how much of a concession traditional chivalrous behavior represents—a sporting kind of reparation to allow the subordinate female certain means of saving face. While a palliative to the injustice of woman's social position, chivalry is also a technique for disguising it. One must acknowledge that the chivalrous stance is a game the master group plays in elevating its subject to pedestal level. Historians of courtly love stress the fact that the raptures of the poets had no effect upon the legal or economic standing of women, and very little

---

[14] Goode, op. cit., p. 74.

upon their social status.[15] As the sociologist Hugo Beigel has observed, both the courtly and the romantic versions of love are "grants" which the male concedes out of his total powers.[16] Both have had the effect of obscuring the patriarchal character of Western culture and in their general tendency to attribute impossible virtues to women, have ended by confining them in a narrow and often remarkably conscribing sphere of behavior. It was a Victorian habit, for example, to insist the female assume the function of serving as the male's conscience and living the life of goodness he found tedious but felt someone ought to do anyway.

The concept of romantic love affords a means of emotional manipulation which the male is free to exploit, since love is the only circumstance in which the female is (ideologically) pardoned for sexual activity. And convictions of romantic love are convenient to both parties since this is often the only condition in which the female can overcome the far more powerful conditioning she has received toward sexual inhibition. Romantic love also obscures the realities of female status and the burden of economic dependency. As to "chivalry," such gallant gesture as still resides in the middle classes has degenerated to a tired ritualism, which scarcely serves to mask the status situation of the present.

Within patriarchy one must often deal with contradictions which are simply a matter of class style. David Riesman has noted that as the working class has been assimilated into the middle class, so have its sexual mores and attitudes. The fairly blatant male chauvinism which was once a province of the lower class or immigrant male has been absorbed and taken on a certain glamour through a number of contemporary figures, who have made it, and a certain number of other working-class male attitudes, part of a new, and at the moment, fashionable life style. So influential is this working-class ideal of brute virility (or more accurately, a literary and therefore middle-class version of it) become in our time that it may replace more discreet and "gentlemanly" attitudes of the past.[17]

One of the chief effects of class within patriarchy is to set one woman

---

[15] This is the gist of Valency's summary of the situation before the troubadours, acknowledging that courtly love is an utter anomaly: "With regard to the social background, all that can be stated with confidence is that we know nothing of the objective relationships of men and women in the Middle Ages which might conceivably motivate the strain of love-poetry which the troubadours developed." Maurice Valency, *In Praise of Love* (New York: Macmillan, 1958), p. 5.

[16] Hugo Beigel, "Romantic Love," *The American Sociological Review*, Vol. 16, 1951, p. 331.

[17] Mailer and Miller occur to one in this connection, and Lawrence as well. One might trace Rojack's very existence as a fictional figure to the virility symbol of Jack London's Ernest Everhard and Tennessee William's Stanley Kowalski. That Rojack is also literate is nothing more than an elegant finish upon the furniture of his "manhood" solidly based in the hard oaken grain of his mastery over any and every "broad" he can better, bludgeon, or bugger.

against another, in the past creating a lively antagonism between whore and matron, and in the present between career woman and housewife. One envies the other her "security" and prestige, while the envied yearns beyond the confines of respectability for what she takes to be the other's freedom, adventure, and contact with the great world. Through the multiple advantages of the double standard, the male participates in both worlds, empowered by his superior social and economic resources to play the estranged women against each other as rivals. One might also recognize subsidiary status categories among women: not only is virtue class, but beauty and age as well.

Perhaps, in the final analysis, it is possible to argue that women tend to transcend the usual class stratifications in patriarchy, for whatever the class of her birth and education, the female has fewer permanent class associations than does the male. Economic dependency renders her affiliations with any class a tangential, vicarious, and temporary matter. Aristotle observed that the only slave to whom a commoner might lay claim was his woman, and the service of an unpaid domestic still provides working-class males with a "cushion" against the buffets of the class system which incidentally provides them with some of the psychic luxuries of the leisure class.

.   .   .

V. Economic and Educational

One of the most efficient branches of patriarchal government lies in the agency of its economic hold over its female subjects. In traditional patriarchy, women, as non-persons without legal standing, were permitted no actual economic existence as they could neither own nor earn in their own right. Since women have always worked in patriarchal societies, often at the most routine or strenuous tasks, what is at issue here is not labor but economic reward. In modern reformed patriarchal societies, women have certain economic rights, yet the "woman's work" in which some two thirds of the female population in most developed countries are engaged is work that is not paid for.[18] In a money economy where autonomy and prestige depend upon currency, this is a fact of great importance. In general, the position of women in patriarchy is a continuous function of their economic dependence. Just as their social position is vicarious and achieved (often on a temporary or marginal basis) through males, their relation to the economy is also typically vicarious or tangential.

.   .   .

[18] Sweden is an exception in considering housework a material service rendered and calculable in divorce suits, etc. Thirty-three to forty per cent of the female population have market employment in Western countries: this leaves up to two thirds out of the market labor force. In Sweden and the Soviet Union that figure is lower.

Since education and economy are so closely related in the advanced nations, it is significant that the general level and style of higher education for women, particularly in their many remaining segregated institutions, is closer to that of Renaissance humanism than to the skills of mid-twentieth-century scientific and technological society. Traditionally patriarchy permitted occasional minimal literacy to women while higher education was closed to them. While modern patriarchies have, fairly recently, opened all educational levels to women,[19] the kind and quality of education is not the same for each sex. This difference is of course apparent in early socialization, but it persists and enters into higher education as well. Universities, once places of scholarship and the training of a few professionals, now also produce the personnel of a technocracy. This is not the case with regard to women. Their own colleges typically produce neither scholars nor professionals nor technocrats. Nor are they funded by government and corporations as are male colleges and those co-educational colleges and universities whose primary function is the education of males.

In keeping with the inferior sphere of culture to which women in patriarchy have always been restricted, the present encouragement of their "artistic" interests through study of the humanities is hardly more than an extension of the "accomplishments" they once cultivated in preparation for the marriage market. Achievement in the arts and humanities is reserved, now, as it has been historically, for males. Token representation, be it Susan Sontag's or Lady Murasaki's, does not vitiate this rule.

VI. Force

We are not accustomed to associate patriarchy with force. So perfect is its system of socialization, so complete the general assent to its values, so long and so universally has it prevailed in human society, that it scarcely seems to require violent implementation. Customarily, we view its brutalities in the past as exotic or "primitive" custom. Those of the present are regarded as the product of individual deviance, confined to pathological or exceptional behavior, and without general import. And yet, just as under other

---

[19] We often forget how recent an event is higher education for women. In the U.S. it is barely one hundred years old; in many Western countries barely fifty. Oxford did not grant degrees to women on the same terms as to men until 1920. In Japan and a number of other countries universities have been open to women only in the period after World War II. There are still areas where higher education for women scarcely exists. Women do not have the same access to education as do men. The Princeton Report stated that "although at the high school level more girls than boys receive grades of 'A,' roughly 50% more boys than girls go to college." *The Princeton Report to the Alumni on Co-Education* (pamphlet), Princeton, N.J. 1968, p. 10. Most other authorities give the national ratio of college students as two males to one female. In a great many countries it is far lower.

total ideologies (racism and colonialism are somewhat analogous in this respect) control in patriarchal society would be imperfect, even inoperable, unless it had the rule of force to rely upon, both in emergencies and as an ever-present instrument of intimidation.

Historically, most patriarchies have institutionalized force through their legal systems. For example, strict patriarchies such as that of Islam, have implemented the prohibition against illegitimacy or sexual autonomy with a death sentence. In Afghanistan and Saudi Arabia the adulteress is still stoned to death with a mullah presiding at the execution. Execution by stoning was once common practice through the Near East. It is still condoned in Sicily. Needless to say there was and is no penalty imposed upon the male corespondent. Save in recent times or exceptional cases, adultery was not generally recognized in males except as an offense one male might commit against another's property interest. . . .

.   .   .

Excepting a social license to physical abuse among certain class and ethnic groups, force is diffuse and generalized in most contemporary patriarchies. Significantly, force itself is restricted to the male who alone is psychologically and technically equipped to perpetrate physical violence.[20] Where differences in physical strength have become immaterial through the use of arms, the female is rendered innocuous by her socialization. Before assault she is almost universally defenseless both by her physical and emotional training. Needless to say, this has the most far-reaching effects on the social and psychological behavior of both sexes.

. . . In rape, the emotions of aggression, hatred, contempt, and the desire to break or violate personality, take a form consummately appropriate to sexual politics. . . .

.   .   .

VII. Anthropological: Myth and Religion

Evidence from anthropology, religious and literary myth all attests to the politically expedient character of patriarchal convictions about women. One anthropologist refers to a consistent patriarchal strain of assumption that "woman's biological differences set her apart . . . she is essentially inferior," and since "human institutions grow from deep and primal anxieties and are shaped by irrational psychological mechanisms . . . socially organized attitudes toward women arise from basic tensions expressed by

---

[20] Vivid exceptions come to mind in the wars of liberation conducted by Vietnam, China, etc. But through most of history, women have been unarmed and forbidden to exhibit any defense of their own.

the male."[21] Under patriarchy the female did not herself develop the symbols by which she is described. As both the primitive and the civilized worlds are male worlds, the ideas which shaped culture in regard to the female were also of male design. The image of women as we know it is an image created by men and fashioned to suit their needs. These needs spring from a fear of the "otherness" of woman. Yet this notion itself presupposes that patriarchy has already been established and the male has already set himself as the human norm, the subject and referent to which the female is "other" or alien. Whatever its origin, the function of the male's sexual antipathy is to provide a means of control over a subordinate group and a rationale which justifies the inferior station of those in a lower order, "explaining" the oppression of their lives.

The feeling that woman's sexual functions are impure is both worldwide and persistent. One sees evidence of it everywhere in literature, in myth, in primitive and civilized life. It is striking how the notion persists today. The event of menstruation, for example, is a largely clandestine affair, and the psycho-social effect of the stigma attached must have great effect on the female ego. There is a large anthropological literature on menstrual taboo; the practice of isolating offenders in huts at the edge of the village occurs throughout the primitive world. . . .

Primitive peoples explain the phenomenon of the female's genitals in terms of a wound, sometimes reasoning that she was visited by a bird or snake and mutilated into her present condition. Once she was wounded, now she bleeds. Contemporary slang for the vagina is "gash." The Freudian description of the female genitals is in terms of a "castrated" condition. The uneasiness and disgust female genitals arouse in patriarchal societies is attested to through religious, cultural, and literary proscription. In preliterate groups fear is also a factor, as in the belief in a castrating *vagina dentata.* The penis, badge of the male's superior status in both preliterate and civilized patriarchies, is given the most crucial significance, the subject both of endless boasting and endless anxiety.

The Pandora myth is one of two important Western archetypes which condemn the female through her sexuality and explain her position as her well-deserved punishment for the primal sin under whose unfortunate consequences the race yet labors. Ethics have entered the scene, replacing the simplicities of ritual, taboo, and mana. The more sophisticated vehicle of myth also provides official explanations of sexual history. In Hesiod's

---

[21] H. R. Hays, *The Dangerous Sex, the Myth of Feminine Evil* (New York: Putnam, 1964). Much of my summary in this section is indebted to Hays's useful assessment of cultural notions about the female.

tale, Zeus, a rancorous and arbitrary father figure, in sending Epimetheus evil in the form of female genitalia, is actually chastising him for adult heterosexual knowledge and activity. In opening the vessel she brings (the vulva or hymen, Pandora's "box") the male satisfies his curiosity but sustains the discovery only by punishing himself at the hands of the father god with death and the assorted calamities of postlapsarian life. The patriarchal trait of male rivalry across age or status line, particularly those of powerful father and rival son, is present as well as the ubiquitous maligning of the female.

The myth of the Fall is a highly finished version of the same themes. As the central myth of the Judeo-Christian imagination and therefore of our immediate cultural heritage, it is well that we appraise and acknowledge the enormous power it still holds over us even in a rationalist era which has long ago given up literal belief in it while maintaining its emotional assent intact.[22] This mythic version of the female as the cause of human suffering, knowledge, and sin is still the foundation of sexual attitudes, for it represents the most crucial argument of the patriarchal tradition in the West.

The Israelites lived in a continual state of war with the fertility cults of their neighbors; these latter afforded sufficient attraction to be the source of constant defection, and the figure of Eve, like that of Pandora, has vestigial traces of a fertility goddess overthrown. There is some, probably unconscious, evidence of this in the Biblical account which announces, even before the narration of the fall has begun—"Adam called his wife's name Eve; because she was the mother of all living things." Due to the fact that the tale represents a compilation of different oral traditions, it provides two contradictory schemes for Eve's creation, one in which both sexes are created at the same time, and one in which Eve is fashioned later than Adam, an afterthought born from his rib, peremptory instance of the male's expropriation of the life force through a god who created the world without benefit of female assistance.

The tale of Adam and Eve is, among many other things, a narrative of how humanity invented sexual intercourse. Many such narratives exist in preliterate myth and folk tale. Most of them strike us now as delightfully funny stories of primal innocents who require a good deal of helpful instruction to figure it out. There are other major themes in the story: the loss

---

[22] It is impossible to assess how deeply embedded in our consciousness is the Eden legend and how utterly its patterns are planted in our habits of thought. One comes across its tone and design in the most unlikely places, such as Antonioni's film *Blow-Up*, to name but one of many striking examples. The action of the film takes place in an idyllic garden, loaded with primal overtones largely sexual, where, prompted by a tempter with a phallic gun, the female again betrays the male to death. The photographer who witnesses the scene reacts as if he were being introduced both to the haggard knowledge of the primal scene and original sin at the same time.

of primeval simplicity, the arrival of death, and the first conscious experience of knowledge. All of them revolve about sex. Adam is forbidden to eat of the fruit of life or of the knowledge of good and evil, the warning states explicitly what should happen if he tastes of the latter: "in that day that thou eatest thereof thou shalt surely die." He eats but fails to die (at least in the story), from which one might infer that the serpent told the truth.

But at the moment when the pair eat of the forbidden tree they awake to their nakedness and feel shame. Sexuality is clearly involved, though the fable insists it is only tangential to a higher prohibition against disobeying orders in the matter of another and less controversial appetite—one for food. Róheim points out that the Hebrew verb for "eat" can also mean coitus. Everywhere in the Bible "knowing" is synonymous with sexuality, and clearly a product of contact with the phallus, here in the fable objectified as a snake. To blame the evils and sorrows of life—loss of Eden and the rest—on sexuality, would all too logically implicate the male, and such implication is hardly the purpose of the story, designed as it is expressly in order to blame all this world's discomfort on the female. Therefore it is the female who is tempted first and "beguiled" by the penis, transformed into something else, a snake. Thus Adam has "beaten the rap" of sexual guilt, which appears to be why the sexual motive is so repressed in the Biblical account. Yet the very transparency of the serpent's universal phallic value shows how uneasy the mythic mind can be about its shifts. Accordingly, in her inferiority and vulnerability the woman takes and eats, simple carnal thing that she is, affected by flattery even in a reptile. Only after this does the male fall, and with him, humanity—for the fable has made him the racial type, whereas Eve is a mere sexual type and, according to tradition, either expendable or replaceable. And as the myth records the original sexual adventure, Adam was seduced by woman, who was seduced by a penis. "The woman whom thou gavest to be with me, she gave me of the fruit and I did eat" is the first man's defense. Seduced by the phallic snake, Eve is convicted for Adam's participation in sex.

Adam's curse is to toil in the "sweat of his brow," namely the labor the male associates with civilization. Eden was a fantasy world without either effort or activity, which the entrance of the female, and with her sexuality, has destroyed. Eve's sentence is far more political in nature and a brilliant "explanation" of her inferior status. "In sorrow thou shalt bring forth children. And thy desire shall be to thy husband. And he shall rule over thee." Again, as in the Pandora myth, a proprietary father figure is punishing his subjects for adult heterosexuality. It is easy to agree with Róheim's comment on the negative attitude the myth adopts toward sexuality: "Sexual maturity is regarded as a misfortune, something that has robbed

536   Political Philosophy

mankind of happiness . . . the explanation of how death came into the world."

What requires further emphasis is the responsibility of the female, a marginal creature, in bringing on this plague, and the justice of her suborned condition as dependent on her primary role in this original sin. The connection of woman, sex, and sin constitute the fundamental pattern of western patriarchal thought thereafter.

VIII. Psychological

The aspects of patriarchy already described have each an effect upon the psychology of both sexes. Their principal result is the interiorization of patriarchal ideology. Status, temperament, and role are all value systems with endless psychological ramifications for each sex. Patriarchal marriage and the family with its ranks and division of labor play a large part in enforcing them. The male's superior economic position, the female's inferior one have also grave implications. The large quantity of guilt attached to sexuality in patriarchy is overwhelmingly placed upon the female, who is, culturally speaking, held to be the culpable or the more culpable party in nearly any sexual liaison, whatever the extenuating circumstances. A tendency toward the reification of the female makes her more often a sexual object than a person. This is particularly so when she is denied human rights through chattel status. Even where this has been partly amended the cumulative effect of religion and custom is still very powerful and has enormous psychological consequences. Woman is still denied sexual freedom and the biological control over her body through the cult of virginity, the double standard, the prescription against abortion, and in many places because contraception is physically or psychically unavailable to her.

.   .   .

When in any group of persons, the ego is subjected to such invidious versions of itself through social beliefs, ideology, and tradition, the effect is bound to be pernicious. This coupled with the persistent though frequently subtle denigration women encounter daily through personal contacts, the impressions gathered from the images and media about them, and the discrimination in matters of behavior, employment, and education which they endure, should make it no very special cause for surprise that women develop group characteristics common to those who suffer minority status and a marginal existence. A witty experiment by Philip Goldberg proves what everyone knows, that having internalized the disesteem in which they are held, women despise both themselves and each other.[23] This simple test consisted of asking women undergraduates to respond to the scholarship

---

[23] Philip Goldberg, "Are Women Prejudiced Against Women?" *Transaction*, April 1968.

in an essay signed alternately by one John McKay and one Joan McKay In making their assessments the students generally agreed that John was a remarkable thinker, Joan an unimpressive mind. Yet the articles were identical: the reaction was dependent on the sex of the supposed author.

As women in patriarchy are for the most part marginal citizens when they are citizens at all, their situation is like that of other minorities, here defined not as dependent upon numerical size of the group, but on its status. "A minority group is any group of people who because of their physical or cultural characteristics, are singled out from others in the society in which they live for differential and unequal treatment." Only a handful of sociologists have ever addressed themselves in any meaningful way to the minority status of women. And psychology has yet to produce relevant studies on the subject of ego damage to the female which might bear comparison to the excellent work done on the effects of racism on the minds of blacks and colonials. The remarkably small amount of modern research devoted to the psychological and social effects of masculine supremacy on the female and on the culture in general attests to the widespread ignorance or unconcern of a conservative social science which takes patriarchy to be both the status quo and the state of nature.

What little literature the social sciences afford us in this context confirms the presence in women of the expected traits of minority status: group self-hatred and self-rejection, a contempt both for herself and for her fellows—the result of that continual, however subtle, reiteration of her inferiority which she eventually accepts as a fact.[24] Another index of minority status is the fierceness with which all minority group members are judged. The double standard is applied not only in cases of sexual conduct but other contexts as well. In the relatively rare instances of female crime too: in many American states a woman convicted of crime is awarded a longer sentence.[25] Generally an accused woman acquires a notoriety out of proportion to her acts and due to sensational publicity she may be tried largely for her "sex life." But so effective is her conditioning toward passivity in patriarchy, woman is rarely extrovert enough in her maladjustment to enter upon criminality. Just as every minority member must either apologize for the excesses of a fellow or condemn him with a strident enthusiasm, women are characteristically harsh, ruthless and frightened in their censure of aberration among their numbers.

·   ·   ·

[24] My remarks on the minority status of women are summarized from all the articles listed, and I am particularly indebted to an accomplished critique of them in an unpublished draft by Professor Marlene Dixon, formerly of the University of Chicago's Department of Sociology and the Committee on Human Development, presently of McGill University.
[25] See The Commonwealth v. Daniels, 37 L.W. 2064, Pennsylvania Supreme Court, 7/1/68 (reversing 36 L.W. 2004).

Perhaps patriarchy's greatest psychological weapon is simply its universality and longevity. A referent scarcely exists with which it might be contrasted or by which it might be confuted. While the same might be said of class, patriarchy has a still more tenacious or powerful hold through its successful habit of passing itself off as nature. Religion is also universal in human society and slavery was once nearly so; advocates of each were fond of arguing in terms of fatality, or irrevocable human "instinct"—even "biological origins." When a system of power is thoroughly in command, it has scarcely need to speak itself aloud; when its workings are exposed and questioned, it becomes not only subject to discussion, but even to change.

50

Men Are Not Free

William T. Blackstone (1931–77) was a professor of philosophy and chairman of the department of social sciences at the University of Georgia. Among his works are *The Problem of Religious Knowledge* (1963), *Meaning and Existence* (1971), and *Political Philosophy* (1973).

Blackstone differentiates the woman's movement into four separable groups: the traditionalists, the liberals, the Marxists, and the radicals. He then raises the issue of whether or not the following alleged restraints are actually so: (1) capacity to bear children; (2) sexual classification; and (3) marriage and the family.

TO STUDY

1. Can the four alleged positions within the women's movement be definitely differentiated?
2. Which of the three alleged constraints do you believe to be the least constraining?

The women's liberation movement is a complex phenomenon. Within it there are widely different views of the causes of the oppression of women and, consequently, widely different views of what is required to overcome that oppression. Put in a different way, the movement includes widely different views of what constitutes a free person in the social and political sense and, hence, different views of the sort of society required to assure freedom. The full range of political philosophies are represented in this movement. In this paper I want to focus briefly on some of the more radical claims made in the feminist movement. In order to make my target clear, I will sketch in very general terms several positions within or on the feminist movement.[1]

1. The traditionalist stance can hardly be classified as being *within* the women's liberation movement, but it has many advocates and it constitutes one of the parameters on this issue. The traditionalist holds that everything is all right the way it is (or at least it was all right before the feminists came along). Women are different from men and, in many ways, inferior; they are passive, submissive, and are meant to perform different roles. Sex-differentiated labor, sex stereotyping, and the restriction of females in terms of opportunities and roles are not oppression but the fulfillment of women's nature and necessary for family and social cohesion. Women's real freedom and equality are found within these restrictions, and the state should in no way interfere with those social conventions and practices.

2. The liberal, on the other hand (and I have in mind those like Betty Friedan in *The Feminine Mystique* and John Stuart Mill in *The Subjection of Women*), argues that sex-role stereotyping results in great social injustice, that if a woman wants to be a housewife and mother and perform these traditional roles it is perfectly all right, but she should not be systematically excluded from other alternatives or options on account of her sex. If there are relevant differences between men and women which prevent women from filling certain roles or from performing certain roles well, then discriminatory treatment may be justified, but if there are no relevant differences, then discrimination against women is unjust. Women should have equal rights with men—social, economic, political, and legal—the liberal holds, and equal responsibilities. They should be judged as individuals and on the basis of their ability and performance— just as men. To permit this freedom and equality, men must be prepared to assume more responsibility in child rearing; and the state, or private enterprise (some liberals are more laissez faire than others!), must assist in providing some of the conditions required for genuine freedom and

---

[1] Detailed accounts of various positions within the feminist movements are found in Juliet Mitchell's *Woman's Estate* (Baltimore: Penguin Books, 1966); Leslie B. Tanner, ed., *Voices from Women's Liberation* (New York: Signet Books, New American Library, 1970); V. Gornick and B. Moran, *Women in Sexist Society* (New York: Signet Books, New American Library, 1971); and an excellent unpublished essay by Alison Jaggar, "Four Views of Women's Liberation," which was presented at the American Philosophical Association meeting, Western Division, May 4–6, 1972.

Source: William T. Blackstone, "Freedom and Women," *Ethics,* Vol. 85, No. 3 (April 1975), pp. 243–248. Reprinted by permission of The University of Chicago Press and the author.

equality for women—day-care centers, for example. The liberal does not require the abolition of all traditional sex roles, nor does he (she) challenge traditional family values, though he insists on other options as life-styles.

3. Whereas the liberal thinks freedom can be had by reforming the system, the radical argues that freedom is possible only with the overthrow of the political system, and the political system is seen in very broad terms.[2] Marriage and the family are political institutions which oppress women. They must go, as well as the more overt social and legal rules. Radical feminists cover a wide spectrum, but those with leftist leanings believe, with Marx, that the state must "wither away" before genuine freedom is possible and that the economic system of capitalism and the class system which it presupposes must be abolished, for that system is the fundamental cause of all oppression. The oppression of women, in other words, cannot be overcome independently of other oppressions. It is part of a package which must be disposed of altogether. As Margaret Bengsten, a radical leftist feminist, puts it, women in a capitalist system are defined "as that group of people who are responsible for the production of simple use-values in those activities associated with the home and family."[3] She continues: "The material basis for the inferior status of women is to be found in just this definition of women. In a society in which money determines value, women are a group who work outside the money economy. Their work is not worth money, is therefore valueless, is therefore not even real work. And women themselves, who do this valueless work, can hardly be expected to be worth as much as men, who work for money."[4] The means of production must be socialized; there must be "a reintroduction of the entire female sex into public industry," as Engels claims; goods and services must be distributed on the basis of needs; and society as a whole, *not* the family, must be made responsible for the welfare of children, as for everyone else. The radical feminist advocates total revolution, then, not mere reform within the system.

4. Some radical feminists do not buy the entire Marxist line, and they should be accorded a category of their own. I have in mind Shulamith Firestone and her followers. I quote: "There is a level of reality that does not stem directly from economics. . . ."[5] Firestone attempts to de-

[2] Margaret Bengsten is an example of a radical leftist feminist; see her "Political Economy of Women's Liberation," *Monthly Review,* vol. 21 (September 1969), reprinted in *Voices from Women's Liberation* (see n. 1). Mitchell (n. 1) spells out in detail the leftist feminist position.

[3] Bengsten, p. 281.

[4] Ibid., p. 282.

[5] Shulamith Firestone, *The Dialectic of Sex* (New York: Jonathan Cape, 1971), p. 6.

velop "a materialist view of history based on sex itself," arguing that "for feminist revolution we shall need an analysis of the dynamics of sex war as comprehensive as the Marx-Engels analysis of class antagonism was for economic revolution. More comprehensive. For we are dealing with a larger problem, with an oppression that goes back beyond recorded history to the animal kingdom itself."[6] Firestone sees economic class analysis of social injustice as secondary to sex analysis. The biological differences between men and women—the general physical strength of men plus the weakness of women due to childbearing—made men dominant and women dependent. Oppression resulted. Liberation for females is possible only by overcoming these biological differences through technology. Contraception and "artificial reproduction" will free women from their biological inequalities and, subsequently, from social inequalities. Liberation requires the abolition of the whole sex-role system (including childbearing), marriage, and the family. It requires, to quote Firestone, "freedom from sexual classification altogether rather than merely an equalization of sex roles."[7] Freedom and equality, within this radical picture, preclude even the choice of a traditional female role.

Within these four inadequately sketched positions, there is wide disagreement on the meaning of freedom (and equality) for women and on what is required to attain it.

Feminist critics, it seems to me, are in general correct in their claim that women in our society (and others) are oppressed as a class. Many of our laws and our extralegal practices discriminate unfairly against women. I will not attempt to provide the data for that assessment here. The sex-based discrimination of many state laws is well known[8]—laws which permit women to be imprisoned for three years for habitual drunkenness while restricting the penalty for the same offense to thirty days for males; laws which "excuse" all women from jury duty; which permit the withholding of credit from married women on the assumption that they are all financially dependent on their husbands; which permit the plea of "passion" killing for wronged husbands but not wronged wives; which make the father, not the mother or the parents, the "natural guardian" of children; which give the husband right of action in divorce in cases of adultery but not the wife; and work practices in which women are paid less than men for the same work; and so on.

Rather than focus on those feminist evaluations which seem so obvi-

---

[6] Ibid., p. 2.

[7] Shulamith Firestone, "On American Feminism," in *Woman in Sexist Society* (see n. 1), p. 686, n. 4.

[8] See, for example, Diane B. Schulder, "Does the Law Oppress Women?" in *Sisterhood Is Powerful,* ed. Robin Morgan (New York: Random House, 1970), pp. 139–157.

ously correct, I will examine some of the more philosophically controversial evaluations and theses in the feminist movement. I beg off on those expressed in (3) above. Any treatment of the Marxist feminist position would require an assessment of the cluster of factual and valuational assumptions of the political philosophy of communism.[9] I will focus briefly on only a few of the claims in (4) which can stand independently of these assumptions: the theses that childbearing is a restraint on the freedom of women, that it is an unjustified restraint, and that freedom (and equality or social justice) for women requires biological equality, the total abolition of sexual classification, and the abolition of the traditional institutions of marriage and the family. There are other factual and normative theses within (4) which I will not examine, including the claim that "pregnancy is barbaric";[10] the belief that technology not only will be developed to perform the childbearing function but will also free all humans from the necessity to work;[11] the thesis that all sexual repression ought to cease and will cease with the demise of the biological family (everyone, including children, will be permitted "to do whatever they want sexually. . . . humanity could finally revert to its natural 'polymorphously perverse' sexuality"),[12] the claim that wealth should be distributed on the basis of need; and the belief that a communist anarchy is the proper form of government for liberated persons.

First, is childbearing or the capacity to bear children a restraint? The capacity to bear children is a natural capacity which females possess and males do not. We would not say that males are under a restraint because they cannot bear children. Would we say that females are because they can? In neither case is the capacity or incapacity something which is imposed by the social and legal structure. The decision to exercise that capacity for some women may be imposed via an inculcated stereotype image, and that inculcation may properly be seen in some circumstances as a restraint, just as one might view the inculcation of exclusive sex roles in child rearing. These restraints should be lifted or modified and the duties of child rearing shared equitably by men, the liberal believes. But is the capacity to bear children, or the incapacity, itself a restraint? If we stretch the word "restraint" or "unfree" to include the existence or nonexistence of such natural capacities, then clearly anything could

---

[9] I would not write off entirely the Marxist analysis of the oppression of women, but I am not at all convinced that private property is the root of all social evils. If we look at historical realities, unfreedom and oppression (including that of women) are at least as possible under socialist systems as they are under capitalist ones.

[10] Firestone, The Dialectic of Sex, p. 226.

[11] Ibid., p. 235.

[12] Ibid., pp. 236–237.

be counted as a restraint or unfreedom to someone or something, and
the concept of restraint or unfreedom would be functionless, at least in
the sense of permitting the attribution of responsibility for restraints or
unfreedoms. Justified or unjustified complaints about restraints or inabilities presuppose and require that those restraints or inabilities be due to
social and legal arrangements controlled (or controllable) by human beings. Consequently, the biological inequalities or differences between men
and women cannot be viewed as restraints in the responsibility-attributing
sense. They may be viewed as restraints in the sense that they are natural
conditions which limit possibilities and which are present in contexts in
which there is male domination and oppression of women. One can hardly
say, however, that the biological inequalities or differences are responsible
for the social inequalities. Granted, if there were no biological differences
between men and women there would be no social inequalities between
them. This is tautologically true, because there would be no women (or
no men, however one wishes to state this). But it is an extreme solution
to the problem of unjust discrimination against women to obliterate either
the biological differences between men and women (which Firestone does
not propose) or the different biological functions of men and women
(which Firestone does propose). Even if freedom could be purchased
only at the cost of one's sexuality—which is certainly not the case—
this would be a terrible price to pay and, in fact, would vitiate a basic
purpose for which social and political systems are devised, namely, self-
preservation and the fulfillment of each person's interests. For surely a
"self" and "interests" cannot be defined completely apart from sex, sexuality, or biological traits—at least not in the world we know. Perhaps
they could in some possible world, and Shulamith Firestone may be urging
on us this other possible world—in which case we must be prepared to
calculate the advantages and disadvantages of that world as compared
with our own. In our world, the key factors responsible for oppression
are not biological traits but social, economic, political, and legal options
or choices. The oppression due to such choices could exist even under
conditions in which some biological differences are minimized (strength,
for example) or in which certain biological functions (childbearing) are
not performed by women but by machines. Rather than desexualize or
asexualize our world through technology (if indeed this is possible), we
need to change social and legal systems which discriminate irrelevantly
on the basis of sex.

   A second radical feminist thesis which is questionable is that freedom
for women requires "freedom from sexual classification altogether." As
with any claim, everything hangs on its interpretation. If what is meant
is that laws and policies which discriminate solely and arbitrarily on

the basis of sex (and not on the basis of capacities or abilities to do or become something) are unjust and that a society which has such laws oppresses women (and men), this claim is quite acceptable and follows from the basic democratic commitment to equal rights and equal freedom for all.

However, "freedom from sexual classification altogether" may mean much more than freedom from irrelevant classification based on sex or freedom from unjustified differential treatment based on sex. It may require that sex or sexual characteristics be totally ruled out as ever being relevant to the differential treatment of persons or to according equality of treatment. It may require a system of social justice in which sex and sexually associated characteristics (if they exist and whatever they may be) cannot in principle be invoked. Such a system would increase some freedoms by ridding us of some injustices, for there are many institutionalized practices which discriminate arbitrarily on the basis of sex. At the same time, it would lead to some social injustice *if* there were some differences between the sexes which in certain contexts justified differential treatment. The liberal feminist does not want to rule out such possible differences. Abilities or inabilities due to natural capacities (physical strength or weakness, high or low IQ, blindness, and so on) justify differential treatment in our egalitarian ethic. Firestone rules out such differential treatment with respect to gender in the very name of egalitarianism. Her position on this point would be correct only if all relevant facts, characteristics, or circumstances which could in principle justify differential treatment were independent of gender. One must admit that not all the data are in—perhaps very little which can be trusted—and further that many differences between men and women are enculturated. One might go further and agree that most of the relevant grounds for the differential treatment of persons are independent of gender. But I am leery about prejudging the question before a great deal more research is conducted, and in fact there seem to be differences between men and women (which hold in general) which, whether genetically or culturally caused, justify differential treatment (I am thinking primarily of physical strength).

A third radical feminist thesis which seems to me to be mistaken is that freedom for women requires the utter abolition of the traditional institutions of marriage and the family. There is no doubt that these institutions have oppressed women and continue to do so. But Firestone argues that a free society must preclude the traditional sex-differentiated role for women as a possible option.

However, even if technology will one day permit test-tube babies, even if the state could adequately serve as the custodian of all children, and even if society could function without marriage and the family, the ruling out of traditional options decreases freedom to that extent. Even if freedom were kept as a value (in the sense of the total range of options) distinct from social justice (the proper distribution of goods and services) as a value (though, of course, these values are related), her type of society would limit the range of human options in certain directions and expand it in others. An assessment of her type of society would require a comparative assessment of the range of the options given up and those acquired and the social justice or equality purchased at the cost of limiting human options in her way. Here the liberal feminist's response to the radical is that both social justice for women and the expanded range of options can be had without the preclusion (though not without some alternation) of traditional options (marriage and the family). Marriage and role divisions within marriage are not inherently exploitive and oppressive, though they may be oppressive if predicated on psychological, social, and economic oppression and exploitation (and, of course, many marriages and role divisions are). There is, in other words, no necessary conflict between freedom to choose from a range of options, including traditional roles, and equality or social justice for women. And, with proper modification, the family as an institution need not be a perpetuator of sexist discrimination—though other sorts of inequalities perpetuated by the family as an institution (those stressed in literature from Plato's *Republic* to the Coleman report on *Equality of Educational Opportunity*)[13] are not as easily modified.[14]

Readings

Freedom

1. Adler, Mortimer J. *The Idea of Freedom,* 2 vols. Garden City, N.Y.: Doubleday, 1958–1961. Summarizes the results of research done by the staff of the Institute for Philosophical Research. Volume I examines conceptions of freedom. Volume II examines controversies about freedom.

2. Chafee, Z. *Free Speech in the United States.* Cambridge: Harvard Univ. Press. 1940. An excellent book on free speech and its history.

---

[13] James S. Coleman et al., *Equality of Educational Opportunity* (Washington, D.C.: Government Printing Office, 1966).

[14] See my "Human Rights, Equality, and Education," *Educational Theory,* vol. 19, no. 3 (1969), for discussion.

3. Cranston, Maurice. *Freedom: A New Analysis.* London: Longmans, Green, 1953. A three-part study dealing with the meaning of freedom, the ambiguity of liberalism, and the freedom of the will.

4. Manning, Clarence A. "The Grand Inquisitor," *American Theological Review,* XV (January 1933), 16–20.

5. Muller, Herbert J. *Issues of Freedom: Paradoxes and Promises.* New York: Harper, 1960. Concerned with the meanings of freedom, the assumptions made in holding a view of freedom, and the basic cultural factors relevant to freedom.

6. ———. "Freedom and Justice in History" in D. Bidney, ed., *The Concept of Freedom in Anthropology.* New York: Humanities Press, 1963. A short history of freedom and justice including their relation to "The Grand Inquisitor."

7. Ramsey, Paul. "No Morality Without Immortality: Dostoevski and the Meaning of Atheism," *Journal of Religion,* XXXVI (April, 1956), 90–108.

Civil Liberties

1. Abraham, Henry. *Freedom and the Court.* New York: Oxford V. P., 1972.

2. Barker, Lucius J., and Twiley W. Barker, Jr. *Freedom, Courts, Politics: Studies in Civil Liberties.* Englewood Cliffs: Prentice-Hall, 1965. The problem of civil liberties is examined in six areas including religion, free speech, and obscenity through illustrative Supreme Court cases and decisions.

3. Barth, Alan. *The Price of Liberty.* New York: Viking, 1961.

4. Brant, Irving. *The Bill of Rights: Its Origin and Meaning.* Indianapolis and New York: Bobbs-Merrill, 1965. A study of the origins of our constitutional liberties and a stress on the freedoms of religion, speech, press, assembly, petition, and association.

5. Commager, Henry Steele, *et al. Civil Liberties under Attack.* Ed. by Clair Wilcox. Philadelphia: U. of Pennsylvania Press, 1951. (Swarthmore College, William J. Cooper Foundation.) Six specialists discuss different aspects of the problem of freedom and civil rights. Clear and readable.

6. Hook, Sidney. "Neither Blind Obedience nor Uncivil Disobedience," *New York Times Magazine* (June 5, 1966), pp. 52–53, 122,124, 126,128.

7. *Cornell Studies in Civil Liberty.* Ed. by Robert E. Cushman. Ithaca: Cornell U. Press. A series of books including: *Security, Loyalty, and Science,* Walter Gellhorn, 1950; *The House Committee on Un-American Activities,* Robert H. Carr, 1952; *The States and Subversion,* edited by Walter Gellhorn, 1952; *The Federal Loyalty-Security Program,* Eleanor Bontecou, 1953. These and other books in the series deal with special problems in the area of the civil liberties. They are well documented.

8. Muller, Herbert J. *Issues of Freedom.* New York. Harper, 1960. A small book, in the World Perspective series, edited by Ruth Nanda Anshen. It considers freedom in relation to culture: Part One, "The Premises of Inquiry"; Part Two, "The Basic Cultural Factors."

9. Rossiter, Clinton. *Conservatism in America, The Thankless Persuasion.* 2nd ed. New York: Knopf, 1966. The conservative tradition in American history defined, described, and brought up-to-date with a forecast for the future.

Women and Freedom

1. de Beauvoir, Simone. *The Second Sex.* Trans. H. M. Parshley. New York: Bantam, 1961.

2. de Rougement, Denis. *Love in the Western World.* Greenwich, Conn.: Fawcett, 1966. Especially good on the inter-relationship of love and war; author relies heavily on Freudian psychology.

3. Densmore, Dana. *Sex Roles and Female Oppression—A Collection of Articles.* Boston: New England Free Press, 1969.

4. Lifton, Robert Jay, ed. *The Woman in America.* Boston: Beacon, 1967. Includes essays by Erik H. Erikson, Diana Trilling, Alice S. Rossi, and others.

5. Reed, Evelyn. *Problems of Women's Liberation: A Marxist Approach.* New York: Merit, 1969.

four

What Is the
Best Government?

51

Communism

Karl Marx (1818–1883) was born in Germany and lived in London after 1850. He wrote his Ph.D. thesis (1842) on Greek atomistic philosophy. Marx was the editor of *Rheinische Zeitung* (1842) which was suppressed in 1843. He joined **Frederick Engels** in Paris to develop the theory of socialism. He criticized Proudhon (1847) and founded the First International Workingmen's Association (1864). He is the author of *Communist Manifesto* (1847), *Das Kapital* (1867), *Civil War in France* (1871), *Critique of Political Economy* (1859).

There are many types of political and economic systems among the nations of the world. The economic systems range from almost complete free enterprise to an almost total state economic control. The political systems range from the democratic to the dictatorships. These economic and political systems are seen in almost every possible combination. Among the best known are communism, which nearly always combines a state economic system with a dictatorship; fascism, which is a modified capitalism with a dictatorship; and democracy, which most often is a combination of political democracy with capitalism, although it is also often combined with a modified government-controlled economy such as in the European socialist countries

The program of communism was set forth in 1848 by Marx in the famous *Communist Manifesto,* in which he applies his principles of materialism and dialectical method to the problems of society. It contains a general theory of history, an analysis of the ills of European society, a program of revolutionary action, and finally a plea for the union of the laboring classes.

---TO STUDY

1. Into what groups does Marx divide the history of man?
2. Into what groups does he divide present society? How are these groups defined?
3. What characteristics and social actions does Marx attribute to the bourgeoisie?
4. What economic acts does Marx attribute to the bourgeoisie? How does the bourgeoisie overcome its economic crises?
5. Who created the proletariat? How is it defined?
6. What happens to the middle class?
7. Why is the bourgeoisie unfit to rule?
8. What "measures" will the proletariat use to wrestle the capital from the bourgeoisie, etc.? How many of these measures are incorporated in American life? Which would you like to see realized? Which removed?

A spectre is haunting Europe—the spectre of Communism. All the Powers of old Europe have entered into a holy alliance to exorcise this spectre: Pope and Czar, Metternich and Guizot, French Radicals and German police spies.

Where is the party in opposition that has not been decried as Communistic by its opponents in power? Where the Opposition that has not hurled back the branding reproach of Communism, against the more advanced opposition parties, as well as against its reactionary adversaries?

Two things result from this fact.

I. Communism is already acknowledged by all European Powers to be itself a Power.

II. It is high time that Communists should openly, in the face of the whole world, publish their views, their aims, their tendencies, and meet this nursery tale of the Spectre of Communism with a Manifesto of the party itself.

To this end, Communists of various nationalities have assembled in London, and sketched the following Manifesto, to be published in the English, French, German, Italian, Flemish and Danish languages.

Selected from the *Manifesto of the Communist Party* by Karl Marx and Frederick Engels, translated by Samuel Moore in 1888 from the original German text of 1848 and edited by Frederick Engels (Progress Publishers, Moscow). Footnotes have been omitted.

I
Bourgeois and Proletarians

The history of all hitherto existing society is the history of class struggles.

Freeman and slave, patrician and plebeian, lord and serf, guildmaster and journeyman, in a word, oppressor and oppressed, stood in constant opposition to one another, carried on an uninterrupted, now hidden, now open fight, a fight that each time ended, either in a revolutionary re-constitution of society at large, or in the common ruin of the contending classes.

In the earlier epochs of history, we find almost everywhere a complicated arrangement of society into various orders, a manifold gradation of social rank. In ancient Rome we have patricians, knights, plebeians, slaves; in the Middle Ages, feudal lords, vassals, guild-masters, journeymen, apprentices, serfs; in almost all of these classes, again, subordinate gradations.

The modern bourgeois society that has sprouted from the ruins of feudal society has not done away with class antagonisms. It has but established new classes, new conditions of oppression, new forms of struggle in place of the old ones.

Our epoch, the epoch of the bourgeoisie, possesses, however, this distinctive feature: it has simplified the class antagonisms. Society as a whole is more and more splitting up into two great hostile camps, into two great classes directly facing each other: Bourgeoisie and Proletariat.

From the serfs of the Middle Ages sprang the chartered burghers of the earliest towns. From the burgesses the first elements of the bourgeoisie were developed.

The discovery of America, the rounding of the Cape, opened up fresh ground for the rising bourgeoisie. The East-Indian and Chinese markets, the colonisation of America, trade with the colonies, the increase in the means of exchange and in commodities generally, gave to commerce, to navigation, to industry, an impulse never before known, and thereby, to the revolutionary element in the tottering feudal society, a rapid development.

The feudal system of industry, under which industrial production was monopolised by closed guilds, now no longer sufficed for the growing wants of the new markets. The manufacturing system took its place. The guild-masters were pushed on one side by the manufacturing middle class; division of labour between the different corporate guilds vanished in the face of division of labour in each single workshop.

Meantime the markets kept ever growing, the demand ever rising. Even manufacture no longer sufficed. Thereupon, steam and machinery revolutionised industrial production. The place of manufacture was taken by the giant, Modern Industry, the place of the industrial middle class, by industrial millionaires, the leaders of whole industrial armies, the modern bourgeois.

Modern industry has established the world market, for which the discovery of America paved the way. This market has given an immense development to commerce, to navigation, to communication by land. This development has, in its turn, reacted on the extension of industry; and in proportion as industry, commerce, navigation, railways extended, in the same proportion the bourgeoisie developed, increased its capital, and pushed into the background every class handed down from the Middle Ages.

We see, therefore, how the modern bourgeoisie is itself the product of a long course of development, of a series of revolutions in the modes of production and of exchange. . . .

The bourgeoisie, wherever it has got the upper hand, has put an end to all feudal, patriarchal, idyllic relations. It has pitilessly torn asunder the motley feudal ties that bound man to his "natural superiors", and has left remaining no other nexus between man and man than naked self-interest, than callous "cash payment". It has drowned the most heavenly ecstasies of religous fervour, of chivalrous enthusiasm, of philistine sentimentalism, in the icy water of egotistical calculation. It has resolved personal worth into exchange value, and in place of the numberless indefeasible chartered freedoms, has set up that single, unconscionable freedom—Free Trade. In one word, for exploitation, veiled by religious and political illusions, it has substituted naked, shameless, direct, brutal exploitation.

The bourgeoisie has stripped of its halo every occupation hitherto honoured and looked up to with reverent awe. It has converted the physician, the lawyer, the priest, the poet, the man of science, into its paid wage-labourers.

The bourgeoisie has torn away from the family its sentimental zeal and has reduced the family relation to a mere money relation.

The bourgeoisie has disclosed how it came to pass that the brutal display of vigor in the Middle Ages, which Reactionists so much admire, found its fitting complement in the most slothful indolence. It has been the first to shew what man's activity can bring about. It has accomplished wonders far surpassing Egyptian pyramids, Roman aqueducts, and Gothic cathedrals; it has conducted expeditions that put in the shade all former Exoduses of nations and crusades.

The bourgeoisie cannot exist without constantly revolutionising the instruments of production, and thereby the relations of production, and with them the whole relations of society. Conservation of the old modes of production in unaltered form, was, on the contrary, the first condition of existence for all earlier industrial classes. Constant revolutionising of production, uninterrupted disturbance of all social conditions, everlasting uncertainty and agitation distinguished the bourgeois epoch from all earlier ones. All fixed, fast-frozen relations, with their train of ancient and venerable prejudices and opinions are swept away, all new-formed ones become antiquated before they can ossify. All that is solid melts into air, all that is holy is profaned, and man is at last compelled to face with sober senses, his real conditions of life, and his relations with his kind.

The need of a constantly expanding market for its products chases the bourgeoisie over the whole surface of the globe. It must nestle everywhere, settle everywhere, establish connexions everywhere.

The bourgeoisie has through its exploitation of the world market given a cosmopolitan character to production and consumption in every country. To the great chagrin of Reactionists, it has drawn from under the feet of industry the national ground on which it stood. All old-established national industries have been destroyed or are daily being destroyed. They are dislodged by new industries, whose introduction becomes a life and death question for all civilized nations, by industries that no longer work up indigenous raw material, but raw material drawn from the remotest zones; industries whose products are consumed, not only at home, but in every quarter of the globe. In place of the old wants, satisfied by the productions of the country, we find new wants, requiring for their satisfaction the products of distant lands and climes. In place of the old local and national seclusion and self-sufficiency, we have intercourse in every direction, universal inter-dependence of nations. And as in material, so also in intellectual production. The intellectual creations of individual nations become common property. National one-sidedness and narrow-mindedness become more and more impossible, and from the numerous national and local literatures, there arises a world literature.

The bourgeoisie, by the rapid improvement of all instruments of production, by the immensely facilitated means of communication, draws all, even the most barbarian, nations into civilisation. The cheap prices of its commodities are the heavy artillery with which it batters down all Chinese walls, with which it forces the barbarians' intensely obstinate hatred of foreigners to capitulate. It compels all nations, on pain of extinction, to adopt the bourgeois mode of production; it compels them to introduce what it calls civilisation into their midst, *i.e.,* to become bourgeois themselves. In one word, it creates a world after its own image.

The bourgeoisie has subjected the country to the rule of the towns. It has created enormous cities, has greatly increased the urban population as compared with the rural, and has thus rescued a considerable part of the population from the idiocy of rural life. Just as it has made the country dependent on the towns, so it has made barbarian and semi-barbarian countries dependent on the civilised ones, nations of peasants on nations of bourgeois, the East on the West.

The bourgeoisie keeps more and more doing away with the scattered state of the population, of the means of production, and of property. It has agglomerated population, centralised means of production, and has concentrated property in a few hands. The necessary consequence of this was political centralisation. Independent, or but loosely connected, provinces with separate interests, laws, governments and systems of taxation, became lumped together into one nation, with one government, one code of laws, one national class-interest, one frontier and one customs-tariff.

The bourgeoisie, during its rule of scarce one hundred years, has created more massive and more colossal productive forces than have all preceding generations together. Subjection of Nature's forces to man, machinery, application of chemistry to industry and agriculture, steam-navigation, railways, electric telegraphs, clearing of whole continents for cultivation, canalisation of rivers, whole populations conjured out of the ground—what earlier century had even a presentiment that such productive forces slumbered in the lap of social labour?

We see then: the means of production and of exchange, on whose foundation the bourgeoisie built itself up, were generated in feudal society. At a certain stage in the development of these means of production and of exchange, the conditions under which feudal society produced and exchanged, the feudal organisation of agriculture and manufacturing industry, in one word, the feudal relations of property became no longer compatible with the already developed productive forces; they became so many fetters. They had to be burst asunder; they were burst asunder.

Into their place stepped free competition, accompanied by a social and political constitution adapted to it, and by the economical and political sway of the bourgeois class.

A similar movement is going on before our own eyes. Modern bourgeois society with its relations of production, of exchange and of property, a society that has conjured up such gigantic means of production and of exchange, is like the sorcerer, who is no longer able to control the powers of the nether world whom he has called up by his spells. For many a decade past the history of industry and commerce is but the history of the revolt of modern productive forces against modern conditions of production, against the property relations that are the conditions for the existence of the bourgeoisie and of its rule. It is enough to mention the commercial crises that by their periodical return put on its trial, each time more threateningly, the existence of the entire bourgeois society. In these crises a great part not only of the existing products, but also of the previously created productive forces, are periodically destroyed. In these crises there breaks out an epidemic that, in all earlier epochs, would have seemed an absurdity—the epidemic of overproduction. Society suddenly finds itself put back into a state of momentary barbarism; it appears as if a famine, a universal war of devastation had cut off the supply of every means of subsistence; industry and commerce seem to be destroyed; and why? Because there is too much civilisation, too much means of subsistence, too much industry, too much commerce. The productive forces at the disposal of society no longer tend to further the development of the conditions of bourgeois property; on the contrary, they have become too powerful for these conditions, by which they are fettered, and so soon as they overcome these fetters, they bring disorder into the whole of bourgeois society, endanger the existence of bourgeois property. The conditions of bourgeois society are too narrow to compromise the wealth created by them. And how does the bourgeoisie get over these crises? On the one hand by enforced destruction of a mass of productive forces; on the other, by the conquest of new markets, and by the more thorough exploitation of the old ones. That is to say, by paving the way for more extensive and more destructive crises, and by diminishing the means whereby crises are prevented.

The weapons with which the bourgeoisie felled feudalism to the ground are now turned against the bourgeoisie itself.

But not only has the bourgeoisie forged the weapons that bring death to itself; it has also called into existence the men who are to wield those weapons—the modern working class—the proletarians.

In proportion as the bourgeoisie, i.e., capital, is developed, in the same proportion is the proletariat, the modern working class, developed—a class of labourers, who live only so long as they find work, and who find work only so long as their labour increases capital. These labourers, who must sell themselves piecemeal, are a commodity, like every other article of commerce, and are consequently exposed to all the vicissitudes of competition, to all the fluctuations of the market.

Owing to the extensive use of machinery and to division of labour, the work of the proletarians has lost all individual character, and, consequently, all charm for the workman. He becomes an appendage of the machine, and it is only the most simple, most monotonous, and most easily acquired knack, that is required of him. Hence, the cost of production of a workman is restricted, almost entirely, to the means of subsistence that he requires for his maintenance, and for the propagation of his race. But the price of a commodity, and therefore also of labour, is equal to its cost of production. In proportion, therefore, as the repulsiveness of the work increases, the wage decreases. Nay more, in proportion as the use of machinery and division of labour increases, in the same proportion the burden of toil also increases, whether by prolongation of the working hours, by increase of the work exacted in a given time or by increased speed of the machinery, etc.

Modern industry has converted the little workshop of the patriarchal master into the great factory of the industrial capitalist. Masses of labourers, crowded into the factory, are organised like soldiers. As privates of the industrial army they are placed under the command of a perfect hierarchy of officers and sergeants. Not only are they slaves of the bourgeois class, and of the bourgeois State; they are daily and hourly enslaved by the machine, by the overlooker, and, above all, by the individual bourgeois manufacturer himself. The more openly this despotism proclaims gain to be its end and aim, the more petty, the more hateful and more embittering it is.

The less the skill and exertion of strength implied in manual labor, in other words, the more modern industry becomes developed, the more is the labour of men superseded by that of women. Differences of age and sex have no longer any distinctive social validity for the working class. All are instruments of labour, more or less expensive to use, according to their age and sex.

No sooner is the exploitation of the labourer by the manufacturer, so far, at an end, that he receives his wages in cash, than he is set upon by the other portions of the bourgeoisie, the landlord, the storekeeper, the pawnbroker, etc.

The lower strata of the middle class—the small tradespeople, shop-keepers, and retired tradesmen generally, the handicraftsmen and peas-ants—all these sink gradually into the proletariat, partly because their diminutive capital does not suffice for the scale on which Modern Industry is carried on, and is swamped in the competition with the large capitalists, partly because their specialised skill is rendered worthless by new methods of production. Thus the proletariat is recruited from all classes of the population.

The proletariat goes through various stages of development. With its birth begins its struggle with the bourgeoisie. At first the contest is carried on by individual labourers, then by the workpeople of a factory, then by the operatives of one trade, in one locality, against the individual bourgeois who directly exploits them. They direct their attacks not against the bour-geois conditions of production, but against the instruments of production themselves; they destroy imported wares that compete with their labour, they smash to pieces machinery, they set factories ablaze, they seek to restore by force the vanished status of the workman of the Middle Ages.

At this stage the labourers still form an incoherent mass scattered over the whole country, and broken up by their mutual competition. If anywhere they unite to form more compact bodies, this is not yet the consequence of their own active union, but of the union of the bourgeoisie, which class, in order to attain its own political ends, is compelled to set the whole proletariat in motion, and is moreover yet, for a time, able to do so. At this stage, therefore, the proletarians do not fight their enemies, but the enemies of their enemies, the remnants of absolute monarchy, the landowners, the non-industrial bourgeois, the petty bourgeoisie. Thus the whole historical movement is concentrated in the hands of the bourgeoisie; every victory so obtained is a victory for the bourgeoisie.

But with the development of industry the proletariat not only increases in number; it becomes concentrated in greater masses, its strength grows, and it feels that strengh more. The various interests and conditions of life within the ranks of the proletariat are more and more equalised, in proportion as machinery obliterates all distinctions of labour, and nearly everywhere reduces wages to the same low level. The growing competition among the bourgeois, and the resulting commercial crises, make the wages of the workers ever more fluctuating. The unceasing improvement of machinery, ever more rapidly developing, makes their livelihood more and more precarious; the collisions between individual workmen and individual bourgeois take more and more the character of collisions between two classes. Thereupon the workers begin to form combinations (Trades' Unions) against the bourgeois; they club together in order to keep up the rate of wages; they found permanent associations in order to make provision beforehand for these occasional revolts. Here and there the contest breaks out into riots.

Now and then the workers are victorious, but only for a time. The real fruit of their battles lies, not in the immediate result, but in the ever-expanding union of the workers. This union is helped on by the improved means of communication that are created by modern industry and that place the workers of different localities in contact with one another. It was just this contact that was needed to centralise the numerous local struggles, all of the same character, into one national struggle between classes. But every class struggle is a political struggle. And that union, to attain which the burghers of the Middle Ages, with their miserable highways, required centuries, the modern proletarians, thanks to railroads, achieve in a few years.

This organisation of the proletarians into a class, and consequently into a political party, is continually being upset again by the competition between the workers themselves. But it ever rises up again, stronger, firmer, mightier. It compels legislative recognition of particular interests of the workers, by taking advantage of the divisions among the bourgeoisie itself. Thus the ten-hours' bill in England was carried.

Altogether, collisions between the classes of the old society further, in many ways, the course of development of the proletariat. The bourgeoisie finds itself involved in a constant battle. At first with the aristocracy; later on, with those portions of the bourgeoisie itself, whose interests have become antagonistic to the progress of industry; at all times, with the bourgeoisie of foreign countries. In all these battles it sees itself compelled to appeal to the proletariat, to ask for its help, and thus, to drag it into the political arena. The bourgeoisie itself, therefore, supplies the proletariat with its own elements of political and general education, in other words, it furnishes the proletariat with weapons for fighting the bourgeoisie.

Further, as we have already seen, entire sections of the ruling classes are, by the advance of industry, precipitated into the proletariat, or are at least threatened in their conditions of existence. These also supply the proletariat with fresh elements of enlightenment and progress.

Finally, in times when the class struggle nears the decisive hour, the process of dissolution going on within the ruling class, in fact within the whole range of old society, assumes such a violent, glaring character, that a small section of the ruling class cuts itself adrift, and joins the revolutionary class, the class that holds the future in its hands. Just as, therefore, at an earlier period, a section of the nobility went over to the bourgeoisie, so now a portion of the bourgeoisie goes over to the proletariat, and in particular, a portion of the bourgeois ideologists, who have raised themselves to the level of comprehending theoretically the historical movement as a whole.

Of all the classes that stand face to face with the bourgeoisie today, the proletariat alone is a really revolutionary class. The other classes decay and finally disappear in the face of modern industry; the proletariat is its special and essential product.

The lower middle class, the small manufacturer, the shopkeeper, the artisan, the peasant, all these fight against the bourgeoisie, to save from extinction their existence as fractions of the middle class. They are therefore not revolutionary, but conservative. Nay more, they are reactionary, for they try to roll back the wheel of history. If by chance they are revolutionary, they are so only in view of their impending transfer into the proletariat, they thus defend not their present, but their future interests, they desert their own standpoint to place themselves at that of the proletariat.

The "dangerous class", the social scum, that passively rotting mass thrown off by the lowest layers of old society, may, here and there, be swept into the movement by a proletarian revolution; its conditions of life, however, prepare it far more for the part of a bribed tool of reactionary intrigue.

In the conditions of the proletariat, those of old society at large are already virtually swamped. The proletarian is without property; his relation to his wife and children has no longer anything in common with the bourgeois family relations; modern industrial labour, modern subjection to capital, the same in England as in France, in America as in Germany, has stripped him of every trace of national character. Law, morality, religion, are to him so many bourgeois prejudices, behind which lurk in ambush just as many bourgeois interests.

All the preceding classes that got the upper hand, sought to fortify their already acquired status by subjecting society at large to their conditions of appropriation. The proletarians cannot become masters of the productive forces of society, except by abolishing their own previous mode of appropriation, and thereby also every other previous mode of appropriation. They have nothing of their own to secure and to fortify; their mission is to destroy all previous securities for, and insurances of, individual property.

All previous historical movements were movements of minorities, or in the interest of minorities. The proletarian movement is the self-conscious, independent movement of the immense majority, in the interest of the immense majority. The proletariat, the lowest stratum of our present society, cannot stir, cannot raise itself up, without the whole superincumbent strata of official society being sprung into the air.

Though not in substance, yet in form, the struggle of the proletariat with the bourgeoisie is at first a national struggle. The proletariat of each country must, of course, first of all settle matters with its own bourgeoisie.

In depicting the most general phases of the development of the proletariat, we traced the more or less veiled civil war, raging within existing society, up to the point where that war breaks out into open revolution, and where the violent overthrow of the bourgeoisie lays the foundation for the sway of the proletariat.

Hitherto, every form of society has been based, as we have already seen, on the antagonism of oppressing and oppressed classes. But in order to oppress a class, certain conditions must be assured to it under which it can, at least, continue its slavish existence. The serf, in the period of serfdom, raised himself to membership in the commune, just as the petty bourgeois, under the yoke of feudal absolutism, managed to develop into a bourgeois. The modern labourer, on the contrary, instead of rising with the progress of industry, sinks deeper and deeper below the conditions of existence of his own class. He becomes a pauper, and pauperism develops more rapidly than population and wealth. And here it becomes evident, that the bourgeoisie is unfit any longer to be the ruling class in society, and to impose its conditions of existence upon society as an over-riding law. It is unfit to rule because it is incompetent to assure an existence to its slave within his slavery, because it cannot help letting him sink into such a state, that it has to feed him, instead of being fed by him. Society can no longer live under this bourgeoisie, in other words, its existence is no longer compatible with society.

The essential condition for the existence, and for the sway of the bourgeois class, is the formation and augmentation of capital; the condition for capital is wage labour. Wage labour rests exclusively on competition between the labourers. The advance of industry, whose involuntary promoter is the bourgeoisie, replaces the isolation of the labourers, due to competition, by their revolutinary combination, due to association. The development of Modern Industry, therefore, cuts from under its feet the very foundation on which the bourgeoisie produces and appropriates products. What the bourgeoisie, therefore, produces, above all, is its own grave-diggers. Its fall and the victory of the proletariat are equally inevitable.

II
Proletarians and Communists

In what relation do the Communists stand to the proletarians as a whole?

The Communists do not form a separate party opposed to other working-class parties.

They have no interests separate and apart from those of the proletariat as a whole.

They do not set up any sectarian principles of their own, by which to shape and mould the proletarian movement.

The Communists are distinguished from the other working-class parties by this only: 1. In the national struggles of the proletarians of the different countries, they point out and bring to the front the common interests of the entire proletariat, independently of all nationality. 2. In the various stages of development which the struggle of the working class against the bourgeoisie has to pass through, they always and everywhere represent the interests of the movement as a whole.

The Communists, therefore, are on the one hand, practically, the most advanced and resolute section of the working-class parties of every country, that section which pushes forward all others; on the other hand, theoretically, they have over the great mass of the proletariat the advantage of clearly understanding the line of march, the conditions, and the ultimate general results of the proletarian government.

The immediate aim of the Communists is the same as that of all the other proletarian parties: formation of the proletariat into a class, overthrow of the bourgeois supremacy, conquest of political power by the proletariat. . . .

The proletariat will use its political supremacy to wrest, by degrees, all capital from the bourgeoisie, to centralise all instruments of production in the hands of the State, i.e., of the proletariat organised as the ruling class; and to increase the total of productive forces as rapidly as possible.

Of course, in the beginning, this cannot be effected except by means of despotic inroads on the rights of property, and on the conditions of bourgeois production; by means of measures, therefore, which appear economically insufficient and untenable, but which, in the course of the movement, outstrip themselves, necessitate further inroads upon the old social order, and are unavoidable as a means of entirely revolutionising the mode of production.

These measures will of course be different in different countries.

Nevertheless in the most advanced countries, the following will be pretty generally applicable.

1. Abolition of property in land and application of all rents of land to public purposes.

2. A heavy progressive or graduated income tax.

3. Abolition of all right of inheritance.

4. Confiscation of the property of all emigrants an rebels.

5. Centralisation of credit in the hands of the State, by means of a national bank with State capital and an exclusive monopoly.

6. Centralisation of the means of communication and transport in the hands of the State.

7. Extension of factories and instruments of production owned by the State; the bringing into cultivation of waste-lands, and the improvement of the soil generally in accordance with a common plan.

8. Equal liability of all to labour. Establishment of industrial armies, especially for agriculture.

9. Combination of agriculture with manufacturing industries; gradual abolition of the distinction between town and country, by a more equable distribution of the population over the country.

10. Free education for all children in public schools. Abolition of children's factory labour in its present form. Combination of education with industrial production, &c., &c.

When, in the course of development, class distinctions have disappeared, and all production has been concentrated in the hands of a vast association of the whole nation, the public power will lose its political character. Political power, properly so called, is merely the organised power of one class for oppressing another. If the proletariat during its contest with the bourgeoisie is compelled, by the force of circumstances, to organise itself as a class, if, by means of a revolution, it makes itself the ruling class, and, as such, sweeps away by force the old conditions of production, then it will, along with these conditions, have swept away the conditions for the existence of class antagonisms and of classes generally, and will thereby have abolished its own supremacy as a class.

In place of the old bourgeois society, with its classes and class antagonisms, we shall have an association, in which the free development of each is the condition for the free development of all. . . .

The Communists disdain to conceal their views and aims. They openly declare that their ends can be attained only by the forcible overthrow of all existing social conditions. Let the ruling classes tremble at a Communistic revolution. The proletarians have nothing to lose but their chains. They, have a world to win.

WORKING MEN OF ALL COUNTRIES, UNITE!

————————————————————— THINK ABOUT

1. Distinguish between right, left, and center in social and political philosophy, and indicate where you stand and why. List specific groups in society that you think can reasonably be placed under each of these headings.

2. Indicate why you agree or disagree with the following statement by Samuel Eliot Morison in *Freedom in Contemporary Society* (Boston: Little, Brown, 1956), p. 29:

    In my opinion, the growth of democracy in the United States has not contributed to the growth of political freedom. And the reasons, I think, are clear: (1) Political education has never caught up with political power. (2) The religious sanction to government has declined, with commensurate loss of public virtue; character and intelligence are losing the race to greed and selfishness. It is only by comparison with totalitarian governments, where the religious sanction is wholly wanting, and where free rein is given to cruelty and other abominable traits of human nature, that we are reconciled to the milder ills and supportable disadvantages of democracy.

3. Adherents of the two great contrasting systems cast the same reproaches at each other. The one party considers economic freedom as one of the fundamental rights of the individual, and believes that it is in fact the very condition upon which the material and the moral health of a society depends. Therefore, it denounces economic planning as a form of tyranny which must be fought

against in the name of the sacred value of liberty. The other party asserts that the liberation of individuals can be guaranteed only by an economic structure devoid of the faults of individual profit-seeking. . . .

4. "An appeal to principles is the condition of any considerable reconstruction of society, because social institutions are the visible expression of the scale of moral values which rules the minds of individuals, and it is impossible to alter institutions without altering that valuation."

R. H. Tawney (1920)

5. "It is not the business of government to make men virtuous or religious, or to preserve the fool from the consequences of his own folly. Governments should be repressive no further than is necessary to secure liberty by protecting the equal rights of each from aggression on the part of others. . . . Out of the principle that it is the proper end and purpose of government to secure the natural rights and equal liberty of the individual, grows the principle that it is the business of government to do for the mass of individuals those things which cannot be done, or cannot be so well done, by individual action."

Henry George (1883)

52

Fascism

Benito Mussolini (1883–1945) was an Italian dictator from 1922 to 1943 and founder of the Fascist Party. In 1932 he published *The Doctrine of Fascism.*

Fascism is a totalitarian government system led by a dictator and emphasizing an aggressive nationalism. Mussolini was the leader of the Italian fascist government from 1922 until his death in 1945. His famous article on the philosophy of fascism brings out its three elements: the absolute authoritarianism, in which the dictator is the law; the organistic state, in which the interest of the state is above the interest of any particular member; and finally an attitude of irrationalism, which emphasizes social myths which are often related to nationalistic feelings.

TO STUDY

1. According to Mussolini, what does every concept of the state involve?

2. In what sense does the Fascist state have a spiritual existence?

3. In what sense is Fascism an historical conception?

4. What is the relation of the individual to the state? How does it differ from classical liberalism?

5. What is the nature of liberty in the Fascist state?

6. Why is Fascism opposed to democracy?

7. In what sense is Fascism totalitarian?

8. In what sense is the state an organic person?

1. Like every sound political conception, Fascism is both practice and thought; action in which a doctrine is immanent, and a doctrine which, arising out of a given system of historical forces, remains embedded in them and works there from within. Hence it has a form correlative to the contingencies of place and time, but it has also a content of thought which raises it to a formula of truth in the higher level of the history of thought. In the world one does not act spiritually as a human will dominating other wills without a conception of the transient and particular reality under which it is necessary to act, and of the permanent and universal reality in which the first has its being and its life. In order to know men it is necessary to know man; and in order to know man it is necessary to know reality and its laws. There is no concept of the State which is not fundamentally a concept of life: philosophy or intuition, a system of ideas which develops logically or is gathered up into a vision or into a faith, but which is always, at least virtually, an organic conception of the world.

2. Thus Fascism could not be understood in many of its practical manifestations as a party organization, as a system of education, as a discipline, if it were not always looked at in the light of its whole way of conceiving life, a spiritualized way. The world seen through Fascism is not this material world which appears on the surface, in which man is an individual separated from all others and standing by himself, and in which he is governed by a natural law that makes him instinctively live a life of selfish and momentary pleasure. The man of Fascism is an individual who is nation and fatherland, which is a moral law, binding together individuals and the generations into a tradition and a mission, suppressing the instinct of a life enclosed within the brief round of pleasure in order to restore within duty a higher life free from the limits of time and space: a life in which the individual, through the denial of himself, through the sacrifice of his own private interests, through death itself, realizes that completely spiritual existence in which his value as a man lies.

3. Therefore it is a spiritualized conception, itself the result of the general reaction of modern times against the flabby materialistic positivism of the nineteenth century. Anti-positivistic, but positive: not sceptical, nor agnostic, nor pessimistic, nor passively optimistic, as are, in general, the doctrines (all negative) that put the centre of life outside man, who with his free will can and must create his own world. Fascism desires an active man, one engaged in activity with all his energies: it desires a man virilely conscious of the difficulties that exist in action and ready to face them. It

From *The Social and Political Doctrines of Contemporary Europe*, ed. Michael Oakeshott (New York: Cambridge University Press, 1939), pp. 164–181. Reprinted by permission of the publisher.

conceives of life as a struggle, considering that it behoves man to conquer for himself that life truly worthy of him, creating first of all in himself the instrument (physical, moral, intellectual) in order to construct it. Thus for the single individual, thus for the nation, thus for humanity. Hence the high value of culture in all its forms (art, religion, science), and the enormous importance of education. Hence also the essential value of work, with which man conquers nature and creates the human world (economic, political, moral, intellectual).

4. This positive conception of life is clearly an ethical conception. It covers the whole of reality, not merely the human activity which controls it. No action can be divorced from moral judgement; there is nothing in the world which can be deprived of the value which belongs to everything in its relation to moral ends. Life, therefore, as conceived by the Fascist, is serious, austere, religious: the whole of it is poised in a world supported by the moral and responsible forces of the spirit. The Fascist disdains the "comfortable" life.

5. Fascism is a religious conception in which man is seen in his immanent relationship with a superior law and with an objective Will that transcends the particular individual and raises him to conscious membership of a spiritual society. Whoever has seen in the religious politics of the Fascist regime nothing but mere opportunism has not understood that Fascism besides being a system of government is also, and above all, a system of thought.

6. Fascism is an historical conception, in which man is what he is only in so far as he works with the spiritual process in which he finds himself, in the family or social group, in the nation and in the history in which all nations collaborate. From this follows the great value of tradition, in memories, in languages, in customs, in the standards of social life. Outside history man is nothing. Consequently Fascism is opposed to all the individualistic abstractions of a materialistic nature like those of the eighteenth century and it is opposed to all Jacobin utopias and innovations. It does not consider that "happiness" is possible upon earth, as it appeared to be in the desire of the economic literature of the eighteenth century, and hence it rejects all teleological theories according to which mankind would reach a definitive stabilized condition at a certain period in history. This implies putting oneself outside history and life, which is a continual change and coming to be. Politically, Fascism wishes to be a realistic doctrine; practically, it aspires to solve only the problems which arise historically of themselves and that of themselves find or suggest their own solution. To act among men, as to act in the natural world, it is necessary to enter into the process of reality and to master the already operating forces.

7. Against individualism, the Fascist conception is for the State; and

it is for the individual in so far as he coincides with the State, which is the conscience and universal will of man in his historical existence. It is opposed to classical Liberalism, which arose from the necessity of reacting against absolutism, and which brought its historical purpose to an end when the State was transformed into the conscience and will of the people. Liberalism denied the State in the interests of the particular individual; Fascism reaffirms the State as the true reality of the individual. And if liberty is to be the attribute of the real man, and not of that abstract puppet envisaged by individualistic Liberalism, Fascism is for liberty. And for the only liberty which can be a real thing, the liberty of the State and of the individual within the State. Therefore, for the Fascist, everything is in the State, and nothing human or spiritual exists, much less has value, outside the State. In this sense Fascism is totalitarian, and the Fascist State, the synthesis and unity of all values, interprets, develops and gives strength to the whole life of the people.

8. Outside the State there can be neither individuals nor groups (political parties, associations, syndicates, classes). Therefore Fascism is opposed to Socialism, which confines the movement of history within the class struggle and ignores the unity of classes established in one economic and moral reality in the State; and analogously it is opposed to class syndicalism. Fascism recognizes the real exigencies for which the socialist and syndicalist movement arose, but while recognizing them wishes to bring them under the control of the State and give them a purpose within the corporative system of interests reconciled within the unity of the State.

9. Individuals form classes according to the similarity of their interests, they form syndicates according to differentiated economic activities within these interests; but they form first, and above all, the State, which is not to be thought of numerically as the sum-total of individuals forming the majority of a nation. And consequently Fascism is opposed to Democracy, which equates the nation to the majority, lowering it to the level of that majority; nevertheless it is the purest form of democracy if the nation is conceived, as it should be, qualitatively and not quantitatively, as the most powerful idea (most powerful because most moral, most coherent, most true) which acts within the nation as the conscience and the will of a few, even of One, which ideal tends to become active within the conscience and the will of all—that is to say, of all those who rightly constitute a nation by reason of nature, history or race, and have set out upon the same line of development and spiritual formation as one conscience and one sole will. Not a race, nor a geographically determined region, but as a community historically perpetuating itself, a multitude unified by a single idea, which is the will to existence and to power: consciousness of itself, personality. . . .

10. Above all, Fascism, in so far as it considers and observes the future and the development of humanity quite apart from the political considerations of the moment, believes neither in the possibility nor in the utility of perpetual peace. It thus repudiates the doctrine of Pacifism—born of a renunciation of the struggle and an act of cowardice in the face of sacrifice. War alone brings up to their highest tension all human energies and puts the stamp of nobility upon the peoples who have the courage to meet it. All other trials are substitutes, which never really put a man in front of himself in the alternative of life and death. A doctrine, therefore, which begins with a prejudice in favour of peace is foreign to Fascism; as are foreign to the spirit of Fascism, even though acceptable by reason of the utility which they might have in given political situations, all internationalistic and socialistic systems which, as history proves, can be blown to the winds when emotional, idealistic and practical movements storm the hearts of peoples. Fascism carries over this anti-pacifist spirit even into the lives of the individuals. The proud motto of the *Squadrista*, "Me ne frego", written on the bandages of a wound is an act of philosophy which is not only stoical, it is the epitome of a doctrine that is not only political: it is education for combat, the acceptance of the risks which it brings; it is a new way of life for Italy. Thus the Fascist accepts and loves life, he knows nothing of suicide and despises it; he looks on life as duty, ascent, conquest: life which must be noble and full: lived for oneself, but above all for those others near and far away, present and future.

11. The "demographic" policy of the regime follows from these premises. Even the Fascist does in fact love his neighbour, but this "neighbour" is not for him a vague and ill-defined concept; love for one's neighbour does not exclude necessary educational severities, and still less differentiations and distances. Fascism rejects universal concord, and, since it lives in the community of civilized peoples, it keeps them vigilantly and suspiciously before its eyes, it follows their states of mind and the changes in their interests and it does not let itself be deceived by temporary and fallacious appearances.

12. Such a conception of life makes Fascism the precise negation of that doctrine which formed the basis of the so-called Scientific or Marxian Socialism: the doctrine of historical Materialism, according to which the history of human civilizations can be explained only as the struggle of interest between the different social groups and as arising out of change in the means and instruments of production. That economic improvements—discoveries of raw materials, new methods of work, scientific inventions—should have an importance of their own, no one denies, but that they should suffice to explain human history to the exclusion of all other factors is absurd: Fascism believes, now and always, in holiness and in heroism, that

is in acts in which no economic motive—remote or immediate—plays a part. With this negation of historical materialism, according to which men would be only by-products of history, who appear and disappear on the surface of the waves while in the depths the real directive forces are at work, there is also denied the immutable and irreparable "class struggle" which is the natural product of this economic conception of history, and above all it is denied that the class struggle can be the primary agent of social changes. Socialism, being thus wounded in these two primary tenets of its doctrine, nothing of it is left save the sentimental aspiration—old as humanity—towards a social order in which the sufferings and the pains of the humblest folk could be alleviated. But here Fascism rejects the concept of an economic "happiness" which would be realized socialistically and almost automatically at a given moment of economic evolution by assuring to all a maximum prosperity. Fascism denies the possibility of the material-istic conception of "happiness" and leaves it to the economists of the first half of the eighteenth century; it denies, that is, the equation of prosperity with happiness, which would transform men into animals with one sole preoccupation: that of being well-fed and fat, degraded in consequence to a merely physical existence.

13. After Socialism, Fascism attacks the whole complex of democratic ideologies and rejects them both in their theoretical premises and in their applications or practical manifestations. Fascism denies that the majority, through the mere fact of being a majority, can rule human societies; it denies that this majority can govern by means of a periodical consultation; it affirms the irremediable, fruitful and beneficent inequality of men, who cannot be levelled by such a mechanical and extrinsic fact as universal suffrage. By democratic regimes we mean those in which from time to time the people is given the illusion of being sovereign, while true effective sovereignty lies in other, perhaps irresponsible and secret, forces. Democ-racy is a regime without a king, but with very many kings, perhaps more exclusive, tyrannical and violent than one king even though a tyrant. This explains why Fascism, although before 1922 for reasons of expediency it made a gesture of republicanism, renounced it before the March on Rome, convinced that the question of the political forms of a State is not pre-eminent to-day, and that studying past and present monarchies, past and present Republics it becomes clear that monarchy and republic are not to be judged *sub specie aeternitatis,* but represent forms in which the political evolution, the history, the tradition, the psychology of a given country are manifested. Now Fascism overcomes the antithesis between monarchy and republic which retarded the movements of democracy, burdening the former with every defect and defending the latter as the regime of perfec-tion. Now it has been seen that there are inherently reactionary and absolu-

tistic republics, and monarchies that welcome the most daring political and social innovations. . . .

14. In face of Liberal doctrines, Fascism takes up an attitude of absolute opposition both in the field of politics and in that of economics. . . . But the Fascist repudiations of Socialism, Democracy, Liberalism must not make one think that Fascism wishes to make the world return to what it was before 1789, the year which has been indicated as the year of the beginning of the liberal-democratic age. One does not go backwards. The Fascist doctrine has not chosen De Maistre as its prophet. Monarchical absolutism is a thing of the past and so also is every theocracy. So also feudal privileges and division into impenetrable and isolated castes have had their day. The theory of Fascist authority has nothing to do with the police State. A party that governs a nation in a totalitarian way is a new fact in history. References and comparisons are not possible. Fascism takes over from the ruins of Liberal Socialistic democratic doctrines those elements which still have a living value. It preserves those that can be called the established facts of history, it rejects all the rest, that is to say the idea of a doctrine which holds good for all times and all peoples. If it is admitted that the nineteenth century has been the century of Socialism, Liberalism and Democracy, it does not follow that the twentieth must also be the century of Liberalism, Socialism and Democracy. Political doctrines pass; peoples remain. It is to be expected that this century may be that of authority, a century of the "Right", a Fascist century. If the nineteenth was the century of the individual (Liberalism means individualism) it may be expected that this one may be the century of "collectivism" and therefore the century of the State. That a new doctrine should use the still vital elements of other doctrines is perfectly logical. No doctrine is born quite new, shining, never before seen. No doctrine can boast of an absolute "originality". It is bound, even if only historically, to other doctrines that have been, and to develop into other doctrines that will be. Thus the scientific socialism of Marx is bound to the Utopian Socialism of the Fouriers, the Owens and the Saint-Simons; thus the Liberalism of the nineteenth century is connected with the whole "Enlightenment" of the eighteenth century. Thus the doctrines of democracy are bound to the *Encyclopédie*. Every doctrine tends to direct the activity of men towards a determined objective; but the activity of man reacts upon the doctrine, transforms it, adapts it to new necessities or transcends it. The doctrine itself, therefore, must be, not words, but an act of life. Hence, the pragmatic veins in Fascism, its will to power, its will to be, its attitude in the face of the fact of "violence" and of its own courage. . . .

15. The Fascist State is a will to power and to govern. In it the tradition of Rome is an idea that has force. In the doctrine of Fascism

Empire is not only a territorial, military or mercantile expression, but spiritual or moral. One can think of an empire, that is to say a nation that directly or indirectly leads other nations, without needing to conquer a single square kilometre of territory. For Fascism the tendency to Empire, that is to say, to the expansion of nations, is a manifestation of vitality; its opposite, staying at home, is a sign of decadence: peoples who rise or re-rise are imperialist, peoples who die are renunciatory. Fascism is the doctrine that is most fitted to represent the aims, the states of mind, of a people, like the Italian people, rising again after many centuries of abandonment or slavery to foreigners. But Empire calls for discipline, co-ordination of forces, duty and sacrifice; this explains many aspects of the practical working of the regime and the direction of many of the forces of the State and the necessary severity shown to those who would wish to oppose this spontaneous and destined impulse of the Italy of the twentieth century, to oppose it in the name of the superseded ideologies of the nineteenth, repudiated whatever great experiments of political and social transformation have been courageously attempted: especially where, as now, people thirst for authority, for leadership, for order. If every age has its own doctrine, it is apparent from a thousand signs that the doctrine of the present age is Fascism. That it is a doctrine of life is shown by the fact that it has resuscitated a faith. That this faith has conquered minds is proved by the fact that Fascism has had its dead and its martyrs.

Fascism henceforward has in the world the universality of all those doctrines which, by fulfilling themselves, have significance in the history of the human spirit.

53

Democracy

John Dewey (1859–1952) was professor of philosophy at Columbia University. He is the author of a number of works, including *Essays in Experimental Logic* (1916); *Reconstruction in Philosophy* (1920).

Dewey brings out that democracy is more than a special political form. He says it is the necessity for the participation of every mature human being in the formation of the values that regulate the living of men together. He further maintains that it is faith in human intelligence, the belief that all men are entitled to equality of treatment by the law, and the distribution of power among the members.

──────────────────────────────────────TO STUDY

1. According to Dewey, what is the difference between democracy as a political form and its broader notion?
2. How did political democracy develop? What kinds of coercion are there?
3. What is the foundation of democracy?
4. In what sense are all institutions educational?
5. What is the best way to produce power? What is the relation between power and responsibility?
6. Under what conditions is political democracy insecure?

Jus prius

. . . Democracy is much broader than a special political form, a method of conducting government, of making laws and carrying on governmental administration by means of popular suffrage and elected officers. It is that, of course. But it is something broader and deeper than that. The political and governmental phase of democracy is a means, the best means so far found, for realizing ends that lie in the wide domain of human relationships and the development of human personality. It is, as we often say, though perhaps without appreciating all that is involved in the saying, a way of life, social and individual. The key-note of democracy as a way of life may be expressed, it seems to me, as the necessity for the participation of every mature human being in formation of the values that regulate the living of men together: which is necessary from the standpoint of both the general social welfare and the full development of human beings as individuals.

Universal suffrage, recurring elections, responsibility of those who are in political power to the voters, and the other factors of democratic government are means that have been found expedient for realizing democracy as the truly human way of living. They are not a final end and a final value. They are to be judged on the basis of their contribution to end. It is a form of idolatry to erect means into the end which they serve. Democratic political forms are simply the best means that human wit has devised up to a special time in history. But they rest back upon the idea that no man or limited set of men is wise enough or good enough to rule others without their consent; the positive meaning of this statement is that all those who are affected by social institutions must have a share in producing and managing them. The two facts that each one is influenced in what he does and enjoys and in what he becomes by the institutions under which he lives, and that therefore he shall have, in a democracy, a voice in shaping them, are the passive and active sides of the same fact.

The development of political democracy came about through substitution of the method of mutual consultation and voluntary agreement for the method of subordination of the many to the few enforced from above. Social arrangements which involve fixed subordination are maintained by coercion. The coercion need not be physical. There have existed, for short periods, benevolent despotisms. But coercion of some sort there has been; perhaps economic, certainly psychological and moral. The very fact of exclusion from participation is a subtle form of suppression. It gives individuals no opportunity to reflect and decide upon what is good for them. Others who are supposed to be wiser and who in any case have more power decide the question for them and also decide the methods and means by

Selected from an address delivered to the National Education Association, February 22, 1937, and published under the title "Democracy and Educational Administration" in *School and Society*, XLV (April 3, 1937), 457–467.

which subjects may arrive at the enjoyment of what is good for them. This form of coercion and suppression is more subtle and more effective than is overt intimidation and restraint. When it is habitual and embodied in social institutions, it seems the normal and natural state of affairs. The mass usually become unaware that they have a claim to a development of their own powers. Their experience is so restricted that they are not conscious of restriction. It is part of the democratic conception that they as individuals are not the only sufferers, but that the whole social body is deprived of the potential resources that should be at its service. The individuals of the submerged mass may not be very wise. But there is one thing they are wiser about than anybody else can be, and that is where the shoe pinches, the troubles they suffer from.

The foundation of democracy is faith in the capacities of human nature; faith in human intelligence and in the power of pooled and cooperative experience. It is not belief that these things are complete but that if given a show they will grow and be able to generate progressively the knowledge and wisdom needed to guide collective action. Every autocratic and authoritarian scheme of social action rests on a belief that the needed intelligence is confined to a superior few, who because of inherent natural gifts are endowed with the ability and the right to control the conduct of others; laying down principles and rules and directing the ways in which they are carried out. It would be foolish to deny that much can be said for this point of view. It is that which controlled human relations in social groups for much the greater part of human history. The democratic faith has emerged very, very recently in the history of mankind. Even where democracies now exist, men's minds and feelings are still permeated with ideas about leadership imposed from above, ideas that developed in the long early history of mankind. After democratic political institutions were nominally established, beliefs and ways of looking at life and of acting that originated when men and women were externally controlled and subjected to arbitrary power, persisted in the family, the church, business and the school, and experience shows that as long as they persist there, political democracy is not secure.

Belief in equality is an element of the democratic credo. It is not, however, belief in equality of natural endowments. Those who proclaimed the idea of equality did not suppose they were enunciating a psychological doctrine, but a legal and political one. All individuals are entitled to equality of treatment by law and in its administration. Each one is affected equally in quality if not in quantity by the institutions under which he lives and has an equal right to express his judgment, although the weight of his judgment may not be equal in amount when it enters into the pooled result to that of others. In short, each one is equally an individual and entitled to equal opportunity of development of his own capacities, be they large or small in range. Moreover, each has needs of his own, as significant to him as those of others are to them. The very fact of natural and psychological inequality is all the more reason for establishment by law of equality of opportunity, since otherwise the former becomes a means of oppression of the less gifted.

While what we call intelligence be distributed in unequal amounts, it is the democratic faith that it is sufficiently general so that each individual has something to contribute, whose value can be assessed only as enters into the final pooled intelligence constituted by the contributions of all. Every authoritarian scheme, on the contrary, assumes that its value may be assessed by some *prior* principle, if not of family and birth or race and color or possession of material wealth, then by the position and rank a person occupies in the existing social scheme. The democratic faith in equality is the faith that each individual shall have the chance and opportunity to contribute whatever he is capable of contributing and that the value of his contribution be decided by its place and function in the organized total of similar contributions, not on the basis of prior status of any kind whatever.

I have emphasized in what precedes the importance of the effective release of intelligence in connection with personal experience in the democratic way of living. I have done so purposely because democracy is so often and so naturally associated in our minds with freedom of *action,* forgetting the importance of freed intelligence which is necessary to direct and to warrant freedom of action. Unless freedom of individual action has intelligence and informed conviction back of it, its manifestation is almost sure to result in confusion and disorder. The democratic idea of freedom is not the right of each individual to *do* as he pleases, even if it be qualified by adding "provided he does not interfere with the same freedom on the part of others." While the idea is not always, not often enough, expressed in words, the basic freedom is that of freedom of *mind* and of whatever degree of freedom of action and experience is necessary to produce freedom of intelligence. The modes of freedom guaranteed in the Bill of Rights are all of this nature: Freedom of belief and conscience, of expression of opinion, of assembly for discussion and conference, of the press as an organ of communication. They are guaranteed because without them individuals are not free to develop and society is deprived of what they might contribute.

It is a disputed question of theory and practice just how far a democratic political government should go in control of the conditions of action within special groups. At the present time, for example, there are those who think the federal and state governments leave too much freedom of independent action to industrial and financial groups, and there are others who think the government is going altogether too far at the present time. I do not need to discuss this phase of the problem, much less to try to settle it. But it must be pointed out that if the methods of regulation and administration in vogue in the conduct of secondary social groups are non-democratic, whether directly or indirectly or both, there is bound to be unfavorable reaction back into the habits of feeling, thought and action of citizenship in the broadest sense of that word. The way in which any organized social interest is controlled necessarily plays an important part in forming the dispositions and tastes, the attitudes, interests, purposes and desires, of those engaged in carrying on the activities of the group. For illustration, I do not need to do more than point to the moral, emotional and intellectual effect upon both employers and laborers of the existing industrial system. Just what the effects specifically are is a matter about which we know very little. But I suppose that every one who reflects upon the subject admits that it is impossible that the ways in which activities are carried on for the greater part of the waking hours of the day; and the way in which the share of individuals are involved in the management of affairs in such a matter as gaining a livelihood and attaining material and social security, can not but be a highly important factor in shaping personal dispositions; in short, forming character and intelligence.

In the broad and final sense all institutions are educational in the sense that they operate to form the attitudes, dispositions, abilities and disabilities that constitute a concrete personality. The principle applies with special force to the school. For it is the main business of the family and the school to influence directly the formation and growth of attitudes and dispositions, emotional, intellectual and moral. Whether this educative process is carried on in a predominantly democratic or non-democratic way becomes, therefore, a question of transcendent importance not only for education itself but for its final effect upon all the interests and activities of a society that is committed to the democratic way of life.

. . . there are certain corollaries which clarify the meaning of the issue. Absence of participation tends to produce lack of interest and concern on the part of those shut out. The result is a corresponding lack of effective responsibility. Automatically and unconsciously, if not consciously, the feeling develops, "This is none of our affair; it is the business of those at the top; let that particular set of Georges do what needs to be done." The countries in which autocratic government prevails are just those in which there is least public spirit and the greatest indifference to matters of general as distinct from personal concern.

. . . Where there is little power, there is correspondingly little sense of positive responsibility. It is enough to do what one is told to do sufficiently well to escape flagrant unfavorable notice. About larger matters, a spirit of passivity is engendered. In some cases, indifference passes into evasion of duties when not directly under the eye of a supervisor; in other cases, a carping, rebellious spirit is engendered. . . . habitual exclusion has the effect of reducing a sense of responsibility for what is done and its consequences. What the argument for democracy implies is that the best way to produce initiative and constructive power is to exercise it. Power, as well as interest, comes by use and practice. . . . It is also true that incapacity to assume the responsibilities involved in having a voice in shaping policies is bred and increased by conditions in which that responsibility is denied. I suppose there has never been an autocrat, big or little, who did not justify his conduct on the ground of the unfitness of his subjects to take part in government.

. . . I conclude by saying that the present subject is one of peculiar importance at the present time. The fundamental beliefs and practices of democracy are now challenged as they never have been before. In some nations they are more than challenged. They are ruthlessly and systematically destroyed. Everywhere there are waves of criticism and doubt as to whether democracy can meet pressing problems of order and security. The causes for the destruction of political democracy in countries where it was nominally established are complex. But of one thing I think we may be sure. Wherever it has fallen it was too exclusively political in nature. It had not become part of the bone and blood of the people in daily conduct of its life. Democratic forms were limited to Parliament, elections and combats between parties. What is happening proves conclusively, I think, that unless democratic habits of thought and action are part of the fiber of a people, political democracy is insecure. It can not stand in isolation. It must be buttressed by the presence of democratic methods in all social relationships. The relations that exist in educational institutions are second only in importance in this respect to those which exist in industry and business, perhaps not even to them.

Readings

Communism

1. Bober, M. M. *Karl Marx's Interpretation of History.* Cambridge: Harvard University Press, 1950.

2. Cole, G. D. H. *A History of Socialist Thought,* vol. 1, *The Forerunners, 1789–1850.* London: Macmillan Company, 1953.

3. Hook, Sidney. *From Hegel to Marx: Studies in the Intellectual Development of Karl Marx.* New York: Humanities Press, 1950.

4. Lindsay, A. D. *Karl Marx's Capital: An Introductory Essay.* London: Geoffrey Cumberlege, 1947.

5. Sweezy, Paul. *The Theory of Capitalist Development: Principles of Marxian Political Economy.* New York: Oxford University Press, 1942

Fascism

1. Gentile, G. "The Philosophical Bases of Fascism," *Foreign Affairs* (1928).

2. Germino, Dante. *The Italian Fascist Party in Power.* Minneapolis: Univ. of Minnesota Press, 1959.

3. Groth, P. "The 'isms' in Totalitarianism," *American Political Science Review* (1964).

4. Nolte, E. *Three Faces of Fascism.* New York: New American Library, 1969

Democracy

1. Benn, S. I., and R. S. Peters. *Social Principles and the Democratic State.* London, 1959. Reissued as *Principles of Political Thought.* New York: Free Press, 1964.

2. Dahl, R. A. *Preface to Democratic Theory.* Chicago: Univ. of Chicago Press, 1956. A formal analysis of types of democratic theory.

3. Pennock, J. R. *Liberal Democracy: Its Merits and Prospects.* New York, 1950. Includes an extensive bibliography.

4. Spitz, D. *Patterns of Antidemocratic Thought.* New York: Free Press, 1949.

5. Wollheim, R. "Democracy," *Journal of the History of Ideas,* Vol. 19 (1958), 225–242. Includes brief history and bibliographical references.

8

Aesthetics

one

Are Artistic Judgments
Subjective?

54

There Can Be No Disputing of Tastes

Curt Ducasse (1881–1969) was President of the American Philosophical Association in 1936. His works include *Nature, Mind, and Death* (1951) and *Truth, Knowledge, and Causation* (1968)

Can differences in artistic tastes be disputed? You may like Beethoven, but I prefer folk rock. Is one better than the other? Is Rembrandt better than Norman Rockwell? This question is one constantly debated by people. Ducasse maintains that the basic function of art is to express emotions rather than create beauty, but at the same time he holds that beauty is a legitimate standard in the criticism of works of art. He says that the choice of a standard is ultimately an expression of personal preference, and that taste is subjective and relative. There is, he concludes, no disputing among tastes for either the naive or the sophisticated.

─── TO STUDY

1. What is Ducasse's definition of beauty? Why does he believe there is no such thing as authoritative opinion concerning beauty?
2. Why can't beauty be proved by appeal to consensus, test of time, or to type of person who experiences it?
3. Why can't beauty be proved by appeal to technical principles?
4. Can one criticize art objects in ethical terms?
5. Regarding beauty, to what does ultimate analysis unavoidably lead?
6. Can taste be refined?

Beauty Is Relative To the Individual Observer

Beauty, it will be recalled, was defined as the capacity of an object aesthetically contemplated to yield feelings that are pleasant. This definition cannot
be characterized simply either as objective, or as subjective. According to
it, "beautiful" is an adjective properly predicable only of objects, but what
that adjective does predicate of an object is that the feelings of which it
constitutes the aesthetic symbol for a contemplating observer, are pleasurable. Beauty being in this definite sense dependent upon the constitution of
the individual observer, it will be as variable as that constitution. That is
to say, an object which one person properly calls beautiful will, with equal
propriety be not so judged by another, or indeed by the same person at a
different time.

*There is, then, no such thing as authoritative opinion concerning the
beauty of a given object.* There is only the opinion of this person or that;
or the opinion of persons of some specified sort. When one has stated the
opinion and mentioned the person or class of persons who hold it, one has
gone as far as it is possible to go in the direction of a scientifically objective
statement relating to the beauty of the object. When some matter (as that
of beauty) is not of the sort which "is so," or "not so," in an *absolute* sense,
the nearest approach that one can make to the wished-for absoluteness lies
in furnishing, as fully as possible, the data to which the matter in question
is *relative;* and this is what one does in the case of beauty when one indicates
just who it happens to be that judges the given object beautiful or the
reverse.

All that was said above concerning aesthetic connoisseurship, i.e.,
concerning superior capacity for experiencing difference in aesthetic feeling —
in the presence of slight differences in the aesthetic object, applies equally
here, where differences in the pleasantness of the feelings are particularly
in question. There are connoisseurs of beauty, or, more often, of particular
sorts of beauty; but their judgments of beauty are "binding" on no one.
Indeed it is hard to see what could possibly be meant by "binding" in such
a connection, unless it were an obligation on others to lie or dissemble
concerning the aesthetic feelings which in fact they have or do not have
on a given occasion. There is, of course, such a thing as good taste, and
bad taste. But good taste, I submit, means either my taste, or the taste of
people who are to my taste, or the taste of people to whose taste I want
to be. There is no objective test of the goodness or badness of taste, in the

From *The Philosophy of Art* by Curt J. Ducasse (New York: Dover Publications, Inc., 1929),
Chap. 15. Reprinted through the permission of the publisher.

sense in which there is an objective test of the goodness or badness of a person's judgment concerning, let us say, the fitness of a given tool to a given task.

Beauty Cannot Be Proved by Appeal to Consensus, or to the "Test of Time," or to The Type of Person Who Experiences It in a Given Case

In the light of what precedes, it is obvious that the familiar attempts to prove the beauty of certain works of art by appeal to the consensus of opinion, or to the test of continued approval through long periods of time in the life either of society or of the individual, are, like the appeal to the connoisseur's verdict, entirely futile. Such tests cannot possibly prove the object's beauty to those who do not perceive any in it; and to those who do, they are needless. They prove nothing whatever, except that beauty is found in the object . . . by such as do find it there.

We might attempt to rank beauties on the basis of the particular aspect of human nature, or type of human being, that experiences aesthetic pleasure in given cases. This would lead to a classifying of beauties as, for instance, sentimental, intellectual, sexual, spiritual, utilitarian, sensuous, social, etc. We might well believe in some certain order of worth or dignity in the human faculties respectively concerned, but this would not lead to any aesthetically objective ranking of beauties. To suggest it would be as ludicrous as a proposal to rank the worth of various religions according to the average cost of the vestments of their priests. For a ranking of beauties, there are available only such principles as the relative intensity of the pleasure felt, its relative duration, relative volume, and relative freedom from admixture of pain. These principles, however, do not in the least release us from the need of relying upon the individual's judgment; on the contrary their application rests wholly upon it.

Beauty Cannot Be Proved by Appeal to Technical Principles or Canons

It may yet be thought, however, that there are certain narrower and more technical requirements in the various fields of art, without the fulfilling of which no work can be beautiful. Among such alleged canons of beauty may be mentioned the rules of so-called "harmony" in music; various precepts concerning literary composition; unity; truth to nature; such requirements as consistency, relevance, and unambiguity; and so on. There are indeed "rules" or "principles" of that sort, some of which are, I will freely declare, valid for me; so that when I find myself confronted by flagrant violations of them, I am apt to feel rather strongly, and to be impatient or sarcastic about "that sort of stuff." And indeed, on occasions when I have found myself inadvertently guilty of having drawn some line or written some sentence in violation of my own aesthetic canons, I have at times felt as ashamed of the line or the sentence as I should of having picked somebody's pocket. I admit having pronounced opinions about the beauty or ugliness of various things, and what is more, in many cases I am able to *give reasons* for my opinions.

But of what nature are those reasons? They are, ultimately, of the same nature as would be that offered by a man arguing that my pen had to fall when I let go of it a moment ago, *because of gravitation.* Gravitation is but the name we give to the general fact that unsupported objects *do* fall, and at a certain rate; but it is not a reason, or cause, or proof of that fact. To say that something always happens, is not to give any reason why it ever does. Therefore when I say that a certain design is ugly because it is against the "law of symmetry," I am not giving a reason why it *had* to give me aesthetic displeasure, but only mentioning the fact that it resembles in a stated respect certain others which as a bare matter of fact also do displease me. This character which displeases me and many persons, may, however, please others. And, what is more directly to the point, it not only may but it does,—jazzy or uncouth though I may call the taste of such persons. But what most obstinately drives me to the acquisition of a certain, at least abstract, sense of humor concerning the ravening intolerance and would-be-authoritativeness of my own pet canons of beauty, is the fact that they have changed in the past, and that I see no reason why they should not change again in the future. For all I can see to prevent it, I may well to-morrow, next year, or in some future incarnation, burn what I aesthetically adore to-day, and adore what I now would burn. If this happens, I have no doubt at all that I shall then smugly label the change a progress and a development of my taste; whereas to-day I should no less smugly describe the possibility of a change of that sort in me, as a possibility that my taste may go to the devil. And, let it be noted, the sole foundation upon which either of the two descriptions would rest, would be the fact that the describer *actually* possesses at the time the sort of taste which he does. Tastes can be neither proved nor refuted, but only "called names," i.e., praised or reviled.

Certain limited and empirical generalizations have been found possible concerning factors upon which the aesthetic pleasure of most people, or of some kinds of people, appears to depend. Precarious generalizations of this sort may be found for instance in manuals of design and of pictorial composition, where they are often dignified by the name of "principles." People familiar with them may then be heard to say that a given picture, perhaps, is well composed and why; or that the tones, the masses, or the values are, as the case may be, well or ill balanced, and so on. Other statements that we may hear and which also imply "principles," would be that the color is clean, or else muddy; that the drawing is, perhaps, distorted; that the surfaces are well modelled; that the lines are rhythmical; that the color combinations are impossible; that the masses lack volume or solidity, etc. The words beauty and ugliness may not occur once, but it is nevertheless obvious that all such statements are not merely descriptive, but *critical.* They are not direct assertions of aesthetic value or disvalue, viz., of beauty or ugliness, but, taking it as an obvious fact, they attempt to trace it to certain definite sorts of features in the work. The more intelligent and better informed kind of art-criticism is of this analytical and diagnostic sort, and there is nothing beyond this that the art-critic could do.

All such comments, worded in the technical jargon of the particular craft, have the imposing sound of expert judgments based upon authoritative principles, and are likely to make the lay consumer of art feel very small and uninitiated. Therefore it cannot be too much emphasized here that a given picture is not ugly because the compositon of it, or the color combinations in it, are against the rules; but that the rule against a given type of compositon or of color combination is authoritative only because, or if, or for whom, or when, compositions or combinations of that type are *actually* found displeasing. All rules and canons and theories concerning what a painting or other work of art should or should not be, derive such authority as they have over you or me or anyone else, solely from the capacity of such canons *to predict to us* that we shall feel aesthetic pleasure here, and aesthetic pain there. If a given rule predicts this accurately for a given person, that person's *actual* feeling of aesthetic pleasure or displeasure then, proves that this rule *was* a valid one so far as *he is* concerned. That is, the feeling judges the rule, not the rule the feeling. The rule may not be valid for someone else, and it may at any time cease to be valid for the given person, since few things are so variable as pleasure. The *actual* experience of beauty or ugliness by somebody is the final test of the validity of all rules and theories of painting, music, etc., and that test absolutely determines how far, and when, and for whom any given rule or theory holds or does not hold.

The difference between the criticisms of the professionals, and those of the people who, having humbly premised that they "know nothing about art," find little more to say than that a given work is in their judgment beautiful, or as the case may be, ugly or indifferent;—the difference, I say, between the criticisms of professionals and of laymen is essentially that the former are able to trace the aesthetic pleasure or displeasure which they feel, to certain features of the object, while the latter are not able to do it. From this, however, it does not in the least follow that the evaluations of the professionals ultimately rest on any basis less subjective and less a matter of individual taste than do those of the layman. Indeed, so far as the non-professionals really judge at all, i.e., do not merely echo an opinion which they have somehow been bluffed into accepting as authoritative, their judgment is based on the fact that they actually feel something. The artists and professional critics, on the other hand, are exposed to a danger which does not threaten people who know nothing of the factors on which aesthetic pleasure or displeasure has in the past been found to depend for most people, or for some particular class of people,—the danger, namely, of erecting such empirical findings into fixed and rigid rules, and of judging the work of art no longer by the aesthetic pleasure it actually gives them, but by that which they think it "ought" to give them according to such rules. This danger is really very great, especially for the artist, who, in the nature of the case, is constantly forced to give attention to the technical means by which the objective expression of his feeling is alone to be achieved. Having thus all the time to solve technical problems, it is fatally easy for him to become interested in them for their own sake, and, without knowing it, to be henceforth no longer an artist expressing what he feels, but a restless virtuoso searching for new stunts to perform. This may be the reason why so many of the pictures displayed in our exhibits, although well-enough painted, make one feel as though one were receiving a special-delivery, registered, extra-postage letter, . . . just to say, perhaps, that after Thursday comes Friday

Listening to the comments of artists and of some critics on a picture will quickly convince one that, strange as it sounds, they are as often as not almost incapable of seeing the picture about which they speak. What they see instead is brush work, values, edges, dark against light, colored shadows, etc. They are thus often not more but less capable than the untrained public of giving the picture *aesthetic* attention, and of getting from it genuinely aesthetic enjoyment. The theory that *aesthetic* appreciation of the products of a given art is increased by cultivating an amateur's measure of proficiency in that art, is therefore true only so far as such cultivation results in more intimate and thoroughgoing *aesthetic* acquaintance with the products of that art. This is likely to be the case in an interpretative art like music (not music-composing). But in an art which, like painting, is not so largely interpretative, and is at the same time dependent on rather elaborate technical processes, the amateur practitioner's attention is from the very first emphatically directed to these processes; and, when it is directed to extant works of art it is directed to them as examples of a technique to be studied, not as aesthetic objects to be contemplated. The danger is then that such technical matters will come to monopolize his attention habitually, and that even in the face of nature he will forget to look at her, wondering instead whether the water or the sky be the brighter, or what color would have to be used to reproduce the appearance of a given shadow. Attention to technique is of course indispensable to the acquisition of it; and mastery of technique is in turn necessary to the production of art on any but the most humble scale. The risk is that the outcome of technical training will be not mastery of technique, but slavery to it. This risk disappears only when the technical apparatus has become as intimately a part of the artist as the hand is of the body for ordinary purposes, and is used without requiring attention. The attention can then turn from the means to the ends of art, viz, to the objective expression of feeling. But the stage at which technique has so become second-nature as to be forgotten, is not often fully reached. With most artists, what we may call their technical *savoir-faire* creaks more or less, as does the social *savoir-faire* of people who have become emilyposted but lately. Like the nouveaux gentlemen, such artists are too conscious of their technical manners, and forget what they are for.

Criticism of Aesthetic Objects in Ethical Terms

Instead of asking whether a work of art or other aesthetic object is beautiful or ugly, i.e., whether the feeling obtained in aesthetic contemplation of it is pleasant or unpleasant, we may on the contrary disregard this and ask whether the feeling so obtained by a person is or may become connected with the rest of his life, and in what manner it may affect it for good or ill. The ethical or the religious worth of the feelings obtained in aesthetic contemplation of works of art, it will be recalled, would have been made by Plato and by Tolstoi the ruling standard in terms of which to judge art as good or bad. It is worth noting, however, that standards of evaluation cannot themselves be evaluated, except in terms of some standard not itself in any way vindicated but only dogmatically laid down. And any standard evaluated in this manner may itself equally well be laid down in turn as absolute, and be used to evaluate the standard which before was evaluating it. Arguments about the relative worth of various standards of worth are therefore wholly futile, inasmuch as, in the very nature of the logical situation, every such argument must to begin with beg as its premise the point essentially at issue. Ultimately, then, a given standard can only be sympathized with and adopted, or the reverse; and logic can come in only *after* this has occurred. Plato's and Tolstoi's choice of the ethical or religious nature of the aesthetic feelings imparted, as ruling standard for the evalua-

art was evaluated according to political function

tion of art, is legitimate, but it constitutes only a manifestation of their own ruling interest, and a different choice of ruling standard is equally legitimate by anyone else whose ruling interest happens to be different. With these remarks concerning the permissibility, but the arbitrariness, of describing any one standard of worth as "supreme" or "ruling," we may leave the matter, and now simply consider the question raised, namely, whether the feelings obtained in aesthetic contemplation may affect the rest of one's life, and how.

The value other than aesthetic that aesthetic feelings may have depends upon the fact that if, when a feeling has been obtained through aesthetic contemplation, the aesthetic attitude is then given up and replaced by the practical, that which had up to that moment the status of aesthetic feeling now assumes that of impulse.

So long as our state is properly describable as aesthetic feeling, its value is immediate and intrinsic, and consists in the pleasantness or unpleasantness of the state. But when our state comes to be properly describable as impulse, then its value is as usual to be measured in terms of the eventual significance of the impulse. An impulse is a seed of conduct, and an aesthetic feeling is at least a potential seed of impulse; the terms in which we commonly appraise conduct are therefore potentially applicable to it.

The impulse or embryonic conduct resulting from the transmutation of an aesthetic feeling through a shift to the practical attitude, may be either a novel impulse in the life of the individual or not. If it is an impulse of a sort already experienced and more or less established with characteristic modes of manifestation in the life of the person concerned, then the reëxperiencing of it as aftermath of aesthetic contemplation will not affect the individual's life qualitatively, but only quantitatively. It will be simply fuel to an engine already existing and functioning; it will add to the intensity of some aspect of life but will not alter it in kind, except perhaps indirectly if the changes of intensity involved are such as to upset an equilibrium previously existing, and thus force the recasting of life in a different qualitative pattern.

If however the impulse is a novel one in the life of the individual, then it constitutes directly the seed of a change in the kind of life that has been his. The evolution (whether towards good or evil) of the will-aspect of man's nature does not take place merely through increases in his knowledge of the facts and relations that constitute the field of action of his will, but also through the advent in him of qualitatively novel impulses. Indeed, it might well be argued that mere increase in the quantity as distinguished from the nature of one's knowledge and experience, only furnishes one with new means for the service of old ends, or makes one better aware of the ends to which one's hitherto blind impulses tended; but that, however such increase of knowledge may transform the manifestations of existing long-ings or impulses, it does not of itself alter their intrinsic nature. Transformation in the nature of the impulses themselves (apart from maturation) seems traceable to experiences of two sorts. One of them is awareness by the individual of the presence of a practically real situation novel in kind in his life. This may call forth in him an impulse hitherto foreign to him. The other is what we might call the surreptitious implantation of the impulse itself in him, through the transmutation which we are now considering of an aesthetic feeling into an impulse, by a shift to the practical attitude.

The aesthetic contemplation of nature and of various aspects of life is, through such a shift of attitude, a source of germs of new impulses and of food for old ones. Some persons are known to the writer, in whom the contemplation for the first time of the ocean, or of great mountains, seems to have produced feelings comparable in point of novelty and depth to those reported by the mystics, and the aftermath of impulse due to which gave to life a different pattern, somewhat as does a religious conversion. But art is capable of being as much more effective in the sowing of such seeds of novel impulse, as, for instance, the study of existing records is more effective than personal investigation in acquiring a knowledge of geography. For one thing, art is usually easier than nature to contemplate, being, we might almost say, made for that. Again, when nature was its model, art may be described as at least a drastic editing of nature, supplying what she forgot, omitting what was irrelevant, accenting her here or there into unambiguity. The work of art, being created specifically to give objective expression to a given feeling, is likely to have a pointedness of feeling-import which nature matches only by accident. The work of art, moreover, can be contemplated at length and returned to again and again, whereas natural facts and the aspects they show us are mostly beyond our control. They come and go heedless of the conditions which alone would make it possible for us to contemplate them adequately. But lastly, art, although in some ways it falls short of nature, has in another way a range of resources far greater than nature's, for it has at its command the boundless resources of the imagination. What it cannot present it often can represent, and thus set up before our attention objects of contemplation never to be found in nature. It can lead us into new worlds, in the contemplation of which our feeling-selves spontaneously burgeon and bloom in all sorts of new ways. Some poems, some music, some statues and pictures, have had in an extraordinary degree this power to bring to birth in people qualities of feeling that had remained latent in them. One such work of art is Leonardo's *Mona Lisa*. Art theorists whose fundamental dogma is that the end of painting is the representation of plastic form, and who find that picture but indifferently successful in this respect, cannot understand why the theft of it a few years ago should have

aesthetic art can intensify feelings or create new feelings been deemed a world-calamity. Their only explanation is the aesthetic ineptitude of mankind at large. They cannot see that design and the representation of plastic form is not the whole of the art of painting, but is rather a means which may be used to the ends of art, *when it is important to those ends.* Not the aesthetic ineptitude of mankind, therefore, but the sophomoric character of the measuring-rod by which such theorists would judge Leonardo's picture, is the lesson of the effect produced by that famous theft. There are doubtless people who, in a similar way, would insist on characterizing Socrates essentially as a Greek who was not a "good provider."

Liberalism in Aesthetics

The principal standards in terms of which works of art and aesthetic objects may be criticized have been considered above, and the general nature of the conclusions reached concerning the significance and validity of such criticisms may now be summarily characterized.

Judgments of mediate or instrumental value are capable of being proved or disproved. Their truth or falsity is objective, in the sense that it is not conferred upon them by the individual's taste, but is a matter of connections in nature independent of the critic's taste. But the *relevance* or importance, if not the truth, of any judgment of mediate value, is a matter of the individual critic's taste or constitution, since for any such critic that relevance depends on a judgment of immediate value by him.

As regards judgments of immediate value, and in particular of beauty and ugliness, it seems to me that here as in other fields, ultimate analysis leads unavoidably to *the particular constitution of the individual critic* (no matter how he may have come by it); as the necessary and sufficient ground for all such judgments. The constitutions of numbers of individual critics may, of course, happen to be alike in some respects; or they can be made more or less alike by subjecting them to the sort of psychological pressure appropriate to the causation of such a result. If a number of critics are constituted alike in some respects, then any one of them will be able to formulate value judgments with which will agree as many of the other critics as are constituted like him in the respects needed for such agreement! I cannot see that "objective validity" in the case of a judgment of immediate value, means anything whatever but this; namely, several people judge alike because they are constituted alike. But whether a given taste be possessed by one person only, or by a thousand alike, the maxim that *de gustibus non est disputandum* holds with regard to it.

Is there then no such thing as the refining and educating of taste? Certainly there is,—and there is also such a thing as perversion and depravation of taste. But the question in any given case is, which is which? No one so far as I know has yet pointed out any way of answering this question otherwise than arbitrarily and dogmatically, i.e., otherwise than in terms of the taste actually possessed by some person or other, usually oneself, *arbitrarily* taken as standard. That question, indeed, is hardly ever frankly faced. Those who have approached it at all seem always to have labored under the strange delusion that if only they succeeded in showing that the tastes of a large number or a majority of people were alike, the question was answered; whereas the truth is on the contrary, as just pointed out, that mere numbers have no bearing whatever on the question. Taking a vote is only a device for ascertaining in advance what would be the outcome of a fight between two groups of people, if every person were as strong as every other and strength alone counted. "Proof" by appeal to a vote is obviously but a civilized form of the *argumentum ad baculum.*

It may be asked, however, whether in the absence of any standard of immediate value objectively valid in any sense other than that described above, it is not possible at least to point to some respects in which the (immediate) value judgments of all people whatever, would agree. Nobody whatever, it may be urged, likes great hunger or thirst or cold, or cuts and burns, etc. Now it may be granted that certainly not many do, but after all there are masochists and ascetics and martyrs. It may be true because tautologous that nobody likes pain; but we must keep in mind that pain and pleasure are the predicates, not the subjects, of immediate-value-judgments. Their subjects are things, situations, experiences. The question is thus not whether painfulness is ever pleasurable, but whether there are any *situations* or *experiences* which everybody without exception finds, for instance, painful. And this is very doubtful. We can probably say only that with regard to some situations or experiences, the dissentients are very few. And as we have just seen, numbers mean nothing at all in such a matter.

This brings us to what may be called a dogmatico-liberalistic position. Neither I nor anyone can refute anyone else's judgments of immediate value,—here, of beauty and ugliness; nor can anyone refute mine. This is the liberalistic aspect of the situation. The fullest insight into it, however, constitutes no reason whatever why any one should hold to his own immediate valuations any the less strongly. That our own opinion must in the nature of such matters be dogmatic is no reason why it should not be honest, vigorous, and unashamed.

55

Tastes Can Be Disputed

Monroe Beardsley (1915–   ) was elected President of the American Society for Aesthetics in 1956. His works include *Practical Logic* (1950), *Aesthetics* (1958), and *Aesthetics: A Short History* (1966).

Beardsley disagrees with Ducasse and maintains that one can and does dispute about tastes. He says that when a person critically comments on a work of art, he gives his reasons for saying that a work of art is good or bad. He points out those features of the work which are evidence of its ability or inability to provide the audience with a deep aesthetic experience.

TO STUDY

1. What is the chief use of the maxim: "There is no disputing about taste"? To what areas is the maxim most significantly applied?

2 Why do we believe there is no disputing about art, but there can be about political matters?

3 What is the theory of the aesthetic skeptic? How does Beardsley criticize this? Cite his reasons.

4. What is the value of works of art? Explain fully.

We are assured by an old and often-quoted maxim,[1] whose authority is not diminished by its being cast in Latin, that there can be no disputing about tastes. The chief use of this maxim is in putting an end to disputes that last a long time and don't appear to be getting anywhere. And for this purpose it is very efficacious, for it has an air of profound finality, and it also seems to provide a democratic compromise of a deadlocked issue. If you can't convince someone that he is wrong, or bring yourself to admit that he is right, you can always say that neither of you is more wrong than the other, because nobody can be right.

Remarks that serve to close some people's debates, however, are quite often just the remarks to start a new one among philosophers. And this maxim is no exception. It has been given a great deal of thought, some of it very illuminating; yet there is still something to be learned from further reflection upon it. Nor is it of small importance to know, if we can, whether the maxim is true or false, for if it is true we won't waste time in futile discussion, and if it is false we won't waste opportunities for fruitful discussion.

The question whether tastes are disputable is one to be approached with wariness. The first thing is to be clear about what it really means. There are two key words in it that we should pay particular attention to.

The first is the word "taste." The maxim is perhaps most readily and least doubtfully applied to taste in its primary sensory meaning: some people like ripe olives, some green; some people like turnips, others cannot abide them; some people will go long distances for pizza pies, others can hardly choke them down. And there are no disputes about olives: we don't find two schools of thought, the Ripe Olive School and the Green Olive School, publishing quarterly journals or demanding equal time on television—probably because there simply isn't much you can say about the relative merits of these comestibles.

But we apply the word "taste," of course, more broadly. We speak of a person's taste in hats and neckties; we speak of his taste in poetry and painting and music. And it is here that the *non disputandum* maxim is most significantly applied. Some people like Auden and others Swinburne, some enjoy the paintings of Jackson Pollock and others avoid them when they can, some people are panting to hear Shostakovitch's latest symphony and others find no music since Haydn really satisfying. In these cases, unlike the olive case, people are generally not at a loss for words: there is plenty you can say about Shostakovitch, pro or con. They talk, all right; they may

From *Swarthmore College Alumni Bulletin,* LVI (October 1958), 1–5. Reprinted by permission of the publisher and author.
[1] *De gustibus non est disputandum*—"Matters of taste aren't disputable."

justify position with reasons not emotions

praise, deplore, threaten, cajole, wheedle, and scream—but, according to the maxim, they do not really dispute.

This brings us, then, to the second key word. What does it mean to say that we cannot *dispute* about tastes in literature, fine arts, and music, even though we can clearly make known our tastes? It certainly doesn't mean that we cannot disagree, or differ in taste: for obviously we do, and not only we but also the acknowledged or supposed experts in these fields. Consider James Gould Cozzens' novel, *By Love Possessed,* which appeared in August, 1957; consult the critics and reviewers to discover whether it is a good novel. Being a serious and ambitious work by a writer of standing, and also a best seller, it provoked unusually forthright judgments from a number of reviewers and critics—as may be seen in the accompanying quotations. "Masterpiece . . . brilliant . . . distinguished . . . high order . . . mediocre . . . bad;" that just about covers the spectrum of evaluation.

The International Council of the Museum of Modern Art recently took a large collection of American abstract expressionist paintings on tour in Europe. Its reception was reported in *Time.* In Spain some said, "If this is art, what was it that Goya painted?" and others cheered its "furious vitality" and "renovating spirit." In Italy one newspaper remarked, "It is not painting," but "droppings of paint, sprayings, burstings, lumps, squirts, whirls, rubs and marks, erasures, scrawls, doodles and kaleidoscope backgrounds." In Switzerland it was an "artistic event" that spoke for the genius of American art. And of course all these judgments could be found in this country too.

Not a dispute? Well, what is a dispute? Let us take first the plainest case of a disagreement (no matter what it is about): two people who say, " 'Tis so!" and " 'Taint so!" Let them repeat these words as often as they like, and shout them from the housetops; they still haven't got a dispute going, but merely a contradiction, or perhaps an altercation. But let one person say, " 'Tis so!" and give a *reason* why 'tis so—let him say, "Jones is the best candidate for Senator because he is tactful, honest, and has had much experience in government." And let the other person say, " 'Taint so!" and give a reason why 'taint so—"Jones is not the best candidate, because he is too subservient to certain interests, indecisive and wishywashy in his own views, and has no conception of the United States' international responsibilities." *Then* we have a dispute—that is, a disagreement in which the parties give reasons for their contentions. Of course this is not all there is to it; the dispute has just begun. But we see how it might continue, each side giving further reasons for its own view, and questioning whether the reasons given by the other are true, relevant, and compelling.

It is this kind of thing that counts as a dispute about the possibility of getting to the moon, about American intervention in the Middle East, about a Supreme Court decision, or anything else. And if we can dispute about these things, why not about art?

But here is where the *non disputandum* maxim would draw the line. We do not speak (or not without irony) about people's tastes in Senatorial candidates or missile policies (if the President replied to critics by saying, "Well, your taste is for speeding up the missile program and spending money, but that's not to my taste," we would feel he ought to back up his opinion more than that). Nor do we speak of tastes in international affairs, or laws, or constitutions. And that seems to be because we believe that judgments on these matters can be, and ought to be, based on good reasons—not that they always are, of course. To prefer a democratic to a totalitarian form of government is *not* just a matter of taste, though to like green olives better than ripe olives is a matter of taste, and we don't require the green olive man to rise and give his reasons, or even to *have* reasons. What kind of reasons could he have? "Green olives are better because they are green" would not look like much of a reason to the ripe olive devotee.

The question, then, is whether a preference for Picasso or Monteverdi is more like a preference for green olives or like a preference for a Senatorial candidate: is it *arguable?* can it be *reasoned?*

When we read what critics and reviewers have to say about the things they talk about, we cannot doubt that they do not merely praise or blame, but defend their judgments by giving reasons, or what they claim to be reasons. The judgments of *By Love Possessed,* here quoted out of context, are supplied with arguments, some of them with long arguments dealing in detail with the plot, style, characterization, structure, underlying philosophy, attitudes towards Catholics, Jews, and Negroes, and other aspects of the novel. Collect a number of these reviews together and it certainly *reads* like a dispute. Or here is one person who says, "Mozart's Quintet in E Flat Major for Piano and Winds (K. 452) is a greater piece of music than Beethoven's Quintet in E Flat Major for Piano and Winds (Op. 16) because it has greater melodic invention, subtlety of texture, a more characteristic scoring for the wind instruments, and a more expressive slow movement." And here is his friend, who replies, "The Beethoven quintet is greater because it has richer sonority, greater vigor and vitality, and a more powerful dynamic spirit." There's a dispute, or something that looks very much like one.

But according to the Aesthetic Skeptic—if I may choose this convenient name for the upholder of the "no disputing" doctrine—this is an illusion. The apparent reasons are not genuine reasons, or cannot be compelling reasons, like the ones we find in other fields. For in the last analysis they rest upon sheer liking or disliking, which is not susceptible of rational discussion. The defender of the Mozart Quintet, for example, seems to be trying to prove his point, but what he is actually doing (says the Skeptic) is better put this way: *"If* you like subtle texture and expressiveness in slow movements, *then* you (like me) will prefer the Mozart quintet." But what if his friend cares more for vigor and vitality? Then the so-called "argument" is bound to leave him cold. He can only reply, *"If* you like vigor and vitality, as I do, *then* you would prefer the Beethoven quintet." But this is no longer a dispute; they are talking completely at cross purposes, not even contradicting each other.

The Aesthetic Skeptic would analyze all apparent disputes among critics in these terms: the critic can point out features of the novel, the abstract expressionist painting, the quintet for winds, but when he does this he is taking for granted, what may not be true, that you happen to like these features. You can't, says the Skeptic, argue anybody into liking something he doesn't like, and that's why there's no disputing about tastes; all disputes are in the end useless.

Now this view, which I have here stated in a fairly rough way, can be worked out into a sophisticated and impressive position, and if it is mistaken, as I believe it is, its mistakes are not childish or simple-minded. Consequently, I cannot pretend to give here an adequate treatment of it. But I should like to consider briefly some of the difficulties in Aesthetic Skepticism, as I see it, and point out the possibility of an alternative theory.

The Skeptical theory takes people's likes and dislikes as ultimate and unappealable facts about them; when two people finally get down to saying "I like X" and "I don't like X" (be it the flavor of turnip or subtlety of texture in music), there the discussion has to end, there the dispute vanishes. But though it is true that you can't change a disliking into a liking by arguments, that doesn't imply that you can't change it at all, or that we cannot argue whether or not it *ought* to be changed. . . . But the fact remains that one person can give reasons to another why he would be better off if he *could* enjoy music or painting that he now abhors, and sometimes the other person can set about indirectly, by study and enlarged experience, to change his own tastes, or, as we say, to improve them. There is not just your taste and mine, but better and worse taste; and this doesn't mean just that I have a taste for my taste, but not yours—I might in fact have a distaste for the limitations of my own taste (though that is a queer way to put it). It is something like a person with deep-rooted prejudices, to which he has been conditioned from an early age; perhaps he cannot quite get rid of them, no matter how he tries, and yet he may acknowledge in them a weakness, a crippling feature of his personality, and he may resolve that he will help his children grow up free from them.

The Skeptic does not allow for the possibility that we might give reasons why a person would be better off if he liked or disliked *By Love*

Possessed in the way, and to the degree, that it deserves to be liked or disliked. Sometimes, I think, he really holds that it would not be worth the trouble. After all, what does it matter whether people like green olives or ripe olives? We can obtain both in sufficient supply, and nothing much depends upon it as far as the fate of the world is concerned. That's another reason why we ordinarily don't speak of Senatorial candidates as a matter of taste—unless we want to be disparaging, as when people speak of the President's choice in Secretaries of State, to imply that he has no good reason for his choice. It does matter who is Senator, or Secretary of State—it matters a great deal. . . .

ad. Hominem argument

Now of course, if we are thinking of our two musical disputants about the relative merits of the two quintets, this is a dispute we may safely leave alone. Both quintets are of such a high order that it perhaps doesn't matter enormously which we decide to rank higher than the other, though there's no harm in trying to do this, if we wish. But the question about *By Love Possessed* is whether it is a "masterpiece" or "bad"; and the question about the paintings is whether they ought to be shown abroad at all. It may not matter so very much whether a person on the whole admires Mozart or Beethoven more, but what if he cannot make up his mind between Mozart and Strauss, or between Beethoven and Shostakovitch?

The fact is that the prevailing level of taste in the general public matters a great deal to me, for it has a great deal to do with determining what I shall have the chance to read, what movies will be filmed, shown, or censored, what music will be played most availably on the radio, what plays will be performed on television. And it has a great deal to do with what composers and painters and poets will do, or whether some of them will do anything at all. But more than that, even: if I am convinced that the kind of experiences that can only be obtained by access to the greatest works is an important ingredient of the richest and most fully-developed human life, then do I not owe it to others to try to put that experience within their reach, or them within its reach? It might be as important to them as good housing, good medical and dental care, or good government.

But here is another point at which the Skeptic feels uneasy. Isn't it undemocratic to go around telling other people that they have crude tastes—wouldn't it be more in keeping with our laissez-faire spirit of tolerance, and less reminiscent of totalitarian absolutism and compulsion, to let others like and enjoy what they like and enjoy? Isn't this their natural right?

There are too many confusions in this point of view to clear them all up briefly. But some of them are worth sorting out. Of course it is a person's right to hear the music he enjoys, provided it doesn't bother other people too much. But it is no invasion of his right, if he is willing to consider the problem, to try to convince him that he should try to like other things that appear to deserve it. . . .

The distinction that many Skeptics find it hard to keep in mind is this: I may hold that there *is* a better and a worse in music and novels without at all claiming that *I know for certain* which are which. Those critics and reviewers who pronounced their judgments on *By Love Possessed* are not necessarily dogmatic because they deny that it's all a matter of taste (even though some of them were more positive than they had a right to be). They believe that some true and reasonable judgment of the novel is in principle possible, and that objective critics, given time and discussion, could in principle agree, or come close to agreeing, on it. But they do not have to claim infallibility—people can be mistaken about novels, as they can about anything else. Works of art are complicated. There need be nothing totalitarian about literary criticism, and there is nothing especially democratic in the view that nobody is wrong because there is no good or bad to be wrong about.

It would help us all, I think, to look at the problem of judging works of art in a more direct way. These judgments, as can easily be seen in any random collection of reviews, go off in so many directions that it sometimes seems that the reviewers are talking about different things. We must keep our eye on the object—the painting, the novel, the quintet. Because the composer's love affairs were in a sorry state at the time he was composing, people think that the value of the music must somehow be connected with this circumstance. Because the painter was regarding his model while he painted, people think that the value of the painting must depend on some relation to the way she really looked, or felt. Because the novelist is known to be an anarchist or a conservative, people think that the value of the novel must consist partly in its fidelity to these attitudes. Now, of course, when we approach a work of art, there are many kinds of interest that we can take in it, as well as in its creator. But when we are trying to judge it *as* a work of art, rather than as biography or social criticism or something else, there is a central interest that ought to be kept in view.

A work of art, whatever its species, is an object of some kind—something somebody made. And the question is whether it was worth making, what it is good for, what can be done with it. In this respect it is like a tool. Tools of course are production goods, instrumental to other instruments, whereas paintings and musical compositions and novels are consumption goods, directly instrumental to some sort of experience. And their own peculiar excellence consists, I believe, in their capacity to afford certain valuable kinds and degrees of aesthetic experience. Of course they do not yield this experience to those who cannot understand them, just as a tool is of no use to one who has not the skill to wield it. But we do not talk in the Skeptical way about tools: we do not say that the value of a hammer is all a matter of taste, some people having a taste for hammering nails, some not. No, the value resides in its capability to drive the nail, given a hand and arm with the right skill, and if the need should arise. And this value it would have, though unrealized, even if the skill were temporarily lost

So with works of art, it seems to me. Their value is what they can do to and for us, if we are capable of having it done. And for those who do not, or not yet, have this capacity, it is not a simple fact that they do not, but a misfortune, and the only question is whether, or to what extent, it can be remedied. It is because this question sometimes has a hopeful answer that we dispute, and must dispute, about tastes. When the political disputant gives his reasons for supporting one Senatorial candidate over another, he cites facts about that candidate that he knows, from past experience, justify the hope of a good performance—the hope that the candidate, once elected, will do what a Senator is supposed to do, well. When the critic gives his reasons for saying that a work of art is good or bad, he is not, as the Skeptic claims, trying to guess whom it will please or displease; he is pointing out those features of the work—its qualities, structure, style, and so on—that are evidence of the work's ability or inability to provide qualified readers, listeners, or viewers, with a deep aesthetic experience.

THINK ABOUT

1. Plato, Tolstoy, and others have raised the question of the relation of art to morals. Is the production and enjoyment of art subject to the principles of ethics, or are art and morality two separate and autonomous fields? In your discussion, comment on the following:
   (a) "Art for art's sake."
   (b) "Art, like other interests, can flourish only in a sound and whole society, and the law of soundness and wholeness in life is morality."—Ralph Barton Perry
   (c) "Just as physical things cannot exist without the support of a physical environment, so moral life cannot go on without the support of a moral environment."—John Dewey

2 Should there be any censorship of art? Some groups vigorously oppose any type of censorship; others favor some censorship. Is censorship desirable? Give your reaction to the view that if censorship is ever tolerated it should be limited to cases of obscenity

not necessary to artistic effect and the depicting of crime and vice in such a way as to stimulate brutality.

3. Pablo Picasso, when asked to explain modern art, is said to have replied: "Do you require an explanation for the song of a bird?" Discuss this reply with some care.

two

What Is the Function of Art?

56

To Communicate
Emotions

Leo Tolstoy (1828–1910) was a Russian novelist and re-
former. His great novels, including *War and Peace* (1863–
69) and *Anna Karenina* (1873–77) were written in the earlier
period of his creative life. During the later period, he was
principally concerned with religious, ethical and aesthetic
subjects.

Some aestheticians believe that the function of art is to express emotions.
These writers maintain that art is the "language" of emotions. Tolstoy
asks two questions: first, are the emotions of the artist put into effective
communicable form? and second, are the emotions worthwhile? Tolstoy
believes that because art is so important in molding human attitudes it
should express simple and universal feelings which all men can appreciate,
especially the feelings engendered by Christianity.

TO STUDY

1. How does Tolstoy criticize the theory that art is founded on
   beauty?
2. What is his criticism of Schiller? Can you give an example?
3. What is his criticism of Veron?
4. What is his criticism of Sully's Theory?
5. Upon what is the activity of art based?
6. Of what is art a means?

7. What are the many art objects? How does one recognize real art? Better art?

8. Upon what does the degree of infectiousness depend?

9. How, in the subject matter of art, are we to decide what is good and what is bad?

10. What is the religious perception of our time?

There is no objective definition of beauty. The existing definitions . . . amount only to one and the same subjective definition, which is (strange as it seems to say so), that art is that which makes beauty manifest, and beauty is that which pleases (without exciting desire). Many estheticians have felt the insufficiency and instability of such a definition, and in order to give it a firm basis have asked themselves why a thing pleases. And they have converted the discussion on beauty into a question of taste, as did Hutcheson, Voltaire, Diderot, and others. But all attempts to define what taste is must lead to nothing, as the reader may see both from the history of esthetics and experimentally. There is and can be no explanation of why one thing pleases one man and displeases another, or *vice versa*; so that the whole existing science of esthetics fails to do what we might expect from it as a mental activity calling itself a science, namely, it does not define the qualities and laws of art, or of the beautiful (if that be the content of art), or the nature of taste (if taste decides the question of art and its merit), and then on the basis of such definitions acknowledge as art those productions which correspond to these laws and reject those which do not come under them. But this science of esthetics consists in first acknowledging a certain set of productions to be art (because they please us), and then framing such a theory of art as all these productions which please a certain circle of people can be fitted into. There exists an art-canon according to which certain productions favored by our circle are acknowledged as being art,—the works of Phidias, Sophocles, Homer, Titian, Raphael, Bach, Beethoven, Dante, Shakespeare, Goethe, and others,—and the esthetic laws must be such as to embrace all these productions. In esthetic literature you will constantly meet with opinions on the merit and importance of art, founded not on any certain laws by which this or that is held to be good or bad, but merely on consideration as to whether this art tallies with the art-canon we have drawn up. . . .

So that the theory of art founded on beauty, expounded by esthetics and in dim outline professed by the public, is nothing but the setting up as good of that which has pleased and pleases us, that is, pleases a certain class of people.

In order to define any human activity, it is necessary to understand its sense and importance; and in order to do this it is primarily necessary to examine that activity in itself, in its dependence on its causes and in connection with its effects, and not merely in relation to the pleasure we can get from it.

If we say that the aim of any activity is merely our pleasure and define it solely by that pleasure, our definition will evidently be a false one. But this is precisely what has occurred in the efforts to define art. . . .

What is art if we put aside the conception of beauty, which confuses the whole matter? The latest and most comprehensible definitions of art, apart from the conception of beauty, are the following:—(1) *a*, Art is an activity arising even in the animal kingdom, and springing from sexual desire and the propensity to play (Schiller, Darwin, Spencer), and *b*, accompanied by a pleasurable excitement of the nervous system (Grant Allen). This is the physiological-evolutionary definition. (2) Art is the external manifestation, by means of lines, colors, movements, sounds, or words, of emotions felt by man (Véron). This is the experimental definition. According to the very latest definition (Sully), (3) Art is "the production of some permanent object or passing action which is fitted not only to supply an active enjoyment to the producer, but to convey a pleasurable impression to a number of spectators or listeners, quite apart from any personal advantage to be derived from it."

Notwithstanding the superiority of these definitions to the metaphysical definitions which depended on the conception of beauty, they are yet far from exact. The first, the physiological-evolutionary definition (1), *a*, is inexact, because instead of speaking about the artistic activity itself, which is the real matter in hand, it treats of the derivation of art. The modification of it, *b*, based on the physiological effects on the human organism, is inexact because within the limits of such definition many other human activities can be included, as has occurred in the neo-esthetic theories which reckon as art the preparation of handsome clothes, pleasant scents, and even of victuals.

The experimental definition, (2), which makes art consist in the expression of emotions, is inexact because a man may express his emotions by means of lines, colors, sounds, or words and yet may not act on others by such expression—and then the manifestation of his emotions is not art.

The third definition (that of Sully) is inexact because in the production of objects or actions affording pleasure to the producer and a pleasant emotion to the spectators or hearers apart from personal advantage, may be included the showing of conjuring tricks or gymnastic exercises, and other activities which are not art. And further, many things the production of which does not afford pleasure to the producer and the sensation received from which is unpleasant, such as gloomy, heart-rending scenes in a poetic description or a play, may nevertheless be undoubted works of art.

The inaccuracy of all these definitions arises from the fact that in them all (as also in the metaphysical definitions) the object considered is the pleasure art may give, and not the purpose it may serve in the life of man and of humanity.

In order to define art correctly it is necessary first of all to cease to consider it as a means to pleasure, and to consider it as one of the conditions of human life. Viewing it in this way we cannot fail to observe that art is one of the means of intercourse between man and man.

Every work of art causes the receiver to enter into a certain kind of relationship both with him who produced or is producing the art, and with all those who, simultaneously, previously, or subsequently, receive the same artistic impression.

Speech transmitting the thoughts and experiences of men serves as a means of union among them, and art serves a similar purpose. The peculiarity of this latter means of intercourse, distinguishing it from intercourse by means of words, consists in this, that whereas by words a man transmits his thoughts to another, by art he transmits his feelings.

The activity of art is based on the fact that a man receiving through his sense of hearing or sight another man's expression of feeling, is capable of experiencing the emotion which moved the man who expressed it. To take the simplest example: one man laughs, and another who hears becomes merry, or a man weeps, and another who hears feels sorrow. A man is excited or irritated, and another man seeing him is brought to a similar state of mind. By his movements or by the sounds of his voice a man expresses courage and determination or sadness and calmness, and this state of mind passes on to others. A man suffers, manifesting his suffering by groans and spasms, and this suffering transmits itself to other people; a man expresses his feelings of admiration, devotion, fear, respect, or love, to certain objects, persons, or phenomena, and others are infected by the same feelings of admiration, devotion, fear, respect, or love, to the same objects, persons, or phenomena.

And it is on this capacity of man to receive another man's expression of feeling and to experience those feelings himself, that the activity of art is based.

If a man infects another or others directly, immediately, by his appearance or by the sounds he gives vent to at the very time he experiences the feeling; if he causes another man to yawn when he himself cannot help yawning, or to laugh or cry when he himself is obliged to laugh or cry, or to suffer when he himself is suffering—that does not amount to art.

Art begins when one person with the object of joining another or others to himself in one and the same feeling, expresses that feeling by certain external indications. To take the simplest example: a boy having experienced, let us say, fear on encountering a wolf, relates that encounter, and in order to evoke in others the feeling he has experienced, describes himself, his condition before the encounter, the surroundings, the wood, his own lightheartedness, and then the wolf's appearance, its movements, the distance between himself and the wolf, and so forth. All this, if only the boy when telling the story again experiences the feelings he had lived through, and infects the hearers and compels them to feel what he had experienced—is art. Even if the boy had not seen a wolf but had frequently been afraid of one, and if wishing to evoke in others the fear he had felt, he invented an encounter with a wolf and recounted it so as to make his hearers share the feelings he experienced when he feared the wolf, that also would be art. And just in the same way it is art if a man, having experienced either the fear of suffering or the attraction of enjoyment (whether in reality or in imagination), expresses these feelings on canvas or in marble so that others are infected by them. And it is also art if a man feels, or imagines to himself, feelings of delight, gladness, sorrow, despair, courage, or despondency, and the transition from one to another of these feelings, and expresses them by sounds so that the hearers are infected by them and experience them as they were experienced by the composer.

The feelings with which the artist infects others may be most various—very strong or very weak, very important or very insignificant, very bad or very good: feelings of love of one's country, self-devotion and submission to fate or to God expressed in a drama, raptures of lovers described in a novel, feelings of voluptuousness expressed in a picture, courage expressed in a triumphal march, merriment evoked by a dance, humor evoked by a funny story, the feeling of quietness transmitted by an evening landscape or by a lullaby, or the feeling of admiration evoked by a beautiful arabesque—it is all art.

If only the spectators or auditors are infected by the feelings which the author has felt, it is art.

To evoke in oneself a feeling one has once experienced and having evoked it in oneself then by means of movements, lines, colors, sounds, or forms expressed in words, so to transmit that feeling that others experience the same feeling—this is the activity of art.

Art is a human activity consisting in this, that one man consciously by means of certain external signs, hands on to others feelings he has lived through, and that others are infected by these feelings and also experience them.

Art is not, as the metaphysicians say, the manifestation of some mysterious Idea of beauty or God; it is not, as the esthetic physiologists say, a game in which man lets off his excess of stored-up energy; it is not the expression of man's emotions by external signs; it is not the production of pleasing objects; and, above all, it is not pleasure; but it is a means of union among men joining them together in the same feelings, and indispensable for the life and progress towards well-being of individuals and of humanity.

As every man, thanks to man's capacity to express thoughts by words, may know all that has been done for him in the realms of thought by all humanity before this day, and can in the present, thanks to this capacity to understand the thoughts of others, become a sharer in their activity and also himself hand on to his contemporaries and descendants the thoughts he has assimilated from others as well as those that have arisen in himself; so, thanks to man's capacity to be infected with the feelings of others by means of art, all that is being lived through by his contemporaries is accessible to him, as well as the feelings experienced by men thousands of years ago, and he has also the possibility of transmitting his own feelings to others.

If people lacked the capacity to receive the thoughts conceived by men who preceded them and to pass on to others their own thoughts, men would be like wild beasts, or like Kasper Hauser.[1]

And if men lacked this other capacity of being infected by art, people might be almost more savage still, and above all more separated from, and more hostile to, one another.

And therefore the activity of art is a most important one, as important as the activity of speech itself and as generally diffused.

As speech does not act on us only in sermons, orations, or books, but in all those remarks by which we interchange thoughts and experiences with one another, so also art in the wide sense of the word permeates our whole life, but it is only to some of its manifestations that we apply the term in the limited sense of the word.

We are accustomed to understand art to be only what we hear and see in theaters, concerts, and exhibitions; together with buildings, statues,

---

[1] "The foundling of Nuremberg," found in the marketplace of that town on 23rd May 1828, apparently some sixteen years old. He spoke little and was almost totally ignorant even of common objects. He subsequently explained that he had been brought up in confinement underground and visited by only one man, whom he saw but seldom.

poems, and novels. . . . But all this is but the smallest part of the art by which we communicate with one another in life. All human life is filled with works of art of every kind—from cradle-song, jest, mimicry, the ornamentation of houses, dress, and utensils, to church services, buildings, monuments, and triumphal processions. It is all artistic activity. So that by art, in the limited sense of the word, we do not mean all human activity transmitting feelings but only that part which we for some reason select from it and to which we attach special importance. . . .

There is one indubitable sign distinguishing real art from its counterfeit—namely, the infectiousness of art. If a man without exercising effort and without altering his standpoint, on reading, hearing, or seeing another man's work experiences a mental condition which unites him with that man and with others who are also affected by that work, then the object evoking that condition is a work of art. And however poetic, realistic, striking, or interesting, a work may be, it is not a work of art if it does not evoke that feeling (quite distinct from all other feelings) of joy and of spiritual union with another (the author) and with others (those who are also infected by it).

It is true that this indication is an *internal* one and that there are people who, having forgotten what the action of real art is, expect something else from art (in our society the great majority are in this state), and that therefore such people may mistake for this esthetic feeling the feeling of diversion and a certain excitement which they receive from counterfeits of art. But though it is impossible to undeceive these people, just as it may be impossible to convince a man suffering from color-blindness that green is not red, yet for all that, this indication remains perfectly definite to those whose feeling for art is neither perverted nor atrophied, and it clearly distinguishes the feeling produced by art from all other feelings.

The chief peculiarity of this feeling is that the recipient of a truly artistic impression is so united to the artist that he feels as if the work were his own and not some one else's—as if what it expresses were just what he had long been wishing to express. A real work of art destroys in the consciousness of the recipient the separation between himself and the artist, and not that alone, but also between himself and all whose minds receive this work of art. In this freeing of our personality from its separation and isolation, in this uniting of it with others, lies the chief characteristic and the great attractive force of art.

If a man is infected by the author's condition of soul, if he feels this emotion and this union with others, then the object which has effected this is art; but if there be no such infection, if there be not this union with the author and with others who are moved by the same work—

then it is not art. And not only is infection a sure sign of art, but the degree of infectiousness is also the sole measure of excellence in art.

The stronger the infection the better is the art, as art, speaking of it now apart from its subject-matter—that is, not considering the value of the feelings it transmits.

And the degree of the infectiousness of art depends on three conditions: (1) On the greater or lesser individuality of the feeling transmitted; (2) on the greater or lesser clearness with which the feeling is transmitted; (3) on the sincerity of the artist, that is, on the greater or lesser force with which the artist himself feels the emotion he transmits.

The more individual the feeling transmitted the more strongly does it act on the recipient; the more individual the state of soul into which he is transferred the more pleasure does the recipient obtain and therefore the more readily and strongly does he join in it.

Clearness of expression assists infection because the recipient who mingles in consciousness with the author is the better satisfied the more clearly that feeling is transmitted which, as it seems to him, he has long known and felt and for which he has only now found expression.

But most of all is the degree of infectiousness of art increased by the degree of sincerity in the artist. As soon as the spectator, hearer, or reader, feels that the artist is infected by his own production and writes, sings, or plays, for himself, and not merely to act on others, this mental condition of the artist infects the recipient; and, on the contrary, as soon as the spectator, reader, or hearer, feels that the author is not writing, singing, or playing, for his own satisfaction—does not himself feel what he wishes to express, but is doing it for him, the recipient—resistance immediately springs up, and the most individual and the newest feelings and the cleverest technique not only fail to produce any infection but actually repel.

I have mentioned three conditions of contagion in art, but they may all be summed up into one, the last, sincerity; that is, that the artist should be impelled by an inner need to express his feeling. That condition includes the first; for if the artist is sincere he will express the feeling as he experienced it. And as each man is different from everyone else, his feeling will be individual for everyone else; and the more individual it is—the more the artist has drawn it from the depths of his nature—the more sympathetic and sincere will it be. And this same sincerity will impel the artist to find clear expression for the feeling which he wishes to transmit.

Therefore this third condition—sincerity—is the most important of the three. It is always complied with in peasant art, and this explains why such art always acts so powerfully; but it is a condition almost entirely absent from our upper-class art, which is continually produced by artists actuated by personal aims of covetousness or vanity.

Such are the three conditions which divide art from its counterfeits, and which also decide the quality of every work of art considered apart from its subject matter.

The absence of any one of these conditions excludes a work from the category of art and relegates it to that of art's counterfeits. If the work does not transmit the artist's peculiarity of feeling and is therefore not individual, if it is unintelligibly expressed, or if it has not proceeded from the author's inner need for expression—it is not a work of art. If all these conditions are present even in the smallest degree, then the work even if a weak one is yet a work of art.

The presence in various degrees of these three conditions: individuality, clearness, and sincerity, decides the merit of a work of art as art, apart from subject matter. All works of art take order of merit according to the degree in which they fulfil the first, the second, and the third, of these conditions. In one the individuality of the feeling transmitted may predominate; in another, clearness of expression; in a third, sincerity; while a fourth may have sincerity and individuality but be deficient in clearness; a fifth, individuality and clearness, but less sincerity; and so forth, in all possible degrees and combinations.

Thus is art divided from what is not art, and thus is the quality of art, as art, decided, independently of its subject matter, that is to say, apart from whether the feelings it transmits are good or bad. . . .

How in the subject matter of art are we to decide what is good and what is bad?

Art like speech is a means of communication and therefore of progress, that is, of the movement of humanity forward towards perfection. Speech renders accessible to men of the latest generation all the knowledge discovered by the experience and reflection both of preceding generations and of the best and foremost men of their own times; art renders accessible to men of the latest generations all the feelings experienced by their predecessors and also those felt by their best and foremost contemporaries. And as the evolution of knowledge proceeds by truer and more necessary knowledge dislodging and replacing what was mistaken and unnecessary, so the evolution of feeling proceeds by means of art—feelings less kind and less necessary for the well-being of mankind being replaced by others kinder and more needful for that end. That is the purpose of art. And speaking now of the feelings which are its subject matter, the more art fulfils that purpose the better the art, and the less it fulfils it the worse the art.

The appraisement of feelings (that is, the recognition of one or other set of feelings as more or less good, more or less necessary for the well-being of mankind) is effected by the religious perception of the age.

In every period of history and in every human society there exists an understanding of the meaning of life, which represents the highest level to which men of that society have attained—an understanding indicating the highest good at which that society aims. This understanding is the religious perception of the given time and society. And this religious perception is always clearly expressed by a few advanced men and more or less vividly perceived by members of the society generally. Such a religious perception and its corresponding expression always exists in every society. If it appears to us that there is no religious perception in our society, this is not because there really is none, but only because we do not wish to see it. And we often wish not to see it because it exposes the fact that our life is inconsistent with that religious perception.

Religious perception in a society is like the direction of a flowing river. If the river flows at all it must have a direction. If a society lives, there must be a religious perception indicating the direction in which, more or less consciously, all its members tend.

And so there always has been, and is, a religious perception in every society. And it is by the standard of this religious perception that the feelings transmitted by art have always been appraised. It has always been only on the basis of this religious perception of their age, that men have chosen from amid the endlessly varied spheres of art that art which transmitted feelings making religious perception operative in actual life. And such art has always been highly valued and encouraged, while art transmitting feelings already outlived, flowing from the antiquated religious perceptions of a former age, has always been condemned and despised. All the rest of art transmitting those most diverse feelings by means of which people commune with one another was not condemned and was tolerated if only it did not transmit feelings contrary to religious perception. Thus for instance among the Greeks, art transmitting feelings of beauty, strength, and courage (Hesiod, Homer, Phidias) was chosen, approved, and encouraged, while art transmitting feelings of rude sensuality, despondency, and effeminacy, was condemned and despised. Among the Jews, art transmitting feelings of devotion and submission to the God of the Hebrews and to His will (the epic of Genesis, the prophets, the Psalms) was chosen and encouraged, while art transmitting feelings of idolatry (the Golden Calf) was condemned and despised. All the rest of art—stories, songs, dances, ornamentation of houses, of utensils, and of clothes—which was not contrary to religious perception, was neither distinguished nor discussed. Thus as regards its subject matter has art always and everywhere been appraised and thus it should be appraised, for this attitude towards art proceeds from the fundamental characteristics of human nature, and those characteristics do not change.

I know that according to an opinion current in our times religion is a superstition humanity has outgrown, and it is therefore assumed that no such thing exists as a religious perception common to us all by which art in our time can be appraised. I know that this is the opinion current in the pseudo-cultured circles of today. People who do not acknowledge Christianity in its true meaning because it undermines their social privileges, and who therefore invent all kinds of philosophic and esthetic theories to hide from themselves the meaninglessness and wrongfulness of their lives, cannot think otherwise. These people intentionally, or sometimes unintentionally, confuse the notion of a religious cult with the notion of religious perception, and think that by denying the cult they get rid of the perception. But even the very attacks on religion and the attempts to establish an idea of life contrary to the religious perception of our times, most clearly demonstrate the existence of a religious perception condemning the lives that are not in harmony with it.

If humanity progresses, that is, moves forward, there must inevitably be a guide to the direction of that movement. And religions have always furnished that guide. All history shows that the progress of humanity is accomplished no otherwise than under the guidance of religion. But if the race cannot progress without the guidance of religion—and progress is always going on, and consequently goes on also in our own times— then there must be a religion of our times. So that whether it pleases or displeases the so-called cultured people of today, they must admit the existence of religion—not of a religious cult, Catholic, Protestant, or another, but of religious perception—which even in our times is the guide always present where there is any progress. And if a religious perception exists amongst us, then the feelings dealt with by our art should be appraised on the basis of that religious perception; and as has been the case always and everywhere, art transmitting feelings flowing from the religious perception of our time should be chosen from amid all the indifferent art, should be acknowledged, highly valued, and encouraged, while art running counter to that perception should be condemned and despised, and all the remaining, indifferent, art should neither be distinguished nor encouraged.

The religious perception of our time in its widest and most practical application is the consciousness that our well-being, both material and spiritual, individual and collective, temporal and eternal, lies in the growth of brotherhood among men—in their loving harmony with one another.

This perception is not only expressed by Christ and all the best men of past ages, it is not only repeated in most varied forms and from most diverse sides by the best men of our times, but it already serves as a clue to all the complex labor of humanity, consisting as this labor does on the one hand in the destruction of physical and moral obstacles to the union of men, and on the other hand in establishing the principles common to all men which can and should unite them in one universal brotherhood. And it is on the basis of this perception that we should appraise all the phenomena of our life and among the rest our art also: choosing from all its realms and highly prizing and encouraging whatever transmits feelings flowing from this religious perception, rejecting whatever is contrary to it, and not attributing to the rest of art an importance that does not properly belong to it. . . .

Whatever the work may be and however it may have been extolled, we have first to ask whether this work is one of real art, or a counterfeit. Having acknowledged, on the basis of the indication of its infectiousness even to a small class of people, that a certain production belongs to the realm of art, it is necessary on this basis to decide the next question, Does this work belong to the category of bad exclusive art opposed to religious perception, or of Christian art uniting people? And having acknowledged a work to belong to real Christian art, we must then, according to whether it transmits feelings flowing from love of God and man, or merely the simple feelings uniting all men, assign it a place in the ranks of religious art, or in those of universal art.

Only on the basis of such verification shall we find it possible to select from the whole mass of what in our society claims to be art, those works which form real, important, necessary, spiritual food, and to separate them from all the harmful and useless art and from the counterfeits of art which surround us. Only on the basis of such verification shall we be able to rid ourselves of the pernicious results of harmful art and avail ourselves of that beneficent action which is the purpose of true and good art, and which is indispensable for the spiritual life of man and of humanity.

From *What Is Art?* (1896; translated 1905 by Aylmer Maude).

57

To Communicate
Political Views

Meredith Tax (1940–   ) writes about the women's movement. Currently she lives in New York and is a free lance
writer.

Tax perceives the matter of culture and its meaning to be politically
significant. She claims that all art, from "All in the Family" to Wagner's
music, serves someone's political interest: the poor or blacks are often
presented as stupid; the omission of certain difficult problems on, say,
television is a political act, etc. Recall Worsham's famous statement,
"The function of mass culture is to maintain public morale." Thus, Rome
had its circuses, and we have mass sports and television to maintain
public morale. Tax sees art as the only means of teaching people to
take control over their own lives.

TO STUDY

1. What is Tax's thesis? Explain what she means.
2. Tax argues that to "refrain from mentioning genocide, racism,
   . . . is itself a political act." Explain and discuss whether or not
   you agree.
3. What is Tax's main thesis regarding the contrast between the
   poems of Brecht and Yeats?
4. According to Tax, what happens to art in a capitalist society?
5. Is she correct as to the central ideas of the art of the modern
   period?

6. Explain: "this art . . . is the opium of the people."
7. What positive things does she claim about counter-culture art?

The thesis I wish to present here is that culture is not neutral politically, and that it is as impossible for it to be so as it is impossible for any other product of human labour to be detached from its conditions of production and reception. All culture serves someone's interest. Cultural products which present foreign wars as the heroic effort of a master race to ennoble mankind are, to the degree that they are successful as art, objectively in the interests of imperialists, who are people who make foreign wars against other races for profit. Cultural products that present people who have no money or power as innately stupid or depraved, and thus unworthy of money or power, are in the interests of the ruling class and the power structure as it stands. Cultural products which present women who do not want to be household slaves or universal mothers or sex objects as bitches or sexual failures objectively aid male supremacy.

Some writers are overtly political—though to be so in America has taken more courage or vision than most writers since the Second World War have had. Most writers avoid mentioning overtly political issues. But this does not mean they are disengaged from them. In our times, to refrain from mentioning genocide, racism, cultural schizophrenia, sexual exploitation, and the systematic starvation of entire populations is itself a political act. For no one in our time can be awake enough to write and have avoided noticing these phenomena—though he may not recognize them for what they are. As our bankrupt civilization draws to its close, and as the violence of the powerful against the weak, of the rich against the poor, of the few against the many, becomes more and more apparent, until it becomes impossible to watch a news broadcast and remain unaware of it for a second—as this situation becomes exacerbated, to refrain from mentioning it becomes more and more clearly a political act, an act of censorship or cowardice.

Yet very few of our establishment writers and artists, let alone of our literary critics, think these things are important enough to mention in their work. They may bear witness as private individuals, but they do not allow their private concern to interfere with business as usual. Let us paraphrase any well-adjusted academic critic's attitude toward the poet's method of dealing with this problem.

From Meredith Tax, "Introductory: Culture is not Neutral, Whom Does it Serve," in *Radical Perspectives in the Arts,* edited by Lee Baxandall (New York and London: Penguin Books, 1972), pp. 15–29. Reprinted with permission of the editor and author.

"A poet's job is to do his thing," he will say. "Naturally he will write about what is important or central to him personally, and who am I to interfere with another man's system of values? If Wallace Stevens chooses to write about arpeggios and pineapples rather than about racial tensions in Hartford or the practices of the insurance company he was vice-president of in regard to people on welfare, this was his decision; what's it to me? And as for the implication that his position as a member of the ruling class may have governed his perception of the importance of such problems, or led him to fear dignifying them by the poetic process, why, I think that's extremely unfair and full of all kinds of critical fallacies."

And, perhaps, considered from the strictly *professional* point of view of keeping up standards within the criticism business, and not rocking the boat, this may be so. But let us, for the moment, consider the problem from a *human* rather than a *professional* point of view.

Bertolt Brecht, a German Communist poet, wrote an essay in 1935 entitled: "Writing the Truth: Five Difficulties." In it he states:

> Nowadays, anyone who wishes to combat lies and ignorance and to write the truth must overcome at least five difficulties. He must have the *courage* to write the truth when truth is everywhere opposed; the *keenness* to recognize it, although it is everywhere concealed; the *skill* to manipulate it as a weapon; the *judgement* to select those in whose hands it will be effective; and the *cunning* to spread the truth among such persons. These are formidable problems for a writer living under Fascism, but they exist also for those writers who have fled or been exiled; they exist even for writers working in countries where civil liberty prevails.

Brecht goes on to discuss the problem of *what* truths are worth telling, a problem of peculiar relevance to us.

> First of all we strike trouble in determining *what* truth is worth the telling. For example, before the eyes of the whole world one great civilized nation after the other falls into barbarism. Moreover, everyone knows that the domestic war which is being waged by the most ghastly methods can at any moment be converted into a foreign war which may well leave our continent a heap of ruins. This, undoubtedly, is one truth, but there are others. Thus, for example, it is not untrue that chairs have seats and that rain falls downward. Many poets write truths of this sort. They are like a painter adorning the walls of a sinking ship with a still life. . . . Those in power cannot corrupt them, but neither are they disturbed by the cries of the oppressed. . . . At the same time, it is not easy to realize that their truths are truths about chairs or rain; they usually sound like truths about important things. For it is the nature of artistic creation to confer importance. But upon closer examination it is possible to see that they say merely: a chair is a chair; and: no one can prevent the rain from falling down.

I went through a respectable liberal education, one purpose of which was to outfit me as a literary critic and teacher of literature. We studied a great many monuments of culture in my classes. We discussed the form of these works, either in itself, or in relation to other things written at the time; we occasionally speculated as to whether there were any eternal truths concealed in these works; or whether they had any relation to works of art in other genres; but mostly we just discussed the form of these works in exhaustive detail—the words, how they operated in tension with each other, the length of the poetic line, the use of symbols, etcetera.

The one thing we never discussed about any cultural monuments was their *meaning*—just their barefaced everyday philistine literal meaning. I think that if any of us had thought to bring this problem up we would have been laughed at. Of course, none of us ever did bring it up, because we wanted the approval of our teachers, and because we had never heard that one should take literature seriously enough to worry about what it meant in terms of one's own life. At most, we had heard that form and content were the same in great works, so that there was clearly no importance to discussing anything but form.

And so we went through all the great works of literature, works which were often, at least until the modern period, passionately ideological, as if we had blinkers on. It is indeed a characteristic of the modern period that reality in it is so intolerable that most artists and critics cannot bear to deal with it directly. But some of them, at least, allude to it if not confront it. Take, for instance, the poem "Easter 1916" by Yeats, a poem frequently studied in school.

> We know their dream; enough
> To know they dreamed and are dead;
> And what if excess of love
> Bewildered them till they died?
> I write it out in a verse—
> MacDonagh and MacBride
> And Connolly and Pearse
> Now and in time to be,
> Wherever green is worn,
> Are changed, changed utterly:
> A terrible beauty is born.

What are the political implications of this verse? What does it mean? What is he trying to get us to think or to do? And how is it that such questions so seldom arise in the consideration of a poem?

What Yeats is getting at becomes clearer when his poem is put next to Brecht's "To Posterity," another great poem, which is however never taught in literature classes. Brecht's poem ends:

> You, who shall emerge from the flood
> In which we are sinking,
> Think—
> When you speak of our weaknesses,
> Also of the dark time
> That brought them forth.
> For we went, changing our country more often than our shoes,
> In the class war, despairing
> When there was only injustice and no resistance.
> For we knew only too well:
> Even hatred of squalor
> Makes the brow grow stern.
> Even anger against injustice
> Makes the voice grow harsh. Alas, we
> Who wished to lay the foundations of kindness
> Could not ourselves be kind.
> But you, when at last it comes to pass
> That man can help his fellow man,
> Do not judge us
> Too harshly.

Brecht and Yeats are talking of the same phenomena, of what happens to people who commit themselves to revolutionary politics. Their ordinary life is transformed; and personal values, as trivially defined, become less important to them than the good of all people. This involves certain kinds of sacrifice that often seem bizarre or incomprehensible to people who do not get the point. Brecht speaks of this, and of what he has missed out on in his personal life, in an earlier stanza of the same poem:

> I ate my food between massacres.
> The shadow of murder lay upon my sleep.
> And when I loved, I loved with indifference.
> I looked upon nature with impatience.
> So the time passes away
> Which on earth was given me.

Yeats is talking about the same withdrawals and austerities in his central metaphor of the stone in the midst of the living stream:

> Hearts with one purpose alone
> Through summer and winter seem

Enchanted to a stone
To trouble the living stream.
The horse that comes from the road,
The rider, the birds that range
From cloud to trembling cloud,
Minute by minute they change;
A shadow of cloud on the stream
Changes minute by minute;
A horse-hoof slides on the brim,
And a horse plashes within it;
The long-legged moor-hens dive,
And hens to moor-cocks call;
Minute by minute they live:
The stone's in the midst of all.

Too long a sacrifice
Can make a stone of the heart.

Brecht devoted his life and his work to making sure, to the best of his ability, that certain things happened in the world. He ends his poem by looking ahead with absolute confidence to a time after the revolution, when people will have changed, when circumstances will have ceased to require that they be as hard and purposeful as he needed to be. This is what is important to him, that the quality of life will change, and that people will cease to have to be deformed by their environment as he was.

In Yeats's poem, what is important is not whether the revolutionaries he writes about win or lose, not whether their political ideas are right or wrong, but whether individual heroism and aesthetic beauty are the products of their struggle. "O when may it suffice?" he asks of their sacrifice, and answers, leave it to heaven, we can't know; our job is to make verses which tell how they have been personally ennobled.

We know their dream; enough
To know they dreamed and are dead . . .
Are changed, changed utterly:
A terrible beauty is born.

What does this mean but that, in the end, aesthetic values are the most important; and beauty of a certain noble kind is more important than success? And what is this but to focus on a few heroes, as if the whole meaning of the struggle dwelt in their features, and forget the thousands that followed behind them, peasants, workers, not aristocrats, and less beautiful than themselves, but to whom an end of colonialism was literally a matter of life or death. Their lives do not come into the poem; and this fact determines its political meaning—it is a beautiful expression of a certain kind of romantic élitism, and a betrayal of the Irish Revolution.

The ideas that aesthetic values are primary, and that personal heroism is the kind to focus on, are typical of late bourgeois poetry, in that they express the privatization of bourgeois life, and the divorcement of modern art from the base of society.

Let us take a longer look at the philosophy of art-for-art's-sake: that is, at the ideology that art is justified by its existence, that it does not and should not serve any social purpose, that it frequently has no reference to anything outside itself, and that it is expressive of the vision of the individual poet, if of anything. The accompanying critical doctrine is that any criticism of a poem in terms other than these is an importation of irrelevant values: "A poem should not mean but be."

The thing we tend to forget is that this aesthetic philosophy developed at a certain historical moment—it didn't always exist, and is in fact fairly recent. "Art-for-art's-sake" was the response of the producers of art to a market which was as mysterious and alienating to them as it was to the producers of other commodities. In most cultures prior to that of industrial capitalism, artists have had a well-defined and clearly understood relation to some part of their society, some group of consumers. In a primitive tribe or collective, art is the expression of the whole tribe—later, some people may be specially good at it, or hereditarily trained to it, and take on the production of artifacts as their work, but they work surrounded by the community, and work for the community's immediate and obvious benefit. In other periods of history, the artist has produced for a court, for a personal patron, for a religious sect, or for a political party. It is only with the dominance of the capitalist system that the artist has been put in the position of producing for a *market,* for strangers far away, whose life styles and beliefs and needs are completely unknown to him, and who will either buy his works or ignore them for reasons that are equally inscrutable and out of his control.

In the sphere of production, Marxists call the attitude that results from this process "commodity fetishism." The processes of production and distribution—that is: the gathering of raw materials, the inventing of machines and processes, the organization of labour into successive stages of work on the different stages of manufacture, distribution, marketing, advertising, and all the rest—all make up a process so infinitely complex that neither the consumer who buys the finished product nor the producer of any one stage of it, has any clear idea what is going on. You buy a chair. You have no idea who made it, what the materials in it are and where they came from and what they originally cost, how much the labour in it cost, and how much the price of the chair has been jacked up by profit and by waste like advertising. All of this is no more mysterious to you than it is to the factory worker who made one ingredient of the plastic that the seat of the chair is made of. In this kind of economy, objects are regarded as though they had originated by magic and appeared in the shops, not as if they were made by people for other people to use.

Most critical theory as currently practised is an extension of this commodity fetishism into the realm of culture. A poem is not thought of as something made by a man for other men to use—it is thought of as having come about by some incomprehensible process, and for no clear end but its own existence. It is thought of in this way even by its producer, the poet. Like the factory worker he sends his product out into an unfriendly void. The use of his product, if any, is conjectural; he probably thinks it has none to anyone but himself. How can he be other than alienated from his work? How can he justify its existence, when he cannot *see* or *know* the people who use it, except by making its clear lack of relation to his society into an artistic creed, which becomes in its turn a critical dogma?

Art has not always been isolated in this way. An Italian fresco painter knew exactly who he was decorating a church for—who would pay him and what families would worship in that church. Voltaire knew who he wanted to reach with *Candide,* and what he wanted them to think. Even Samuel Richardson managed to get in touch with a circle of correspondents, whose reaction to his books he could judge as he went along and thus determine whether he was achieving the desired moral effects. And contemporary Soviet poets are in touch with mass audiences who will flock to hear them read their latest. Writers in conditions like these are not alienated from their own work to the extent that they think it isn't good for anything, and isn't meant to reach anyone but a few friends.

In the period of bourgeois culture that is drawing to a close, two kinds of art have been produced: "high-brow" and "low-brow" as they are often called. Both have served the political end of pacifying or immobilizing parts of the population potentially hostile to the system as it stands.

"High-brow" culture is directed at the upper middle class, students, and intellectuals, who tend to take jobs such as teachers, health workers, social workers, etc., whose social function in our society is to control the lives and minds of others. This form of culture militates against the perception of the political solutions of political problems by purveying ideas which are in their implications and social use, if not in the motives of the people who produced them, reactionary. These are the central ideas of the art of the modern period, expressed in its form as well as its content. Some of them are:

1. That life is absurd, meaningless.

2. That we are all victims, and to be conscious is to despair.
3. That any communication or understanding between human beings is *a priori* impossible because the human condition is one of quintessential isolation.
4. That one's perception of reality is both subjective and uncontrollably fragmented; that there is no way of integrating the different parts of one's experience and the external world.
5. That most of life and most people are disgusting, vulgar and stupid. The class bias inherent in the word 'vulgar' is quite conscious in this formulation.
6. That there are no real objective truths, including the above.

This is what most serious modern literature teaches us. It's no accident. The extreme inhumanity of our civilization—its class system, its racism, its gross commercialism, its male chauvinism, its institutionalized violence, its imperialist wars—all these factors make consciousness almost unbearable to people who have not looked behind these symptoms to their causes and cure, who do not see that they make up the fabric of a particular social and economic system which is different from those of the past and can be superseded in the future. What has been made by people can, in the long run, be understood and changed by them.

The other kind of culture purveyed in our society is "low-brow" or mass culture—a kind we are taught to despise as we are taught to despise those who consume it. This art, in fact, expresses nothing about the people who consume it but their deprivation. It is a mass-produced means of social control by manipulation of the national fantasy life. It is no more a product of any working-class culture than are the can-openers and Fords produced in our factories. I'm talking about TV, Westerns, Mickey Spillane and Erle Stanley Gardner, drugstore romances, sexy novels, Mantovani and Muzak, Norman Rockwell and the Keuhns. This is proletarianized art: it implicitly expresses its consumers' consciousness of their oppression, while at the same time preventing them from changing it. Christopher Caudwell described it thirty years ago in his book *Illusion and Reality:*

> Because art's role is now that of adapting the multitude to the dead mechanical existence of capitalist production, in which work sucks them of their vital energies without awakening their instincts, where leisure becomes a time to deaden the mind with the easy fantasy of films, simple wish-fulfilment writing, or music that is mere emotional massage—because of this the paid craft of writing becomes as tedious and wearisome as that of machine-minder . . . [this art] is at once an expression of real misery and a protest against the real misery. This art, universal, constant, fabulous, full of the easy gratifica-

tions of instincts starved by modern capitalism, peopled by passionate lovers and heroic cowboys and amazing detectives, is the religion of today, as characteristic an expression of proletarian exploitation as Catholicism is of feudal exploitation. It is the opium of the people; it pictures an inverted world because the world of society *is* inverted.

But times are changing. And in certain small ways, art is beginning to reflect these changes. For the first time since the Industrial Revolution it has become possible for artists to define themselves against the values of capitalist society and at the same time have an audience, a definite and large subgroup of the population, that they are producing for, an audience that also defines itself in opposition to the dominant culture. We have the makings of a revolutionary culture, that tells the truth about our society, demonstrates opposition to what is going on, and sometimes even poses alternatives. I'm not saying this *is* a revolutionary culture yet—you don't get a revolutionary culture until you get a revolution. But something is happening here.

There are three things about this new counter-culture that I find especially interesting and positive in terms of the social values they imply.

The first is that this culture is in many cases the product of collective effort rather than of bourgeois individualism. Rock groups, street theatre groups, poster workshops, art crews for demonstrations—all of these are forms of creativity that are social and shared.

The second thing is that many of these cultural forms are conceived of as participatory; these would include a lot of theatre which demands audience participation and response; poetry which demands being read out loud; and music that needs dance to fulfil it, and which is participated in by people who dance.

The third thing is that many of these new art expressions mix media and genres to a new extent. The rock groups that combine posters, slides, light shows, music, poetry, dance and special effects are one example. Such art breaks down very old divisions of labour; and any breakdown of the division of labour in the arts seems a hopeful sign of our growing ability to integrate different kinds of experience.

This new art is often explicitly political, political in a sense that embraces all of experience, not just the narrow realm defined by poli. sci. Take for instance The Cream's song called "Politician," which begins, "Come on, baby, get into my big black car, I'm going to show you just what my politics are."

The conditions of production and even more of distribution of this poetry are a long way from being ideal. Rock performers are exploited by their merchandisers and preyed upon by their public to a degree unusual even in the mass performing arts. There is much that is religious about mass art, and some rock performers have become to some degree human sacrifices; the confusion between the demands of their art, of their public, and of the business, and the confusion between their public-performing and private selves is alienating in the extreme. But this very alienation, in artists that can hold out (and most groups are short-lived) produces a degree of political consciousness and explicitness that is incredible when you realize that it is marketed by the very forces it is battling against, and that it is accepted wholeheartedly by millions of people. Bob Dylan is the most striking example of this consciousness. He writes for kids in a language they can understand, that is hip and full of symbols of the things that oppress all of us. As in "Subterranean Homesick Blues":

Johnny's in the basement
Mixing up the medicine
I'm on the pavement
Thinking about the government
The man in the trenchcoat
Badge out, laid off
Says he's got a bad cough
Wants to get paid off
Look out kid
It's something you did
God knows when
But you're doin' it again . . .

Ah, get born, keep warm
Short pants, romance, learn to dance
Get dressed, get blessed
Try to be a success
Please her, please him, buy gifts
Don't steal, don't lift
Twenty years of schoolin'
And they put you on the day shift
Look out kid they keep it all hid
Better jump down a manhole
Buy yourself a candle, don't wear sandals
Try to avoid the scandals
Don't wanna be a bum
You better chew gum
The pump don't work
Cause the vandals took the handles.

Dylan is a mass poet. People follow his work and wait for his latest releases with an eagerness that no poet has received in this country since at least the Industrial Revolution. People talk about his work and his changes as if they had participated in them. They see his poetry as a *process* —a living, growing thing—not as a mysterious product in an aesthetic universe apart from life.

This sense of art as process is crucial to the revitalization of it. As politics must teach people the ways and give them the means to take control over their own lives, art must teach people, in the most vivid and imaginative ways possible, how to take control over their own experience and observations, how to link these things with theory, and how to connect both with the experience of others.

This essay is deeply indebted to two books, *Illusion and Reality* by Christopher Caudwell, and *Art and Revolution* by John Berger. Everyone interested in such things should read both.

Readings

1. Beardsley, Monroe. *Aesthetics, From Classical Greece to the Present.* New York: Macmillan, 1966. A short history of aesthetics that brings the discussion down to contemporary developments.

2. ———. *Aesthetics: Problems in the Philosophy of Criticism.* New York: Harcourt, Brace, 1958, Chap. 12, "The Arts in the Life of Man."

3. Ducasse, Curt John. *The Philosophy of Art.* New York: Dover, 1966. A comprehensive and clear presentation and an elaboration of the author's view that art is the language of feeling. See also his earlier *Art, the Critics, and You.*

4. Hofstadter, Albert. *Truth and Art.* New York: Columbia U. Press, 1965. An evaluation of a number of recent philosophies of art.

5. Jarrett, James L. *The Quest for Beauty.* Englewood Cliffs: Prentice-Hall, 1957. A general book dealing with aesthetics and art that brings in a considerable amount of illustrative material.

6. Osborne, Harold. *Aesthetics and Criticism.* London: Macmillan, 1956.

7. Sibley, Frank. "Aesthetics and Nonaesthetics." *Philosophical Review,* 74 (April 1965), 135–159.

8. Stolnitz, Jerome. *Aesthetics.* Boston: Houghton Mifflin Co., 1958.

Art and Society

1. Baxandall, Lee. *Radical Perspectives in the Arts.* Baltimore: Penguin, 1972.

2. Berger, John. *Art and Revolution.* New York: Scribners, 1970.
3. Caudwell, Chris. *Studies in a Dying Culture.* London: Lawrence and Wishart, 1965.
4. Newton, Eric. *The Meaning of Beauty.* Baltimore: Penguin, 1962.

three

Why Do We Laugh?

58

Because of
Non-Life Actions

Henri Bergson (1859–1941) dominated French philosophy for a considerable part of the twentieth century. His philosophy focused on evolutionary process and interpreted it in terms of a fundamental life force; it had wide international influence. Among his books are: *Creative Evolution* (1944); *The Two Sources of Morality and Religion* (1935); *Time and Free Will* (1950); *Introduction to MetaPhysics* (1949); and *Matter and Memory* (1950).

One usually thinks of comedy as dealing with what is funny and therefore everything connected with it as pleasing. This, however, is often not the case. Thurber once said, "The closest thing to humor is tragedy." This is borne out by the fact that comic figures like Charlie Chaplin and Red Skelton often hide a tragic situation. A comic figure often has a tragic mask. He finds himself in situations of defeat and frustration, and he begins events which he cannot control and by which he is overwhelmed. Consequently the comic is often very close to the tragic.

But comedy is much more than a mask to the tragic. This is because there are so many different kinds of comedy. There are farces, satires, as well as humor based on wit, word play, *et cetera*. Hence it is very difficult to come up with a theory of comedy which covers all cases, but there have been many theories devised which explain many aspects of comedy. This section contains theories about the comic as devised by Bergson and Styan.

Henri Bergson was one of the few major philosophers who wrote a theory of comedy. It was based on his metaphysics which conceived realitv as vital, spontaneous, irreversible, changing organisms. The vital, flowing, natural life is real. We laugh at that which is the opposite, namely that which is static, awkward, and mechanical. For example, tension and elasticity are two natural forces of life. Hence the inelastic is unnatural, and social groups respond to it with the social gesture of laughter because this inelasticity is contrary to a successful life. Thus Bergson's theory of comedy has this pragmatic element as well.

<hr>

— TO STUDY

1. How is Bergson going to treat laughter?

2. What are Bergson's three fundamental observations concerning the comic? Towards what point do these three observations converge?

3. Why do people laugh at a man who stumbles along a street?

4. Why is absent-mindedness often comic? What general law does Bergson formulate out of such cases?

5. Why do we find the comic in situations of violence?

6. What does life and society require of each of us? What two forces are involved? Why does society become suspicious of all inelasticity of character?

7. Finally, what must laughter be? Explain.

What does laughter mean? What is the basal element in the laughable? What common ground can we find between the grimace of a merry-andrew,[1] a play upon words, an equivocal situation in a burlesque and a scene of high comedy? What method of distillation will yield us invariably the same essence from which so many different products borrow either their obtrusive odour or their delicate perfume? The greatest of thinkers, from Aristotle downwards, have tackled this little problem, which has a knack of baffling every effort, of slipping away and escaping only to bob up again, a pert challenge flung at philosophic speculation.

Our excuse for attacking the problem in our turn must lie in the fact that we shall not aim at imprisoning the comic spirit within a definition.

<hr>

From the book *Comedy,* copyright © 1956 by Wylie Sypher, which contains "Laughter," by Henri Bergson. Reprinted by permission of Doubleday & Company, Inc.
[1] A buffon (ED.).

We regard it, above all, as a living thing. However trivial it may be, we shall treat it with the respect due to life. We shall confine ourselves to watching it grow and expand. Passing by imperceptible gradations from one form to another, it will be seen to achieve the strangest metamorphoses. We shall disdain nothing we have seen. Maybe we may gain from this prolonged contact, for the matter of that, something more flexible than an abstract definition,—a practical, intimate acquaintance, such as springs from a long companionship. And maybe we may also find that, unintentionally, we have made an acquaintance that is useful. For the comic spirit has a logic of its own, even in its wildest eccentricities. It has a method in its madness. It dreams, I admit, but it conjures up in its dreams visions that are at once accepted and understood by the whole of a social group. Can it then fail to throw light for us on the way that human imagination works, and more particularly social, collective, and popular imagination? Begotten of real life and akin to art, should it not also have something of its own to tell us about art and life?

At the outset we shall put forward three observations which we look upon as fundamental. They have less bearing on the actually comic than on the field within which it must be sought.

I

The first point to which attention should be called is that the comic does not exist outside the pale of that which is strictly *human.* A landscape may be beautiful, charming and sublime, or insignificant and ugly; it will never be laughable. You may laugh at an animal, but only because you have detected in it some human attitude or expression. You may laugh at a hat, but what you are making fun of, in this case, is not the piece of felt or straw, but the shape that men have given it,—the human caprice whose mould it has assumed. It is strange that so important a fact, and such a simple one too, has not attracted to a greater degree the attention of philosophers. Several have defined man as "an animal which laughs." They might equally well have defined him as an animal which is laughed at; for if any other animal, or some lifeless object, produces the same effect, it is always because of some resemblance to man, of the stamp he gives it or the use he puts it to.

Here I would point out, as a symptom equally worthy of notice, the *absence of feeling* which usually accompanies laughter. It seems as though the comic could not produce its disturbing effect unless it fell, so to say, on the surface of a soul that is thoroughly calm and unruffled. Indifference is its natural environment, for laughter has no greater foe than emotion. I do not mean that we could not laugh at a person who inspires us with pity, for instance, or even with affection, but in such a case we must, for the moment, put our affection out of court and impose silence upon our pity. In a society composed of pure intelligences there would probably be no more tears, though perhaps there would still be laughter; whereas highly emotional souls, in tune and unison with life, in whom every event would be sentimentally prolonged and re-echoed, would neither know nor understand laughter. Try, for a moment, to become interested in everything that is being said and done; act, in imagination, with those who act, and feel with those who feel; in a word, give your sympathy its widest expansion: as though at the touch of a fairy wand you will see the flimsiest of objects assume importance, and a gloomy hue spread over everything. Now step aside, look upon life as a disinterested spectator: many a drama will turn into a comedy. It is enough for us to stop our ears to the sound of music in a room, where dancing is going on, for the dancers at once to appear ridiculous. How many human actions would stand a similar test? Should we not see many of them suddenly pass from grave to gay, on isolating them from the accompanying music of sentiment? To produce the whole of its effect, then, the comic demands something like a momentary anesthesia of the heart. Its appeal is to intelligence, pure and simple.

This intelligence, however, must always remain in touch with other intelligences. And here is the third fact to which attention should be drawn. You would hardly appreciate the comic if you felt yourself isolated from others. Laughter appears to stand in need of an echo. Listen to it carefully: it is not an articulate, clear, well-defined sound; it is something which would fain be prolonged by reverberating from one to another, something beginning with a crash, to continue in successive rumblings, like thunder in a mountain. Still, this reverberation cannot go on for ever. It can travel within as wide a circle as you please: the circle remains, none the less, a closed one. Our laughter is always the laughter of a group. It may, perchance, have happened to you, when seated in a railway carriage or at *table d'hôte,* to hear travellers relating to one another stories which must have been comic to them, for they laughed heartily. Had you been one of their company, you would have laughed like them, but, as you were not, you had no desire whatever to do so. A man who was once asked why he did not weep at a sermon when everybody else was shedding tears replied: "I don't belong to the parish!" What that man thought of tears would be still more true of laughter. However spontaneous it seems, laughter always implies a kind of secret freemasonry, or even complicity, with other laughers, real or imaginary. How often has it been said that the fuller the theatre, the more uncontrolled the laughter of the audience! On the other hand, how often has the remark been made that many comic effects are incapable of translation from one language to another, because they refer to the customs and ideas of a particular social group! It is through not understanding the importance of this double fact that the comic has been looked upon as a mere curiosity in which the mind finds amusement, and laughter itself as a strange, isolated phenomenon, without any bearing on the rest of human activity. Hence those definitions which tend to make the comic into an abstract relation between ideas: "an intellectual contrast," "a patent absurdity," etc., definitions which, even were they really suitable to every form of the comic, would not in the least explain why the comic makes us laugh. How, indeed, should it come about that this particular logical relation, as soon as it is perceived, contracts, expands and shakes our limbs, whilst all other relations leave the body unaffected? It is not from this point of view that we shall approach the problem. To understand laughter, we must put it back into its natural environment, which is society, and above all must we determine the utility of its function, which is a social one. Such, let us say at once, will be the leading idea of all our investigations. Laughter must answer to certain requirements of life in common. It must have a *social* signification.

Let us clearly mark the point towards which our three preliminary observations are converging. The comic will come into being, it appears, whenever a group of men concentrate their attention on one of their number, imposing silence on their emotions and calling into play nothing but their intelligence. What, now, is the particular point on which their attention will have to be concentrated, and what will here be the function of intelligence? To reply to these questions will be at once to come to closer grips with the problem. But here a few examples have become indispensable.

II

A man, running along the street, stumbles and falls; the passers-by burst out laughing. They would not laugh at him, I imagine, could they suppose that the whim had suddenly seized him to sit down on the ground. They laugh because his sitting down is involuntary. Consequently, it is not his sudden change of attitude that raises a laugh, but rather the involuntary element in this change,—his clumsiness, in fact. Perhaps there was a stone on the road. He should have altered his pace or avoided the obstacle. Instead of that, through lack of elasticity, through absentmindedness and a kind of physical obstinacy, *as a result, in fact, of rigidity or of momentum,* the muscles continued to perform the same movement when the circumstances of the case called for something else. That is the reason of the man's fall, and also of the people's laughter.

Now, take the case of a person who attends to the petty occupations of his everyday life with mathematical precision. The objects around him, however, have all been tampered with by a mischievous wag, the result being that when he dips his pen into the inkstand he draws it out all covered with mud, when he fancies he is sitting down on a solid chair he finds himself sprawling on the floor, in a word his actions are all topsy-turvy or mere beating the air, while in every case the effect is invariably one of momentum. Habit has given the impulse: what was wanted was to check the movement or deflect it. He did nothing of the sort, but continued like a machine in the same straight line. The victim, then, of a practical joke is in a position similar to that of a runner who falls,—he is comic for the same reason. The laughable element in both cases consists of a certain *mechanical inelasticity,* just where one would expect to find the wideawake adaptability and the living pliableness of a human being. The only difference in the two cases is that the former happened of itself, whilst the latter was obtained artificially. In the first instance, the passer-by does nothing but look on, but in the second the mischievous wag intervenes.

All the same, in both cases the result has been brought about by an external circumstance. The comic is therefore accidental: it remains, so to speak, in superficial contact with the person. How is it to penetrate within? The necessary conditions will be fulfilled when mechanical rigidity no longer requires for its manifestation a stumbling-block which either the hazard of circumstance or human knavery has set in its way, but extracts by natural processes, from its own store, an inexhaustible series of opportunities for externally revealing its presence. Suppose, then, we imagine a mind always thinking of what it has just done and never of what it is doing, like a song which lags behind its accompaniment. Let us try to picture to ourselves a certain inborn lack of elasticity of both senses and intelligence, which brings it to pass that we continue to see what is no longer visible, to hear what is no longer audible, to say what is no longer to the point: in short, to adapt ourselves to a past and therefore imaginary situation, when we ought to be shaping our conduct in accordance with the reality which is present. This time the comic will take up its abode in the person himself; it is the person who will supply it with everything—matter and form, cause and opportunity. Is it then surprising that the absent-minded individual—for this is the character we have just been describing—has usually fired the imagination of comic authors? When La Bruyère came across this particular type, he realised, on analysing it, that he had got hold of a recipe for the wholesale manufacture of comic effects. As a matter of fact he overdid it, and gave us far too lengthy and detailed a description of *Ménalque,* coming back to his subject, dwelling and expatiating on it beyond all bounds. The very facility of the subject fascinated him. Absent-mindedness, indeed, is not perhaps the actual fountain-head of the comic, but surely it is contiguous to a certain stream of facts and fancies which flows straight from the fountain-head. It is situated, so to say, on one of the great natural watersheds of laughter.

Now, the effect of absentmindedness may gather strength in its turn. There is a general law, the first example of which we have just encountered, and which we will formulate in the following terms: when a certain comic effect has its origin in a certain cause, the more natural we regard the cause to be, the more comic shall we find the effect. Even now we laugh at absentmindedness when presented to us as a simple fact. Still more laughable will be the absentmindedness we have seen springing up and growing before our very eyes, with whose origin we are acquainted and whose life-history we can reconstruct. To choose a definite example: suppose a man has taken to reading nothing but romances of love and chivalry. Attracted and fascinated by his heroes, his thoughts and intentions gradually turn more and more towards them, till one fine day we find him walking among us like a somnambulist. His actions are distractions. But then his distractions can be traced back to a definite, positive cause. They are no longer cases of *absence* of mind, pure and simple; they find their explanation in the *presence* of the individual in quite definite, though imaginary, surroundings. Doubtless a fall is always a fall, but it is one thing to tumble into a well because you were looking anywhere but in front of you, it is quite another thing to fall into it because you were intent upon a star. It was certainly a star at which Don Quixote was gazing. How profound is the comic element in the over-romantic, Utopian bent of mind! And yet, if you reintroduce the idea of absentmindedness, which acts as a go-between you will see this profound comic element uniting with the most superficial type. Yes, indeed, these whimsical wild enthusiasts, these madmen who are yet so strangely reasonable, excite us to laughter by playing on the same chords within ourselves, by setting in motion the same inner mechanism, as does the victim of a practical joke or the passer-by who slips down in the street. They, too, are runners who fall and simple souls who are being hoaxed— runners after the ideal who stumble over realities, child-like dreamers for whom life delights to lie in wait. But, above all, they are past-masters in absentmindedness, with this superiority over their fellows that their absentmindedness is systematic and organised around one central idea, and that their mishaps are also quite coherent, thanks to the inexorable logic which reality applies to the correction of dreams, so that they kindle in those around them, by a series of cumulative effects, a hilarity capable of unlimited expansion.

Now, let us go a little further. Might not certain vices have the same relation to character that the rigidity of a fixed idea has to intellect? Whether as a moral kink or a crooked twist given to the will, vice has often the appearance of a curvature of the soul. Doubtless there are vices into which the soul plunges deeply with all its pregnant potency, which it rejuvenates and drags along with it into a moving circle of reincarnations. Those are tragic vices. But the vice capable of making us comic is, on the contrary, that which is brought from without, like a ready-made frame into which we are to step. It lends us its own rigidity instead of borrowing from us our flexibility. We do not render it more complicated; on the contrary, it simplifies us. Here, as we shall see later on in the concluding section of this study, lies the essential difference between comedy and drama. A drama, even when portraying passions or vices that bear a name, so completely incorporates them in the person that their names are forgotten, their general characteristics effaced, and we no longer think of them at all, but rather of the person in whom they are assimilated; hence, the title of a drama can seldom be anything else than a proper noun. On the other hand, many comedies have a common noun as their title: *l'Avare, le Joueur,* etc. Were you asked to think of a play capable of being called *le Jaloux,* for instance, you would find that *Sganarelle* or *George Dandin* would occur to your mind, but not *Othello: le Jaloux* could only be the title of a comedy. The reason is that, however intimately vice, when comic, is associated with persons, it none the less retains its simple, independent existence, it remains the central character, present though invisible, to which the characters in flesh and blood on the stage are attached. At times it delights in dragging them down with its own weight and making them share in its tumbles. More frequently, however, it plays on them as on an instrument or pulls the strings as though they were puppets. Look closely: you will find that the art of the comic poet consists in making us so well acquainted with the particular vice, in introducing us, the spectators, to such a degree of intimacy with it, that in the end we get hold of some of the strings of the marionette with which he is playing, and actually work them ourselves; this it is what explains part of the pleasure we feel. Here, too, it is really a kind of automatism that makes us laugh—an automatism, as we have already remarked, closely akin to mere absentmindedness. To realise this more fully, it need only be noted that a comic character is generally comic in proportion to his ignorance of himself. The comic person is unconscious. As though wearing the ring of Gyges with reverse effect, he becomes invisible to himself while remaining visible to all the world. A character in a tragedy will make no change in his conduct because he will know how it is judged by us; he may continue therein even though fully conscious of what he is and feeling keenly the horror he inspires in us. But a defect that is ridiculous, as soon as it feels itself to be so, endeavours to modify itself or at least to appear as though it did. Were Harpagon to see us laugh at his miserliness, I do not say that he would get rid of it, but he would either show it less or show it differently. Indeed, it is in this sense only that laughter "corrects men's manners." It makes us at once endeavour to appear what we ought to be, what some day we shall perhaps end in being.

It is unnecessary to carry this analysis any further. From the runner who falls to the simpleton who is hoaxed, from a state of being hoaxed to one of absentmindedness, from absentmindedness to wild enthusiasm, from wild enthusiasm to various distortions of character and will, we have followed the line of progress along which the comic becomes more and more deeply imbedded in the person, yet without ceasing, in its subtler manifestations, to recall to us some trace of what we noticed in its grosser forms, an effect of automatism and of inelasticity. Now we can obtain a first glimpse—a distant one, it is true, and still hazy and confused—of the laughable side of human nature and of the ordinary function of laughter.

What life and society require of each of us is a constantly alert attention that discerns the outlines of the present situation, together with a certain elasticity of mind and body to enable us to adapt ourselves in consequence. *Tension* and *elasticity* are two forces, mutually complementary, which life brings into play. If these two forces are lacking in the body to any considerable extent, we have sickness and infirmity and accidents of every kind. If they are lacking in the mind, we find every degree of mental deficiency, every variety of insanity. Finally, if they are lacking in the character, we have cases of the gravest inadaptibility to social life, which are the sources of misery and at times the causes of crime. Once these elements of inferiority that affect the serious side of existence are removed—and they tend to eliminate themselves in what has been called the struggle for life—the person can live, and that in common with other persons. But society asks for something more; it is not satisfied with simply living, it insists on living well. What it now has to dread is that each one of us, content with paying attention to what affects the essentials of life, will, so far as the rest is concerned, give way to the easy automatism of acquired habits. Another thing it must fear is that the members of whom it is made up, instead of aiming after an increasingly delicate adjustment of wills which will fit more and more perfectly into one another, will confine themselves to respecting simply the fundamental conditions of this adjustment: a cut-and-dried agreement among the persons will not satisfy it, it insists on a constant striving after reciprocal adaptation. Society will therefore be suspicious of all *inelasticity* of character, of mind and even of body, because it is the possible sign of a slumbering activity as well as of an activity with separatist tendencies, that inclines to swerve from the common centre round which society gravitates: in short, because it is the sign of an eccentricity. And yet, society cannot intervene at this stage by material repression, since it is not affected in a material fashion. It is confronted with something that makes it uneasy, but only as a symptom—scarcely a threat, at the very most a gesture. A gesture, therefore, will be its reply. Laughter must be something of this kind, a sort of *social gesture*. By the fear which it inspires, it restrains eccentricity, keeps constantly awake and in mutual contact certain activities of a secondary order which might retire into their shell and go to sleep, and in short, softens down whatever the surface of the social body may retain of mechanical inelasticity. Laughter, then, does not belong to the province of esthetics alone, since unconsciously (and even immorally in many particular instances) it pursues a utilitarian aim of general improvement. And yet there is something esthetic about it, since the comic comes into being just when society and the individual, freed from the worry of self-preservation, begin to regard themselves as works of art. In a word, if a circle be drawn round those actions and dispositions—implied in individual or social life—to which their natural consequences bring their own penalties, there remains outside this sphere of emotion and struggle—and within a neutral zone in which man simply exposes himself to man's curiosity—a certain rigidity of body, mind and character that society would still like to get rid of in order to obtain from its members the greatest possible degree of elasticity and sociability. This rigidity is the comic, and laughter is its corrective.

Still, we must not accept this formula as a definition of the comic. It is suitable only for cases that are elementary, theoretical and perfect, in which the comic is free from all adulteration. Nor do we offer it, either, as an explanation. We prefer to make it, if you will, the *leitmotiv* which is to accompany all our explanations. We must ever keep it in mind, though without dwelling on it too much, somewhat as a skilful fencer must think of the discontinuous movements of the lesson whilst his body is given up to the continuity of the fencing-match. We will now endeavour to reconstruct the sequence of comic forms, taking up again the thread that leads from the horseplay of a clown up to the most refined effects of comedy, following this thread in its often unforeseen windings, halting at intervals to look around, and finally getting back, if possible, to the point at which the thread is dangling and where we shall perhaps find—since the comic oscillates between life and art—the general relation that art bears to life.

THINK ABOUT

1. "The function of comedy is to correct men's views. Nothing will reform men better than a depiction of their faults. Men are willing to be mean, but they never like to be ridiculed."

2. "Laughter comes from the idea of one's own superiority."

3. "The most comic of animals are the most serious—e.g. the monkey."

4. "One excellent test of the civilization of a country is the flourishing of the comic idea."

5. "In considering Chaplin we must not overlook the basic things about so universal a comedian. First he is short—and therefore he is *low*."

6. "Comedy is a game that imitates life."

7. "The absurd is more than ever inherent in Human Existence. The world stands on absurdities."

8. "Laughter is man's way of showing his fangs."

59

There Are Many Reasons for Laughter

John Louis Styan (1923–   ) is presently Senior Staff Tutor in literature and drama at the University of Hull. His works include *The Elements of Drama* (1960), *The Dark Comedy* (1962), *Television Drama in Contemporary Theatre* (1962), *Shakespeare's Sense of the Stage* (1964), and *Dramatic Experience* (1965).

Styan argues that because laughter arises from so many sources it is impossible to bring all the types of comedy under a single theory. Even Bergson's theory cannot account for much of Shakespearian comedy. Nonetheless, a sense of incongruity with the resulting release of tension seems to be always present in comedy.

TO STUDY

1. Why does the diagnosis of comedy present difficulties?
2. According to Hazlitt, what is the essence of the laughable?
3. According to Meredith, what is the test of true comedy?
4. What is Styan's criticism of Bergson's theory of laughter?
5. What are the recurrent elements in the comic coming out of these various theories?
6. What are the traditional uses of comedy?
7. How does the best comedy function?

641

The recognized theories of comedy do not help us any the more to understand the characteristic drama of the twentieth century. Ideas about the comic have never been expressed as abundantly as those about tragedy, both because the seriousness of comedy has not been as evident to writers as its more impressive high-toned counterpart, and because the ways and intentions of comedy may be more tiresome to explain. Up to the beginning of this century, comedy suffered a hardening in its arteries and its critics had grown further and further away from the practice on the stage. Certainly, no theorist seemed capable of putting forward an explanation sufficiently all-embracing, and the philosophical and the psychological approaches have both been wanting.

The diagnosis of comedy presents many difficulties. Laughter, a recurring and therefore an evidently important ingredient, seems to arise from a great variety of sources: we laugh at other people's bad luck, or at relief from embarrassment, or at a little flattery, or even when we do not want to laugh. We laugh heartily, or smile gently, or at some comedy we may not laugh at all. There are so many uses to which laughter can be put, from the promotion of a cold vindictive sarcasm to that of the empty gaiety of knock-about. There is considerable discrepancy between the things we find comic in life and those contrived on the stage: a man falling on his face in the street may be an object of pathos, but on the stage an object of derision. There is confusion between the techniques of comedy designed to raise laughter and the use to which the laughter is put: why should an anticlimax make us happy, or a clown make us sad? There are too many 'types' of the comic, and we plague ourselves by trying to sort comedy from burlesque, satire and farce, notwithstanding that in Shakespearian comedy elements of each seem to be present, and the points where they overlap are none too clearly defined. We are often at a loss to assess a total impression: even where in Molière the play's parts have been largely sweet and farcical, the whole when swallowed can leave a bitter taste in the mouth.

We find that when a joke is dissected, it abruptly ceases to be funny, which is disconcerting to say the least. It is also notorious that a 'sense of humour' is an unreliable quality, and what will seem laughable to an English audience will not necessarily seem so to a Scottish. As a psychologist has written, 'If members of a social group observe that their own objects of laughter do not produce laughter in another social group they are inclined to express this fact by saying that the second group has "no sense of humour" '.[1] From the world of the theatre we might add that what will

---

From *The Dark Comedy* by J. L. Styan (New York: Cambridge University Press, 1962), pp. 42–52. Reprinted by permission of the publisher and author.

[1] R. H. Thouless, *General and Social Psychology* (London, 2nd ed., 1937), p. 209.

seem laughable on Monday may be damned on Tuesday. It is, moreover, a nuisance that what is comic to one age is not to another: Shylock was a butt for the Elizabethans, but not for the Victorians; Richard III was played for comedy by Irving, but for pathos by Olivier. Fashions in laughter change too readily, and we are in some doubt today whether to laugh at or sympathize with a Falstaff or a Tartuffe or a Sir Peter Teazle. Furthermore, should we begin by studying crowd psychology or the particular successes of a particular writer? And if we are to set our standards by one author, who shall it be?—Aristophanes, Shakespeare, Molière, Shaw?

For Hazlitt[2] the essence of the laughable was 'the incongruous', a distinction between 'what things are and what they ought to be'. This happily enough explains what we may call 'satirical' laughter, the laughter by which the spectator refuses to acknowledge the propriety of the fop and the coquette in Restoration comedy, when he recognizes the affectation in their gesture and speech, or by which he knows to ridicule the seriousness with which the characters in *The Importance of Being Earnest* pursue their absurd ends. But Hazlitt lets fall a damning admission: 'It is perhaps the fault of Shakespeare's comic muse that it is too good-natured and magnanimous. We sympathize with his characters more often than we laugh at them.' It is a *fault!*

For Meredith[3] 'the test of true Comedy is that it shall awaken thoughtful laughter', but he too can only comfortably explain the *raison d'être* of the 'high' comedy of intellect: 'The laughter of Comedy is impersonal and of unrivalled politeness. . . . It laughs through the mind, for the mind directs it.' And though in another place he suggests, attempting to distinguish between comedy and humour, 'The stroke of the great humourist is world-wide, with lights of Tragedy in his laughter', he will not admit that this quality can also appear in the greatest forms of comedy. Shakespeare is again the stumbling-block: because Shakespeare paints 'humanity' rather than 'manners', he does not begin to explain Shakespeare's eye for the comic. 'Jaques, Falstaff and his regiment, the varied troop of Clowns, Malvolio, Sir Hugh Evans and Fluellen—marvellous Welshmen! —Benedick and Beatrice, Dogberry, and the rest, are subjects of a special study in the poetically comic.' So we move on to safer ground with Molière, some of whose success he can account for.

After Meredith has named this glittering variety of the ostensibly comic, should he not have tried to understand them? Neither Hazlitt nor Meredith can explain the warm comic success of these and others like

---

[2] Hazlitt, Introduction to *The English Comic Writers* (1818).
[3] Meredith, 'On the Idea of Comedy and of the Uses of the Comic Spirit', a lecture delivered in 1877.

Rosalind and Touchstone and Quince and Bottom and that great host of Shakespeare's comic creation which reflects so closely the 'English' sense of humour. Moreover, they cannot help us to sense the nature of the achievement in plays like *The Wild Duck, The Cherry Orchard, Major Barbara* and *Waiting for Godot,* ambiguous plays of the modern theatre which challenge our laughter, as we shall see.

Bergson[4] with every good intention turned to example after example to establish his precepts, but concerned himself too much with first causes and with the detail of technique rather than the odd results produced in the theatre. He further remained rather parochial in drawing too much on the kind of comedy which has so admirably set the standard for the French comic stage, that of Molière. It is noticeable that his examples are drawn chiefly from the farces and farcical moments of Molière and Labiche (author of such plays as *Le Voyage de M. Perrichon* and *Un Chapeau de paille d'Italie*) or the comical-absurd of such works as *Don Quixote.* He diagnoses comedy as arising from the incongruity of 'something mechanical encrusted on the living': 'the attitudes, gestures, and movements of the human body are laughable in exact proportion as that body reminds us of a mere machine'. He thus cites as laughable the forms and movements of the puppet, and in the same way Molière's Sganarelle and his kind. Sganarelle, *The Doctor in Spite of Himself,* is enjoying his new-found power as a man of medicine, when he is accused by Géronte of reversing the position of the heart and the liver:

> Géronte . . . the heart should be on the left side, and the liver on the right.
> Sganarelle Yes, it used to be so, but we have changed all that.

Likewise, Dr Bahis of *Love's the Best Doctor,* provides an excellent example of professional automatism when he advises that 'It's better [for a patient] to die through following the rules than to recover through violating them'. This argument of course helps us to explain the fun in much of Molière, and the comedy of snobbery in Lady Bracknell, and how in Fry's *The Lady's Not for Burning* Tyson's pomposity as mayor is belied by his having a frightful cold in the head. It explains all manner of caricature in character and action on the stage. It explains the prohibition of much emotionality from the comic theatre. It does not explain the force of its *presence,* and emotion is often present to great purpose in comedy. Bergson declares rigidly 'laughter is incompatible with emotion', when we know well enough from experience, if not from countless moments on the comic stage, that we *do* have the faculty of laughing and feeling at one and the same time.

---

[4] Bergson, *Laughter, An Essay on the Meaning of the Comic,* trans. C. Brereton and F. Rothwell (London, 1921), first French ed. 1889.

It must exclude Shakespeare once again, and, what is more, it cannot approach our true sense of Molière's greatest achievement, *The Misanthrope*. Bergson's laughter is a 'social corrective', as Meredith's was an 'agent of civilization', but it trades on the debased and degraded in human nature and cannot respond to the warmth of comic humanity which remains after the eccentricities have been skimmed off.

The argument was not quite over. Freud[5] arbitrarily narrowed his field to include only what he pleased to call 'wit', and satisfactorily explains to us, after much belabouring, that wit serves as an escape from authority just as nonsense serves as an escape from critical reason (with occasional help from alcohol). Having said this at great length, he has said little that we did not know already. Others have since taken up the challenge, and J. B. Priestley's essay on humour[6] was a hopeful advance on his predecessors. Where Freud started from minimal instances, with little wish to move into the wider world of comedy, Priestley saw all the limitations and difficulties and perhaps would embrace too much. He would admit Shakespeare into the ranks, and goes some way to explaining his humour as the product of the close observation of human character and behaviour in its incongruities.

Among all the hints offered by these writers, certain recurring elements in the comic stand out. A sense of incongruity, with a resulting release of tension, is felt within the mind. Whether by the laughter of success or of failure, whether arising from the recognition of a friend or a tune, or from Santayana's 'little triumph' of the mind when it receives an illumination, whether by the laughter that follows upon bathos or upon the loss of a lady's dignity when her hat is blown off by the wind, some bulwark of our natural resistance, little or big, is broken down, and a weapon of unquestionable power is in the hands of the one who can effect this artificially. The comedian is suddenly free to pour his shafts through the gap, rebuffing us with mockery or drawing us with tears. Whatever the technique he employs he has his audience captive.

On the other hand, that a comedy *should* make you laugh is not admissible as an argument: incongruity is not necessarily laughable. There are too many plays, patently not tragedies, which clearly evoke no laughter, or little that is perceived as laughter; too many fine plays end in questions and by sobering us, from *Troilus and Cressida* and *The Misanthrope* to the comedies of Pirandello. The interested reader should look into that excellent discussion initiated by L. J. Potts in a more recent essay on our subject.[7] Where it does arise laughter can be a means to a greater end than itself,

---

[5] Freud, *Wit and its Relation to the Unconscious,* trans. Brill (London, undated, ?1906).
[6] J. B. Priestley, *English Humour* (London, 1929).
[7] L. J. Potts, *Comedy* (London, 1948), esp. pp. 18–22.

creating the conditions for the dramatic achievement of other things. The values of the comic attitude appear only when we measure the *uses* to which it is put. Nor should we deceive ourselves into thinking that its uses are not infinitely variable. The evidence suggests that the conventions of the comic stage readily admit an admixture of seemingly extraneous elements like the tragic and the pathetic, whereas tragedy has its fabric dangerously stretched to admit the comic or the farcical. What then are the traditional uses of comedy?

Broad comedy has contrived the release of laughter for partly satirical purposes by a relatively uncomplicated incongruity. Just as we laugh at the clown who sacrifices his self-respect by wearing trousers that are excessively too big for him, or at Charlie Chaplin for his exaggerated delight in a 'house' whose wall afterwards collapses when he leans on it, so we laugh at Harpagon, grotesque in his avarice, faced with the costly processes of being in love; or we laugh at the newly honoured Lord Foppington's airs and graces as he incongruously rehearses his part for the evening's *levée* while still in his nightgown: 'Well, 'tis an unspeakable pleasure to be a man of quality— Strike me dumb—My Lord—Your lordship—My Lord Foppington. . . .' Of course, it is the situation which the dramatist may complicate, and the wink at the audience can be very much more subtle when, say, Lady Bracknell finally succumbs to hard cash in lieu of the desirable attributes of an elegant lineage, or when Volpone the fox out-foxes himself. The bookworm is funnier and more like a bookworm on a dance-floor than in a library, the flirt funnier and more of a flirt in a library than on a dance-floor.

Even at the level of the near-farcical, where the merely physical sensationalism of the laugh is uppermost in the playwright's mind, such drama can sometimes justify itself morally by being acutely pointed in its object of derision. The contrivance of derisive laughter by the exaggeration of some affectation of human behaviour is a time-honoured method used since the days of Aristophanes. Thus the learned Meton of *The Birds* arrives in Cloudcuckooland to 'subdivide the air into square acres':

> Meton   Observe:
> The conformation of the air, considered as
> a total entity, is that of a conical damper.
> Very well. At the apex of this cone we apply
> the ruler, bracketing in the dividers to allow
> for the congruent curve. Q.E.D. . . .

But his notions are not received as gratefully as he expected:

> Pisthetairos . . . we've passed a law
> that charlatans shall be whipped in tne public square

Meton   Oh. Then I'd better be going.
Pisthetairos   You're almost too late.
    Here's a sample, God help you!   (*Knocks him down.*)
Meton   My head! My head![8]

One would not of course think that there were a majority of learned mathematicians in the Greek audience to make the satirical and corrective point of this very far-reaching. Nor would Molière have expected to find too many hypochondriacs like Argan in the court of Louis XIV. These comedies can nevertheless give us, perhaps incidentally, many tiny and momentary insights into human nature through the agency of puppets like Meton and Argan. We all share a little of Meton's desire to make order of fantasy, to stiffen what should be flexible. Even if we would not confess to being, each of us, a little of the hypochondriac with a natural fear for our health, we must feel just a touch of fellow-feeling for Argan when M Purgon the doctor wreaks his rage like this:

M. Purgon   I foretell that within four days you'll be in an incurable condition.
Argan   Oh mercy!
M. Purgon   You'll fall into a state of bradypepsia.
Argan   M. Purgon!
M. Purgon   From bradypepsia into dyspepsia.
Argan   M. Purgon!
M. Purgon   From dyspepsia into apepsia.
Argan   M. Purgon!
M. Purgon   From apepsia into diarrhoea and lientery.
Argan   M. Purgon!
M. Purgon   From lientery into dysentery.
Argan   M. Purgon!
M. Purgon   From dysentery into dropsy.
Argan   M. Purgon!
M. Purgon   And from dropsy to autopsy that your own folly will have brought
    you to.
Argan   Oh my God! I'm dying.[9]

Here character, situation and dialogue are artificial' and the playing demands a special degree of stylized speech and movement, all apparently earnest in manner. The characters' behaviour tends to puppetry, and the situations, though still recognizable, may be outrageous: the ways of the actors are deliberately shown at some 'distance' from normal behaviour in order that the spectator can freely laugh across the gap at what he believes

---

[8] Aristophanes, *The Birds*, version by D. Fitts (London, 1958).
[9] Molière, *the Imaginary Invalid*, in *The Misanthrope and Other Plays*, trans. J. Wood (London, 1959).

different from his own. The classical methods of comedy, whether broad
and low, romantic and pastoral, or high and mannered, have always been
anti-naturalistic. A stage extravagant in word and deed permitted those
excesses which still compel us to deride certain characters and their attitude
to life. To talk of 'stylization' equally to cover *As You Like It, Volpone,
The Way of the World, The School for Scandal, The Importance of Being
Earnest* and *Man and Superman* is perhaps an impertinence, but in each
of these plays the dramatist invented a world to different degrees fantastic
the better to compare our own. Artificial characters in an artificial situation
gained him more freedom and more force for his dramatic effects. It is only
after we have laughed spontaneously that we perhaps perceive that the
laugh has rebounded upon us, and that the artificiality was all a snare. In
the same way a simple verbal witticism can leave some permanent mark
upon us—if it includes some quality of illuminating humour too.

Thus the best comedy teases and troubles an audience: it *can* be painful. Comic method can serve to create an imaginative but dispassionate
attitude; to create the conditions for thinking; to free the dramatist in his
attempt to tap certain rational resources of mind in his audience. Derisory
laughter may be used for this and it may arise from this; it may not. Clearly
it must do so in mannered comedy like Shaw's *Arms and the Man* or
Heartbreak House, where we are encouraged for the most part to keep our
critical distance from the central characters Raina and Ellie the better to
recognize their whole significance. It may do so in surrealistic comedy like
Samuel Beckett's *Waiting for Godot,* where the slapstick convention of the
play deceives us most of the time into thinking that we are not looking at
ourselves. It probably will not do so in *King Lear,* where an ironic joke
from the Fool, laughable out of its context, is the more caustic in context
because we feel our sympathies are too directly its butt. The urgent fact
remains that, whether we laugh or not, the 'comic' attitude may be present
in any genre of play. The best jokes are not only compatible with the most
solemn intention, but are likely to be the best jokes for that reason.

As the gap narrows so that what remains incongruous is still funny,
but too close to the bone to laugh at, then we move swiftly across the
frontier into the realms of the tragic. We have seen that plays with large
measures of sympathy felt through the laughter, like Shakespeare's romantic comedies, were inconvenient to the theorists. Similarly, plays which
came near to closing the gap between the normality of the audience and
the abnormality of the stage, plays like *Measure for Measure* or *The Misanthrope,* have been regarded as on the suspect fringe of the comic tradition,
unwelcome exceptions to the rule. The presence of the comic eye in the
midst of tragedy, as in *King Lear* or *Hamlet,* was put down to the licence
of genius. Now, in the work of Chekhov, Pirandello and Anouilh, and many

other, it is the rule and not the exception to mingle the laughter and the tears; large numbers of plays today merely *use* the mechanism of laughter without granting its expected release of tension.

Readings

1. Corrigan, Robert W. "Comedy and the Comic Spirit," in *Comedy, Meaning, and Form,* Robert W. Corrigan, ed. San Francisco: Chandler Pub. Co., 1965, pp. 1–11.

2. Feibleman, James K. "The Meaning of Comedy," *Aesthetics.* New York: Humanities Press, 1949.

3. Langer, Susanne. "The Comic Rhythm," in *Feeling and Form.* New York: Charles Scribner's Sons, 1953, pp. 326–350.

4. Lauter, Paul, ed. *Theories of Comedy.* New York: Doubleday, 1964.

5. Sypher, Wylie. "The Meanings of Comedy," in *Comedy,* Wylie Sypher, ed. Garden City, N.Y.: Doubleday, 1956, pp. 193–258.

four

Why Do We Enjoy
the Tragic?

60

The Catharsis Theory

Aristotle (385/4–322 B.C.) wrote the *Poetics* about 330 B.C. It is probably the most influential work ever written in aesthetics.

The world's great tragedies, notably those of the Greeks, Sophocles and Euripides, and of Shakespeare, are considered to be among the supreme works of art by many people. *Oedipus Rex, Hamlet, Macbeth*—these creations are hardly surpassed by anything else in literature or indeed in any other work of art. The surprising fact is that we enjoy these tragedies, yet each is full of misery and suffering. This gives rise to the "paradox" of tragedy. Why is it that we enjoy these spectacles which are so full of misery? Consider *Hamlet,* for example. In this play Ophelia dies, Polonius dies, and even Hamlet himself is killed, yet many people consider this to be the supreme work of art. In modern times, such a play as Miller's *Death of a Salesman* is considered to be among the greatest of twentieth-century works, and yet this too is filled with suffering. There have been many attempts to answer this paradox.

In Aristotle's *Poetics,* from which the following selection is taken, he analyzes the structure of tragedy, the nature of the tragic hero, and finally the paradox of tragedy itself. Aristotle explains the paradox with his doctrine of *catharsis,* which states that tragedy provokes emotions of pity and fear to the extent that they are purged from the individual, who takes pleasure in that purgation. His answer to the paradox of tragedy, then, is that there is a kind of pleasure that results from the purging of the emotions. Hence we enjoy these depictions of suffering.

TO STUDY

1. What is Artistotle's definition of tragedy? What are the six elements of tragedy? Which of them is most important?
2. What is the proper structure of the plot?
3. Why is poetry "a higher thing than history"? Give an example.
4. What are some elements of a perfect tragedy?
5. Discuss the role of pity and fear and their relation to pleasure in tragedies.

VI [*Definition of tragedy. Six elements in tragedy. Plot, or the representation of the action, is of primary importance; character and thought come next in order.*]

Tragedy, then, is an imitation of an action that is serious, complete, and of a certain magnitude; in language embellished with each kind of artistic ornament, the several kinds being found in separate parts of the play; in the form of action, not of narrative; through pity and fear effecting the proper purgation of these emotions. By "language embellished," I mean language into which rhythm, "harmony," and song enter. By "the several kinds in separate parts," I mean, that some parts are rendered through the medium of verse alone, others again with the aid of song.

Now as tragic imitation implies persons acting, it necessarily follows, in the first place, that Spectacular equipment will be a part of Tragedy. Next, Song and Diction, for these are the medium of imitation. By "Diction" I mean the mere metrical arrangement of the words: as for "Song," it is a term whose sense everyone understands.

Again, Tragedy is the imitation of an action; and an action implies personal agents, who necessarily possess certain distinctive qualities both of character and thought; for it is by these that we qualify actions themselves, and these—thought and character—are the two natural causes from which actions spring, and on actions again all success or failure depends. Hence, the Plot is the imitation of the action:—for by plot I here mean the arrangement of the incidents. By character I mean that in virtue of which we ascribe certain qualities to the agents. Thought is required wherever a statement is proved, or, it may be, a general truth enunciated. Every Tragedy, therefore, must have six parts, which parts determine its quality—namely, Plot, Character, Diction, Thought, Spectacle, Song. Two of the

From *The Poetics*, trans. by Butcher.

parts constitute the medium of imitation, one the manner, and three the objects of imitation, and these complete the list. These elements have been employed, we may say, by the poets to a man; in fact, every play contains Spectacular elements as well as Character, Plot, Diction, Song, and Thought.

But most important of all is the structure of the incidents. For Tragedy is an imitation, not of men, but of an action and of life, and life consists in action, and its end is a mode of action, not a quality. Now character determines men's qualities, but it is by their actions that they are happy or the reverse. Dramatic action, therefore, is not with a view to the representation of character: character comes in as subsidiary to the actions. Hence the incidents and the plot are the end of a tragedy; and the end is the chief thing of all. Again, without action there cannot be a tragedy; there may be without character. The tragedies of most of our modern poets fail in the rendering of character; and of poets in general this is often true. It is the same in painting; and here lies the difference between Zeuxis and Polygnotus. Polygnotus delineates character well: the style of Zeuxis is devoid of ethical quality. Again, if you string together a set of speeches expressive of character, and well finished in point of diction and thought, you will not produce the essential tragic effect nearly so well as with a play which, however deficient in these respects, yet has a plot and artistically constructed incidents. Besides which, the most powerful elements of emotional interest in Tragedy—Peripeteia or Reversal of the Situation, and Recognition scenes—are parts of the plot. A further proof is, that novices in the art attain to finish of diction and precision of portraiture before they can construct the plot. It is the same with almost all the early poets.

The Plot, then, is the first principle, and, as it were, the soul of a tragedy: Character holds the second place. A similar fact is seen in painting. The most beautiful colors, laid on confusedly, will not give as much pleasure as the chalk outline of a portrait. Thus Tragedy is the imitation of an action, and of the agents mainly with a view to the action.

Third in order is Thought,—that is, the faculty of saying what is possible and pertinent in given circumstances. In the case of oratory, this is the function of the political art and of the art of rhetoric: and so indeed the older poets make their characters speak the language of civic life; the poets of our time, the language of the rhetoricians. Character is that which reveals moral purpose, showing what kind of things a man chooses or avoids. Speeches, therefore, which do not make this manifest, or in which the speaker does not choose or avoid anything whatever, are not expressive of character. Thought, on the other hand, is found where something is proved to be or not to be, or a general maxim is enunciated.

Fourth among the elements enumerated comes Diction; by which I mean, as has been already said, the expression of the meaning in words; and its essence is the same both in verse and prose.

Of the remaining elements Song holds the chief place among the embellishments.

The Spectacle has, indeed, an emotional attraction of its own, but, of all the parts, it is the least artistic, and connected least with the art of poetry. For the power of Tragedy, we may be sure, is felt even apart from representation and actors. Besides, the production of spectacular effects depends more on the art of the stage machinist than on that of the poet.

VII [*The plot must be a whole, complete in itself, and of adequate magnitude.*]

These principles being established, let us now discuss the proper structure of the Plot, since this is the first and most important thing in Tragedy.

Now, according to our definition, Tragedy is an imitation of an action that is complete, and whole, and of a certain magnitude; for there may be a whole that is wanting in magnitude. A whole is that which has a beginning, a middle, and an end. A beginning is that which does not itself follow anything by causal necessity, but after which something naturally is or comes to be. An end, on the contrary, is that which itself naturally follows some other thing, either by necessity, or as a rule, but has nothing following it. A middle is that which follows something as some other thing follows it. A well-constructed plot, therefore, must neither begin nor end at haphazard, but conform to these principles.

Again, a beautiful object, whether it be a living organism or any whole composed of parts, must not only have an orderly arrangement of parts, but must also be of a certain magnitude; for beauty depends on magnitude and order. Hence a very small animal organism cannot be beautiful; for the view of it is confused, the object being seen in an almost imperceptible moment of time. Nor, again, can one of vast size be beautiful; for as the eye cannot take it all in at once, the unity and sense of the whole is lost for the spectator; as for instance if there were one a thousand miles long. As, therefore, in the case of animate bodies and organisms a certain magnitude is necessary, and a magnitude which may be easily embraced in one view; so in the plot, a certain length is necessary, and a length which can be easily embraced by the memory. The limit of length in relation to dramatic competition and sensuous presentment, is no part of artistic theory. For had it been the rule for a hundred tragedies to compete together, the performance would have been regulated by the water-clock,—as indeed we are told was formerly done. But the limit as fixed by the nature of the drama itself is this:—the greater the length, the more beautiful will the piece be by reason of its size, provided that the whole be perspicuous. And to define the matter roughly, we may say that the proper magnitude is comprised within such limits, that the sequence of events, according to the law of probability or necessity, will admit of a change from bad fortune to good, or from good fortune to bad.

VIII [*The plot must be a unity. Unity of plot consists not in unity of hero, but in unity of action. The parts must be organically connected.*]

Unity of plot does not, as some persons think, consist in the unity of the hero. For infinitely various are the incidents in one man's life which cannot be reduced to unity; and so, too, there are many actions of one man out of which we cannot make one action. Hence the error, as it appears, of all poets who have composed a Heracleid, a Theseid, or other poems of the kind. They imagine that as Heracles was one man, the story of Heracles must also be a unity. But Homer, as in all else he is of surpassing merit, here too—whether from art or natural genius—seems to have happily discerned the truth. In composing the Odyssey he did not include all the adventures of Odysseus—such as his wound on Parnassus, or his feigned madness at the mustering of the host—incidents between which there was no necessary or probable connection: but he made the Odyssey, and likewise the Iliad, to center round an action that in our sense of the word is one. As therefore, in the other imitative arts, the imitation is one when the object imitated is one, so the plot, being an imitation of an action, must imitate one action and that a whole, the structural union of the parts being such that, if any one of them is displaced or removed, the whole will be disjointed and disturbed. For a thing whose presence or absence makes no visible difference, is not an organic part of the whole.

IX [*(Plot continued.) Dramatic unity can be attained only by the observance of poetic as distinct from historic truth; for poetry is an expression of the universal; history of the particular. The rule of probable or necessary sequence as applied to the incidents. The best tragic effect depends on the combination of the inevitable and the unexpected.*]

It is, moreover, evident from what has been said, that it is not the function of the poet to relate what has happened, but what may happen—what is possible according to the law of probability or necessity. The poet and the historian differ not by writing in verse or in prose. The work of

Herodotus might be put into verse, and it would still be a species of history, with meter no less than without it. The true difference is that one relates what has happened, the other what may happen. Poetry, therefore, is a more philosophical and a higher thing than history for poetry tends to express the universal, history the particular. By the universal I mean how a person of a certain type will on occasion speak or act, according to the law of probability or necessity; and it is this universality at which poetry aims in the names she attaches to the personages. The particular is—for example— what Alcibiades did or suffered. In Comedy this is already apparent: for here the poet first constructs the plot on the lines of probability, and then inserts characteristic names—unlike the lampooners who write about particular individuals. But tragedians still keep to real names, the reason being that what is possible is credible: what has not happened is manifestly possible: otherwise it would not have happened. Still there are even some tragedies in which there are only one or two well-known names, the rest being fictitious. In others, none are well known—as in Agathon's Antheus, where incidents and names alike are fictitious, and yet they give none the less pleasure. We must not, therefore, at all costs keep to the received legends, which are the usual subjects of Tragedy. Indeed, it would be absurd to attempt it; for even subjects that are known are known only to a few, and yet give pleasure to all. It clearly follows that the poet or "maker" should be the maker of plots rather than of verses; since he is a poet because he imitates, and what he imitates are actions. And even if he chances to take an historical subject, he is none the less a poet; for there is no reason why some events that have actually happened should not conform to the law of the probable and possible, and in virtue of that quality in them he is their poet or maker.

Of all plots and actions the episodic are the worst. I call a plot "episodic" in which the episodes or acts succeed one another without probable or necessary sequence. Bad poets compose such pieces by their own fault, good poets, to please the players; for, as they write show pieces for competition, they stretch the plot beyond its capacity, and are often forced to break the natural continuity.

But again, Tragedy is an imitation not only of a complete action, but of events inspiring fear or pity. Such an effect is best produced when the events come on us by surprise; and the effect is heightened when, at the same time, they follow as cause and effect. The tragic wonder will then be greater than if they happened of themselves or by accident; for even coincidences are most striking when they have an air of design. We may instance the statue of Mitys at Argos, which fell upon his murderer while he was a spectator at a festival, and killed him. Such events seem not to be due to mere chance. Plots, therefore, constructed on these principles are necessarily the best.

XIII [*(Plot continued.) what constitutes tragic action. The change of fortune and the character of the hero as requisite to an ideal tragedy. The unhappy ending more truly tragic than the "poetic justice" which is in favor with a popular audience, and belongs rather to comedy.*]

A perfect tragedy should, as we have seen, be arranged not on the simple but on the complex plan. It should, moreover, imitate actions which excite pity and fear, this being the distinctive mark of tragic imitation. It follows plainly, in the first place, that the change of fortune presented must not be the spectacle of a virtuous man brought from prosperity to adversity: for this moves neither pity nor fear; it merely shocks us. Nor, again, that of a bad man passing from adversity to prosperity: for nothing can be more alien to the spirit of Tragedy; it possesses no single tragic quality; it neither satisfies the moral sense nor calls forth pity or fear. Nor, again, should the downfall of the utter villain be exhibited. A plot of this kind would, doubtless, satisfy the moral sense, but it would inspire neither pity nor fear; for pity is aroused by unmerited misfortune, fear by the misfortune of a man like ourselves. Such an event, therefore, will be neither pitiful nor terrible. There remains, then, the character between these two extremes—that of a man who is not eminently good and just, yet whose misfortune is brought about not by vice or depravity, but by some error or frailty. He must be one who is highly renowned and prosperous—a personage like Oedipus, Thyestes, or other illustrious men of such families.

A well-constructed plot should, therefore, be single in its issue, rather than double as some maintain. The change of fortune should be not from bad to good, but, reversely, from good to bad. It should come about as the result not of vice, but of some great error or frailty, in a character either such as we have described, or better rather than worse. . . .

In the second rank comes the kind of tragedy which some place first. Like the Odyssey, it has a double thread of plot, and also an opposite catastrophe for the good and for the bad. It is accounted the best because of the weakness of the spectators; for the poet is guided in what he writes by the wishes of his audience. The pleasure, however, thence derived is not the true tragic pleasure. It is proper rather to Comedy, where those who, in the piece, are the deadliest enemies—like Orestes and Aegisthus—quit the stage as friends at the close, and no one slays or is slain.

XIV [*(Plot continued.) The tragic emotions of pity and fear should spring out of the plot itself. To produce them by scenery or spectacular effect is entirely against the spirit of tragedy.*]

Fear and pity may be aroused by spectacular means; but they may also result from the inner structure of the piece, which is the better way, and indicates a superior poet. For the plot ought to be so constructed that, even without the aid of the eye, he who hears the tale told will thrill with horror and melt to pity at what takes place. This is the impression we should receive from hearing the story of the Oedipus. But to produce this effect by the mere spectacle is a less artistic method, and dependent on extraneous aids. Those who employ spectacular means to create a sense not of the terrible but only of the monstrous, are strangers to the purpose of Tragedy; for we must not demand of Tragedy any and every kind of pleasure, but only that which is proper to it. And since the pleasure which the poet should afford is that which comes from pity and fear through imitation, it is evident that this quality must be impressed upon the incidents. . . .

XV [*The element of character in tragedy. The rule of necessity or probability applicable to character as to plot. The "deus ex machina." How character is idealized.*]

In respect of Character there are four things to be aimed at. First, and most important, it must be good. Now any speech or action that manifests moral purpose of any kind will be expressive of character: the character will be good if the purpose is good. This rule is relative to each class. Even a woman may be good, and also a slave; though the woman may be said to be an inferior being, and the slave quite worthless. The second thing to aim at is propriety. There is a type of manly valor; but valor in a woman, or unscrupulous cleverness, is inappropriate. Thirdly, character must be true to life: for this is a distinct thing from goodness and propriety, as here described. The fourth point is consistency: for though the subject of the imitation, who suggested the type, be inconsistent, still he must be consistently inconsistent. As an example of motiveless degradation of character, we have Menelaus in the Orestes: of character indecorous and inappropriate, the lament of Odysseus in the Scylla, and the speech of Melanippe: of inconsistency, the Iphigenia at Aulis—for Iphigenia the suppliant in no way resembles her later self.

As in the structure of the plot, so too in the portraiture of character, the poet should always aim either at the necessary or the probable. Thus a person of a given character should speak or act in a given way, by the rule either of necessity or of probability; just as this event should follow that by necessary or probable sequence. It is therefore evident that the unravelling of the plot, no less than the complication, must arise out of the plot itself, it must not be brought about by the *Deus ex Machina*—as in the Medea, or in the Return of the Greeks in the Iliad. The *Deus ex Machina* should be employed only for events external to the drama—for antecedent or subsequent events, which lie beyond the range of human knowledge, and which require to be reported or foretold; for to the gods we ascribe the power of seeing all things. Within the action there must be nothing irrational. If the irrational cannot be excluded, it should be outside the scope of the tragedy. Such is the irrational element in the Oedipus of Sophocles.

Again, since Tragedy is an imitation of persons who are above the common level, the example of good portrait-painters should be followed. They, while reproducing the distinctive form of the original, make a likeness which is true to life and yet more beautiful. So too the poet, in representing men who are irascible or indolent, or have other defects of character, should preserve the type and yet ennoble it. In this way Achilles is portrayed by Agathon and Homer. . . .

THINK ABOUT

1. "The tragic is an essential element of the universe itself."
2. Tragedy has always appeared at the mature period of a culture not at its beginning.
3. "Tragedy must make life seem worth while."
4. Miller's *Death of a Salesman* consists in the hero's glad acceptance of the conditions of life which will lead to his own annihilation.
5. "Americans have a kind of armor against tragic experience. It is due to our optimistic attitude and our lack of heroes."

61

The Catharsis Theory Is Inadequate

DeWitt Parker (1885–1949) studied at Harvard under Josiah Royce, William James, and George Santayana. He taught two years at the University of California, but spent most of his life at the University of Michigan. His creative work centered on the philosophy of value, including aesthetics and the philosophy of art. He is the author of *The Principles of Aesthetics* (1920), *Experience and Substance* (1941).

Parker views life as essentially tragic in that it involves a continual warfare with circumstances from nature or from social-political interests. Parker's solution to the paradox of tragedy is that we identify with the hero, making his will ours because we agree with his values. We find a "special value in his courage, which, we feel, compensates for the evil of his suffering, defeat, or death."

TO STUDY

1. According to Parker, what are the characteristics of tragedies?
2. Why do we accept tragedies?
3. What is the difference between pathos and tragedy, and why do we enjoy the reception of pathos?
4. What was Hegel's theory of tragedy and on what grounds does Parker reject it?
5. What is Parker's view regarding the Protestant theory of tragedy?
6. What is Parker's criticism of Aristotle's theory of tragedy?

What any one may mean by tragic is largely a matter of personal definition or tradition; yet there is, I think, a common essence upon which all would agree. First, tragedy always involves the manful struggle of a personality in the pursuit of some end, at the cost of suffering, perhaps of death and failure. The opposition may come from nature, as in *The Grammarian's Funeral;* from fate, as in the *Oedipus;* from social and political interests, as in *Antigone;* that is of little moment; it is important solely that the battle be accepted and waged unflinchingly to the issue. In this ultimate sense, most of human life is tragic; because it involves a continual warfare with circumstances, which the majority of people carry on with a silent heroism. Originally, only the glorious and spectacular conflicts of great personalities were deemed worthy of representation in art; but with the growth of sympathy the range of tragic portrayal has gradually been extended over almost the whole human life. The peasant in his struggle for subsistence against a niggardly soil, or the patient woman who loses the bloom of her youth in the unremitting effort to maintain her children, are tragic figures.

Second, it is part of the essence of tragedy that the conflict should be recognized as necessary and its issue as inevitable. In one form or another, whether as Greek or Christian or naturalistic, fatality has remained an abiding element in the idea of tragedy. The purpose of passion or sentiment which impels the hero to undertake and maintain the struggle must be a part of his nature so integral that nothing else is possible for him. "Ich kann nicht anders" is the cry of every tragic personality. And the opposition which he meets from other persons, from social forces or natural circumstances, must seem to be equally fateful—must be represented as issuing from a counter determination or law no less inescapable than the hero's will. Even when the catastrophe depends upon some so-called accident, it must be made to appear necessary that our human purposes should sometimes be caught and strangled in the web of natural fact which envelops them.

The reasons for our acceptance of tragedy are not difficult to find and have been noted, with more or less clearness, by all students. We accept it much as the hero accepts his own struggle—he believes in the values which he is fighting for and we sympathetically make his will ours. Moreover, we discover a special value in his courage which, we feel, compensates for the evil of his suffering, defeat, or death. So long as we set any value on life, it is impossible for us not to esteem courage; for courage is at once the defense against attack of all our possessions and the source, in personal

From *The Principles of Aesthetics* by DeWitt H. Parker. Second Edition. Copyright 1946. Reprinted by permission of the publishers Appleton-Century Crofts, Educational Division, Meredith Corporation.

initiative and aggressive action, of newer and larger life. And any shrinking that we may feel against the sternness of the struggle is quenched both by the hero's example and by our recognition of its necessity. Since we are not participants in it, we should be as foolish as we should be weak, not to recognize that the Will which opposes us is as inflexible as our own—"such is life"—that is our ultimate comment. An appreciation of tragedy involves, therefore, a sure discernment of the essential disharmony of existence, yet at the same time, a feeling for the moral values which it may create; neither the optimist nor the utilitarian can enter into its world.

There are, however, works of art in which sheer evil, without any compensating development of character, is portrayed; where indeed the struggle may even cause decay of character. In Zola's *The Dram Shop*, for example, the story is the tale of the moral decline, through unfortunate circumstances and vicious surrounding, of the sweet, pliant Gervaise. Instead of developing a resistance to circumstances which would have made them yield a value even in defeat, she lets herself go and is spoiled beneath them. She has no friend to help or guardian angel to save. We do not blame her, for, with her soft nature, she could not do otherwise than crumble under the hard press of fate; neither can we admire her, for she lacks the adamantine stuff of which heroes are made. This is pathos, not tragedy. And just as most of human life involves tragedy in so far as it develops a strength to meet the dangers which threaten it, so likewise it involves pathos, in so far as it seldom resists at every point, but gives way, blighted without hope. Many a man or woman issues from life's conflicts weaker, not stronger; broken, not defiant; petulant, not sweetened; and at the hour of death there are few heroes. Yet there may be beauty in the story of this human weakness and weariness. Whence comes it? How can the representation of this sheer evil become a good? The principle involved is a simple one. Announced first, as far as I know, by Mendelssohn, it has been much more scientifically and penetratingly analyzed by Lipps, although wrongly applied by him to the tragic rather than the pathetic.[1]

It is a familiar and generally recognized experience, as Lipps has observed, that any threat or harm done to a value evokes in us a heightened appreciation of its worth. Parting is a sweet sorrow because only then do we fully realize the worth of what we are losing; the beauty of youth that dies is more beautiful because in death its radiance shines the brighter in our memory. A good in contemplation comes to take the place of a lost good in reality. Just as we hold on the more tightly to things that are slipping away from us in a vain effort to keep them, so to save ourselves from utter sorrow, we build up in the imagination a fair image of what we

---

[1] Cf. Lipps: *Der Streit Über die Tragödie,* and *Aesthetik,* Bd. I, S. 559.

have lost, free of the dust of the world. This makes the peculiar charm of the delicate and fragile, of weak things and little things, of the transient and perishable; they awaken in us the tender, protective impulse while they last, and when they are gone they suffer at our hands an idealization which the strong and enduring can never receive. Our pity for them mediates an increased love of them; we mock at fate which deprives us of them by keeping them secure and fairer in our memory.

As in life, so in art. Beneath and around the pictured destruction and ruin there opens up to us a brighter vision of the loveliness of what was or might have been. At the end of *The Dram Shop*, when Gervaise sinks into ruin, we inevitably revert to the beginning and see again, only more intensely, the gentle girl that she was, or else, going forward, we imagine what she might have been, if only she had been given a chance. The form of a possible good rises up from under the actual evil. The story of oppression becomes the praise of freedom; the picture of death, a vision of life. I know of no finer example of this in all literature than Sophocles' *Ajax*. Ajax has offended Athena, so he, the hero of the Grecian host, is seized with the mad desire to do battle with cattle and sheep. In lucid intervals he laments to his wife the shameful fate which has befallen him. How glorious his former prowess appears lost in so ridiculous a counterfeit! And his despair creates its magic.

In almost all so-called tragedies, true tragedy and pathos are intermingled; for we feel both pity and admiration, and the pity intensifies the admiration. The danger that threatens or the disaster that overwhelms the values which the hero embodies make us realize their worth the more. Throughout the *Antigone* we admire the heroine's tragic course of devotion; but it is at the point when, just before her death, she laments her youth and beauty that shall go fruitless—

ἀλεχιρον, ἀνυμέναιον, οὖτε του γαμου
μερος ταχοῦσαν οὖτε παιδειον τρο φῆς*

that we feel the fullness of strength that was needed for the sacrifice. One might perhaps think this lament a blemish of weakness in a picture of fortitude; but the impression is just the opposite, I believe; for force is measured by what it overcomes.

There are so many different theories of tragedy that it would be impossible, were it worth while, to embark on a criticism of all of them. There are certain ones, however, which, because of their wide acceptance, demand some attention at our hands. First, it is often assumed that a tragedy should

---

* Unwedded, without nuptial song, neither of marriage having a part nor nature of a child [ED.].

represent the good as ultimately triumphing, despite suffering and failure. But how can the good triumph when the hero fails and dies? Only, it is answered, if the hero represents a cause which may win despite or even because of his individual doom; and it is with this cause, not with him, that we chiefly sympathize. This was Hegel's view, who demanded that the tragic hero represent some universal interest which, when purged of the one-sidedness and uncompromising insistence of the hero's championing, may nevertheless endure and triumph in its genuine worth. In the *Antigone,* Hegel's favorite example, the cause of family loyalty finds recognition through the punishment of Creon for the girl's death; while at the same time the principle of the sovereignty of the state is upheld through her sacrifice. There are many tragedies which conform, at least partially, to this scheme; but not all, hence it cannot be a universal norm. In *Romeo and Juliet,* although the death of the young people serves to bring about a reconciliation of their families, the real principle for which they suffered— the right of private choice in matters of love—is in no way furthered by the outcome of the play. And, although it is always possible to universalize the good which is sought by any will, it is not possible to deflect upon a principle the full intensity of our sympathy, away from the individual, concrete passion and action. Whenever a great personality is represented, it is his personal suffering and fortitude that win at once our pity and our admiration. For private sorrows, for the ruin of character, for the death of those whom we love, there can be no complete atonement in the universal; because it is with the individual that we are chiefly concerned. No; the reconciliation lies where we have placed it—in tragedy, in the personal heroism of the strong character; in pathos, in the vision, not in the triumph, of the good.

The ordinary Protestant theological theory of tragedy is even more inadequate than the Hegelian. For, by assuming that there is no genuine loss in the world, that every evil is compensated for in the future lives of the heroes, it takes away the sting from their sacrifice and so deprives them of their crown of glory. It makes every adventure a calculation of prudence and every despair a farce. It is remote from the reality of experience where men stake all on a chance and, instead of receiving the good by an act of grace, wring it by blood and tears from evil.

On much the same level of thinking is the moralistic theory which requires that the misfortunes of the hero should be the penalty for some fault or weakness. This view, which has the authority of Aristotle, is also based on the doctrine of the justice of the world-order. It was pretty consistently carried out in the classical Greek drama; although there suffering is not exacted as an external retribution, but as the inevitable consequence of the turbulent passions of the characters; for even the punishment for offenses against the gods is of the nature of a personal revenge which they take. Later, when the gods retreated into the background of human life, retributive justice was conceived more abstractly. Now, it must be admitted, I think, that this idea, so deeply rooted in the popular mind, has exerted a profound influence on the drama; yet it cannot be applied universally without sophistry. To be sure, in *Romeo and Juliet*, the young people were disobedient and headstrong; in *Lear*, the old father was foolishly trustful of his wicked daughters; these frailties brought about their ruin. But did they deserve so hard a fate as theirs? Did not Lear suffer as much for his folly as his daughters for their wickedness? This is always true in life, and Shakespeare holds the mirror up to nature—but is it consistent with the theory of retributive justice? One can usually trace back to some element of his nature, physical or moral, the misfortunes that befall an individual; even those which we call accidents, as Galton claimed, are often due to some inherent defect of attention which makes us fail to respond protectively at the right moment. If we take the self to include the entire organism, then it remains true that we co-operate as a partial cause in all that happens to us. Ophelia's weak and unresisting brain must share with the stresses which surrounded her the responsibility for her madness. In this sense, and in this sense only, do we deserve our fate, be it good or ill. Yet, when interpreted in this broadest meaning, retributive justice loses all ethical significance. And the cosmic disharmony appears all the more glaring. It ceases to be chargeable to an external fate or God, to the environment or convention, which might perhaps be mastered and remolded; and is seen pervading the nature of reality itself, no accidental circumstance, but essential evil, ineradicable. The greatest tragic poets see it thus. And then blame turns to understanding and resentment to pity.

Retributive justice, as the motive force of tragedy, has for us lost its meaning. We no longer feel the necessity of justifying the ways of God to man, because we have ceased to believe that there exists any single, responsible power. The good is not a pre-ordained and automatically accomplished fact, but an achievement of finite effort, appearing here and there in the world when individuals, instead of contending against each other, co-operate for their mutual advantage.

―――――THINK ABOUT

1. Because art's role is now that of adapting the multitude to the dead mechanical existence of capitalist production, in which work sucks them of their vital energies without awakening their instincts, where leisure becomes a time to deaden the mind with the easy fantasy of films, simple wish-fulfilment writing, or music

that is mere emotional massage—because of this the paid craft of writing becomes as tedious and wearisome as that of machine-minder . . . (this art) is at once an expression of real misery and a protest against the real misery. This art, universal, constant, fabulous, full of the easy gratifications of instincts starved by modern capitalism, peopled by passionate lovers and heroic cowboys and amazing detectives, is the religion of today, as characteristic an expression of proletarian exploitation as Catholicism is of feudal exploitation. It is the opium of the people; it pictures an inverted world because the world of society *is* inverted.

2. Nobody seriously questions the principle that it is the function of mass culture to maintain public morale, and certainly nobody in the mass audience objects to having his morale maintained.

3. Poetry is a more philosophical and a more serious thing than history; for poetry is chiefly conversant about universal truth, history about particular.

4. Once again I want to emphasize that literature does not present us with propositions which are empirically verifiable like those of science and history; few if any statements in novels, that is, depicting the action or thought of a fictional character, can be verified in the way that informative propositions can. And yet they are true-*to*-human-nature as we know it. Thus in a way we *can* verify what the artist has presented; we can verify his insights in our own further observations of people and actions.

5. The artist picks out of reality something which we, owing to a certain hardening of our perceptions, have been unable to see ourselves.

6. The emotions which admit of being thus played upon for purposes of amusement are infinitely various; we shall take a few examples only. Sexual desire is highly adaptable to these purposes; easily titillated, and easily put off with make-believe objects. Hence the kind of amusement art which at its crudest and most brutal is called pornography is very common and very popular.

Readings

1. Else, Gerald F. *Aristotle's Poetics: The Argument.* Cambridge, Mass.: Harvard University Press, 1957.

2. Jarrett, James. *The Quest for Beauty.* Englewood Cliffs, N.J.: Prentice-Hall, Inc., 1957, pp. 291–299.

3. Henn, Thomas. *The Harvest of Tragedy.* London: Farber and Farber, 1956. Excellent summaries of main theories.

4. Mandel, Oscar. *A Definition of Tragedy.* New York: New York University Press, 1961.

5. Parker, DeWitt H. *The Principles of Aesthetics.* New York: Appleton, 1946.

6. Santayana, George. *The Sense of Beauty.* New York: Scribners, 1896.

7. Stolnitz, Jerome. *Aesthetics and the Philosophy of Art Criticism.* Boston: Houghton Mifflin, 1960.

8. Wellek, Rene. *A History of Modern Criticism.* Vols. I & II. London: Macmillan, 1955. Excellent survey from Dryden to Schopenhauer.

Appendix

General References

1. *Concise Encyclopedia of Western Philosophy and Philosophers.* Edited by J. O. Urmson. New York: Hawthorne, 1960.
2. *Dictionary of Philosophy and Psychology.* Edited by James Mark Baldwin. New York: Peter Smith, 1901–1905.
3. *Encyclopedia of Philosophy.* 8 vols. Edited by Paul Edwards. New York: Macmillan, 1967. Excellent.
4. *A Critical History of Western Philosophy.* Edited by D. O'Connor. Glencoe: Free Press, 1964.
5. Runes, D. *The Dictionary of Philosophy.* New York: Philosophical Library, 1937.

Index